Panama Handbook

D0581821

Richard Arghiris

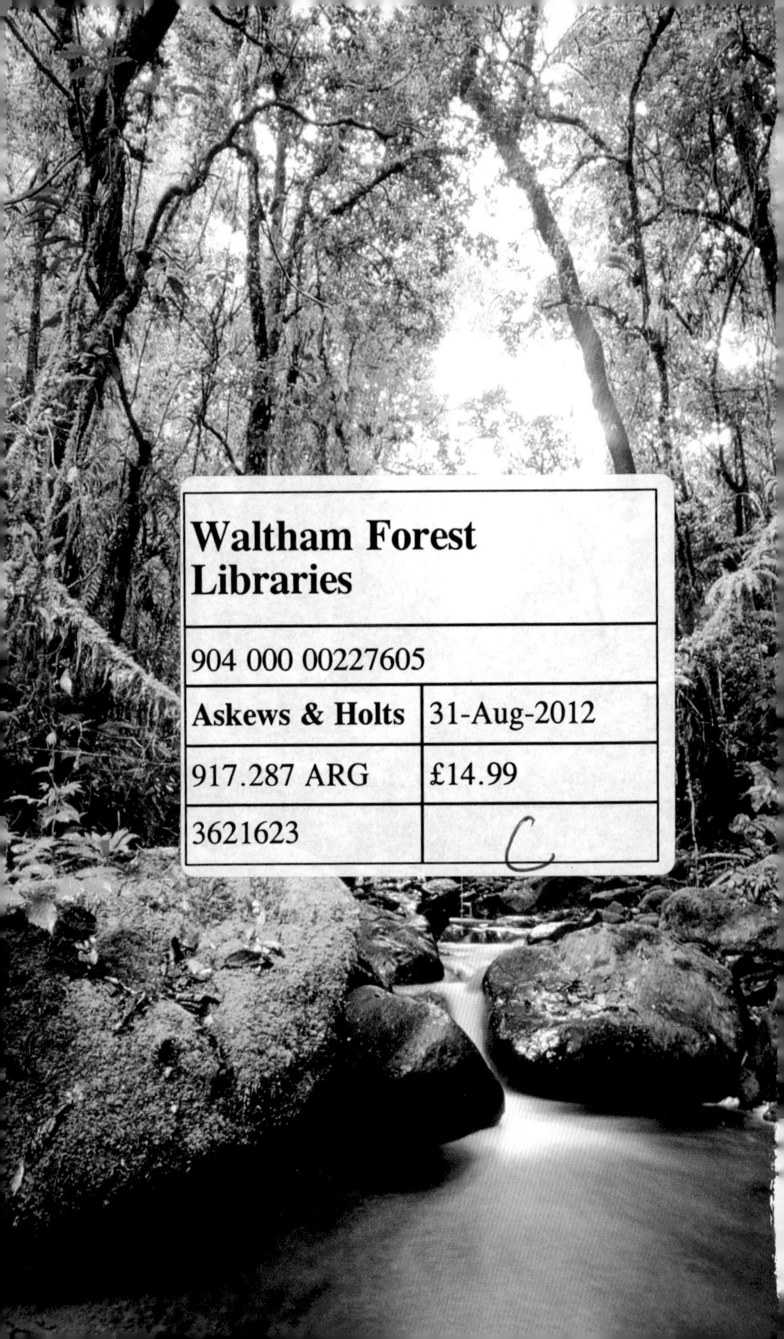

On the edge of the world stage and at the heart of global capitalism, the isthmus of Panama is a paradoxical place. It has long been a conduit for powerful international forces, but it is also a peripheral Central American state and home to some of the most remote wilderness on the planet. As a nation, it is both globally and locally orientated, forever gazing outward to the world and inward to its own soul. It is bound by patriotism, but sustained by foreign influence; united under the flag, but fragmented into a multitude of cultural forms.

Throughout world history, the isthmus has played a key role in facilitating dramatic shifts in geopolitical power. When Spanish conquistadors washed up in the Americas in the 16th century, Panama became a base for their expansive colonial enterprise – the birthplace of the world's first truly global empire. Centuries later, the country's fate as a transnational crossroads was sealed when the United States carved out the Panama Canal and joined the oceans as one.

Today, the isthmus is a fiercely multi-ethnic place, blending vibrant flavours from Europe, Asia, Africa and indigenous America. As a bridge between the continents, it is a bastion of ecological diversity too. A third of the national territory is an officially protected area with tropical rainforests, wetlands, rivers, mountains, cloud forests, offshore islands and coral reefs playing host to some of the most biologically varied and brilliantly coloured wildlife anywhere.

But as Panama's economy powers forth into the 21st century, the nation's outstanding natural spaces are under threat from uncontrolled development. The coming years will be critically important. Will Panama embrace sustainability? Or will it sell out to big business and heavy polluters? There has never been so much to gain – or so much to lose. Panama, the great crossroads of the world, has arrived at its own urgent and ethical crossroads.

THIS PAGE Neotropical vegetation in the immense virgin rainforests of the Parque Nacional Darién
PREVIOUS PAGE Strings of brightly coloured beads (*winis*) are part of traditional Guna dress

Don't miss...

1 **San Felipe** ➤ page 43
Wander the colonial plazas of Panama City's historic quarter.

2 **Miraflores Locks** ➤ page 91
Admire the engineering marvel of the giant lock operations.

3 **Rainforest Center** ➤ page 96
Enjoy close encounters with sloths, monkeys and toucans.

4 **Portobelo** ➤ page 113
Live out your swashbuckling fantasies in the old Spanish treasure forts.

5 **Parque Nacional Darién** ➤ page 143
Explore the great frontier wilderness of the Darién rainforest.

6 **Santa Fe** ➤ page 191
Take to the hills for pristine forests, waterfalls and farming communities.

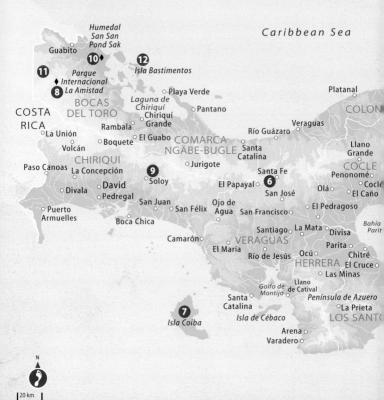

7 **Isla Coiba** ▶▶ page 196
Observe big fish, whales, dolphins and dazzling coral reefs.

8 **Parque La Amistad** ▶▶ page 232
Spot resplendent quetzals and other cloud forest creatures.

9 **Soloy** ▶▶ page 240
Learn about indigenous culture at this new community tourism project.

10 **San San Pond Sak** ▶▶ page 249
Meet the manatees and observe nesting sea turtles.

11 **Naso Kingdom** ▶▶ page 249
Immerse yourself in the fascinating world of the indigenous Naso.

12 **Isla Bastimentos** ▶▶ page 261
Soak up the Caribbean vibe and kick back on the beach.

The steamy metropolis of Panama City overlooks passing ships at the entrance to the Panama Canal

Itineraries for Panama

Many first-time visitors to Panama are astounded at how much there is to see and do. For such a small country, it offers an astonishing variety of adventures. Fortunately, it is also a very compact place and, for the most part, easy to navigate. If you're short on time, Panama City makes a great base with scores of attractions within easy reach. West of the capital, the road network is in very good shape, with frequent intercity bus services. Many travellers like to hire their own vehicle; the well-plied Interamericana highway connects most parts of the country and is a joy to drive. Eastern Panama is much more remote and tricky to explore. It is home to large areas of rainforest, far-flung indigenous communities and few paved roads. Domestic flights are an option, but costs add up quickly. Plan ahead.

ITINERARY ONE: 7-10 days
Transisthmian trails

Take a day or two to experience the multi-cultural throng of Panama City, including the colonial quarter of San Felipe and the old Canal Zone township of Balboa. A trip to see the workings of the Panama Canal is obligatory, as is a hike in one of the nearby rainforests reserves, including the Parque Nacional Soberanía. If time is on your side, consider a trip to the central provinces, where you'll find laid-back Pacific beaches, such as Santa Clara

and the verdant highland spa town of El Valle. For island paradise, you can't do much better than the stunning Islas Perlas. A stay in Panama City wouldn't be complete without a journey across the isthmus, if only for cultural contrast. You can reach the Caribbean coast by bus or car, but the most enjoyable way is on the Panama Canal Railway, which spirits passengers from coast to coast in just one hour. If time and money are not factors, it is also possible to transit the Panama Canal by boat, but plan well ahead. On the

Caribbean side, intrepid urban explorers may be drawn to the crumbling city of Colón, sadly deprived but rich in history and intrigue. If tropical decay doesn't interest you, swing west to the mighty Gatún Locks, the old Spanish fortress of San Lorenzo and the remote fishing communities of the Costa Abajo. The area is fascinating, but is also challenging to explore without your own vehicle. Many travellers instead prefer to head east to the Costa Arriba, a bastion of history and feisty Afro-colonial traditions. The old fortresses of Portobelo, straight from the era of pirates and swashbucklers, are not to be missed. Further east, the offshore retreat of Isla Grande is a great place to conclude your journey. You can choose to relax in a lazy beach-side hammock or, if it's the weekend, crack open a bottle of rum with new friends.

ITINERARY TWO: 10-14 days
The road less travelled

It's easy to reach the stunning Caribbean archipelago of Guna Yala from the capital with direct flights to several islands. Alternatively, you can take private over-land transport to Cartí and go from there. The Guna maintain strict control over their semi-autonomous territory and it can be complicated getting around without your own boat. After a few days lolling on the beaches, snorkelling in coral reefs, eating fresh seafood and exploring interesting indigenous villages, most visitors find they need to fly back to Panama City before continuing on to the remote Darién province. Conveniently, the Interamericana highway is now fully paved as far as Yaviza, taking you into the heart of the region. From there, it's easy to arrange boat transport to El Real and guides onwards to the Parque Nacional Darién. It's worth spending a few nights in the rangers' station to explore several different trails and really soak up the neotropical grandeur of the rainforest.

Handsome Caribbean houses line the water's edge on the colourful islands of Bocas del Toro

Returning to the Interamericana highway, you could turn south at Metetí and catch a boat to Darién's sultry capital, La Palma. From there, you can make excursions to Emberá and Wounaan communities.

ITINERARY THREE: 3-4 weeks
The best of the west

From Panama City, head west along the Interamericana highway and into the rolling rural landscapes of Panama's central provinces. It's worth stopping at the provincial market town of Penonomé to stock up on cigars and sombreros, or otherwise make a detour to the lush hills of the Reserva Privada Tavida. Back on the Interamericana highway, you'll pass a string of interesting sites, including the modest archaeological ruins of El Caño, the ancient church of Natá and the salt-producing town of Aguadulce. At the junction of Divisa, swing south into the Azuero Peninsula, where you could easily spend a week exploring the network of Old World colonial towns and friendly farming communities. Don't miss the relaxed city of Chitré, the surf beaches of Pedasí, the coral reefs of Isla Iguana and, if in season, the remote turtle nesting site of Isla Caña. If you can tear yourself away from the region, head west in the lesser-visited province of Veraguas. Nestled beneath the continental divide, the highland town of Santa Fe is a burgeoning new outdoors mecca with superb birdwatching and hiking trails. On the coast, the surf town of Santa Catalina offers access to some of the best waves in Central America, as well as the spectacular ecological jewel of Isla

Panama's rural central provinces are bastions of rugged scenery and equally rugged lifestyles

Coiba, a world-class dive site that's not be missed. Continuing west on the highway into Chiriquí province, intrepid travellers head to the Comarca Ngäbe-Buglé, an isolated indigenous reserve of intriguing communities and barely explored mountain scenery. In the lowlands, the offshore islands near Boca Chica are disarmingly beautiful and a welcome respite from the rigours of the road. Chiriquí's capital, David, is a useful stopover that provides highway access to the popular mountain resort of Boquete, where there's enough in the surrounding countryside to keep you busy for days. Depending on your level of fitness, you can hike to the peak of the highest mountain in Panama, Volcán Barú, ride some whitewater rapids, soar through the air on a zip-line, or simply relax in wonderfully rustic, piping-hot springs. Don't leave the area without travelling to the other side of the volcano,

TRAVEL TIP
It is easy to hop between passing buses on the Interamericana highway, but few services run after dark.

where the towns of Volcán and Cerro Punta offer access to excellent birdwatching sites, including the cloud forests of the Parque Internacional La Amistad. Once you're ready to leave the Pacific, the journey across the continental divide is singularly beautiful. At the conclusion of your journey, you will arrive in the province of Bocas del Toro, where you'll be rewarded with a string of stunning Caribbean islands. Unwind on the beaches, go searching for neon frogs, or visit the intrepid communities of the indigenous Naso and Ngäbe – it's up to you. It's at least a 15-hour bus journey back to the capital, but you can fly it in about an hour.

The offshore reefs are filled with multicoloured corals and other dazzling sea creatures

ix

Map 1 Panama West

Las Delicias
La Tablas
La Mesa
California
La Mesa
Guabito
Changuinola
El Silencio
Bonyic

Humedal San San Pond Sak
Isla de los Pájaros
Isla Caranero
Isla Colón
Archipiélago Bocas del Toro
Isla Solarte
Isla Bastimentos
Parque Nacional Marino Isla Bastimentos

Tibite
Almirante

Isla San Cristóbal
Isla Popa
Quebrada Pastor
Tierra Oscura
Traicionera
Bosque Protector Palo Seco
Silico Creek

Kusapin
Isla Cayo Agua
Playa Verde
Tobobe
Isla Escudo de Veragua

Laguna de Chiriquí
Punta Róbalo
Bahía Grande
Playa Rojo
Pantano
Punta Cricamola
Humedal de Importancia Internacional Damani-Guarivia

Parque Internacional La Amistad

Rio Teribe

COSTA RICA

BOCAS DEL TORO

Miramar
Chiriquí Grande
Ballena
Bisira
Quebrada Tula
Rambala
Malí
El Guabo
Calante
Kakintú
Boca del Río Chiriquí
San Pedro Arriba

Las Nubes
Cerro Punta
La Unión
Río Sereno
Volcán
Bijao
Barriles
Parque Nacional Volcán Barú
San Ramón
Boquete
Alto Boquete
Caldera
Mutari
Bosalituvite

COMARCA NGÄB

Cañas Gordas
Los Planes
Plaza de Caisán
Dominical
San Andrés
Cuesta de Piedra
Nueva Esperanza
Chiriquicito
Los Planes
Bella Vista
Reserva Forestal Fortuna
Sabana de Huso
Jurigote
C

Gómez
CHIRIQUÍ
Paso Canoas
Chuchupate
Garichė Marto
El Santo
La Concepción
Bagalá
Dolega
Gualaca
Los Algarrobos
Las Lomas
Boca de Balsa
Rincón
Veladero
Soloy
Gasparillo
Algarrobo
Cerro Puerco
Cerro Miel
Cerro Nance
Bajo So

La Victoria
Divala
San Martín
Mostrenco
David
La Pita
Las Huacas
Boca de Monte
Hato Jobo
Hato Juli
San Valentín
Finca Corredor
Palo Grande
Pedregal
Chiriquí
San Lorenzo
Cianagurita
Hato Juli
San Félix
Tolé
Veladero
El Palmar
Paja Blanca
Isla Mono
Boca Chica
San Juan
Santa Cruz
Las Lajas
El Nancito
Guabir

Puerto Armuelles
Refugio de Vida Silvestre Playa de la Barqueta Agrícola
Isla Chapala
Isla Sevilla
Isla Boca Brava
Bahía de San Lorenzo
Refugio de Vida Silvestre Playa de Boca Vieja
Isla de Porcada
Camarón

Guanábano
Limónes
Quebrada del Medio
Bahía de Charco Azul
Isla Pariída
Isla Bolaños
Parque Nacional Marino Golfo de Chiriquí
Isla de Silva de Afuera
Puerto Vidal

Islas Secas

Pajarón
Punta Pixva

Pacific Ocean

Isla Canal de Afuera
Isla Rancher

Parque Nacional Coiba
Former Penal Colony
Isla Coiba
Bahía Damas

Canal de Jicarón
Isla Jicarón
Isla Jicarita

Legend

Pan-American Highway
Primary road, paved
Secondary road
Trail
National park
Provincial boundary

N

20 km
20 miles

A B C
1 2 3

Caribbean Sea

Golfo de Mosquitos

COLON

Fort San Lorenzo
Piña
Los Camarones
Miguel de Diego La Borda
Nuevo Paraíso
Platanal
Coclé del Norte
Nuevo Veraguas
Boca del Congal
Sabanita Verde
Boca de Toabré
El Coquillo
Valle de San Miguel

Bosque Protector San Lorenzo
Achiote
El Guabo
Chorillo
Ciricito
Arenosa
El Nancito
Tres Hermanus
El Gasperillal
El Aguacate
La Gaita Arriba
Cirí Grande
Caimit
El Cacao

Veraguas
Concepción
Río Guázaro
Calovébora
Ciudad Romero
Collecito
Cutiva
Mollejón
Guacamayo
Limón
Cascajal
Boca de Tucué
Llano Grande
Tambo
Caimito

Pedrito Abajo
Santa Catalina
Río Luis
Calle Larga
Las Tablas
El Espino
Bella Vista
El Cócal
El Valle

GLE
Alto Ortiga
Cerro Galcra

Cordillera Central
Camarón
Antonio
El Papayal
El Común
Alto Ibala
Chumico
El Bale
El Perú
Hatillo

Parque Nacional Omar Torrijos
La Pintada

COCLÉ

Parque Nacional Santa Fe
Santa Fe
Reserva Forestal La Yeguada
El Puente
Las Huacas Del Quije
Vueltas Larga
Los Mendozas
San José
La Honda
Cañazas

Olá
Coclé
El Caño
El Caño
Natá
Los Corralitos
El Gago
El Espino
Penonomé
El Limón
Pueblo Nuevo
Palo Verde
El Hato
Farallón
El Espino
Quebrad

Juan Hombrón

Monumento Natural Los Pozos de Calobre
Calobre
El Naranjal

San Francisco
El Pedragoso
Cerro Redondo
Boquerón
El Balso
El Espino
El Anón
El Pedernal

Aguadulce
Membrillar
Ciénaga de las Macanas
Bahía de Parita

Cerro Mangote
Refugio de Vida Silvestre Cenegón del Mangle

El Perú
Los Valdeses
La Mesa
Llano de Los Muertos
María
VERAGUAS
La Pira
Piedras Negras
El Pilón
Río de Jesús
Puerto Mutis
Soná
Cirón
La Mata
El Círuelito
Tara
Caratales
Santiago
Quebrada de Agua

El Rincón
Santa María
Divisa
Parque Nacional Sarigua

Parita
Chitré
Los Santos

La Soledad
Guaramal
El Tigre
Humedal de Importancia Internacional Golfo de Montijo
Isla Leones
Tebario
Golfo de Montijo
Isla de Cébaco

Cirbulaco
Sabanera
Cerro Largo
El Toro
Los Pozos
HERRERA
Ocú
El Hatillo
Valle Rico
Chumical
Las Minas
Pesé

Agua Buena
Villa Lourdes
Llano Abajo
Macaracas
Santa Marta
El Cruce
Guararé
Las Tablas

Llano de Catival
Tolú Abajo
La Prieta
Reserva Forestal El Montuoso
El Cedro
Bombachito
Mogollón
Bayano
Guera
LOS SANTOS
La Miel
Los Asientos
El Cacao
Cañas
Las Cabezas

La Laja
El Muñoz
Pocrí
La Laguna
El Canafístulo
Refugio de Vida Silvestre Isla Iguana

Pedasí
Punta Mala
Playa Los Destiladeras
Venado

Santa Catalina
La Loma
Malena
Torio
Flores Nuevo
Arenas
Varadero
Parque Nacional Cerro Hoya
Reserva Forestal Tonosí
Tonosí
Reserva de Vida Isla Silvestre Isla Caña
Cambutal
Ave María

Península de Azuero

A **B** **C**

4 **5** **6**

Map 2 Panama East

Caribbean Sea

a Yala (San Blas)

Maguebganti

Irgandí
Isla Yalatuma
Isla Yantupo
Playón Isla Monos
Chico
Isla Nustupo

GUNA YALA
(SAN BLAS)

Isla Ulurtupo
Bahía de Masargandí
Serranía de Darién Punta Mosquito

Punta Navagandí

Isla Pino

Río Uala
Rubén Puerto
Limón Pigandecito Isla Soskatupo
tí Isla Cuba
Playa Isla Soletupo
Chuzo
Punta Escocés
atanilla Agua Fría
Carrero
El Tirao Punta Carreto
Anachakuna Puerto
Pueblo Nuevo Quebrada Obaldía La Miel
Santa Fe Honda Canán Cerro Bell
arriales Puerto Lara (1046 m)
Alto del Cristo Nuevo
Cucunatí Punoloso Santa Rosa
Puerto Metetí Tortugo
Quimba Bosque Protector
onzalo Isla Sansoncito Alto Darién
squez El Encanto
Río Congo Quebrada Félix
La Palma La Esperanza
Isla Iguana Canglón La Pulida
olfo de Reserva Nazareth
n Miguel Punta Alegre Forestal Canglón Punta Boca de
umedal de Importancia Mogué Grande Río Tigre
Internacional
Punta Patiño Yaviza
Reserva Natural
Pueblo Nuevo Punta Patiño DARIEN El Real Vista Alegre
Ensenada de
Garachiné Reserva Capetí
nta Bárbara Forestal Camogantí Boca de Cupé
achine Chepigana Pirre Field Station Bajo Grande Púcuro
Calle Larga (ANAM Station)
Sambú Bajo Lepe El Balsal
Boca de Tigre Río Sambú Paya
Manené
Playa de Muerto
Parque Nacional Darién
Pueblo Nuevo
Santa Cruz Boca de
de Cana Punusa

Serranía del Sapo

COLOMBIA
Puerto Piña

Bahía Piña
Jaqué

Serranía de Jungurudo
Altos de
Aspavé

Cordillera
de Jurado

Panama's jungle-shrouded waterways are vital transit routes for the Emberá people, who use punted long-boats called *piraguas*

Slow-moving three-toed sloths are a common sight in Panama's tropical forests, even in Panama City's Parque Metropolitano

Contents

Contents

Footprint features

Essentials

Planning your trip

Best time to visit Panama

Panama enjoys year-round temperatures of 21-32°C and two distinct seasons – wet and dry. The dry season, known locally as *verano* (summer), runs from December to April and broadly corresponds with tourist high season, when airfares and hotel prices are higher. In the Pacific lowlands, the *verano* is characterized by bright, cloudless days that get hotter and hotter until the rains finally break in May. In the highlands, early morning mists or brief periods of drizzle are a common and welcome blessing. On the Caribbean, short bouts of rainfall can occur spontaneously at any time, making it significantly humid year round. The dry season is the best time for most activities, including hiking, diving and surfing on the Pacific (Caribbean surfing is less predictable).

The wet season, known as *invierno* (winter), runs from May to November and corresponds to tourist low season, when prices drop considerably (the exception is the US summer vacation period of June to August). You should expect extreme humidity in the lowlands accompanied by changeable skies and short, heavy downpours in the early afternoon. Occasionally it can be overcast and showery for a few days at a time. Meanwhile, the highlands often experience cold, driving rain for several hours a day. It is usually much wetter during the later months of September, October and November, and downpours can persist into late December. Hiking is not recommended in the wet season owing to widespread flooding. The *invierno* is the best time for whitewater rafting, however. Note that Bocas del Toro province in western Panama enjoys its own microclimate: February to March and September to October are the dry months.

What to do in Panama

For such a tiny country, Panama boasts a staggering diversity of natural landscapes. Teeming rainforests, rugged mountains, wave-swept beaches, dazzling underwater coral gardens and thousands of untouched islands – all are the settings for some phenomenal outdoor adventures. As a natural land bridge between the Americas, Panama is also one of the most biologically diverse places on the planet. More than 25% of its national territory is an officially protected area and the opportunities for nature tourism are outstanding – for comprehensive advice on visiting reserves, see page 302. For specialist tour operators, please see individual chapters.

Archaeology

Human occupation of the isthmus appears to date back to 10,000-8000 BC, but there are few very ancient ruins in Panama and no evidence of the kinds of monumental city-states that characterized Mexico and other Central American countries further north. The modest sites of El Caño in Coclé province and Los Barriles in Chiriquí contain the most extensive evidence of urban development. However, many of their most interesting pieces have been relocated to museums, or worse, looted. Elsewhere, a scattering of archaeological fragments has been uncovered throughout Panama's interior, especially in the Azuero Peninsula. The lion's share of Panama's archaeological treasure is guarded by the

The #**1** Essential Travel Download[*]
Get TripAdvisor Mobile - **FREE**

- Browse millions of traveller reviews, photos & maps
- Find hotels, restaurants & things to do
- See what's nearby
- Apps available for iPhone, Android, Nokia, Palm Pre, & Windows Mobile

[*] From "iPhone Travel Apps: 10 Essential Downloads" on Frommers.com

Six of the best: cultural odysseys

Emberá villages

For those who can't make it out to the Darién, scores of Emberá communities can be found in the rainforests just outside Panama City. Most of them are geared towards tourism and welcome visitors on almost a daily basis. Activities include guided hikes in the surrounding forests, traditional dance presentations, and the chance to purchase superb handmade crafts, including carved cocobolo wood statues and fine baskets woven from palm fibres. See page 94.

Costa Arriba

The Costa Arriba is the heartland of Panama's so-called 'Afro-colonial' people, who are directly descended from escaped slaves called *Cimarrones*. Their culture is an intriguing fusion of distinct and largely disparate foreign traditions. The adoration of a black Christ known as 'El Nazareno' is a clear manifestation of Spanish Catholicism. Other customs, such as the Congo dance, are straight from the continent of Africa. See page 113.

Río Sambú

Snaking through the remote frontier lands of the Darién, the jungle-shrouded Río Sambú is home to a handful of the region's Emberá and Wounaan communities, whose striking appearances and way of life are strongly reminiscent of the Amazon. Their traditional culture includes scores of vivid dances and songs, as well as striking adornments of colourful flowers, beads and copious temporary tattoos. Page 146.

Azuero Peninsula

Often celebrated as Panama's cradle of folklore, the Azuero Peninsula is a bastion of ancient Spanish and European traditions. Throughout its network of sleepy colonial villages, Catholic-tinged festivals revel in unique modes of music, song and dance. Unsurprisingly, the region also boasts vibrant artisan traditions, including robust forms of pottery, mask-making and fine needlework. See page 168.

Comarca Ngäbe-Buglé

Encompassing vast swathes of mountains and remote Caribbean shoreline, the Comarca Ngäbe-Buglé is the largest of Panama's semi-autonomous *comarcas*. Few roads or power lines penetrate the region, a rolling wilderness of rugged mule trails and isolated villages. The indigenous population are necessarily resilient, but a beautiful tranquillity pervades their homeland – a world punctuated by desolate peaks, rivers, waterfalls and cloud forests. See page 237.

Naso Kingdom

Settled along the banks of the mighty Río Teribe, the 3500-strong indigenous Naso maintain one of Latin America's last remaining monarchies. Masters of bushcraft and herbal medicine, their shamans guard unparalleled cultural knowledge of the surrounding rainforests. Sadly, the kingdom is under ongoing threats from hydroelectric projects, but they welcome independent travellers keen to learn more about Naso culture. See page 249.

Reina Torres museum in Panama City, but at the time of press, most of the collection was in storage. Petroglyphs depicting a range of stylized motifs – human, animal and geographical – can be found on rocks and boulders throughout the country, especially in highland areas. Elsewhere, there are several ruins dating back to the colonial era, including the 16th-century settlement of **Panamá La Vieja** in Panama City and the fortresses of **San Lorenzo** and **Portobelo** on the central Caribbean coast.

Six of the best: island escapes

Isla Barro Colorado

Owned and maintained by the prestigious **Smithsonian Tropical Research Institute**, Isla Barro Colorado is one of the world's oldest protected areas and a centre of scientific study for nearly a century. Artificially created with the flooding of Lake Gatún, the island provides refuge to an astonishing array of Neotropical plant and animal species. See page 98.

Isla Grande

If you like to party, head to Isla Grande. Located just a few hours from the capital, this friendly Caribbean island sees crowds of revellers wash up on its shores every Friday afternoon. The festivities last all weekend and few places are as lively or welcoming. If you want to sleep, better come during the week when the island is deserted. See page 117.

Guna Yala

They say there's an island for every day of the year in Guna Yala. In fact, the remote semi-autonomous *comarca* boasts some 400 dazzling offshore atolls, most of them blissfully uninhabited. Governed by the indigenous Guna people, who have outlawed intensive development in the region, the islands are as rustic, tranquil and culturally unique as it gets. See page 125.

Isla Coiba

Few destinations are as stunning as Isla Coiba, Panama's largest and most pristine island. Blanketed by virgin rainforest and mercifully free of human development, Coiba is earning a reputation as one of the world's hottest diving sites. When it comes to viewing really large pelagic species – including formidable shoals of hammerhead sharks, sailfish, marlin and tuna – the Pacific waters offshore are second to none. See page 196.

Isla Boca Brava

The sleepy hideaway of Isla Boca Brava looks destined for great things. Hidden in a quiet enclave in the Bay of Chiriquí, the island has a remote and isolated feel, despite its close proximity to the city of David. Just beyond its shores lie the pristine atolls of the Parida Archipelago, replete with deserted beaches and untouched forests. Surfing, snorkelling, fishing and swimming can all be enjoyed in healthy quantities. See page 210.

Bocas del Toro

Nestled in a remote bay near Panama's northwest border, the secluded islands of the Bocas del Toro archipelago are a true bastion of Caribbean style. Few can resist the lure of white-sand beaches, lazy hammocks and rum-soaked sunsets, but the archipelago is equally celebrated for its lavish natural beauty. Teeming coral reefs, rainforests and mangroves all await exploration. See page 255.

Beaches

Panama is home to mile upon mile of rambling coastline, not to mention thousands of offshore islands, all accented by scores of beautiful sandy beaches. The **Pacific coast** between Penonomé and Panama City features long, wide, golden stretches with strong waves and a high concentration of resorts. By contrast, the **Caribbean coast** is less built up. For truly remote 'desert island' beach time, you can't do better than the **Guna Yala** archipelago. Other hotspots include **Isla Bastimentos**

Tips for observing wildlife

- **Come prepared** Bring binoculars, walking boots, a notepad, a compact umbrella or raincoat, and lightweight cotton clothing in muted or dark colours. Point-and-shoot cameras are useless for wildlife photography – you'll need an SLR with telephoto lenses and a compact tripod. Field guides are useful, but heavy to carry around. Avoid strong perfumes or colognes, pack for stealth, and remember: 'the early bird catches the worm'.
- **Be still, be patient** It is better to confine your search to a relatively small area. Wildlife will usually come to you if you wait for long enough in the same spot. Observing wildlife is often down to luck. Be patient. Some days will be better than others.
- **Be quiet, look and listen carefully** Most animals have an acute sense of hearing, so tread slowly and carefully. At the same time, listen out for sounds that may indicate their nearby presence, such as twigs breaking, rustling in the underbrush or bird calls. Most animals will be camouflaged. Run your eyes slowly over the foliage and look for any changes or movements. Also keep an eye out for signs of recent activity, such as paw-prints, shredded bark or scat.
- **Consider joining a tour group** A professional tour is often the easiest and most reliable way to observe wildlife. The most important aspect of any group is its leader. Professional biologists may be able to supply lots of information about the ecosystem, but they are not necessarily familiar with the area. Local naturalists are often more skilled at spotting animals. The size of the group doesn't matter as long as you are allowed to wander.

in Bocas del Toro, **Islas Paridas** in Chiriquí province, the **Costa Abajo** in Colón province, the **Islas Perlas** archipelago and the beaches around Pedasí in the **Azuero Peninsula**.

Birdwatching

Home to 976 species of avifauna, including 12 endemic and 20 endangered species, Panama is one of the world's most stunning birdwatching destinations. The **Audubon Society of Panama** has identified 88 sites as Important Bird Areas (IBAs) and over half of them have global importance. Thanks to its fortuitous geographic location, Panama represents the range limit for numerous species from both North and South America, as well as a vital migratory path for scores of others. The annual raptor migration, Oct-Dec, sees the skies filled with over a million vultures and hawks – a truly awesome natural spectacle. A complete list of birdwatching sites in Panama would fill an entire book, but the lowland forests around the Panama Canal

are a particularly fruitful and easy-to-access region. Home to an astonishing two-thirds of Panama's avifauna, the area includes a north–south biological corridor of protected nature reserves. Among them, the Parque Nacional Soberanía is home to the world-class **Pipeline Trail**, where the Audubon Society of Panama famously counted a record-breaking 357 species in one morning. If you want to get up close to the park's chattering canopy, the **Rainforest Discovery Centre** has a 32-m-high tower with a viewing platform. In Panama's highlands, the bucolic village of Santa Fe, Veraguas province, has been well known to the Audubon Society for years. In western Chiriquí, 2 national parks – the **Parque Internacional La Amistad** and the **Parque Nacional Volcán Barú** – are among the last nesting sites of the rare resplendent quetzal, seen in flocks during breeding season, March to May. The forests of Darién, eastern Panama, have particularly high rates of endemism and are home to some spectacular species, including four types of macaw, the golden-headed quetzal and the harpy eagle. The region is remote and challenging, and many prime birdwatching locations, including the world-class Cana Field Station, can be accessed only by private plane. For this reason, many birders prefer to visit the Darién with the safety and convenience of a tour operator, such as ANCON.

Community tourism

Grassroots community tourism projects offer a unique and intimate opportunity to experience life in an indigenous or *campesino* village. Scores of communities across Panama have opened their doors to travellers and most offer informative guided tours of the surrounding region. Some indigenous communities offer workshops where you can learn how to make *artesanías* or speak the local language. Others have their own forms of dance and music, which they are happy to demonstrate. Wherever you choose to go, spending time in a rural community – preferably with a host family – can be one of the most rewarding and transformative experiences of any trip to Panama. Don't miss it.

Diving and snorkelling

Diving is the most developed sport on the isthmus and there are a staggering variety of dive sites off both coasts, many of them 'undiscovered'. The **Bocas del Toro** archipelago has very sheltered waters and is a great spot for learners or inexperienced divers looking to bolster their skills. Expect to see colourful Caribbean reefs typical of Central America (but nothing as spectacular as Belize). There are some more reefs off the coast of **Portobelo** in Colón province, as well as some interesting sunken ships and planes. The **Guna Yala** archipelago has scores of pristine coral reefs, but diving in the region is outlawed, leaving snorkelling as the only option. The Pacific is a much more challenging dive zone. Due to greater

tidal ranges, differing water temperatures and densities, it contains a wide variety of ecosystems. It is the place to see large pelagic species, including sharks, whales and dolphins. The diving off **Isla Coiba** is second to none, but it comes at a price. **Isla Cébaco** is a cheaper alternative. Inland, it is possible to dive in **Lake Gatún** where there is an old train carriage dating from the construction of the Panama Canal. However, the lake is reported to be infested with crocodiles – take care!

Fishing

Panama means 'abundance of fish', and freshwater angling is possible in many of the country's 480 rivers. In the highlands, this can be as simple as finding a spot and casting a line. In the Panama Canal area, **Lake Gatún** is presently overstocked with peacock bass and you should be able to pull several from the water without any problems. Big game fishing is a popular pursuit off the Pacific coast. Prize marlin, tuna, sailfish, dorado and others can be snagged in the waters around **Isla Parida**, **Isla Coiba** and the **Isla Perlas** archipelago. The most celebrated sports fishing in Panama is off **Punta Patina** in the Darién, where international **Game Fish Association** world records are broken year on year. However, lodging and expeditions with the Tropic Star Lodge – the only facility in the region – come at world-class prices. The Caribbean boasts great fishing too, but tourist infrastructure is generally less developed. You can rely on local boatmen to take you out, otherwise head to the tourist haunt of **Bocas Town**, where a professional tour operator should be able to hook you up.

Hiking

Panama's mountains and forests provide ample opportunities for hiking, including a few spectacular trails that are among the finest in Central America. Most hikers gravitate to the bucolic **Cordillera de Talamanca** in western Chiriquí, home to Volcán Barú (3475 m), the country's highest peak. The surrounding countryside is criss-crossed by an endless variety of trails, including the famous **Sendero Quetzales**, which connects the towns of Boquete and Cerro Punta. Near Panama City, the famous **Camino Real** is an old colonial gold road that crosses the continental divide to arrive on the Caribbean coast 3-5 days later. If that sounds too athletic, the capital is the jumping-off point for several rainforest trails that can be hiked unguided in a few hours or less – head for the Panama Canal watershed. The spa town of **El Valle**, just 2½ hrs from the capital, offers a taste of the highlands with its rolling pastures, dark peaks and crashing waterfalls, all very accessible. Further west into the rolling expanse of the Cordillera Central, the tiny village of **Santa Fe** is just awakening to its vast eco-touristic potential. For those with true grit, a track wends all the way to the Caribbean coast village of **Calovébora**. The indigenous **Comarca Ngäbe-Buglé** is a particularly remote highland region which promises unforgettable experiences for those determined enough to tackle it – a knowledgeable guide and a strong spirit of adventure are essential. The rainforests of **Darién** are a highly rewarding (if hard-core) wilderness that should not be undertaken lightly – they've claimed many a lost explorer over the centuries.

Spectator sports

Baseball Panamanians love baseball more than any other sport and the provincial championships are an exciting part of the national sporting calendar. In a testament to Panama's skill in the stadium, many of its finest players get snapped up by the United States – to date, there have been no less than 46 Panamanians playing in major league teams. As of 2012, Panama's national team ranked 16th in the world. In Panama City, you can catch national league games at the **Estadio Nacional Rodney Carew**, Vía Ricardo J Alfaro, www.estadionacional.com.pa.

Boxing Panama has produced many notable prize fighters, including several world championship winners. The most famous is Roberto Durán – nicknamed Manos de Piedra (Stone Hands) – staunchly celebrated as a national hero and widely regarded as one of the greats. There are boxing clubs all over the country, but the big fights often take place at the **ATLAPA Convention Centre**, www.atlapa.gob.pa, in Panama City.

Cockfighting Cockfighting is a particularly popular Sun afternoon diversion in the rural villages of Panama's interior. The event is very male orientated and invariably accompanied by copious quantities of alcohol, gambling and good-natured rowdiness. Although frequently bloody and gruesome, the contests are not usually fought to the death.

Football Panamanians do not regard soccer with the same sense of devotion as other Latin American nations. It's popular, but not as popular as baseball. The highest league is the **Liga Panameña de Fútbol** with an annual season divided into 2 major tournaments. Some of the country's best players hail from the ghettoes of El Chorillo, Panama City, which has no less than 2 high-ranking teams. Panama's national football stadium is the **Estadio Rommel Fernández**, Av José Agustín Arango y Calle 121 Este.

Surfing

Panama has huge surfing potential and many awesome breaks are still waiting to be discovered. The rambling and often rugged Pacific coast has fair surf at most major beaches, but for really outstanding action you should head to the burgeoning mecca of **Santa Catalina**, Veraguas province, where the waves can reach up to 4 m from Feb-Mar. Nearby, on the Azuero Peninsula, the beaches around Pedasí, particularly **Playa Venado**, are earning a formidable reputation for their vast and powerful breaks. If you're out on the islands – including **Isla Boca Brava**, **Isla Coiba** or the **Islas Perlas** archipelago – most boatmen will know some secret places. Otherwise nothing beats loading up a 4WD and discovering the Pacific coast for yourself. On the other side of the country, in the Caribbean province of Bocas del Toro, you'll find the legendary Hawaiian-style waves of **Silverbacks**, along with some more sedate breaks to suit beginners.

Whitewater rafting

Chiriquí province, western Panama, is a land of rugged mountains and feisty whitewater rapids, promising some of the most exciting rafting in Central America. Numerous Grade III-IV stretches can be accessed year-round, but they are increasingly under threat from the government's sale of hydroelectric concessions – experience them while you can. Boquete is the centre of operations for most specialized rafting companies, which lead regular expeditions on the **Río Chiriquí** and the **Chiriquí Viejo**, among others. Alternatively, the indigenous **Comarca Ngäbe-Buglé** is developing its options. The community of Soloy, just 1½ hrs from David, offers exciting and highly rewarding trips on the **Río Fonseca**.

Getting to Panama

Air

In Panama City, **Tocumen International Airport (PTY)**, www.tocumenpanama.aero, is the country's main international flight hub, with arrivals from the United States, Central America, Mexico, South America and a handful of European destinations. Three regional airports also offer short-haul connections with Costa Rica, including **'Enrique Malek' International Airport (DAV)** in David, **Isla Colón International Airport (BOC)** in Bocas del Toro, and **Albrook 'Marcos A Gelabert' International Airport (PAC)** in Panama City.

When searching for a fare, you can check general costs and availability on airline websites. The best deals are available Monday to Thursday in the low season. Many airlines also offer 'unpublished fares' (cheaper than official fares), which are available through travel agencies only – call around or check some of the price comparison websites below. If time is not an issue, flying into Costa Rica and travelling overland to Panama can often prove substantially cheaper than a direct flight to Panama City.

From Europe

There are no direct flights from the UK to Panama, although **British Airways** is rumoured to be considering a new service. At the time of press, most routes demanded at least one stopover in the United States. Transatlantic carriers with on-going services to Panama include **American Airlines** and **Delta Airlines** (see below). Schedules from Europe are generally more restrictive, but an alternative option is to fly via Madrid with **Iberia** or Amsterdam with **KLM** (see below). Return flights from London to Panama City via the US/Europe cost around US$1400 in the high season; US$1000 in the low season.

There are very few direct flights from mainland Europe to Panama, and most travellers will find themselves routed via the US. Exceptions are **Iberia**, which operates a few weekly flights from Madrid, and **KLM**, with comparable services from Amsterdam. Return flights are roughly US$1300 in the high season; US$900 in the low season.

From USA and Canada

The US is a major gateway to Panama and direct flights depart from a range of cities including Atlanta, Dallas, Houston, Fort Lauderdale, Los Angeles, Miami, New York, Newark and Washington DC. Several airlines offer comparable services (see below), but the very cheapest is **Spirit Airlines**, which operates out of Fort Lauderdale, Florida, with return fares as low as US$400 in the high season, US$250 in the low season. From Canada, flights depart directly from Toronto with **Air Canada** at a rough cost of US$800 in the high season, US$600 in the low season.

From Australia and New Zealand

There are no direct flights to Panama from Australia or New Zealand and most journeys demand at least one stopover in the US, usually in Los Angeles. From Australia, some airlines make the trans-Pacific crossing and connect with their own onward services, including **American Airlines** and **Delta Airlines**, otherwise most flights are with **Qantas** or **United Airlines**.

From Mexico, Central and South America

The national airline, **Copa**, connects the capital with a wide range of destinations including Mexico, Guatemala, Costa Rica, El Salvador, Honduras, Colombia, Chile, Perú, Venezuela and Argentina. Colombian airline **Avianca** is now partnered with Grupo Taca – a trade group composed of several independent Central American airlines – and they offer direct and connecting services from numerous Latin American cities. For short flights from Costa Rica, try **Air Panama** or **Nature Air**.

Airport information

Tocumen International Airport, www.tocumenpanama.aero, is the busiest airport in Central America and its passenger traffic has roughly doubled over the past decade. To meet increasing demands, the airport has undergone significant improvement and modernization since 2006. Nonetheless, it remains small and easy to navigate. Amenities include car hire, a small duty-free zone, ATMs, telephones, toilets, restaurant, café, internet and a health clinic for emergency treatment. A new phase of expansion is underway which includes the creation of a new terminal with 12 additional gates. Parking is available at Tocumen for US$1.80 for the first hour, US$1.20 for the second to fifth hour, US$0.60 per hour thereafter.

Road

In years gone by, adventurous trekkers could cross the jungles of the Darién Gap and enter Panama from Colombia, but this is no longer possible because of the threat of armed paramilitaries and drug-traffickers. Consequently, Panama has just three official border crossings, all of them with Costa Rica. On the Pacific side, the main point of entry is **Paso Canoas**, a frenetic border town located on Panama's main highway, the Carretera Interamericana (Panamerican Highway). In the Chiriquí highlands, **Río Sereno** is a quiet rural crossing, but tricky to reach without your own vehicle. On the Caribbean side, **Sixaola-Guabito** is the gateway to the remote province of Bocas del Toro.

Bus

Ticabus, www.ticabus.com, is the main international bus line and it connects Panama with Costa Rica, Nicaragua, Honduras, El Salvador, Guatemala and Mexico. Expect time-consuming formalities (two to four hours) at Paso Canoas, where you'll have to queue for stamps and undergo rigorous security checks with your fellow passengers. On-board amenities include reclining seats, toilet, movies and icy air-conditioning (bring a sweater). Regular and executive services are broadly similar: the extra dollars buy you a simple meal. International buses usually (but not always) take a break at Santiago, roughly halfway between David and Panama City. If you need to exit before then, you should be able to hop out on the highway at Paso Canoas (for Volcán and Cerro Punta) or David, but give the driver advance warning. If luggage is light, consider using local rather than international buses, as you will be able to avoid lengthy processing at the border – if you're very lucky, you can cross in less than 10 minutes. Aim to arrive 1000-1600 and skip customs entirely if you have nothing to declare. If you wish to enter Panama at Río Sereno or Guabito-Sixaola, you will have no choice but to use local buses.

Car

The drive from the US to Panama may be long and expensive, but it's also an unforgettable experience that takes in seven or more different nations. On entering Panama, all foreign-plated vehicles are automatically granted a 90-day temporary import permit – you will require a valid driver's licence, proof of ownership and insurance. Border formalities are smooth compared with other Central American countries but you can always hire a helper (*tránsito*) to guide you through the process, around US$5. The first step is to take your passport to the immigration windows and receive the appropriate exit and entrance stamps. Next take your passport and vehicle papers to the *aduana* and pay US$5 for a *tarjeta de circulación* (vehicle control card). Finally get your car inspected and pay US$1 for a fumigation.

Sea

Panama is a hub for cargo ships from all over the world. Although an interesting way to travel, they're not necessarily a cheap means to reach the country – you'll have to pay food and board for every day you're at sea. You may, however, get to transit the Panama Canal. Most commercial cruise-ships arrive in Panama via Colón. They include an obligatory trip to the Free Trade Zone before crossing the canal and docking on the outskirts of Panama City.

From Colombia In May 2012 **Panamerican Seaways** launched a new ferry service from Cartagena to Colón with departures every Tuesday, Friday and Sunday. Fares for the 12-hour journey start at around US$100. A more expensive, leisurely and scenic route uses private yachts, passing the stunning islands of Guna Yala en route. Services are not public or scheduled, but offered privately. To find a captain, make enquiries at the port in Cartagena or look for flyers in youth hostels. Like any significant sea journey, the trip should not be taken lightly. Do your research before selecting a vessel and never be pressured into anything. As a minimum, be sure that your captain is qualified, experienced and trustworthy. Check how many other passengers are taking the trip and that there are sufficient life vests. Ask to see the living quarters and try to assess the general sea-worthiness of the vessel. Also determine whether meals are included and if you'll be expected to work for them. You can expect to pay around US$350-450 for the five- to seven-day trip.

Transport in Panama

Air

Domestic flights are a good idea if you're short on time and a very practical option if you want to reach some remote destinations. **Albrook 'Marcos A Gelabert' International Airport** (PAC), 1.5 km from the centre of Panama City, is the country's main domestic airport. Since **Aeroperlas** ceased operations in February 2012, Panama has just one domestic Airline, **Air Panama**, www.flyairpanama.com, which which flies to David, Bocas del Toro, Changuinola and Isla Contadora and also serves numerous regional airports in Guna Yala and Darién.
➤➤ *For a complete schedule, please see Transport, Panama City, page 74.*

Baggage restrictions, date changes and refunds
A checked luggage limit of 25 lb (11.3 kg) applies to all domestic flights. The exceptions are Panama–David/Bocas del Toro routes, where the standard limit is 30 lb (13.6 kg). Hand-luggage should not exceed one piece and 5 lb (2.27 kg) on Air Panama flights. You will be charged US$1 for each pound (0.45 kg) of excess weight. Fees for surfboards range from US$10-30 – consult the airline before travelling. Tickets are valid for 90 days from the first travelling date; penalties for no show are 100% of all applicable fares, taxes and surcharges. Tickets can be changed in advance of travel (up to a maximum of four times) for US$10.

Rail

The United Fruit Company managed extensive railway networks in the provinces of Bocas del Toro and Chiriquí during the 20th century, but these have long since closed. Today, Panama's only surviving passenger railway is the **Panama Railroad**, which crosses the isthmus from Panama City to Colón. The train makes one journey a day in each direction and carries mostly tourists and executives working at the Colón Free Trade Zone. In Panama City, construction work on an underground **Metro** system has recently begun, but it will be several years before it reaches completion.

River and sea

Rivers are the main transport network in some remote areas, including mainland Bocas del Toro, the Chagres National Park and the Darién. Note that currents and water levels are dramatically affected by seasonal rainfall. Passage along some waterways may be very slow or impossible in the height of the dry season, or fraught with dangerous rapids in the wet season. Traditional riverboats known as *piraguas* are long, flat-bottom vessels dug out from a ceiba tree trunk – they may be punted with a long stick or powered by an outbound motor. Modern fibre-glass *pangas* are also common. Riverboat services are not usually scheduled and private charters are costly.

The coast of Panama is punctuated by thousands of islands, making travel by sea a distinct possibility. Popular haunts, such as Isla Taboga and Isla Contadora, have scheduled ferries and catamarans, but in other places you'll have to rely on water-taxis, tour operators or the services of freelance boatmen. In the Bocas del Toro archipelago, it's easy to zip between islands on *pangas* equipped with high-powered outboard motors. The rates are set and average US$3-5 for a 10- to 20-minute journey. In the Guna Yala archipelago, local transport is usually in wooden *cayucos*, also fitted with outboard motors. Chartering a boat for the day is expensive due to the cost of gasoline. Exact rates vary with the boat, distance, load and type of motor, but a *panga* equipped with 75 hp four-stroke engine is best for the ocean. Unsurprisingly, Panama is a favourite destination among yachters and there are numerous excellent marinas along both coasts.

Road

Bus

All major towns and cities are served by an affordable and efficient bus network. Most intercity buses are 28-seater air-conditioned 'coasters', often enlivened with high-volume salsa or reggaeton. Seats are usually comfortable but can be a squeeze due to overloading (those with long legs should avoid sitting over the wheel and try to grab a space next to the driver). There is limited luggage space at the back, but strapping bags to the roof is an option. If departing from Panama City, buy your ticket at one of the booths before boarding. Elsewhere, an assistant will collect fares shortly after departure. Designated bus stops usually consist of a concrete shelter by the roadside. To get off, simply inform the assistant of your desired destination or yell '*Parada*' (stop) for immediate effect. Buses making the haul between Panama City and David are comfortable, modern coaches. By contrast, rickety *diablos rojos* (red devils) are converted US school buses, usually pimped with gaudy artwork and disco lights – they operate mainly in Panama City, along the Caribbean coast and on a handful of rural routes, although they are being phased out. Particularly remote destinations are served by converted trucks with hard wooden benches and plastic rain covers – a great way to rub shoulders with the locals. Note that buses operating within city limits usually require payment on boarding.

Bicycle

Imported bike parts are impossible to find outside Panama City so buy everything you need before you leave home. Most towns have a bicycle shop of some description, but it is best to do your own repairs whenever possible. Due to highway traffic, it is usually more rewarding to keep to the smaller roads. Watch for oncoming and overtaking vehicles, as well as protruding or unstable loads on trucks. Make yourself conspicuous by wearing bright clothing and a helmet. You are strongly advised to forego cycling in the capital, where drivers are among the most aggressive in the western hemisphere. The climate is very tough – take care to avoid dehydration.

Car

Panama boasts one of the best road networks in Central America. Its main highway, the Carretera Interamericana, links five of the nation's 10 provinces from Paso Canoas to Yaviza. Various small highways cross the isthmus from the Pacific to the Caribbean, including the Corredor Norte, which connects Panama City to Colón. West of the capital, most secondary and many minor roads are now paved, but if you intend to get off the beaten track a 4WD will be required, especially in the wet season, when dirt roads are often washed out and treacherous. Driving in the capital is a nightmare best avoided. Speed restrictions of 100 kph apply on highways, 60 kph on secondary roads and 45 kph in urban areas, unless otherwise indicated. If you are involved in an accident, don't move your vehicle as the police first have to assess the situation and issue a report. Flashing lights by the side of the road may indicate a speed trap or road restriction ahead. Always carry your passport and driver's licence – police stops are common, especially near the international border. Note that speed lanes are rarely observed but traffic outside Panama City is usually courteous and overtaking is quite normal. Drivers and passengers must wear seatbelts at all times.

Car hire Car hire agencies are widespread in Panama City and David, with most offices concentrated in the airports – please see individual chapters for listings. You will need a credit card (or cash deposit, usually US$1000), a valid passport and driver's licence to get going. Most agencies enforce an age restriction of 25, but this will often be waived to 21. Before signing anything, make a very thorough inspection of any existing damage to the car – no matter how minor – and ensure that it is noted in your rental agreement. Prices are comparable to other Central American countries – the base rate for a simple automatic is around US$30 per day. Shop around: deals are often available.

Hitchhiking

Hitchhiking is not very common on major highways and not recommended at all for solo travellers, especially lone women. As ever, the practice carries risks and you should listen to your instincts before getting into any vehicle. Long-distance trucks ply the Interamericana in both directions, but it may be quicker, safer and easier to jump on a bus. In very remote areas where public transport is non-existent, hitching a ride in the back of a pickup truck is common and acceptable. Some form of payment is usually expected, so always offer something or ask how much at the end.

Taxi

Taxis are a convenient way to get around sprawling urban areas, and most journeys rarely exceed US$2. Many drivers will be happy to take you to hard-to-reach attractions out of town but negotiate a fee and a collection time before setting out. It's worth taking the phone number of a particularly helpful *taxista* for such excursions. Sadly, Panama City taxi drivers are often temperamental and prone to overcharging. Speaking Spanish helps.

Maps

The **Autoridad de Turismo Panamá (ATP)** ① *Av Samuel Lewis y Calle Gerardo Ortega, Edificio Central, T526-7000, www.atp.gob.pa,* has produced some basic country maps. For detailed topographical maps head to the **Instituto Geográfico Nacional** ① *Calle 57 y Av 6a Norte, T507-9684, www.ignpanama.anati.gob.pa.* Maps produced internationally include an Adventure map by **National Geographic** and a 1:800,000 colour country map by International Travel Maps, www.itmb.com. Useful tourist maps are available in souvenir shops – look for a handy range by **Mapi**, www.mapiamericas.com.

Where to stay in Panama

Hotels and hospedajes

Hotels are widespread in all major towns and cities, but less prevalent in villages and small communities. They usually represent good value for couples and small groups. Most hotel rooms come with their own bathroom, running hot water, cable TV, a fan, writing desk, and now, Wi-Fi. Air-conditioning will often ratchet up the price by an extra

US$20. The very cheapest rooms have a shared bathroom with no hot water. Hotel rates vary with the seasons' and 'gringo prices' based on your appearance and command of Spanish are not uncommon. Many hotels have a few cheap and very basic rooms set aside from their standards, so if your budget is tight it is always worth enquiring. *Hospedajes* are guesthouses, usually quite basic and family-run. They may or may not have sunlight, television or running hot water. *Empujes* are 'love motels', usually found on highways and designed with discretion in mind. Although comfortable, their rates tend to be hourly.

Hostels
More and more hostels are springing up in Panama, most of them in Panama City, David, Boquete and Bocas Town. They remain a cheap and sociable option for international backpackers, and useful for those who want to get together groups for tours. Every hostel has a different character, but most offer a reliable range of amenities including free coffee, lockers, Wi-Fi, tourist information and tours. Private rooms in hostels are not always a good deal compared to hotels, but dorm accommodation, around US$10-15 a night, is the best bet for solo travellers on a budget.

Nature lodges
Panama's nature lodges are famed for their romantic settings and access to areas of outstanding natural beauty, including rainforests, cloud forests, mountains and beaches. They are among the world's best places for wildlife observation, especially for birds. Although nature lodges are comparatively expensive – most fall in the $$$ and $$$$ range – they promise a unique and intimate experience of the wilderness that is sure to leave lasting impressions. Everyone should consider splashing out at least once.

Resorts
All-inclusive resorts are concentrated on the Pacific coast between Farallón and Punta Chame. They're a good option for families or hard-working professionals who like to be pampered. Most resorts have beach access, as well as pools, restaurants and a small army of staff to cater to your needs. Although convenient and reassuring, a resort will also minimize your experience of the real world outside.

Homestays
Homestays are a great way to learn about local culture, but they aren't for everyone. Options tend to be rural and situated in remote indigenous comarcas. Expect very rustic conditions, including an outdoor toilet, little or no electricity, and cold running water (or just a bucket and wash bowl). If a Peace Corps volunteer is working in the village, they should be able to hook you up with a host. Otherwise ask at the nearest store or eating establishment. Simple meals are often included in the rates.

Campsites
There are no official campsites in Panama but camping is generally tolerated. In some national parks, simple rangers' station offer rustic lodging in cots. Bring your own food and water and some warm bedding – the rainforest can get quite chilly in the early hours.

Price codes

Where to stay

$$$$ over US$150 $$$ US$66-150
$$ US$30-65 $ under US$30
Unless otherwise stated, prices are for two people sharing a room in the high season, including taxes and service charges.

Restaurants

$$$ over US$12 $$ US$6-12 $ under US$6
Prices refer to the cost of a meal for one person with a drink, not including service charge.

Food and drink in Panama

Food

Panamanian cuisine echoes the unfussy style of its Central American neighbours – it's generally comforting, filling and rich in carbohydrates. A typical main dish consists of beef, chicken, pork or fish, that's either *asado* (baked), *frito* (fried), *a la parrilla* (grilled) or *guisado* (braised). Rice is the standard side dish, usually accompanied by beans or lentils. Meat-lovers should look out for *bistec* (steak) or *chuleta* (pork chop). *Mondongo* is stewed tripe, less spicy than Mexican versions. *Ropa vieja* (literally old clothes) consists of stewed and shredded beef served on rice. *Sancocho* is a tasty chicken and vegetable stew. Panama is blessed with miles of rambling shorelines and its kitchens are well stocked with a bounty of freshly caught fish, shrimp, octopus, crab and, in certain seasons, lobster. On the Caribbean coast, coconut plays a big role in local recipes and is used to flavour everything from tasty sauces to rejuvenating fish chowders. There are as many ceviche recipes as there are chefs, but most are based on raw *corvina* (sea bass) or shellfish seasoned with spicy peppers, onion and lemon juice – tasty, with a sharp kick. Maize is a very ancient and endlessly versatile local staple and the principal ingredient in numerous dishes. Panamanian tortillas are not the flatbread variety common to Mexico, but crispy deep-fried cornmeal cakes, usually served at breakfast. *Almojabonos* are similar, except fashioned into rolls. *Hojaldres*, also a breakfast accompaniment, are pieces of deep-fried corn bread. *Empanadas* are fried corn patties filled with minced meat – great for a snack or lunch on the go. *Tamales* consist of cornmeal mixed with spiced meat or chicken, wrapped in a plantain leaf and boiled. All kinds of delicious fruits grow in Panama, but *plátano* (plantain) is one of the most important. When cut into slices, dipped in batter and deep-fried, it becomes *patacones* – a popular alternative to *papas* (chips). *Tajadas* are thin, lengthways slices fried like crisps, great for a quick snack. *Plátano en tentación* is simply caramelized plantain in sugar and cinnamon. *Maduro*, the slightly larger, tougher cousin of plantain, is also popular and can be served grilled or sautéed in oil. Numerous root vegetables form part of the traditional Panamanian diet, including *yuca* (cassava) , with a similar taste and consistency to potato. It is often cut into chips and fried or, better still, fashioned into *caramiñolas* – delicious rolls with a minced meat filling.

Drink

A mouthwatering array of delicious fresh fruits – including mango, *naranja* (orange), *guayaba* (guava), papaya, *piña* (pineapple), *melón*, *maracuyá* (passion fruit) and *sandía* (watermelon) – are the basis for numerous traditional beverages. *Chicha dulce* is simply fruit juice blended with water or milk. *Chicha fuerte* is an alcoholic variation usually containing fermented corn or rice, popular in the countryside but rarely very strong. *Chicheme* is a non-alcoholic drink made from blended sweetcorn, cinnamon, vanilla and milk or water. A *licuado* (shake) is similar to *chicha dulce*, but thicker and often sweetened with sugar. Carbonated soft drinks are called *sodas* and always cheaper in glass bottles. Coffee is excellent in Panama, with numerous award-winning beans grown in the highlands. There are a few national *cervezas* (beers) worth trying, all light-bodied lagers, including **Atlas**, **Panamá** and **Balboa**. Local rum, namely **Carta Vieja**, is not too bad. *Seco* is distilled sugar cane that's quite popular in rural areas where it's taken *con leche* (with milk). It's a feisty tipple and not to be underestimated – look for **Herrerano**, the cherished national brand.

Restaurants in Panama

Excellent international fare is available in the capital, but tastes become simpler as you head into the interior. For breakfast, *panaderías* (bakeries) offer a selection of cheap baked goods, sweet or savoury, best washed down with a sugary black coffee or fruit juice. For lunch, budget travellers should head to *cafeterías*, where they can fill up on cheap buffet food or order a set meal known as a *comida corriente* (or *casado*), which usually consists of a meat, chicken or fish main served with rice, beans and plantain, and a drink. Dinner tends to be à la carte in a sit-down restaurant and the most expensive meal of the day. Reservations are unnecessary, except at the most upscale Panama City joints.

Entertainment in Panama

Panama City is the epicentre of the country's nightlife, with scores of venues catering to all music tastes, from techno and salsa to reggae and rock. Most dance clubs are showy affairs where you'll need good shoes and impeccable decorum to get in. Bars run the gamut from grungy to *ye-ye* (yuppie) (see Panama City, page 67). Outside the capital, options for drinking and dancing are far more limited. There is a youthful party scene in Bocas Town and neighbouring Isla Caranero, but it's dominated by foreign tourists and expats. All towns and villages have some form of dingy *cantina*, but outsiders – and women, unless they're prostitutes – are not necessarily welcome. *Discotecas*, complete with frenetic strobe lights and gallons of dry ice, are fairly widespread and these can be cheesy, seedy or quite fun depending on their location and clientele. Expat bars of varying repute can be found in Boquete, Panama City and Bocas Town. Sadly, Panama's arts scene is not as developed as it could be and most cultural entertainment is confined to the capital, where plays and concerts are regularly performed at a number of venues. Cinemas in David and Panama City tend to feature the latest Hollywood releases.

Festivals in Panama

Panama is a very festive place and it boasts a vibrant calendar filled with diverse musical rhythms, dances, costumes and widespread revelry. Blending Spanish, African and indigenous roots, celebrations run the gamut from solemn religious processions to decadent village fiestas. A handful of solid parties are celebrated nationwide, but many of the country's most interesting events are strictly local affairs. The Azuero Peninsula is a special hotbed of activity where you might witness traditions reminiscent of medieval Spain. By contrast, the festival life of the Caribbean is distinctly African-flavoured and filled with driving drum beats. If you're stuck for a party, remember that every town and village in Panama has its own patron saint's day – something is always being celebrated somewhere. Consult individual chapters for listings.

February/March
Carnaval Commencing 4 days before Shrove Tuesday, few festivals are as staunchly celebrated as Panama's 5-day Carnaval. Even hardened party animals will find it a challenge keeping up. Marked by widespread inebriation and raucous over-indulgence, the festivities include numerous resplendent parades, fights with water cannons, beauty contests, music, singing and dancing. Carnaval is at its most debauched in the city of Las Tablas, which sees thousands of festival-goers every year. Many report wild, beautiful and overwhelming experiences.

March/April
Semana Santa Running from Palm Sunday to Easter Sunday, Semana Santa (Holy Week) is the most important festival in the Catholic calendar. Traditional celebrations tend be strongest in Panama's interior, particularly in the Azuero Peninsula, where festivities include a theatrical re-enactment of Christ's Passion, numerous religious processions, church services and the presentation of exuberant floral displays. Many Panamanians, of course, use the occasion to get away to the beaches.

May/June
Corpus Christi Few celebrations are as colourful and intriguing as the Azuero Peninsula's interpretation of Corpus Christi, attended with vigour 40 days after Easter. The festivities, which are rich in colonial undertones, celebrate the founding of the Eucharist with untold pageantry and theatrical performances. The action focuses on the city of Villa de Santos, where

'dirty devil' dance troops descend with wonderfully gruesome masks and costumes.

October
Festival of the Black Christ Portobelo's 'miraculous' Black Christ is honoured every year on 21 Oct, when tens of thousands of pilgrims arrive to pay their respects. Many attendees will walk over 100 km across the isthmus from Panama City, some covering the final stretch on their hands and knees. The normally sleepy Caribbean village throngs with religious fervour throughout the day, reaching an emotional climax towards dusk, when 'El Nazareno' is brought out in procession.

Public holidays

Banks, government offices and businesses are often closed on public holidays (*días feriados*), with the sale of alcohol prohibited for up to 24 hrs. You should avoid travelling on major holidays such as Christmas, Easter and New Year, when buses are oversubscribed or infrequent.
1 Jan New Year's Day
9 Jan Martyr's Day
Mar/Apr Good Friday, Easter
1 May Labour Day
12 Oct Hispanic Day
1 Nov National Anthem Day
2 Nov All Souls' Day
3 Nov Independence Day (from Colombia)
4 Nov Flag Day
5 Nov Colón Day
10 Nov First call for Independence
28 Nov Independence Day (from Spain)
8 Dec Mother's Day
25 Dec Christmas

Shopping in Panama

What to buy

Panama's indigenous peoples produce a diverse range of unique and highly collectible *artesanías*. *Molas* are embroidered multi-layered cloth panels traditionally worn by Guna women. They feature colourful cultural motifs – including parrots, turtles, dolphins and other exotic creatures – as well as more traditional geometric designs. Prices start at US$10, but *molas* of quality cost US$20-100 (see box, page 129). The Emberá and Wounaan of central and eastern Panama are known for their extremely attractive, high-quality woven baskets. A great deal of work goes into them and they can fetch top dollar on the international market. The baskets are handwoven from *chunga* palm and *nahuala* bush leaves and prices start at around US$20. The Emberá and Wounaan also produce carved cocobolo wood statues and small figurines fashioned from tagua nuts. From western Panama, Ngäbe-Buglé *artesanías* include very sturdy, practical bags called *chakras* and bead necklaces called *chakiras*. *Huacas* are a type of pre-Colombian gold jewellery featuring shamans, power animals and other ancient magical emblems. They are no longer produced by Panama's indigenous people, but some innovative jewellers in Panama City have revived their art. The campesino artisans of Panama's interior are also highly celebrated for their crafts, especially in the Azuero Peninsula, where the country's finest mask-makers produce ferocious-looking and brilliantly coloured devil masks. The Azuero is also the fabled home of the *pollera* – Panama's highly ornate national dress – which features numerous embroidered skirts, all sewn by hand over several months. Prices begin at US$150, but unsurprisingly, the very best can fetch thousands of dollars. *Sombreros pintados* are traditional straw hats and are still widely worn by many *interioranos*. They are produced in the province of Coclé and widely available on roadside stalls. So-called 'Panama hats' are available in Panama City, but they in fact originated in Ecuador – the tighter the weave, the better the quality. Excellent cigars, produced in Coclé by **Joyas de Panamá**, can be picked up in the capital too. Some of the world's best coffee is grown in the Chiriquí highlands.

Tips

The most rewarding and economical way to buy *artesanías* is directly from their makers. You will avoid costly mark-ups and know that every cent you spend goes directly to the communities who need it. Additionally, the artist will be able to answer questions about the manufacture and design of your chosen purchase. Of course, it is not always practical to visit the communities where *artesanías* are made. The next best places are craft markets and street stalls in Panama City (see Shopping, page 71); in most cases, you will still be buying directly from indigenous artists or from their relatives. Souvenir shops are widespread throughout the capital and while their selection is often broad, prices are marked up. The wares in the boutique shops in San Felipe often represent very high quality but they are also marketed to cruise-ship passengers straight off the boat.

Responsible travel in Panama

Tourism is booming in Panama. In recent years, growth in the hospitalities industry has forged thousands of new jobs and funnelled millions of dollars into the economy. Nonetheless, Panama's burgeoning tourist scene has not always worked to the benefit of local communities – or the natural environment. Fortunately, there are some very dedicated environmentalists working in tourism and lobbying the government for greater awareness and change. As a visitor, you can make a significant difference at this critical stage in the country's development. To learn more about sustainable tourism in Panama, visit the Asociación Panameña de Turismo Sostenible, www.aptso.org.

10 ways to be a responsible traveller

There are some aspects of travel that you have to accept are going to have an impact, but try to balance the negatives with positives by following these guidelines to responsible travel.

· **Cut your emissions** Plan an itinerary that minimizes carbon emissions whenever possible. This might involve travelling by train, hiring a bike or booking a walking or canoeing tour rather than one that relies on vehicle transport. See opposite page for details of carbon offset programmes. Visit www.seat61.com for worldwide train travel.

· **Check the small print** Choose travel operators that abide by a responsible travel policy (if they have one it will usually be posted on their website). Visit www.responsibletravel.com.

· **Keep it local** If travelling independently, try to use public transport, stay in locally owned accommodation, eat in local restaurants, buy local produce and hire local guides.

· **Cut out waste** Take biodegradable soap and shampoo and leave excess packaging, particularly plastics, at home. The countries you are visiting may not have the waste collection or recycling facilities to deal with it.

· **Get in touch** Find out if there are any local schools, charities or voluntary conservation organizations that you could include in your itinerary. If appropriate, take along some useful gifts or supplies; www.stuffyourrucksack.com has a list of projects that could benefit from your support.

· **Learn the lingo** Practise some local words, even if it's just to say 'hello', 'thank you' and 'goodbye'. Respect local customs and dress codes and always ask permission before photographing people – including your wildlife tour guide. Once you get home, remember to honour any promises you've made to send photographs.

· **Avoid the crowds** Consider travelling out of season to relieve pressure on popular destinations, or visit a lesser-known alternative.

· **Take only photos** Resist the temptation to buy souvenirs made from animals or plants. Not only is it illegal to import or export many wildlife souvenirs, but their uncontrolled collection supports poaching and can have a devastating impact on local populations, upsetting the natural balance of entire ecosystems.
  CITES, the Convention on International Trade in Endangered Species (www.cites.org) bans international trade in around 900 animal and plant species, and controls trade in a further 33,000 species.

Several organizations, including WWF, TRAFFIC and the Smithsonian Institution have formed the Coalition Against Wildlife Trafficking (www.cawtglobal.org).

• **Use water wisely** Water is a precious commodity in many countries. Treating your own water avoids the need to buy bottled water which can contribute to the build-up of litter.

• **Don't interfere** Avoid disturbing wildlife, damaging habitats or interfering with natural behaviour by feeding wild animals, getting too close or being too noisy. Leave plants and shells where you find them.

Code green for hikers
• Take biodegradable soap, shampoo and toilet paper, long-lasting lithium batteries and plastic bags for packing out all rubbish.
• Use a water filter instead of buying bottled water and save fuel at remote lodges by ordering the same food at the same time. Only take a hot shower if the water has been heated by solar power.
• If no toilet facilities are available, make sure you are at least 30 m from any water source.
• Keep to trails to avoid erosion and trampling vegetation. Don't take short cuts, especially at high altitude where plants may take years to recover.

Code green for divers and snorkellers
• Help conserve underwater environments by joining local clean-ups or collecting data for Project AWARE (www.projectaware.org).
• Choose resorts that properly treat sewage and wastewater and support marine protected areas.
• Choose operators that use mooring buoys or drift diving techniques, rather

than anchors, which can damage fragile marine habitats such as coral reefs.
• Never touch coral. Practise buoyancy-control skills in a pool or sandy area before diving around coral reefs, and tuck away trailing equipment.
• Avoid handling, feeding or riding on marine life.
• Never purchase marine souvenirs.
• Don't order seafood caught using destructive or unsustainable practices such as dynamite fishing.

How should I offset my carbon emissions?
Carbon offsetting schemes allow you to offset greenhouse gas emissions by donating to various projects, from tree planting to renewable energy schemes. Although some conservation groups are concerned that carbon offsetting is being used as a smoke-screen to delay the urgent action needed to cut emissions and develop alternative energy solutions, it remains an important way of counterbalancing your carbon footprint.

For every tonne of CO_2 you generate through a fossil fuel-burning activity, such as flying, you pay for an equivalent tonne to be removed elsewhere through a 'green' initiative. There are numerous online carbon footprint calculators (such as www.carbonfootprint.com). Alternatively, book with a travel operator that supports a carbon offset provider like TICOS (www.ticos.co.uk) or Reduce my Footprint (www.reducemyfootprint.travel).

It's not all about tree-planting schemes. Support now goes to a far wider range of climate-friendly technology projects, ranging from the provision of energy-efficient light bulbs and cookers in the developing world to large-scale renewable energy schemes such as wind farms.

Essentials A-Z

Accident and emergency

Ambulance: 911
Fire: 103
Police: 104
Directory assistance: 102

Children

It's all about the family in Panama and travellers with young children are likely to be warmly welcomed wherever they go. Only a handful of foreign-owned establishments enforce a restrictive 'no children' policy. Meanwhile, Panama's comparatively well-developed infrastructure tends to facilitate family travel quite well, although those with youngsters under the age of 7 may find the safety, convenience and on-hand amenities of an established resort their best option. The **Gamboa Rainforest Resort** (see page 97) is geared towards families and, although it does not offer beach access, it is perched on the edge of the rainforest. The challenges of Panama's more remote destinations – including the Darién and Kuna Yala – are not recommended for children. Elsewhere, parents should prepare for harsh sun, mosquitoes and the possibility of upset stomachs. Due to the risk of diseases and vaccinations, travelling with very young infants is not recommended. Most supermarkets and pharmacies in the capital are well stocked with baby supplies. If hiring a car, ensure it is fitted with a safety seat. All high-end and most mid-range hotels should be able to arrange babysitters.

Customs and duty free

Panama permits duty free imports of up to 500 cigarettes or 50 cigars or 500 g of tobacco; 3 bottles of alcoholic beverage; 3 bottles of perfume or eau de cologne.

Do not import any fruit, vegetable or meat products. Please do not try to export exotic pets or archaeological objects.

Disabled travellers

Panamanians are helpful by nature and happy to assist whenever they can, but unfortunately facilities for disabled travellers are severely lacking in Panama, especially in rural areas. Pavements in towns and cities are often in poor repair, and while it is now mandatory for all public buildings to be fitted with wheelchair ramps, in practice this requirement is not always met. The best available facilities will be found in major resorts and upscale hotels, but you should make thorough enquiries to check on the details. For example, disabled parking spaces and wheelchair ramps are reasonably common, but handrails are not. If you require assistance at the airport – including help with luggage, check-in, transport, embarking and disembarking – notify your airline at least 48 hrs in advance. For inspiration, try reading *Nothing Ventured*, edited by Alison Walsh (HarperCollins), which gives personal accounts of worldwide journeys for disabled travellers, plus listings and advice.

Useful websites

Access-Able, www.access-able.com. A comprehensive disabled travel resource with listings, links, resources, tips, advice and feature articles.
Disabled Travelers, www.disabledtravelers. com. A broad-reaching resource that includes listings of specialized travel agents and tour operators.
Instituto Panameño de Habitalición Especial, www.iphe.gob.pa. The IPHE is a government body dedicated to advancing rights and facilities for the disabled in Panama. Spanish only.

Drugs and the law

Drugs Depending on your appearance, you may be offered drugs in Bocas del Toro or Panama City, but their use is heavily outlawed and you will face severe penalties if caught in possession. In the event that you're arrested for anything, call your embassy immediately. They may or may not be sympathetic to your plight, but they should be able to recommend a good local lawyer.

Smoking Since 2008, Law 13 has effectively outlawed smoking in most public spaces, including hotels, restaurants and any outdoor area where people are congregated. The cost of cigarettes is around US$4 per pack.

Electricity

120V or 220V AC in the capital; 110V AC, 60 Hz everywhere else. Plugs are US-style. If you require converters for your chargers, bring them from your home country (especially UK adapters). Note electricity supply may be non-existent or limited to evenings in very remote areas.

Embassies and consulates

A comprehensive directory of Panamanian embassies and consulates abroad can be found at **Panama Tramita**, www.panama tramita.gob.pa. In Panama, foreign embassies and consulates are concentrated in Panama City. For a complete list, see www.embassypages.com/panama.php or embassy.goabroad.com.

Gay and lesbian travellers

Panama is generally tolerant of homosexuality but, as in most Latin American countries, attitudes in the countryside tend to be conservative. Nonetheless, times are changing and the macho cowboy town of Antón recently surprised the nation by hosting a well-attended gay parade. Panama City, meanwhile, is home to a thriving and quite open gay community, which hosts a colourful Gay Pride Festival every year. A highlight of the event is the presentation of the Great Pink Egg Award to the country's most homophobic person or institution. Gay bars, clubs and saunas are relatively easy to find in the capital, but are usually underground and tricky to locate elsewhere. Interestingly, the indigenous Guna are quite tolerant of homosexuality and their beautiful offshore islands are often a popular stop on gay cruises. Panama's main gay and lesbian organization is the **Asociación Hombres y Mujeres Nuevos de Panamá**, ahmnp@yahoo.com.

Useful websites
Ciudad Pride, www.ciudadpride.com. A well-developed Spanish-language site featuring regularly updated news and reviews for Panama's gay and lesbian community.
Farra Urbana, www.farraurbana.com. A guide to gay Panama featuring listings of bars, clubs and upcoming events. Spanish only.
International Gay and Lesbian Travel Association, www.iglta.org. The leading organization in the worldwide gay and lesbian tourism industry.

Health

Before you go
See your doctor or travel clinic at least 6 weeks before your departure for general advice on travel risks, **malaria precautions** and **vaccinations**. Make sure you have travel insurance, get a dental check (especially if you are going to be away for more than a month), know your own blood group and, if you suffer from a long-term condition such as diabetes or epilepsy, make sure someone knows or that you have a **Medic Alert** bracelet/necklace with this information on it, preferably in Spanish and English (www.medicalert.org.uk).

Vaccinations

There are no required vaccinations for Panama, but medical professionals often recommend jabs for tetanus-diphtheria, hepatitis A and typhoid. If you're planning on visiting Darién or Kuna Yala, yellow fever is also recommended – you will need a vaccination certificate if you are coming from or going to an infected area. Hepatitis B vaccine is recommended for some long-term travellers and those working with animals should be protected against rabies.

A-Z of health risks
Bites and stings

To prevent mosquito bites wear clothes that cover the arms and legs, use effective insect repellent and a mosquito net treated with insecticide. Repellents containing 30-50% DEET (Di-ethyltoluamide) are recommended when visiting particularly infested areas (eg wetlands or rainforest). If you are a popular target for insect bites, use antihistamine tablets and apply a cream such as hydrocortisone. If you are unlucky (or careless) enough to be bitten by a venomous snake, spider, scorpion or sea creature, try to identify the culprit, without putting yourself in further danger (ie do not try to catch a live snake). Scorpions are relatively common in rural areas, so avoid leaving piles of laundry on the floor and check your shoes before putting them on. Ticks can carry diseases but are usually just a painless annoyance – use tweezers to carefully remove them and never twist. Snake bites can be particularly frightening, but are in fact rarely poisonous. Victims should be taken to a hospital or a doctor without delay.

Dengue fever

Dengue fever, also known as 'break-bone fever', is a viral disease spread by mosquitoes that tend to bite in urban areas during the day. The symptoms are fever and intense joint pain and some people also develop a rash. Symptoms last about a week but it can take a month to recover fully. Dengue can be difficult to distinguish from malaria so it is important to get your blood tested as soon as possible. There are no effective vaccines or antiviral drugs. Rest, plenty of fluids and paracetamol (never aspirin, which can cause fatal complications in some strains) are the recommended treatment.

Diarrhoea

It is not uncommon to contract a short but unpleasant bout of diarrhoea while your body adjusts to changes in diet, climate and temperature. Bacterial diarrhoea is different and usually transmitted through contaminated food and drinking water. Be wary of salads, reheated foods or food that has been left out in the sun having been cooked earlier in the day. Avoid all unpasteurized dairy products. Adults can use medication such as loperamide to control the symptoms of diarrhoea, but only for up to 24 hrs. Keep well hydrated and eat bland foods only. Oral rehydration sachets are useful. If your diarrhoea persists for more than 5 days – or is accompanied by blood, fever and/or vomiting – seek medical attention immediately. Travellers to rural areas sometimes contract parasites, which can cause medical complications if left untreated. Amoebas are the usual culprits and if you suspect an infection, go straight to your nearest lab for stool tests. Note that it can take 5 consecutive days of testing to get a positive result.

Hepatitis

Hepatitis means inflammation of the liver. The most obvious symptom is a yellowing of your skin or the whites of your eyes. However, prior to this all that you may notice is itching and tiredness. There are vaccines for hepatitis A and B (the latter is spread through blood and unprotected sexual intercourse, both of which can be avoided).

Malaria

The key advice is to guard against contracting malaria by taking the correct antimalarials and finishing the recommended course. There are currently around 800 confirmed cases of malaria in Panama each year, although this figure jumped to 5000 in 2005. Transmission rates are highest in the Darién and all areas east of Panama City. Malaria can cause death within 24 hrs and can start as something resembling an attack of flu. You may feel tired, lethargic, headachy or feverish; or, more seriously, you may develop fits, followed by coma and then death. Have a low index of suspicion because it is very easy to write off vague symptoms, which may actually be malaria. If you have a temperature, visit a doctor as soon as you can and ask for a malaria test. On your return home, if you suffer any of these symptoms, have a test as soon as possible. Even if a previous test proved negative, this could save your life. Remember **ABCD: Awareness** (of whether the disease is present in the area you are travelling in), **Bite avoidance**, **Chemoprophylaxis**, **Diagnosis**.

Rabies

Rabies is quite rare in Panama and vampire bats, common to the Darién, are the main carriers. Rabies vaccination before travel can be considered for those intending to visit areas more than a day's journey from hospital facilities. If bitten always seek urgent medical attention – whether or not you have been previously vaccinated – after first cleaning the wound and treating with an iodine-based disinfectant or alcohol. Avoid handling wild or feral animals.

Sun

The sun is extremely fierce in Panama and over-exposure can quickly lead to sunburn and, in the longer term, skin cancers and premature skin aging. The best advice is simply to cover exposed skin, wear a hat and stay in the shade if possible, particularly between late morning and early afternoon. Apply a high-factor sunscreen (greater than SPF15) and be sure it screens against UVB. A further danger in tropical climates is heat exhaustion or, more seriously, heatstroke. These can be avoided with good hydration, which means drinking water past the point of simply quenching thirst. If you cannot avoid heavy exercise it is also a good idea to increase salt intake. Note that cloud coverage does not mitigate the dangers posed by ultraviolet light – continue covering up and using sun block even if the weather is overcast.

Water

Panama boasts one of the cleanest water systems in Central America and tap water is safe to drink in most populated places, including Panama City. Exceptions are the remote provinces of Darién, Guna Yala and Bocas del Toro. If you intend to get off the beaten track, bottled water may not be available and you should certainly purify whatever else is available. Dirty water must first be strained through a filter bag or coffee filter and then boiled or treated. When boiling, bring the water to a rolling boil for several minutes. Chemical sterilizers usually contain chlorine or iodine compounds. Their unpleasant taste can often be neutralized with additional products. In an emergency situation, add 3-5 drops of bleach to a litre of water and let it stand for 30-60 mins.

Other diseases

There is a range of other insect-borne diseases that are quite rare, but worth researching if going to particularly remote destinations, including the Darién. These include sleeping sickness, river blindness and leishmaniasis. Fresh water can also be a source of diseases such as bilharzia and leptospirosis and it is worth investigating whether these are a danger before bathing in lakes and streams. Remember that unprotected sex always carries multiple risks.

Useful websites

The National Travel Health Network and Centre (NaTHNaC) www.nathnac.org. **World Health Organisation**, www.who.int.

Insurance

Insurance is highly recommended for all travellers. It's best to buy this before you leave as few companies will insure you once you are travelling. Shop around and check some online reviews before settling on a provider. If you have financial restraints, the most important aspect of any policy is medical care and repatriation. Conveniently, at the time of research, everyone entering Panama via Tocumen Airport was entitled to free non-renewable medical insurance for up to 30 days; pick up a brochure and user card at the tourist information desk in the immigration section. Ideally you will want to be covered for personal items too. Most policies have strict limits regarding the total value of lost or stolen items – as well as an excess – so if you are carrying digital cameras, laptops or other expensive equipment you may have to insure these separately. Adventure activities such as trekking, diving and whitewater rafting usually add cost to a policy. Before you leave, read all the small print and take digital photos of your valuables and their receipts, including serial numbers. Store all these images in a secure online facility (eg Dropbox) along with electronic copies of your passport and insurance policy. If you need to make a claim, call your provider immediately to determine which documents (eg medical or police reports) they will require. Keep hard and digital copies of everything and always have the number of your insurance provider to hand in case of an emergency.

Internet

Internet shops, known as *cibers*, are widespread in all but the most remote places – expect to pay around US$1 per hr for surf time. In large towns and cities connections are usually fast enough for Skype or video streaming, but access can be painfully slow in rural areas. Many cibers offer printing, scanning and CD burning. An increasing number of hotels and hostels also offer Wi-Fi, and travelling with a laptop can make a lot of sense.

Language

→ *For a list of useful words and phrases in Spanish, see page 308.*

Spanish is the official language of Panama and there is a wide range of regional dialects. English is spoken by many people in the capital thanks to historical ties with North America. Beautifully honeyed Creole English is spoken in the Afro-Antillean communities of the Caribbean coast, including a unique Bocas del Toro dialect called Guari-Guari, which blends Spanish, English and indigenous elements. Several complex and interesting languages are spoken by Panama's indigenous people, including Ngabere (Ngobe), Buglere (Buglé, Bokota), Teribe (Naso), Bribri, 2 variants of Kuna, 3 variants of Emberá and Woun Meu (Wounaan). Panama's staunch multiculturalism means numerous other languages are spoken across the country, including Chinese Yue and Hakka.

Local customs

Clothing
Panamanians like to look good and dress well, whatever their level of income. This is taken to an extreme in Panama City, where designer labels are de rigueur. Generally, however, a moderately well-groomed appearance will suffice. Scruffy, tattered or unwashed travellers may elicit looks of disdain or pity, especially in the conservative countryside. Note that the only place men are permitted to strip off their tops is on the beach – try it elsewhere and the police may stop you. Topless bathing for women is prohibited everywhere. Always dress respectfully when entering rural churches or attending Mass.

Photography
Always ask permission before taking photographs, especially in indigenous communities.

Media

Newspapers

Panama has 5 daily newspapers, all heavily politicized and printed in Panama City. One of the best is *La Prensa*, www.prensa. com, founded in 1980 as a voice of dissent against the guardia dictatorship. Despite several violent attempts to shut it down, it has survived its enemies and remains one of the country's most authoritative news sources. Also popular, *El Panamá América*, www.panamaamerica.com.pa, is a right-leaning publication with serious features and analysis. *El Siglo*, www.elsiglo. com, was founded in 1985 and boasts the largest circulation in the country. *La Estrella*, www.laestrella.com.pa, was founded in 1849 and is the oldest daily in Panama. *La Crítica*, www.critica.com.pa, is a sensationalist and well-read tabloid with violent crime stories and smutty pictures. There are a handful of newspapers distributed in Panama City only, including *Día a Día* and *Mi Diario*.

Radio and TV

There are scores of radio stations on the FM and MW dials, running the gamut from news to talk shows to non-stop reggaeton. Since the advent of cable technology, television has become equally pluralistic, although **Televisora Nacional Panamá (TVN)** retains its role as the country's only state-run broadcaster. Most cable selections include a range of English and Spanish entertainment, as well as news programmes from **CNN** and the **BBC**.

Blogs and websites

Panama's online community is very bitterly divided. In the past, feuds between bloggers have erupted into public scandals involving lawsuits, high-speed car chases and a disturbing incident concerning a stun gun. Nonetheless, a handful of very useful websites continue to provide insightful and thought-provoking discourse on Panamanian news and issues.

Panama News, www.thepanamanews. com. Eric Jackson has been writing about current affairs in Panama for decades. His site features in-depth and critical analyses of all the latest happenings. Highly recommended. **Bananama Republic**, www.bananama republic.com. Biting satire from Dutch journalist Okke Ornstein, who previously ran the **Noriegaville News**. Close to the bone, unapologetic and very funny.

Money

Currency

The unit of currency in Panama is the **balboa** and it is pegged directly to the US dollar. The country does not issue paper money; US bank notes are used instead. One balboa is made up of 100 **centavos** or **centésimos** and Panamanian coins come in denominations of 1, 5, 10, 25 (*'cinco reales'*) and 50 (*'peso'*) centavos. They are practically identical to US coins (which are also standard tender). Since 2011, a new 1 balboa coin has also entered circulation. Owing to counterfeiting, US$50 and US$100 dollar notes are not widely accepted – you will need to sign a register and present identification if you want to spend them. Carry cash in denominations of US$20 or less if possible.

Exchange

The **Banco Nacional de Panamá** in Tocumen Airport is reportedly the only bank prepared to exchange foreign currency. Elsewhere, you will have to rely on *casas de cambio*, which can only be found in the capital. *Casas de cambio* generally accept euros and UK pounds, but it is recommended that you do not bring foreign currency at all; if possible, buy all US dollars before you leave home.

Debit and credit cards

Debit and credit cards can be used to make cash withdrawals from ATMs and ideally you should carry at least one of each. However, do not rely on making payments solely with credit cards. **Visa** and **MasterCard** are widely accepted in resorts and high-end establishments in Panama City, but beyond these places it's strictly cash only. Before leaving home, ensure you have all the necessary contact numbers to report any lost or stolen cards.

ATMs

ATMs are widespread throughout Panama's towns and cities. Most of them accept debit and credit cards on all the major networks including **Plus**, **Cirrus**, **MasterCard**, **Visa** and **American Express** – look for the red '**Sistema Clave**' sign. In addition to any fees levied by your own bank, expect a charge of US$3 for each withdrawal you make. Daily limits are US$200-500. Because of high levels of money laundering in Panama, it is not unusual for some foreign banks to put a temporary freeze on ATM withdrawals (usually fixed with a phone call to the bank). ATMs are rare to non-existent in most remote areas. Consult individual chapters and plan ahead if you intend to get off the beaten track.

Traveller's cheques

Traveller's cheques (TCs) provide peace of mind against theft but are not accepted by most Panamanian businesses. It's wise to keep a small reserve/emergency fund in TCs, but don't rely on them exclusively as only a few banks will change them. Keep the original purchase slip in a separate place to the TCs and make a photocopy/digital copy of it for security. You will need a passport and record of purchase to exchange your cheques for cash and you will be charged a commission of 1-2.5%. **American Express** dollar TCs are recommended as the most widely accepted type.

Cost of travelling and living

Tourism is booming in Panama and hotel rates have risen sharply in response. Good-value accommodation is increasingly hard to find in Panama City, El Valle, Boquete and Bocas Town, where the cost of a simple hotel room for 2 people starts at US$35. In the lesser-visited interior, you can still find a good bargain. Food remains reasonable value, if more expensive in the capital. A simple sit-down meal in a local café costs around US$3-5. More sophisticated international fare is available for around US$10-15 per meal, inclusive of drinks and tip. Thankfully, beer remains cheap at US$1-2 per bottle. Transportation is more costly than in most other Central American countries, but also more comfortable. Prices vary with routes, but expect to pay around US$2 for every hour of travel. A sensible daily budget – including 3 meals a day, the occasional tour, overland transport and accommodation – would be US$60-100 per person. Very thrifty backpackers who stay in hostels and don't mind slinging a hammock might scrape by on US$30 per day. The long-term cost of living in Panama has also risen in recent years. Most expats report monthly expenditure of at least US$600, but often double or more in the capital.

Opening hours

Banks Mon-Fri 0830-1500, some open Sat 0900-1200.
Businesses Mon-Fri 0800-1200, 1330-1700.
Convenience/grocery stores 0730-2000, some supermarkets open 24 hrs.
Government offices and post offices Mon-Fri 0800-1600.
Restaurants Breakfast 0700-1000, lunch 1200-1500, dinner 1800-2200. Many close on Sun.

Post

Panama's national postal service is the **Correos y Telégrafos de Panamá (COTEL)**, www.correospanama.gob.pa. It operates post offices in all major towns. COTEL is not recommended for sending or receiving valuable items – use a company like Mail Boxes Etc instead and make sure your items are insured against loss. Couriers like **UPS** can be found in Panama City and David, but they are comparatively expensive. If sending a package through COTEL, do not seal it until a customs form has been completed and stamped. Airmail to Europe takes around 2 weeks to arrive; to the US about 1 week. Stamps are available only in post offices and there are no post boxes on the street. Mail is not delivered door to door in Panama but held in collection boxes. You can receive mail at any Panamanian post office. They will hold it for 30 days and you must present a passport on collection. The sender should clearly address the mail 'República de Panamá' and access the COTEL website to locate the *Código* (code) and *Nombre de Estafeta* (branch name) – click on 'Punto de Servicio Estafetas' for a list. The full address format is as follows: Name of recipient; 'Entrega General'; Nombre de Estafeta + Código; Town + Province; 'República de Panamá'.

Safety

Most places in Panama are no more dangerous than any major city in Europe or North America and the people, if anything, are friendlier and more open. You should be quite safe in most provincial towns and places of interest. The major exceptions are a handful of sketchy and neglected neighbourhoods in Panama City, most areas of Colón, and the thickly forested no-man's land of the Darién Gap. Please see individual chapters for more details.

Theft and muggings
Where crime exists, it is mostly of the opportunistic kind. The following tips, endorsed by travellers, are meant to forewarn, not alarm. To guard against muggers and pickpockets, keep all documents secure and hide your cash and cards in different places under your clothes. Hidden pockets, money-belts, neck or leg pouches are a sensible idea. Pouches worn outside the clothes are not safe. Keep cameras in bags and don't wear fancy wrist-watches or jewellery, especially at night. In cities, carry your small day pack in front of

you, not on your back. It is best, if you can trust your hotel, to leave any valuables you don't need in a safe-deposit. Always keep an inventory. If you don't trust the hotel, lock everything in your pack and secure that in your room. If you do lose valuables, you will need to report the incident to the police for insurance purposes. Listen to your gut when walking around. If you find yourself in a bad neighbourhood, stay calm and act confident – appearing lost or scared will only attract unwanted attention. If walking on quiet streets after dark, walk in the road, not on the pavement. Maintain particular vigilance in market places, bus stations or any other crowded locale. Never resist a robbery, your assailants may well be armed.

Scams
Street scams are quite rare in Panama. A number of distraction techniques such as strangers' remarks like 'What's that on your shoulder?' are designed to distract you for a few critical moments in which time your bag may be grabbed. A few crooks are known to wander the streets of Panama City pretending to be tourists who have lost all their money. As ever, you should think carefully before handing over cash to someone you don't know. Professional con-artists are a breed apart and an entire book could be written about some of the dubious characters operating in Panama. If you are looking to make a serious financial investment in the country you should proceed cautiously and beware any opportunity that looks too good to be true – it almost certainly is.

Outdoor safety
Never underestimate the wilderness and always take thorough precautions before setting out. Whether hiking alone or in a group, it's best to inform your hotel or a park ranger of your intentions, ie where you are going and for how long. For most hikes, seek advice about the state of the trails, as heavy rains can leave paths obscured or

impassable. Unless you have wilderness training, you should always use a guide if ANAM (see page 33) recommends it. Pack plenty of water and, if you intend to camp, warm clothes. On the coast, swimmers should take particular care with rip tides, which, tragically, have drowned several travellers in recent years. If you find yourself pulled out to sea, swim sideways or at a 45° angle until you are free, then head back to shore. Never swim directly against a rip tide.

Senior travellers

Seniors are held in high regard in Panama and you can expect courteous treatment wherever you go – you may even find yourself ushered to the front of queues. Discounts on a wide range of attractions are available, so keep your ID handy. Panama's infrastructure is well developed by Central American standards and travel between the major sights is easy if you're savvy and know a smattering of Spanish. Seniors should take care with the health risks posed by extreme sun, heat and humidity, however. Many prefer the relatively cool, lush surroundings of highland destinations like El Valle, Boquete, Volcán and Cerro Punta, although Panama City does make a modern and convenient base. Growing numbers of seniors are choosing to retire in Panama. If you receive a pension of US$1000 or more and are looking to settle, you are entitled to apply for a *Pensionado Visa*, which delivers healthy benefits including discounts on transport, hotels, medical bills and more.

Student travellers

If you are in full-time education you are entitled to an **International Student Identity Card** (ISIC), which is distributed by student travel offices and travel agencies in over 100 countries. ISIC gives you special prices on all forms of transport and a variety of other concessions and services as well. Contact **International Student Travel Confederation**

(ISTC), Herengracht 479, 1017 BS Amsterdam, Netherlands, T+31-20-421 2800, www.isic. org. Student cards must carry a photograph if they are to be of any use in Panama. The ISIC website provides a list of card-issuing offices around the world and a searchable database of current discounts and offers.

Taxes

A 10% tax is added to hotel rooms and 7% to restaurant bills (sometimes with an additional and non-obligatory 10% service charge). A 7% sales tax is applicable to most goods and services, with the exception of food and medicine. You will be charged an exit tax of US$40 if you leave Panama by plane, although this is often included in the price of your ticket. Border crossings are subject to a US$1 *alcaldía* tax.

Tipping

A 10% service charge is often added to restaurant bills, especially in Panama City. Elsewhere, tipping is not expected, but in budget eateries a small gratuity of US$0.50-1 per person – handed directly to the server – is often appreciated. Bell boys and luggage handlers expect a tip of around US$1 per bag. Taxi drivers do not expect tips unless they've been particularly helpful or informative.

Telephone

Country code: T507; **International dialling code**: T00; **Directory enquiries**: T102; **International operator**: T106.

Cable & Wireless operate Panama's telephone system. Local numbers have 7 digits; mobile phone numbers have 8 digits and commence with '6'. There are no local area codes. Payphones are widespread in all populated areas and they accept 5c, 10c, 25c and 50c coins. Alternatively, buy a calling card at any convenience store or kiosk. Sometimes street vendors operate an impromptu phone service. Pre-pay mobile phones are reasonably cheap and start at US$20. Networks include **Movistar**, **Claro** and **+ Movil** (Cable & Wireless) and **Digicel** (recommended); bring your passport when purchasing. You can buy top-up credit at convenience stores and supermarkets from US$2. Internet cafés often double up as call shops and offer competitive rates on international calls, especially to the US. An alternative is calling through the internet on **Skype**, www.skype.com. You will need a headset or a USB phone to use the software – sometimes internet cafés have these, but not always. Bring them from home if possible.

Time

GMT -5 hrs.
Panama's close proximity to the equator means the length of days and nights are consistent throughout the year. The sun will typically rise around 0600 and set around 1800. Don't forget to change your watch if travelling to or from Costa Rica, which is 1 hr behind.

Toilets

Public toilets are few and far between – try the nearest bus station, market or fast-food joint, where you'll normally be charged 25c for the privilege of their use. In very rural areas, facilities are often limited to a wooden out-house. Never flush toilet paper or other objects as this will block the drain; use the little wastepaper basket instead.

Tour operators

For tour operators within Panama, please see individual chapters.

UK
Explore Worldwide, 55 Victoria Rd, Farnborough, Hampshire, GU14 7PA, T0844-499 0901, www.explore.co.uk.

Journey Latin America, 12-13 Heathfield Terrace, London, W4 4JE, T020-8747-8315, www.journeylatinamerica.co.uk.
Last Frontiers, The Mill, Quainton Rd, Waddesden, Buckinghamshire, HP18 0LP, T01296-653000, www.lastfrontiers.com.
Rainbow Tours, Layden House, 76-86 Turnmill St, London EC1M 5QN, T020-7666 1260, www.rainbowtours.co.uk.
Select Latin America, 3.51 Canterbury Court, 1-3 Brixton Rd, Kennington Park, London, SW9 6DE, T020-7407 1478, www.selectlatinamerica.com.
Tucan Travel, 316 Uxbridge Rd, London, W3 9QP, T020-8896 1600, www.tucantravel.com.

North America
Exito Travel, 108 Rutgers Av, Fort Collins, CO 80525, T800-655 4053, www.exitotravel.com.
G Adventures, 19 Charlotte St, Toronto, Ontario, M5V 2H5, T1-416-260-0999, www.gadventures.com.
Mila Tours, 100 S Greenleaf Av, Gurnee, Il 60031, T1-800-367-7378, www.milatours.com.
S and S Tours, 4250 S Hohokam Dr, Sierra Vista, AZ 85650, T866-780-2813, www.ss-tours.com.

Tourist information

Panama's tourist board is the **Autoridad de Turismo Panamá** (ATP), www.atp.gob.pa, formerly known as the Instituto Panameño de Turismo, IPAT. They have offices in most towns and cities but are not always prepared for public visits – it helps if you have specific questions in mind. Staff usually speak Spanish only. Online, the ATP operates a visitors' website, www.visitpanama.com. If you intend to do any serious trekking in protected areas, always contact the environment agency in advance, **Autoridad Nacional del Ambiente** (ANAM), www.anam. gob.pa; they have offices in most towns.

Tourist publications
The Visitor, www.thevisitorpanama.com, is a weekly English-language newspaper

with lightweight news, events and listings. It's marketed to tourists and widely available in Panama City and beyond.

Focus Panamá, www.focuspublicationsint. com, is a free glossy book worth looking out for. It's produced twice a year and contains listings, adverts and articles in English; also available online.

Visas and immigration

All visitors to Panama must have a passport valid for a minimum of 6 months, an onward/return ticket and proof of sufficient funds for their stay (US$500 cash or a credit card). Depending on your country of origin, you may or may not require a stamped visa (see below). The latest presidential decree states all visitors are entitled to a maximum stay of 180 days, no renewals (visas 90 days). However, if your stamp/tourist card expires, you can renew it by leaving the country for 72 hrs and re-entering. Panama's immigration laws are in a state of flux and official websites (and even some offices) may not have up-to-date information.

Entry requirements

Citizens of the United States, Canada, Australia, New Zealand, most European (including the United Kingdom), Caribbean, South American, Central American and some Asian countries do not need a visa – simply hand over your passport and receive your entry stamp. Citizens of Egypt, Peru, Dominican Republic, many African, Eastern European and Asian countries require a visa, which must be arranged in advance of travel – check with Panama's **Migración** office, www.migracion.gob.pa, for more information. If you are a non-US citizen travelling to Panama via the USA, you are strongly advised to check your individual entry requirements ahead of travel. If you are eligible for a visa waiver, you are required to register in advance with the **Electronic System for Travel Authorization (ESTA)**, https://esta.cbp.dhs.gov/esta/.

Women travellers

As in most Latin countries, some unaccompanied Western women will be at times subject to intense curiosity and attention, usually in the form of cat-calls, honking horns, solicitous smiles and chat-up lines. Don't be unduly scared, simply ignore them. To help minimize unwanted interest, consider your clothing choices. When travelling on buses, sit next to another woman. If accepting an invitation from new friends or acquaintances, make sure that someone else knows the address you are going to and the time you left. Ask if you can bring a friend (even if you do not intend to do so). Use common sense and err on the side of caution until you are adjusted to the local culture. Never disclose to strangers where you are staying. If a man won't take a hint, shouting something along the lines of '*Déjame en paz*' (Leave me alone) will usually get rid of them.

Working in Panama

Paid work is hard to find and technically requires a permit. Qualified English teachers may find casual hours in Panama City where there is a high demand for business English. The cost of living in the capital is very high, however, and many struggle to make ends meet. Two main areas provide opportunities for unskilled volunteers: childcare – often at orphanages or schools – and nature projects. Be warned: spontaneous volunteering is becoming more difficult. NGOs that use volunteers often plan their personnel needs, so you may be required to make contact before you visit. Some developed countries have their own national volunteer programmes working in Panama. The **US Peace Corps**, Paul D: Coverdell Peace Corps Headquarters, 1111 20th St NW, Washington, DC 20526, T1-800-424 8580, www.peacecorps.gov, is the most prominent, placing US citizens on 2-year assignments throughout rural Panama.

Contents

Footprint features

Panama City & Central Pacific Islands

At a glance

⊖ **Getting around** Use taxis and buses to get around the city. The Metro, when finished, should prove useful. Planes, ferries, catamarans and high-speed *pangas* are common forms of transport offshore.

✪ **Time required** 5-10 days.

☀ **Weather** Day-time temperatures in Panama City rarely fall below 32°C. Dec-Apr are generally dry months; May-Nov are cloudy with heavy downpours in the early afternoon.

✖ **When not to go** The city is uncomfortably humid in the wet season, but a/c is almost ubiquitous. Beach time may be hampered by prolonged storms during the wetter months, Sep-Nov.

Founded five centuries ago as the Pacific terminus of Spain's pioneering transcontinental trade routes, Panama City has always thrived on the flow of commerce and imperial power. Today, perched at the entrance to the Panama Canal, its multinational banks and corporate headquarters are driving rapid development across the isthmus. Extravagant high-rise condos, boutique shopping malls, luxury car dealerships, showy international bars, restaurants and nightclubs all cater to the city's booming nouveau riche, who make no apologies for their ostentatious displays of wealth. Gentrification advances with a prodigious zeal in the city's most historic neighbourhoods, where lavish colonial mansions and elegant public plazas are receiving multimillion dollar renovations. Elsewhere, brand new mass transit systems, bold contemporary architecture, convention centres and a slew of modern festivals dedicated to music, food, dance, film and fashion all signal Panama City's emergence as a dynamic regional player. But beyond the optimism of the moment, significant challenges lie ahead if the city is to transform itself into a truly world-class destination. Haphazard urban planning has left its avenues clogged with traffic and overheated tempers, while the pervasive influence of mass consumerism has stifled more nuanced and authentic cultural enterprises. In many parts of the city, the 'economic miracle' has failed to happen at all. As the financial towers compete for a piece of the ever-diminishing skyline, many working-class Panamanians are left wondering what the view must be like from way up there; inevitably, scenes of hustle and wilful urban decay are reflected in the façades of glass and steel. Panama City's shameless love affair with capitalism has today transformed it into a sweltering economic powerhouse, but many travellers find its energy chaotic and overwhelming. Fortunately, the urban jungle can be easily traded for more sedate destinations, including the Central Pacific Islands, bastions of verdant tranquillity and tropical indolence.

Arriving in Panama City → *Colour map 2, A1.*

Getting there

Air Tocumen International Airport, www.aeropuertotocumen.aero, is located 35 km east of Panama City. A taxi to the centre costs US$25 for two people, 30-45 minutes, or one to two hours in rush hour. Buses depart from the opposite side of the highway every 15-20 minutes – take a **Metrobus** that uses the Corredor Sur, US$1.25, one hour, or you might spend hours trundling through the suburbs. Panama's domestic airport is Marcos A Gelabert Airport, better known as **Albrook Airport**. It is located roughly 2 km outside the city centre (taxi US$3).

Bus Panama City's bus terminal, the **Gran Terminal de Transportes**, is located 2 km northwest of the city centre in the suburb of Albrook. It is the hub for all long-distance and international buses, including Ticabus. The terminal is clean and modern with numerous amenities including fast food, ATMs, pharmacies and a shopping mall. Local buses run to all parts of the city from the road outside. A taxi to the city centre should cost no more than US$3.

Getting around

On foot Some parts of the city are conducive to strolling, including the historic quarter of San Felipe, but generally the capital is not very pedestrian friendly. Drivers are highly aggressive and there are few designated crossing points. Walking from one side of the city to the other is not really feasible, except along the new **Cinta Costera**, which skirts the Pacific Coast from Punta Paitilla to San Felipe. This walk is best achieved in the early morning or late afternoon, when the heat is less intense.

Bus Set to be phased out in 2012, Panama City's traditional public buses *diablos rojos* (red devils), consist of crowded old US school buses pimped with gaudy neon lights, go-fast tassels and colourful artwork. **Metrobuses**, are modern, air-conditioned and decidedly more conservative in appearance. Routes are long and complex, but most begin in the **Gran Terminal de Transporte** and fan east along major arteries. Fares are pre-paid using electronic top-up cards, available from kiosks or shops for US$2 – look for the orange logo. Routes within the city are US$0.25 (expected to soon rise to US$0.45), or US$1.25 for routes on the Corredor Sur and Corredor Norte.

Taxi Taxis are an efficient way to get around but finding one is not always as simple as you might hope. State your destination before getting in and don't be offended if the driver turns you down with a scowl or some other unfriendly gesture. Many *taxistas* are fussy about where they go, or otherwise temperamental and prone to fits of insanity. Fares are not metered but based on a zone system. Overcharging is very common. For short trips in the centre, hand the driver US$2 on arrival and look like you expect change. Fares for longer trips should be agreed in advance. Never use tourist taxis that wait outside large hotels – their rates are four or five times higher. Speaking Spanish helps.

Car Driving in the capital is not recommended. Roads are confusing, poorly signed and often heavily congested. Panama City motorists are also among the most belligerent in the western hemisphere and their interpretation of local driving laws is liberal at best. If you must drive, a good map and steady nerves are essential. Two toll roads – the **Corredor**

Norte and **Corredor Sur** – are the fastest way to get from end to end. Avoid travelling during rush hours 0700-0930 and 1600-1830.

Metro Construction of Panama City's new Metro, www.elmetrodepanama.com, officially began in 2011 with **Línea Uno**. Scheduled to open in 2014 it will connect Albrook with the suburb of Los Andes, passing through many neighbourhoods on the way, including Calidonia, Bella Vista, El Cangrejo and Pueblo Nuevo. Other lines are planned for the coming years.

Tourist information

For general information, head to the central offices of Panama's tourist board, the **Autoridad de Turismo Panamá (ATP)** ⓘ *Av Samuel Lewis y Calle Gerardo Ortega, Edificio Central, 1st floor, Obarrio, T526-7000, www.atp.gob.pa or www.visitpanama.com*. Additional ATP offices can be found in Tocumen and Albrook airports. The environment agency, the **Autoridad Nacional del Ambiente (ANAM)** ⓘ *Calle Broberg, Albrook, T500-0855, www.anam.gob.pa*, is a crucial stop for anyone wishing to visit remote national parks or protected areas.

1 Panama City

➡ **Panama City maps**
1 Panama City, page 38
2 San Felipe (Casco Viejo), page 44
3 Calidonia, page 50
4 Area Bancaria & around, page 52
5 Panamá La Vieja, page 54

500 metres
500 yards

Where to stay 🛏
Riande Aeropuerto **3**

Don't miss …

Safety

You should strictly avoid the neighbourhoods of **Curundú**, **El Chorrillo** and **Hollywood**, where the risk of robbery is extremely high. The security situation in **San Felipe** has greatly improved in recent years; but stay alert and avoid flashy jewellery. Nearby, **Santa Ana** has barely begun to gentrify and you should avoid its backstreets, including run-down areas around Chinatown. In both districts, take particular care at night. Many cheap hotels are concentrated in **Calidonia**, but the area is seedy after dark with lots of prostitutes and unsavoury types. The streets of **Bella Vista** and the **Area Bancaria** are generally safe to wander until midnight, but are poorly policed and deserted after dark. Use registered taxis wherever possible. Tourist police on mountain bikes are present in San Felipe during the day, but curiously enough, most of them don't speak English.

Background

The rise and fall of Panamá La Vieja

In 1515, Captain Antonio Tello de Guzmán was conducting explorations of the newly discovered Pacific coast when he encountered an indigenous fishing village called Panamá. Recently unearthed archaeological evidence suggests the site was probably inhabited for several centuries before his arrival. In 1517, under orders from Pedro Arias Dávila (aka Pedrarias the Cruel), Gaspar de Espinosa established a garrison in the village. Two years later, on 15 August 1519, the town of

Birds in the city

With the exception of rats and vultures, it seems unfathomable that any creature could flourish in the harsh urban jungle of Panama City. But tropical nature, if anything, is resilient. Closer inspection of the capital's steamy streets reveals a metropolis surprisingly rich in avian fauna, much of it straight from the rainforest. In the residential district of El Cangrejo, Vía Argentina is normally known for its popular restaurant scene. But head there towards dusk and you'll be rewarded with the spectacle of thousands of chattering green parrots returning home to roost. Birds of prey are always impressive and the Cinta Costera is the place to glimpse a caracara, a variety of falcon that inhabits the capital in great numbers – scan high-up locations for potential perches and listen out for its piercing cry. For colourful keel-billed toucans, who emit a throaty frog-like call, try the large trees around Ancón and Balboa. Pelicans, virtually tame, can be seen in great numbers around the fish market in Santa Ana. Between the dust and noise of the city's building sites, you'll often see small patches of wasteland, home to yellow flycatchers and small passerines. Just off the shores of Panamá La Vieja, the vast mudflats at low tide draw scores of waders, terns and herons, all very easy to spot. Predictably, urban parks such as Parque Urracá are great places to see a variety of species, including hummingbirds, woodpeckers and brightly coloured tanagers.

If you would like to learn more about Panama City's birds, the Smithsonian Institute have published *A guide to the common birds of Panama City* (2004) by Jorge Ventocilla, available from their offices in Ancón.

Panamá – officially Nuestra Señora de la Asunción de Panamá – was founded by Pedrarias himself. It was the first European colony on the Pacific and it soon grew in stature as a major port and embarkation point for expeditions to Peru, Chile and Mexico.

As the conquest of the New World advanced, plundered mineral wealth began arriving in volume to be dispatched along the Camino Real – an old indigenous walking trail that crossed the isthmus to the Caribbean. Second only to Mexico City and Lima, the city of Panamá expanded exponentially. In 1620 an earthquake struck, followed by a devastating fire in 1644, which claimed no less than 83 religious structures, including the cathedral. Sadly, worse catastrophes were to come when the city's reputation as a Spanish treasure house drew the interest of Welsh privateer Henry Morgan. On 28 January 1671, he launched an unprecedented attack from which the city never recovered. Consumed by fires of uncertain cause, Panamá fell into ruin and was eventually rebuilt at a new location several kilometres away. The ruins of Panamá La Vieja have now been partially restored and are one of the city's most popular attractions (see page 53).

Rebirth, Independence and nationhood

Established on 21 January 1673, the new Panama City – today's San Felipe district – occupied a defensive position on an ocean-swept promontory. It was heavily fortified with towers and sea walls, but the threat from pirates was destined to recede. By the 18th century, the Spanish had ceased transporting gold across the isthmus, instead rounding Cape Horn. Panama City's importance began to wane and by the time Panama gained Independence from Spain in 1821, there were just 5000 inhabitants left. Incorporated as

Rise of the Cocaine Towers

Panama City's slew of skyscrapers are a palpable symbol of the country's power-driven success. But when night descends on the Area Bancaria, its streets fall eerily quiet. The lights do not turn on in its glitzy apartment blocks, which stand as dead and empty as spent champagne bottles. Nonetheless, the city's construction boom continues to advance with an almost religious zeal – some 18,000 new units were completed in 2008-2010 alone. Rents are soaring and, as the real estate sector boasts prodigious double-digit growth, what exactly is fuelling this tremendous and apparently invincible property bubble? Colombian drug cartels, seeking legitimate business fronts through which to launder their profits, are long thought to have been driving the transformation of Panama City's urban skyline. Even back in the 1970s, cynical commentators had wryly christened the new skyscrapers the 'Cocaine Towers'.

Panama's long and notorious involvement with the cartels reached a jittery high during the tenure of Manuel Noriega, who turned a healthy profit feeding voracious North American appetites for the white stuff. The heady days of the *guardia* (and direct government involvement in drug trafficking) are long gone, but the country remains an attractive proposition for a broad spectrum of criminal organizations. Specifically, Panama's lax business laws allow for the virtually instantaneous creation of multiple shell corporations, through which a person or persons can orchestrate anything from tax avoidance to money laundering. Corporate ownership, too, can be easily concealed with 'bearer shares', which assign legal proprietorship on the sole basis of possessing physical share titles.

The freedom to conceal ownership and operate obscure interconnected webs of shell corporations – along with the country's prime geographic location between the Americas, its absence of visa restrictions for Colombian nationals, its dollar-based economy, its free trade zone, its loosely regulated gaming industry and its massive ports and maritime sectors – is the reason why Colombian gangs are drawn so persistently to Panama. It is not known how many of Panama City's registered businesses are engaged in illicit activities but, according to Public Citizen's 2009 Panama Tax Evasion Report, the city is home to an astonishing 350,000 corporations. In recent years, the government has committed its banking industry to greater openness and transparency by signing tax information exchange agreements. However, if the national economy is structurally dependent on cartel money – as some commentators suspect – the government is unlikely to take serious steps towards cleaning up its construction sector. For now, Panama's coke-fuelled economic euphoria is showing no sign of a crash.

a provincial outpost of Gran Colombia, the city famously hosted the Congress of Panama in 1826. Headed by the liberator Simón Bolívar, the event drew leaders from all the newly independent nations of Latin America with the aim of forging a single federal government. The idea initially gained traction, but was doomed to fail. By 1830, both Venezuela and Ecuador had split from Gran Colombia to strike out as independent states.

In 1848, the California gold rush signalled boom times for Panama City. A massive influx of Yankee 49ers brought new wealth and investment, including the construction of the Panama railroad. Social change brought social tensions and in 1856 a dispute over a slice of watermelon erupted into a full-scale riot. In 1882, the French arrived on the scene to much fanfare and jubilation. Their plan to build a trans-isthmian canal was destined to end ingloriously, but they left behind numerous elegant French mansions as part of their legacy. In 1903, the United States took up the challenge and provided military support to enable Panama to separate from Colombia. The city grew exponentially thereafter. The Americans are credited with drastically improving the capital's sanitation and constructing several new neighbourhoods, including Ancón, Balboa and Amador, which all fell under the jurisdiction of the US-controlled Canal Zone. Waves of immigrant workers arrived, particularly from Barbados, and social tensions rose once again. In 1964, Panamanian anger at six decades of American occupation sparked riots in the capital.

Dawn of the narco-hub

In the 1970s and 1980s, Panama City's skyline mushroomed as it gained prominence as a centre of offshore banking and international cocaine trafficking. General Manuel Noriega and his Colombian business associates enjoyed several years of criminal prosperity until US President George Bush initiated a full-blown invasion on 20 December 1989. The historic quarter of El Chorrillo was virtually destroyed and riots broke out in the aftermath, causing damage to many local businesses. The year 1999 signalled the handover of the Panama Canal and the final incorporation of all Canal Zone townships into Panama's national territory. In recent years, the city has experienced unprecedented levels of economic growth as well as a new influx of migrants from both North and South America. The accelerated pace of change combined with poor urban planning has put significant strain on the city's infrastructure. Recent presidents, including Ricardo Martinelli, have instigated several ambitious city makeovers, such as the overhaul of the public transit system. Developers continue to construct new tower blocks and gated communities at a breathless pace.

Places in Panama City

Buffered by the Panama Canal and the protected forests of its watershed, Panama City has evolved on a narrow lateral trajectory, skirting the bays and promontories of the Pacific coast in its perpetual search for new ground. The best part of the capital is framed by two wave-swept points. In the west, the historic district of San Felipe, also known as Casco Viejo, is the opulent symbol of Old Panamá, boasting a mix of newly restored colonial mansions and elegant public squares, chic new guesthouses and upmarket eateries. In the east, the burgeoning Area Bancaria is the dynamic reality of New Panamá, home to luxury condos and high-rise office blocks, frenetic urban boulevards and rapidly evolving horizons. Beyond and between these two points lies an intriguing patchwork of disparate and self-contained neighbourhoods. The working-class districts of Santa Ana and Calidonia are places to glimpse the barter and hustle of authentic Panamanian street life. The planned community of Balboa – unique to the capital's development as a crossroads destination – is home to a slew of functional canal-zone architecture. Although Panama City is the most urban destination in the country, the exuberance of tropical nature is never far off. Breezy Ancón Hill and thickly forested Metropolitan Park are places to escape the city's relentless noise and movement and soak up some restful natural ambience. ➤➤ *For listings, see pages 60-77.*

San Felipe (Casco Viejo) → *For listings, see pages 60-77.*

A UNESCO World Heritage Site since 1997, the historic district of San Felipe – popularly known as Casco Viejo or Casco Antiguo (Old Compound) – occupies a strategic headland overlooking the bay of Panama. Built in 1673 after the pirate Henry Morgan destroyed Panamá La Vieja, 'the city from within' remained a heavily fortified and somewhat impenetrable compound until the mid-19th century, when its defensive walls and sentry towers were finally dismantled. Today, diverse architectural influences find expression in San Felipe's compact grid of narrow streets and plazas, including baroque, art deco, neoclassical, Spanish and French colonial styles. Although it is one of the most aesthetic historic quarters in Latin America, many of its most beautiful edifices fell into disrepair during the 20th century. In 1992, a long overdue restoration campaign was initiated and San Felipe now boasts an intriguing blend of fine renovated mansions and visually compelling colonial ruins.

Plaza Independencia
Plaza Independencia is the geographic and spiritual heart of San Felipe, where Independence from Spain was declared in 1821, and Independence from Colombia in 1903. Filled with shady trees, benches, pathways and bronze busts of the republic's founders, the plaza is the site of occasional civic ceremonies and public fiestas. Numerous notable buildings overlook the plaza, including several remodelled mansions and the city's cathedral, from which the plaza derives its alternative name, **Plaza Catedral**. On the east side stands the former **Hotel Central** (1884), once the most luxurious lodging in Central America. At the time of research, it was in ruins but undergoing restoration.

Catedral de Nuestra Señora de la Asunción
Work on Panama City's cathedral began in 1688 and was not completed until 1794, over a century later. The building features a classical façade with attractive multi-toned stone

work. Its towers, partially encrusted with mother-of-pearl from the Islas Perlas, house three bells from the city's original (now ruined) cathedral in Panamá La Vieja. Despite being one of the largest churches in Central America, the cathedral has an underwhelming interior. Some ecclesiastical remains are buried in an area to the left of the altar, including Saint Aurelio, or so it is rumoured. On the other side is the sealed entrance to various disused subterranean passages which criss-cross San Felipe's underworld.

Museo del Canal Interoceánico
ⓘ *Plaza Independencia, T211-1649, www.museodelcanal.com. Tue-Sun 0900-1700, US$2. Nearly all exhibits are in Spanish, but English audio-guides are available, US$5.*

Opened in 1997, the comprehensive Museo del Canal Interoceánico chronicles the social and political history of the Panama Canal. The building, which dates from 1874, was originally the opulent Grand Hotel, which later served as the headquarters of both French

2 San Felipe (Casco Viejo)

→ Panama City maps
1 Panama City, page 38
2 San Felipe (Casco Viejo), page 44
3 Calidonia, page 50
4 Area Bancaria & around, page 52
5 Panamá La Vieja, page 54

N
100 metres
100 yards

Where to stay 🛏
Canal House 3
Casa Sucre 1
Casco Antiguo 6
Hospedaje Casco Viejo 5
Las Clementinas 7

Los Cuatro Tulipanes 2
Luna's Castle 4

Restaurants 🍴
Café Coca Cola 1
Casablanca 6

Cedros Grill & Tavern 2
Ciao Pescao 5
Diablo Rosso 9
Ego y Narciso 10
Granclement 4
Las Bóvedas 3

and North American canal companies. Commencing with Panama's pre-Columbian past, exhibits include a modest collection of archaeological relics, including funerary urns, zoomorphic bowls, dishes, masks and statues. Progressing in a methodical fashion through first European contact, conquest, colonization and the age of piracy, subsequent displays emphasize Panama's historic role as a bridge between the oceans. No telling of the canal's history would be complete without a treatment of the ill-fated French effort, illustrated here by scores of canal company share certificates that ultimately proved worthless to the bearers. American involvement in the canal is particularly well treated on the museum's second floor, where expositions document daily life in the Canal Zone – a world of crisp white linen suits and silver tea sets, at least in part. Later exhibits relate the US handover of the canal and include the fabled 1977 Torrijos-Carter treaty.

Manolo CARACOL **8**
Mostaza **7**
Super Gourmet **11**

Bars & clubs 🎵
Habana Panamá **12**

La Casona de las Brujas **13**
Mojitos sin Mojitos **14**
Platea Jazz Bar **15**
Relic Bar **16**
Vieja Habana **17**

Museo de Historia de Panamá

ⓘ *Plaza Independencia, T228-6231, Mon-Fri 0800-1600, US\$1.*

The small but diverting museum of Panamanian history is housed in the neoclassical **Palacio Municipal**, where the historic Separation Act of Panama from Colombia was signed on 3 November 1903. The building was designed by Italian architect Genaro Ruggierri and features a smiling, wave-lapped nude sculpture by Enrico Biago, said to symbolize the nation of Panama. The museum's exhibits comprise a small, subtle but precious collection of artefacts from significant moments in Panama's history. They include one of the original Panamanian flags stitched by María Ossa de Amador in 1903, a plan for the fort of Portobelo, chains from the *bóvedas* (dungeons), and an old key to the Puerta de Tierra – for centuries the only land gate into the highly fortified San Felipe compound.

Plaza Bolívar

The popular and often buzzing evening haunt of Plaza Bolívar is named after the liberator, Símon Bolívar, who chaired the historic Congress of Panama in 1826 (see Background, page 40). Although his plans for a federal union failed, history would honour the Venezuelan revolutionary with a statue by Mariano Benillure. Standing upright at the centre of the plaza, Bolívar is depicted in civilian attire and surrounded by flowing capes and condors. The plaza has been heavily restored in recent years and is now home to numerous restaurants and terraced cafés. The old Hotel Colombia is a particularly handsome structure.

Iglesia y Convento de San Francisco
Originally built in 1678, San Felipe's Church of San Francisco was destroyed by fires in 1737 and 1756. Rebuilt by Leonardo Villanueva Meyer in 1918, the church is adorned with angelic statues who encircle the bell-tower and dome. Next door, the Convent of San Francisco is the largest of San Felipe's religious buildings, although little of it is original. Today it houses the ministry for foreign affairs and the Salón Bolívar, which you can visit for glimpses of wood-panelled finery, embossed leather benches and paintings belonging to the Bolívar Society. There is a replica of the liberator's jewel-encrusted sword on display. The rest of the building is worth a stroll, mainly to admire the views of the sea from the glass-fronted inner courtyard.

Iglesia de San Felipe Neri
Located just off the southwest corner of Plaza Bolívar, the church of San Felipe Neri is one of the city's oldest structures. Built by Lucas Fernández de Piedrahita in 1684, it was originally intended as an oratory house and hospital for poor local priests and itinerant clergy. It was damaged by fires in the 18th century and completely restored in 1913. It served as a seminary thereafter, until 1941, when it was occupied by various religious missions, including the Pious Missionary Sisters of the Miraculous Medal. It closed in 1996 for seven years of restoration. Its tower is beautifully laden with mother-of-pearl.

Teatro Nacional
① *T262-2535, open 0800-1700, US$1, including explanations in Spanish.*
Panama's national theatre was commissioned by the republic's first president, Dr Manuel Amador Guerrero, who rightly declared that no independent nation should be without proper national arts facilities. Built by Genaro Ruggieri, the theatre occupies the site of an old 18th-century convent. It opened in 1908 with a performance of Verdi's *Aida*. The auditorium, although compact, is quite sumptuous and operatic. The main ceiling features a dramatic and spiritually charged fresco by Roberto Lewis, which was restored in 2004 after damage from heavy rains. The theatre's exterior features French-influenced sculptures, including the muses of literature and music, and medallions commemorating legends such as Shakespeare and Cervantes. Throughout the early 20th century, the national theatre was a haunt of the city's high society. After the 1930s, the theatre's popularity – and state of repair – began to quickly decline. A major restoration was required in 1974 and Dame Margot Fonteyn, who had married into the prominent Panamanian Arias family, danced for the public during the subsequent re-inauguration.

Palacio Presidencial
① *The street is heavily policed and you will be asked to present your passport. The public are not normally permitted to enter the building, but the Alcaldía can grant permission on an individual basis. Ask a tour guide to arrange this in advance.*
The opulent Presidential Palace was built in 1673 as a residence for colonial governors and auditors. It overlooks the water at the site of the former Puerta Mar, the city's ancient sea-gate. Originally made of wood, the building was renovated in 1922 under the presidency of Belisario Porras, who added several new rooms and patios. After the project's completion, the president received a gift of nine herons, said to symbolize the nine provinces of

Panama. He allowed them to wander freely around the palace and it was subsequently nicknamed **El Palacio de las Garzas** (Herons' Palace). Today there are only two herons and you can sometimes spot them as they gobble fish from the fountains. The president does not now live in the palace, but it is still used for government purposes.

Plaza de Francia

Perched at the southern tip of San Felipe, Plaza de Francia is surrounded by remnants of the city's old sea walls. For many years it was the site of a notorious dungeon, and grizzly stories recall the fate of prisoners who were left to drown when the high tide flooded their cells. Today, *las bóvedas* (the vaults) serve much less sinister purposes: one has been converted into a French restaurant, while another is used as a small contemporary art gallery by the **Instituto Nacional de Cultura**. The plaza itself is well restored and beautified with fiery poinciana trees. In memory of the first failed attempt to build the canal, a large central monument was donated by the French government: it features a series of commemorative plaques and a large obelisk designed by Leonardo Villanueva provides a lofty perch to a rooster wearing a crown – *le coq gaulois*, symbol of the Gallic nation.

Instituto Nacional de Cultura

Dedicated to the documentation, promotion and preservation of Panamanian culture, the Instituto Nacional de Cultura stands on the north side of Plaza de Francia. Built in 1931 by Gennaro Ruggieri, the building originally served as the Supreme Court and was partially damaged during the bombings of Operation Just Cause (see page 283). Since then, the old courtroom has been converted into the **Anita Villalaz Theatre**, renowned for its innovative and alternative performances. The rest of the institute's facilities are not open to casual visitors, but you can admire dramatic murals by Esteban Palomino in the reception area. The building was used in the James Bond film, *Quantum of Solace*.

Paseo de las Bóvedas

From Plaza de Francia, the Paseo de las Bóvedas follows an old sea wall around the southeast corner of San Felipe. It provides expansive views over the bay and sections of it are ablaze with bougainvillea. Sadly, at the time of press, the Martinelli administration was planning to construct a grotesque highway around it and ruin the Paseo's ambience forever. As you exit on the north side, close to the junction of Avenida A and Calle Primera, look out for the former **Club Unión** building, which has been quietly crumbling for years. During its heyday, Panama's oligarchy entertained themselves in its ballrooms and banquet halls. In the 1980s, the building was commandeered by General Noriega, who transformed it into the tawdry **Club de Clases y Tropas**, a favourite haunt of drug lords, arms dealers, CIA operatives and other assorted deviants. It is now being restored and converted into a swanky new hotel.

Casa Góngora

ⓘ *Av Central and Calle 4a, T212-0338, Mon-Fri 0800-1600, free.*

Casa Góngora is reputed to be one of the oldest houses in the city. Built in 1756 by a Spanish pearl merchant, Captain Paul Góngora de Caceres, it has been repaired and restored several times thanks to the work of a local preservation group, The Board of Friends of Casa Góngora. The interior is plain and simple, and previously contained many oil paintings by Roberto Lewis. Now home to a small cultural centre, the house occasionally hosts art exhibitions or concerts – drop by to see if anything is happening.

Iglesia y Convento de Santo Domingo

ⓘ *Av A and Calle 3a, Tue-Sat 0800-1600, US$1. The church and museum were closed for restoration at the time of research.*

The Church and Convent of Santo Domingo were built in 1673 and razed by fires in 1737 and 1756. A single original feature survived the infernos – the legendary **Arco Chato** (Flat Arch). In the early 20th century, when America was debating where to build a transoceanic canal, propagandists famously used an image of the arch to illustrate the geological stability of Panama. The arch was so well constructed and resilient it remained upright for over 300 years, until 2003, when it tragically collapsed in a heap of dust and rubble. It has since been rebuilt in its original location but, for obvious reasons, it's not the same. Next door to the now heavily restored convent, the Iglesia de Santo Domingo has been converted into the **Museo de Arte Religioso Colonial**. Its treasures include a precious gold altar, a delicate spiral staircase, silver relics, wooden sculptures from Lima and Mexico, 19th-century engravings of the city, and the skeleton of a woman found during the excavation of the church.

Iglesia de San José

ⓘ *Av A, between Calle 8a and Calle 9a, Mon-Sat 0500-1200 and 1200-2000, Sun 0500-1200 and 1700-2000.*

The church of San José is home to the famous **Altar de Oro**, a massive baroque altar carved from mahogany and veneered with gold. It is one of the few treasures of Panamá La Vieja to have survived Henry Morgan's attack. Different legends recall how it was concealed from the gold-hungry pirates. Some say it was whitewashed by the priest, others that it was covered in mud by nuns, or covered in oil, or completely boarded up. Whatever the truth, a remark attributed to Morgan hints he was not deceived: "I think you are more of a pirate than I", he reportedly said to the priest.

Plaza Herrera

Perched on the western fringe of San Felipe, ramshackle Plaza Herrera gives an idea of how things looked before the developers moved into the area. Surrounded by the dilapidated grandeur of ruined French mansions, local street life here remains authentic and brazen. Historically, the area was the site of an important 50-man military post. The ruins of **Tiger's Hand Bulwark** – the point where the city's defensive wall ended and a landward moat began – are located just off the west side of the plaza. The plaza itself did not exist until 1781, when a fire devastated the city block and it was rebuilt as a small park. West of Plaza Herrera, the city crumbles away into the slums of El Chorrillo, which you are strongly advised to avoid.

Santa Ana → *For listings, see pages 60-77.*

The gritty working-class district of Santa Ana grew up as a suburb of San Felipe. It has not yet been gentrified and it retains an artfully dishevelled air, with crumbling historic architecture and some unsightly modern construction too. Life gravitates to the **Parque Santa Ana**, a popular gathering place for political rallies and protests. On a typical afternoon the park is bustling with itinerant salesmen, shoe-shiners and elderly gentlemen, who gather on the benches to play chess or engage in animated discussions. The **Iglesia Santa Ana**, built in 1764, overlooks the plaza with a modest interior of marbled pillars and frescoes. The park is a major hub for local buses.

La Peatonal

Just off Parque Santa Ana, a large gateway marks the entrance to La Peatonal, a thronging and unpretentious pedestrianized shopping street. It lurches for nearly a kilometre with thrifty store fronts, fast-food joints, cut-price clothing stalls and booming loud speakers. Between the drab parade of modern commercial outlets, there are a handful of architectural treasures, all in various states of dilapidation. Check out the building next to the **Banco Nacional**, which features interesting tile work dating from the canal era. Even if you're not into bargain shopping, La Peatonal is a great place to observe the authentic day-to-day bustle of the city.

Barrio Chino

A block east of Parque Santa Ana, a narrow street called **Bajada Salsipuedes** (Get-out-if-you-can) heads east off La Peatonal. The street is packed with a mildly diverting array of cramped market stalls which informally flog everything from herbal medicines to school text books. A block from the seafront, a side road turns east into the city's Barrio Chino, or Chinatown, established in the 1850s by Chinese railway workers. Encompassing just a few small streets, the quarter is not as vibrant as it used to be, and architecturally there is little to distinguish it from other poor neighbourhoods. Aside from a large red gate at the barrio's eastern entrance, you'll have to make do with the authentic aroma of Chinese spices as evidence you're in an ethnic enclave. The barrio is very sketchy – please take care.

Mercado Municipal

① *Av B and Calle 15 Este.*

The city market has occupied a former railway terminal and customs building since 2006. As markets go, it's not particularly exciting, but it is well ordered, easy to navigate and secure for tourists. There are various sections selling meat, vegetables and dry food. If you're hungry, there are food stalls dishing up very economical, freshly cooked high-carb delights. Nearby, there is a **Mercado de Mariscos** (seafood market), opened in 1995, where you can pick up good fresh fish, lobster, shrimps and squid. Don't miss the ceviche!

Plaza 5 de Mayo and around

La Peatonal emerges at Plaza 5 de Mayo, a busy junction full of roaring traffic and frenetic activity. At the centre of the plaza, a large obelisk honours firemen who died in a gunpowder explosion at El Polvorín munitions house in May 1914. To the east stands the former terminus of the Panama railway, inaugurated in 1912. It served as an anthropology museum for many years but it is now occupied by a theatre school. Just north of 5 de Mayo, a small exhaust-choked plaza honours Mahatma Gandhi with a bronze statue donated by the city's Hindu community in 1969. To the west, an important monument honours slain President José Antonio Remón Cantera, who met his demise under a hail of machine-gun fire in 1955. Those responsible for his assassination at the Panama City racetrack have never been caught, but many fingers point to mobster Lucky Luciano. The monument, entitled *The Allegoric Frieze of Justice*, was designed by Peruvians Juan Pardo de Zela and Joaquín Roca Rey. It includes 17 bronze figures backed by fountains and a large commemorative monolith. Behind the monument lies the **Palacio Legislativo Justo Arosemena** – headquarters of the legislative assembly and the focus of regular public protests.

Calidonia → *For listings, see pages 60-77.*

Beyond Santa Ana, Calidonia's grid of broad avenues march east along the Bay of Panama, bridging the old and new in a distinctive district that is neither deeply historic nor especially modern. Several diverse neighbourhoods lend the area a shifting character that can be sketchy, drab, bustling or regal by turns. In the west, the barrios of **San Miguel** and **Marañón** directly border **Plaza 5 de Mayo** and teem with traffic, decay and low-grade criminality. In the north, **Perejil** is commercial, lively and poor. In the centre, a procession of gloomy casinos and cheap hotels lend the district a terminally grey ambience. In the east, **La Exposición** commemorates the famous 1915 Exposition with a slew of grand civic architecture and historic monuments. Finally, to the south, the newly constructed **Cinta Costera** is enjoying a boom of high-rise towers.

Avenida Central

Enclosed in a dense shroud of awnings, Avenida Central exits Plaza 5 de Mayo and proceeds in helter-skelter fashion through the heart of Calidonia. As a major thoroughfare and shopping street, it throngs with a commotion of pedestrians, traffic and vociferous street vendors. Stalls hawk everything from mobile phones to running shoes and fake Rolexes. Kiosks sell fresh fruit and vegetables, stacks of flowers and weird medicinal roots.

3 **Calidonia**

➡ **Panama City maps**
1 Panama City, page 38
2 San Felipe (Casco Viejo), page 44
3 Calidonia, page 50
4 Area Bancaria & around, page 52
5 Panamá La Vieja, page 54

Where to stay	Las Tablas 12	Restaurants
Arenteiro 1	Lisboa 13	Café Boulevard Balboa 1
Centro Americano 6	Pensión Monaco 14	El Sabor Interiorano 7
Costa Inn 5	Residencial Volcán 18	Rincón Tableño 4
Dos Mares 10	Venecia 3	Romanaccio Pizza 5
Hostel Mamallena 2	Veracruz 4	

200 metres
200 yards

Music seems to blast from every direction at once. The rough-and-ready entrepreneurial zeal of Avenida Central promises some fascinating close-up encounters with street life, but it's also a mean place, so watch your pockets and take care.

Museo Afro-Antillano

ⓘ *Calle 24 Este y Av Justo Arosemena, T262-5348, www.samaap.org, Tue-Sat 0830-1630, US$1.*
Inaugurated in 1980, the Museo Afro-Antillano is dedicated to the Afro-Antillean migrant workers who were charged with the most physical, dangerous and punishing tasks of the Panama Canal's construction. The museum is housed in an old Christian Mission Chapel, a traditional Caribbean clapboard structure built by Barbadian immigrants in 1910. Exhibits include a collection of historic photographs that chronicle the life and times of Panama's Afro-Antillean community, starting with the construction of the Panama railway in the 1850s. Antique furniture, household tools, musical instruments and other period pieces complement exhibitions that explore different dimensions of West Indian culture, including education, religion and the family. In 2011, the UN's 'International Year of Peoples of African Descent', photographer Rose Marie Cromwell donated a series of contemporary images of West Indian life. The museum is located in the poor neighbourhood of Marañón, formerly a bastion of Afro-Antillean culture.

Parque Belisario Porras

At the heart of **La Exposición** is a plaza commemorating the pioneering liberal and thrice-elected president Dr Belisario Porras. The good doctor's progressive vision transformed the site of his famous 1915 Exposition – an internationally acclaimed science and technology fair – into the tidy, stately place it is today. Since its foundation in the early 20th century, the neighbourhood has functioned as a hub of government offices, embassies, hospitals and other civic services. Dedicated to Porras after his death in 1942, the plaza features a large monument built by Spaniard Victorio Macho. Sumptuous mansions flank the east and west sides, including the Spanish Embassy and various halls of power. The **National Archives** are housed in a particularly impressive neoclassical edifice designed by Leonardo Villanueva, a block west of the plaza on Avenida Perú.

Cinta Costera

Commissioned by President Martín Torrijos in 2007, the Cinta Costera is a major new highway designed to alleviate the heavy congestion on Avenida Balboa. Completed in 2009 at a cost of US$189 million, the project included the reclamation of some 25 ha of land and extensive dredging of the bay. Today, the *cinta* roars alongside the Pacific Ocean with no less than 10 lanes of traffic, engulfing a statue of Balboa that once occupied a more commanding position by the water's edge. Fortunately, the builders of the highway have complemented their thoroughfare with plentiful palm trees, cycle lanes, basketball courts, cafés and park space. The *cinta* is popular place with strollers, joggers and roller-bladers. Sunday evening is a good time to soak up the family atmosphere, or simply admire the skyscrapers illuminated against the evening sky.

Area Bancaria and around → *For listings, see pages 60-77.*

Panama City's Area Bancaria (banking area) encompasses several modern localities and boasts the highest property prices in the city. The construction boom of the last two decades has radically transformed its energy and appearance, and a thriving high-rise

⁴ Area Bancaria & around

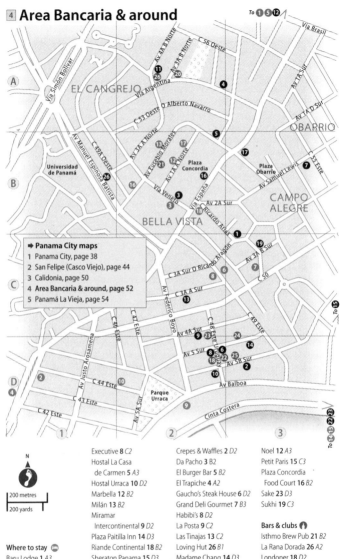

Via Brasil
To ① ⑤ ⑫

A

Via Simón Bolívar
EL CANGREJO
Via Argentina
C 56 Oeste
Av 4A B Norte
Av 3A B Norte
⑪ ⑳
⑳
④
Av 1A Sur
C 53 Oeste O Alberto Navarro
OBARRIO
Av 1A D Sur

B

Universidad de Panamá ㉖
Av Manuel Espinoza Batista
C 4A Oeste
⑬ ⑰
Av Eugenio Morales
⑫ ㉑
Plaza Concordia
⑯
⑯
⑤
Plaza Obarrio
⑰
C 57 Este
⑦
Av Samuel Lewis
CAMPO ALEGRE
Via Veneto
Via España
③ ⑱
Av 2A Sur
BELLA VISTA
Via Ricardo Arias
①
⑲
Av 3A B Sur
⑦
C 50
C
⑥
⑧
C 3A Sur O Ricardo Aragón
C 3A Sur
C 56 Este
C 47 Este
Av Justo Arosamena
⑬
Av Federico Boyd
Av 4A Sur
② ㉓
C 48 Este
C 49 Este
㉔
To ⑮
⑧ ⑥ ⑭
⑱ ㉕
Av 5A Sur
⑩
Av 5B Sur
②
Av Balboa
⑩
C 44 Este
Parque Urraca
⑨
C 43 Este
Cinta Costera
To ⑭ ⑯ ⑰ ㉒ ㉑
C 42 Este
De Ville ⑦

Panama City maps
1 Panama City, page 38
2 San Felipe (Casco Viejo), page 44
3 Calidonia, page 50
4 Area Bancaria & around, page 52
5 Panamá La Vieja, page 54

① ② ③

N
↑
200 metres
200 yards

Where to stay 🛏
Baru Lodge 1 A3
Bristol 6 C2
California 2 D1
De Ville 7 C3
El Panamá 3 B2
Euro 4 D1

Executive 8 C2
Hostal La Casa
 de Carmen 5 A3
Hostal Urraca 10 D2
Marbella 12 B2
Milán 13 B2
Miramar
 Intercontinental 9 D2
Plaza Paitilla Inn 14 D3
Riande Continental 18 B2
Sheraton Panama 15 D3
Torres de Alba 16 B2
Toscana Inn 17 B2

Restaurants 🍴
Beirut 1 C3

Crepes & Waffles 2 D2
Da Pacho 3 B2
El Burger Bar 5 B2
El Trapiche 4 A2
Gaucho's Steak House 6 D2
Grand Deli Gourmet 7 B3
Habibi's 8 D2
La Posta 9 C2
Las Tinajas 13 C2
Loving Hut 26 B1
Madame Chang 14 D3
Marina Marina 22 D3
Market 10 D2
New York Bagel
 Café 11 A2
Niko's Café 17 B3

Noel 12 A3
Petit Paris 15 C3
Plaza Concordia
 Food Court 16 B2
Sake 23 D3
Sukhi 19 C3

Bars & clubs 🍸
Isthmo Brew Pub 21 B2
La Rana Dorada 26 A2
Londoner 18 D2
Pavo Real 20 A2
People Ultra Lounge 22 D3
Privé & S6IS 23 C2
Pure 24 D3
Starlight 25 D3

financial sector now couches the sprawl of exclusive residential neighbourhoods. The Area Bancaria is the busiest, most populous and densely built area of the city. It throngs with a fierce international atmosphere that can be enthralling at best and exhausting at worst. Dense traffic, air pollution and the almighty dollar reign.

Bella Vista

The district of Calidonia rolls almost imperceptibly into the residential neighbourhood of Bella Vista, a lightly faded middle-class enclave with a scattering of 1930s art deco mansions. As Avenida Central advances, its name changes to **Vía España**. The streets immediately south and east are leafy and prosperous, particularly around the verdant **Parque Urraca**, a good spot for a picnic. To confuse matters, Bella Vista is the official name of a large *corregimiento* (district) that broadly corresponds to the entire Area Bancaria. Ask a taxi driver for Bella Vista, however, and they're likely to take you to the small neighbourhood bordering Calidonia.

El Cangrejo and around

As Vía España continues northeast, it passes the **Iglesia del Carmen** (1955) with its neo-Gothic spires and Byzantine-style altar. It is one of the city's most popular churches but, owing to its location next to the **Hotel El Panamá**, it did not install any bells until 1999. The Vía España grows lively with billboards, department stores and other commercial imagery as it enters El Cangrejo, a neighbourhood which first evolved as an entertainment district for American soldiers. The residential areas north and west are filled with a web of back roads, including **Vía Argentina**, which boasts a high concentration of good international restaurants and bars. Nearby, just off Vía España, the gaudily illuminated **Vía Veneto** is home to a major casino, plentiful souvenir shops and a low-key red-light district. South and east of Vía España, the neighbourhood of **Obarrio** is punctuated by an ordered grid of roads. On **Avenida Samuel Lewis**, look out for the mock-colonial **Santuario Nacional**, built by Claretian missionaries in 1947. Two blocks south, Calle 50 is a major boulevard flanked by offices, banks, imposing skyscrapers and corporate headquarters.

Marbella, Punta Paitilla and Punta Pacífica

Southeast of Obarrio, three prestigious neighbourhoods – Marbella, Punta Paitilla and Punta Pacífica – sit side-by-side on the Pacific waterfront. All three areas are characterized by upscale residences, exclusive shops, shimmering skyscrapers and gleaming business hotels. Marbella, buffered by Bella Vista to the west, is the most down-to-earth of the three and notable as the epicentre of Panama City's thumping party scene. The action is focused on and around **Calle Uruguay**, also a great area for eating out.

Panamá La Vieja

ⓘ *Vía Cincuentenario, T226-8915, www.panamaviejo.org. Most of the area is free to stroll, but access to the museum and cathedral is restricted to Tue-Sun 0830-1800, adults US$6, children US$2. A taxi to the ruins should cost US$3-4. Buses depart from Vía Israel outside the multi-plaza, 30 mins, US$0.25. For safety reasons, avoid visiting at night.*

The weathered archaeological ruins of Panamá La Vieja, sometimes referred to as Panamá Viejo, are a UNESCO World Heritage Site and all that remains of the original Panama City founded in 1519. Sadly, its burnt-out edifices have suffered centuries of damage and vandalism with their bricks looted for building materials. Today, it's hard to believe that the site's crumbling old walls and broken foundation stones once belonged to one of the finest cities in the Spanish Empire. Nonetheless, Panamá La Vieja is an atmospheric location with a highly photogenic quality. A handful of its structures have been restored to a measure of their former glory, including the cathedral tower.

The ruins

Built in 1607, **Puente del Matadero** (Slaughterhouse Bridge) crosses the Río Agarroba at the point where Henry Morgan and his men entered the city. It is named after a local slaughterhouse. Nearby stand the crumbling walls of **Fuerte de la Natividad**, a small fortress that evidently provided little defence against the marauding pirates. Just beyond it stands the modern **Centro de Visitantes de Panamá Viejo** with compelling exhibits (Spanish only) on the site's social and historical development. Further up the road lie the scattered rocks of the **Iglesia y Convento de la Merced**, founded by monks in 1522. The structure managed to escape the blaze of 1671 and was used by Morgan as a makeshift jail. The church was later dismantled and its stones used in the façade of a new temple.

Further along the main road are the modest remains of one of the largest churches in Panamá La Vieja, the **Iglesia y Convento San Francisco**, constructed by Franciscan monks over several decades. Nearby, the **Hospital San Juan de Dios** was founded in the 16th century. The surviving walls were probably part of its main hall. The **Convento de las Monjas de la Concepción** was founded by nuns in 1597 and is one of the best-preserved structures in the whole site. Under the direction of Beatriz de Silva, a noble Spanish woman who would later be canonized, the nuns were the first such group to establish themselves in the Americas. The convent has been the focus of significant restoration work since 2001.

5 Panamá La Vieja

➡ Panama City maps
1 Panama City, page 38
2 San Felipe (Casco Viejo), page 44
3 Calidonia, page 50
4 Area Bancaria & around, page 52
5 Panamá La Vieja, page 54

Colonial road to Portobelo

Pacific Ocean

N

Not to scale

Puente del Rey/King's Bridge **1**
Convento de San José **2**
Main Plaza **3**
Cathedral **4**
Cabildo **5**
Convento de Santo Domingo **6**
Casa Alarcón **7**
Slaves' House/
  House of the Genovese **8**

Royal Houses **9**
Emperor's Bridge **10**
Dungeons **11**
Kitchens **12**
Meat Market **13**
Convento de la Compañía
  de Jesús **14**
Convento La Concepción **15**
Church of La Concepción **16**

Hospital San Juan de Dios **17**
Convento de San Francisco **18**
Convento de la Merced **19**
La Natividad Fort **20**
Puente del Matadero/
  Slaughterhouse Bridge **21**

The pillage of Panamá La Vieja

When Henry Morgan arrived in Panama City on 28 January 1671, he beheld the crowning prize of his buccaneering career, or so he believed. For nearly two centuries, the city had grown fat on prodigious mineral wealth and boasted fine mansions, churches, convents and storehouses. A wealthy elite of merchants and landlords lorded over the city's 10,000-strong population, guarding untold treasures and riches. When Morgan's men arrived at the gates to the city, they were tired, hungry and afflicted by all kinds of tropical diseases. Nonetheless, they easily slaughtered the inexperienced militia who stood in their way. Days of carnage ensued, but Morgan found little treasure in the city. A week earlier, its inhabitants had been warned of Morgan's approach and had spirited away their valuables on ships. Highly

displeased, Morgan remained in the city for a month, beating and torturing its citizens in a vain attempt to locate the whereabouts of the loot. When he finally left the scene with a fraction of his promised treasure, his crew mutinied. But Morgan managed to stash the plunder and escape, so it is said, after getting the mutineers so drunk that they passed out. Upon his return to England in 1672, Morgan was arrested for having violated a peace treaty signed in 1670 between England and Spain. He was tried, proved innocent and eventually knighted for his efforts by King Charles II. He returned to Jamaica to assume the post of Lieutenant Governor, living out his final years in peace and prosperity. His attack on Panama La Viejá is remembered as a singularly audacious act, even if it didn't go to plan.

Nearby, the **Iglesia y Convento de la Compañía de Jesús** was dedicated to evangelizing the natives. Originally constructed of wood in the late 16th century, it was eventually upgraded to stone and the ruins visible today were part of the main church and cloister.

As Vía Cincuentenario rounds a corner, you can cross over to arrive at the once-wealthy **Casas Oeste** (west houses), now nothing more than a few foundation stones. Nearby, you'll see the partial walls of some houses commissioned by Francisco Terrín, which have survived the ages in slightly better form. The large space to the east is the site of the former **Plaza Mayor** (Main Plaza), which measured 69 m by 57 m and formed the social heart of the city. On its north side, the iconic stone tower of the **Catedral** is the most prominent and archaeologically significant structure in the whole site. Built between 1619 and 1626 under Bishop Francisco de Cámara, it represents the third version of the city's main church, built in the classic shape of a crucifix. The tower stands 27 m high and has survived the rigours of time thanks to its solid foundations. Nonetheless, several conservation projects have been initiated in recent years to secure the structural integrity of its walls. A recently installed internal staircase permits visitors to climb to the top for good views over the site.

To the south stand the very meagre remains of the **Casas Reales** (Royal Houses), once separated from the main city by a moat. Before reaching their current sorry state, the structures were home to important government buildings, including a royal court, counting offices, prison and governor's residence. The **Casa Alarcón**, one of the best-preserved and largest colonial houses in Panamá La Vieja, stands to the north of the cathedral. It was formerly the property of Pedro de Alarcón, a wealthy and powerful nobleman who helped fund the building of the cathedral. To the east, the **Casa de los Genoveses** served as the city's slave market, housing some 3000 slaves in 1610, each one valued at 300 pesos. Further north stands the **Iglesia y Convento de Santo Domingo**, founded in 1571 and originally built of wood. At the exit of the site, the **Puente del Rey** (1620) marks the beginning of three trails across the isthmus, including the Camino Real.

Parque Natural Metropolitano

ⓘ *Between Av Juan Pablo II and the Camino de la Amistad, along the Río Curundú, T232-5552, www.parquemetropolitano.org, visitor centre Mon-Fri 1030-1630, park Mon-Sun 0600-1700, US$2. A taxi from the city centre costs US$3-4.*

The 232-ha Parque Natural Metropolitano is one of the last remaining patches of Pacific tropical dry forest in Central America. It is home to some 208 bird species, including crimson-crested woodpeckers, keel-billed toucans and squirrel cuckoos, all very easy to spot. During the migratory months, May to September, an additional 53 species can be seen, including yellow and blackburnian warblers, barn swallows and Baltimore orioles. Mammals are prolific too: bats, capybaras, agoutis, monkeys, armadillos, racoons, squirrels, sloths and silky anteaters are among the 45 species, all relatively common. The park's amphibians include numerous frogs and toads, while boas, turtles and green iguanas are among the 36 species of reptile. There are literally hundreds of thousands of insect species in the Parque Metropolitano, many of them unidentified, but Azteca and leaf-cutter ants are easily seen, as are termites and striking blue morpho butterlies. The park's public services are exemplary and include tours, workshops, internships, volunteering opportunities and a very decent environmental library, the **Biblioteca Ambiental Corotú**. For unrivalled views of the canopy, an ascent in the Smithsonian construction crane is highly recommended – reserve in advance through the visitor centre or Smithsonian Institute (see page 58).

The trails

The park has four easy trails and an old road which can be casually explored in a few hours. The **Sendero Momotides**, named after the blue-crowned motmot bird, is a simple 0.7-km circular route that begins on the opposite side of the road to the visitor centre. It is very flat, easy and particularly recommended for elderly visitors. The 1.1-km **Sendero Caobos**, which starts near the visitor centre, is similarly undemanding. The **Sendero Roble** is a useful trail that connects with some of the more demanding areas of the park. It runs north from the visitor centre passing a turtle-filled pond and bonsai nursery before arriving at a junction marked by a security station. The 1.1-km **Sendero La Cienaguita**, the park's first and best trail, bears left and gently climbs through the forest. It concludes at the summit of **Cedar Hill**, where you can glimpse the Calzada Amador, Panama Canal and Bridge of the Americas. From Cedar Hill, the Mono Tití Road gently descends past a viewing platform, **Los Trinos**, where it's possible to spot numerous birds. After bearing south, it reconnects with Sendero Roble close to a derelict Second World War US aircraft workshop known as 'El Castillo'.

Museo Antropológico Reina Torres de Araúz

ⓘ *Av Ascanio Villalaz, Altos de Curundú, a 5-min walk from the park, T501-4743, Tue-Fri 0900-1600, US$2.*

Named after the pioneering Panamanian anthropologist, Reina Torres de Araúz, this excellent museum is home to a really stunning archaeological collection, including dazzling gold huacas and eerie statues from the country's pre-Columbian sites. Unfortunately, most of it was in storage at the time of research as the museum building does not have the correct ambient conditions for displaying archaeological pieces. Instead, it was hosting changing exhibitions on diverse national themes, but they're not worth a special trip. Ask at the ATP if the situation has been rectified.

Cerro Ancón → *For listings, see pages 60-77.*

The verdant slopes of Ancón Hill overlook the capital from the west, a welcome refuge from the heat and chaos of the city streets. The Panamanian flag billows proudly at the hill's summit, where visitors enjoy refreshing breezes and commanding vistas. To the east, you can breathe in superlative views of the Bay of Panama, the Amador Causeway, Casco Viejo and the Area Bancaria. To the west, you can observe the Panama railway, canal, locks and port operations. During the colonial era, the hill supplied San Felipe with spring water and was a popular place of weekend rest and recreation. After the establishment of the Canal Zone, Cerro Ancón fell under the jurisdiction of the US military, who barred public access to the site for over 60 years.

To the summit
The 2-km road to the summit starts in Quarry Heights, where much of the stone to build the canal's locks was mined. The walk is moderately strenuous and best accomplished in the early morning or late afternoon. It takes 30 to 40 minutes to ascend; bring plenty of water. Along the way there are good chances of spotting tamarins, agoutis, sloths, butterflies and a variety of birdlife. You will also pass many attractive US-style Canal Zone-era houses, including the offices of the environmental organization ANCON. If you prefer, a taxi can take you up, US$3-4 from downtown.

Museo de Arte Contemporáneo
ⓘ *Av de los Mártires, Calle San Blas, T262-8012, www.macpanama.org, Tue-Sun 0900-1600, US$3.*
Housed in a former masonic lodge, Panama's museum of contemporary art is privately owned by an NGO and is the only gallery of its kind in the country. It contains a small but diverting collection of work by national and international artists, including paintings, sculptures, ceramics and photography. Most of the permanent collection hails from Latin America. The gallery also hosts good temporary exhibitions and past themes include 'Evolution', 'Geometrics and abstraction' and 'Landscapes'. Art students should check out the library of contemporary visual art and make enquires about workshops, which include marquetry, silk-screening and engraving.

Mi Pueblito
ⓘ *Av de los Mártires, T228-9785, Tue-Sun 0900-2100, US$1.*
Created by Mayin Correa, a former Panama City mayor, Mi Pueblito offers a touristy but not unpleasant glimpse of village life in Panama. Essentially an ethnic theme park, Mi Pueblito features a series of cheesy but good-natured replica settlements. The village plaza from the Azuero Peninsula comes complete with a missionary church and adobe houses. The Afro-Antillean settlement boasts a wooden Anglican chapel reminiscent of Jamaica. Each village has a traditional restaurant allowing you to sample the local cuisine. Numerous guides are on hand – inevitably clad in traditional village attire – to answer any questions you might have.

The Smithsonian Tropical Research Institute (STRI)

ⓘ *Av Roosevelt, Tupper Building 401, T212-8000, www.stri.si.edu, Mon-Fri 0900-1700, guided tours of the arboretum Wed and Fri 1230, free.*

Dedicated to the study of biological diversity, the Smithsonian Tropical Research Institute is one of the world's leading centres of scientific research. It has programmes in behaviour, conservation, ecology, evolution, archaeology and anthropology. The STRI headquarters in Ancón feature an **arboretum** where you can see examples of native flora including numerous trees, shrubs, orchids and epiphytes. The **Tupper Research and Conference Centre** is located next to the main office and it contains numerous offices and laboratories, including a digital imaging lab, electron microscope, auditorium, gallery and café. Seminars are led by resident or visiting scientists every Tuesday (1600-1700, free; see their website for a schedule). The building is also home to the excellent **Tupper Tropical Sciences Library**, with over 66,000 volumes. The collection covers mostly biology, but there are numerous titles on social science and history too. Their website contains an online catalogue. There is a fine bookstore with ecological literature and souvenirs. The STRI maintains biological stations all over Panama, including **Barro Colorado Nature Monument** (see page 100), **Isla Colón Research Station** in Bocas del Toro (see page 258), the marine exhibits at **Punta Culebra Nature Center** (see page 59) and the **Galeta Marine Laboratory** in Colón province.

Balboa → *For listings, see pages 60-77.*

Nestled between Cerro Ancón and the quays of the Panama Canal, the township of Balboa enjoys an illustrious history as the former capital of the Canal Zone. Designed and built by the United States, Balboa was home to canal staff and their families for over six decades, boasting its own schools, banks, police station, churches, cinema and baseball stadium. Ordered, sterile and efficient, it was a typical American answer to the wilfulness and riot of the tropics. Since the dissolution of the Canal Zone and incorporation of Balboa into the rest of the city, most of the town's apartment blocks have been converted to office space. The area retains its fascinating utilitarian character, however, and the Canal Administration Building continues to function as a centre of canal operations.

The Canal Administration Building

ⓘ *www.pancanal.com, Mon-Fri 1000-1500, free.*

Work on the stately Canal Administration Building began in 1912 under the direction of George Goethals, the canal's chief engineer. It was completed in July 1914 at a total cost of US$879,000, one month before the canal's official inauguration. Designed by Austin Lord of New York, the building features several marbled halls, a large domed ceiling and a series of striking murals by William Van Ingen, who also designed artwork for the Library of Congress in Washington DC. Replete with drama and heroism, the murals depict the great engineering trials of the canal's construction, including the excavation of Culebra Cut, the construction of flood gates, the building of Gatún Dam and Miraflores Locks. Behind the building, a large flight of stairs leads to a monolithic marble monument commemorating Goethals himself. It features a frieze dedicated to David du Bose Gaillard, who was charged with the immense challenge of cutting through the continental divide. Designed by sculptor James Earle Fraser, the frieze was originally fixed to the mountainside at Culebra Cut.

El Prado

Lined with trees and rows of lightly weathered Canal Zone apartment blocks, the Prado proceeds in an orderly fashion south of the Goethals monument. Just east of its entrance stands the former **Balboa Elementary School**. On the west stands the former **High School**, the site of an eternal flame honouring 21 fallen martyrs who died during the flag riots of 1964. The infamous conflict was sparked when Canal Zone police prevented Panamanian students from raising their national flag. The building now houses a small collection of historical artefacts including weathered old tools, maps and household items. The Prado concludes at a dull monument dedicated to John Stevens, the canal's chief engineer from 1905 to 1907.

Calle Balboa

Opposite the John Stevens Monument stands the art deco **Balboa Theatre**, formerly a cinema. It was turned over to Panamanian control in 1979 and is now home to the National Symphony Orchestra. South on Calle Balboa, the **Balboa Union Church** stands out with its imposing neo-Gothic grandeur. Further along is an interesting sculpture dedicated to the ill-fated nationalist President Arnulfo Arias Madrid, who was thrice elected and thrice overthrown in military coups. The monument was crafted by Colombian sculptor Héctor Lombana in 2002 and is called *Homage to Democracy*. Beyond it, Calle Balboa connects with the thoroughfare of **Avenida del los Mártires**.

Calzada Amador → *For listings, see pages 60-77.*

Faintly reminiscent of Miami, the Calzada Amador (Amador Causeway) extends 2 km across the Bay of Panama with a palm-fringed boulevard, glitzy nightclubs, bars, restaurants, boutique malls, an international marina and a cruise-ship terminal. Built in 1911 using rubble acquired from the excavation of Culebra Cut, the causeway joins the mainland with three tiny offshore islets – Naos, Perico and Flamenco – and acts as a buffer preventing the build up of sediments at the canal's entrance. In 1913, the US established one of the world's most expensive and important military installations on Isla Flamenco – Fort Grant – complete with secret tunnels, bomb shelters and massive artillery weapons intended to fend off invaders. Defensive operations were significantly scaled back after the Second World War, but the causeway remained an important strategic post for many years. After it reverted to Panamanian control in 1979, the Panama Defence Forces established their headquarters at Fuerte Amador, close to the mainland. It was seized by US forces during the 1989 invasion and was finally returned to Panama in 1994. Since then, the causeway has been rigorously developed for tourism, business and conventions.

Punta Culebra Nature Center

ⓘ *Punta Culebra, Isla Naos, www.stri.si.edu, Tue-Fri 1300-1700, Sat-Sun 1000-1800. General admission US$5, children and retirees US$1. Signs are in Spanish and English, guides are available.*

The Punta Culebra Nature Center is owned and managed by the excellent Smithsonian Tropical Research Institute. It maintains a diverse range of exhibits intended to educate, raise awareness and promote conservation of Central and South American marine environments. Aquariums feature colourful specimens from the Caribbean and the Pacific, as well as several hawksbill turtles and nurse sharks. Children will enjoy the 'touching pools' where they can handle starfish, sea cucumbers and other aquatic fauna. Changing exhibits explore themes such as marine diversity, the relationship of humans and sea, coral reefs, fishing and sustainability. A small walking trail leads past some mangroves and concludes in a patch of tropical dry forest where you might spot numerous birds, iguanas or even an armadillo. There is an observation area outside with telescopes for watching the ships enter the canal.

Bridge of Life Biodiversity Museum

ⓘ *www.biomuseopanama.org, tours on request.*

The long-awaited (and heavily delayed) Bridge of Life Biodiversity museum was still under construction at the time of research, but promises to be world class once completed. Designed by acclaimed architect Frank Gehry – whose previous works include the Guggenheim Museum in Bilbao, Spain, and the MIT Stata Center in Cambridge, Massachusetts – the museum will explore the natural history of Panama and its important role as a major ecological crossroads. A range of interactive and technological exhibits have been developed by Bruce May Design, along with botanical gardens by New York specialist Edwina von Gal, addressing themes such as evolution, migration and interdependency. Labelled a learning centre and "hub of interchange of nature, culture, the economy and life", the Bridge of Life Biodiversity Museum is already being trumpeted as the city's most iconic and cutting-edge new development.

◉ Panama City listings

For sleeping and eating price codes and other relevant information, see pages 16-19.

● Where to stay

Tocumen International Airport *p37*
$$$$-$$$ Riande Aeropuerto, near Tocumen Airport (5 mins), T290-3333, www.hotelesriande.com. Conveniently located for fliers, with free transport to the airport. Rooms are dated and, in some cases, shabby. Amenities include pool (loud music all day), tennis courts and casino. Poor value, mixed reports.

San Felipe *p43, map p44*
A slew of very elegant and expensive boutique hotels have opened in the district, the epitome of colonial grandeur. Despite the moneyed pretensions of San Felipe, development is patchy. Take care after dark.
$$$$ The Canal House, Av A and Calle 5, T228-1907, www.canalhousepanama.com. Housed in a handsome 19th-century town house, this exclusive boutique hotel has received praise in *The New York Times* and

other international press. It has 3 crisp, elegant suites, all immaculately presented. Private, professional and personalized service. Not cheap.
$$$$ Los Cuatro Tulipanes, Casa las Monjas Apt. 2A, Av Central between Calle 3a y 4a (above Granclement ice cream parlour) T211-0877, www.loscuatrotulipanes.com. Several tastefully attired apartments in the heart of Casco Viejo, including studios and 1- and 2-bedroom properties. Well equipped, charming, comfortable and often recommended.
$$$$-$$$ Casa Sucre Hotel, Calle 8 and Av B, T6679-7077, www.casasucreboutique hotel.com. This restored 1873 guesthouse is another reliable boutique option. It has 4 bedrooms and 3 apartments, all well equipped with Wi-Fi, cable TV, fridge, microwave, balcony, fully fitted kitchens and great stonework. A reasonable deal for groups.
$$$$-$$$ Las Clementinas, Calle 11 and Av B, T228-7613, www.lasclementinas.com. This tastefully furnished 4-floor townhouse has 6 comfortable, modern suite-apartments

with fully fitted kitchens, high-speed internet, cable TV and safe. A European atmosphere with good views from the rooftop patio. Same owners as The Canal House.

$$-$ Hotel Casco Antiguo, Calle B and Calle 12, T228-8510, www.hotelcasco antiguo.com. Built in 1915, this historic landmark hotel has a Moorish tiled lobby and an antique hand-operated lift. Lodgings comprise 45 clean, simple rooms in various states of restoration; those with a/c and hot water are twice the price. Wi-Fi and breakfast included. Take care on the surrounding streets.

$ Hospedaje Casco Viejo Calle 8, in front of San José church, T211-2027, www. hospedajecascoviejo.com. A mix of simple rooms at this backpackers' hostel, with private and shared bathrooms, and dorms too. A safe, quiet spot with outdoor terrace, kitchen and internet access. They have good travel advice for Panama and moving on.

$ Luna's Castle, 9a Este, between Av B and Av Alfaro, T262-1540, www.lunascastle hostel.com. A very popular, busy backpacker hostel in a beautiful old colonial mansion. Amenities include comfortable communal spaces, Wi-Fi, table tennis, guitars, book exchange, movie room and a kitchen. Dorms and private rooms available, rates include pancake breakfast. Often packed, book ahead.

Calidonia *p50, map p50*
If your standards are modest, there are plentiful cheap hotels in this area. It is insalubrious after dark, however, and a favourite haunt of prostitutes. Always check a room before accepting.

$$$ Costa Inn, Av Perú y Calle 39, T225-1522, www.hotelcostainn.com. A sparklingly clean and comfortable hotel right on the edge of Bella Vista. Double rooms feature 2 bathrooms, and the rooftop pool has great views of the city. Scheduled transport to the airport and other places. Breakfast included.

$$ Arenteiro, Calle 30 Este y Av Cuba, T227-5883, www.hotelarenteiropanama.

com. Some of these simple, functional rooms are on the small side, but they're all clean and have hot water, cable TV, telephone and a/c. There's a popular bar/ restaurant downstairs. Recommended.

$$ Centro Americano, Av Justo Arosemena y Av Ecuador, T227-4555, www.hotelcentro americano.com. The 61 rooms here are very clean, smart and well appointed, with Wi-Fi, hot water, plasma screen cable TV. Some have balconies and views of the bay. Restaurant, business centre and parking available. Recently remodelled and recommended.

$$ Dos Mares, Calle 30 between Perú and Cuba, T227-6149, dosmares@cwpanama. net. This hotel has a good rooftop pool with views across the city. Some rooms are more 'renovated' than others, so ask to see a few. Otherwise generally clean and comfortable, with a/c, hot water, cable TV and phone as standard. There's internet service and a restaurant. Popular with Ticos.

$$ Lisboa, Av Cuba y Calle 31, T227-5916. The rooms at this hotel are nice and big, but avoid those overlooking the main road below. The usual amenities include a/c, hot water and cable TV, with a restaurant downstairs. Well established. An old favourite.

$$ Venecia, Av Perú, between Calle 36 and 37, T227-5252, www.hvenecia.com. This hotel is fading, but still going strong. Some rooms are better than others; ask to see a few. The good ones are large and have a fridge. All have cable TV, bath, hot water and a/c. Wi-Fi in the lobby, restaurant-bar attached. Courteous.

$$ Veracruz, Av Perú y Calle 30, T227-3022, www.hotelveracruz.com.pa. This friendly old hotel has an elegant reception area, but some of the rooms are noisy and in need of renovation. It has a very good restaurant, helpful staff, sea views, Wi-Fi, jacuzzi and sauna.

$ Las Tablas, Av Perú y Calle 29 Este. Rooms here are equipped with fan and national TV. They're a good deal for experienced budget travellers, but the hotel interior is a bit dark and gloomy. Opposite is **El Machetazo** supermarket, food for cheap meals. Chatty owner.

$ Mamallena, Casa 7-62, Calle Primera, T6676-6163, www.mamallena.com. A backpacker hostel with private rooms and dorms, kitchen and plenty of places to hang out. Often full. They've done their research, and have details about sail boats to Colombia on the website.

$ Pensión Monaco, Av Cuba y Calle 29, T225-2573. This large, echo-filled place has big, comfortable rooms; some have good views. Cable TV, hot water and a/c are standard, private parking available. Worth a look.

$ Residencial Volcán, Calle 29 y Av Perú, T225-5263. A good option for budget travellers, although lots of '1-hour' guests passing through. Rooms have a/c or fan, and cable TV. Guests have access to the rooftop pool at **Covadonga**, next door. Not bad for the price.

Area Bancaria and around *p51, map p52*

Most hotels are glitzy, well appointed and marketed to high-end travellers. Budget accommodation is scarce with the exception of a few hostels.

Bella Vista

$$$$ Miramar Intercontinental, Av Balboa, T206-8888, www.miramarpanama. com. These illustrious glass towers on the bay have a wealth of amenities, including 3 restaurants, a huge pool, gym, Wi-Fi and exclusive marina. Former guests include President Bush, who hired 120 rooms here during his visit to Panama. Bold and classy.

$$ California, Vía España y Calle 43, T263-7736, www.hotelcaliforniapanama.net. A good, clean, professional hotel with friendly, English-speaking staff. Rooms are modern, with a/c, cable TV, Wi-Fi and hot water. There's a restaurant attached and gym upstairs. Good value and recommended.

$$ Euro Hotel, Vía España 33, T263-0802, www.eurohotelpanama.com. Located on a busy street on the edge of Calidonia district, this hotel has over 100 large, comfortable rooms with a/c, hot water and cable TV. There's also a pool, restaurant and bar. OK.

$$-$ Hostal Urraca, Calle 44 Este, T391-3971, www.hostalurraca.com. A cheery new hostel nestled in the heart of Bella Vista, just minutes from leafy Parque Urraca. They have a range of simple but comfortable rooms (**$$**) and dorm beds (**$**). Amenities include free Wi-Fi, kitchen, BBQ, free continental breakfast and a relaxing outdoor patio with hammocks and tables. Spanish, English and Italian spoken.

El Cangrejo and around

$$$$ El Panamá, Vía España 111, T215-9182, www.elpanama.com. Built in 1951, this landmark hotel boasts intriguing 'tropical art-deco' architecture, huge rooms, fabulous pool, disco and a vast Vegas-style casino. A bit inefficient and perhaps overpriced, but generally worthy. Often hosts interesting events.

$$$$ Hotel Bristol, Av Aquilino de la Guardia, T264-0000, www.thebristol.com. The interior of the **Bristol Panama** is a paragon of style and luxury. Guests are assigned a personal 24-hr butler to meet their every need, while elegantly attired guestrooms include fine Frette linens, Molton Brown toiletries and Hungarian goose down pillows.

$$$$-$$$ Riande Continental, Vía España and Ricardo Arias, T263-9999, www.continentalhotel.com. Sister hotel to the **Riande Aeropuerto** and a striking 1970s landmark. There are over 300 rooms and amenities include gym, jacuzzi, business services, casino, travel agency, 24-hr café and parking.

$$$$-$$$ Sheraton Panama, Vía Israel y Calle 77, T305-5100, www.starwoodhotels. com. This reputable chain hotel has 4 restaurants, 1 with an excellent view over the bay. Other facilities include casino, sports bar and outdoor swimming pool. Located next to the **Atlapa Convention Centre** in San Francisco, good for conference groups but not a great location for tourists.

$$$ Baru Lodge, Calle 2a Norte, El Carmen, T393-2340, www.barulodge.com. An oasis of calm and balance. Rooms are classy, comfortable and minimalist, and include a kitchen area with a fridge and microwave. The real draw is the garden, complete with bubbling fountain, koi pond and lush vegetation. A great place to unwind after the frenetic challenges of the city. Recommended.

$$$ Executive Hotel, Calle 52 y Aquilino de la Guardia, T265-8011, www.executive hotel-panama.com. Marketed to business travellers, as the name might suggest. Rooms are clean, comfortable and functional, if uninspiring, and include writing desk, coffee-maker and 42" plasma TVs. After a hard day brokering deals, executive guests can unwind in the bar, sundeck or fitness centre.

$$$ Hotel De Ville, Calle 50 y Beatriz M De Cabal, T206-3100, www.devillehotel.com. pa. Recalling the elegance and opulence of a bygone era, **Hotel De Ville** is adorned with fine antique furniture imported from former French colonies. Tasteful rooms and suites have a simple, romantic air but also enjoy modern amenities like Wi-Fi and DVD.

$$$ Torres de Alba, Calle Eusebio Morales 55, T269-7770, www.torresdealba.com.pa. Slick, stylish, self-contained apartments with a minimalist touch. Some have great views over the city and all are equipped with a fully fitted kitchen, lounge, sofas, plasma TVs, internet and a/c. There's also a pool, gym and a so-so buffet breakfast, if you desire. Ask for a suite in the new tower, worth the extra dollars. Generally good value, comfortable and recommended.

$$$ Toscana Inn, Vía España y Calle D, T265-0018, www.toscanainnhotel.com. A comfortable and reliable option with lots of good reports from former guests. Rooms are clean, modern and well equipped with a/c, cable TV, minibar and Wi-Fi.

Other amenities include computer and business centre, conference room and café. Professional service, friendly, tasteful and highly recommended.

$$ Hostal La Casa de Carmen, Calle 1a, El Carmen, Casa 32 (from Vía España and Vía Brasil, 1 block north, 1 block east), T263-4366, www.lacasadecarmen.net. 3 friendly Panamanian ladies run this good-value option close to the action. Rooms have a/c and come with or without private bath. Dorms are also available (**$**). The garden provides blissful refuge from the city. Popular and recommended.

$$ Hotel Milán, Calle Eusebio A Morales 31, T263-6130, www.hotelmilan.com.pa. A reliable and economical option conveniently located. Rooms are clean, functional, comfortable and quiet, and include a/c, cable TV and Wi-Fi. They are currently expanding their premises. Unexciting but safe and good value. Lots of satisfied reports.

$$ Marbella, Calle D, between Calle 55 and Calle Eusebio A Morales, T263-2220, www.hmarbella.com. Clean, tidy, adequate rooms with a/c, cable TV and private bath. Located in a safe, central area of town, on a quiet backstreet. Friendly with good reports, if a touch spartan.

Marbella, Punta Paitilla and Punta Pacífica

$$$ Plaza Paitilla Inn, Vía Italia, T208-0600, www.plazapaitillainn.com. Once the tallest building in Panama City, the **Plaza Paitilla Inn** is today dwarfed by its high-rise neighbours. Nonetheless, its junior suites are comfortable and clean and provide commanding views over the bay. A memorable option, and good value for its location. Recommended.

Cerro Ancón p57

$$$ La Estancia, Casa 35, Calle Amelia Denis de Icaza, Quarry Heights, T314-1581, www. bedandbreakfastpanama.com. Managed by the hospitable Tammy Liu and Gustavo Chan, **La Estancia** is one of Panama's City's finest B&Bs. It enjoys refreshing breezes and lush surroundings from its commanding position up on Ancón Hill and wildlife sightings are frequent. Comfortable standard rooms and suites are available, all with Wi-Fi, complementary tea, coffee and fruit. Rates include a hearty cooked breakfast served on a tranquil balcony. Lots of good reports, recommended.

Balboa *p58*
A quiet, residential neighbourhood. Good if you want to access the canal, the causeway or even the national parks further north, but a trip downtown requires a taxi.
$$$ Canal Inn, Casa 7, Calle Ernesto Castillero, T314-0112, www.canal-inn.com. A bright, friendly, comfortable B&B with an attractive courtyard, leafy garden and pool. Amenities include satellite TV, a/c, Wi-Fi and a good cooked breakfast. Quiet, cosy and hospitable. Good for couples.
$$-$ Hostal Amador Familiar, Casa 1519, Calle Akee, T314-1251, www.hostalamadorfamiliar.com. A handsome Canal Zone-era house in the heart of leafy Balboa. Amenities include internet, kitchen, tourist information and a relaxing garden complete with hammocks and tables. Dorms and private rooms (**$$**) are available.

Calzada Amador *p59*
$$$ Country Inn and Suites Amador, Av Amador y Av Pelícano, T211-4500, www.countryinns.com. Perched at the foot of the causeway, the **Country Inn Amador** has 159 rooms and suites, most with enchanting views over the entrance to the canal. Rooms are clean, tidy and well equipped with whirlpool bath, Wi-Fi, coffee-maker and all the usual mod-cons. Other amenities include a gym, business centre, excellent pool and hot tub. Well appointed and reliable.

❼ Restaurants

The website **Oferta Simple**, www.ofertasimple.com, often features great discounts for Panama City restaurants. For reviews, try **Degusta**, www.degustapanama.com.

San Felipe *p43, map p44*
The restaurant scene in San Felipe takes itself a bit seriously and is increasingly aimed at upmarket clientele. Reservations may be necessary for dinner, especially at weekends.
$$$ Casablanca, Plaza Bolívar, T212-0040, www.restaurantecasablanca.com. Long established and popular, **Casablanca** occupies the handsome premises of the former Hotel Colombia. It has scores of tables set out in the picturesque plaza and serves average meat, pasta, salad and seafood. The food is overpriced, but the al fresco setting is great.
$$$ Ego y Narciso, Calle 3a y Plaza Bolívar, T262-2045. Dinner daily, lunch Mon-Fri only. **Ego y Narciso** has stood the test of time and is now celebrated as one of San Felipe's finest and most popular restaurants. Their menu is eclectic and includes lots of Spanish tapas, Italian pasta and Peruvian-style seafood. The interior is modern and comfortable, but nothing beats the romance and atmosphere of dining outdoors on the plaza, especially after dark.
$$$ Las Bóvedas, Plaza de Francia, T228-8058. Mon-Fri 1800-2300, Sat 1200-2300. Located in the converted dungeons at the seaward end of Casco Viejo, this long-standing and very atmospheric restaurant serves up French cuisine beneath intimate, arched stone ceilings. An interesting spot, with an adjoining art gallery and live jazz Fri-Sat.
$$$ Manolo Caracol, Av Central y Calle 3a, T228-4640, www.manolocaracol.net. No lunch on Sat. This respected San Felipe institution serves tapas and seafood, uses the freshest ingredients and draws culinary inspiration from the owner's homeland – Andalusia, Spain. The interior

is warm and rustic, and is often packed with diners, thanks to the restaurant's on-going popularity.

$$$ Mostaza, Av A y Calle 3a, T228-3341. Closed Sun. **Mostaza** is an oft-praised and intimate little establishment with a romantic setting in the shadow of the Arco Chato ruins. Its Argentine-inspired menu features excellent beef cuts, steaks and immaculately seasoned seafood. Live music at the weekends. Good atmosphere and service.

$$ Cedros Grill and Tavern, Av Central, between Calle 4a and 5a, T228-6797. This American-style grill house is a casual and easygoing addition to the scene. They serve decent burgers, excellent pizzas and other wholesome pub grub, best washed down with a cold beer or two. Friendly and fun, with outdoor seating and sports TV.

$$ Ciao Pescao, Plaza Bolívar, T262-3700. Closed Mon. A funky little joint on the plaza. They serve a broad range of excellent Peruvian-style ceviche and over 30 varieties of international beer – the perfect accompaniment. Skip the interior and sit outside.

$$ Diablo Rosso, Av A y Calle 7a, T228-4833, www.diablorosso.com. Tue-Sat. Injecting some much-needed creativity into the local scene, kitsch and bohemian **Diablo Rosso** is a breath of fresh air. Its premises are a multifunctional artistic space, serving as a gallery, concept store and colourful café. Tue night is film night, when you can enjoy a dose of alternative cinema and tasty international food. Recommended.

Bakeries, delis and ice cream parlours

Granclement, Av Central y Calle 3a, T228-0737, www.granclement.com. Fantastic gourmet ice cream to soothe your soul and take your taste buds to another level. Not cheap, but delicious. Recommended.

Super Gourmet, Av A y Calle 6a, T212-3487, www.supergourmetcascoviejo.com. A haven for foodies with a delectable range of imported cheeses, fruits, fine wines and other delicious fare. There are also gourmet

sandwiches, salads and tasty breakfasts, such as eggs Benedict. Wi-Fi available.

Santa Ana p48

Most eateries are geared towards locals, with a few bakeries and passable snack bars on the pedestrian Peatonal.

$$-$ Mercado de Mariscos, Av Balboa y Av Eloy Alfaro. The Japanese-built fish market is the place to sample Panama's rich and varied seafood offerings. Stalls downstairs sell a staggering array of ceviche for a little over US$1 a tub. Upstairs, a bustling and unpretentious restaurant offers delicious sit-down meals, including crab, lobster, fish fillet and more. It doesn't get any fresher than this. Highly recommended.

$ Café Coca Cola, Av Central and Plaza Santa Ana. A bustling, friendly little locals' haunt with good coffee, breakfasts and reasonably priced set lunches. Opened in 1875, **Café Coca Cola** is the oldest café in the city and something of an institution, boasting numerous Panamanian politicians and Che Guevara among its former diners. Great neighbourhood colour. Recommended.

Calidonia p50

Many hotels have restaurants attached but dining in Calidonia is generally mediocre. If you're cash-strapped, there are lots of kiosks selling street food, particularly around Parque Belisario Porras – pick one that's clean and popular.

$$ Café Boulevard Balboa, Calle 33 and Av Balboa. Mon-Sat. One of the few bay-side eateries that hasn't been demolished for new skyscrapers. This historic Panamanian diner has been around since the 1950s and continues to serve reasonable breakfasts, lunches and dinners, as well as coffee and snacks (avoid the sandwiches). OK.

$$-$ Romanaccio Pizza, Calle 29, between Av Cuba and Av Perú. Mon-Sat. Good, tasty Italian-style pizzas with authentic crusts, but forget the burgers. Dining is casual and down-to-earth. Takeaways available.

$ El Sabor Interiorano, Calle 37, between Av Central and Av Perú. Mon-Fri 1200-1500. A cosy, unassuming little locals' haunt serving affordable staples and Panamanian fare.

$ Rincón Tableño, Av Cuba No 5 y Calle 31. Lunchtimes only. This popular restaurant serves typical national fare and good *comida criolla* and it's always bustling with working-class Panamanians. Economical, filling and assuredly no frills.

Area Bancaria and around *p51*
El Cangrejo and around

$$ Beirut, Calle 52, T214-3815. Daily 1200-2300. Beirut stands out as the city's best Lebanese restaurant with really good hummus, falafels, kebabs and other wholesome Middle Eastern fare. The decor is overdone, but service is prompt, friendly and professional. There's also some seating on a balcony overlooking the street where you can enjoy a mint tea, smoke a hookah and watch the world go by. Recommended.

$$ Da Pacho, Vía Veneto. Mon-Sat 1200-2230, Sun 1800-2200. The place for decent and completely authentic Napolitan-style pizzas and other Italian fare. Slick decor and a buzzing ambience with a handful of booth tables overlooking the street. Takeaway available. Popular and recommended.

$$ El Burger Bar, Mini-mall, Av Eusebio Morales, www.elburgerbar.com. Tue-Sun 1200-2200. Bright and bold sports-themed joint where you can enjoy wholesome gourmet burgers, sugary drinks and occasionally discounted beer and cocktails. Racy music and icy a/c. Not bad.

$$ El Trapiche, Vía Argentina 10, T221-5241. This popular restaurant specializes in classic Panamanian fare, including some of the best *caramiñolas* in the country. They often host traditional music and dance programmes; call for information.

$$ Las Tinajas, on Calle 51, near Ejecutivo Hotel, T263-7890. Mon-Sat. Panamanian cuisine and traditional entertainment, including dance, music and costumes (Tue and Thu-Sat from 2100). A little touristy, but the food is very good and authentic. There's also a craft shop attached.

$$ Sukhi, Calle Beatriz M Cabal, next to the Marriott, T395-6081, www.sukhionline.com. Mon-Sat 1200-2230. **Sukhi** offers excellent, authentic and affordable southeast Asian cuisine, including tasty Vietnamese summer rolls, spicy Penang curry and Teriyaki noodles. So delicious it's almost addictive.

$ Loving Hut, Calle Manuel Espinosa Batista, www.lovinghut.com/pa. Open 1200-2000. Very fresh, tasty and affordable vegan and vegetarian buffet food with an Oriental twist. A clean, simple interior and friendly service. Excellent fruit juices (try the *maracuyá*) and free fresh jasmine tea. Highly recommended for budget travellers.

$ Niko's Café, Vía España near El Rey supermarket, T264-0136. Open 24 hrs. Cheap, reliable fast food, including burgers, subs and sodas. Nothing special, but good for a snack in the early hours. Several other locations around the city, including El Dorado Shopping Centre, Paitilla and Balboa.

$ Plaza Concordia Food Court, Vía España. Mon-Fri. Head to the back of the arcade to find this large, unpretentious food court with several cheap restaurants serving fresh, wholesome buffet fare. One of the few places in the Area Bancaria where you can eat for under US$5 and packed with workers 1230-1330. Highly recommended for budget travellers.

Cafés and bakeries

Grand Deli Gourmet, Av Samuel Lewis. Swish deli in the swanky neighbourhood of Obarrio. They sell cheese, cooked meats, coffee, salads, tasty *empanadas* and fresh bread. A good spot for casual lunch, but often packed with office workers in the week.

New York Bagel Café, Plaza Einstein, off Vía Argentina, T390-6051, www.newyorkbagel cafe.com. A popular spot for coffee and bagels, as the name suggests. There's also Wi-Fi, soft sofas and a great bakery selling fresh bread and brownies. Service can be poor during busy times.

Noel, Vía Porras, between Av1a C Norte and Av 2a C Norte, El Carmen. One of the city's best bakeries and great for a cheap breakfast or lunch. They offer *empanadas*, good fresh bread, cookies, cakes and sweet treats. Highly recommended.

Marbella, Punta Paitilla and Punta Pacífica

$$$ Gaucho's Steak House, Calle Uruguay. Choose your own cut at this buzzing Argentine steakhouse in Marbella, a must for meat lovers. The kitchen uses prime beef imported from the US and a range of interesting sauces, including spicy chimichurri. Servings are huge and fit for a king.

$$$ Marina Marina, Plaza Pacífica, next to Super 99, T390-1010, www.marina marina.com. Marina Marina is pushing the boundaries of contemporary Panamanian cuisine with interesting mains like plantain-crusted pork tenderloin and pineapple-rum skirt steak. They also offer daily fixed-price specials for around US$12. Good reports.

$$$ Sake, Torre de las Américas, also in the Metro Mall. The best sushi in the city, including some particularly tasty white tuna sashimi. The surroundings are clean, calm and contemporary. Excellent, but quite pricey.

$$$-$$ La Posta, Calle 49 y Calle Uruguay, T269-1076, www.lapostapanama.com. La Posta is one of Panama City's great culinary pioneers. It boasts a creative menu of mostly meat, seafood and pasta, including temptations like jumbo prawns and passion fruit served with smoked bacon and hearts of palm, or organic wood oven roasted chicken with lemon, herbs and polenta. The interior is smart and tasteful, but not fussy.

$$$-$$ Madame Chang, Av 5 Sur, between Calle 48 and Calle 49. One of the city's better Chinese restaurants, although culinary standards aren't always consistent. A diverse menu sporting Peking duck and other tasty oriental fare. Set meals may be better than individual items.

$$$-$$ Market, Calle 47 y Calle Uruguay, T264-9401, www.marketpanama.com. Market has a smart brick and tile interior reminiscent of a New York steakhouse. They serve superb prime Angus beef burgers and enormous mouth-watering steaks, as well as really delicious desserts, such as coconut pavlova and key lime pie. Buzzing ambience and attentive service. Affordable and highly recommended.

$$ Crepes & Waffles, Calle 47, also at Multiplaza and Albrook malls. As the name suggests, appetizing crêpes and waffles with a range of sweet and savoury fillings, some of them quite creative. For a final course, there's an entire mouth-watering menu devoted to ice cream. A hit with families and couples and very popular with middle-class Panamanians. Recommended.

$$ Habibi's, Calle Uruguay y Calle 48. Tasty, full-flavoured Middle Eastern and Mediterranean food served in a converted mansion. It can get busy on Fri and Sat night when revellers occupy the upper floors. There's also outdoor seating on the patio where you can soak up the Calle Uruguay vibe and maybe smoke a hookah or two. Good hummus and kofta kebabs. Not bad.

Cafés and bakeries

Petit Paris, Calle 50 Este, www.petitparis panama.com. You can enjoy the taste of Paris at this French-style café. Crunchy baguette sandwiches, artisan bread, cappuccinos, chocolate éclairs and other fine euro fare are on offer. Tasty, but not cheap.

🎭 Entertainment

Bars, clubs and live music

Panameños love a good party and Panama City's nightlife is as vibrant and varied as it gets. Pounding dance clubs, slick lounge-bars, swinging salsa halls, boozy pubs and bohemian jazz haunts are among the venues. When visiting night clubs, you should dress to impress and keep a healthy stock of dollars to hand – most places charge a cover of US$10-25. No trainers or shorts, please. For listings, check www.eventostoppanama.com.

San Felipe

San Felipe is a great place to go bar hopping and definitely worth checking out. Most places are casual.

Habana Panamá, Calle Eloy Alfaro y Calle 12 Este, www.habanapanama.com. You'll enjoy astounding glimpses of old Cuba at this swinging bastion of style and 1950s elegance. Live salsa music is performed at weekends by smartly attired bands. Pass through the red velvet curtains to the dance floor or head upstairs to sit in one of the red booths. Very cool and highly recommended. Smart attire only, including shoes.

La Casona de las Brujas, end of Calle 5, just off Av A, www.enlacasona.com. La Casona is a cultural centre featuring local art work and occasional events in the day. It occupies a space on the water's edge and its patio out back is the scene of DJs and live music most weekend evenings. Off-beat and bohemian.

Mojitos sin Mojitos, Av A y Calle 9a, Plaza Herrera, www.mojitossinmojitos.com. An atmospheric outdoor patio surrounded by crumbling old city walls and tropical plant life. Laid back and hospitable, great for a cold beer and meeting new friends. They do BBQ burgers too. Occasional live music. Recommended.

Platea Jazz Bar, Calle 1a, opposite the old Club Unión, T228-4011, www.scenayplatea. com. An intimate and well-established San Felipe bar, widely celebrated for its live music sets. Jazz plays on Thu, live salsa, complete with spirited dancing, on Fri, and rock on Sat. Check the website to see what's new.

Relic Bar, Calle 9a, www.relicbar.com. Relic Bar is a hugely popular place that sees an eclectic mix of foreign travellers. It's located in the distinctive stone-walled cellars of Luna's Castle, a backpackers' hostel well known for its party-loving clientele (see page 61). There's a garden with outdoor seating where you can enjoy the tropical night.

Vieja Habana, Av B y Calle 5a. This relaxed Cuban bar boasts handsome dark-wood furnishings and an extensive selection of fine rum, much of it straight from the homeland. A great place for an ice cold Mojito or, if you're hungry, a *cubano* sandwich.

El Cangrejo and around

Most of the action is concentrated on or around Vía Argentina, a good place for warming up. Laid back, sociable and generally unpretentious.

El Pavo Real, Vía Argentina and José Martí, www.elpavoreal.net. A good old-fashioned British-owned pub where you can enjoy a pint of lager and a plate of fish and chips. Naturally, a pool table and dart board are available, and you can sometimes catch live music at the weekends. Popular with locals and expats alike.

Istmo Brew Pub, Av Eusebio Morales, www.istmobrewpub.com. In addition to several national and imported beers, Istmo Brew Pub offers a range of tasty artisan beers from Chiriquí, Coclé, Colón, Veraguas and beyond. There's a pool table, outdoor seating and light snacks. A relaxed and convivial pub experience. Recommended.

La Rana Dorada, Plaza Einstein, just off Vía Argentina. Another popular pub-style drinking establishment in Cangrejo. This one is Irish-owned and it boasts a great terrace for watching the world go by. Aside from the usual refreshing beers, good pub food is available, including excellent burgers.

Marbella, Punta Paitilla and Punta Pacífica

Marbella is home to Calle Uruguay, the heart of Panama City's nightclub scene. Establishments come and go quite frequently, so just turn up, chat to fellow revellers and find out what's in vogue.

The Londoner, Calle Uruguay. A popular pub-restaurant where you can enjoy a low-key English-style pint and some grub. Fun and popular with locals. A good place to warm up before hitting the dance floor.

People Ultra Lounge, Calle Uruguay. A big, thumping disco where you can let loose on the dance floor, or alternatively, chill out in the VIP lounge. A favourite haunt of students and energetic young whipper-snappers. Fun and reasonably informal.

Privé, Calle Uruguay. **Privé** is a classy lounge-style club with modern, minimalist decor and an exclusive clientele, including local celebrities and wealthy Panameños. The ambience is low-key and friendly. Good DJs and cocktails.

Pure, Calle Uruguay y Calle 48, www.pure clubpanama.com. **Pure** club is one of the city's best-established venues and it plays a broad range of music, from house to hip hop and R&B. It boasts a large outdoor terrace, a pounding dance floor and a sophisticated white-leather lounge. Often recommended.

S6IS, Calle Uruguay, upstairs from Privé, www.bars6is.com. Pronounced 'Seis', this intimate club features electronic music and fabulous decor, but it's often more drinking than dancing. Among the finest and most exclusive venues in the city. Swish, young and beautiful.

Starlight, Calle 47, just off Calle Uruguay, opposite **Crepes & Waffles**, www.starlight. com.pa. An ambient lounge and karaoke bar where you can glug cocktails and sing your favourite pop songs. Good fun.

Calzada Amador

The Calzada has something for everyone, but most options are big, bold and commercial. Alternatively, you can mingle with the yachters and the beautiful people.

Zona Viva, Calzada. A complex of several different nightclubs and bars. The crowds and flavours vary, but most joints are flashy. The best thing you can do is wander around and see what takes your fancy. For security purposes, bring your ID to gain entry.

Gay and lesbian venues

Panama City has a thriving gay scene. There are several specialized clubs and saunas that gay men will want to check out, but sadly no lesbian-only establishments. For more on gay and lesbian travel in Panama, see page 25.

BLG, Vía Transístmica, Edificio Bonivel, opposite Ford Autos. **BLG** is one of the most popular and well known of Panama's gay clubs, featuring DJs, dancing, events and occasional open bars. Young and energetic.

Lips, Av Manuel Espinoza Batista, next to Café Durán, Lava Auto Splash, 2nd floor. Great dance club featuring house, reggaeton and regular drag shows. Youthful and fun.

Xscape Bar, opposite the Selecta, Calle Camino de la Amistad, next to Pizza Hut. Tue-Sat. A recent addition to the gay scene, **Xscape** is an intimate space featuring 2 floors and bars and lounge seating.

Cinema

Plenty of cinemas, but most of them show trashy Hollywood flicks. For listings, consult www.cinespanama.com. For alternative cinema, consider dinner and movie night at Diablo Rosso (see Restaurants, page 65).

Alhambra, Vía España, El Cangrejo, T264-6585.

Cinemark, Multicentro Mall, Punta Paitilla, T208-2507, www.cinemarkca.com. Additional screens in Albrook Mall and Centro Comercial Los Pueblos 2000.

Cinépolis, Multiplaza Mall, Punta Pacífica, T302-6262, www.cinepolis.com.pa. Additional screens in Metro Mall.

Extreme Planet, Av Balboa, Punta Paitilla, T214-7022, www.extremeplanetpanama.com.

Theatre

Panama's theatre scene is surprisingly vibrant, including everything from amateur plays to symphony concerts. *La Prensa* and other newspapers publish daily programming (*cartelera*) of cultural events.

Teatro ABA, Vía Transístmica, opposite Riba Smith supermarket, T260-6316, www.teatroaba.com. A small, contemporary theatre managed by the ABA artistic group. They offer highly regarded acting classes.

The Panama Jazz Festival

Each year in January, the capital's theatres and music halls come alive to the trumpets, trombones, pianos, flutes, saxophones and syncopated rhythms of the city's annual jazz festival. Established in 2003 by Grammy-winning pianist and composer Danilo Pérez, the event draws an eclectic crowd of 25,000 music lovers and some of the most talented names in jazz. Thanks to Pérez, who is a Fulbright scholar and world-renowned educator, the festival has a deeply educational ethos. Some of the world's most prestigious music institutes attend to offer workshops and master-classes, or otherwise award scholarships to bright young music students. Pérez's own institute, the **Fundación Danilo Pérez**, www.fundaciondaniloperez.com, is based in San Felipe and enjoys an admirable reputation for educating disadvantaged teenagers from poor neighbourhoods; it offers year-round private classes in ethnomusicology, composition and improvization, among others. The six-day Panama Jazz Festival concludes with a popular open-air concert in San Felipe, where the combination of swinging melodies, convivial company and fine colonial architecture conspire to create an unbeatable ambience.

To learn more about the Panama Jazz Festival, including schedules and audition opportunities, see www.panamajazzfestival.com.

Teatro Anayansi, in the ATLAPA Convention Centre, Vía Israel, San Francisco. Has a 3000-seat capacity, good acoustics, regular recitals and concerts.
Teatro Anita Villalaz, Plaza de Francia, San Felipe, T211-4020. Located in the former Supreme Court of Justice, this small theatre is part of the National Institute of Art and Culture. It has 250 seats and hosts regular folklore presentations, plays and workshops.
Teatro Balboa, Av Arnulfo Arias Madrid, Edif 727-C, near Steven's Circle and post office in Balboa, T228-0327. A fantastic art deco building which originally served as a Canal Zone cinema. It is the headquarters of the National Symphony Orchestra.
Teatro en Círculo, Av 6C Norte, near Vía Transístmica, Urbanización Herbruger, T261-5375. The Teatro en Círculo theatre group was formed in 1961 and since 1979 they have managed this intimate 242-seat space.
Teatro La Quadra, Calle D, El Cangrejo, T214-3695, www.teatroquadra.com. Teatro La Quadra believes that access to culture and artistic expression is a human right. They stage interesting alternative productions and provide regular workshops.
Teatro Nacional, Av B y Calle 3a, T262-3525. Panama's elegant National Theatre stages folklore sessions every other Sun and monthly National Ballet performances when not on tour. Check press for details. For more information on the theatre, see page 46.
Theatre Guild of Ancón, next to the judicial police headquarters, Ancón, T212-0060, www.anconguild.com. The **Theatre Guild of Ancón** opened its doors in 1950 and continues to host English-language productions that prove very popular with the city's expats.

✹ Festivals

Jan Panama City's annual 6-day **Jazz Festival**, www.panamajazzfestival.com, takes place at various locations around the city. It draws crowds of 25,000 and is one Central America's finest live music events – don't miss it! For more information, see box, above.
Feb/Mar **Carnaval** is staunchly celebrated in the capital, Sat-Tue before Ash Wed.

Stages are set up all over the city, including the Cinta Costera, where you can catch live music and dance. Colourful parades, which culminate in the crowning of a Carnival Queen, occur most days. Meanwhile, there is much drinking and abandon in the streets and, traditionally, revellers often enjoy a soaking from water cannons. Pace yourself, as the party goes on late into the evenings at most bars and clubs. Keep your passport handy to enter some parts of the festivities.
3 Nov Independence Day, practically the whole city – or so it seems – marches in a colourful and noisy parade through the old part of the city lasting over 3 hrs. Another parade takes place the following day.
Dec Annual Christmas parade, with US influence much in evidence, rather than the Latin American emphasis on the *Nacimiento* and the Three Kings.

✪ Shopping

Artesanías
Artesanías are widely available in specialized craft markets, street stalls, and souvenir and boutique shops. For a complete discussion of Panama's artistic offerings, see page 21.
Centro Artesanal Antiguo YMCA, Av Arnuldo Arias Madrid y Av Amador, Balboa. Located inside the old YMCA building in Balboa, a small selection of crafts, not to be confused with the bigger site in the yellow building behind it.
Centro Municipal de Artesanías, Av Arnulfo Arias Madrid (Calle Balboa), a few blocks behind the old YMCA, Balboa. A small, intimate market run by Kuna women. Specializes in *molas*.
Flory Salzman, Vía Veneto, El Cangrejo, at the back of **Don Lee**, T223-6963, www.florymola.com. The best place outside Guna Yala for *molas*, a huge selection sorted by theme. Recommended.
La Ronda, Calle 1a, San Felipe. An attractive little store that stocks a range of quality *artesanías* from all over the country. One of several in the historic quarter.

Mercado Artesanal de Balboa, Av Arnuldo Arias Madrid y Av Amador, Balboa, just behind the YMCA building. One of the city's largest and best-stocked craft markets. A very comprehensive range of *artesanías* from all over the country. Recommended.
Mercado de Artesanías Panamá Viejo, Vía Cincuentenario, by the visitor centre, T222-0612. A small, clean, easy-to-navigate craft market with products sourced from indigenous Kuna, Emberá, Wounaan and Ngäbe communities. Convenient if visiting the ruins.
Mercado de Buhonería, behind the old Museo Antropológico on Plaza 5 de Mayo, Calidonia. A small, friendly market selling indigenous and Azuero crafts, hammocks and artefacts from neighbouring countries. Worth a look.

Books
El Hombre de la Mancha, Calle 52, Bella Vista, www.bookshombredelamancha.com. Commercial bookstore with a café and a selection of English-language titles. Additional branches at Albrook airport, Amador causeway, Multiplaza and Multicentro malls.
Exedra books, Vía Brasil and Vía España, www.exedrabooks.com. A large, modern bookstore with a small selection of English-language titles, including guides and novels. Coffee shop upstairs.
Gran Morrison, Vía España, T269-2211, and 4 other locations around the city. Paperback novels, travel guides (not Footprint) and magazines in English.
Librería Argosy, Vía Argentina, El Cangrejo, T223-5344. A very good selection of literature in English, Spanish and French, but not cheap. Also sells tickets for musical and cultural events. Recommended.
Librería Cultural Panameña, SA, Vía España opposite Calle 1a, Perejil, T223-5628, www.libreriacultural.com. Mon-Fri 0900-1800, Sat 0900-1700. Excellent, mostly Spanish bookshop with obscure Panamanian inprints as well as regular titles and very helpful staff.

National University Bookshop, on campus between Av Manuel Espinosa Batista and Vía Simón Bolívar, T223-3155. Mon-Fri 0800-1600. For an excellent range of specialized books on Panama, national authors, social sciences and history. Highly recommended.
Smithsonian Tropical Research Institute, see page 58. Mon-Fri 0800-1600. Has a bookshop and the best English-language scientific library in the city.

Jewellery

Av Samuel Lewis in Obarrio is the place to shop for high-quality jewellery. Particularly recommended is:
Reprosa, Av Samuel Lewis y Calle 54, T269-0457, www.reprosa.com. A unique collection of pre-Columbian gold artefacts reproduced in sterling silver and gold vermeil. They offer interesting tours of their workshop in Panamá Viejo where you can learn about the production process, daily US$10.

Malls and shopping centres

The spirit of consumerism is alive and well in Panama City. Scores of gaudy shopping centres, commercial plazas and US-style malls cater to your wanton material needs, including:
Albrook Mall, next to the Terminal de Transporte in Albrook, www.albrookmall.com. Squarely marketed to the masses with a vast array of affordable shops, cinema and a food court. Packed at weekends.
Flamenco Shopping Plaza, Isla Flamenco, Calzada Amador. Duty-free shopping at the cruise-ship terminal on the causeway. Bring your passport to enter.
Los Pueblos, Vía Tocumen. A vast US-style strip mall near Tocumen Airport featuring 150 stores, including numerous boutiques and shoe shops. Often free from crowds.
Multicentro Mall, Av Balboa, near Punta Paitilla, www.multicentropanama.com.pa. The largest mall in Central America, featuring youthful shops, a food court, casino and cinema and other entertainment venues.

Multiplaza Mall, Punta Pacífica, www.multiplaza.com. The most upmarket mall in the country with brand names like **Calvin Klein**, **Lacoste**, **Apple** and more.

⏾ What to do

Adventure and extreme sport

Hiking is offered by most tour operators. The agencies below offer a broad range of specialist outdoor activities, including biking, rafting and climbing.
Aventuras Panamá, Calle 63 Oeste, Tumba Muerto, T260-0044, www.aventuras panama.com. Specialists in hiking, rock climbing and canyoning. Very knowledgeable about Darién and the old colonial roads. Many trips focus on the nearby Chagres National Park including the 'Jungle Challenge' which involves rappelling off a series of waterfalls. For all your adventuring and extreme sport needs.
Panama Pete Adventures, Av Miguel Brostella, Plaza Camino de Cruces No 35, next to **Country Inn & Suites El Dorado**, T231-1438, www.panamapeteadventures.com. All the adventure options available in Panama, including biking, hiking, caving, fishing and kayaking.

Birding and wildlife

The following are particularly recommended for their specialist knowledge of wildlife:
Advantage Tours, T6676-2466, www.advantagepanama.com. Founded by a group of biologists, **Advantage Tours** offers a range of reliable birding and wildlife tours, including expeditions to Darién. All guides are experienced and usually have a background in biology or tourism. Sponsors of the **Audubon Society**.
Ancon Expeditions, Calle Elvira Méndez, Edificio Dorado, next to **Marriott Hotel**, T269-9415, www.anconexpeditions.com. This is the tour operator of the famous environmental NGO, Ancón. Excellent guides and service, with highly recommended trekking programmes in

the Darién region (Cana Valley and Punta Patiño). One of the best.

Birding Panama, T393-5728, www.panama birding.com. Run by birders for birders, **Birding Panama** offers quality birdwatching and custom-designed natural history tours to hotspots throughout the country, including the Pipeline Rd, Chiriquí Highlands and Darién. Responsible and reputable.

Panama Audubon Society, Casa 2006-B, Llanos de Curundú, T232-5977, www. audubonpanama.org. Panama's oldest and most prestigious bird conservation society. They run regular fieldtrips as well as lectures and reasonably priced tours of the Parque Metropolitano and Parque Soberanía. Don't miss their Christmas bird count. Highly recommended.

Diving

See also individual listings for Bocas del Toro, Colón province (Costa Arriba) and Veraguas, all endowed with excellent sites.

Panama Dive Adventure, Miguel Brostella Av, Edif Don Manuel 2a, opposite **TGI Fridays**, El Dorado, T279-1467, www.dive.com.pa. Diving and technical courses, including deep diver. Tours to sites around Portobelo on the Central Caribbean coast as well as equipment sales, rental, repair and service.

Scubapanama, Urbanización El Carmen, Av 6 Norte y Calle 62a No 29-B, T261-3841, www.scubapanama.com. Respected local dive operator. Offers dives in the Caribbean (near Portobelo), Pacific and the Canal. One option includes all 3 areas in 1 day. Certification courses available.

Fishing

Panama Canal Fishing, T669-0507, www. panamacanalfishing.com. A very reputable and experienced operation headed by Rich and Gabby Cahill. They offer fishing trips on world-class Lago Gatún where you can catch abundant peacock bass and snook (see also page 97). They claim to reel in 20-30 per person. All equipment, food and drinks included. Recommended.

Kayaking

Expediciones Tropicales, T317-1279, www.xtrop.com. Headed by conservationists and indigenous leaders, **Expediciones Tropicales** is fiercely committed to the preservation of Panama's natural and cultural heritage. They boast exclusive access to several remote areas and offer kayak trips in the Chagres River, Panama Canal, Guna Yala and others. Recommended.

Sailing

For transits of the Panama Canal, see also page 92.

Panama Yacht Tours, T314-1000, www.panamayachttours.com. Private charters, canal transit, sunset cruises, parties and fishing trips, including services to both coasts.

San Blas Sailing, T314-1800, www.sanblas sailing.com. The first and oldest **San Blas Sailing** charter offers crewed yacht tours of the Guna Yala archipelago and Central Caribbean coast from 4 to 21 days. They have an impressive fleet of monohulls and catamarans.

Tour operators

Arian's Tours, Vía España, Plaza Concordia, Oficina 143A, T213-1172, www.arianstours pty.com. This agency offers a wide range of cultural and ecological tours including birdwatching, visits to indigenous communities and hiking in national parks.

Eco Circuitos, Albrook Plaza, 2nd floor No 31, Ancón, T315-1305, www.ecocircuitos. com. Expertly run with conservation and sustainability an utmost priority, **Eco Circuitos** offers a broad range of creative tours to destinations across the country. Activities include hiking, cultural exchange and educational programmes. A founding member of Panamanian Association of Sustainable Tourism. Highly recommended.

Emberá Tours Panama, T6519-7121, www.emberatourspanama.com. Managed by Garceth Cunampio, an English-speaking Emberá guide who leads adventurous trips to his home community. Options include journeys in dugout canoes, trips to see shamans, hiking and cultural presentations. Professional service and lots of good reports. Recommended.

Margo Tours, Plaza Paitilla, ground floor, in front of Banco General, Oficina 36, T264-8888, www.margotours.com. Specializes in tourism for small groups with an emphasis on using local guides. Professional and well established with over 30 years' experience.

Xplora Eco-Adventures, Calle 50 y Vía Brasil, Plaza 50 Building, ground floor, T6674-6050, www.panamatraveltours.com. A strong emphasis on ecology and good reports from past clients. They offer day trips and multi-day tours to a wide range of destinations including the Panama Canal, Bayano Caves, Guna Yala and Isla Grande.

⊖ Transport

Air

International flights Tocumen International Airport (PTY), www.tocumen panama.aero. Official taxi fare is US$25 for 2 passengers, or US$10 per person for 3 or more, 30-45 mins, or 1-2 hrs in rush hour. For fast transit, insist on the Corredor Sur toll road. To get to the airport on public transport, take a 'Tocumen' Metrobus from the Cinta Costera or Terminal de Transporte, every 15-30 mins, 45 mins, US$1.25. To get to the city from the airport, walk out of the terminal and cross the highway to the bus shelter. Metrobuses are much faster and less crowded than the *diablos rojos*, which are only practical if you're light on luggage. Allow plenty of extra time if travelling during rush hour.

Domestic flights Panama's domestic flight hub is Marcos A Gelabert International Airport, commonly known as Albrook Airport. There is no convenient bus service; a taxi costs US$3, beware overcharging.

Panama now has just 1 domestic airline. **Air Panama**, Albrook International Airport,

T316-9000, www.flyairpanama.com, flies to a wide range of regional airports and has a downtown office at Edificio Balboa, beside Laboratory Laser, Av Balboa, T269-3214.

Tickets Buy tickets direct from the airline, travel agents or tour operators at least 48 hrs prior to travel, or 3 weeks prior during peak holiday periods including Christmas and New Year (for more information on ticketing and restrictions, see page 14). The schedules below are subject to frequent change. All fares are one way and exclusive of taxes and charges, approximately an additional 25%.

Schedules Air Panama: To **Achutupo**, daily 0600, 1 hr, US$46. To **Bahía Piñas**, Mon and Fri 1030, 1 hr, US$56. To **Bocas del Toro**, Mon-Sat 0630, Sun 0800, daily 1530, 1 hr, US$80. To **Changuinola**, Mon-Sat 0630, 1530, 1½ hrs, US$80. To **Corazón de Jesús**, Mon-Sat 0600, ½ hr, US$40. To **David**, Mon-Fri 0700, Mon-Sat 0915, Sun 0830, daily 1620, 1 hr, US$80. To **El Porvenir**, daily 0600, ½ hr, US$38. To **Garachine**, Tue, Thu, 1030, 1 hr, US$46. To **Isla Contadora**, Mon-Sat 1000, Fri, Sun, 1630, ½ hr, US$35. To **Isla San José**, Mon-Sat 0930, Fri and Sun 1630, 20 mins, US$36. To **Isla San Miguel**, Tue, Thu and Sat, 1030, 20 mins, US$36. To **Jaque**, Mon and Fri, 1030, 1¼ hrs, US$54. To **Mulatupo**, daily 0600, 1 hr, US$38. To **Ogobsucum**, daily, 0600, 1 hr, US$35. To **Playón Chico**, daily, 0600, 50 mins, US$44. To **Puerto Obaldía**, Tue, Thu and Sun 0830, 1 hr, US$58. To **Sambu**, Tue and Thu 1030, 45 mins, US$48. To **San José** (Costa Rica), Mon, Wed and Fri 0915, US$146.

Bus

Local Most city buses depart from 1 of 3 zones outside the Gran Terminal de Transporte in Albrook. Outbound (east) buses travel along Av Perú in Calidonia before fanning out to their various destinations. Inbound (west) buses usually travel along Vía España and Av Central. The basic fare is US$0.25; outlying areas, including the Corredor Sur (Cinta Costera), US$1.25.

Metrobuses no longer accept cash: buy a top-up card from a kiosk or shop, US$2. The highly polluting but colourful *diablos rojos* are on their way out but offer a gritty shoulder-to-shoulder experience of city life.

Long distance All long-distance buses depart from the Gran Terminal de Transporte in Albrook, T303-3030, www.grantnt.com. To get there, take a bus from Vía España or Av Central, 20 mins, US$0.25; a taxi costs US$2-3. Inside the terminal, ticket offices are arranged in a line – simply look for your destination on the signs. For journeys of under 5 hrs, it's normally fine to just turn up. For longer trips (including David), or if travelling during holiday periods, you should allow 1-2 hrs for queuing and waiting. There is a 5 cent turnstile charge for accessing the platforms. No left luggage.

Bus schedules: To **Bocas del Toro** (including Almirante and Changuinola), 2000, 2030, 9 hrs, US$28; to Chame/San Carlos, every 15 mins, 0530-2000, US$2.60; to **Chitré**, hourly, 0600-2300, 4 hrs, US$9.05; to **Colón**, every ½ hr, 0330-2130, 2 hrs, US$3.15 (expreso); to **David**, hourly, 0530-2400, 7 hrs, US$15.25 (express 2245, 2400, 6 hrs, US$18.15); to El Valle, every ½ hr, 0600-2100, 2½ hrs, US$4.25; to **Las Tablas**, hourly, 0600-1900, 5 hrs, US$9.70; to Metetí, 5 daily, 1230-1645, 6 hrs, US$9; to **Penonomé**, every 15 mins, 0445-2245, 2 hrs, US$5.25; to **Santiago**, every ½ hr, 0400-2100, 3½ hrs, US$9.10; to Yaviza, hourly, 0300-1130, 7 hrs, US$14. For the former Canal Zone, including Miraflores locks and Gamboa, take a **SACA** bus, every 1-2 hrs, US$0.50-1.

International Buses going north through Central America get booked up so reserve a seat at least 4 days in advance in low season (or 1-3 months if travelling during Dec).

Ticabus, T314-6385, www.ticabus.com, is the main international carrier. It runs daily buses to **San José** at 1100 (executive class) arriving 0200 the next morning, US$45

one way; economy class departs 2300 and arrives 1600 the following afternoon, US$35 one way. Services continue to **Managua**, US$88 executive, US$60 economy; **Tegucigalpa**, US$103 executive, US$80 economy; **San Pedro Sula**, US$115 executive, US$92 economy; **Guatemala City**, US$133 executive, US$113 economy; as far as **Tapachula** in Mexico, US$152 executive, US$132 economy. Tickets are refundable and pay on the same day, minus 15%. Dates are open and easily changed.

Expreso Panama (formerly known as Panalines) also runs daily buses to **San José** from the Gran Terminal de Transporte, T314-6837, departing at 2300 and arriving 1500 the next day, US$35. Finally, you can travel with **Padafront**, T314-6263, Panama City–Paso Canoas then change to **Tracopa** or other Costa Rican buses for **San José** (or other destinations en route to the Costa Rican capital).

Boat and ferry
'Calypso' ferries to **Isla Taboga** depart from the Playita de Amador on the Causeway, just behind the Smithsonian Marine Center, T314-1730, Mon-Thu 0830, Fri 0830, 1500, Sat-Sun 0800, 1030, 1600, 1-1½ hrs, US$12 return, children US$7. Arrive 30 mins prior to departure to be assured a seat. Taxi to the causeway, US$5-6. For return schedules, see page 82. The journey to the island is pleasant and interesting. To the **Islas Perlas**, Sea Las Perlas, www.sealasperlas. com, T391-1424, operate a catamaran from Brisas de Amador, Isla Périco on the Amador Causeway. It departs Mon, Thu-Sun, 0800, 1½ hrs, US$42 one way, US$80 same day return. A flight is roughly the same price and it will get you there in just 20 mins.

Car rental
Avis, Calle D, El Cangrejo, T264-0722, www. avis.com.pa; additional offices at Tocumen Airport, Albrook Airport and Transístmica. **Budget**, Vía España, Calle Gabriela Mistral, entrada a la Cresta, T294-2300,

www.budgetpanama.com; additional offices in Tocumen Airport, Albrook Airport, Hotel El Panamá, Hotel Sheraton, Metromall and Multiplaza.

Dollar, Vía Veneto, Torre de Alba Hotel, El Cangrejo, T214-4725, www.dollarpanama. com. Additional offices at Tocumen Airport, Albrook Airport, Tumba Muerto, Vía Israel.

Hertz, Calle 55, El Cangrejo, T301-2699, www.rentacarpanama.com. Additional offices at Tocumen Airport, Albrook Airport, Hotel Marriott, Costa del Este, Vía Porras, Transístmica.

National, Edificio PH Universal, Calle 50, Obarrio, T265-2222, www.nationalpanama. com. Additional offices at Tocumen Airport, Albrook Airport, El Cangrejo.

Taxi

Taxis can be scarce during peak hours. Many drivers have little clue where some streets are so it's good to have a rough idea of the address location. Voluntary sharing is common but not recommended after dark. If a taxi already has a passenger, the driver will ask your destination to see if it coincides with the other passenger's. If you do not wish to share, waggle your index finger or say '*No, gracias*'. Similarly, if you are in a taxi and the driver stops for additional passengers, you may refuse politely. Overcharging is very common and official fares are based on a zone system: US$1.25 for 1 passenger within 1 zone, US$0.25 for each additional zone. If you get into a dispute, ask to see the driver's zone map. Hourly hire, advised for touring dubious areas, US$10 per hr. After dark, radio taxis summoned by telephone are recommended. They are listed in yellow pages under 'Taxis'; try Radio Taxi Italia, 270-0563; Radio Taxi Metro, T223-0942; or Taxi Nacional, T224-1132.

Train

A train runs daily from Corozal Passenger Station in Panama City to **Colón** US$22 one way, US$44 return, 0715, returns 1715,

1 hr. Turn up on the day or book in advance through tour operators. More details available at www.panarail.com. A taxi to the station costs US3. For more information on the Panama Canal Railway, see page 92.

🅞 Directory

Dentists

Most dentists are fluent in English, but always agree the price before any check-up. Beware overcharging and seek a second opinion for 'essential' or costly surgical treatments. Recommended practitioners include:

Dr Luis Bartres, Centro Especializado Paitilla, Av Balboa and Calle 53, opposite Paitilla Hospital, T263-8220, www.panamadentalcare.com.

Dr Ramón Vallarino, Clínica Dental Vallarino, Centro Comercial La Colmena, Offices 13 and 14, between Calle 50 and Vía Israel, T264-0237, www.dentalvallarino.com.

Doctors, clinics and hospitals

There are over a dozen hospitals in Panama City, both public and private. Some facilities are world class, but not necessarily cheap – insurance is a must. Health clinics are widespread and most doctors speak English. Ask your hotel for a local recommendation.

Centro Médico Paitilla, Calle 53 and Av Balboa, T265-8800, www.centromedico paitilla.com, has US-trained doctors and is one of the best established private hospitals in the city.

Clínica Einstein, Vía Argentina, El Cangrejo, T264-7110. Prompt, professional services, including an on-site laboratory for blood and other tests. Basic consultation around US$35.

Hospital Nacional, Av Cuba, between Calle 38 and Calle 39, T306-3300, www.hospital nacional.com, is an 80-bed facility with over 100 specialists. They accept many international health care plans.

Hospital Punta Pacífica, Blvd Pacífica y Vía Punta Darién, T204-8000, www.hospital puntapacifica.com, is the newest and most expensive of the city's hospitals. Great care if you can afford it.

Immigration
Migración y Naturalización, Av Cuba y Calle 28, Calidonia, T507-1800, www. migracion.gob.pa. Mon-Fri 0730-1530, for visas, permits and extensions. For more information, see page 34.

Language schools
Spanish Panama, Vía Argentina, El Cangrejo, T213-3121, www.spanishpanama. com, offers small group or flexible one-to-one classes with options for volunteering, homestays and/or cultural activities.
ILERI Language Institute, Altos de Betania, Av 17C Norte, house 20H, El Dorado, T392-40-86, www.ileripanama.com, is a small, friendly school located 20 mins from downtown. They have a range of programmes and can organize homestay.

Laundry
In Panama, *lavamáticos* are launderettes and *lavanderías* are dry cleaners. Expect to pay around US$2-3 to wash and dry a medium load. In San Felipe, you'll find a *lavamático* at Calle 7 Central. In Calidonia, head to **Lavandería y Lavamático América**, Av Justo Arosemana and Calle 27. In the banking district, try **Vía Veneto** y Av 3A Norte in El Cangrejo. Alternatively, many hotels offer affordable laundry service.

Libraries
Biblioteca Nacional de Panamá, inside Parque Recreativo Omar, Vía Belisario Porras, San Francisco, www.binal.ac.pa. Mon-Fri 0900-1800, Sat 0900-1700. Panama's national library has a formidable collection with many titles in English. Search its catalogue online.
Earl S Tupper Tropical Sciences Library, Av Portobelo, Ancón, T212-8113, www.sil. si.edu/libraries/stri. Mon, Wed-Fri 0900-1700, Tue 0800-1700, Sat 0900-1200. Superb biology texts and life-science resources.

Central Pacific Islands

Steeped in blazing sunsets and sugar-white beaches, over a hundred islands and islets bask in the remote Pacific waters off the Bay of Panama. If you're looking for a quick escape, none are as popular or easy to reach as the weekend retreat of Isla Taboga, just 19 km offshore. The island's flowery village streets and languorous ambience are a world apart from the cloistered mayhem of the capital. Further afield, the Islas Perlas are an archipelago of diverse offshore atolls in various stages of development. The most pristine are thickly forested and rich in wildlife, devoid of human settlement and complemented by a dazzling underwater world of coral reefs. The more touristic of the islands play host to million-dollar vacation homes, exclusive gated communities and lavish resorts with select clientele and prices to match.
▶▶ *For listings, see pages 81-82.*

Isla Taboga → *Colour map 2, A1.*

Draped in swathes of colourful bougainvillea, richly scented jasmine and other brightly coloured flora, Isla Taboga has a faintly Mediterranean feel. The artist Paul Gauguin was so taken with the place when he visited in 1887 that he tried to buy land there. He couldn't afford it, however, and worked for some months on the Panama Canal instead. Dubbed the 'Island of Flowers', Taboga is well known for its super-sweet pineapples, mangoes, lazy beaches, pelicans and an ancient church, one of the oldest in the Americas. The island's tiny whitewashed village, San Pedro, is terminally sleepy most of the time, but hides a turbulent history rich in tales of piracy.

Arriving on Isla Taboga
Ferries to Isla Taboga depart two or three times a day from La Playita de Amador, behind the Smithsonian Marine Center on the Amador Causeway, 45 minutes, US$12 (see page 75 for a complete schedule). A taxi to the pier costs US$5-6. There are no ATMs on Taboga, so bring all the cash you will need.

Background
Vasco Nuñez de Balboa was the first European to set foot on Isla Taboga. He originally named it San Pedro, but it was later dubbed Taboga after the indigenous word 'aboga', which means 'many fish'. In 1524, Padre Fernando de Luque founded the colonial village of San Pedro, including a church and numerous pineapple plantations. It is said that the ruthless conquistador, Francisco Pizarro, planned the destruction of Perú in San Pedro and that the padre gave him his blessing before he departed. For many years, Isla Taboga was targeted by pirates, Henry Morgan and John Illingworth among them. In the 19th century, the island served as a major deep-water port. The Pacific Steamship Navigation Company set up shop with ship repair facilities and coaling stations, employing hundreds of Irishmen, many of whom remained on the island for the rest of their lives. In the 1880s, during the French attempt to build the canal, Isla Taboga was home to a yellow fever sanatorium. During the Second World War, the United States trained soldiers on the tiny neighbouring islet of El Morro and practised artillery on a nearby hill. There is rumoured to be a great deal of buried treasure in the ground of Isla Taboga, partially confirmed by 1000 pieces of silver unearthed during the construction of Taboga's health clinic in 1998.

San Pedro village

Originally built of wood in the 16th century, the tiny whitewashed **Iglesia de San Pedro**, situated on the main plaza, is believed to be the second oldest church in the western hemisphere. Nearby, there's a plaque commemorating Gauguin and a small garden with a shrine to the island's patron saint, **Nuestra Señora del Carmen**, who is honoured with a procession and ceremonial boat ride around the island on 16 July every year. Legend holds that she once fended off a gang of marauding pirates. The would-be attackers reported seeing an enormous and terrifying army led by a strikingly beautiful woman, so the story goes, forcing them to beat a retreat.

Playa Restinga

There are a few pleasant beaches on Isla Taboga, but they're nothing spectacular. Most people head to Playa Restinga, around 150 m north of the main pier, where you will be quickly approached with offers of sun loungers and umbrellas, US$5-10 per day. Nearby, a small spit of sand emerges at low tide to join Playa Restinga to a tiny islet, **El Morro**. A bit of casual snorkelling is possible around the islet, but more interesting underwater experiences can be had in the caves on the west side of the island; hire a fisherman to take you over, around US$20-30.

Cerro de la Cruz

A good hike leads to Cerro de la Cruz with its commanding ocean views and fresh sea breezes. There are two routes to the top. The shorter, harsher path begins on the south side of the island on the edge of the village. The longer, more scenic route begins just south of the pier – ask a local how to get to **Las Tres Cruces**, a marker of three white crosses indicating where three slain pirates are buried. From the crosses, the path ascends **Cerro del Vigía** before winding south towards Cerro de la Cruz. Roughly 30% of the island is a wildlife refuge for brown pelicans: **El Refugio de Vida Silvestre Islas Taboga y Urabá**. The pelicans can be seen on the hill in their thousands from January to June, and particularly in May, their nesting season. Note the heat can be fierce, so don't set out without adequate supplies of water and sunscreen.

Islas Perlas → *Colour map 2, B2.*

Known for their prolific pearl fishing in colonial times, the Islas Perlas are a scattered archipelago of over 100 islands and islets, most of them unnamed and blissfully uninhabited. Pearls are less common than they used to be, but the surrounding waters remain rich in marine life. Pacific mackerel, red snapper, corvina, sailfish, marlin, shark and many species of game fish are a consistent draw for sea anglers and sports fishermen. In recent years, many of the Pearl Islands have been snapped up by foreign developers with their eye on wealthy investors. Still, there is great scope for adventure travel if you have the time and funds to get around independently. Thick rainforests and deserted beaches have made the islands a favourite among some adventurers, and indeed, the producers of many 'Survivor' TV shows.

Arriving on Islas Perlas

The Pearl Islands are located 75 km southeast of Panama City. **Air Panama** flies to Isla Contadora one or two times daily, 20 minutes, US$70 return (excluding taxes). At roughly the same price, ferries and catamarans call at Isla Contadora and Isla Saboga, 1½ hours. See page 74 for a complete transport schedule. Only a fraction of the archipelago's islands are inhabited and there are no ATMs, so bring all the cash you will need.

Background

Although the explorer Vasco de Nuñez Balboa was the first Spaniard to set eyes on the Pearl Islands, their immense riches were not to be his. Lacking the arms or troops to subdue the local population, he sailed on, leaving the way open to Gaspar de Morales, a close friend of the notoriously cruel Pedro Arias de Avila. Morales launched a swift and brutal extermination campaign and within two years he had eradicated the entire indigenous population, including 20 chiefs who he personally fed to his dogs. Slaves were subsequently brought in from Africa to harvest the local oysters and it is their descendants who populate the islands today. Touristic development on the Pearl Islands began in the 1960s and 1970s. They earned some international notoriety in 1979, when the former Shah of Iran took exile on Isla Contadora.

Isla Contadora → *Colour map 2, B2.*

Isla Contadora is the historic headquarters of Panama's now-declining pearl industry. Its name means 'counter' (or 'accountant') and refers to the island's former role as a counting station for harvested pearls. It is today a wealthy island resort, popular with rich Panameños and crowds of Canadian, Spanish, US and Italian holidaymakers. It is not as peaceful or affordable as it once was, but remains the most developed and visited place in the archipelago. Island infrastructure includes a runway, a marina, a dive shop, numerous upscale hotels and scores of wealthy villas. Although it is one of the smallest islands in the archipelago (it has an area of just 1.2 sq km), Isla Contadora boasts no less than 13 powdery white beaches. Many of them – such as **Playa Cacique** and **Playa Galeón** – are flanked by colourful coral gardens, great for diving or snorkelling. **Playa Larga** is the longest and most popular stretch, but the beaches on the southern side of the island are much quieter and more secluded. If you have naturist inclinations, you're in luck, as **Playa Suide** is Panama's only nudist beach. To see the former home of the last Shah of Iran, Mohammed Rezá Pahlaví, head to **Playa Ejecutiva** and ask around for the house called 'Puntalara'. The Shah spent some months in residence at the invitation of Omar Torrijos. He and his wife were reportedly quite unhappy there, but most visitors to Contadora, by contrast, seem to enjoy their trip.

Isla Saboga → *Colour map 2, B2.*

Isla Saboga is home to approximately 700 inhabitants, including many workers who commute to hospitality jobs on neighbouring Contadora. The island – recently slated for touristic and residential development – covers an area of 3 sq km, most it consumed by rainforest. Trails to various secluded beaches fan out from the island's main settlement, **Pueblo Nuevo**, which is also home to a very old church. For now, Isla Saboga represents an affordable and down-to-earth alternative to upscale Contadora. It's possible to rent rooms in houses or simple hotel accommodation on the island, but be warned, times are changing.

Isla San José → *Colour map 2, B2.*

Isla San José is a private island with waters rich in marine life, especially black marlin. It attracts wealthy sports fishers keen to snag a world record – no less than 16 have been bagged here already. The island is situated next to a continental plate where the seabed drops suddenly by 2750 m at a point nicknamed **The Explosives** (perhaps due to the local

US military practice of dumping explosives at sea). It remains a prime spot for fishing, as does a site called **Three Monks**, where underwater mountains converge. At 43.5 sq km, the island is the second largest in the archipelago and home to rugged terrain, including numerous coves, rainforests, crashing waterfalls, rivers and natural springs. Turtles often nest on the island's isolated black-sand beaches while some 3000 wild pigs roam free. Unfortunately, the island is as exclusive as it is beautiful – the only lodging is an upmarket resort, **Hacienda del Mar** (see page 82), and the only way in is by chartered plane. Isla San José was formerly a testing ground for chemical weapons by US, Canadian and British forces, but don't let that put you off.

Other islands

Isla Viveros is a particularly idyllic spot filled with turquoise lagoons and white-sand beaches. Unfortunately, it is also home to a new housing development sure to destroy the island's tranquillity. **Isla San Telmo** is one of the more pristine islands in the archipelago, home to lush primary forests, prolific bird species and nesting turtles. **Isla del Rey** is the second largest island in Panama after Isla Coiba. It is home to several towns and fishing villages, including **San Miguel** and **San José**, as well as numerous rivers and waterfalls. Unfortunately, it too is slated for development. If you're looking to buy pearls, head for **Isla Casaya** and **Isla Casayeta**, 12 km south of Contadora – your hotel should be able to arrange transit. Closer to the mainland, **Isla Taborcillo** is home to John Wayne's hotel, www.isla-taborcillo.com.

◉ Central Pacific Islands listings

For sleeping and eating price codes and other relevant information, see pages 16-19.

● Where to stay

Isla Taboga *p78*
$$$ Cerrito Tropical, T6489-0074, www.cerritotropicalpanama.com. Managed by Cynthia and Hiddo Mulder from Canada and the Dutch Caribbean, Cerrito Tropical is a short walk from the village and boasts nice views from its balcony. Accommodation includes clean, simple, comfortable rooms and apartments. Lots of good information.
$$$ Hotel Vereda Tropical, T250-2154, www.veredatropicalhotel.com. Perched on a cliff by the water's edge, Hotel Vereda Tropical is steeped in flowers and has a charming plant-draped courtyard. Rooms are clean, quiet and comfortable, some with sea views.

Isla Contadora *p80*
$$$ Casa del Sol, T250-4212, www.panama-isla-contadora.com. Casa del Sol offers a range of comfortable B&B accommodation, as well as apartment, villa and house rental (**$$$$**). Amenities include Wi-Fi, a/c, fridge, fan, hot water. Knowledgeable owners can hook you up with reputable guides and other services.
$$$ Contadora Island Inn, T250-4161, www.contadoraislandinn.com. This attractive B&B in a spacious remodelled home offers several clean, tidy, tastefully decorated rooms and suites with private bath, hot water, a/c and orthopaedic mattresses. Good reports.
$$$ Perla Real Inn, T250-4095, www.perla real.com. This attractive villa-style inn is nestled in the heart of the island's residential district. Rooms are very comfortable and come with a/c, hot water and all modern amenities. Suites are additionally equipped with a kitchen. Tranquil and tasteful with a touch of old Spain.
$$$ Punta Galeón Resort, T250-4221, www.puntagaleonhotel.com. A bit over-priced, but the setting is extremely handsome with superb sea views and direct

access to the beach. Amenities include 2 pools and a restaurant. They can help with activities, including diving, fishing and sailing.

Isla San José *p80*

$$$$ Hacienda del Mar, T269-6613, www.haciendadelmar.net. A very beautiful and exclusive resort set on the private retreat of Isla San José. Accommodation consists of secluded beach-front cabins complete with a/c, hot water and fine balconies overlooking the ocean or jungle canopy. A host of other amenities include pool, restaurant and gym. Romantic and remote, and not cheap either.

● What to do

Islas Perlas *p79*
Diving and snorkelling

Coral Dreams, opposite Isla Contadora Airport, T6536-1776, www.coral-dreams.com. Snorkelling and diving trips to a variety of sites close to Contadora, including caves, coral reefs and interesting plateaux. Tuna, reef sharks, rays and parrot fish are common. PADI certification up to dive master is available.

Fishing

Several agencies in Panama City can arrange sports fishing tours in the waters around Isla Perlas, including **Panama Yacht tours** (see page 73). On Isla Contadora itself, try: **Las Perlas Fishing and Snorkelling**, Isla Contadora, T6689-4916. This Italian-run operation offers custom-designed fishing expeditions on their 200-HP fishing boat,

including ambitious deep-sea excursions. They also offer snorkelling, birdwatching and general marine tours.

⊖ Transport

Isla Taboga *p78*
Boat and ferry

For outbound schedules, please see Panama City transport, page 75. Return services to Panama City with 'Calypso' ferries depart Mon-Thu 1630, Fri 0930, 1630, Sat-Sun 0900, 1500, 1700, 1-1½ hrs, US$12 return, children US$7. Schedules are subject to seasonal changes, confirm times locally or call ahead T314-1730.

Islas Perlas *p79*
Air

The fares below are one way and exclude tax. All schedules are subject to change, for outbound times, see page 74. From Isla Contadora to **Panama City** with Air Panama, daily 1000, Fri, Sun, 1700, 20 mins, US$35. From Isla San José to **Panama City** with **Air Panama**, daily 1020, Fri, Sun, 1720, 20 mins, US$36. From Isla San Miguel to **Panama City** with Air Panama, daily Tue, Thu, Sun, 0930, 20 mins, US$36.

Boat and ferry

For outbound services, see page 75. The *Sea Las Perlas* catamaran, T391-1424, returns from Isla Contadora to **Panama City** on Mon and Thu-Sun, 1445, 1½ hrs, US$42 one way, US$80 same day return.

Contents

At a glance

⊖ **Getting around** The coast-to-coast journey across the isthmus can be made by bus, boat or train, although rugged types like to go on foot. SACA buses and taxis are best for reaching attractions within the watershed, followed by *piragua* or river boat where necessary.

⊛ **Time required** 2-5 days.

☀ **Weather** The forest canopy provides slight relief from intense daytime temperatures, but humidity is high year-round. Dec-Apr are generally dry but sporadic rainfall can occur at any time. May-Nov are extremely wet.

⊗ **When not to go** The height of the wet season, Sep-Nov, when the region is beset by torrential downpours, thick mud and occasional floods.

The Panama Canal & around

Few achievements can match the bravado of cutting a passage between the oceans and the completion of the Panama Canal in 1914 heralded a bold new era of American ascendancy and international trade. Words like 'fortitude', 'ingenuity', 'perseverance' and 'bravery' became permanently inscribed in the US national narrative. But the canal was key in forging Panamanian identity too. Formerly a prized province of Colombia, the isthmus of Panama was wrestled free in a US-backed bloodless revolution in 1903. The price of American military intervention included the creation of a sovereign 'Canal Zone' – a state within a state – owned and operated by the US in perpetuity. Thus the Republic of Panama began life as a divided and colonized outpost of the United States, until treaty revisions saw the Canal Zone's complete dissolution in 1999. Today, the canal is the sole property of Panama and a source of immense national pride – its handover symbolized the true beginnings of autonomy and nationhood. Standing at its edge, watching the vast ocean-going vessels transit its length, it's hard not to be impressed by the scale of the project, or its extraordinary ambition. Impenetrable rainforests, raging rivers, malaria-infested swamps and an entire mountain range were among the obstacles facing its builders, who perished by their thousands in a mire of torrential rain, mud and disease. Today, vast regions of the landscape that so troubled the canal's architects have been preserved as a vital natural watershed. In addition to draining all the water necessary for the canal's operations, the protected forests of central Panama provide a refuge for untold flora and fauna, including hundreds of species of brilliantly coloured neotropical birds. The canal stands as a testament to human fortitude, but it will always be framed by the fierce power and beauty of nature.

Panama Canal

The Panama Canal is a key component in the world trade system and a crowning endeavour of the age of engineering. It runs for 80 km from deep water to deep water, crossing the isthmus to connect the Port of Balboa in Panama City with the Port of Cristóbal in Colón. Unlike the canal in Suez, the Panama Canal is not a sea-level canal; it employs a series of enormous mechanized locks to raise and lower ships between the oceans and its channels. Prodigious quantities of water are required for their operation. Each time a ship transits, approximately 197 million litres are flushed out to sea. At present, some 13,000 ships transit the canal annually, requiring an astonishing 2.5 trillion litres of H_2O – an impossible demand were it not for Panama's tremendous levels of rainfall. All the water required for the canal's day-to-day operations is stored in the vast man-made lakes of Gatún and Alajuela, whose levels are controlled by dams. In recent years, the growing populations of Panama City and Colón – which are serviced with drinking water from the lakes – have created concerns about the canal's long-term water supplies. The Panama Canal – currently undergoing an ambitious expansion to meet 21st-century shipping needs – represents the final manifestation of a transcontinental trade route that began over 400 years ago with a simple overland mule trail. ▸▸ For listings, see page 92.

Background

Overland trails

Following the instructions of an indigenous chief who had reported a shining ocean beyond the forests of Panama's interior, the Spanish explorer Vasco Núñez de Balboa set forth into the Darién on 1 September 1513. Travelling from the colony of Santa María La Antigua, he emerged from the jungle on 25 September and became the first European to set eyes on the Pacific coast of the Americas. He immediately constructed a crude road for the transport of his ships to the Pacific, which were subsequently used in the conquest of Peru. The road itself was abandoned to the forest.

In 1515, Captain Antonio Tello de Guzmán located a well-worn indigenous trail leading from the Gulf of Panama to the Caribbean coast. Pedro Arias de Avila ordered the trail to be expanded and paved – a work entrusted to Gaspar de Espinosa, who used some 4000 indigenous slaves in the task. The Camino Real, as it became known, was used to transport plundered indigenous gold across the isthmus. In 1533, owing to safety and security issues with the trail, which was highly treacherous in the wet season, Gaspar de Espinosa established a new route. The Camino Las Cruces ran from Panama City to the village of Las Cruces on the Río Chagres, where cargo was packed onto boats and sailed downstream. At San Lorenzo, where the Chagres emptied into the Caribbean, goods were dispatched to the coastal fortress of Porto Bello. For centuries, the Camino Las Cruces served as the main trade route across Panama.

The Panama railway

The demand for cheap passage across the isthmus was massively catalysed by the California gold rush. In 1848, an American entrepreneur, William H Aspinwall, dispatched the famous adventurer John Lloyd Stevens to Bogota, Colombia, to negotiate a concession for a Panama railway. He was granted an exclusive concession for 49 years and the railway was incorporated in New York on 7 April 1849. Six months later they established the town of Aspinwall on the Caribbean Coast, which would later be renamed Colón. Construction

Don't miss ...

of the railway began in August 1850 close to Monkey Hill. Progress was slow and by October 1851 just 12 km of track had been laid at a cost of US$1 million.

The share value of the company declined until December 1851, when 1000 passengers were ferried from Colón to the end of the line. Some US$7000 was collected in fares, causing the value of the company to rise exponentially; US$4,000,000 in stock was sold, providing the capital necessary to continue construction. The world's most expensive per-kilometre railway was completed on 27 January 1855 at a cost of US$6,564,522. Over 12,000 construction workers had lost their lives in the process, most to yellow fever and malaria. In 1869, the completion of the First Transcontinental Railroad at Promontory, Utah, marked the start of decline for the old Panama route. By 1877, the railway – which had once been the highest priced stock on the New York Stock Exchange – had plummeted to just US$52 per share. It was forced to file for bankruptcy.

The French attempt

Following the glittering success of the Suez Canal, completed in 1869 under the direction of former French diplomat Ferdinand de Lesseps, La Société Internacionale du Canal Interocéanique was created in 1876 with the noble ambition of building a transoceanic canal in Panama. De Lesseps, who was a celebrated national hero, was placed in charge of the project. He soon proved an adept fund-raiser and public relations man. In 1879, he headed an international engineering congress in Paris to discuss the project and establish a plan of action. Tellingly, it contained more politicians, speculators and personal friends of de Lesseps than actual engineers. The congress approved proposals for a sea-level canal that would have a uniform depth of 9 m and a width of 27.5 m. The design was impossible to accomplish for a variety of technical reasons, but this would not stop de Lesseps' stubborn insistence upon it.

Construction of the Panama Canal began on 1 January 1882 to much popping of champagne corks. Great mansions were erected for the company directors and a huge labour force was assembled, mostly from the West Indies. There was great optimism, but it was not to last. Soon yellow fever and malaria swept through the work camps, while heavy rain and landslides inundated the construction sites. The engineers were confounded by the challenges of the task, including the levelling of Panama's rugged mountainous spine, which rose to 110 m at the continental divide. Year after year, the death toll rose and the value of the company declined. By 15 May 1889, some 22,000 workers lay dead and France itself teetered on the brink of bankruptcy. The company admitted defeat, with less than half of the canal completed. An investigation into its handling of affairs subsequently found 104 French legislators guilty of corruption. De Lesseps himself was heavily fined and narrowly escaped imprisonment. He died broken and disgraced on 7 December 1894.

Blood on the tracks: the Isthmian Guard

It was the California gold rush and business was booming in the vice-ridden frontier town of Yankee Chagres. A steady stream of adventurers poured back and forth across the isthmus, supplying local enterprises with a generous new source of revenue. But the mass transit of 49ers – many of them returning home with bags of Californian gold – also attracted the unwanted attention of bandits, who loitered like hungry vultures in the bars, brothels and billiard halls. The forested trails of the isthmus were soon awash with murder and robbery and Panama's reputation for lawlessness began to undermine its promising economic growth. By 1850, the **Howland and Aspinwall Company**, who were in the process of constructing the Panama Railway, decided enough was enough. The services of a professional, a lawman, would be required. A former Texas ranger, Randolph Runnels, was contracted for the role. After establishing a mule and transportation agency as a cover for his crime-fighting activities, Runnels proceeded to form a secret vigilante army of about 40 assorted gun-slingers. They were dubbed 'The Isthmian Guard'. Runnels immediately set about gathering intelligence on the local underworld, sending his guards on undercover missions to the *cantinas* and other dens of delinquency. They returned with snippets of information which he meticulously recorded in a black leather ledger. For his own part, Runnels would frequent the gambling halls of the **La Vista** hotel, a popular haunt for high-ranking criminal bosses. One calm summer evening in 1852, under direct orders from the US consul, the Isthmian Guard set out to round up 37 known offenders, including a few wealthy 'businessmen' and local dignitaries. Dragged from their beds and bar stools, they were cordially hanged en masse and left by the sea walls for the public to mull over. The isthmus enjoyed an unprecedented period of calm and Runnels earned the nickname 'El Verdugo' (the executioner). Six months later he was called on again and this time 41 more criminals were found hanging. The Isthmian Guard remained in Panama until 1856, resolving scores of incidents from murders to riots and labour disputes. Runnels was feared and feted wherever he went and lived out his final years as an American consul in Nicaragua.

The Isthmian Canal Commission

In a bid to save shareholders from complete bankruptcy, a new French canal company was formed in 1894 – the Compagnie Nouvelle de Panama – but it failed to gather momentum, mainly due to US speculation. In 1899, President William McKinley established the US Isthmian Canal Commission to explore possibilities for an American-built canal. It twice recommended Nicaragua's Río San Juan as the best site, unless the French would sell their company for US$40,000,000. In 1901, President Theodore Roosevelt resolved to press ahead. In a protracted debate, US senators argued the relative merits of the competing sites in Panama and Nicaragua. A defining moment came when Frenchman Philippe Bunau-Varilla – a major shareholder in the failed French canal company – cunningly distributed postage stamps depicting an eruption of Volcán Momotombo in Nicaragua. Although the proposed canal passed nowhere near the volcano, it persuaded senators that Nicaragua was simply too unstable for the project. The US drafted the Herran-Hay Treaty with Colombia, but Miguel Antonio Caro and Juan Pérez-Soto of the Colombian Conservative Party led a movement to block it.

The Canal Zone: an American dream?

At the height of its glory, the US-controlled Canal Zone appeared to have accomplished utopia. An American, small-town utopia … all hard-working, contented and adoringly draped in stars and stripes. Theirs was a world of marching bands and baseball games, swinging dance halls and well-attended protestant sermons. Citizens of the zone – affectionately called 'Zonians' – wanted for nothing. Yet the ideological foundation of this very Anglo-Saxon utopia was not free market capitalism, but state-sponsored socialism. Chaired by a Washington-appointed governor, the **Panama Canal Company** was responsible for the provision of all civic amenities, including law enforcement, entertainment, education, housing, media, utilities and health care. In a land where free enterprise was virtually outlawed, Zonians shopped in company stores using company vouchers. Home ownership was strictly forbidden. Democratic participation was nil. Beyond the trim green lawns and whitewashed façades, the zone nurtured a deeply autocratic and disturbingly Orwellian streak. If the Soviet Union had won the Cold War, it's quite possible that the United States might today resemble the now defunct but admirably efficient Panama Canal Zone.

The French treaty was due to expire in October 1904, returning the canal to Colombian ownership, and their hope was to acquire the project, sell directly to the US and cut France out of the deal.

Bunau-Varilla was furious and immediately allied himself with a Panamanian separatist movement led by Dr Manuel Amador Guerrero. Roosevelt privately insinuated that any uprising against the Colombian government would be supported by the US. On 2 November 1903, the *USS Nashville* arrived off the shores of the isthmus. The next day, Panama declared Independence from Colombia and enjoyed the full military support of US marines. Bunau-Varilla subsequently negotiated a canal treaty with the US on behalf of the newly forged Panamanian government. Under its terms and conditions, Panama would be paid a lump sum of US$10,000,000 plus US$250,000 annually. Controversially, the treaty also stipulated the creation of a Canal Zone that extended 8 km on either side of the canal. The US was granted complete ownership of the zone in perpetuity.

The work and construction of the canal

The US took formal control of the French company and all its assets on 4 May 1904. John Findlay Wallace was appointed chief engineer and he inherited some severely dilapidated infrastructure. The Panama railway was particularly decayed and many of the French buildings were in complete disrepair. Frustrated by red tape and Washington bureaucracy, he resigned just over a year later. His replacement, John Frank Stevens, initiated a major programme to improve and modernize the Canal Zone's housing and infrastructure. He also initiated a recruitment drive of West Indian workers and persuaded Washington to commit to a lock-based canal. Most importantly, Stevens authorized an extensive sanitation programme. Colonel William Crawford Gorgas, appointed head of hospitals and sanitation in 1904, oversaw an ambitious mosquito-eradication drive. Standing water was eliminated house by house in the cities of Panama and Colón, swamps and wetlands were drained, ponds and streams were oiled, leaving no place for larvae to flourish. The programme was controversial because there was resistance to the newly formulated theory that mosquitoes carried diseases. The results spoke for themselves: in 1906, only one case of yellow fever was reported.

In 1907, Stevens resigned from his position. He was replaced by Major George Washington Goethals, who separated his team into three broad divisions. The Atlantic division was charged with building the Caribbean approach channel, the immense Gatún Dam and its locks. The Pacific division was ordered to construct a 4.8-km breakwater in the Panama bay, the Pacific approach channel, and the Miraflores and Pedro Miguel locks. The Central division, under the command of Major David du Bose Gaillard, had the hardest job of all – cutting through the continental divide to a height of 12 m. By the time the canal had been completed, nearly 205 million cubic metres of earth had been excavated, 2.5 million barrels of concrete had been poured and some 27,000 tonnes of dynamite detonated. The Canal broke the record for the world's largest earthen dam, largest canal locks, largest man-made lake and most expensive construction project. Over the course of 10 years, 75,000 workers had contributed to its construction. The opening of the Panama Canal was celebrated on 15 August 1914. Owing to the start of the Great War in Europe, it was a relatively subdued event. The *SS Ancon* was the first ship to traverse the canal's length.

Handover and expansion

The Canal Zone was an ongoing point of tension in US-Panama relations for decades, notoriously erupting into violent riots on 9 January 1964. In 1977, the Torrijos-Carter Treaty addressed long-standing grievances by scheduling the withdrawal of the US military. On 31 December 1999, the US relinquished complete control of the canal to Panama and it is now managed by the Autoridad del Canal de Panamá. But it is currently operating near its maximum transit capacity. Facing competition from alternative routes in Nicaragua and Colombia, ambitious plans for its expansion were approved in a national referendum on 22 October 2006. They include the excavation of new access channels, the widening of existing channels and the elevation of Lake Gatún to its highest operating level. Large new locks – 427 m long, 55 m wide and 18.3 m deep – will be able to accommodate so-called post-Panamax ships, which exceed the dimensions of the existing locks.

Scheduled for completion in 2014 – the centenary of the canal's opening – the expansion is predicted to triple container traffic. President Martín Torrijos, who initiated the project, claimed it will reduce national poverty by 30% and turn Panama into a first-world country within a generation. But the project is not without critics or controversy. According to the trade union Frenadeso, opponents of the project were censored in the run-up to the referendum. They also say that fewer than half of the 5000 jobs promised during the 'yes' campaign have materialized. The canal authority itself has also admitted its projected costs are too low, yet it continues to use old figures in public discussions. Independent engineers argue that the current lock scheme is overly expensive and complex. Furthermore, it is expected to salinate Lake Gatún, gravely affecting the urban water supply.

Transiting the canal → *For listings, see page 92. Colour map 2, A1.*

Around 30-40 ships pass through the canal each day. Although a complete transit requires only eight hours, most will spend 16 hours or more queuing in canal waters. From the Pacific, ships enter near the **Amador Causeway** and sail directly under the iconic **Bridge of the Americas**. After passing the port of Balboa, they arrive in **Miraflores Locks** where they are raised 16.5 m to man-made **Miraflores Lake**. Shortly after, they meet with **Pedro Miguel Locks** and are lifted a further 9.5 m. **Culebra Cut**, formerly known as Gaillard Cut, is a narrow rock gorge that crosses the continental divide to **Lake Gatún**. On the other side of Lake Gatún, ships are lowered 26.5 m to sea level and exit the canal near the city of Colón. The transit occurs with the aid of tug-boats and is a remarkably quiet affair. If you would like to experience it, a range of companies offer canal tours (see What to do, page 92). Most people find a partial transit, four or five hours, is quite sufficient. They typically run from Gamboa to the Amador Causeway, or from the Amador Causeway to Lake Miraflores, and are offered on a weekly basis, usually Saturdays. Full transits depart once a month from either Colón or Panama City. Book your journey well in advance.

Train crossings: The Panama Canal Railway

ⓘ *Corozal One West, Panama City, T317-6070, www.panarail.com; departs from Panama City Mon-Fri 0715; returns from Colón 1715; US$22 one way.*

In 1998, the Panama Canal Railway Company – a subsidiary of Kansas City Southern Lines – acquired a 50-year concession to operate and improve the old Panama railway. They invested US$80 million, repairing the damaged lines and purchasing new rolling stock, including 10 3250-horsepower Amtrak locomotives, five remodelled passenger coaches with a 50-person capacity, and one 1938 Southern Pacific Dome Car with a transparent ceiling. A passenger service was launched in 2001 and is highly recommended as an affordable alternative to a ship transit. Rushing past jungle foliage and the misty morning waters of Lake Gatún, you'll cross the isthmus in just one hour. Return services from Colón don't depart until the late afternoon, giving you several hours to explore the Caribbean coast.

The locks → For listings, see page 92.

The canal uses three sets of locks to lift and lower ships. Each lock consists of a large chamber with sluice gates and valves that allow it to be filled with (and emptied of) water. Gatún has three chambers running in steps; Miraflores has two and Pedro Miguel has one. They all measure 33.5 m wide and 320 m long, determining the maximum size of ships that can use them. When a ship needs to be lifted, it enters

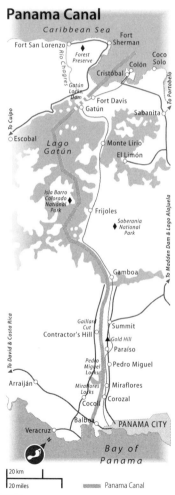

Panama Canal

Caribbean Sea

Fort San Lorenzo
Fort Sherman
Coco Solo
Forest Preserve
Colón
Cristóbal
Gatún Locks Dam
Fort Davis
Gatún
Sabanita
To Cuipo
Escobal
Lago Gatún
Monte Lirio
El Limón
Isla Barro Colorado National Park
Frijoles
Soberania National Park
To Portobelo
To Madden Dam & Lago Alajuela
Gamboa
To David & Costa Rica
Gaillard Cut
Contractor's Hill
Summit
Gold Hill
Paraíso
Pedro Miguel Locks
Pedro Miguel
Arraiján
Miraflores Locks
Miraflores
Cocolí
Corozal
Balboa
PANAMA CITY
Veracruz
Bay of Panama
20 km
20 miles
Panama Canal

the chamber with the help of a tug-boat and towing locomotives called mules. Once inside, the watertight gates are closed behind it and the valves are opened, causing water to flow from the adjacent chamber or 'step'. The chamber fills and the water level rises, eventually equalizing with the adjacent chamber and lifting the ship one step. When a ship needs to be lowered, the reverse happens: water is emptied from the ship's chamber into the adjacent one.

Miraflores Locks → *Colour map 2, A1.*

ⓘ *www.pancanal.com, daily 0900-1700, restaurant 1200-2300, full entrance US$8, students US$5; partial entrance including ground terrace, snack bar, restaurant and gift shop, US$5, students US$3. A taxi to the locks is around US$10, beware overcharging.*

Completed in 1913, the two-step Miraflores Locks have a lift of 16.5 m and are supported by two dams with a concrete spillway. Receiving more than 300,000 visitors each year, Miraflores boasts an excellent **observation deck** complete with running commentary in Spanish and English. Its museum is spread over four floors, starting with the 'History Hall', which includes exhibits on the French era and numerous intricate models of antiquated dredgers. The next hall, 'Water: Source of Life', deals with the hydrology of the canal's watershed and includes specimens of grasshoppers, tarantulas, butterflies, bees, wasps, scorpions and cockroaches that live in the forests around the canal. The 'Canal in Action' hall chronicles the canal's day-to-day operations with expositions on marine traffic control, a simulated pilot's bridge and a topographical model depicting its route across the isthmus. The final hall, 'The Canal and The World', explores international trade. Additional facilities include a cinema screening documentaries in Spanish or English, a gift shop, event hall and snack bar. The restaurant upstairs is quite smart and features a daily buffet (**$$$**) with commanding views of the ships.

Pedro Miguel Locks

Around 4 km north of Miraflores, the one-step Pedro Miguel Locks offer a poor man's experience of the canal. It's free to watch the ships as they transit, but you'll be peering through a wire fence and won't get anything like the views at Miraflores. The Pedro Miguel Locks have a lift of 9.5 m and are overlooked by the **Centenario Bridge**, completed in 2004. To reach the locks, take a SACA bus from Panama City, or a taxi, US$10-15.

Gatún Locks → *Colour map 2, A1.*

ⓘ *10 km south of Colón, daily 0800-1600, US$5. To get there, take a 'Costa Abajo' bus from Colón, 20 mins, US$1.50; or a taxi, US$20 return, groups US$50-60 for a 'tour'. Gatún Dam is located 2-3 km from locks on the opposite bank; follow the road over the swing bridge.*

Gatún Locks on the Caribbean side are the largest of the canal's three sets. Spanning a length of 1.5 km, a staggering 1.82 million cubic metres of concrete were used in their construction. Although less visited than Miraflores, Gatún offers the best views, with an observation deck that's right up close to the action. The locks integrate three steps and lift ships 29.5 m; duplicate flights allow ships to pass in opposite directions simultaneously. The passage takes around one hour. Gatún Dam adjoins the locks and is no less impressive, particularly if you see the spillway unleashing millions of litres of water. Built in 1908, the dam served an important engineering function by blocking the Río Chagres and transforming it into the enormous Lake Gatún.

For sleeping and eating price codes and other relevant information, see pages 16-19.

✪ What to do

Transiting the Canal *p89*
Tour operators
Nearly all tours depart from Playita de Amador on Isla Flamenco, Amador Causeway. Services aren't luxurious, but they do include food, drinks and bilingual guide. Additionally, bring sun-block, hat, umbrella, binoculars and, for full transits, a warm sweater. Both companies below accept online bookings.

Canal and Bay Tours, Playita de Amador, Calzada Amador, or look for a stand at Multiplaza Mall, T209-2002, www. canal andbaytours.com. Full transit of the canal on the 1st Sat of the month, 0730, adults US$165, children US$75. Partial transit every Sat, 0900, adults US$115, children US$60. They also run various tours around the Bay of Panama, including an evening tour with bar and calypso. Their fleet includes *Fantasía del Mar, Tuira II*, and a particularly handsome wooden vessel, *Isla Morada*.

The Panama Canal Railway Company, Corozal Passenger Station, Corozal One West, Building T376, Ancón, T317-6070, www. panarail.com. Operates the legendary service from Panama City to **Colón**, US$22 one way, US$44 return. It departs Mon-Fri 0715 and returns 1715, 1 hr. Turn up on the morning or book in advance through tour operators. The station is located near the Terminal de Transportes in Albrook and a cab from downtown Panama City costs around US$3. Under no circumstances go wandering the streets of Colón, including the area around the train station. Plan your day in advance and take a taxi to wherever you want to go. **Panama Marine Adventures**, T226-8917, Vía Porras y Calle Belén 106, www.pmatours.

net. Full transit of the canal is usually offered once a month on the *Pacific Queen*, adults US$165, children US$75, call for schedule. Partial transit Jan-Mar Thu-Sat; Apr-Nov Fri and Sat, adults US$115, children US$65, 4-5 hrs. All schedules are subject to change. Transport departs from Isla Flamenco, Calzada Amador. Alternatively, an adventure tour on the exclusive *Discovery* takes in the Darién and Pearl Islands before crossing the canal and exploring the Caribbean coast, US$5000. Good reports, recommended.

⊖ Transport

Miraflores and Pedro Miguel locks *p90*
Bus
Beaten up old **SACA** buses travel from **Panama City** to the former Canal Zone, passing Miraflores and Pedro Miguel locks en route. They depart from Terminal de Transportes, Albrook, every 1-2 hrs, 0500-2230, US$0.35-1. For Miraflores, ask the driver to drop you at 'Las Esclusas de Miraflores', from where it's a 5-min walk.

Taxi
A taxi to Miraflores locks should cost under US$10 from downtown **Panama City**, but overcharging is common, especially on the return trip. Bargain hard and try to avoid unscrupulous *taxistas* by hailing a cab from the highway, not the Miraflores car park. Fares to/from Pedro Miguel, a few mins further on, are comparable.

Gatún Locks *p91*
Gatún Locks are best accessed from the city of Colón on the Caribbean coast. A taxi from **Colón** should cost around US$20 return, but many *taxistas* will try to sell you a 'tour' for US$50. 'Costa Abajo' buses pass the locks, every 1-2 hrs, ½ hr, US$0.50. For more information on Colón, see page 103.

Panama Canal watershed

The untamed and deeply luxuriant Panama Canal watershed drains the vast quantities of rain and groundwater necessary for the canal's daily functioning. Under the Panamanian constitution, the area is strictly managed by the Panama Canal Authority, which is closely assisted by several government bodies, including the environment agency ANAM, who have established no less than four national parks in the region. Swathes of pristine tropical forests blanket the watershed from north to south, concealing some of Central America's finest hiking and birdwatching trails. Remnants of the old colonial gold routes can even be ascertained in the thickets and undergrowth. Between the teeming pockets of natural exuberance, the watershed is populated by numerous Emberá communities whose multi-hued traditions and communal way of life offer a vivid and welcome contrast to the aggressive hustle of the capital, less than 100 km away. Fishing, boating, kayaking and diving are all possible in the canal watershed, home to scores of rivers, streams and lakes, not least the mighty Río Chagres and expansive freshwater sea of Lago Gatún. ▸▸ *For listings, see pages 99-100.*

Parque Nacional Camino de Cruces → *Colour map 2, A1.*

ⓘ *US$5 Guides and maps available from the visitors' centre. To get there, take a SACA bus from Panama City, every 1-2 hrs, 40 mins, US$0.50. A taxi should cost US$15 one way.*

Replete with grand ceiba, nance and fig trees, the gently rolling terrain of the Parque Nacional Camino de Cruces includes 4590 ha of protected rainforest. Positioned between the Parque Metropolitano and the Parque Nacional Soberanía, the park plays a vital role in the biological corridor linking Panama's Caribbean and Pacific coasts. The Parque Nacional Camino de Cruces derives its name from the old Spanish mule trail used to transport gold and other riches across the isthmus. It has been partially reconstructed and can be followed into neighbouring Parque Nacional Soberanía (see below).

Parque Nacional Soberanía → *For listings, see pages 99-100. Colour map 2, A1.*

ⓘ *Administrative offices at the intersection of the Carretera Gaillard (also known as Av Omar Torrijos) and the Carretera Madden, T232-4192, www.anam.gob.pa/soberania, US$5. To get there from Panama City, take a SACA bus or a taxi.*

The Parque Nacional Soberanía encompasses 19,545 ha of teeming lowland rainforest. It is one of the most accessible and easily explored national parks anywhere, rife with wildlife and not be to be missed. Enclosing the eastern bank of the canal from Bahía Limón on Lago Gatún to the town of Paraíso on the Gaillard Highway, Soberanía reaches into both provinces of Colón and Panamá. Swathed in exuberant foliage, the park is home to some 1300 recorded plant species including prolific orchids and epiphytes. Out of 105 mammals, the most commonly sighted are monkeys, raccoons, sloths, deer, peccaries and agoutis. Jaguars and other big cats are resident but rarely encountered. Reptiles are prolific, with 79 species including caimans and snakes, easily spotted on a night tour. Toads and salamanders are among the 55 types of amphibian, commonly seen on the banks of the Chagres River or Lake Gatún. It is the park's avian life, however, that makes it so special. The 525 bird species are too many to list, but on a single visit you're likely to see parrots, woodpeckers, wrens, manakins, toucans and aracaris. Arrive at dawn for an unforgettable display of colourful plumage and birdsong.

Community tourism: Emberá and Wounaan villages

For the past 60 years, external pressures have forced groups of Emberá and Wounaan from their traditional homelands in the Darién, eastern Panama, into the comparatively sheltered rainforests of the Panama Canal watershed. Illegal loggers, aggressive colonists, drug traffickers, Colombian guerrillas and vast, state-approved mega-projects – especially hydroelectric dams – have all featured in this sad, on-going story of indigenous displacement. Struggling to maintain a balance between modernity and the preservation of their traditional culture, many of the newly settled communities in central Panama have opened their doors to tourism, and with great success.

Although each village has a different flavour, they all offer broadly similar options. An explanation of the community's history and culture is a typical starting point, usually followed by traditional dances and music, in which you may be invited to participate. Birdwatching, jungle hikes and trips along the river in dugout *piraguas* are all popular options, as are strolls through the botanical garden with a knowledgeable shaman or village elder. Stay for lunch and you'll be presented with a traditional meal – usually fresh fish or chicken served with *patacones*. Most visits conclude with a presentation of *artesanías*, including baskets, masks and carved cocobolo and tagua wood statuettes. Remember, if you decide to get a *jagua* tattoo, the ink can stay on your skin for up to two weeks!

Most of the Emberá and Wounaan villages listed here are less than two hours from the capital and make an easily organized day trip (if you lack the basic Spanish to get around, you should rely on the guidance of a tour operator). Be aware that tourism is a vital source of income for some communities. A few villages receive very high numbers of visitors, so much of the life you'll see – although beautiful and intriguing – is staged solely for their benefit. If you're seeking authenticity, get as far from Panama City as possible. It's best to contact the community in advance

The trails

Soberanía has six different trails of varying length and difficulty. They are generally well maintained, but sometimes subject to flood damage. It's worth checking their status with ANAM before setting out. Note that some of the trailheads are far from the administrative offices; if travelling by taxi, ask it to wait while you pay entrance fees. If you arrive before office hours, you should be able to pay upon exit.

The Pipeline Road 17 km, eight hours round-trip, access from Gamboa (see page 97). The Pipeline Road (Camino Oleoducto) is one of the world's finest birding trails. The **Panama Audubon Society** hosts a count on the trail each Christmas and has broken world records for 19 consecutive years. In 1996 they spotted 357 species in a single 24-hour period. Built as an access road for a Second World War oil pipeline (a guarantee of free-flowing oil in the event of the canal's obstruction), the trail is flat, paved and moderately strenuous. The first 6 km are secondary forest. A guide is recommended to make the most out of your bird sightings; try **ANCON** in Panama City, or the **Rainforest Discovery Centre**, 1.5 km from the trailhead (see page 96).

of your visit. Bring a swimming costume, towel, insect repellent, sunscreen and, during the wet season, rubber boots. Please tip kindly.

Many Emberá and Wounaan communities are situated on rivers inside protected national parks. In the remote Parque Nacional Chagres, the community of **Emberá Purú** lies on the banks of the Río San Juan de Pequení and has been receiving visitors for over a decade – it even boasts a few English speakers. For the truly intrepid, they offer rustic overnight accommodation and the option of spear fishing. Also in the Chagres area, located at the confluence of the Río Chagres and Río Indio, is the village of **Tusípono Emberá**; to visit, contact Antonio Tócamo, T6539-7918, www.emberatusipono09.blogspot.com. **Emberá Drua**, founded in 1975 by Emilio Caisamo, is another popular and often recommended option, T216-7765, www.trail2.com/embera. To get to the Chagres villages, take a bus to Las Cumbres, followed by a taxi to the dock at **Corotú**

on Lake Alajuela. Get there early to catch a public boat; chartered boats, US$20-30.

For those in the Gamboa area, the Emberá community of **Ella Purú**, and its Wounaan neighbour, **San Antonio**, are easily reached by chartered boat from the main pier in town. On the Caribbean side of the watershed, the village of **Ella Drua**, www.elladruaembera.com, has made great strides to develop its tourism programme. Situated on the banks of the Río Gatún, the community was established in 1973 by a single family who found the beauty and tranquillity of the location irresistible. Today it is home to 120 inhabitants and remains one of the best places to experience authentic Emberá village life. To get there, take the Corredor Norte towards Colón, turn off at Panama Centro exit and drive for seven minutes. Cross Puente Gatún and turn immediately left. Follow the road until you arrive at a dock marked Ella Drua and Emberá Communities. A day of activities costs US$40 per person for a group of one to 10, excluding transport.

The Plantation Trail 13 km, four hours round-trip, access from the Gaillard Highway, near the entrance to the Canopy Tower. The moderately strenuous Plantation Trail began life as an access road for local coffee and cacao plantations. It was later used for military training. Wildlife is relatively easy to spot and you can also connect with the Camino de Cruces.

Camino de Cruces 10 km, six to seven hours, access from the Plantation Trail or Madden Highway; look for the parking area with picnic tables. The old 16th-century Spanish gold route connects with a longer trail running south into Camino de Cruces National Park. It is a tough hike that concludes near the ruins of Venta de Cruces, where treasure was packed on riverboats and spirited to San Lorenzo on the Caribbean coast.

Spirit of the Forest 1.7 km, one-hour round-trip, access from opposite the administrative offices. The park's newest trail is an easy stroll that includes plenty of interpretive signage.

El Charco 0.8 km, 20 minutes, access from Gaillard Highway. A very tame and easy trail that leads to waterfalls and swimming holes. There is a family picnic area.

Cicloruta 17.5 km. This road commences 2 km from the administrative office on the Madden Highway. It is designed for mountain bikes.

Summit Botanical Gardens and Zoo

ⓘ *Carretera Gaillard, T232-4854, 0900-1700, US$1.There are food stalls, but the zoo is a great place for a picnic.*

First known rather functionally as the 'Experimental Gardens of the Canal Zone', the Summit Botanical Gardens were created by the Canal company in 1923, originally for the study of plants. Animals were added in 1962 and when Panama took control of the facility in 1985, it was renamed the 'Summit Municipal Park and Botanical Gardens'. Today, the site houses some 40 species of animal, including tapirs, jaguars, deer, monkeys and crocodiles. The star attraction is the harpy eagle enclosure, where the zoo worked with the **Peregrine Fund** (www.peregrinefund.org) for many years, breeding and releasing new eagles into the forests of Soberanía. The zoo has some great plant specimens too, including plentiful bamboo and one of the world's largest palm collections.

Canopy Tower

ⓘ *Semaphore Hill, signed off the Gaillard highway, T264-5720, www.canopytower.com.*

Perched atop Semaphore Hill with commanding views of the rainforest, the Canopy Tower began life in 1965 as a US Air Force radar tower. By 1969 it was jointly used by the Federal Aviation Administration and Panama Canal Commission, until 1988, when it became 'Site One' in the Caribbean Basin Radar Network – a radar unit used to track planes suspected of carrying drugs. The tower retired in 1995 and was transferred to Panamanian control in 1996. When businessman Raúl Arias de Para acquired the site in 1997, he set about converting the former military structure into one of Central America's finest ecolodges. Day visitors are welcome (contact in advance), but to really appreciate the forested surroundings, an overnight stay and early rise is recommended. Amenities include a great library with field guides, a communal restaurant and observation deck equipped with Leica 77-mm scopes. All guides are bilingual and some of them are able to call the birds directly. ►► *For more information see listings, page 99.*

Panama Rainforest Discovery Center

ⓘ *Pipeline Rd, 1.6 km from entrance, access from Gamboa, T6588-0679, www.pipelineroad. org, 0600-1600, US$20 peak hours (0600-1000), US$15 off peak; 20% reduction if booked 48 hrs in advance.*

Managed by the **Fundación Avifauna Eugene Eisemann** (www.avifauna.org.pa), this ecologically aware and socially responsible interpretive centre specializes in environmental education. The central attraction is a 32-m-high observation tower with intimate views of the forest canopy, which is often teeming with birds, monkeys and sloth. There's also a well-maintained 1.2-km circuit of forest trails, gift shop and a viewing deck on the banks of Calamito Lake, where you might spot caimans and aquatic birds. The centre conducts an annual 'raptor count', 1 October-15 November, when vultures, hawks and other birds of prey fill the skies. They also belong to the Mesoamerican study network and conduct Monitoring of Winter Survival (MOSI) with mist nets during the dry season. Possibly their most exciting research project is a study exploring the feasibility of reintroducing green macaws to the area. True to its principles, the building is equipped with solar panels and is energetically self-sustained.

Gamboa and around → *For listings, see pages 99-100. Colour map 2, A1.*

Located roughly halfway across the isthmus, the sleepy township of Gamboa was constructed in 1911 to house a few hundred Canal Zone employees. Its population grew exponentially after 1936, when the Panama Canal Company decided to base its Dredging Division in town, reaching over 3000 by 1942. A civic centre, golf course, cinema and other modern amenities sprang up to service its affluent and mostly North American residents but, after the handover of the canal in 1999, all such services closed. Today, Gamboa is still home to the Dredging Division, but its population is comparatively sparse and many of its buildings lie empty. The Smithsonian Tropical Research Institute maintains some laboratories and residential accommodation in town, along with a small pier for the transportation of scientists, visitors and supplies to its research station on Isla Barro Colorado.

Arriving in Gamboa
A small wood and iron bridge leads into Gamboa at the point where the Chagres, Culebra Cut and Lake Gatún meet. SACA buses leave from Panama City every one to two hours, and drop passengers 6 km before town. A taxi from Panama City, US$25 one way, is highly recommended if you're meeting the STRI ferry; it won't wait for late arrivals. Hitching on the Gaillard Highway is possible, but not recommended for lone women.

Gamboa Rainforest Resort
The long-running Gamboa Rainforest Resort is a hit with families and those seeking tame adventures within the safe confines of a resort development. An orchid nursery, serpentarium, butterfly house, freshwater aquarium and staged Emberá village are among its draws, but the star attraction is a cable-car ride over the forest canopy. The trip is fun and great for kids, but not the best way to observe wildlife. The resort also offers a wide range of tours including freshwater fishing, birdwatching, night safari, river trips on the Chagres and kayaking on the Panama Canal. ▸▸ *For more information, see page 99.*

Lago Gatún → *Colour map 2, A1.*
Serene Lake Gatún was formed by the damming of the Río Chagres near the village of Gatún, 10 km from its mouth on the Caribbean coast. Some 422 sq km were permanently flooded, washing away abandoned villages and transforming hilltops into islands. At the time of its creation, it was the world's largest man-made lake. Today, Gatún supplies Colón and Panama City with drinking water and acts as the main reservoir for the canal. Damage to the watershed from deforestation and increased canal traffic means levels are not as consistently high as they once were. Ships follow a fixed route across the lake, but some small vessels are eligible for a short-cut channel called 'Banana Cut'.

Gatún is home to a very large population of peacock bass known locally as *sargentos* (sergeants) due to the stripes on their sides. They originate from South America and are believed to have been artificially introduced to the lake by a Panamanian aquarist and doctor. They are prized game fish, aggressive and, owing to their numbers, easy to snag. **Rich Cahill** ① *T6678-2653, www.panamacanalfishing.com*, offers reputable expeditions to Gatún; alternatively get to the pier at Gamboa before dawn and you should be able to find a boatman to take you out on the lake, US$75-100 for three to four hours. After mid-morning the fish don't bite. **Diving** is also interesting, with an old Belgian locomotive and ruined towns resting in the murky depths. However, the lake is also crocodile-infested, so please seek up-to-date advice from a professional dive outfit. There are numerous islands on Lake Gatún, some of them home to rescue monkeys; please approach with a qualified naturalist only.

Monumento Isla Barro Colorado → *Colour map 2, A1.*

ⓘ *T212-8951, www.stri.org, office hours 0800-1500, tour US$70. Boats to the island depart Tue, Wed, Fri 0715; Sat-Sun 0800 – be on time, the boat won't wait. The dock in Gamboa is on a gravel track just past the dredging dock. Taxi from Panama City, US$25 one way.*

Isla Barro Colorado is the largest island in Lake Gatún and one of the most studied places on earth. It is home to 1316 species of plant, 384 species of bird, 30 species of frog and 255 species of ant, to name a few. A centre of study since 1923, Isla Barro Colorado is the site of a world-class field station that sees over 200 visiting scientists per year. Facilities include labs, growing houses, insectaries and dark rooms. Long-term and short-term research is conducted at various sites, including a 50-ha forest plot that's part of the **Center of Tropical Science's 'Earth Observatory'** (www.sigeo.si.edu) – an ambitious project that explores the dynamics of tropical forests on three different continents. Visitors to the island will experience a tour of the facilities, a guided walk on a two- to three-hour interpretative trail and lunch. Places are limited so you are advised to organize your trip well in advance, two to three weeks if possible, directly through the Smithsonian Institute or a Panama City tour operator.

Parque Nacional Chagres → *Colour map 2, A2.*

ⓘ *US$5. The park is remote and access requires own vehicle or a tour operator. There are various entry points, the best is via Cerro Azul, north of the Interamericana before Tocumen Airport. Visit ANAM in Panama City before setting out; they can advise on guides, trails, transport, etc. It's also possible to enter the park by river boat on the Chagres.*

Encompassing 129,000 ha of challenging terrain, the Parque Nacional Chagres is one of Panama's largest and most important reserves. Mountains, valleys, rivers, rainforests and cloud forests are among the park's diverse landscapes, all home to scores of rare animals, including jaguars, tapirs and harpy eagles. The reserve's watershed supplies 40% of the water required to keep the canal functioning, much of it stored by **Lago Alajuela**, an artificial reservoir created by Madden Dam. The reservoir's levels are highest in early January, at the end of the wet season, when local communities take advantage of the occasion by hosting a **Feria Campesina** (Farmers' Fair). If you're in the area, you can partake in boat rides, witness traditional dances and stock up on fresh fish, honey and other local produce. The **Río Chagres** also passes through the park, which has some Grade II/III rapids, tame but diverting nonetheless.

Places in the Parque Nacional Chagres

ANAM maintains two short trails that can be easily traversed in under an hour or so: **Sendero El Cuipo**, 1.5 km, and **Sendero Las Grietas**, 2.3 km. Both trails snake through deciduous dry and evergreen forest to panoramic views of Lago Alajuela. They are both popular with birders. True adventurers, however, may prefer to traverse the **Camino Real**, the oldest and toughest of the old colonial trade routes. You will need a few days and a strong constitution to follow its entire length from coast to coast. The park is home to several scalable peaks, including **Cerro Jefe** (1007 m), **Cerro Bruja** (974 m), **Cerro Brewster** (899 m) and **Cerro Azul** (771 m), which houses a refuge and warder's station. Seek advice from ANAM before setting out.

◉ Panama Canal watershed listings

For sleeping and eating price codes and other relevant information, see pages 16-19.

● Where to stay

Parque Nacional Soberanía *p93*
$$$$ Canopy Tower Ecolodge,
Semaphore Hill, off Gaillard Highway, signposted after Summit Gardens, T264-5720, www.canopytower.com. One of the world's finest birdwatching lodges. Rooms in this converted radar tower are simple but comfortable. They include several singles with shared bath, 5 doubles with private bath, and 2 suites, including the excellent Blue Cotinga suite with its balcony. Rates include excellent buffet meals, wine, Wi-Fi and 1 introductory tour. The views over the canopy from the observation deck are stunning. A range of tours are available, including various multi-day packages with a focus on birds, mammals, culture or nature photography. An unforgettable experience. Highly recommended.

Gamboa *p97*
$$$$ Gamboa Rainforest Resort,
Goethals Blvd, 1st right after crossing the bridge into Gamboa, T206-8888, www.gamboaresort.com. This looming green and white resort is built on the vast, rambling grounds of an old American golf course. Rooms are large, comfortable and well attired. They include excellent 'deluxe' rooms with views over the Río Chagres and some very elegant 'historic apartments' that are great for families. Facilities include spa, restaurant business centre and pool. Tours are available to non-residents. Resort standards, just as the name suggests.
$$$ Canopy B&B, Harding Av and Jadwin Av, T264-5720, www.canopytower.com. Part of the prestigious Canopy Tower group, **Canopy B&B** is a very attractive 1930s Canal Zone-era building that has been artfully restored to its former glory. It has just 5 rooms, all very comfortable, quiet and cosy, some with great views over the surrounding vegetation. Staff are very helpful and hospitable. Numerous tours available.
$$ Ivan's B&B, 111 Jadwin Av, T314-9436, www.gamboaecotours.com. Quiet and homely bed and breakfast accommodation in lush, tranquil surroundings. Rooms are clean, comfortable and cosy, and the owner, Iván Ortiz, is very knowledgeable about birds and the surrounding area. He offers a range of tours, including birding, fishing, Emberá villages and Caribbean coast. Relaxed and hospitable. Good reports.
$$ Mateo's B&B, Calle Humberto Zarate, Casa 131A, T6690-9664, www.gamboabedandbreakfast.com. Friendly, welcoming, down-to-earth B&B accommodation with a host of visiting wildlife in the garden, including agoutis, hummingbirds and monkeys. Simple rooms and cabins are available, along with a 2-room apartment for longer-term visitors. Meals can be arranged for US$6. Very tranquil and easy-going. Staying with Mateo and Beatrice is like staying with your grandparents. Recommended.

◉ Transport

Bus

Exploring the area by bus is possible, but it can involve long waits on empty highways. SACA buses depart from the Terminal de Transportes in Albrook, every 1-2 hrs, 0500-2230, US$0.35-1, and travel through the former Canal Zone, passing Ciudad de Saber, Miraflores, Pedro Miguel and Paraíso, before branching west onto Av Omar Torrijos to the Parque Soberanía, Summit gardens, Canopy Tower and finally Gamboa. It may be possible to hitch, but take the usual precautions. Bus services are reduced on Sun, always check the destination on the windscreen as not all of them terminate in Gamboa.

Car hire

Hiring a vehicle is highly recommended. Traffic is light and roads are generally in good condition with most destinations 10-50 mins outside of the capital.

Taxi

Taxis are a good option for groups. Sample fare to Gamboa, US$25 one way.

Contents

Footprint features

Colón & the central Caribbean coast

At a glance

⊖ **Getting around** Buses and taxis for most parts of the coast; boats and 4WD for really remote stretches. A passenger train connects Colón with the capital.

✪ **Time required** 3-7 days.

☀ **Weather** The wet season officially runs May-Nov, but the Caribbean coast receives nearly twice as much rain as the Pacific and downpours are possible at any time of the year. Jan-Mar are the driest months.

✖ **When not to go** The worst of the wet season, Sep-Nov, when the region can sometimes experience bad flooding.

The Caribbean coast of Panama has always been valued as a strategic link between the Old World and the New. During the colonial era, it was the scene of opulent international trade fairs where the wealth of the Spanish Empire changed hands. Today, at the point where the Panama Canal empties into the Bay of Limón, the historic city of Colón is home to a sprawling and heavily fortified Free Trade Zone – the largest in the Americas, where every product imaginable is bought and sold. But, despite Colón's important role in facilitating global trade, life on Panama's 'other side' is often marked by economic hardship. Unemployment remains stubbornly high and decades of underinvestment have left local infrastructure in a weary state. Fortunately, the region's lack of development does not detract from its easy-going ambience or lavish natural beauty. Punctuated by deserted beaches and lost-in-time fishing villages, the Caribbean coast is a world of few roads and fewer worries. Part of its special appeal lies in its swaggering sense of history. For over 250 years, the region was the focus of intense international intrigue, beset by pirates and cut-throats keen to plunder Spain's wealthy fleets and treasure houses. Today, a string of well-preserved Spanish fortresses recall the days when Francis Drake and Henry Morgan plied the waters offshore. The coast's swashbuckling history is well complemented by a sizzling fusion of cultures that hail predominantly from Africa. Raucous festivals recall the era of colonial slave trading with feisty Congo dances and fervent drum beats. English-speaking Afro-Antilleans, who are credited with constructing the Panama Canal, add lilting calypso music and delicious cooking that's straight from the islands of Barbados, Jamaica and Trinidad. Rambling drowsily along the shores, ramshackle and content, few places are as distinct or romantic as Panama's Caribbean coast.

Colón and around

Sadly, there is no shortage of horror stories about Colón, the Panama Canal's dilapidated Caribbean coast terminus. The city began life in the 19th century as a lawless and dismal frontier town, impressively branded 'the wickedest city in the Americas'. In many respects, little has changed. Despite historic moments of affluence – first as a terminal for the Panama railway, more recently as a hub for the nation's maritime industries – Colón has failed to shake off its negative image. Decades of neglect have left swathes of the city in disrepair, riddled with violence and crime, its population terminally deprived and marginalized. The scenes of destitution and urban decay are the legacy of Panama City elitism, for the vast wealth generated by Colón's Free Trade Zone is funnelled straight to the capital, never reaching the streets outside. Despite its problems, there is much to celebrate about Colón. Beyond the ghettoes, it boasts lively pockets of colour and, in some places, there are optimistic signs of gentrification. It is hoped that, in the not-too-distant future, Colón will once again rise to glory. For now, it is assuredly off the tourist trail, but a fascinating destination nonetheless.
▸▸ *For listings, see pages 111-112.*

Arriving in Colón → *Colour map 2, A1.*

Getting there
Colón's **bus station**, Avenida Bolívar and Calle Terminal, receives regular buses from the capital and nearby coastal villages. The **train station** sees one daily return from Panama City and is situated on Avenida Bolívar on the south side of town. The **Panamerican Seaways** *Nissos Rodos* arrives in the cruiseship terminal, Colón 2000, on the eastside. All areas are sketchy and you should use a taxi upon arrival. If driving from Panama City, the **Corredor Norte** connects with a rapid four-lane toll highway, Ruta 3.

Getting around
Located on Isla Manzanillo, the city of Colón is connected to the mainland by two main arteries: Avenida Amador Guerrero and Avenida Bolívar. Although walking around the city is not recommended, it's useful to remember that streets are laid out in a compact grid with numbered *calles* running east–west and named *avenidas* running north–south. Most taxis charge US$1-2 for destinations within the city. Please use them.

Tourist information
There is an **ATP office** in Colón 2000, T475-2300, 0800-1600, and a **CEFATI office** on Paseo Washington, T448-2200, 0800-1600. Any decent hotel will also be able to offer advice and information on visiting the Colón Free Trade Zone.

Safety
Colón is a dangerous place and the risk of robbery (or worse) is extremely high. You are strongly advised to use a taxi when visiting the sights below. If you must walk, stick to the main thoroughfares, leave all valuables in your hotel and strictly avoid deserted areas and backstreets. Stay alert and under no circumstances go walking at night. Sadly, Colón is not for the faint of heart and less experienced travellers may want to skip it altogether.

Don't miss ...

Background

Foundations

During his fourth and final exploration of the Americas, Columbus arrived at a small, swampy, mosquito-infested island in the Bay of Limón, took a look and decided it was no fit place to build a settlement. Isla Manzanillo, as it would later be dubbed, was ignored for three centuries until the California gold rush sparked demand for passage across the isthmus. In 1850, the island was selected as the unlikely Caribbean terminus of the new Panama railway, not because it was technically advantageous, but because a land speculator, George Law, had bought up most of the prime real estate on the coast. Forging a camp from the pestilent backwater of Isla Manzanillo proved a major challenge for the early engineers, who spent the first months of the project living in an old sailing ship anchored in the bay. On 29 February 1852, the cornerstones of the new passenger station and office were laid in a grand ceremony. Colombian diplomat Dr Victoriano de Diego Paredes baptized the burgeoning new settlement 'Aspinwall', after the president of the railway company. The government in Bogotá subsequently objected and said the town should be called Colón (Columbus), after the island's 'discoverer'. The railway company refused and years of confusion ensued as both names went into common usage. In 1890, the government ordered all post marked 'Aspinwall' to be returned to sender, forcing 'Colón' to stick.

The Panama railway

As work on the railway progressed, Colón emerged out of the swamp. Its population burgeoned with Chinese and Afro-Antillean labourers, but living conditions were grim and unsanitary. Garbage was dumped in the streets or at the end of piers and the barely fluctuating Caribbean tides never carried it far. Rainwater was collected in catch basins that were often alive with larvae and protozoa. The city lacked any proper form of sewage disposal or drainage and, unsurprisingly, intestinal complaints and cholera were common. By the time the railway had been completed in 1855, over 12,000 workers had died from malaria, yellow fever and other tropical maladies. Nonetheless, Colón enjoyed over a decade of boom time. Crowds of 49ers flowed through the city, spurred by dreams of gold and glory. Scores of new businesses opened to service their needs, including prolific saloons, gambling houses and brothels. Venereal disease was common, and so was murder, and few commentators had anything complimentary to say about the city. HH Bancroft noted, "...searching for the specialty in which Aspinwall excelled, we found it in her carrion birds, which cannot be surpassed in size or smell."

The Silver People: Afro-Antillean legacies

In a massive recruitment drive that focused on Barbados, Jamaica and Trinidad, the Panama Canal Company dispatched a secret weapon to entice young men to the isthmus: 'The Panama Man'. Recently returned from Central America, a local boy done good, the smooth-talking Panama Man was always loaded with cash and impeccably attired in a crisp white suit. He'd spin enviable tales of life on the mainland, where beautiful women and easy prosperity awaited. On the plantation islands of the West Indies, where jobs were scarce and pay was low, the finely dressed Panama Man symbolized not just a shot at the good life but, in many cases, survival itself. Over 30,000 migrants left for the isthmus, but the reality of life in Panama bore little resemblance to the company recruitment pitch.

Workers were expected to conform to a harsh regimen of physical labour, toiling for 10 hours a day under the fierce tropical sun. Living conditions were unsanitary and overcrowded. Hundreds of lives were lost in landslides or badly timed dynamite explosions. Thousands more were lost to yellow fever, cholera and malaria. Worst of all, a system of racial segregation ensured that no West Indian ever rose above his rank, which was always subordinate to the white man. Under the direction of Washington DC, white North Americans received 'Gold Roll' status, including generous wages, sick pay, vacation leave and clean, comfortable housing.

By contrast, black West Indians were assigned to the 'Silver Roll' and received considerably lower wages, no welfare privileges and inferior social amenities. Echoing the Jim Crow laws of the southern states of America, many public services – including company stores – were fiercely segregated along 'Gold' and 'Silver' lines.

For the unsung 'silver people' of the Canal Zone – who led lives filled with struggle and danger – there was an unpleasant irony to the company motto: 'the land divided, the world united.' Some returned home empty-handed, often to ridicule. A famous Jamaican folksong recalls a pretentious 'Colón Man', finely dressed but penniless. "So fast he leave the island," goes the song. "So quickly he come back". In fact, very few Afro-Antilleans made their fortunes in the mire of the company work-camps, but those who stayed succeeded in building one of the great wonders of the world, and in the process, a bold new community bound by collective purpose. Panama's Afro-Antilleans can forever point to the Panama Canal and claim with dignity 'We made this'. The true 'Panama Man' was no smooth-talking player in a zoot suit – he was a dedicated family man, a disciplined worker and, above all else, a survivor.

Afro-Antilleans in Panama are continuing to campaign for recognition of their historic contribution to the nation. To learn more about their struggle, visit www.thesilverpeoplechronicle.com.

French and American eras

Following the completion of the US Transcontinental Railway in 1869, the Panama railway became obsolete. Colón entered a period of decline and its population dwindled as many departed in search of new opportunities. The city's fortunes turned in 1879, when Ferdinand de Lesseps arrived in town on a Lafayette steamer heralding plans to build a canal. The French engineers soon discovered Colón was too small for their needs and set about constructing a new settlement, Cristóbal, where they built rows of neat cottages for their technicians. The French era was widely regarded as a lavish time, when the brothels and gambling houses flourished. Wine and champagne were consumed in great quantities and words like 'Bacchanalian orgy' were uttered in the international press. The high death rate – which plagued the doomed French canal effort from start to finish – was attributed to moral decadence. In 1889, France admitted defeat, but its contribution to Colón, including numerous French colonial buildings, would not be forgotten. The city entered another phase of obscurity until the Americans took over in 1904. Under the direction of William Gorgas, the US Canal Company installed waterworks and sewers, drained the swamps, sanitized the area and paved the streets. They expanded Cristóbal and built scores of new houses, hospitals and social facilities. After the completion of the canal, Colón and Cristóbal continued to develop with the construction of New Cristóbal, an American residential zone near the north shores of the island. In 1948, the Colón Free Trade Zone was completed.

Colón today

From the mid-1950s, many of Cristóbal's inhabitants moved to new settlements, such as Margarita and Coco Solo and, in accordance with the 1977 Torrijos-Carter Treaty, the territorial boundaries of the Canal Zone soon began to diminish. The rule of the Guardia Nacional, however, generally paralleled a protracted period of depression, when many of Colón's fine buildings fell into ruin. The canal handover in 1999 signalled the final incorporation of former US territories into Panama, including the port and township of Cristóbal, which has now completely merged with the city of Colón. Today, Colón boasts two cruise-ship terminals – Colón 2000 and Pier 6 – and several ports, including Manzanillo International. Despite these useful developments, the city remains one of the most polarized and impoverished places in the country.

Places in Colón

Avenida Bolívar is one of Colón's main commercial streets and a great place to witness the bustle of day-to-day life. The crowded *avenida* is home to lots of weathered old stores and hotels and enters the city from the southwest, heading directly north until it concludes at the ocean-front **Paseo de Washington** (see below). A few blocks east, **Avenida Central** features lots of palm trees and small gardens, as well as historic statues, including one of Columbus and an indigenous girl, a gift from the Empress of France. Colón's French-influenced **cathedral**, Calle 5 y Avenida Herrera, has an attractive altar and stained-glass windows. The **public market** is on Calle 11 and is worth a quick visit for its mercantile buzz and array of local produce, including the fieriest hot sauce anywhere.

Paseo de Washington

Paseo de Washington fronts the Atlantic Ocean in the north and offers fine views of the ships waiting to enter the canal. The surrounding neighbourhood, known as **Nuevo Cristóbal**, is currently becoming gentrified and is home to numerous handsome old structures dating from the early 20th century. Among them is the historic **Washington Hotel**, constructed in 1913 on the site of an old railway building. Although extensively remodelled and well past its prime, the hotel still manages to conjure an air of romance and faded elegance. Just west of the hotel lies **Fuerte de Lesseps**, a former American artillery post. Today it's a gated community for some of the city's wealthiest inhabitants, but it still bears the sign 'Battery Morgan'. The old **Episcopal Church**, known locally as the Church-by-the-Sea, is located directly opposite the hotel. It was built in 1865 for the railway workers and was formerly the only Protestant church in Colombia.

Port of Cristóbal

In southwest Colón, the old Port of Cristóbal overlooks the Panama Canal with a sea of containers. It is the first and largest of the city's ports, but now faces stiff competition from Manzanillo Port in Coco Solo on the mainland. Inside the port area, agents for many of the world's great shipping lines are located in colonial-style Caribbean buildings dating from

Colón

Fuerte de Lesseps

Episcopal

C1
C2
C3
C Lesseps
C4
C5
C6
C7
C8
C9
C10
C11
C12
C13
C14
C15
C16

Av del Frente
Av Balboa
Av Bolívar
Av Justo Arosemena
Paseo del Centenario
Amador Guerrero
Av Herrera
Av Central
Av Meléndez
Av Santa Isabel
Av Roosevelt

Cathedral

To Colón 2000 &

Old (disused) Railway Station

Dollar rent-a-computer

Explonet

Bahía de Limón

Taxis & Car Hire

Stadium

Capitanía del Puerto

CRISTOBAL

ZONA LIBRE

Calle Tobago

Calle Canal

Río Folk

To Rainbow City & Gatún Locks

To Panama City, France Field Air Base, Coco Solo & Portobelo

N

200 metres
200 yards

Where to stay 🛏
Andros 1
Four Points Colón 2
Meryland 3

Nuevo Washington 7
Radisson Colón 2000 4

Restaurants 🍴
Grand Café 1
Café Andros 2

1914; you will require permission from the Port Authority security officer to enter. For over eight decades, Cristóbal Port was also the site of the famous **Panama Canal Yacht Club**, which was dramatically demolished during a surprise eviction in February 2009. Heading north from the port, **Avenida del Frente** faces the Bahía de Limón and has many historic buildings, most of them terribly dilapidated. During the 1950s and 1960s, the avenue was a prestigious commercial centre, but it is now ghettoized and home to squatters.

Colón Free Trade Zone

ⓘ *For an overview of stores, see www.colonfreetradzone.com. Note you will not be able to leave the zone with your purchases. They will be forwarded to Tocumen International Airport where you can collect them on leaving the country. Bring your passport to gain entry.*

Established in 1948, the 400-ha Colón Free Trade Zone is a major distribution hub for shipments throughout the Americas. It receives 250,000 visitors annually and boasts imports and exports valued at over US$5 billion. A city within a city, the zone is home to some 1750 commercial outlets, including purveyors of fine perfume and liquor, designer clothing, jewellery, electronics and more. Virtually all trade, however, is wholesale. The Colón Free Trade Zone is celebrated as a pillar of the national economy and also criticized as a hub of money-laundering and other illicit activities.

Colón 2000

Attached to Colón's Home Port and second cruise-ship terminal, Colón 2000 is a well-guarded shopping and entertainment complex. Although lacking in personality, this touristic enclave is one of the safest and most-visited places in the whole city, home to numerous bars, restaurants, duty-free shops, cafés, a supermarket, ATM and taxi stand. For many cruise-ship passengers, Colón 2000 will be their only experience of Colón. At the time of research, a very large shopping mall was in construction nearby, opening up the options slightly.

Around Colón

The old School of the Americas

From Colón, Avenida Bolívar heads south to the colourful old Canal Zone township of **Margarita**, where an access road braches east to Lake Gatún and the former military base of Fuerte Espinar, now the five-star **Hotel Melia**. Prior to its handover in the 1980s, Fuerte Espinar was a US training camp known as Fort Gulick or, more infamously, the **School of the Americas (SOA)**. The facility was responsible for training scores of brutal Latin American dictators, General Manuel Noriega among them. Today, the school continues to operate on US soil at Fort Benning, Georgia, under the guise of the Western Hemisphere Institute for Security Cooperation. For years, the activist group **SOA Watch**, www.soaw. org, have been campaigning for its closure and they maintain an astonishing list of past graduates on their website.

Gatún → *Colour map 2, A1.*

South of Margarita, a paved road continues to the township of Gatún, its impressive locks (for more information on visiting Gatún Locks, see page 91) and the former installation of Fort Davis (now the Colón campus of the Technological University of Panama). From the locks, a swing bridge crosses over the Panama Canal, but it is often closed for long periods when canal traffic is high. On the opposite bank, the road divides. One route heads south and skirts the shores of Lake Gatún, offering access to the protected forests of San Lorenzo, and eventually, the remote coast-road of the **Costa Abajo**. A northbound branch heads to **Fort Sherman** (now an international marina) and the ruined Spanish fortress of **San Lorenzo**.

Bosque Protector San Lorenzo → *Colour map 2, A1.*

Covering an area of 9653 ha, the lush Protected Forest of San Lorenzo encompasses 12 varieties of forest, including plentiful mangroves, semi-deciduous woodland and rainforests. Squeezed between the Caribbean Sea and Lake Gatún, the park also includes 15 km of rambling coastline and coral reefs, along with the ruined Spanish fortress of San Lorenzo. From 1953-1999, the whole area served as a training ground for the US Defense Department's Jungle Operation Training Battalion at Fort Sherman, which readied US soldiers for the war in Vietnam. Consequently, there are plentiful trails snaking through the undergrowth, great for observing the region's wildlife, which includes over 400 species of bird and 81 mammals. The park is poorly served by buses and it helps if you have your own vehicle, preferably 4WD.

Fuerte San Lorenzo → *Colour map 2, A1.*
ⓘ *0800-1600, free. The fort is situated about 1 hr from Colón on a winding road. To get there, go to Gatún, cross over the bridge and turn north. There is no public transport to the fort. A taxi from Colón should cost US$40-60 return – bargain hard.*

Perched on a cliff-top promontory overlooking the coast, Fuerte San Lorenzo is one of the oldest and best-preserved Spanish fortifications in the Americas, although it has been destroyed and rebuilt several times since its foundation in 1595. Situated close to the outlet of the Río Chagres, the fort was designed to protect the **Camino Las Cruces,** a transisthmian trade route which brought gold, silver and other riches from the Pacific (see page 85). In 1596, the Englishman Sir Francis Drake launched a 23-ship attack on San Lorenzo and destroyed it. He proceeded up the Chagres but failed to reach Panama City. In 1671, Henry Morgan fought a bloody 11-day battle to take the fort as a prelude to his decisive swoop on Panamá La Vieja. In 1860, the fort was rebuilt on a higher part of the cliff, but despite its solid new masonry, it was unable to withstand an attack by Edward Vernon in 1740.

Engineer Hernández spent seven years strengthening the garrison, but the threat to San Lorenzo gradually receded as Spanish galleons were diverted to the Cape Horn route. The last royalist soldiers left the fort in 1821 as Panama declared its Independence from Spain. It subsequently served as a Colombian prison, a campsite for gold miners and an English post office. Today, the site has undergone an extensive UNESCO renovation programme and is well worth a visit. It boasts well-preserved moats, cannons and arched rooms, and promises commanding views of the Chagres and Caribbean Sea. Like Portobelo, most of the fortress is constructed from cut coral. The earliest artillery sheds can be seen on the lower cliff level but most of the bulwarks, stone rooms and lines of cannons are from the 18th century. There is a picnic area and a tiny beach is accessible from a steep path down the cliff.

Achiote → *Colour map 2, A1.*
Shade-grown coffee and livestock are the traditional economies of Achiote, a rural hamlet of around 500 inhabitants. Set in a flowery valley close to the forests, Achiote is

Raising the dead

In recent years, marine archaeologists have uncovered a slew of lost treasure off Panama's Caribbean coast. In 2008, a team led by Texas State University began conducting meticulous surveys of the seabed around the mouth of the Río Chagres. Three years later, in 2011, they announced the discovery of what are believed to be the remains of Henry Morgan's lost fleet, including his flagship, the *Satisfaction*. The remains are thought to date from 1671, when Morgan attacked Panama City and managed to crash five ships on the Las Lajas reef near San Lorenzo. Archaeologists have successfully recovered several cannons, assorted cargo boxes, chests and a section of a hull, which are now under the protection of the Patronato Panamá Viejo. Gold and silver are predictably absent from the finds, but the ships themselves are a priceless piece of historic patrimony.

Equally intriguing were the remains of two ships discovered off the coast of Portobelo in 2011, which are believed to be the vessels of Sir Francis Drake – the *Elizabeth* and the *Delight* – scuttled after his death in 1596. Under the sponsorship of Pat Croce – a well-known sports entrepreneur, US TV celebrity and self-confessed pirate fanatic – a team of marine archaeologists discovered three sections of hull with fire damage. But, despite the use of powerful new technology, the team failed to locate the remains of Drake himself, who was dispatched to the ocean floor in a lead coffin. Basing their research on the journals of Thomas Maynard, a crew-member on the *Defiance*, they believe that the casket is located somewhere within a league (5.5 km) of the wrecks. In true swashbuckling spirit, Croce and the team have vowed to return.

a great place to organize birdwatching or hiking expeditions. For information on trails – including the famous Achiote Road – visit **El Tucán Visitor Centre** ⓘ *www.sanlorenzo. org.pa*, founded and maintained by ACEASPA, an excellent NGO dedicated to sustainable development and environmental education. To get to Achiote from Colón, first travel to Gatún, cross over the canal, bear south and follow the shore of Lake Gatún until you see the turning on your right. On public transport, take a Costa Abajo bus and ask the driver to drop you at 'el Centro El Tucán de Achiote'.

Costa Abajo

The Costa Abajo is a remote and sparsely populated stretch of Caribbean shoreline with an end-of-the-world ambience and friendly Afro-Antillean inhabitants. To get there, follow the Achiote Road to the languorous village of **Piña**, where you'll find a long sandy beach and the start of a rugged coast road. The road connects a string of palm-fringed fishing villages, including **Nuevo Chagres** and **Palmas Bellas**, before finally petering out around **Miguel de la Borda**. You'll need a sturdy 4WD to continue to the communities beyond, which include historic **Río Belén**, where one of Columbus's ships was abandoned in 1502. There are few restaurants or other facilities on the Costa Abajo, so come prepared with your own supplies of food and water. While it is possible to use public buses to get around, it's much better to have your own vehicle.

For sleeping and eating price codes and other relevant information, see pages 16-19.

◉ Where to stay

Colón *p103, map p107*
There are lots of dirt-cheap pensiones in Colón, but security is an issue and none have been recommended here.
$$$$-$$$ Four Points Colón, Millennium Plaza, Av A Waked, Corredor Zona Libre, T447-1000, www.starwoodhotel.com/fourpoints. A comfortable business-class hotel complete with gym, restaurant and business centre. Rooms are well appointed, but internet costs extra, US$10 per day. Located on the southern entrance to town, close to the Colón Free Trade Zone. One of the best. Good reports.
$$$ Radisson Colón 2000, Paseo Gorgas, Calle 13, T446-2000, www.radisson.com/colonpan. A decent hotel, popular with cruise-ship passengers and people conducting business in the Free Trade Zone. Amenities include restaurant, bar, pool, sauna and casino. Conveniently located in the Colón 2000 cruise-ship terminal with access to shops and restaurants.
$$$-$$ Meryland, Calle 7a y Santa Isabel, T441-7128, www.hotelmeryland.com. A clean, secure and professional hotel in a safe part of town. It has 80 comfortable rooms, each with telephone, a/c and hot water. Amenities include an internet room and a good restaurant.
$$$-$$ Nuevo Washington, Calle 1ra, Paseo Washington, T441-7133, www.newhotelwashington.net. An interesting old hotel with lots of history and character, but definitely past its prime. The garden has a pool and good views of ships entering the canal. Other amenities include restaurant, bar and casino. Rooms vary, ask to see a few.
$$ Andros, Av Herrera, between Calle 9a y 10a, T441-0477, www.hotelandros.com. Located in downtown Colón, Hotel Andros has 60 clean, comfortable, modern rooms equipped with TV, a/c, hot water and Wi-Fi. Good service and reasonable value. Recommended.

Fuerte San Lorenzo *p109*
$$$ Marina Hotel, 30 Butner St, Fort Sherman, T433-0471, www.shelterbaymarinahotel.com. Affiliated with the modern yachting marina at Fort Sherman, the **Marina Hotel** is located a short drive from the ruins of San Lorenzo. It has 11 rooms complete with satellite TV, efficient a/c and hot water. A quiet spot in attractive surroundings.

Achiote *p109*
$ Centro El Tucán, Achiote, www.sanlorenzo.org.pa, arrange your visit through CEASPA, T226-4529. The Toucan Centre is a community project with 2 dormitories and a total capacity for 20 people. Amenities include toilets, showers, drinking water, outdoor terrace, dining room and kitchen. The grounds are green and peaceful and filled with coffee and banana plants. Unrivalled access to the Achiote Rd birdwatching trail.

◉ Restaurants

Colón *p103, map p107*
There are plenty of cheap eateries offering locally flavoured *comida criolla* – ask a taxi driver for recommendations. Otherwise head to the Colón 2000 terminal, the safest place in the city, where you'll find a range of mid-range restaurants to satisfy most tastes. All the hotels listed above have reasonable restaurants attached.
$$ Café Andros, Av Herrera and Calle 9. Passable buffet food served in drab, Soviet-style surroundings. Open till 2000 with a security guard posted at the door. A convenient downtown location.

$$ Grand Café, Colón 2000, Calle 11 and Av Roosevelt. Excellent, authentic Lebanese cuisine including tasty falafels, humus, Turkish coffee and kofte kebabs. A very safe location with a pleasant outdoor terrace. Highly recommended.

⊖ Transport

Colón *p103, map p107*
Bus
Bus station is on Av Bolívar and Calle Terminal, use a taxi to get there. To **Panama City**, every 20 mins, express (recommended) US$3.15, 1½ hrs; to **La Guaira** (including Puerto Lindo), 5 daily, 2 hrs, US$3.20; to **Portobelo**, every 30 mins, US$2.80, 1½ hrs; to the Costa Arriba (including Portobelo and Nombre de Dios, but check final destination with driver), hourly, 1-4 hrs, US$1-5; to the **Costa Abajo** (including Gatún Locks and Achiote), every 1-2 hrs, 1-3 hrs, US$1-3. Note if travelling from Panama City to Portobelo, you can skip Colón entirely by changing buses in Sabanitas.

Car rental
Europcar, Millennium Plaza, inside Four Points Sheraton, T447-1408, www.europcar.com. **Hertz**, T441-3272, Plaza Colón 2000, www.hertzpanama.com.pa.

Ferry
The Greek-operated *Nissos Rodos* sails to **Cartagena** from Colón 2000 every Mon, Thu and Sat, 12 hrs, US$100-500, with space for vehicles. This is a new service with fares and schedules subject to change. Return sailings depart form Cartagena every Tue, Fri and Sun.

Taxi
Because of safety concerns, a taxi is highly recommended for getting around the city. Tariffs vary; US$1 in Colón, US$1.25 to outskirts, US$10 per hr.

Train
US$22 one way to **Panama City**, leaves 1715, station on west side of town just south of the centre. For more information, see page 76.

Costa Arriba

East of Colón, the Costa Arriba calmly unravels with a succession of sheltered bays and secluded villages. Some come to relax and soak up the unhurried atmosphere. Others come to explore the pristine natural landscapes, which become increasingly remote as the coast road advances east. Inland, the exuberant forests of the Parque Nacional Portobelo are replete with challenging hiking trails, brilliantly coloured birds, rugged peaks, copious waterfalls and rivers. Offshore, the clear Caribbean waters conceal an intriguing underwater world of old shipwrecks and coral reefs. Steeped in legends of piracy, the Costa Arriba is a bastion of historical drama. The tangible legacy of Spain's imperial authority survives in the awesome ruined fortifications at Portobelo. But living vestiges of Afro-colonial culture have survived the ages too, and the Costa Arriba is the heartland of Panama's Cimarrón population, who are directly descended from escaped African slaves. Their traditional music, dances and stories add spice to a region already packed with adventure and intrigue. ▸▸ *For listings, see pages 119-121.*

Sabanitas to Portobelo

If you're heading from Panama City to the Costa Arriba, you can skip Colón altogether by exiting at the town of Sabinatas, 13 km south of Colón on the main highway. Buses to Portobelo and other coastal destinations pass outside the Rey Supermarket every 30 minutes. When returning to the capital, simply cross over the highway and wait at the shelter by the footbridge. The coast road from Sabanitas to Portobelo takes around an hour to traverse. Some 15 km east of Sabinitas, just beyond the village of **María Chiquita**, you'll pass the turning for the adrenalin-charged zip-lines of **Panama Outdoor Adventures**, www.panamaoutdooradventures.com (see page 121). A kilometre further on, **Playa Langosta** is one of the best beaches in the area.

Portobelo → *For listings, see pages 119-121. Colour map 2, A1.*

Now no more than a large village, Portobelo was once the affluent Caribbean coast terminus of Spain's lucrative transcontinental trade routes. At the height of its glory in the 17th century, bars of gold were piled up like firewood in the Royal Customs House. Although Spain took serious measures to protect its treasure, constructing vast fortifications that were considered virtually impregnable, it didn't stop marauding pirates from launching periodic attacks (some of them even succeeded in breaking through). Today, wrapped in tropical torpor, Portobelo is a poor and sleepy settlement of just a few thousand inhabitants. The ruined fortresses, designated a UNESCO World Heritage Site in 1980, offer tentative glimpses of Portobelo's swashbuckling past, but beyond its history and romance, the village is a fierce bastion of Caribbean culture, a raucous place during festival time and the gateway to a host of natural attractions, including several diverting dive sites.

Arriving in Portobelo

Buses travel from Colón to Portobelo every 30 minutes, passing Sabanitas en route. The village is very small and easily explored on foot. The ATP, just west of the square behind the Alcaldía, can supply guides, schedules of Congo dances and other performances, as well as comprehensive information about many local points of interest.

Background

Rodrigo de Bastidas was the first Spaniard to lay eyes on the protective bay of Portobelo, but he did not care to name it – that privilege went to Christopher Columbus, who, on his fourth and final voyage, took refuge in the bay for seven days. He named it 'Puerto Bello' – beautiful port. Several years later, in 1509, Diego de Nicuesa landed in Puerto Bello during his ill-fated search for the gold fields of Veraguas, but was soon routed by indigenous attackers. In 1518, Captain Diego de Albites attempted to colonize Puerto Bello before relocating to Nombre de Dios. For the next 70 years, Puerto Bello was ignored while Nombre de Dios flourished. In 1596, Sir Francis Drake burned Nombre de Dios to the ground, retreating to the bay of Puerto Bello where he died of dysentery. Following the destruction of Nombre de Dios, a colonization drive pushed settlers to Puerto Bello, which was officially founded as San Felipe de Puertobelo in 1597. Puertobelo – later contracted to Portobelo – was built in a crescent shape around the bay.

By the beginning of the 17th century, several fortresses had been built from coral stone, which was a lightweight material, easy to cut when wet and hard as granite when dry. El Castillo de San Felipe de Todo Fierro – nicknamed 'the iron castle' – was built at the base of a large hill. It was equipped with 35 cannons and a garrison of 50 soldiers. A smaller fort named Santiago was built on the other side of the harbour. It had five cannons and a garrison of 30 soldiers. In the east, they built the fortress of San Jerónimo. There were many other small garrisons controlling the approach to the city. Assigned the role of Spanish treasure house, Portobelo flourished. Gold, silver and other treasures from the New World piled up in its warehouses. An annual trade fair – for which 300 soldiers were garrisoned – brought crowds of international travellers. The fair of 1637 saw so much material change hands that, according to the Englishman Thomas Gage, it took 30 days for the loading and unloading to be completed.

Inevitably, Portobelo's wealth made it a target for pirates. In 1602, William Parker slipped into the bay, torched the district of Triana and marched on Portobelo, looting 10,000 ducats from the royal treasure house. In June 1668, Henry Morgan, the ever-ambitious Welsh privateer, sacked the settlement entirely. Commanding a force of nine ships and 500 men, he destroyed the Castillo San Jerónimo and took the town the next day. Morgan stayed for a week and plundered 260,000 pesos and large quantities of silk and other precious merchandise. He burned whatever buildings he could and destroyed the cannons he could not steal. In 1739, Admiral Edward Vernon attacked Portobelo with a formidable force of six ships, 370 cannons and 2735 men. He bombarded the forts non-stop until the inhabitants were forced to surrender. The fortifications were rebuilt, but were never again seriously challenged. The re-routing of trade routes around Cape Horn spelled the end of Portobelo's illustrious and eventful career.

Ruined fortresses

The ruined forts of Portobelo overlook the bay with crumbling walls and wistful old cannons – with enough imagination, you can make out the treasure ships in the distance. Perched on the coast road on the western outskirts of town, **Fuerte Santiago** was constructed after Admiral Vernon's devastating attack in 1739. It boasts security-conscious 3-m-thick walls, officers' quarters, a sentry box, barracks, watchtowers and artillery sheds. Nestled on the bay at the centre of town, Portobelo's largest and most impressive fortress is **Fuerte San Jerónimo**. It features an impressive gateway, officers' quarters, barracks and guardroom, as well as 18 cannon embrasures where some cannons have not been moved since the Spanish left in 1821. Across the bay, **Fuerte San Fernando** was built to

The Cimarrones

During the 16th and 17th centuries, Panama's Caribbean coast was the dark heart of Spain's colonial slave trade. The great fairs of Portobelo and Nombre de Dios saw thousands of African prisoners change hands every year. Occasionally, however, groups of captives would escape into the wilderness. These so-called *Cimarrones* intermarried with indigenous tribes, learning precious survival skills and founding their own outlaw communities, or *palenques*. Over time, the *Cimarrones* organized themselves into distinct kingdoms with their own monarchs and systems of kinship. They were both dreaded and celebrated as formidable warriors.

Few *Cimarrones* were as feared and respected as the unruly King Bayano, a West African Mandinko who was spirited to Panama in 1552 along with 400 others. When their ship sank offshore, the group swam to freedom and elected Bayano their leader. As ruthless as he was fierce, King Bayano fought the Spanish for nearly five years, plundering mule trails and murdering Spanish soldiers with complete audacity. The fearsome conquistador Pedro de Ursúa was finally sent to subdue him, but he soon realized there was no defeating Bayano on the battlefield. Instead, he initiated peace talks, and in

1556, during a round of negotiations, slyly poisoned 32 of Bayano's men. The *Cimarrón* king was promptly clapped in irons and forced to sign a peace treaty. He was later exiled to Peru, then Spain, where he is reported to have died a wealthy and successful man.

The remaining *Cimarrones* signed an official treaty granting them clemency, but peace did not reign long. During his tentative explorations of Castillo de Oro, Sir Francis Drake noted the existence of at least two nations of *Cimarrones* – a people he described as 'valiant'. Like many buccaneers before him, he decided to forge an alliance with the locals, exchanging iron tools and weapons for *Cimarrón* expertise and military support. In 1573, a band of *Cimarrones* helped Drake attack two different mule trails and the British began to regard them as key to toppling Spain's power in the New World. In February 1577, the *Cimarrones* assisted John Oxenham in raiding ships travelling from Peru and the Pearl Islands. For the Spaniards, this was the final insult and they responded by attacking *Cimarrón* settlements with unrestrained ferocity. The *Cimarrones* surrendered in 1579, agreeing to settle in one large pueblo and ending direct British involvement in the region.

---

replace Fuerte San Felipe and San Diego, also destroyed by Vernon. Much of the structure was dismantled to build the breakwater at the northern end of the canal, but it remains intriguing nonetheless. You need a boat to get there, US$5 return. A small tower, **Mirador Perú**, overlooks Fuerte Santiago from a hill. It features steps carved into the hillside and promises commanding views over the village.

Iglesia de San Felipe

Built in 1814, the Iglesia de San Felipe is a historic national landmark and the most important church in Portobelo. It is home to the highly revered Black Christ – also known as **El Nazareno** – a 17th-century cocobolo-wood statue that draws over 50,000 pilgrims each year on 21 October. El Nazareno is said to be able to work miracles and there are at least three different legends regarding its origin. One account recalls how fishermen found it floating in the sea during a cholera epidemic. After it was brought ashore, the epidemic miraculously began to wane and the statue was venerated. Another version explains how the image was on its way to Cartagena when the ship put into Portobelo for supplies. Upon trying to leave, the ship was thwarted by rough weather until the crew decided to jettison the statue. It eventually floated ashore to be rescued by locals. A third account tells how the Black Christ was originally destined for Isla Taboga in the Pacific, but a mistake in the shipment's labelling sent it to Portobelo. Despite numerous attempts to dispatch it to its correct destination, it somehow remained.

Museo del Cristo Negro de Portobelo
ⓘ *Behind the Iglesia de San Felipe, T448-2024, daily 0900-1700, US$1.*
Located inside the Iglesia de San Juan de Dios, the Museo del Cristo Negro is home to a collection of over 60 of the Black Christ's ceremonial robes. Red-coloured robes are for the Black Christ Festival on 21 October; purple ones are for Holy Week. Some of the robes are over a century old and boast lavish materials and ornate needlework. Others are more thrifty and simple. Panamanian boxing hero, Roberto 'Manos de Piedra' Durán, is among previous donors, although most of the robes on display have been given anonymously. The Black Christ of Portobelo is evidently an extravagant character – he wears each of his robes just once.

Real Aduana de Portobelo
ⓘ *Calle Principal, T448-2024, Tue-Sun 0800-1600, US$1.*
Built 1630-1634, Portobelo's Royal Customs House is a very handsome colonial structure painstakingly restored to glory in 1998. It originally served as the king's counting house, where careful inventories for Portobelo fairs were made and hundreds of guards were posted for security. Today, the Customs House is home to a good local museum with expositions on Portobelo's turbulent past and its historic role as an imperial port. There is a collection of antique weaponry and, on the second floor, interesting photos and illustrations of the village in its heyday. Cultural exhibits explore the lives and customs of the village's Cimarrón inhabitants. The bronze cannon at the entrance of the museum was found on a sunken galleon in the bay.

Parque Nacional Portobelo
Created in 1976, the Parque Nacional Portobelo encompasses the Costa Arriba all the way from Buena Ventura to Isla Grande. Covering a total area of 35,929 ha, the park climbs to the continental divide to merge with neighbouring **Parque Nacional Chagres**. The region's relatively high rainfall (4800 mm annually) and complex topography have bestowed upon it a variety of exuberant forests, all rich in flora and fauna and easily hiked with the assistance of a guide. Popular routes include two hills, **Cerro Cross** and **Cerro Bruja**, and a trail that adjoins the demanding **Camino Real**. The park also embraces 112 km of coastline and protected waters, including several offshore islands, coral reefs, mangroves and deserted beaches. Diving and snorkelling are worthwhile, but visibility can sometimes be an issue. Aside from rich marine life, you can explore numerous shipwrecks and a crashed plane in Portobelo's remote coastal waters. ▸▸ *For more information on dive shops, see page 121.*

Beaches around Portobelo
Playa Blanca is a great swimming beach. It's located on a peninsula just northeast of Portobelo Bay and the only way to get there is by boat, 20 minutes from Portobelo, around

US$5 per person. The beach is surrounded by forests and there are some good coral reefs just offshore. **Playa La Huerta** is a small, sheltered cove flanked by thick vegetation. It's a very calm spot and dive shops sometimes use the area to train students. To get there, hire a boatman from the dock in Portobelo, around US$5 per person. **Puerto Francés** has also been recommended for swimming. In all cases, pay the boatman on return and take adequate supplies of food and water with you.

Puerto Lindo

Beyond Portobelo, the coastal highway strikes inland for several kilometres before branching north into the heart of the Parque Nacional Portobelo. Around 6 km before **La Guaira** – the jumping off point for Isla Grande (see below) – the road forks near Puerto Lindo, a tiny fishing village hidden inside a bay. Puerto Lindo is becoming an increasingly popular stopover for vessels travelling to the fabled islands of Guna Yala and beyond, to Colombia. A small but vibrant backpackers' scene has emerged offering a handful of cheap lodgings. It's easy to arrange excursions to nearby attractions, including blissful **Isla Mamey**.

Isla Grande → *For listings, see pages 119-121. Colour map 2, A1.*

It would be a stretch of imagination to call Isla Grande 'paradise', but it is a popular and agreeable destination boasting palm-fringed beaches and a tropical island ambience. Despite its name, it is not a big place – just 5 km long and 1.5 km wide. Most of the action is concentrated on the south side of the island, where a ramshackle village clings to the shore with a string of hotels, restaurants and holiday homes. If you like to party, head over at the weekend, when the place is thronging to capacity with feisty revellers from the capital. If you like it quiet, come in the week, when it's virtually deserted. Aside from tourism, the island's 300 inhabitants make a living from fishing and coconut cultivation.

Arriving in Isla Grande

Isla Grande lies just a few hundred metres off the coast, with *lanchas* departing from the tiny village of La Guaira, 10 minutes, US$3. Buses to La Guaira depart five times daily from Colón, US$3.20, passing through Sabanitas and Portobelo. A taxi from Portobelo to La Guaira costs US$10.

Around Isla Grande

The best and only really feasible beach is **La Punta**. Head left after landing on the pier and you'll discover it beyond a spit of sand at the island's southwest tip. The beach enjoys the shade of palms and other exuberant vegetation, but unfortunately, a large hotel also overlooks it. They shouldn't charge you for accessing the beach, which is free by law. If you fancy a short stroll, 10-20 minutes, a steep path commences on the northeast side of the island and leads to a mirador and French-built **lighthouse**. It once contained a lamp designed by Gustav Eiffel (now in the canal museum in Casco Viejo) and brave souls can climb it for fine views of the rocky shores and surrounding waters. There are plenty of **coral reefs** around Isla Grande, but those closest to the island are reportedly damaged. Discuss the options before committing to any snorkel or dive trip. Surfers should head to the east side of the island, where they'll find a **reef bottom break** with three peaks.

Nombre de Dios and beyond → *For listings, see pages 119-121. Colour map 2, A2.*

The deserted mainland beaches continue as the coast road heads east to Nombre de Dios, a tiny end-of-the-earth village that boasts an extraordinary and turbulent history. For over 60 years it served as Spain's foremost Caribbean coast trading hub, seeing more than half the commerce between the Crown and its colonies pass through. By the end of the 16th century, however, the settlement had been abandoned for Portobelo. Many years later, the English buccaneer William Dampier would describe Nombre de Dios as "only a name… everything is covered by the jungle with no sign that it was ever populated…" Not much has changed since then.

Background

In 1509, the Spanish nobleman Diego de Nicuesa sailed from Hispañola to Tierra Firme (Panama) with a view to exploiting the newly discovered mineral wealth of Veraguas. He failed to locate the gold fields that had been charted by previous explorers, instead unravelling into an ill-fated debacle that left him shipwrecked for several months. When he finally acquired a new vessel and set sail up the coast, 520 of his 800-strong crew had been lost to starvation and disease. Upon arriving in a sheltered harbour some leagues east of Puerto Bello, the bedraggled Nicuesa is reported to have cried out, "Paremos aquí, en el nombre de Dios!" (Let's stop here, in the name of God!). Thus Nicuesa set about establishing Tierra Firme's first Spanish colony, Nombre de Dios. His efforts were not very successful and after a few months just 60 members of his crew were still alive. Meanwhile, the more fruitful colony of Santa María Antigua de Darién had been founded some distance away. When its inhabitants heard of the settlement at Nombre de Dios, they sent a scout party to investigate.

Nicuesa was cheered by the arrival of outsiders, who brought food, wine and a cordial invitation to join them in Antigua. Nicuesa accepted but began haughtily proclaiming his rights over the new colony, which he intended to rule with an iron fist. When he and 17 of his men finally arrived in the Darién, they were arrested and sent into exile in a broken boat, never to be seen again. Nicuesa's short-lived colony at Nombre de Dios fell into ruin thereafter, until 1519, when Diego de Albites revived it. As the northern terminus for the Camino Real, the settlement grew and prospered. But despite its good fortunes, it earned a reputation for thievery and disease, and was dubbed the 'Graveyard of Spaniards'. On 29 July 1572, Sir Francis Drake attacked and captured Nombre de Dios, but Spanish reinforcements forced him into an early and empty-handed retreat. A year later, he attacked again, capturing a mule train and making off with much treasure. In August 1595, he embarked on an ambitious scheme to take Panama City, but found himself ambushed on the Camino Real. He retreated, burning Nombre de Dios to the ground as he fled, and dying of dysentery soon after. The settlement was abandoned in favour of Portobelo.

Places in Nombre de Dios

There isn't much to see or do in Nombre de Dios itself. There's a good beach, **Playa Damas**, around 1.5 km from town, but it's best to take a boat, as the trail demands you cross a deep river. If you can locate a guide, it's also possible to hike in the surrounding hills and forests, where excavations have revealed parts of the **Camino Real**, a broken cannon and other historical objects.

Beyond Nombre de Dios

The settlements beyond Nombre de Dios become increasingly isolated the further east you travel. The first village you'll pass is **Viento Frío**, a small fishing community with a large beach. Beyond it, **Palenque** is a very remote and unspoilt community with calm waters and mangroves. **Miramar** is the cleanest of the pueblitos on this stretch of coastline and the occasional smuggling boat puts in here. At the end of the road lies **Cuango**, a bit run-down and dusty between the rains. If you want to go any further, you will need to hire a boat. For the very determined, it's possible to reach Guna Yala.

⊙ Costa Arriba listings

For sleeping and eating price codes and other relevant information, see pages 16-19.

⊙ Where to stay

Sabanitas to Portobelo *p113*
$$$ Sierra Llorana Ecolodge, signed from the Santa Arriba turn-off, south of Sabanitas, T6574-0083, www.sierralloranalodge.yola site.com. Nestled in the heart of a 400-ha private nature reserve, the Sierra Llorana is ideal for birdwatchers and other wildlife enthusiasts. Accommodation consists of clean, simple, tastefully adorned suites with balcony. They also have one slightly cheaper room (**$$**). Tours to San Lorenzo and birding sites are available. Recommended.

Portobelo *p113*
Nearly all accommodation is situated west of Portobelo on the highway to Sabanitas.
$$$-$$ Sunset Cabins, Buena Ventura, 5 km west of Portobelo, T261-3841, www. scubapanama.com. Clean, comfortable, brightly coloured bungalows and rooms (**$$**) with a/c, fan and hot water. There's a common room, restaurant-bar, and motor boat tours. Owned by **Scuba Panama**, who do dive trips from here. Recommended.
$$ Coco Plum Cabañas, Buena Ventura, 5 km west of Portobelo, T448-2102, www. cocoplum-panama.com. Colourful, nautically themed rooms adorned with fishing nets and shells. There's a small dive shop attached and they offer snorkelling tours and transit to the beaches. A pretty, relaxing spot, but reports on service are mixed.

$$ Octopus Garden, Can Can, 8 km west of Portobelo, T448-2293, www.octopusgarden hotel.panamadivers.com. A laid-back and sociable diving resort with a range of simple, comfortable rooms with a/c and hot water. Their restaurant serves ultra-fresh seafood and boasts a deck overlooking the water – the perfect place to knock back a beer and enjoy the sunset.
$ Hospedaje Sangui, T448-2204, on the highway in Portobelo, close to the church. Economical and basic quarters with shared bath and cold water.

Puerto Lindo *p117*
$$ Bambu Guest House, Puerto Lindo, T448-2247, www.panamaguesthouse.com. A comfortable guesthouse built on the side of a mountain overlooking the sea. They have a handful of large rooms, all with own bathroom. Can help arrange excursions.
$ Hostel Wunderbar, Puerto Lindo, T448-2433, www.hostelwunderbar.com. This laid-back hostel features a traditional Guna-style 'house of congress' made of cane and thatch. Activities include canoes, cycles and horse riding. This is also the place to enquire about sailing trips to the Guna Yala archipelago and Cartagena, Colombia. All accommodation is in simple dorms.

Isla Grande *p117*
During holidays and dry season weekends, make reservations in advance; prices often double during high season. All hotels have bars and simple restaurants.

$$$$ Bananas Village Resort, north side of the island, usually accessed by boat but also by path over the steep hill, T263-9510, www.bananasresort.com. Relatively discreet luxury hotel on the best beach on the island, with a good but expensive bar. Day use costs US$35 + tax and includes a welcome cocktail and lunch.

$$$ Isla Grande, T225-2798 (reservations), www.hotelislagrande.com, west of the main pier, at the end of the path. Colourful, if slightly run-down cabins overlooking the beach, popular with Panamanians. To keep you entertained, facilities include BBQ, volley ball, ping-pong, pool table, waterslide and restaurant. Not great value.

$$$ Sister Moon, 5-10 mins east of Super Jackson, T6948-1990 (reservations), www.hotelsistermoon.com. Sister Moon occupies a privileged position on a hill overlooking the ocean. It has comfortable, simple cabins with private bath and fan. Amenities include pool, common rooms, terrace, restaurant and billiards room.

$$ Cabañas Jackson, immediately behind main pier, T441-5656. Clean, basic and economical lodgings. Rooms have fan, cold water and spongy beds. Grocery shop attached.

$$ Villa Ensueño, east of the main pier, T448-2964, www.hotelvillaensueno.com. Big lawns (big enough to play football), colourful cabins and picnic tables overlooking the water. There are also hammocks, ping-pong and *artesanías*.

Nombre de Dios *p118*
$$$ Caribbean Jimmy's Dive Resort, 5 km beyond Nombre de Dios, www.caribbean jimmys.com. Colourful, clean, simple *cabañas* with a superb beachfront location. Each has a private bath, a/c and fan. Although Jimmy can arrange spear fishing trips, jungle tours and horse riding, the real reason for coming all this way is to dive. Multi-day dive packages are available with sites including numerous reefs and wrecks.

🍴 Restaurants

Portobelo *p113*
A number of small *fondas* serve coconut rice with fresh shrimps, spicy Caribbean food with octopus or fish, or *fufú* (fish soup cooked with coconut milk and vegetables).

$$ Las Anclas, Buena Ventura, 5 km west on the road to Colón. **Coco Plum's** restaurant is pleasant, brightly decorated and overlooks the waves. They serve breakfasts, lunches and seafood dinners but aren't always open in low season.

$$ Los Cañones, in Buena Ventura, 5 km west on the road to Colón. Good food in a lovely setting by the water, but not cheap. Good reports.

$ La Torre, T448-2039, in La Escucha, 3 km west on the road to Colón. Large wooden structure serving good seafood and burgers. Large portions and highly praised by some.

Isla Grande *p117*
You'll find lots of good fresh fish at a host of places on the waterfront.

$$ Kiosco Milly Mar, just west of landing pier. A cute little place serving excellent fish dishes at moderate prices.

$$-$ Bar-Restaurant Congo, west of the pier. This restaurant juts out over the water on its own small pier. They serve up the usual Caribbean treats, rum, beer and fresh fish.

🎉 Festivals

Portobelo *p113*
Jan-Apr Several important fiestas in the first part of the year provide opportunities to experience the unfolding Congo dramas that run from the Día de los Reyes (6 Jan) until Easter. Unlike the dance of the same name, Congo here refers to the main male participants who are conversant in festival dances, customs and a secret Congo dialect. The various elements of Congo symbolism relate the people's original African religions, their capture into slavery, their conversion to

Catholicism and the mockery of the colonial Spaniards, who are often depicted as gruesome devils. Members of the audience are sometimes 'imprisoned' in a makeshift palisade and have to pay a 'ransom' to be freed (some spare change will do!). The major celebrations of Carnaval and the Patron Saint Day (20 Mar) are good times to witness the exuberant Congo festivities, but none are as lively or well attended as the Festival de los Diablos y Congos, celebrated every 2 years 2 weeks after Carnaval.

21 Oct The miraculous reputation of the **Black Christ** is celebrated annually when tens of thousands of purple-clad pilgrims arrive from all over the country. Some of them will walk great distances and cover the last stretch on their hands and knees. Mass is celebrated at 1800, but you should be inside the church by 1600 if you want to witness it. From 2000, the statue of El Nazareno is paraded through town on pathways strewn with flowers and flickering candles. The procession is led by 80 men who take 3 steps forward and 2 steps back to musical accompaniment. There's feasting and dancing till dawn.

☉ What to do

Sabanitas to Portobelo *p113*
Canopy tours
Panama Outdoor Adventures, Río Piedra, T6605-8171, www.panamaoutdoor adventures, look for the turning by the orange bus stop 5 mins past María Chiquita. One of Panama's best canopy tours. Their circuit features 11 platforms and 9 cables, the longest running 225 m. They also offer a range of outdoor activities, including hiking, horse riding, camping trips and river tubing. Recommended.

Portobelo *p113*
Diving
Panama Divers, Can Can, 8 km west of Portobelo, T448-2293, www.panamadivers. com. Experienced staff and instructors with PADI-certification up to Dive Master. Various

speciality dives available, including deep, drift and wreck dives. Snorkel trips available too. Same owners as **Octopus Garden** (see page 119).
Scuba Panama, Buena Ventura, 5 km west of Portobelo, T261-3841, www.scuba panama.com. PADI-certification up to Dive Master. Snorkelling, fishing, boat tours and trips to Guna Yala archipelago are also available. Same owners as Sunset Cabins (see page 119).

⊖ Transport

Portobelo *p113*
Bus
To **Colón**, hourly, 1½ hrs, US$2.80; to **La Guaira** (including Puerto Lindo), 5 daily, US$1.50, 45 mins (taxi is also a possibility, US$10). To villages further east, take buses marked 'Costa Arriba' from stop at back of square: **Nombre de Dios**, 45 mins US$1.20; **Palenque**, 70 mins, US$1.75; **Miramar**, 80 mins US$2, **Cuango**, 1½ hrs, US$3.50. The road is paved until just beyond Nombre de Dios.

Puerto Lindo *p117*
Boat
Puerto Lindo is an increasingly popular departure point for trips to Guna Yala and Colombia. Enquire at hotels or hostels to see if any captains are moored in the vicinity.

Isla Grande *p117*
Bus
Buses drop you at La Guaira on the mainland from where *lanchas* (motor boats) nip across to the island, US$3. Tell the boatman if you need a particular locale, Bananas Resort, for example. From La Guaira 5 buses per day go to Colón, hourly 0530-0830, the last at 1300, US$3.20. There may be later buses on Sun and you should expect crowding at such times. Hitching with weekend Panamanians is also possible, all the way to **Panama City** if you're lucky!

Contents

Footprint features

At a glance

⊖ **Getting around** Local infrastructure is poorly developed and you will have to rely on a variety of transportation including planes, buses, 4WD, *piraguas* and *pangas*.
✪ **Time required** 7-14 days.
☀ **Weather** The region receives much more rainfall than the Pacific with regular showers at all times of the year, especially in the rainforest.
✖ **When not to go** The worst of the wet season, Oct-Dec, when the Darién is beset by knee-high mud, flood waters and swarms of blood-sucking insects. Jan-Mar are the driest months; rivers can sometimes dry out towards the end, hindering travel.

A last refuge of ethnic and ecological purity, the remote borderlands of eastern Panama are a place where frontiers converge and realities collide. Perched on the margins of modern civilization, the region's impenetrable rainforests and serene desert isles have long divided it from the world outside. Few destinations are so pristine and isolated but, historically, eastern Panama was the first place in the continent to be colonized by European invaders, who waded ashore from Spanish warships in the 16th century. Some conquistadors won their fortunes pillaging local chiefdoms, others disappeared into the consuming vaults of the jungle, never to be seen again. At every turn, the incipient empire threatened collapse under violent tribal skirmishes, feverish epidemics, phenomenal rainfall and the sheer ferocity of tropical nature. The region was ultimately abandoned for a more strategic foothold further west, and the forests were left to bloom unhindered for centuries. Today, eastern Panama is home to vast tracts of virgin wilderness and lost world landscapes filled with giant trees and snaking rivers, mist-swathed mountains and crashing shorelines. Unsurprisingly, it is one of the most biologically diverse places on earth, boasting scores of undocumented plant and animal species. But the region is a bastion of indigenous diversity too, celebrated as the fabled heartland of the Guna, Emberá and Wounaan people, whose cultures have not been broken by the passage of time – or the destructive appetites of colonialism. Ethnically, geographically and ecologically, eastern Panama signifies an adventurous outer limit, a precarious threshold and a fiercely contested space where humanity, nature and a multitude of biological forms fight for survival. Sadly, modernity has brought new and deadly forces to the region in the form of loggers, ranchers and colonists. What the conquistadors could never accomplish with greed alone, humans are now realizing with bulldozers and chainsaws.

Comarca Guna Yala

The Guna are one of Latin America's strongest and most successful indigenous groups. Their homeland, Guna Yala, is a semi-autonomous comarca that encompasses an archipelago of 400 sublime offshore islands (formerly known as the San Blas islands) and a narrow strip of cultivated Caribbean shoreline. It signifies Panama's first self-governing indigenous territory, awarded to the Guna only after years of struggle and revolutionary upheaval. Administration of the comarca and its islands – of which only 40 are permanently inhabited – is strictly controlled. No large-scale developments blight the landscape, no resorts or gated communities. Life is wonderfully pure and simple, conforming to the easy rhythms of tide and harvest: men cast their fishing lines from dugout canoes, children scale coconut trees and women chatter outside cane-and-thatch houses, sewing brilliantly coloured molas. Despite the intrusion of a modern cash economy, Guna society continues to be dominated by the forces of family, community and tradition. The ancient art of storytelling is alive and well, and equally, the Guna remain fiercely politicized and active. ▸▸ *For listings, see pages 132-134.*

Arriving in Guna Yala → *Colour map 2, A3/4/5.*

Getting there

There are several airstrips in Guna Yala, most are accessible with **Air Panama**. Daily flights depart from **Albrook Airport** in Panama City to **El Porvenir**, **Achutupo**, **Mulatupo**, **Playón Chico** and **Ustupo Ogobsucum**; with an additional six flights a week to **Corazón de Jesús**. At the time of press, flights to Río Sidra and Cartí had been suspended. All schedules are subject to change and you should book flights well in advance. Return tickets are strongly recommended to avoid being stranded. It is possible to reach the Comarca by boat, usually as part of a long-haul trip to Cartagena, Colombia. Private charters depart from **Colón**, **Portobelo**, and more frequently, **Puerto Lindo** – see page 121 for more information. There is also a road running over the Serranía de San Blas from **El Llano** to **Cartí**, now in better shape than ever thanks to new paving and a river bridge. At the time of press, access was strictly controlled by the **Guna Congreso General** (see below). Prior permission is absolutely essential if you want to drive to Guna Yala; taxes are also payable, US$6-7 plus US$2 port tax. Alternatively, many hostels in Panama City now offer approved overland transport, US$25-35, but with additional taxes and boat charges you may end up paying little less than for a flight. Very fit and adventurous types can hike over the isthmus in the dry season; contact a tour operator in Panama City for advice.

Getting around

Tourism is strictly controlled in the Comarca. Without your own yacht, moving at will between the islands is not easily accomplished. It is always possible to rent a private *lancha* (motorboat), but costs will be high for anything other than short trips. In all cases, you will be obliged to use a local boatman or guide. Dugout canoes are sometimes available for fun paddles around close-lying islands, but please do not head out to sea in them. Public *lanchas* depart regularly from major settlements, including Cartí, but there's no official schedule. If you have a specific journey in mind, discuss your plans with your hotel or guide. You will have difficulty finding a boatman to travel to the more remote eastern islands (the journey is very rough and dangerous), but you may be able to hitch a ride with a yacht (usual precautions apply). Otherwise, the best way of travelling long distance within the Comarca is by plane.

Information

There are no official tourist information offices in Guna Yala, but the **Guna Congreso General** ⓘ *Calle Crotón, Edif 820-XB, Balboa, Panama City, T314-1293, www.congresogeneralkuna. com*, maintains some modest material on their website, www.turismokunayala.com. The best sources of up-to-date news and information are local hotel owners or guides, who can advise on all the best local attractions. Many of the lodgings listed on page 132 have informative websites.

What to expect

You will not be free to roam unguided and the number of communities open to foreign visitors is limited – expect to be accompanied on most of your journeys. Tax is payable when you land on any island for any length of time, usually US$3-10. Bring a valid photo ID for registration with the *Sahlia* (local chief). There are very few restaurants on the islands and most are attached to hotels. You will be served seafood, seafood and more seafood. Hotels vary and can be very private and secluded or, alternatively, nestled in the heart of bustling communities. It pays to shop around as you are likely to be tied to your chosen lodging for the length of your stay. Most rates include meals and one daily excursion, typically to snorkelling sites, a beach, a Guna museum or a local community. Even the most expensive accommodation is quite rustic. Running water is often unavailable and many toilets consist of latrines over the water. It goes without saying, swimming around populated islands is not a good idea. Electricity may be non-existent or supplied by generators for a few hours after dark – bring a torch. Most communities of any size have simple shops where you can buy snacks and sundries, but it's a good idea to bring some supplies of fresh water from the mainland. There are no ATMs in the region, bring all the cash you need, preferably in lots of small notes. Camping is possible but needs to be cleared with the *Sahlia*. Due to the presence of drug-traffickers in the region, camping on uninhabited islands is not recommended. There are payphones in the larger communities.

Customs and etiquette

The Guna are very conservative people and you will be expected to behave politely and adhere to their rules. Please dress appropriately when visiting communities and avoid exposing too much flesh, except on the beach (women should avoid topless bathing altogether). You must always ask permission before photographing any indigenous people, but the issue is particularly strict in the Comarca. The Guna wish to protect their image from commercial exploitation and you will typically be charged US$1 per subject, but US$1 per photo is not uncommon either. Fees for using video cameras are quite high, sometimes up to US$50.

Background

Origins and colonial history

The Guna language, **Dulegaya**, belongs to the Chibchan family of languages, placing Guna origins in an area corresponding to present-day western Panama. Nonetheless, most Guna trace their roots to the region of Urabá in Colombia, where they were heavily concentrated at the time of European contact. The Guna are thought to have migrated to the Darién following inter-tribal wars in the 16th century. After settling into rainforest communities, they established trade relationships with European pirates and adventurers, or otherwise served as guides and mercenaries in British-led incursions against Spanish outposts. A few

Don't miss ...

chiefs even learned European languages and travelled through the Caribbean. Promising relations were struck with the French in 1740, but when they started growing cacao for export and exploiting the Guna as their workforce, relations deteriorated and they were expelled. By the mid-1800s, the Guna began migrating offshore to the Caribbean islands, where they could escape the insect-borne diseases sweeping across the isthmus. The British, who made a point of forging close partnerships with indigenous and African-descendent tribes throughout Central America, became close trading partners of the Guna. It was the Colombians, however, who proved consistently loyal and profitable – to this day, the Guna continue to export large quantities of lobster and coconut to Colombia.

The Dule Revolution

In 1870, Colombia granted the Guna their own semi-autonomous region, including a large swathe of coast from eastern Colón as far the Gulf of Urabá. In 1903, the nation of Panama was formed and their territorial area dissolved. Under the authority of central government, the region saw an influx of foreigners, including prospectors, fishermen, fruit companies and US Baptist missionaries, who began intermarrying with the Guna. In the 1920s, the Panamanian government launched a programme of forced assimilation, which included the suppression of age-old Guna traditions. On 25 February 1925, two chiefs – **Olgintipipilele** and **Nele Kantule** – led a rebellion against the state, killing several Panamanian policemen and ethnically cleansing non-Guna or mixed-blood children. A few days later, the flag of the **Independent Republic of Dule** was raised, with its orange stripes and black swastika symbolizing the four winds. Panama beseeched the United States for help, but they refused to intervene militarily and instead brokered a peace deal. The accord included the recognition of Guna autonomy and the removal of state police from their territory. In 1938, the **Kuna District of San Blas** was officially recognized as Panama's first self-governing *comarca*. The structures of governance were formalized in a 1948 document, **La Carta Orgánica de San Blas**, and cemented with Law 16 in 1953.

Recent developments

Traditional Guna culture remains fragile and imperilled, partly due to infrastructure improvements which have shattered the Comarca's geographic and cultural isolation. The incursion of non-Guna colonists on the mainland remains a persistent threat, while the flow of Colombian cocaine along the coast is adding pressure for a police presence in the region. Some Guna have also chanced upon abandoned consignments floating in the ocean, with mixed results. Elsewhere, entrenched poverty and infant mortality continue to plague Guna society and almost 50% of their population now dwell in urban settlements, mainly Colón and Panama City. Tourism continues to generate cash, but many are sceptical about its benefits and frown upon the presence of foreigners. There have been some successful attempts at resource management since the 1980s, but Guna fisheries now face collapse with dwindling lobster stocks. Climate change is also threatening to engulf the Guna homeland, with nearly all of their islands lying just above sea level. In 2011, efforts to standardize spellings in the native Dulegaya language saw 'Guna' officially replace the spelling 'Kuna' (there is no equivalent of 'k' in Dulegaya).

Culture and community

Guna communities span the headwaters of the **Río Bayano**, the banks of the **Río Chucunaque**, parts of the Darién and the islands of the Guna Yala archipelago. Settlements range from a single household on a lonely desert isle to bustling townships of several thousand inhabitants. The typical Guna village is a crowded, ramshackle place punctuated by a maze of teetering alleyways. Most homes are built with cane and palm thatch, but concrete is not uncommon, especially in more Westernized communities. Guna society is broadly egalitarian and everyone is expected to participate in the burden of work. Friends, relatives and neighbours often organize into small entrepreneurial groups to co-operate in shared commercial ventures, such as farming a plot, harvesting coconuts, fishing or running a hotel. At the heart of the community lies the **Casa de Congreso** (House of Congress), where meetings take place daily to discuss local issues, recite traditional chants, hold rituals or recall myths and legends of times past. Local chiefs called *Sahilas* are the main community representatives and twice a year they report to the **Congreso General Guna** (Guna General Congress) – the highest authority in the land.

Family and work
Life in the land of the Guna begins and ends with the family. It is not unusual for a single household to shelter large extended families of two or three generations, which are typically presided over by mothers, grandmothers and other powerful female figures. By contrast, men tend to dominate the public and political worlds, but this balance is now shifting. When Guna men marry, they are expected to live in the house of their mother-in-law, work for their father-in-law and contribute to the upkeep of all his relatives. Marriages in Guna society were once arranged by parents and based on the man's capacity for hard work, but this is now rare. Guna children are initially raised by their mothers and grandmothers with the help of other female relatives and will attend school thereafter. When boys reach the age of five, they start embarking on fishing and hunting expeditions, bonding with their fathers and other men in the community. Many children will continue to secondary and high school, and some to university, but most will enter the world of work upon leaving adolescence. Young men will be expected to participate in the farming and fishing that are the mainstay of the Guna economy. Since the 1960s, Guna men have been migrating in search of seasonal employment, mainly in Colón, Panama City and the banana plantations of Changuinola. Women have less opportunity to migrate and tend to remain closer to home, retaining their traditional roles as nannies, cooks, traders, and of course, makers of brightly coloured *molas*. The export of lobster and coconuts is also a major cash earner, as is tourism.

Rituals and traditions
Traditional Guna religion reveres the forces of nature and embraces an unseen spiritual Otherworld. It is called 'Father's Way' and it includes epic songs, dances and ceremonies that transmit social history, reinforce Guna identity and disseminate basic spiritual values.

The mola: a synthesis of modernity and tradition

Molas are a type of reverse appliqué decorative textile made by Guna women. They are traditionally worn as panels on the front and back of a blouse (the word *mola* actually means 'blouse' in the Dulegaya language), but they also make great wall-hangings and cushion covers. The art of *mola*-making is thought to have begun with the arrival of Christian missionaries. Scandalized by the ancient Guna practice of body painting, the moral-minded preachers persuaded them to cover up their skin and instead switch to the medium of cloth. Early *mola* designs replicated the geometric shapes and abstract patterns of their body art, while later productions incorporated psychedelic birds, animals, fish, spirits and other totemic figures. Some of the most modern *molas* feature aeroplanes, flags, political ideas or scenes, which can be quite intriguing. Another recent development is machine-made *molas* with simplistic motifs and gaudy colours. Usually measuring 40 by 33 cm, *molas* are made out of up to seven (but on average three to four) superimposed, differently coloured cloths. Each layer is cut to make up a design element constituted by the unveiled layer beneath it. The ragged hem is folded over and sewn down with concealed stitching and step-by-step, layer-by-layer, the process slowly reveals the design. *Molas* are quintessential souvenirs and have the advantage of being light and small, so they don't take up precious luggage space. It's worth seeking out a good quality one, but be aware that the very best *molas* take months of work and may set you back hundreds of dollars. Generally, most people settle for something in the region of US$20-50 – anything less and the quality starts to suffer. As a rule, the more layers a *mola* has, the higher its cost. Stitching should be fine, even and hidden, and never substituted with tape. Where there is decorative surface stitching, it shouldn't compete with the more graphic cut-away. Some *molas* have appliqué sewn on, as opposed to cut away, and they can create additional depth and enliven the surface. However, try to avoid those with dots, triangles and small circles roughly applied to fill up space. Don't worry about exact symmetry, but do look for fine and even outlines, the narrower the better. Check the quality of the material in the lower layers and run your hand across the surface of the *mola* to make sure the layers don't scrunch up. Finally, beware *molas* that have been left out in the sun for weeks on end as their colours will be bleached. A bit of playful barter is appropriate when making multiple purchases, but generally Guna are astute business people and won't budge too much on prices.

It revolves around two principal deities: **Pab Dummat** (Big Father) and **Nan Dummat** (Big Mother), although some anthropologists argue these figures originated with the Evangelical movements of the 20th century. Nonetheless, generations of effective resistance against Catholic missionaries have left Guna religious life remarkably intact. Their main mythical hero is **Ibeorgun**, who taught the Guna material culture, including how to prepare food, grow crops and build houses, and from which the term 'Guna' is derived. Traditional medicine continues to be widely practised, with shamans or *neles* using herbs and sacred chants to heal the sick, commune with the spirits, or guide departed souls to the underworld. Girls are the focus of many interesting rites of passage, including the 'needle ceremony' or *ikko inna*, when their nose is pierced with a gold ring for the first time. Puberty rites are particularly important and well attended, when a girl's hair is cut short and she is given her full adult name. Women continue to wear traditional clothing too, including head scarves, strings of beads wrapped around the wrists and ankles (*uinis*), colourful *mola* blouses and wrap-around skirts. Death is a particularly vivid occasion in Guna society, when the body of the deceased is dispatched to the mainland for burial and their grave dressed with a host of objects for use in the afterlife. This is a Christian custom, however – traditionally the Guna buried their dead in the place where they slept (usually under their hammock).

The Guna Yala archipelago → *Colour map 2, A3/4/5.*

El Porvenir and around

El Porvenir is the western gateway to the archipelago. It has a small landing strip that sees early-morning traffic from **Air Panama**, a simple grocery store, a basic hotel and a tiny beach. The **Museo de la Nación Kuna** ⓘ *open on demand, US$2*, has some intriguing displays on Guna culture, including exhibitions relating to Guna ceremonial life and some traditional *artesanías*. Apart from that, there's not much to detain you and most travellers head to one of the other nearby islands, including **Isla Wichub-Wala** and **Isla Nalunega** (Red Snapper Island), where you'll encounter vibrant village life first-hand. Both islands have their own Casa de Congreso, as well as a range of simple accommodation, sparsely stocked general stores and basketball courts. Between Wichub-Wala and Nalunega lies the artificial island of **Ukuptupu**, formerly a Smithsonian Institute research station, which operated here for 20 years until 1998. It's now the site of a popular hotel and a great place to watch the comings and goings of yachts, motorboats and dugout canoes. Around 15 to 30 minutes away lie several small islands, often visited as day excursions. They include **Isla Pelícano**, with its gorgeous beach and colourful coral reef, and **Isla Perros**, with its sunken ship that's teeming with marine life and great for snorkelling. **Isla Ogobsibu** is a private island with its own lodgings.

Los Cayos

Around 7 km east of El Porvenir lie the idyllic islands of the **Cayos Chichime**, also known as Wichudup or Wichitupo. The deep-water channel entering the harbour is only 30 m wide with reefs on both sides, requiring extremely careful navigation. The islands are beautiful and inhabited by only a handful of Guna families who survive by fishing, harvesting coconuts and selling *molas* to passing boats. To the northeast of Chichime lies a long chain of sparsely inhabited islands known as **Cayos Holandeses** or Dutch Keys. The islands have no permanent residents, but most have at least one family of Guna harvesting coconuts. Washed by strong Caribbean swells, the *cayos* are quite far from the mainland and have a remote, rugged feel. They harbour abundant marine life inside a large barrier reef and in deep-water channels at either end of the chain. Towards the eastern side, there is excellent protected anchorage known to yachters as the 'swimming pool'. As with Chichime, caution and good navigational charts are required when entering this area – one of the local reefs is called 'wreck reef' for good reason. Other very beautiful uninhabited island cays include **Cayos Grullos**, **Cayos Limonés** and **Cayos Coco Bandero**.

Cartí

The communities of Cartí, south of El Porvenir, consist of several densely inhabited island villages and a mainland settlement with a landing strip and road access to El Llano. **Cartí**

Suitupo is the usual port of call, with its interesting folkloric museum and crowds of *mola* vendors. There are lots of social amenities in this busy community, including a school, post office, library and medical centre. Sadly, it is also quite polluted, particularly around the port. If you're looking for an encounter with traditional Guna culture, this isn't the best place. Many people here have exchanged their traditional clothing for Western-style attire and cruise ships frequently descend on the area, bringing crowds of gawping tourists, which, perversely, is the best time to see the locals dressed like Gunas. If you're looking for a more natural locale, the rather lovely **Isla Aguja** lies nearby, with its beaches, palm trees and handful of inhabitants.

Río Sidra and around

The island of Río Sidra lies around 16 km east of Cartí and it is composed of two densely populated communities: **Marmatupo** and **Urgandí**. The island has some basic amenities, including a telephone and general store, and is mainly used as a departure point for some rather splendid and secluded destinations, including **Isla Kuanidup** which has rustic lodgings, blissful hammocks and beaches. **Isla Nusatupo** is a less visited spot offering access to the **Cayos Los Grullos**, with fine snorkelling around the islands and coral reefs. **Isla Máquina** is a quiet, traditional island that's worth visiting as a day trip, but no tourist facilities exist for longer stays. **Islas Robinson** are a group of islands that are becoming very popular with backpackers, especially **Isla Naranjo Chico**. Jeep transport from the hostels in Panama City usually unloads in Cartí for dispatch directly to the Islas Robinson.

Corazón de Jesús and around → *Colour map 2, A3.*

Around 30 km east of Río Sidra, Corazón de Jesús is the archipelago's main trading centre, home to a large grocery store, airstrip and lots of built-up areas. Connected to Corazón de Jesús by a long footbridge, **Narganá** is the Comarca's administrative centre, with the only courthouse, jail and bank for miles. Both communities are highly Westernized, with concrete being the preferred construction material. Although you won't encounter the kind of 'cane-and-thatch' villages that most people expect from Guna Yala, a visit to these communities is still an intriguing experience, often providing fascinating insights and cultural contrasts. Some 7 km east of Narganá lies the more traditional community of **Isla Tigre**, reportedly very clean and friendly, but best approached with a guide. **Río Azúcar** is a very crowded island, close to the mainland and popular with yachters. There are lots of amenities here, including a hardware and grocery store.

Playón Chico and around

Playón Chico lies around 40 km east of Corazón de Jesús. It is a large inhabited island, relatively modern and the jumping-off point for more idyllic destinations. Nearby, **Isla Iskardarp** is home to the **Sapibenega Kuna Lodge**, widely regarded as the archipelago's premier lodging. **Isla Yandup**, about five minutes from Playón Chico, is also very comfortable. The waters are rough between Corazón de Jesús and Playón Chico, making it hard to reach the area by motorboat; the best way is by plane.

Isla Achutupo and beyond

Isla Achutupo, around 30 km east of Playón Chico, is a very traditional island with its own airstrip and lots of unspoilt culture. Nearby, about a minute away, **Isla Uaguitupo** (Dolphin Island) is home to an upmarket ecolodge. **Isla Ustupo**, 15 km away, is the largest island in the *comarca* with a population of 5000, lots of social amenities and a grocery store.

Isla Ailigandi lies around 35 minutes from Achutupo and has an array of murals and political statues devoted to the Guna nation. Much further east, **Mulatupo** has its own airstrip but is rarely visited by tourists and virtually off the radar. **Puerto Obaldía**, close to the Colombian border, is a very interesting frontier town with lots of sketchy traffic passing through; seek advice before setting out.

◉ Comarca Guna Yala listings

For sleeping and eating price codes and other relevant information, see pages 16-19.

◉ Where to stay

You are strongly advised to book ahead, especially during major holidays when most accommodation is likely to be full. Lodgings below are grouped by point of entry, but many require additional onward transport (assuming you've booked ahead, this should be waiting for you). All rates are per person and all but the very cheapest include meals, transport and excursions.

El Porvenir and around *p130*
$$$ Cabañas Coco Blanco, Isla Ogobsibu, 15 mins from El Porvenir, T275-2853 or T6700-9427, cocoblanco.wordpress.com. Secluded private island with a handful of traditional cane-and-thatch *cabañas* right on the beach. Interestingly, they prepare a lot of Italian food.
$$$ Cabañas Wailidup, Isla Wailidup, 25 mins from El Porvernir, T259-9136 (Panama City) or T6709-4484. Exclusive *cabañas* on a private island, all powered by solar energy. Guests enjoy their own personal beach, bar-restaurant and pier. Sandflies may be an issue during certain months. The owner, Sr Juan Antonio Martínez, also owns **Kuna Niskua** on Wichub-Wala (see below).
$$$ Kuna Niskua, Isla Wichub-Wala, 5 mins from El Porvenir, T259-9136 (Panama City) or T6709-4484, www.kunaniskuahotel.com. Owned by the friendly and knowledgeable Sr Juan Antonio Martínez, who is reportedly an important player in Kuna politics. Basic rooms right in the heart of a thriving Kuna

community. Most rooms have private bath and shower, but some cheaper ones have shared bath.
$$ Cabañas Ukuptupu, Isla Ukuptupu, 5 mins from El Porvenir, T6746-5088, www.ukuptupu.com. Housed in the former Smithsonian Institute research station, these wooden cabins are built on platforms over the water. Some walkways have hammocks and interesting views of the boats arriving at Wichub-Wala. The owner, Don Juan García, speaks some English and is very hospitable. The bathroom is shared with barrel and bucket showers. Recommended.
$$ Hotel Corbiski, Isla Corbiski, T6708-5254, www.hospedajecorbiskikunayala.blogspot. com. Located on a community island near El Porvenir, simple cane-and-thatch cabins with shared bath. English-speaking owner Elias Martínez is a school teacher and very knowledgeable about the community.
$$ Hotel El Porvenir, El Porvenir, T221-1397 (Panama City) or T6692-3542, hotelelporvenir @hotmail.com. Managed by the friendly Miss Oti. Simple, solid rooms close to the airstrip, with a handy grocery store attached. Rates include 3 meals, but lobster is extra. All rooms have a private bathroom. For large groups, call the Panama City number.
$$ Hotel San Blas, Isla Nalunega, 5 mins from El Porvenir. T344-1274 (Panama City) or T6063-6708. Located inside a Kuna community. The traditional cane-and-thatch *cabañas* here are more interesting than the solid brick wall rooms upstairs, which are simple and smallish. The hotel's guide, Lucino, is very friendly and scouts for guests at **El Porvenir** airport; he speaks English and French. There's a small beach out front.

$ Alberto Vásquez's, Nalunega, 5 mins from El Porvenir, T6772-5135. If you would like the experience of staying in a Kuna house, Alberto Vásquez has 2 rooms, each with a 2-person capacity, shared bath, bucket-and-barrel shower. Reasonable rates include 3 meals, but excursions, when available, are US$5 extra. Alberto works for Juan García (Cabañas Ukuptupu) and is a good guide.

Cartí *p130*
$$ Cartí Homestay, T6734-3454, www.carti homestay.info. A new, family-run hostel with a laid-back ambience and backpacker clientele. Lodging is rustic and consists of hammocks, bunks and double beds. The owners also offer transportation to Colombia.

Río Sidra and around *p131*
$$$ Cabañas Kuanidup, Isla Kuanidup, 25 mins from Río Sidra, T6635-6737, www.kuanidup.8k.com. An idyllic, isolated spot with rustic *cabañas*, swaying hammocks, lovely coral reef and achingly picturesque white-sand beaches. The perfect castaway desert island.
$$ Cabañas Narascandub Pipi, Isla Naranjo Chico, T256-6239 or T6501-6033. Rustic cabins and dorm beds by the beach.
$ Robinson Cabins, Isla Naranjo Chico, T6721-9885. A popular backpacker option with lots of chill-out spots. Private cabins and dorms are available.

Corazón de Jesús *p131*
$ Narganá Lodge Hotel, Narganá. A basic hotel and restaurant, El Caprichito, serving good crab dishes.

Playón Chico and around *p131*
$$$$ Sapibenega Kuna Lodge, Isla Iskardup, 5 mins from Playón Chico, T215-1406, www.sapibenega.com. One of the most expensive and exclusive lodgings in the entire *comarca* with solar-powered cane-and-thatch *cabañas* on stilts, all with private baths, balconies and hammocks.

$$$ Yandup Lodge, Isla Yandup, T202-0854 www.yandupisland.com. Situated on a private island and one of the best lodgings in Guna Yala. Isla Yandup boasts its own white-sand beach and offshore coral reefs. Cabins are rustic but comfortable and fully kitted with lights, fans and mosquito nets. Recommended.

Isla Achutupo and beyond *p131*
$$$$ Akwadup Lodge, Isla Akwadup, T396-4805, www.sanblaslodge.com. More private island 'luxury' among the top-end of Guna Yala's accommodation. Lodgings consist of *cabañas* over the water, relatively modern and fully equipped with running water and Wi-Fi. Very comfortable and idyllic, but not cheap.
$$$$ Uaguinega Ecoresort, Isla Uaguitupu, T396-4805 or 6090-8990, www.uaguinega. com. Also known as 'Dolphin Island Lodge'. A range of upmarket wooden cabins and cane-and-thatch *cabañas*. Amenities include bar-restaurant, hammocks and volleyball. This the only hotel in the *comarca* with satellite internet.

⊛ Festivals

All the following fiestas involve dances, games, meals and speeches, and are traditional. Those on Narganá have a stronger Western element (but also typical dancing and food).
25 Feb Anniversary of the Dule Revolution, at Playón Chico, Tupile, Ailigandi and Ustupu.
19 Mar Fiesta patronal on Narganá.
8 Jul Anniversary of Inakiña on Mulatupo.
29-31 Jul Fiesta patronal on Fulipe.
20 Aug Charles Robinson anniversary on Narganá.
3 Sep Anniversary of Nele-Kantule on Ustupo.
11 Sep Anniversary of Yabilikiña on Tuwala.

Air

Air Panama, www.flyairpanama.com, serves all major destinations in Guna Yala and El Porvenir is the main entry/departure point for most visitors, US$37.50 one-way excluding taxes. Costs and schedules vary with the seasons and all flights leave early in the morning, 0600-0700.

Boat

There are occasional private boats to Guna Yala, but services are unscheduled and the trip can be rough depending on the season. Talk to the hostels in Panama City, or try Hostel Wunderbar, www.hostelwunderbar.com, in Puerto Lindo (see page 119).

Shipwrecks are not as uncommon as you might expect, please be careful selecting a captain. Boat transport between the islands is usually private and included as part of your hotel package. **Public boats** depart from Cartí and trips to the backpacker islands around Río Sidra should cost US$20-30 per person one-way.

Car

Overland transport to Cartí is provided by several hostels in Panama City including Luna's Castle, www.lunascastlehostle.com, and Hostel Mamallena, www.mamallena.com. The 2- to 3-hr journey costs US$20-30 (extra fees and charges apply). Driving your own vehicle is not recommended at this time due to restrictions.

The Darién

The Darién is a land of vast rainforests, vibrant cultures and ever-advancing agrarian frontiers. It is the place to witness neotropical nature in all its glory – and to reflect on humanity's reckless relationship with the environment. Despite the sad ongoing loss of biodiversity, the region remains extraordinarily lush and impenetrable. Having traversed the entire North American continent from Alaska to Panama, the Panamerican Highway promptly ends in the Darién. Beyond it, a consuming wilderness sprawls east into Colombia – the so-called Darién Gap – a graveyard of failed explorers, missionaries and colonists. Entering the rainforests of the Darién is like lifting the veil on an alien world. Nature's unbridled energy manifests in a dazzling profusion of weird flora and fauna, and intriguingly, the art and culture of the Emberá and Wounaan are tied to the land in all its diversity. In recent years, the Darién has earned a notorious reputation as a 'no-go' zone and haunt of armed rebels, paramilitaries, drug-traffickers, kidnappers, murderers and other villains. The risks of travelling in the region should not be understated and the overland route to Colombia is presently dangerous and inadvisable. Equally, there are many other areas of the Darién that can be visited safely. Navigating the region requires careful planning, plenty of funds and, ideally, a strong constitution and sense of adventure. ➨ *For listings, see pages 147-148.*

Arriving in the Darién ➔ *Colour map 2, A4-C5.*

Getting there
The cheapest way into the Darién is by road, but some destinations are very isolated and only accessible by plane. Plan thoroughly before setting out. By **bus**, there are several daily departures from Panama City to Yaviza, all before 1130, six to eight hours, US$14. By **plane**, Air Panama flies from Albrook Airport in Panama City to Garachiné, Jaqué, Bahía Piñas and Sambú. **Ancon Expeditions** (see page 147) runs charter flights from Panama City to their field station in Cana, available only as part of their comprehensive tour package.

Getting around

Independent exploration of the Darién is impossible without reasonable Spanish – you will need to talk to locals in order to secure guides or public transport, which is often infrequent, casual and without any fixed schedule. Most river travel is conducted on motorized long-boats called *piraguas*. These can be hired privately with a captain and pole-man, US$10-20 per day, but gasoline is extra. How much you use depends on the horse-power and type of engine, the total cargo/passenger weight, distance covered and type of boat – US$100-150 per day is a rough estimate. If travelling long distances, always enquire about the availability of gasoline en route and pack a barrel or tank for the return leg if necessary. It is possible to hitch rides on cargo boats but arrange a fee before boarding. River travel is always speedier in the wet season when water levels are higher. Hiking between destinations is very common but subject to important safety concerns (see below). Always use a guide and be aware the going is rough and muddy in the wet season. There are very few roads in the Darién – paved or otherwise. You'll need a good 4WD with high clearance if you do want to travel cross-country (not recommended in the wet season when tracks are washed out). The highway to Yaviza is now paved.

Safety and precautions

The Darién is a dangerous wilderness populated by drug-runners, bandits, paramilitaries and other on-the-edge characters. It pays to be cautious. By the same token, many people travel safely to the region each year by following common-sense guidelines and not visiting areas deemed 'no-go'. Broadly speaking, the forests east of **Yaviza**, with a few exceptions, are considered dangerous for foreign visitors, particularly beyond the last-stop frontier town of **Boca de Cupe**, where you may be arrested if you attempt to go any further. Note it has not been safe to cross the Darién Gap into Colombia for many years and you will risk kidnapping and murder if you try. The destinations detailed in this section were 'safe' at the time of research, but it is important to realize that the situation in the Darién is constantly changing. Seek up-to-date information before setting out.

For your safety, it is a legal requirement to present identification at frequent security checkpoints throughout the region. Keep your passport handy and make the local police station your first port of call upon arrival anywhere. A guide is absolutely obligatory if trekking in the rainforest – even if you have years of wilderness experience, the police will demand you hire one. Choose your guides carefully and consult the local ANAM office or other trustworthy persons in the community. Because of banditry, do not discuss your journey or destination with people you don't know. Using an established tour operator will probably not work out cheaper than using your own guides and hired transport, but it will certainly be safer and hassle-free. **Ancon Expeditions** and **EcoCircuitos** are particularly recommended for their Darién expeditions (see page 147).

Conditions in the Darién are generally extreme and you should pack for wet weather, blazing sun, high humidity and blood-thirsty bugs. Malaria is endemic, so take medication well in advance of setting out. Use nets and lashings of repellent to protect against other insect-borne diseases, especially those carried by flies. If trekking, it is recommended you sleep in a zipped tent to avoid unpleasant evening encounters with vampire bats, which are sometimes infected with rabies. If bitten, a course of shots must be administered within 24 hours and there is no guarantee they will work. Venomous snakes pose a further threat, especially at night. If you require antivenin, hospitals can be found in Yaviza, La Palma and Real, along with a string of health centres in smaller settlements. As a precaution, wear boots until you need to sleep and always, always shake them out in the morning. Tap water is not potable in the Darién, so bring purification tablets. Blackouts are common – torches, matches, candles and batteries are essential. There are no banks beyond Yaviza and La Palma, so bring lots of cash, including small notes, and never allow stocks to run out.

Background

An inglorious landing

Following the pioneering voyages of **Rodrigo de Bastidas** and **Cristóbal Colón** (Christopher Columbus), who were the first explorers to chart the coast of Central America, King Ferdinand II of Spain commissioned a series of expeditions to establish new colonies on the mainland. On 12 November 1509, **Alonso de Ojeda** departed from Hispaniola to claim governorship of **Andalusia**, which included all the untamed lands east of the Río Atrato in the Darién. When Ojeda landed on a sheltered beach near the present-day city of Cartagena, Colombia, he was immediately attacked by a group of indigenous warriors. After a brief skirmish, they fled into the darkness of the rainforest and Ojeda and his men pursued, only to be ambushed and assaulted with poison darts and arrows. Many Spaniards were killed and Ojeda himself barely made it out alive. His party packed up and set sail for the Gulf of Darién, where they successfully forged a fortified garrison, **Sebastián**. Sadly, the tone of their colonial enterprise had been set. Subjected to continual attacks from local tribes, they were forced to hide, day and night, within the protected walls of their fort. Unable to plant, hunt, fish or forage, starvation and disease quickly set in. By the time an unscrupulous privateer called **Talavera** arrived – drawn by false rumours of San Sebastián's wealth and riches – the colony was already fading fast. Talavera agreed to provide Ojeda with passage back to Hispaniola, but once they were at sea he took him hostage and confiscated his plundered gold. In a curious twist of fate, the ship was hit by a hurricane and ran aground off the coast of Cuba. The crew spent several months marooned in the wilderness where most of them died, until the remaining survivors were rescued and brought to Jamaica. Talavera was hanged and Ojeda died in Santo Domingo in 1515 following complications from an old war wound.

Santa María de la Antigua del Darién

For two months, the settlers at San Sebastián waited in vain for Ojeda's return; hearing nothing, they eventually abandoned the garrison. By the time **Martín Fernández de Enciso** arrived with reinforcements of 200 men, the colony had been burned to the ground by local tribes. Enciso, who was Ojeda's main financial backer, began scouring the coast for a new place to settle. He was a poor navigator, however, and crashed his ship on a reef, losing all its provisions. Fortunately for him, there was an experienced conquistador among his crew, **Vasco Núñez de Balboa**, who suggested that Enciso take a landing party to explore the opposite side of the gulf. Arriving on the shore in their rowing boats, they were met by a powerful cacique (ruler) called **Cémaco**, who commanded a formidable force of 500 warriors. The Spaniards prepared themselves for battle, donning their armour and praying to the Señora de la Antigua of Seville, promising to dedicate a colony to her if they were victorious. The fight was bloody and harsh, but the Spaniards successfully routed Cémaco, looted his village and set it ablaze. Upon its charred remains they founded the colony of **Santa María de la Antigua**, constructing houses, a church, a town hall and a prison. Enciso, who had been appointed Mayor of Nueva Andalusia in Hispaniola, took up the task of colonial administration. He was a lawyer by trade and began passing countless regulations, including punitive gold taxes and strict restrictions on trade. When there were

Ambassador of the Revolution

When American adventurer Richard Marsh set out into the Darién rainforests in search of a lost tribe of white-skinned Indians, little did he know he would end up playing a lead role in an indigenous uprising. Marsh was an engineer by trade and had his first glimpse of the mysterious tribe while prospecting for rubber in Yaviza in 1923. Seeing a group of white indigenous girls walking through town, he began to wonder if there were more of them, and if they were in fact descended from ancient seafaring Europeans. He resolved to find out and began lobbying the Smithsonian Institute for an organized expedition. In 1924, he led a prestigious team of scientists and specialists in an exploration of the Río Chucunaque. It was the dry season, water levels were low and the river was choked with mud, branches and other debris. Progress was slow and, when rumours began circulating of deadly local tribes, the atmosphere grew tense. Soon the team's agronomist fell ill and was sent back to Panama City where he died shortly afterwards. The Smithsonian anthropologist began to suffer a nasty infection too, but he battled on. The onset of the rains brought new horrors when the party was nearly washed away in a flood. Some of the crew deserted, others came down with malaria and typhoid. Marsh decided to change course and crossed over the mountains into the San Blas region. His anthropologist died soon afterwards and was buried on the beach. The expedition was broken beyond repair

when he finally came into contact with a friendly Guna community. At the time, the Guna were suffering badly under the government's acculturation programme, which had outlawed all forms of traditional culture. The Guna, who had a long history of allying with foreign forces, decided to strike a deal with Marsh: in exchange for presenting their case to the US government, they would introduce him to some of the white Indians he was so desperate to find. Marsh agreed, and when he returned to New York in June 1924, he brought a small group of white-skinned Guna with him, sparking months of public debate. It turned out that the pale-skinned Guna were in fact albinos – a relatively common occurrence in Guna society due to their isolated gene pool (even today, albinos are highly revered as 'Moon Children'). Nonetheless, Marsh pleaded the case for Guna autonomy, but was apparently turned away by Washington. In early 1925, he returned to the San Blas Islands and revolution broke out shortly afterwards. He closely advised the Guna rebels and helped draft their declaration of Independence, which he submitted to the US and Panamanian governments. When a US warship, the *USS Cleveland*, came to the area at the behest of Panama, Marsh was able to successfully negotiate on behalf of the Guna, and in the end, broker a peace deal. He was expelled from Panama thereafter, but lives on in local lore as the white man who played ambassador to the Dule Revolution.

hushed murmurings of an uprising, Balboa intervened, relieved Enciso of his authority and assumed command of the settlement himself.

The subjugation of the Darién

As Governor of Spain's only surviving mainland colony, Balboa set about stamping his authority on the region. He travelled up and down the coast, searching for new allies and treasure to plunder. The powerful **Cacique Careta** was initially hostile to the conquistadors, but later thought better, converted to Christianity and offered Balboa his most beautiful daughter in marriage. **Cacique Comagre** was equally accommodating, awarding the Spaniards 4000 ounces of gold and submitting his own people to mass baptisms. In 1512, Balboa set out in search of an opulent chief, **Cacique Dabaibe**, who, it was said, guarded entire temples fashioned from gold. Travelling along the darkened waterways of the Río Atrato, Balboa discovered the village of **Cacique Abenameche**, which he vigorously looted, hacking off an arm of the chief in the fighting. Nearby, he located the village of **Abibeiba**, which was built high up in the tree-tops, but sadly not immune from the conquistadors' axes. The expedition continued upstream, passing many abandoned villages, but no gold temples. Before returning to Santa María, they launched one final attack on a cacique called **Araiba**, but they were heavily resisted. Thereafter, the three indigenous caciques – Abenameche, Abibeiba and Araiba – decided to join forces and hatched a plan to drive out the Spaniards permanently. Unfortunately, Balboa heard about the plot from one of his indigenous mistresses and counter-attacked, capturing and hanging all the caciques. As a result, vast swathes of the Darién fell under his dominion.

On 1 September 1513, spurred by stories of a shining ocean in the lands to the south, Balboa set forth into the rainforest with 190 men, 1000 slaves and a pack of dogs. It was an eventful journey and he was able to subjugate many chiefs en route, including **Cacique Ponca** and **Cacique Porque**. On 25 September, he climbed to the summit of a mountain and became the first European to set eyes on the eastern Pacific Ocean. On 29 September, he arrived at the shore itself, waded into the water, unfurled his Spanish banner and claimed everything in sight for the Spanish crown. On his return, he subdued yet more caciques, learning about the rich bounty of the Pearl Islands and the great Kingdom of the Incas to the south. The future looked bold and bright for Balboa, but on 30 June 1514, a particularly cruel and clever Spanish nobleman, **Pedro Arias de Avila** (Pedrarias) arrived in Santa María to replace him as governor. Pedrarias kept a watchful eye on Balboa, and in January 1517, had him arrested and executed on false charges of treason. Pedrarias went on to found Panama City in 1519 and within five years it had emerged as the most important colony on the isthmus. In 1524, as power shifted west to Nombre de Dios, Santa María was entirely abandoned, burned to the ground and finally relinquished to the jungle.

The fiasco of New Edinburgh

In the late 17th century, on the other side of the world, the Kingdom of Scotland had fallen on hard times. Years of civil war, famine, failing industry and economic decline were driving mass unemployment and homelessness. Taking the lead from England, their powerful mercantile neighbour to the south, the Scots decided to embark on a bold new international enterprise. The **Company of Scotland** was chartered in 1698 with the aim of launching the country onto the world trade scene. They had originally intended to exploit commerce with Africa, but when a respected financier, **William Paterson**, began rigorously promoting the Darién – a 'land of plenty' he had heard about from a sailor – the company decided to found a colony on the isthmus instead. Unfortunately, the English government, pressured by the English East India Company who wished to maintain a monopoly over their global trade routes, withdrew their support for the scheme and forced European investors to do the same. The Company of Scotland was thus made to seek backing from Scotland itself. Fired with nationalistic pride, many loyal Scottish families, rich and poor, handed over their life savings to Paterson. In July 1698, under threat of reprisals from the English navy, the Scottish expedition slipped out of Leith harbour under the cover of darkness. Their fleet included five ships, 1200 passengers and a large ex-military contingent headed by a former soldier called **Thomas Drummond**.

On 2 November, the convoy arrived in a large bay in the Darién, which they renamed **New Caledonia**. Under the direction of Drummond, the colonists began clearing the forests, building houses and constructing a defensive fortress. The settlement was baptised **New Edinburgh**, but it was not destined for great things. The local tribes, although friendly, had no interest in trading the colonists' useless European merchandise, which included hand-mirrors, combs and wigs. There were few passing ships and, in any case, the English had imposed a strict embargo on the colony, partly as a deferent gesture to Spain. The wet season intensified the colonists' problems, as crops failed, food stocks spoiled and tropical diseases bloomed. They began perishing in great numbers, and by July 1699, amid rumours of an imminent Spanish strike, the 200 or so survivors packed up and fled. Meanwhile, a second expedition of 1000 men had already set sail; it arrived in November to find a ruined colony. They picked up where their predecessors had left off and quickly slumped into a torpor of disease and low morale. A third expedition brought the skilled leadership of **Alexander Campbell of Fonab**, but in January 1700, he foolishly fired the wrath of Spain during a pre-emptive attack against their forces in Toubacanti. They reacted by laying siege to New Edinburgh for a month, until the Scots negotiated a surrender and finally abandoned the settlement. The few survivors who made it home were reviled for the rest of their lives, while Scotland, economically crippled by the fiasco, was forced to enter the union of the United Kingdom of Great Britain just seven years later.

The end of the line: the Darién today

The second half of the 20th century has seen the extension of the Panamerican Highway deep into the Darién, along with the opening of new agrarian frontiers, intensive deforestation and waves of colonization. In the face of persistent guerrilla activity, the highway has stopped short of crossing into Colombia. Today, the forests of the Darién remain lawless and dangerous, effectively torn between rebels from the **Revolutionary Armed Forces of Colombia (FARC)**, right-wing paramilitaries, drug-runners, Colombian security forces, Panamanian border police and, allegedly, American mercenaries working on behalf of private security corporations. The FARC are often criticized for their role in regional drug-trafficking and are reported to force Emberá and Wounaan villagers to act as guides and mules. They have also been guilty of kidnapping international tourists and missionaries, and in some cases, murdering them. By the same token, right-wing militia – who make an uneasy political ally of the Colombian government – have also committed atrocities in the Darién.

In recent years, skirmishes between Panamanian police and FARC drug-runners have become more frequent, with President Martinelli pledging extra funds and new bases in the region. There is some limited evidence to suggest the existence of American-owned aero-naval bases from which spy drones are launched, but there is no official confirmation of this. Meanwhile, the Panamanian border police, who resemble armed troops and were created specifically to deal with the Darién, maintain tight control over regional transport. In a bid to starve the FARC, they have begun blocking vital shipments of food to small river communities. This strategy – along with the wider violence of the Darién conflict – is having a highly detrimental impact on indigenous communities, who are also contending with flooding, climate change, deforestation, oil exploration and aggressive colonizers. Entire villages are now being abandoned. At the same time, the police are heavily outnumbered by the FARC, and utterly underequipped. When the Colombian cartels boast a war-chest of billions of dollars (and have in any case infiltrated Panama's government), stopping the movement of cocaine through the Darién may be an impossible task.

Culture and community

The Darién's riverine interior is home to numerous communities of Emberá and Wounaan, who maintain their own self-governing Comarca, which is divided into two districts – **Cémaco** in the north and **Sambú** in the south. The two indigenous groups are linguistically distinct but culturally homogenous and are believed to have originated in the Amazon rainforests. The Emberá and Wounaan tend to live in small villages of several households clustered on riverbanks. Prior to the 20th century, their society lacked any formal political structure, instead operating on broadly egalitarian lines with shamans and elders maintaining the highest authority. Equally, their settlement patterns consisted of dispersed semi-permanent households with most inhabitants leading nomadic hunter-gatherer lifestyles. In 1963, an adventurer called **Harold Baker Fernández** spent a considerable time with the Emberá and informed them that by settling into villages they could petition the government for schools, clinics and other social amenities. They subsequently constructed their political life around the Guna model, which includes a hierarchy of local and regional caciques, as well as communal decision-making through a Casa de Congreso (House of Congress). Numerous local committees are also important in Emberá and Wounaan municipal affairs.

Family and work

The Emberá and Wounaan are traditionally polygamous, but this arrangement is now rare and monogamy is the norm. Most households are headed by a male and include one extended family. Traditionally, houses are built on stilts to protect against flooding or wild animals. Most have a simple notched log for a ladder, thatched roofing and one or more sides open to the air to allow a through breeze. Some modern houses have zinc roofing as a sign of status, but this can be hot and impractical. Subsistence farming of plantain, banana, yucca, palm, manioc and other staples is highly prevalent, with plantations rather than rainforests now surrounding many communities. All land is communally owned and worked with additional cash input from *artesanía* production and seasonal labour in other parts of the country. The hunting of wild game is still common practice among the Emberá and Wounaan, although they have replaced their poison darts and arrows with modern rifles, shot-guns and traps. Spear-fishing remains popular among young men, along with line-and net-fishing. Rivers are the principal arteries and large dugout canoes called *piraguas*, driven by motors or punted with long sticks, are the main form of transport.

Rituals and traditions

Traditional dress codes are maintained by many Emberá and Wounaan women, including brightly coloured wrap-around skirts, intricate bead jewellery, silver bracelets, anklets and necklaces fashioned from flattened coins. Men are usually attired in Western clothing, but traditional loin cloths are often donned for formal or ceremonial occasions. The Emberá and Wounaan are not squeamish about nudity – women are usually bare-chested and most children go naked until puberty. Both sexes like to paint themselves with copious semi-permanent tattoos using juice from inedible *jagua* fruits. Etched on the skin with a bamboo stick, designs often include intricate geometric lines or dark blocks, bands and zig-zags. Sometimes they cover nearly the entire body, including parts of the face, and will last up to two weeks until they are fully exfoliated. Unfortunately, the traditional art of Emberá and Wounaan ceramics has now been lost, but both groups continue to create excellent baskets (see box, page 144) and carved ornaments from cocobolo wood and tagua nuts. Traditional music includes the use of drums, flutes and conches, frequently accompanied by dances that mimic the movements of wild animals. Traditional religion is broadly animistic and based on a belief in natural spirits. Sadly, there has been some disruptive and divisive missionary influence since the 1950s, but many aspects of Emberá and Wounaan spiritual life remain unchanged. Shamans, who guard considerable knowledge about the medicinal properties of rainforest plants, remain important community figures, although their expertise is becoming supplanted by modern health centres. At the heart of traditional Emberá and Wounaan philosophy are two opposing forces – **Ewandama**, the good creator god, and his evil rival, **Tiauru**.

Panama City to Yaviza → *For listings, see pages 147-148.*

The Interamericana is now paved as far as Yaviza and passes through a string of sleepy towns en route to its conclusion in the jungle. Until the 1970s, everything east of Chepo, 50 km from Panama City, was thickly forested and considered part of the Darién Gap. Not so today. Actually located in Panamá province, **Chepo** itself is a reasonably large town and has useful modern amenities including an ATM, stores and a hospital. About 18 km east of Chepo, you'll pass the 30-km-long **El Llano–Cartí** highway, which crosses over the continental divide and into Guna Yala. It has also been recently paved and offers access to the reputable **Burbayar Lodge**, an upmarket but pleasantly rustic ecolodge with good forest trails and some of the world's best birding (see Where to stay, page 147).

Lago Bayano → *Colour map 2, A3.*
Back on the Interamericana, the town of **Cañita**, 10 km further east, has good, if not better provisions than Chepo. Expansive Lago Bayano lies another 12 km ahead. Created in 1976 with the damming of the Bayano River, the 350-sq-km lake displaced thousands of Guna and Emberá, many of whom relocated to the banks of the Río Chagres in what is today the Parque Nacional Chagres (see page 98). On the south side of Lake Bayano, which is named after the famous Cimarron (escaped African slave) warrior, are the atmospheric, bat-filled **Bayano Caves**. To visit, you need to charter a boat, US$50. Once inside, cover your mouth to avoid inhaling nasty particles and do not swim in the water – it is reportedly home to crocodiles and carnivorous fish.

Ipetí
Beyond Bayano, the highway rolls east towards the provincial border with Darién, closely flanked by the folded ridges of the **Serranía de Majé** to the south. The settlement of Ipetí, which is composed of three ethnically distinct Guna, Emberá and Latino townships, is worth a stop if you have time. The Emberá contingent have established a community tourism project where you can experience village life, hike in the surrounding forests, swim in waterfalls, take canoe trips or get beautified with *jagua* temporary tattoos. Continuing east on the highway, you'll pass the towns of **Torti** and **Cañazas**, both with basic amenities (including hotels in Torti), before crossing into Darién at **Agua Fría No 1**.

Santa Fe → *Colour map 2, B4.*
The 6000-strong town of Santa Fe lies 3 km off the Interamericana, roughly 25 km east of the Panamá–Darién border. In former times, the settlement prospered thanks to its river

connections with the Pacific Ocean. Today, there's not much to see beyond some basic stores and small hotels. About 10 km east of the Santa Fe turn-off lies **Quebrada Honda**. If you have a 4WD, you can turn south here and head 11 km on a bumpy track to the excellent community tourism project of **Puerto Lara**, www.puertolara.com. This friendly Wounaan village offers a host of fun activities including body painting, traditional dancing, hiking and fishing. They are also among the finest basket-weavers in Panama. Taxi pick-up available, book in advance.

Meteti → *Colour map 2, B4.*

It's another 26 km on the Interamericana until you arrive at Meteti, a major town and stopover just 50 km from the end of the highway. It is home to convenience stores, restaurants, hotels and many colonists from other parts of the country, mostly from Chiriquí province in the west. Many people pass through Meteti on their way to La Palma, the capital of the Darién (see page 145). Public boats depart from **Puerto Quimba**, 20 km away on the Río Iglesias (0730-1830, 30 minutes, US$3). To get to the port, catch a local bus (US$1.50) or a taxi (US$10). Should you need to stay overnight in Meteti, there are a

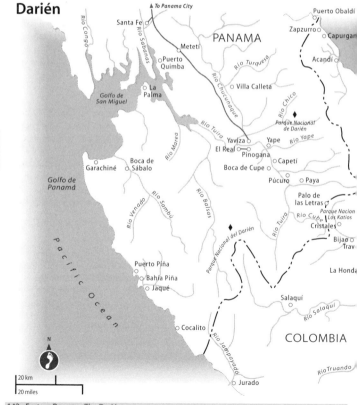

Darién

few cheap, basic hotels and one outstanding option – the **Filo de Tallo** ecolodge ⓘ *www.panamaexoticadventures.com* (see Where to stay, page 147). In nearly every way, Metetí is a preferable place to Yaviza, which is insalubrious at the best of times.

Yaviza → *Colour map 2, B5.*

Rough-and-ready Yaviza is the end of the road. Like many frontier towns, it throngs with criminal undertones. There are numerous cheap hotels, stores, restaurants and seedy bars, along with a police station where you must check in immediately. If you intend to visit the Parque Nacional Darién, you must also register with **ANAM** and pay park entrance fees. From Yaviza, it's possible to hire a boat to **El Real** (one hour, US$60-80). You can also hitch on a public cargo boat (US$5-10), but finding one is a matter of luck and persistence. If you find yourself stuck in Yaviza, the sights are modest. On the banks of the Río Chucunaque you'll find the crumbling remains of the **Fuerte San Jerónimo de Yaviza**, an old Spanish fort used to protect gold shipments from the mines at Cana. The port, too, makes a worthy distraction. Otherwise, the best thing you can do is start drinking.

Parque Nacional Darién → *For listings, see pages 147-148. Colour map 2, C5.*

The Parque Nacional Darién encompasses 579,000 ha of pristine wilderness along the Panama–Colombia border. It is the largest protected area in Central America and a UNESCO Biosphere Reserve since 1983. The park is punctuated by diverse natural features including vast lowland rainforests, cloud forests, mountain ranges, rambling coastline, rugged ravines and gorges. Dispersed Guna, Emberá, Wounaan and African-descended settlements lie within the park, mostly along the banks of river systems such as the Tuira, Balsas, Sambú and Jaqué rivers. Unsurprisingly, the Parque Nacional Darién is one of the world's premier nature and wildlife destinations. Some 450 bird species are known to inhabit the park, including harpy eagles, macaws, parakeets, quetzals and the virtually ubiquitous toucans. Resident mammals include rare jaguars, peccaries, bush dogs, tapirs, capybaras, anteaters, agoutis, coatis, deer and scores of different monkeys. Botanists, too, will find plenty to inspire them in the primeval forests, which are home to towering virgin trees and untold species of orchid.

The art of rainforest baskets

Decorative Emberá and Wounaan baskets, known as *hösig di* in the Wounaan language, are among the most beautiful and sought-after indigenous art in the world. They are extremely labour intensive, each piece requiring several months of painstaking effort. The principal raw material in their production is a spiny palm tree called *chunga* (*Astrocaryum standleyanum*), which is also used in the construction of houses, medicinal preparations, shamanic healing ceremonies and traditional bows, arrows and blow-pipes. Due to the Darién's regional insecurity, the trek to harvest the tree is often long and dangerous. Once gathered, stacked and dried, the *chunga* leaves are carefully stripped of their fibres by women basket-makers. The practice of dying the threads to achieve complex designs began in the 1980s, when anthropologist Richard Binder encouraged local artisans to improve upon their work, bringing examples of fine Colombian baskets to fire their imaginations. Today, *hösig*

di incorporate a broad range of motifs, including pictorial representations of birds, plants and other natural emblems, as well as more traditional geometric shapes and patterns, which may be shamanic in origin. As a rule, only natural dyes are used, including brown colours from cocobolo wood, yellow from turmeric, red from achiote and dark blue from *jagua* juice. Processing and boiling the fibres is very time-consuming and occasionally several different rainforest plants must be carefully blended in order to achieve just the right tone. The fibres are woven in a coil and spiralled upwards from the base. The tricky part is achieving a symmetrical shape with all the coloured threads in the right places. Baskets can be woven into a vase, bowl or plate shape. The tighter and finer the weave, the higher the quality of the work. The very best rainforest baskets can fetch thousands of dollars and represent an extremely potent cash income for an otherwise marginalized and disadvantaged group of people.

Tourist information

Park entrance fees US$5. It is not possible to visit the park alone ; you will require a guide and the permission of ANAM before you proceed.

Pirre Field Station (Rancho Frío) → *Colour map 2, C5.*

The Pirre Field Station is managed by **ANAM** (T299-6965 in El Real) and offers very rustic accommodation on fold-out cots (**$**), a simple dining area and cooking facilities. Camping and hammocks are an option if you bring your own gear. There are a couple of good trails in the vicinity, including a forested loop trail that passes some waterfalls (do not scale them, highly dangerous!) and the more strenuous **Cerro Pirre Trail**, which ascends a stiff mountain ridge (guide essential). You will not be able to buy food at the station, so bring enough for yourself and the guide who leads you there, if he's staying overnight. A little extra will sweeten the guards too, and they might cook for a small fee. Pirre Field Station is located at Rancho Frío, 13 km south of the town of **El Real** – a fairly large frontier settlement that's best accessed from Yaviza (see above). Be aware that El Real is your last chance to pick up supplies, including anti-malarial medicine if you're running low. If you get stuck, there's a rustic *pensión* (**$**) and a few *fondas* for cheap meals. From El Real, you need to hire a guide for the two- to three-hour trek to Rancho Frío; ANAM charges US$20-

30 but other guides may be cheaper. In the wet season the trip can take four hours and you will certainly need rubber boots. If you don't want to walk, you can take a boat up the Río Pirre as far as the Emberá village of **Piji Baisal** (US$75) and hike from there (guide still necessary), one hour.

Cana Field Station → *Colour map 2, C5.*
Cana Field Station is managed by **ANCON**, an environmental NGO based in Panama City. The station occupies a former mining camp in the foothills of the **Pirre** mountain ridge. Years ago, over 20,000 people lived in the area, most of them employed in the local gold mine, but today there's little evidence of that beyond old equipment rusting in the undergrowth. Cana is one of the most isolated places in Central America and one of the most prestigious birding sites in the world. Getting there isn't cheap. In the past, it was possible to follow an old railway line from **Boca de Cupe**, 30 km away – the highly policed and edgy last outpost of 'civilization'. However, the two-day hike is now considered dangerous and must not be attempted. That leaves the landing strip. Flights to Cana are chartered by **Ancon Expeditions** (see page 147) and are included in their reputable Darién package tours. Costs are high but the facilities, which include a stunning cloud forest camp up in the mountains, are certainly a cut above the poor man's shack at Rancho Frío.

La Palma and around → *For listings, see pages 147-148. Colour map 2, B4.*

La Palma, the diminutive capital of the Darién, is perched on the gulf of San Miguel at the place where the first European, Vasco Núñez de Balboa, emerged to 'discover' the Pacific coast of the Americas. Perched on the water's edge, it's a hot, grubby, indolent place that's not exactly friendly or inviting, but interesting to experience nonetheless. Although little more than a few roads, La Palma has the best amenities for miles, including a bank, airstrip, simple hotels, bars, eateries and general stores. If you have time to kill, charter a boat to visit **El Fuerte de San Carlos de Boca Chica** – a ruined fortress on the island of Boca Chica. Built in the mid-19th century, it formed part of the defences for the Cana gold mine.

Reserva Natural Punta Patiño → *Colour map 2, B4.*
Managed by **ANCON**, the Reserva Natural Punta Patiño encompasses 263 sq km of primary and secondary forests, black-sand beaches and extensive Ramsar-listed wetlands, including red and black mangroves around the mouth of the **Río Mogué**. It is the largest private nature reserve in Panama. Scores of birds can be spotted along the waterways, including kingfishers, waders, herons and duck, with scores more in the forests, including harpy eagles. You can also observe large colonies of capybaras, a few crocodiles and, if you're exceptionally lucky, jaguars. The reserve has good trails, including a two-hour loop known as the **Sendero Piedra de Candela** (the Flintstone Trail), so-named for the reddish quartz littered on the trail (it sparks if you strike it with a machete). ANCON manage a very pleasant lodge on a hill inside the park and ferry guests from La Palma as part of their packages. Otherwise you will have to charter your own vessel (one hour, US$60-80); the ride can be choppy.

Mogué → *Colour map 2, B4.*
Perched between jungle and riverbank, the colourful Emberá village of Mogué is a popular excursion for guests of ANCON's Punta Patiño lodge. Around 60 families live in the village, definitely geared towards tourism. Traditional dances, crafts and tattoos are among the

The harpy eagle

The remote rainforests of the Darién play host to one of the world's most magnificent predators – the harpy eagle. Named after the harpies of Greek mythology – fierce winged monsters who spirited condemned souls to the underworld – harpy eagles stand up to 1 m tall with formidable 5-cm talons to rival the claws of a grizzly bear. They are the world's most powerful birds of prey. In comparison to their body, their wingspan is not particularly large (around 2.1 m), allowing them to glide between the trees with exceptional stealth and agility, searching for their favourite prey of monkeys and sloths. Harpies can lift up to three-quarters of their own body weight and they occasionally carry off large animals such as young deer or capybaras. The eagles tend to nest high up in the tallest trees of the forest where they raise one chick every one to three years. In order to survive, they require huge territories with good wildlife populations. Sadly, their numbers are now declining due to deforestation, but many indigenous guides are expert at locating them nonetheless. Appropriately, the fearsome harpy eagle is the national bird of Panama.

offerings, along with trips to find harpy eagles. If you want to stay overnight, bring a tent or hammock. There's a large wooden shelter and communal kitchen for guests, but it's best to book your visit through a tour operator. Mogué is about 1½ hours from La Palma, or 30 minutes from Punta Patiño.

Río Sambú → *Colour map 2, C4.*

A journey up the jungle-shrouded Río Sambú – home to several authentic Emberá and Wounaan communities – is one of the most interesting river journeys in Panama. The largest and most important village in the region, **Sambú**, has an airstrip, medical centre, hotels and payphone. It makes a good base for exploring destinations further upstream, including **Puerto Indio** and **Pavarandó**. The best place to stay in town is **Sambú Hause** (see page 147), operated by a friendly American expat who knows the best guides and destinations. Sambú can be reached by thrice weekly *panga* from La Palma (US$20, schedules vary). Expect to pay around US$100 round-trip to travel from Sambú to the furthest communities upstream.

Bahía Piña → *For listings, see pages 147-148. Colour map 2, C4.*

Bahía Piña on the Pacific coast is known for its superb fishing – more **International Game Fish Association** records have broken here than anywhere else in the world. Marlin, sailfish, dorado, tuna and snapper all populate the waters, which are carefully protected from commercial exploitation. The bay owes its large fish population to the **Zane Grey Reef** – a seamount that gathers plankton and attracts large predators. Flush fishermen like to stay at the **Tropic Star Lodge** (see page 147), an upmarket destination that boasts Hollywood filmstars and wealthy politicians among its clientele. Around 8 km from the Tropic Star, lies the very small community of **Jaqué**, home to indigenous refugees who fled the fighting in Colombia. It's possible to catch a boat from Jaqué to Buenaventura in Colombia, US$100, but it's a rough trip and you may have to wait five days for an available passage. As ever, check on current safety before setting out.

For sleeping and eating price codes and other relevant information, see pages 16-19.

⊜ Where to stay

Panama City to Yaviza *p141*
$$$$ Burbayar Lodge, Llano–Cartí highway, T236-6061, www.burbayar.com. Rustic and highly regarded ecolodge with 7 secluded wood cabins, restaurant, hammocks and tranquil, leafy grounds. Can arrange tours to indigenous communities, surrounding forests and Bayano Lake. At the heart of a world-class birdwatching zone. Rates are per person and include 3 meals.
$$$$ Filo de Tallo, Metetí, T314-3013 (Panama City booking office), www.panama exoticadventures.com. High-end, rustic accommodation with a natural, peaceful setting and expansive views over the valley. French-run and ecologically aware. Tours of communities and forests available. Rates are per person; book in advance.
$ Hotel 3 Americas, Yaviza, T299-4439. Run-down local lodgings that have been serving stranded travellers for decades. Rooms are plain and simple.

Parque Nacional Darién *p143*
$$$$ Cana Field Station, Santa Cruz de Cana, T269-9415 (Panama City booking office), www.anconexpeditions.com. Formerly the headquarters of the gold mine and now a world-class birding lodge and biological research centre managed by ANCON. The wooden field station has 12 simple, screened bedrooms with battery-powered lamps and single semi-orthopaedic beds. Shared bathrooms have hot water. Limited electricity. If you want to stay, you must purchase an expensive 5- or 8-day tour package.
$ Pirre Field Station, Rancho Frío, T299-6965 (ANAM in El Real). Simple jungle lodgings with cooking facilities and camping space. Basic amenities include cold showers,

flush toilets and limited electricity. Consult ANAM, who manage the station, before setting out. Rates are per person.

La Palma and around *p145*
$$$$ Punta Patiño Lodge, Reserva Natural Punta Patiño, T269-9415 (Panama City booking office), www.anconexpeditions. com. An excellent and very comfortable wildlife lodge managed by ANCON. Cabins are well appointed with a/c, private bath, hot water and sublime views. The complex also includes an early 20th-century chapel. Guests stay as part of all-inclusive packages, not cheap.
$ Hotel Biaquiru Bagara, La Palma, T299-6224. Plain and simple, but comfortable enough. Cheaper with shared bath. There's also a market nearby for supplies.
$ Sambú Hause, Sambú, T6687-4177, www.sambuhausedarienpanama.com. A friendly, comfortable bed-and-breakfast in the jungle. The American owner is very knowledgeable about the area. Rates are per person. Recommended.

Bahía Piña *p146*
$$$$ Tropic Star Lodge, 800-682-3424 (US booking), www.tropicstar.com. Possibly the world's finest fishing resort. Luxury facilities include bar, restaurant and pool. The preferred haunt of moneyed sportsmen. Stays are part of expensive all-inclusive fishing packages.

⊙ What to do

Tour operators
Ancon Expeditions, Calle Elvira Méndez, Edificio Dorado 3, Panama City, T269-9415, www.anconexpeditions.com. One of the best tour operators in Central America. They run a variety of tours to the Darién, including a 2-week birding expedition that concludes in Cana Field Station and a comprehensive 2-week 'Darien Explorer

Trek' that goes almost everywhere. Very specialized and high quality, but not cheap. **Eco Circuitos**, Albrook Plaza, 2nd floor No 31, Ancón, T315-1305, www.ecocircuitos. com. A highly reputable agency with good green credentials and an emphasis on sustainable tourism. They offer specialized tours to the Darién as part of their cultural and wildlife packages.

⊖ Transport

Panama City to Yaviza *p141*
Bus
Several daily departures from **Panama City**'s main bus terminal to Yaviza, 0300-1130, 6-8 hrs, US$14, stops at all towns en route, breaks for meals and snacks.

Metetí *p142*
Boat
From Puerto Quimba to **La Palma**, depart when full, 0730-1830, 30 mins, US$3. Only the first of the day is guaranteed. Interesting journey through tropical rainforest and mangrove thickets.

Bus
To **Puerto Quimba**, every 30 mins, 0600-2100, 30 mins, US$1.50.

Yaviza *p143*
Boat
To **El Real** (for Pirre Station/Rancho Frío), private charter, US$60-80, try ANAM or

Chicho T6539-2007; cargo boat, no schedule, US$5-10 per person.

Bus
To **Panama City**, several daily, 6-8 hrs, US$14.

La Palma *p145*
Boat
To **Puerto Quimba**, depart when full, 0730-1830, 30 mins, US$3. Only the first of the day is guaranteed. To **Reserva Punta Patiño**, 1 hr, organize through ANCON. To **Mogué**, 2½ hrs, private charter US$100-150 (bring extra fuel for the return). To **Sambú**, 3-4 hrs, private charter US$150-200; or thrice weekly private boat, schedules vary, US$20.

Río Sambú *p146*
Air
Services are subject to change. From Sambú to **Panama City**, Air Panama, Mon, Wed, Fri, 1 hr, US$47.50 excluding taxes.

Boat
To **La Palma**, 3-4 hrs, private charter US$100-150; or thrice weekly private boat, schedules vary, US$20.

Bahía Piña *p146*
Air
Tropic Star Lodge includes a charter flight to the region as part of the package. Alternatively: Bahía Piña/Jaque to **Panama City**, Air Panama, Mon, Wed, Fri, 1½ hrs, US$55.50 one-way, excluding taxes.

Contents

Footprint features

Central provinces

At a glance

○ **Getting around** The central provinces boast everything from rugged mountains to remote offshore islands. Buses, trucks, boats, 4WD and horses are all common forms of transport.

● **Time required** 7-14 days.

☼ **Weather** The Azuero Peninsula and Pacific coast of Coclé fall under Panama's *arco seco* (dry arch), with scorching hot weather in the dry season, Dec-Apr, and the country's lowest levels of rainfall in the wet season, May-Nov.

✕ **When not to go** Where you choose to go will be largely determined by what activities you want to pursue. You should avoid hiking in the highlands during the worst of the wet season, Sep-Nov. Hotel rates on the coast can sky-rocket during Christmas, New Year and Semana Santa.

Panama's central provinces – Coclé, Herrera, Los Santos and Veraguas – were the first areas of the isthmus to be settled after the foundation of Panama City in the 16th century. Home to ancient colonial churches and lost-in-time villages, they remain a bastion of traditional folklore and old-world Spanish charm. Feisty, gregarious, conservative and proud, this is Panama's bucolic heartland, the geographic and spiritual centre of the nation, where more Panamanian presidents have been born than anywhere else, and where sugar, cigars, seco and genuine Panama hats are the chief exports. Around the Interamericana highway, centuries of agricultural activity have left a landscape punctuated by rolling cattle pastures and sweltering fields of sugar cane, sleepy cowboy towns and bustling farming communities. Climbing towards the lonely peaks of the continental divide, the roads and settlements grow increasingly remote, before finally surrendering to a wilderness of tropical forests and thriving ecological splendour. If anything, Panama's central provinces are geographically diverse, but they maintain a seamless cultural character grounded in the style and history of the region. Panamanians call it *típico* – a rustic brand of national expression that permeates the campesino way of life from lowlands to highlands. The best way to experience it is during a fiesta, when terminally sleepy village plazas spark to life with explosions of music, dance, fireworks and pageantry. The scenes of revelry are as distinctive as they are impassioned. Ox-carts make poignant processions laden with fresh produce, flowers and exuberant ornamental displays. Bands of itinerant musicians recount ancient folksongs dutifully passed down the generations. Troupes of dancers perform in traditional costumes, masks and flowing *polleras*. Travelling in Panama's hospitable central provinces, one cannot help feeling far removed from the modern world, and at the same time, at the heart and soul of everything.

Coclé

The cleanliness and prosperity of Coclé province is often a welcome relief after the madness and hustle of the capital. A mere two hours from Panama City, the region has long been a popular retreat for well-to-do urbanites. Its Pacific coastline, among the most visited in the country, rambles westward from Punta Chame to Farallón with a procession of ocean-front communities and upmarket beach resorts. In the mountains, the flower-festooned spa town of El Valle overlooks a rolling landscape of verdant highland forests and thundering waterfalls. Further west, the bustling market town of Penonomé is the down-to-earth provincial capital of Coclé. It is the gateway to a host of destinations including magnificent nature reserves, intriguing pre-Columbian ruins, ancient churches and a cigar factory.
➤ *For listings, see pages 162-167.*

West on the Interamericana: the central Pacific coast → *For listings, see pages 162-167.*

The well-plied Interamericana highway heads west out of Panama City and into the heart of Panama's rural interior. The first place of any size you'll encounter is the virtual suburb of **Arraiján**, closely followed by the bustling and unpretentious township of **La Chorrera**, around 34 km from the capital. Beyond a procession of sterile planned communities and aggressive commercial billboards, the highway arrives at **Campana**, where a 4-km side road climbs to the **Parque Nacional Altos de Campana**. Created in 1966, it is the country's first national park and home to striking tropical forest backed by mountainous volcanic rock. A few kilometres further, the Interamericana aligns with the Pacific coast to connect a string of popular beach communities. The region is a consistent hit with surfers, foreign tourists, Panama City weekenders, Floridian retirees and, unfortunately, large-scale real estate and resort developers. If you're looking for quick and easy beach time, the salt-and-pepper sands are generally well serviced, consumer-orientated and convenient. However, they are not necessarily the country's most beautiful or endearing beaches.

Arriving at the central Pacific coast
The Interamericana is plied with scores of buses travelling in both directions – simply hop on board and inform the driver of your intended destination. Most of the places below will require an additional taxi ride (or a long walk) to reach the beach areas. It is possible to visit the coast as a day trip from the capital, but you are advised to start very early. If travelling at the weekend, during holiday periods or on a Friday evening, you should be aware that many others will have the same idea, causing the potential for traffic and higher hotel rates – book in advance to avoid disappointment.

Punta Chame and around → *Colour map 2, B1.*
The narrow windswept peninsula of Punta Chame is one of the central coast's more remote destinations. It boasts desolate white-sand beaches and far-off views of Taboga Island. From December to May, it receives consistent 15- to 25-knot winds and is a popular spot with kite-surfers; contact **Shokogi** ① *T6921-1532, www.shokogi.com*, if you would like to try it yourself. The turn-off to Punta Chame is just before the town **Bejuco** on the Interamericana; buses to the beach run from the junction, hourly, 20 minutes, US$2. Punta Chame should not be confused with the settlement of Chame, situated further west on the Interamericana.

Don't miss ...

Playa Coronado and around → *Colour map 2, B1.*

Playa Gorgona is a small beachside community with 3 km of salt-and-pepper sand and waves increasing in size from east to west; the turn-off is a few kilometres after Bejuco. The next community, Playa Coronado, is one of the largest and most developed destinations on the Pacific. High-rise condos, gated communities, a resort, golf course and wealthy vacation villas make it a popular haunt of moneyed Panameños and US retirees. Look out for the new mall and shopping complex on the Interamericana, the latest manifestation of Coronado's burgeoning commercial presence.

San Carlos to Playa Corona

Starting with the village of San Carlos, around 10 km from Coronado, a string of quiet communities front the ocean, but most are slated for big, bold developments. They include **El Palmar**, well known for its popular surf camp, and **Río Mar**, also recommended for surfing. Playa Corona is a relaxed place with a slowly growing expat presence.

Santa Clara

Santa Clara is a down-to-earth place, once little more than a small fishing village. But sadly, it too is scheduled for ruin and scores of vacation homes have already sprung up, along with an obscene high-rise building. Fortunately, for the moment, the beach remains empty during the week with just a handful of low-key restaurants, hotels and bars. The turning for Santa Clara is just 11 km west of the turning for El Valle (see page 153) from where it is a 2-km walk to the beach; taxi, US$2.

Farallón and Playa Blanca → *Colour map 1, B6.*

Beyond Santa Clara, the tiny hamlet of Farallón was once a favourite retreat of Manuel Noriega. Today, there's no sign of the difficult dictator and popular resorts have sprung up to service visitors. The famous **Royal Decameron** is a favourite haunt of retired Canadians and package tourists, but it suffered a moment of scandal in 2011 when Colombian gangsters fought a pitched gun battle in the grounds. The nearby powder-white sands of Playa Blanca are marketed at an altogether moneyed clientele and never entertain such riff-raff. As for the original settlement of Farallón, there is almost nothing left of it – a typical example of Panama's liberal development laws favouring construction over environmental protection.

Río Hato and beyond → *Colour map 1, B6.*

The town of Río Hato signifies the gateway to the agricultural heartlands of Coclé province. It has some useful amenities including supermarkets and internet connections, and is also home to a dilapidated army base bombed by US forces during the 1989 invasion. Several kilometres beyond it, you'll pass the cowboy town of **Antón**, a quiet place of rice fields and cattle ranches. It is notable for its annual gay parade – no small feat given the region's conservative inclinations.

El Valle → *For listings, see pages 162-167. Colour map 1, B6.*

Nestled in the crater of an extinct volcano, the cool mountain retreat of El Valle is surrounded by brooding mountain peaks, rumbling rivers, expansive lookout points and mysterious stone petroglyphs. Scintillating flora and fauna abound, including brilliantly coloured birds, eerie golden frogs, curious square trees and a seemingly endless variety of orchids. Hikers, birders, climbers and other outdoor types are well served by an extensive network of trails, along with a well-developed tourist infrastructure that offers everything from rappelling to horse riding and zip-lining. For those seeking rest and relaxation there are plenty of amenities too, including extravagant luxury spas, gourmet restaurants and thermally heated springs. The town itself is quiet, slow-paced, great for strolling and home to a fine craft market and scores of flower-filled gardens. It's hard not to like El Valle.

Arriving in El Valle

From the Interamericana, the access road to El Valle is well signed with hotel billboards. Direct buses depart from Panama City every 30 minutes, 2½ hours, US$4.25. The access road leads directly into the town's main thoroughfare, Avenida Central, from where side roads branch north and south. The town is quite sprawling but patient walkers can explore it on foot. Taxis are recommended for outlying hotels and most fares around town should not exceed US$2-3. Cycling is a good option. To rent a bike, ask at your hotel or at **Don Pepe's**. For information, there is an ATP booth on Avenida Central, which may or may not be open. Hotels themselves are usually well informed and helpful. A good online source of information is www.el-valle-panama.com. As ever, seek up-to-date advice before setting out on trails.

APROVACA orchid nursery

ⓘ *Signed off Av Central, next to ANAM, T983-6472, www.aprovaca.webs.com, entrance, US$2, students US$1, children US$0.75.*

APROVACA – the Asociación de Productores de Orquídeas El Valle y Cabuya – was established in 2001 to protect endangered endemic orchids, which sadly are being threatened by poachers. It manages one of the best nurseries in the country with hundreds of specimens of some 147 species, all for sale or reintroduction to the wild. Their collection of Holy Ghost orchids (Panama's national flower) is particularly stunning. APROVACA is always looking for interns and volunteers to help with fundraising, caring for the orchids, photography, web design and project development. They also offer very affordable tours of El Valle and its attractions and, now, hostel accommodation.

Mercado de Artesanías

El Valle's *artesanía* market draws talent from the nation's diverse artisan and indigenous communities, including Ngäbe, Emberá, Wounaan and Guna. It features a variety of handmade arts and crafts, including soapstone carvings of animals, ghoulish masks, painted gourds (*totumas*), carved wooden tableware, pottery, *molas*, palm baskets, ceramic flowerpots and traditional Panama hats. Delicious fresh fruit, flowers and other local produce are also widely available. The market is located on Avenida Central. Although open daily, it is at its most vibrant and well attended on Sunday mornings. For more information on Panamanian *artesanías*, see page 21.

Los Pozos de Aguas Termales (hot springs)
ⓘ *Daily 0800-1700, entrance US$2, children US$1. Bring small notes or exact money. During busy times, bathing sessions may be restricted to 20 mins.*

El Valle

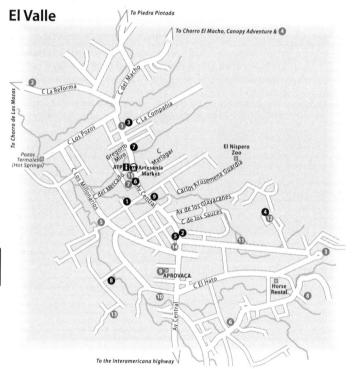

Where to stay ⬜
Anton Valley 1
Cabañas Potosí 2
Campestre 3
Canopy Lodge 4
Crater Valley Adventure 6
Don Pepe 7
Golden Frog Inn 8
Hostal Cariguana 5
Hostel Orchid 9

La Casa de Juan 10
Los Capitanes 11
Los Mandarinos 12
Park Eden B&B 13
Pensión Niña Delia 14
Residencial El Valle 15

Restaurants 🍴
Artash Fresh Choice 1
Bambucillo 2

Bruschetta 3
Casa de Lourdes 4
El Valle Gourmet
  & Coffee Shop 5
Mar de Plata 6
Restaurante Massiel 7
Rincón Vallero 8
Ty's Sports Grill 9

Know your Panama hat

Favoured by socialites at summer garden parties, Al Capone and English cricket spectators, the cream-coloured Panama hats of public imagination actually hail from Ecuador. Woven from the leaves of the *toquilla* plant, the hats first arrived on the isthmus in the 19th and 20th centuries. They were an instant hit among transient 49ers, who took them home to the US and erroneously called them 'Panamas'. During the construction of the canal, the hats proved an ideal working accessory – lightweight, breathable and perfect for keeping off the sun and rain. In 1906, they became all the rage in Europe and the US when President Roosevelt famously donned one during his historic visit to the canal construction site.

Traditional Panama hats – as worn by the rural populations of Panama's central provinces – are an altogether different garment and commonly known as *sombreros pintados*. Woven from the braided fibres of *junco*, *bellota* and *pita* plants, the hats are a vital element in traditional dress codes and essential for festivals and public gatherings. They are also worn by many on a casual daily basis, as a visit to Panama's interior quickly reveals. Style of *sombrero pintado* varies between villages and artisans, but very simple, coarse versions can be bought for around five dollars and serve as robust working hats – the preferred attire of agricultural labourers. The very best hats require a month or more of careful construction and can fetch several hundred dollars on the local market. If you're interested in acquiring a *sombrero pintado* – fine or coarse – try the stalls on the highway near Penonomé, or travel to a specialized village (for example, La Pintada in Coclé or Ocú in the Azuero Peninsula) to buy directly from an artisan. Prices are based on the number of *vueltas* or lines of braiding along the rim and you should generally look for a fine and even weave. Wearing your *sombrero pintado* is an art in itself. Perhaps the best way (and the way least likely to cause offence) is with the front and back turned up just so, denoting a successful, happy and handsome wearer. Turning up only the back is said to indicate specialized intellectual knowledge, while turning up just the front is said to be the preferred style of a ladies' man. Turning down the front, meanwhile, can be a sign of mourning or unhappiness. Panama staged its first festival dedicated to the *sombrero pintado* in 2011. It was a joyous occasion filled with ox-cart processions, traditional dancing, music and, of course, plentiful hats.

There's no better way to relax after a long hike than soaking in El Valle's mineral-rich, thermally heated hot springs. The water at these public baths has been channelled into two large concrete pools and they lack the rustic charm of some other Panamanian springs, but they are decent and calming nonetheless. Tropical vegetation skirts the grounds where you'll hear birds singing from the branches and occasional lizards scurrying in the undergrowth. Various types of local mud are freely supplied if you wish to indulge in a face mask. The facilities include a picnic area, cold showers and changing rooms.

El Chorro Macho

ⓘ *The waterfall is located on the northeast side of town, a 40-min walk from the centre. General entrance US$3.50.*

El Chorro Macho is a powerful waterfall surrounded by verdant forests and some undemanding walking trails. It's easy to spot birdlife in the trees – trogons, cuckoos and hummingbirds are prolific. Adventurous types may prefer to experience the falls from a high-speed zip-line. Incorporating four elevated platforms and a line that passes directly over the 80-m-high crashing waters, the **Canopy Adventure** ⓘ *T983-6457, www.adventure. panamabirding.com*, US$50, offers a popular and well-established 1½-hour canopy tour.

La Piedra Pintada
ⓘ *The official entrance to the petroglyphs is on the north side of town, US$1.50.*
Ancient petroglyphs are strewn throughout the surrounding countryside, all fashioned by indigenous hands long before the Spanish conquest. None are larger and more interesting than the Piedra Pintada (painted stone), a cliff-face etched with obscure lines and interconnected symbols. Their meaning is hotly debated, but most people agree that they are likely to be a map of some kind. After you've scrutinized the weird symbols, it's worth continuing on the trail for a while to enjoy a series of lively waterfalls.

Los árboles cuadrados
The *árboles cuadrados* (square trees) are a botanical curiosity unique to El Valle and one other location in Costa Rica. Although not technically square, the tree bases do have four sides that measure roughly the same length. The species, currently identified as *Quararibea asterolepis*, is a type of cottonwood and does not usually grow to 'square' dimensions. It is not known whether the shape of El Valle's trees results from environmental conditions or genetic mutation. In a bid to find out, scientists at the University of Florida are growing their own specimens from local seeds. Entrance to the trees is directly behind **Hotel Campestre**, southeast side of town. Be warned, they are bound to impress some people more than others.

El Níspero zoo and gardens
ⓘ *1 km east of Av Central, look for the signs. Open daily 0700-1700, US$3, children US$2.*
Shady pathways punctuate the 2.8-ha grounds of El Valle's zoo, home to some 55 species of captive birds and numerous exotic fauna. The facilities were originally set up over 20 years ago by an agronomist who began caring for sick and injured animals, including some tapirs rescued from Noriega's house in Farallón. Most of the animals seem content enough, but a few of the cages could be larger. Interestingly, El Níspero is home to the excellent **El Valle Amphibian Conservation Center**, which is working with Houston, San Antonio and San Diego zoos to study the local golden frogs. Endemic to the hills around El Valle, the rare frogs are facing extinction from a mysterious bacterial disease. Facilities include aquariums and a reading centre.

Chorro las Mozas
Some three million years ago, a giant volcanic eruption forged the crater of El Valle. It subsequently filled with water and became an enormous lake, but when its banks breached at the site of Chorro las Mozas, the water drained away to form the region's many rivers and streams. Today, there are series of small waterfalls where the prehistoric lake once broke, great for swimming and popular with locals. The area is very accessible and lies roughly 2 km northwest of the town church. Take care not to slip on the rocks.

Hikes around El Valle

A variety of trails criss-cross the hills and pastures around El Valle – some, not all, can be accomplished without a guide. A very popular hike leads to the **India Dormida** (Sleeping Indian), a jagged mountain ridge overlooking the town to the north. The ridge derives its name from a local myth which recalls the story of an indigenous girl who fell in love with a Spanish conquistador. When her father refused to let her marry him, she climbed into the hills and committed suicide. As a mark of respect for her eternal love, the gods transformed her body into the eternally unchanging form of a mountain. Another popular hike leads to **Cerro Gaital Natural Monument** with its stunning views of the Pacific Ocean. A tough trail leads to the summit from behind **Hotel Campestre**, but you will need climbing experience, equipment and a guide. A more moderate trailhead begins 10 km from town close to 'Pollo Toledano'. Numerous other peaks can be scaled including **Cerro Pajita**, **Cerro Guacamayo**, **Cerro Iguana**, **Cerro Tagua** and **Cerro Cara Coral**; seek advice before setting out.

Penonomé and around → *For listings, see pages 162-167. Colour map 1, B6.*

Echoing the style of many Panamanian cities, Penonomé, the conservative capital of Coclé province, is an architecturally inconsistent place that blends functional commercial edifices, modern residences and a handful of much older structures dating from the early republic and colonial era. Perched on the Interamericana highway 144 km west of the capital, the city, which looks and feels like a small town, has long thrived as a hub of local commerce and agriculture. It is a pleasant place with the air of provincial times past, well known for its intellectual traditions and a university that has turned out many formidable thinkers. The surrounding communities are famed for their *sombreros pintados*, or 'painted hats', which are still popular with Coclé's rural population and available for sale on the highway (see box, page 155).

Arriving in Penonomé

Penonomé is situated on the Interamericana and served by numerous buses passing in either direction. Unless Penonomé is their final destination, they will not steer off the highway, so exit at the Esso station, which marks the main access road and commercial strip, **Avenida Juan Demóstenes Arosemena**. Penonomé is very small and easily navigated on foot. Numerous taxis are available and fares rarely exceed US$2. There is no tourist office in town. You can try consulting your hotel for specific enquiries or direct your research to ATP headquarters in Panama City.

Background

Penonomé was a thriving indigenous settlement long before Spanish-born Diego López de Villanueva y Zapata arrived in 1581 to establish a colonial footing. The city is named after an old chief, Nomé, who met his end at the hands of a Spanish executioner. Serving as a kind of colonial ghetto for displaced Indians and slaves, the town remained low key until 1671. After the sacking of Panama City by Henry Morgan, it became Panama's temporary administrative centre while Nueva Panamá was constructed. Penonomé is the birthplace of the outspoken and ill-fated nationalist Arnulfo Arias, who served as president on three occasions and was deposed each time by a military junta.

Places in Penonomé

The city's sights are modest. The **Museo de Penonomé** ⓘ *Calle San Antonio, T997-8490, Tue-Sun 0900-1600, US$1*, is located in San Antonio, the oldest neighbourhood in the city. It contains a small collection of pre-Columbian relics and charts the historical development of the province. The surrounding streets are your best chance of seeing old buildings and getting a feel for the city before it was modernized. Particularly attractive is San Antonio's small white *capilla* (chapel). Elsewhere, the **Plaza Central** is very pleasant and worth a look for its handsome architecture and **cathedral**.

Balneario Las Mendozas

Located 1 km out of town, the Balneario Las Mendozas is a recreational complex built on the edge of a lake. The water is deep, good for swimming and very refreshing on a hot day. Crowds are busiest at the weekends, especially Sunday. Nearby, the **Río Zaratí**, also known as the Santa María, is the site of an annual water carnival. It traditionally commemorates the indigenous people who in times past would do business on the riverbanks. The festivities, always popular and well attended, include colourful parades on rafts, huge displays of fruit and a frequent hosing down of the crowds.

Reserva Natural Privada Tavida

Privately owned and maintained by **Posada Cerro La Vieja** – a reputable spa hotel formerly known as La Trinidad (see Where to stay, page 165) – the Reserva Natural Privada Tavida is an enchanting highland nature reserve located some 45 minutes north of Penonomé. It is replete with thickly forested hills, colourful birdlife and teeming tropical vegetation. A variety of hiking trails lead to petroglyphs, the summit of **Cerro La Vieja**, and to **Cascada Tavida**, a refreshing waterfall with some very romantic cabins close by. To get to **Posada Cerro La Vieja**, take one of the old-fashioned *chivas* marked Chiguirí Arriba; they depart roughly every two hours from behind Penonomé market. If you're visiting on a day trip, it's best to book guides at least 24 hours in advance of your journey.

La Pintada → *For listings, see pages 162-167. Colour map 1, B6.*

Nestled in the foothills 10 km outside of Penonomé, the sleepy village of La Pintada is a good staging post for hiking or horse-riding excursions in the countryside. The **Mercado de Artesanías**, next to the football pitch, is a good place to enquire about local guides or otherwise stock up on *sombreros*. For casual walking, head to the **petroglyphs** 2 km past the cemetery; follow the signs from the plaza. Most visitors to La Pintada can't resist visiting its aromatic cigar factory, highly regarded by international cigar aficionados (see below).

Cigars Joyas de Panamá

ⓘ *La Pintada, www.joyasdepanamacigars.com, tours are free but should be booked for groups of 10 or more. To get there, follow the slip road that's signed near the southern entrance to town. When the road forks, bear right and continue for another 100 m.*
Established in 1982 by Miriam Padilla, who learned her craft from Cuban exiles, Cigars Joyas de Panamá is one of the country's few surviving cigar factories, and probably the best. Their mild- to medium-flavoured cigars come in five sizes, including massive 7-inch Churchills and dainty 5-inch Coronitas. Their flavour has been described as "spicy nutmeg ... blending rich leather with hints of rum and oak". Even non-smokers may find the factory's rich aroma quite delicious. All the cigars are handmade using Cuban seed

The last flight of Omar Torrijos

On 31 July 1981, General Omar Torrijos was en route to the remote highland community of Coclesito when his DeHavilland Twin Otter light aircraft met with inclement weather, grew disorientated and crashed into the slopes of Marta Hill. The pilot, crew and passengers – Panama's Maximum Leader among them – all died instantly. Thus ended 12 years of so-called 'Benevolent Dictatorship' with Torrijos, aged 52, buried in a state funeral on 4 August. An inquiry into the crash, led by the FBI and Panamanian authorities, concluded that "the major cause of this accident was controlled flight into terrain by pilot error due to poor visibility". Nonetheless, rumours continue to circulate that Torrijos was in fact assassinated. Manuel Noriega is a prime suspect in many conspiracy theories, as are the CIA, who worked closely with Noriega throughout his infamous rise to power. John Perkins, author of Confessions of an Economic Hitman, alleges that CIA operatives planted a bomb on the plane inside a tape-recorder. According to Perkins, powerful elements in the US business community were perturbed by the Maximum Leader's refusal to renegotiate the Carter-Torrijos Treaty, and by his dealings with Japanese entrepreneur Shigeo Nagano, who wanted to build a new sea-level canal across the isthmus. His assertion is vaguely supported by some witnesses at Coclesito who claim to have heard two explosions at the time of the crash, but Perkins' general assessment of Torrijos as "a very principled man" seems to suggest a lack of insight. As for Noriega, in 1991, under US custody and facing a pre-trial hearing in Miami, he claimed to be in possession of documents proving CIA assassination attempts against himself and Torrijos. The judge refused to admit them as evidence, however, because they would apparently violate the Classified Information Procedures Act. Whatever the cause of Torrijos' death, its sudden and dramatic manner has certainly elevated him to the status of hero. The grim reality of his tenure was thuggery, corruption, murder and political 'disappearances', but he was, if anything, an astute propagandist who knew how to win the allegiance of the poor. The village of Coclesito continues to mourn his death each year in July, while the area of the crash has been protected as a national park that bears his name. Martín Torrijos, son of the Maximum Leader, assumed the presidency of Panama from 2004 to 2009.

tobacco. The plants are cultivated in Chiriquí, close to the town of La Concepción, and rely wholly on organic methods – no chemicals, machinery or pesticides are used. The cigars are individually rolled at wooden tables and many are exported to the USA where they can sell for over US$200 a box. Visitors to the factory can purchase them individually or in bulk at excellent prices. Day-to-day operations are managed by Miriam's son, Braulio Zurita. He is a fine gentleman with a true enthusiasm for his product.

Parque Nacional Omar Torrijos (El Copé) → For listings, see pages 162-167.
Colour map 1, B5.

Named after General Omar Torrijos – who died in a plane crash in the Coclé mountains in 1981 – the Parque Nacional Omar Torrijos (also known as El Copé) encompasses 25,275 ha of challenging highland terrain. It is punctuated by several formidable peaks, including **Cerro Peña Blanca**, the park's highest at 1314 m. The park's many life zones include lower montane and pre-montane rainforests on the Pacific side and tropical wet forests on the Caribbean – delicate orchids, bromeliads and towering ceiba trees abound. Among its numerous rare (but infrequently sighted) animal species are jaguars, pumas, ocelots and tapirs. Birdlife is prolific and comes in its usual multi-coloured glory. Due to its remoteness, El Copé is rarely visited. Nonetheless, it has good trails and fantastic potential for hiking, climbing, birding and other outdoor adventures.

Arriving at the Parque Nacional Omar Torrijos

To get to the park, first take a bus from Penonomé to El Copé, every 30-60 minutes, one hour, US$2.40. From there, catch a connection to **Barrigón**, 15 minutes, US$0.40, then walk 4 km uphill to the gate. The park is open 0600-2000, entrance US$5. If you wish to stay overnight, there is a rangers' station with four beds and cooking facilities, US$5 per person, bring own food and a warm sleeping bag. Alternatively, basic homestays may be available in Barrigón and La Rica; enquire locally.

Hikes in the Parque Nacional Omar Torrijos

Three interesting trails snake out from the rangers' station inside the park. The shortest and easiest is an undemanding 500-m interpretive trail with signs and information on the local flora. The second trail ascends a mountain ridge and provides panoramic views of both oceans at its summit; one-way journey time is about an hour; you should expect some moderately strenuous hiking. The final trail does not have any definite conclusion. It crosses the continental divide, climbs and falls over various ridges, and finally strikes deep into the rainforests of the Caribbean slopes. A guide is absolutely necessary and you will need to be fit. An alternative entrance to the park is via **La Rica**, a small village two to three hours' walk from Barrigón. You can access several interesting sites from the community, including **Cerro Marta** and **Peñas Blancas**, the waterfalls of **Chorro de Tife** and even the crashed plane of Omar Torrijos, but you will have to stay overnight or camp to reach them. Again, expect tough but highly rewarding hiking.

Natá → *For listings, see pages 162-167. Colour map 1, B5.*

Established on 20 May 1522 by Pedro Arias de Avila, the town of Natá – or Natá de Caballeros – is the oldest surviving colonial settlement in Panama and one of the oldest in all the Americas. Named after a local indigenous chief who once ruled the region, Natá served as a strategic military base for one hundred of Spain's fiercest conquistadors, known as the 'Caballeros' (gentlemen) of the town's namesake. From Natá, the conquistadors were able to wage campaigns against resistant tribes, especially those led by Chief Urracá and Chief Paris, who fought ferociously against the Spaniards for many years. They were also able to plunder the hills for their mineral wealth, extracting large quantities of gold using local slave labour. Today, Natá is a quiet town of 6000 inhabitants. It is situated 31 km west of Penonomé on the Interamericana.

Iglesia de Natá

Work on the town church, the Iglesia de Natá (properly known as the Iglesia de Santiago Apóstol) began in 1522 using indigenous slaves. It is a very old, mysterious structure imbued with an intriguing mix of Catholic and pre-Columbian motifs. For fine examples of religious syncretism, look for the feathered serpents carved into the altars along with the distressed indigenous Cherubim and Seraphim. As one of the oldest churches in the western hemisphere, the Iglesia de Natá is likely to hold many unusual secrets. During restoration work in 1995, three human skeletons were uncovered beneath the floor and their identity remains a mystery. If the church is locked, ask for the key from the houses opposite.

Parque Arqueológico del Caño → *Colour map 1, B5.*

ⓘ *Located about 8 km north of Natá, no buses, a taxi costs US$7. Open Tue-Sat 0900-1600, Sun 0900-1300, US$1.*

El Caño is one of only two archaeological sites in Panama that are open to the public – the other is Los Barriles in Chiriquí province. Although it provides evidence of a well-developed pre-Columbian culture dating to 500 AD, El Caño has suffered heavily due to acts of vandalism. Several important burial mounds were destroyed by tractors before they could be properly excavated, and in the 1920s, an American archaeologist looted numerous precious pieces and sold them to private collectors. Today, you'll find a very modest collection at El Caño. The museum has pottery, arrowheads and other local finds, while numerous stone columns adorn the grounds. However, since 2005, Dr Julia Mayo, a research associate at the Smithsonian Tropical Research Institute, has been uncovering stunning gold jewellery in El Caño's ancient burial pits, most of it dating to around 900 AD. The finds are extremely exciting and recent analyses suggest that the gold used in their production was mined locally. The *National Geographic* featured stunning photographs of Dr Mayo's discoveries in its January 2012 edition.

Aguadulce → *For listings, see pages 162-167. Colour map 1, B5.*

Located 10 km west of Natá, the bustling town of Aguadulce (literally 'Sweet Water') is a wealthy supply centre that evolved from colonial times thanks to its supply of fresh water, traditionally drawn from an old well. For many years, the town prospered as a major salt producer, but its factory closed in 1999 when it could no longer compete with Colombian prices. Fortunately, it retains its crown as Panama's top manufacturer of sugar, evidenced by the miles of sweltering sugar cane in the surrounding environs. The **Museo de la Sal y el Azúcar (Museum of Salt and Sugar)** ⓘ *Parque Central, Mon-Fri 0900-1600, Sat 0900-1200, US$1,* commemorates Aguadulce's traditional economy with exhibits relating to the manufacture of both powdery ingredients. Aguadulce's other major industry – shrimp aquaculture – continues to thrive.

Ingenio de Azúcar Santa Rosa

ⓘ *15 km west of town, open mid-Jan to mid-Mar. Take a bus from Aguadulce, every 15 mins, 20 mins, and ask the driver to drop you at the Ingenio de Azúcar. It's a 1-km walk from the guardhouse to the mill.*

First opened in 1991, the Santa Rosa sugar mill continues to produce prodigious quantities of the white stuff – up to a staggering 675,000 kg per day. During harvest season, mid-January to mid-March, thousands of temporary workers find employment in the plantations where the sugar cane is painstakingly cut by hand. Others toil on the factory floor where the cane is crushed by giant rollers at a ferocious rate of 100 kg per second. Visitors to the Santa Rosa factory can expect a detailed explanation of the manufacturing process from harvest to roasting and beyond. On site you'll find a replica of the original mill-owner's house complete with some antique furniture and displays relating to sugar production.

Salt flats

Aguadulce's old commercial salt flats lie some 9 km south of town on the coast and have been abandoned for over a decade. The area is now a prime birdwatching spot with numerous roaming shore-birds and waders. Sea lions, too, can often be spotted basking in the sun. A good place to begin your explorations is at **Johnny Tapia's**, a popular restaurant located on the flats, take a taxi, US$5. They serve excellent seafood, including locally cultivated jumbo shrimp. Take care when walking out towards the ocean as the high tide rolls in very quickly – turn around immediately if you see it coming. Just before Johnny Tapia's is **Turiscentro**, a rolling-skating and recreation park complete with bikes and paddle boats, US$4.

⊚ Coclé listings

For sleeping and eating price codes and other relevant information, see pages 16-19.

⊜ Where to stay

Punta Chame and around *p151*
$$ Hostal Casa, Amarilla, Punta Chame, T6032-7743, www.hostalcasaamarilla.com. Located about 300 m from the sea in the main village, this is a comfortable B&B with 2 tastefully decorated rooms in the main house (**$$$**), 4 rooms in an annexe and 3 rooms in cabins. Amenities include pool, bar and restaurant serving French, Mediterranean and Creole food. Hospitable and attentive. Good reports.

Playa Coronado and around *p152*
$$$$ Coronado Golf and beach resort, Av Punta Prieta, Playa Coronado, T264-3164, www.coronadoresort.com. A well-established and sprawling resort boasting an 18-hole golf course. Amenities include coffee shop, restaurants, pool, tennis court, playground, spa, stables and games room. Can organize watersports and a range of tours. The beach is 10 mins away.
$$$ El Litoral, Av Punta Prieta, Playa Coronado, T6658-1143, www.litoralpanama. com. A modern and homely B&B with a terrace and small pool, 10 mins from the beach. Rooms are clean, comfortable and agreeably attired. El Litoral offers yoga programmes, massage and very tasty, healthy breakfasts. Great hosts and good

reports. Maximum 2 persons per room and a 2-night minimum stay. Recommended.
$$$ Maple Leaf B&B, Playa Coronado, T6129-6034, mapleleafbb.com. A friendly and comfortable B&B, Canadian-run, as the name might suggest. Rooms have Egyptian cotton sheets, handmade quilts and orthopaedic mattresses. Good food, including a hearty North American breakfast. A 10-min walk to the beach. Good hosts and reports.
$$ Playa Gaviota, Playa Coronado, T240-4526, www.hotelgaviotapanama.com. Perched on the edge of the beach with outdoor palapas, a volleyball court and 2 pools (1 for adults, 1 for children). The rooms are plain, simple and comfortable with a/c, cable TV and private bath. Drinks, buffet and à la carte food is available. Prices rise slightly at weekends.

San Carlos to Playa Corona *p152*
$$$ Bay View Resort, Playa El Palmar, T240-9621, www.bayviewelpalmar.net. A relaxed, family-orientated hotel with tasteful, modern furnishings and direct beach access. Rooms are comfortable, clean and well furnished. Amenities include palapas, pool and restaurant. A lush, green garden and great sunsets. Reservations required.
$$$ Cabañas de Playa Guicci Resort, Playa Corona, T6674-7672, www.guicciresort.com. 6 cute, brightly coloured cabins set in a trimmed green garden. Each comes complete with kitchen, cable TV, Wi-Fi, a/c, fan and an outdoor terrace with a table

and hammock. General amenities include parking, BBQ and a small pool.

$$$-$$ Río Mar Surf Camp, Río Mar, T345-4010, www.riomarsurf.com. A great beachside location with access to the breaks. Amenities include a pool and a mini-ramp for skateboarding. They have 8 rooms with cable TV, Wi-Fi and fan (a/c extra). Board rental, tours and surf lessons available. Good café/restaurant attached.

$$ Palmar Surf Camp, Playa El Palmar, T6615-5654, www.palmarsurfcamp.com. Comfortable rooms and comfortable ocean-front *cabañas* for 2-4 persons, all equipped with cable TV, DVD, private bath and kitchen. Surf board rental, classes and lots of outdoor activities including kayaking, snorkelling, camping and fishing. Relaxing palapas with hammocks. Recommended.

Santa Clara *p152*

$$$$ Sheraton Bijao, Santa Clara, Carretera Interamericana Km 108, T908-3600, www.starwoodhotels.com. A modern, all-inclusive resort with spa, pools, restaurants, volleyball, tennis court and gym. Rooms are generic and comfortable (some with ocean views) and include a 32-in LCD cable TV, CD player, Wi-Fi and coffee-maker. Reliable quality, but not cheap.

$$$ Cabañas Las Sirenas, Santa Clara, T993-3235, www.lasirenas.com. A range of clean, comfortable, well-kept cottages set high up in breezy leafy grounds or, if you prefer, close to the beach. Each is equipped with kitchen, cable TV, Wi-Fi, porch and hammock. Pleasant, with good reports, but not great value.

$$$ Villa Botero B&B, Calle Aviación esq con Arroyo, T993-2708, www.villaboterobb.com. A stylish and comfortable B&B with clean, contemporary, tastefully decorated junior suites, all fitted with living areas, 32-in LCD cable TVs, mini-fridge and a terrace overlooking the pool. Wi-Fi and fully equipped kitchen available. Friendly hosts and good reports.

$$ XS Memories, Santa Clara, T993-3096, www.xsmemories.com. Panama's first full-service RV resort with 22 hook-ups. Accommodation includes simple cabins with fan, a/c and hot water, and cheap camping grounds (**$**). Amenities include pool, palapas, hammocks, bicycles, kayaks and good restaurant with burgers. Friendly and affordable expat-run lodgings.

Farallón and Playa Blanca *p152*

$$$$ Playa Blanca Resort, Zone 7, Farallón, T264-6444, www.playablancaresort.com. Opened in 2003, the increasingly popular all-inclusive resort of Playa Blanca features 219 well-attired rooms, pools, jacuzzis, gym, restaurant and business centre. A few mixed reports about noise, service and cleanliness.

$$$$ Togo B&B, Calle La Venta, Playa Blanca, T264-7845, www.togopanama.com. A very comfortable and stylish boutique B&B with clean, modern, tasteful rooms, all kitted out with contemporary artwork, kitchenette, private balcony and sofa bed. Tranquil and inviting with great hosts and consistently good reports. Recommended.

Río Hato and beyond *p153*

$ Hotel Rivera, Carretera Interamericana, Antón, T987-2245, www.hotelrivera-panama.com. Founded in 1966 and remodelled in 2000, this is a reasonably priced, family-run motel-style lodging on the highway. Rooms are clean and simple with bath, a/c or fan. Good for drivers.

El Valle *p153, map p154*

Accommodation is more expensive and harder to find at weekends; you should definitely book ahead Fri-Sat, especially in high season.

$$$$ Canopy Lodge, on the road to Chorro El Macho, T264-5720, www.canopylodge.com. Part of the excellent 'Canopy family' and a very popular place with birders, including Sir David Attenborough. Rooms are large, comfortable and well equipped, overlooking beautiful tranquil grounds that are invariably fluttering with dazzling local birdlife. Birdwatching packages are available and reservations required. Great reputation, good guides and highly recommended.

$$$$ Crater Valley Adventure Spa, Vía Ranita Dorada, T983-6167, www.crater-valley.com. This small but comfortable hotel offers a range of adventure activities including horse riding, trekking, climbing, biking and rappelling. More sedate types might want to take advantage of the spa options, which include skin treatments, salon services, massage and a great outdoor hot tub. Prices rise at the weekends.

$$$$ Los Mandarinos, Calle El Ciclo, T983-6645, www.losmandarinos.com. Luxury Tuscan-style villas complete with elegant guest rooms, spa, fitness centre, pool and an excellent restaurant serving top-notch Panamanian cuisine. Personal services include tailor-made sports and leisure programmes.

$$$ Anton Valley Hotel, Av Central, T983-6097, www.antonvalleyhotel.com. Comfortable, well-attired lodgings with clean, restful, presentable rooms, all equipped with cable TV, hot water and orthopaedic mattresses. Deluxe rooms and the suite are much more attractive than standards. Good internet rates in low season. Helpful and professional. Recommended.

$$$ Golden Frog Inn, off Calle El Ciclo, T983-6117, www.goldenfroginn.com. You'll find tranquil, beautifully landscaped grounds at the **Golden Frog Inn**. Accommodation includes tasteful Mediterranean-style suites with lush verandas, own kitchens, bedrooms and hammocks. Guestrooms are cheaper (**$$**), but comfortable, with use of shared kitchen and pool. Great hosts and reports. Recommended, but reserve in advance.

$$$ Park Eden B&B, Calle Espave 7, T983-6167, www.parkeden.com. This very romantic country house is set in 1 ha of lush gardens. Look out for lots of colourful birds fluttering around. Hosts Lionel and Monica are very gracious and friendly; rooms are very clean, comfortable and well equipped. Good reports, recommended.

$$$-$$ Hotel Campestre, at the foot of Cara Coral Hill, T983-6146, www.hotel campestre.com. This hotel has 20 comfortable rooms, all with fan, Wi-Fi, hot water and TV. It has a dramatic location at the foot of a mountain and there's a short nature walk that begins in the grounds. Prices include breakfast.

$$$-$$ Los Capitanes, Calle de la Cooperativa, T983-6080, www.los-capitanes.com. Owned and operated by a retired German sea captain, Mr Manfred Koch. The hotel grounds are pretty and well tended, home to 16 rooms including 2 suites with bathtubs. The restaurant serves German cuisine, à la carte food, wines and cocktails.

$$ Cabañas Potosí, Calle La Reforma, T983-6181, cabanas.potosi@elvalle.com.pa. Comfortable, clean, secluded cabins with mini-fridges, porches, hot water and hammocks. Very restful and lots of colourful birds in the well-tended garden. Friendly, helpful hosts Dennis and Mireya can arrange good birdwatching trips or anything else you need. A short way out of town. Lots of good reports. Recommended.

$$ Hotel Don Pepe, Av Principal, T983-6425, www.hoteldonpepe.com. Owned and operated by the gregarious Don Pepe, who can often be found in the well-stocked *artesanía* store below. Rooms are clean and comfortable with hot water and TV. Additional services include internet, laundry and guide. Friendly and recommended.

$$ Hotel Residencial El Valle, Av Central, T983-6536, www.hotelresidencialelvalle.com. There's little between this reasonable option and neighbouring Don Pepe. Rooms are straightforward, simple, comfortable, equipped with hot water and cable TV. There's an *artesanía* store and restaurant below. Friendly, helpful management.

$ Hostal Cariguana, Calle Las Medinas, T983-6269, www.hostalcariguana.galeon.com. Very reasonable budget accommodation with good personal attention. Rooms are simple and comfortable and there's a good shady terrace with relaxing hammocks.

$ Hostel Orchid, Av Central, T983-6472, www.aprovaca.org/en/hostel.html.

Very simple, economical dormitory accommodation in bunk-beds, including hot shower, Wi-Fi and free entry to the excellent APROVACA orchid house. A nice ambience and recommended for thrifty wanderers.
$ La Casa de Juan, Calle Cocorron 4, T6453-9775, www.lacasadejuanpanama.blogspot.com. Friendly budget lodgings with very simple rooms, all equipped with own bath and hot water. Shared facilities include internet, ping-pong, kitchen, treehouse, TV, DVD, billiards. Ultra-cheap for El Valle and a good choice for backpackers.
$ Pensión Niña Delia, Av Central, T983-6425. Spartan quarters for backpackers and budget travellers. No towels or soap provided, but they will look after bags. The restaurant lays on a popular weekend lunch buffet – all you can eat for US$7. Ultra-cheap and ultra-basic.

Penonomé p157
$$ Guacamaya, Carretera Interamericana, near the entrance to town, T991-0117. Clean, comfortable and tidy rooms with hot water, a/c and cable TV. There's a restaurant, bar and casino too. Pleasant enough, if fairly unremarkable.
$$ Hotel La Pradera, Carretera Interamericana, south of town, T991-0106. A large business hotel on the highway with an events room, popular restaurant and pool. Rooms are reasonably new and come equipped with hot water, a/c and cable TV. Not bad, but traffic is noisy; try to get a room at the back. Friendly, helpful staff.
$ Dos Continentes, Carretera Interamericana, near the entrance to town, T997-9325. Large, comfortable rooms with hot showers, cable TV and a/c. There's a good little restaurant downstairs, popular with the locals at most times. Clean and functional. Good value, but avoid noisy rooms facing the main road.

Reserva Natural Privada Tavida p158
$$$ Posada Cerro La Vieja, T6627-4921, www.posadalavieja.com. A beautifully

secluded ecolodge set in the rambling grounds of the reserve. It boasts stunning mountain views and lots of colourful birdlife. Lodgings consist of comfortable rooms and suites with a/c, cable TV and hot water. There's also one superb private cabin overlooking Tavida waterfall (**$$$$**). Additional facilities include a great spa with a hot tub, sauna and steam room. Very tranquil, recommended, but book ahead.

Aguadulce p161
$$ El Interamericano, Carretera Interamericana, T997-4363, www.hotel interamericano.com.pa. Good, clean, comfortable, straightforward rooms with bath, a/c, TV and balcony. Also has a swimming pool and restaurant. A good pit-stop for long-distance drivers.
$ Hotel Sarita, Av Alejandro Tapia, T997-4437. Spartan but reasonably priced quarters for the budget traveller, including TV and a/c. Centrally located.

🍴 Restaurants

El Valle p153, map p154
$$$ La Casa de Lourdes, Calle El Ciclo, next to Los Mandarinos, T983-6450, www.lacasadelourdes.com. The finest restaurant in town, very elegant and romantic. A changing menu includes delicious offerings like shrimps in Grand Marnier and plantain croquettes in goat's cheese sauce. The desserts are to die for. Reservations are required, please dress smartly.
$$ Artash Fresh Choice, Calle La Planta, T6980-2734. Closed Tue. Delicious Asian cuisine, fresh wraps, salads and delicious smoothies served at this intimate little restaurant. A relaxing garden and outdoor patio. Call ahead for dinner reservations. Thai massage and yoga also offered. Recommended.
$$ Bruschetta, Av Central, inside the Antón Valley Hotel, T983-6097, www.antonvalley hotel.com. Open for breakfast, lunch and dinner. Very buzzing and busy on Fri and

Sat evenings, when you should book in advance. They serve an eclectic mix of Italian and international food, including good seafood, salads and, if in season, sublime passion-fruit mousse. Service is helpful but sometimes overstretched.

$$ Rincón Vallero, Calle Espavé, T983-6175, www.hotelrinconvallero.com. Outdoor dining in a fabulous garden complete with a well-stocked carp pool, romantic lighting and singing frogs. They serve a range of Panamanian and international fare, including good seafood – try the *corvina*. A fair wine selection too.

$$ Ty's Sports Grill, Av Central, www.tyssportsgrillpanama.com. A Canadian-owned diner-style sports bar and hub of El Valle's expat scene. They serve burgers, chicken wings and other comfort food. Good for a cold beer and meeting gringos, and a helpful source of information about the area, especially if you're looking to settle.

$ Bambucillo, Av Central. A friendly, laid-back little café-restaurant with a changing menu of wholesome, organic vegetarian treats, including a delicious selection of fresh, refreshing herbal teas. There's a handful of seats in the garden outside and a good *artesanía* shop attached. Recommended.

$ Mar de Plata, Av Central. Cheap and cheerful fare, including chicken, burgers and comida at lunchtime. Also try **Tierra y Mar** next door, very similar in style and offerings.

$ Restaurante Massiel, Av Central. A relaxed and friendly cafeteria serving reliable set meals and Panamanian staples like *ropa vieja* and *sancocho*. Wholesome and economical.

Cafés

El Valle Gourmet & Coffee Shop, Av Central. Look for the big sign by the side of the road, just south of town. They serve aromatic coffee, teas and cake on their patio, a good call after a long day hiking.

Penonomé p157

$$ Sweet Tamarindo, Av Juan Demóstenes Arosemena. This bistro-style eatery is the classiest restaurant in Penonomé and a surprising find. They serve tasty steaks, seafood and creative international fare. Recommended.

$$-$ Jin Foon, on the Interamericana, inside **Hotel Guacamaya**. Reasonable Chinese food and the usual meat, chicken and fish fare, for those who prefer less exciting flavours.

$ Las Tinajas, Carretera Interamericana. Bustling locals' haunt serving reasonable *comida típica*, carb-rich buffet food and set meals. Economical and OK.

Bakeries

Panadería El Paisa, Calle Juan Demóstenes Arosemena. The place for sweet rolls, cakes, coffee and other cheap baked goods.

⊕ Festivals

Río Hato and beyond p153
13-16 Jan Patron Saint Feast in Antón with much traditional dancing and revelry.
13-15 Oct Antón's Toro Guapo festivities.

El Valle p153, map p154
19 Jan El Valle's Patron Saint Feast, dedicated to San José.
Sep The Semana de Campesino is a very typical fiesta, complete with processions, ox-carts and dances.

Penonomé p157
Feb/Mar Carnaval is big in Penonomé with a flotilla on the Río Zaratí.
Dec Penonomé's Patron Saint Feast involves a traditional church service, religious procession and street party; dates change, usually 1st or 2nd weekend of Dec.

Aguadulce p161
Feb/Mar Carnaval is celebrated with great aplomb in Aguadulce.

25 Jul Patron Saint Feast, with widespread drinking and dancing.
18-20 Oct Festivities commemorating the founding of Aguadulce.

○ What to do

El Valle *p153, map p154*
Hiking and birding
Plenty of casual hiking and birdwatching can be done in the hills around El Valle, but more ambitious treks may require a guide. The ATP office on Av Centrral, or your hotel, can usually point you in the right direction. For specialized birding guides, speak to **Ken Allaire**, T6873-1772, **Mario Bernal**, T6693-8213 or **Mario Urriola**, T6569-2676; all speak English and Spanish.

Horse riding
Horses can be hired near **Hotel Campestre** and other locations for around US$5-10 per hr (without guide). Look for signs, 'Alquiler de Caballos'

○ Transport

El Valle *p153, map p154*
Bicycles
Bikes are a great way to get around town and explore the surrounding countryside. Many hotels rent them out on an hourly/daily basis, try **Don Pepe**, Av Central.

Buses
Buses to **Panama City** depart every 30-45 mins, 0630-1830, 2½ hrs, US$4.25. For other destinations, take any bus heading to the Interamericana and change at the El Valle turn-off.

Taxis
Roaming cabs can be found on Av Central, but in the evening it may be best to book in advance. Ask your hotel to make arrangements, or try **Alfredo** T6639-1090 or **Efraín** T6609-0371.

Penonomé *p157*
Buses
Buses to **Panama City** depart from their own bus shelter on the Interamericana, opposite Hotel Dos Continentes, every 20 mins, 2½ hrs, US$5.25. For the **Azuero Peninsula**, take a passing Santiago bus on the Interamericana highway and change at Divisa. For **David**, catch a passing bus or go to Santiago and change. To **La Pintada**, catch a bus at the turn-off on the southwest corner of the Plaza Central, every 15 mins, 20 mins, US$1.35. For short-haul destinations west of Penonomé – including **Aguadulce**, every 15 mins, 30 mins, US$1.80 and **El Copé** (Parque Nacional Omar Torrijos), every 30-60 mins, 1 hr, US$2.40 – wait on the Interamericana or enquire at the chaotic local bus station, south of the plaza near the market. To **Chiguiri Arriba** (including Churquita Grande/Reserva Tavida), every 1-2 hrs, 1-2 hrs, US$1.65, rough rural buses depart from behind the market.

Herrera and Los Santos: Azuero Peninsula

The twin provinces of Herrera and Los Santos comprise the fabled, folkloric heartland of Panama's Azuero Peninsula. Their sprawling network of rural communities is filled with tiny whitewashed churches, soporific plazas and traditional colonial houses. The whole region is revered for its fine artistic output, with entire families specializing in the production of intricate embroidered dresses, devilish masks, fine pottery or musical instruments. Equally, Herrera and Los Santos maintain a staunch devotion to traditional modes of worship. Religious feast days draw crowds of pilgrims and miracle-seekers with dazzling public performances that recall the passion of Christ, the conquest of the Americas, or the trials of the human soul and its descent into purgatory. The scenes of ritual Catholic penitence are matched only by scenes of ritual inebriation, including the wildest Carnival celebrations this side of Río. Thanks to its hazy fruit-filled pastures, the Azuero is often compared to the bucolic backwaters of Italy. Some complain that 500 years of intensive agriculture have left little space for the natural world, but this is not true. The peninsula has long been a refuge for migratory birds and endangered sea turtles, with teeming wetlands, marshes, mudflats, offshore islands and coral reefs among its diverse natural landscapes. Likewise, the Azuero's Pacific shoreline is singularly beautiful and has not gone unrecognized by the international surf crowd. ▸▸ *For listings, see pages 182-189.*

Chitré → *For listings, see pages 182-189. Colour map 1, C6.*

The laid-back city of Chitré is the capital of Herrera province and the largest urban settlement in the Azuero. It boasts a handsome central plaza with a stately cathedral, an affable population and a scattering of historic buildings dating from the 19th and early 20th centuries. It is not a beautiful place, but it is very likeable. Day-to-day life proceeds in a rambling, easy-going fashion and, although the city is rapidly developing as a centre of regional trade, there is no intrusion of the kind of harsh commercialism that has come to characterize some other destinations in Panama. For now, Chitré is refreshingly unpretentious and assuredly low-key. It makes an excellent and inexpensive base for exploring the surrounding communities and countryside.

Arriving in Chitré
The bus station is on the south side of town on Vía Circunvalación, around 1.5 km from Parque Unión. Chitré is relatively small and easily covered on foot. Taxis to most places cost US$1-2. For maps and information, there is a **CEFATI office** ⓘ *2 km out of town in La Arena, Vía Circunvalación, T974-4532, www.chitrenet.net/chitre.html, Mon-Fri 0900-1600.*

Background
Chitré was established on 19 October 1848. Its name, so the story goes, was taken from a powerful indigenous chief, Chitra, who resided on a nearby hill. Recently, some historians have disputed this, claiming that the city's namesake is derived from the word 'Chitreca', which means new or young maize. Whatever its etymology, Chitré was elevated to the status of a provincial capital after the creation of Herrera province in 1915. In 1941, under President Arnulfo Arias Madrid, Los Santos and Herrera provinces were merged with Chitré as the capital (they were separated again under Don Ricardo Adolfo de la Guardia). The city's economy is traditionally grounded in agriculture and the production of clay tiles. Today, it is rapidly expanding and modernizing.

Parque Unión

The spiritual heart of the city is the Parque Unión, beautified with trim green lawns and colourful flowers. On its east side stands the **Catedral de San Juan Bautista**, one of the city's finest historic structures. Inaugurated in 1910, the cathedral was carefully restored to its current condition in the 1980s. Dedicated to John the Baptist, it boasts a restrained but elegant altar of precious woods and sparse gold-leaf finishes. The ceiling features several wrought-iron chandeliers, and a series of stained-glass windows, religious paintings and Catholic icons adorn the walls. The entire structure is beautifully illuminated after dark.

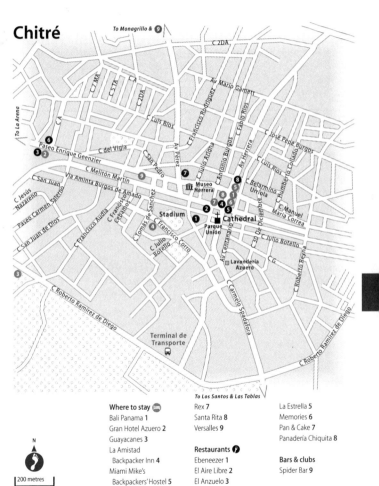

Chitré

Where to stay	Rex 7	La Estrella 5
Bali Panama 1	Santa Rita 8	Memories 6
Gran Hotel Azuero 2	Versalles 9	Pan & Cake 7
Guayacanes 3		Panadería Chiquita 8
La Amistad	Restaurants	
Backpacker Inn 4	Ebeneezer 1	
Miami Mike's	El Aire Libre 2	Bars & clubs
Backpackers' Hostel 5	El Anzuelo 3	Spider Bar 9
Pensión Central 6	El Mesón 4	

N

200 metres
200 yards

Museo Herrera

ⓘ *Paseo Enrique Geenzier, Mon-Sat 0800-1600, US$1. Nearly all signs are in Spanish.*

Housed in the city's elegant old post office, Chitré's only museum is dedicated to local history and anthropology. Exhibits are on the dusty side, but offer a mildly diverting account of the region's development from ancient times to the 20th century. Artefacts include an enormous thigh bone from a giant prehistoric sloth and various pre-Columbian items from the **Sarigua** and **Monagrillo** cultures, including ceramic shards, urns, pots, incense burners, primitive knives, projectiles and *metates* for grinding maize. The reproduction gold *huacas* are the most beautiful items on display. Depicting eagles, jaguars, pelicans, turtles, frogs and other animals, these precious ornaments were typically buried with the bodies of deceased nobles, as the museum's mock-tomb illustrates. Upstairs on the second floor, exhibits have an ethnographic focus. They include several displays of regional costumes, such as the *pollera*, as well as colourful masks. There is particular emphasis on *campesino* culture with Creole violins, *mejoranas* (types of small guitars) and drums, along with agricultural tools and ingenious handmade storage vessels, such as a *chuspa*, a nifty bag fashioned from a bull's scrotum.

Around Chitré → *For listings, see pages 182-189.*

La Arena

The tiny hamlet of La Arena, 2 km west of Chitré, is a renowned pottery centre and a virtual suburb of the city. Rows of workshops flank the **Carretera Nacional**, where you'll find exuberant displays of local craftwork. Giant earthen flowerpots, colourful wind chimes, vases, mushrooms, bells and a menagerie of brilliantly coloured clay geese, macaws, toucans, butterflies and frogs all vie for attention. For ceramic purists, monochrome pre-Columbian reproductions are widely available and among the finest of the community's offerings. Prices are reasonable and if you're in the market for buying, most artisans will be happy to answer questions and show you around their studio. North of the Carretera, there is a diminutive church and plaza that come to life with music and dancing over the Christmas period, 22-25 December. To get to La Arena, walk along the Carretera Nacional for 40 minutes; catch a local bus, five minutes, US$0.25; or take a taxi, US$1.50.

Playa El Aguillito

ⓘ *Get there by frequent bus, 0600-1800, US$0.50, or taxi, US$3.*

The vast tidal mudflats of Playa El Aguillito, 7 km from Chitré, are the site of mass bird migrations. Thousands of terns, egrets, sandpipers and other shore birds – most of them from the western USA and Canada – converge on the beach each year to feed on the tiny shrimps exposed by the low tide. Under the esteemed direction of **Profesor Francisco Delgado** ⓘ *T996-1725, delgadofrancisco2410@gmail.com*, the birds have been scientifically monitored by the Humboldt Ecological Station since the 1980s. Among the station's discoveries is the revelation that the birds return to very specific feeding spots year after year. Sadly, the Humboldt station is no longer operational and Professor Delgado doubts whether it will re-open in the future. He continues to count bird populations on the beach but he is now heavily focused on the migratory habits of butterflies, which he says are connected to the ocean tides. The professor is extremely knowledgeable about the Azuero's natural history, as well as its cultural traditions, and offers excellent and highly recommended private tours to a variety of sites.

Parque Nacional Sarigua → *Colour map 1, C5.*

① 10 km out of town; taxi $5-10. Entrance, US$5.

A protected area since 1984, the Parque Nacional Sarigua is a man-made wasteland that's optimistically peddled as Panama's only desert. Once upon a time, dense tropical forests consumed the park's 4729-ha area, reaching as far as the mangroves and coastline between the Santa María and Parita rivers. Years of intensive farming cleared it of vegetation and exposed the thin topsoil to the elements. Wind, rain and other forces of erosion washed it away, leaving only the nutrient-poor subsoil, which became heavily salinized due to the park's proximity to the ocean. Today, visitors will encounter harsh, arid landscapes of cracked earth and dune-like formations, as striking as they are eerie. Interestingly, sparse life is now beginning to flourish in the park's desolate expanses, including numerous species of cacti and other thorny plants. Life, it seems, always finds a way. Perhaps Sarigua's greatest value, however, is as an archaeological site. The remains of a fishing settlement believed to be 11,000 years old have recently been discovered along with a farming village estimated to be 5000 years old. Ancient arrow heads can also be seen in the park's exposed subsoil. For better or worse, the area's status as a national park means large-scale excavation projects will never be realized.

Parita → *For listings, see pages 182-189. Colour map 1, C5.*

Originally an old Spanish settlement called Santa Elena, the historic and well-preserved colonial town of Parita derives its name from 'Paris', a Spanish nickname for a local indigenous chief properly known as Antataura. Today, the town is home to around 3000 inhabitants and, despite its disarming aesthetic charms, rarely visited by tourists. Semana Santa, Corpus Christi and Carnaval are all attended with great gusto in Parita. Activities focus on the expansive main plaza, a traditional gathering place for bullfights, dances and fireworks displays. Parita's patron saint is **Santo Domingo de Guzmán**, honoured each year in an extensive festival, 26 July to 4 August.

Iglesia de Santo Domingo de Guzmán

Built in 1656, the diminutive church of Santo Domingo de Guzmán is one of the finest colonial structures on the peninsula, declared a historic national landmark in 1926. It's south-facing façade features an interesting bell tower laden with mother-of-pearl. Added to the structure in the mid-18th century, its position directly over the doorway is quite unusual. The church's interior conceals numerous hand-crafted wooden altars dedicated to the Heart of Jesus, the Virgin of the Candle Light, Saint Joseph and Our Lady Carmen, among others. In typically exuberant Churrigueresque style, the altars feature ornately carved Solomonic columns and porticoes complete with wandering vines and other highly wrought details. During Semana Santa, the church hosts many attractive floral displays.

Taller Darío López

① T974-2933.

Darío López is the Azuero's chief mask-maker. He has been crafting brilliantly ghoulish *diablico* masks for almost 50 years now, most of them for Herrera's resplendent Corpus Christi festivities, which sees devilish dance troupes descend en masse (see box, page 174). The masks are made from papier mâché overlaid onto a clay mould. Darío often ships his creations to the international market and is happy to receive visitors at his workshop. Prices vary from a few dollars for a tiny souvenir up to $30-50 for a large mask. To find him, look for the house with masks outside, on the Carretera Nacional on the northern edge of town.

Taller Rodríguez López
ⓘ *Mon-Fri 0900-1600.*
The Rodríguez López workshop specializes in the painstaking restoration of religious art and antiques. There are only a few artisans in Panama with the highly specialized skills for this type of work and, consequently, ancient altars and icons arrive at the workshop from all kinds of far-flung places. Located close to the church, the *taller* is managed by Macario José Rodríguez and José Sergio López, both friendly, interesting and happy to tell you about their profession. Drop in to see what they are working on.

Refugio de Vida Silvestre Cenegón de Mangle → *Colour map 1, B5.*
ⓘ *There are no buses to the reserve; taxi US$20.*
Encompassing the estuary and flood plains of the Río Santa María, the Cenegón de Mangle Wildlife Refuge encompasses 1000 ha of teeming wetlands. The area was previously home to one of the largest colonies of herons on the Pacific, but sadly they have now been exterminated by local shrimp fishermen. The refuge continues to shelter some six different species of mangrove – including prolific red, white and black mangroves – numerous crocodiles, frogs and molluscs. It features a rambling wooden boardwalk for exploring the brackish waters, and boat tours with the ranger are a possibility. The refuge conceals a series of **thermal springs** and a prehistoric cave – **La Cueva de Tigre** – archaeologically significant as a 12,000-year-old human habitation.

Ciénaga de las Macanas → *Colour map 1, B5.*
ⓘ *At the village of Rincón, 3 km after the town of Santa María, turning on the Divisa–Chitré highway. There's a welcome centre in Rincón.*
A watery oasis at the heart of Panama's *arco seco* (dry arc), the 2000-ha Ciénaga de las Macanas Multiple Use Wildlife Reserve is the largest wetland in the Azuero Peninsula. Located on the floodplain of the Santa María River, the reserve is an officially designated Important Bird Area and rich in aquatic wildlife. The region's marshes are thick with spiny plants, hyacinth and lilies, while herons, ducks, waders, storks, doves, ospreys and hawks are all common and easy to spot. The small community of El Rincón forges a modest living fishing the freshwater ponds for shrimp and sardines, as well as farming the surrounding plains with rice, fruit and sugar cane. In recent years it has worked closely with the Peace Corps, the Audubon Society and an excellent NGO, **Grupo Eco Turístico de Macanas**, to improve visitor services and promote the region as a tourist destination. It now boasts an excellent observation deck for birdwatching, several trails and the option of boat tours on the lake, where you might spot green iguanas and boa constrictors on the islands. October and April to May are generally the best months for bird observation.

Pesé → *For listings, see pages 182-189. Colour map 1, C5.*

Steeped in dense sugar-cane plantations, the friendly farming town of Pesé is the proud birthplace of Panama's national tipple, **Seco Herrerano**. Devout drinkers can visit the distillery to learn more about the tasty spirit, but religious devotees may find more interest in the enactment of Christ's Passion, performed on the main plaza every Semana Santa.

The play spans four days, several stages and involves over 100 members of the community. It concludes with a procession, a mock crucifixion and, ultimately, a roaring good fiesta in true Latin spirit. The modest church features contemporary murals of the baptism of Christ and an image of the Virgin that arrived from Quito, Ecuador, in 1783.

Varela Hermanos Seco Factory

ⓘ *T974-9491, www.varelahermanos.com, open Jan-Mar, Mon-Sat 0900-1700, free, but contact well in advance.*

The creation of seco can be credited to a Spanish immigrant, Don José Varela Blanco, who founded Panama's first sugar mill, the Ingenio San Isidro, in Pesé in 1908. Some 28 years later, in 1936, Don José's three eldest sons – José Manuel, Plinio and Julio – encouraged him to distil the sugar-cane juice into a potent liquor. So began a long and lucrative family tradition that today produces one million cases of liquor per year. Each dry season, January to May, over 50,000 tonnes of sugar cane are harvested from 800 ha of company land. Over the wet season, June to December, the cane is weighed and crushed, producing raw juice for fermentation and distillation. The seco is bottled in Pesé while the company's other lines, including Abeulo Rum and Cabillito Gin, are bottled in Panama City.

Ocú → *For listings, see pages 182-189. Colour map 1, C5.*

The town of Ocú, 22 km west of Pesé, is a friendly agricultural community enclosed by hot, sprawling fields of yam, yucca, watermelon and sugar cane. It is chiefly celebrated for its time-honoured customs and cultural life, including its own forms of music, dance, mask-making and, in particular, the manufacture of traditional hats. Although Ocú's fame has recently been eclipsed by its commercial rival Penonomé, many artisans in and around town continue to weave for pleasure and profit. Most trading of Ocú hats – along with distinctive Ocú *polleras* and *montunos* – is done on the **Carretera Interamericana**, reached along the direct northbound road out of town. Alternatively, you are welcome to visit artisans in their workshops. If you're in the region during August, the three-day **Festival de Manito** is a particularly evocative and interesting time (see Festivals, page 188).

Villa de Los Santos → *For listings, see pages 182-189. Colour map 1, C6.*

The Río Villa, 4 km south of Chitré, forms the official boundary between Herrera and neighbouring Los Santos province. Perched on its southern bank, the diminutive Villa de Los Santos is a historic *Santeño* settlement with pastel-shaded colonial architecture and a terminally soporific ambience. It is best known as the birthplace of Panama's Independence movement, where local separatists made the first '*grito*' or cry for freedom from Spain on 10 November 1821. The event is commemorated each year with a presidential visit, a civil parade and much merriment. Villa de Los Santos is also famed for its Corpus Christi celebrations, 40 days after Easter, which are some of the most vivid and fascinating in all Latin America (see box, page 174).

Background

Los Santos was founded on 1 November 1569, All Saints' Day in the Catholic calendar, from which it derives its name. The town's forefathers comprised a rebellious breakaway group of 18 families from the royalist stronghold of Natá. The mayor of Natá, Rodrigo de Zúñiga, had strictly forbidden the establishment of any unauthorized communities

Dancing with the Devil

The Devil and his minions may seem like unwelcome guests at a Christian festival, but the feast of Corpus Christi, 60 days after Easter, sees hordes of diabolical underlings parading through the streets of Villa de Los Santos. The so-called *diablicos sucios* (dirty little devils) descend in great dancing troupes to the explosion of fireworks, the eerie clapping of castanets or, more joyously, a lightly strummed *mejorana*. Clad in grotesque masks and spiky headdresses of brightly coloured macaw feathers, they perform outlandish dance routines before stomping through town in a whirlwind of colour and fury. The *diablicos sucios* derive their unfortunate name from their traditional costume, which in ancient times comprised a grubby blanket painted with stripes of charcoal, mud and achiote. As the dancers grew hot, the blankets would run with sweat and colour, but as if this wasn't unsightly enough, the *diablicos* were also armed with a foul-smelling pig's bladder, which they freely swung as they stamped out their routine. Today, the dirty blanket has been replaced by a clean all-in-one costume of black and red stripes, but the presence of the dirty devils remains as disconcerting as ever. An integral part of Azuero traditions, their dance finds its roots in medieval Spain, where Corpus Christi had unashamedly imperial and conversionary overtones. The Catholic feast may have been originally intended as a celebration of the rite of the Eucharist, but in Iberia, the festival evolved into a grand pageant that symbolized not only the triumph of good over evil, but the victory of righteous Christian believers over non-Christian heretics and, by extension, Spain's militaristic conquest of the New World. Thus the dance of the *diablicos sucios* probably served to indoctrinate its participants on several levels, not least in Catholic notions of cleanliness and sin, salvation and damnation. The evangelical function of Corpus Christi is even more apparent in a narrative performance known as *La Danza de los Diablicos Limpios* (the Dance of the Clean Little Devils), sometimes known as *La Danza de los Gran Diablos* (Dance of the Great Devils). The rendition centres on a human soul clad in a long white gown who is suddenly surrounded by gruesome devils. The so-called *diablicos limpios* are disguised as 15th-century jesters, complete with colourful scarves, bells and rosettes, and their Captain is a particularly horrifying presence with dark black wings and an equally gruesome (if quite comical) wife, *La Diabla*. Thankfully, all is not lost, for the arrival of the Archangel Michael signals the soul's promise of redemption, if only he can overcome the forces of darkness. A prolonged battle ensues in which Michael, perhaps predictably, emerges victorious and frees the soul from its tormentors. Contrary to conventional religious wisdom, Satan never gatecrashes the party – he is always invited, and it wouldn't be the same without him.

and responded by burning down their houses and dragging them and their ringleader, Francisco Gutiérrez, straight to jail. Condemned to death, the group had their sentences overturned after an appeal to the Court of Panamá. They returned to rebuild Los Santos but it would not be granted royal title until 1573, when it was finally recognized after years of legal wrangling. As a political concession to the mainland, the crown accorded Los Santos the status of a diminutive *villa*, rather than a city. Over the centuries, as the town's predilection for liberalism and non-conformity became firmly established, the label became a badge of honour rather than a slight. True to its anti-royal roots, Los Santos was the first town in Panama to issue a call for Independence from Spain. The famous *grito* is said to have originated with a peasant woman, Rufina Alfaro, who is today honoured with a large bust on the edge of town. Some 18 days later, Panama City followed suit and Independence from Spain was officially declared on 28 November 1821.

Iglesia San Atanasio

The Iglesia San Atanasio is regarded as one of Panama's most beautiful churches. Located on the town's main plaza, the **Parque Simón Bolívar**, the church bears the date 1782, although other records suggest it was founded in 1569 by Francisco de Abrego, the Bishop of Panama. The interior features a beautiful vaulted ceiling with painted wooden ribs and rows of geometric patterns that run like a giant gold and turquoise carpet. The baroque-style altar and attendant images are carved from precious woods and gilded with copious gold leaf. A large gold and red archway is particularly magnificent. The church has been a national monument since 1938.

Museo de la Nacionalidad

① *Calle José Vallarino, Tue-Sat 0930-1630, Sun 0930-1300, US$1. All signs in Spanish.*
Panama's Declaration of Independence was signed in this interesting old building in 1821. Formerly occupied by Franciscan monks, prisoners of war and, later, the Vásquez family, it has served as a museum of local history since 1974. Exhibits are quite sparse and it's not worth making a special trip to see them, but if you're already in town you can take a quick browse. Sections are dedicated to pre-Columbian finds, the Spanish conquest, the Independence movement and religious art. There's also a reproduction *campesino* kitchen with interesting old implements and a historic outer courtyard with fine paving stones.

Around Villa Los Santos

There are two modest beaches about 10 km from town, both quite desolate and devoid of people during the week. **Playa El Rompio**, the prettiest, is served by buses from the highway, hourly, 20 minutes, US$0.80; taxi US$5. En route you'll pass a traditional salt factory complete with evaporation pools. **Playa Monagre**, a little further north, is very similar. Neither beach has any facilities, so bring your own food and water. South of Los Santos, the **Reserva Silvestre Peñón de la Onda** is a 3900-ha reserve with beaches, mangroves and dunes. It is rarely visited and you will need your own vehicle to enter the area.

Guararé → *For listings, see pages 182-189. Colour map 1, C6.*

Named after an old indigenous chief, Guarari, the quintessential Azuero town of Guararé stages one of the country's finest annual folkloric festivals, the **Feria de la Mejorana**. The event supplies a wonderfully spirited overview of the region's diverse cultural traditions, with dances, singing, storytelling, plays, beauty contests, bull fighting and ox-cart parades. The town, 6 km north of Las Tablas, is also famed as the birthplace of Roberto 'Manos de Piedra' Durán, Panama's most celebrated prize fighter. There are numerous suburbs around Guararé, all renowned for their production of *polleras*, as well as a couple of less visited beaches, including **Playa Bella Vista** and **Playa El Puerto**.

Museo Profesor Manuel F Zárate
ⓘ *Calle 21 de Enero, T994-5644, Tue-Sat 0900-1600, US$0.75.*

Profesor Manuel F Zárate is credited with establishing the town's first and original **Feria de la Mejorana** in 1949. Originally a chemist by trade, Zárate felt passionately about preserving and promoting the nation's culture. He spent the best part of his life documenting and revitalizing the Azuero's rich folkloric customs, and today a museum honours his life's work in the house where he was born. Exhibits include fine examples of traditional *campesino* clothing, including some very old, intricate and delicate *polleras* from scores of communities across the peninsula. Photos of *mejorana* queens, dirty devil masks, traditional musical instruments – including drums, *mejoranas* and accordians – are among the other effects. Guides are on hand to answer any questions.

Las Tablas and around → *For listings, see pages 182-189. Colour map 1, C6.*

Las Tablas is the fabled capital of Los Santos province and the second largest urban settlement on the peninsula. That's not saying much in the Azuero and it actually feels more like a provincial town than a city. Although Las Tablas is a friendly and laid-back place with a thriving plaza and a smattering of handsome architecture, there isn't much to see or do – until festival time, that is. Las Tablas has a fearsome reputation for the wildest and most debauched Carnaval party in the country, where thousands of revellers descend for several days of non-stop dances, parades and intoxicated grandeur. At other times, the city is feted as the home of one of Panama's most important Catholic icons, **Santa Librada**, and as the birthplace of **Belisarrio Porras**, one of the nation's most revered liberal statesmen.

Arriving in Las Tablas
Las Tablas is situated 31 km south of Chitré on the Carretera Nacional. It served by frequent buses from both Chitré and Panama City. The city centre is compact and easily explored on foot. Taxis to most destinations are US$1-2. There is no tourist information in Las Tablas: the nearest office is in Pedasí.

Background
There are competing accounts of the origins of Las Tablas, but most agree on its official founding date, 20 July 1671. One popular legend tells how a group of Spanish nobles fled Henry Morgan's attack on Panama City, drifted the Pacific Ocean in a battered galleon and landed on the shores of the Azuero, close to the community of La Ermita de Santa Cruz. They began constructing a settlement, dismantling the ship's tables for use in their new houses. Seeing this, their neighbours at Santa Cruz mockingly referred to them as the 'People of the Tables', and the nickname stuck. Another account relates how an image of Santa Librada, the patron saint of Las Tablas, appeared to the shipwrecked Spaniards on a rocky outcrop some distance from their camp. No matter how many times they retrieved the saint, she would always vanish and reappear at the same place. This was a sign, they decided, that Santa Librada wanted them to construct their new settlement at the outcrop. Another more prosaic myth suggests Las Tablas derived its name from a local Spanish judge who was known as 'the man of the tables'. A yet more prosaic and highly probable version suggests 'Las Tablas' comes from an old Spanish word for irrigated crops.

Calle Arriba vs Calle Abajo

The raucous street parties of Carnaval signify one final act of debauchery before the thrift, fasting and atonement of Lent. Few moments in Panama's annual cultural calendar verge so closely on mass hysteria, and few are taken so seriously as by the city of Las Tablas, which sees over 100,000 charged-up visitors for the event. The party commences on the Friday before Ash Wednesday with the ritual crowning of the Carnaval queens, a street procession, fireworks and unfettered drinking and dancing. The festivities continue until Tuesday with almost non-stop alcoholic consumption, music concerts, cultural presentations, ritual soakings by water cannon and endless parades featuring exuberant sequined costumes and incredible feathered headdresses. For Tableños, Carnaval is much more than a spirited annual fiesta – it's a religious and social duty, and a matter of civic pride. But beneath the grand spectacle and revelry, a deep current of rivalry runs through Carnaval. For over 50 years, Las Tablas has maintained a tradition of two opposing Carnaval camps or *tunas* – Calle Arriba and Calle Abajo – each with their own Carnaval queen and band of followers. The *tunas* compete unsparingly for the title of most beautiful and sumptuous queen, the most elegant and impressive parade, the best party, the best musicians, the best dancers, and anything else they can compete over. Throughout the ritual sparring, both sides trade creative insults and colourful jokes. The competition is so fierce and impassioned that, it is said that in Las Tablas, Carnaval can end in broken friendships, family feuds or even divorce. For most, however, the 'Burial of the Sardine' is enough to put bad feelings to rest. In an archaic Spanish ceremony signalling the close of public festivities, a mock funeral procession concludes with the symbolic interment of old ways and habits. Certain that a roaring good time was had by all, the revellers begin the long straggle home, forgetting about their differences and resentments … until next year, that is.

Iglesa Santa Librada

Situated on Las Tablas's main plaza, the baroque Iglesia Santa Librada was built in 1789, damaged by a fire in 1958 and subsequently rebuilt. It boasts an extremely fine gold-leaf altar and several other antique fixtures carved from precious woods. The city's patron saint, **Santa Librada**, is located above her own altar just to the right of the church entrance. She is depicted in crucifixion wearing trademark red and blue robes. Legend holds she was the daughter of a Roman governor, Lucius Castelius Severus, and one of nine sisters, including Marina de Auguas Santas. Born nontuplets, the sisters were deemed an aberration and ordered drowned by their mother. But a servant, Sila, spirited them away and dispersed them among Christian families. Years later, their father discovered their true identity and attempted to entice them from their faith. They refused and were subsequently martyred. Santa Librada's highly spirited official saint's day is 20 July and Las Tablas receives around 25,000 pilgrims for the event.

Museo Belisario Porras

① *Av Belisario Porras, on the main plaza, T994-6326, Tue-Sat 0900-1700, US$1; Spanish-only, includes an informed explanation of all the exhibits.*

A museum dedicated to one of Panama's most esteemed presidents, Belisario Porras, is located in the house where he was born on 27 November 1856. Prior to becoming a statesman, Porras was a journalist and activist in Colombia's Liberal party. His political activities earned him the disdain of Conservative authorities, however, and he was exiled to Nicaragua and El Salvador until 1904, when he returned to newly liberated Panama to serve as a diplomat and, later, as president. Porras was elected to office on no less than three separate occasions and the museum features personal effects and documents relating to his tenure, including numerous historic photographs. Porras is remembered chiefly for his bold contribution to the nation's infrastructure, including the national archives, the Chiriquí railway system and Santo Tomás Hospital in Panama City, then Central America's largest and most modern healthcare facility.

Around Las Tablas

Just out of town, you can visit Belisarrio Porras's former country estate, **El Pausílipo** ⓘ *Tue-Sat 0800-1600, US$0.75; taxi round-trip US$5.* For swimming, try the grey-sand beach of **Playa El Uverito**, 10 km from Las Tablas near the port of Mensabe; taxi US$5. Numerous communities throughout the province retain their traditional practice of *pollera*-making, including Santo Domingo, San José, El Cocal, El Carate and others. For more information on *polleras*, see box, page 187.

Pedasí → *For listings, see pages 182-189. Colour map 1, C6.*

Named after an indigenous chief, the colonial town of Pedasí first appeared on maps in 1785. It has spent most of its sleepy existence ignored by the outside world, but times are fast changing for this remote agricultural community. Feted as a gateway to the Azuero's most pristine and spectacular beaches, the real estate agents have moved in, the gated communities have plotted down and several Hollywood celebrities have even pitched in and bought up vast tracts of land. Fortunately, amid the flurry of speculation, Pedasí has managed to retain its small-town friendliness. For the moment, backpackers can still find cheap accommodation and surfers can still stake claim to miles of deserted coastline. The town's prodigious tourism boom has been partly driven by Panama's first female president, Mireya Moscoso, who was born in Pedasí in 1946. Thanks to her involvement, the town has seen big investments in infrastructure and its recent establishment on the international surf tournament circuit.

Arriving in Pedasí

Pedasí is served by **buses** from Las Tablas, 0600-1900, every 45 minutes, one hour, US$2.40. It is very compact and easily navigated on foot. Public transport to outlying beaches is infrequent and **taxi** charges vary according to distance, US$3-40. For tourist information, the town has a very good **ATP office** ⓘ *just off the main road near the north entrance to town, T995-2339, open 0900-1700.*

Places in Pedasí

Pedasí is a very small place and although it is pleasant rambling up and down its soporific streets, the best of its attractions lie a short distance out of town. A 10-minute drive from the centre, **Playa Lagarto** (also known as Playa Pedasí) is a popular surf spot with good left and right beach breaks; taxi US$3-5. Also good for surfing, **Playa El Toro** has left and right rock bottom point breaks (snorkelling and swimming are not so good); to get there, take a taxi, five minutes, US$3, or walk 30 minutes east from the plaza. **Playa La Garita**, next to El Toro, has rocks and strong currents, little surf or swimming appeal, but it is pleasantly

Pedasí

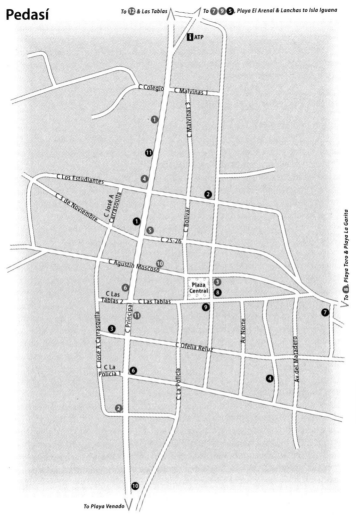

To ⑫ & Las Tablas

To ⑦ ⑨ ⑤, Playa El Arenal & Lanchas to Isla Iguana

ⓘ ATP

C Colegio
C Malvinas 1
C Malvinas 3
C Los Estudiantes
C 3 de Noviembre
C José A Carrasquilla
C Bolívar
C 25-26
C Agustín Moscoso

Plaza Central

C Las Tablas 2
C Las Tablas
C Principal
C José A Carrasquilla
C La Policia 1
C Ofelia Reluz
C La Policia
Av Norte
Av del Matadero

To Playa Toro & Playa La Garita

To Playa Venado

N

Not to scale

Where to stay 🛏
Casa de Campo **1**
Casita Margarita **2**
Corner House **3**
Dim's Hostel **4**
Doña María **5**
Hospedaje Francisca **6**
Hostal Lajagua **7**
La Rosa de los Vientos **8**

Pedasí Sports Club **9**
Pedasito **10**
Residencial Moscoso **11**
Residencial Pedasí **12**

Restaurants 🍴
Bakery **1**
Chili Reef **2**
Dulcería Yely **3**

El Patio **4**
La Granja **5**
Maudy's **6**
Pasta e Vino **7**
Pizzeria Tiesto **8**
Restaurante Ejecutivo **9**
Restaurante Isla Iguana **10**
Smiley's **11**

secluded; to get there, follow the same road towards El Toro, follow the signs and hike the last 100 m through scrub. **Playa El Arenal** (also called El Bajadero) – from where *lanchas* leave to **Isla Iguana** (see below) – is a vast sweeping beach with gold sand and moderately powerful waves. It's the best beach for swimming and usually quite empty except for a few kitesurfers January to April. You can walk there, 30-40 minutes, the access road is near the north entrance to town; or take a taxi, US$3-4.

Around Pedasí → *For listings, see pages 182-189.*

Refugio de Vida Silvestre Isla Iguana → *Colour map 1, C6.*
ⓘ *Boats to the island depart from Playa El Arenal (see above), 30 mins, US$60 return. You will have to wade into the water to board. ANAM entrance fee, US$10. Camping is possible, bring your own supplies and inform ANAM upon arrival.*

The white-sand beaches of Isla Iguana are surrounded by clean, clear tropical waters and 16 ha of dazzling multi-coloured reefs. Diving or snorkelling offshore is fantastic, thanks partly to the island's location near the edge of a continental shelf. Marine fauna includes 11 species of Pacific coral, turtles, hammerhead sharks, humpback whales, dolphins and over 300 species of fish. Established in 1980 in association with the **Council for the International Protection of Birds (CIPA-Panama)**, the 55-ha nature reserve is also home to the largest great frigate colony in Panama, as well as prolific gulls, terns and pelicans. Iguanas and boa constrictors can sometimes be spotted in the island's exuberant jungle foliage, but you should not hike unguided in the undergrowth. Prior to its existence as an idyllic nature reserve, Isla Iguana was used extensively by the US military, and there are rumoured to be unexploded shells in the forests and deep on the ocean floor. Years of bombardment may be part of the reason why some of the island's reefs are today sadly quite damaged. There are two beaches on the island, known locally as **Primera** (officially Playa Cirial) and **Segunda** (Playa El Faro). You will be dropped by the visitor centre on Playa Primera where a path leads across the island to Playa Segunda, which is more secluded and better for snorkelling.

Playa Los Destiladeros and around
A 10-minute drive from Pedasí, the golden sands of Playa Los Destiladeros are backed by low hills and a scattering of high-end hotels and wealthy vacation villas. It is a popular surf spot, with a strong left break known as 'The French', but is not so good for swimming. **Playa Los Panamaes** is hidden just behind Destiladeros with good left and right beach breaks that are best surfed at low or mid tide. **Punta Mala** lies a few kilometres east of Destiladeros. Thanks to its prolific populations of tuna and marlin, it's a popular disembarkation point for sports fishing expeditions.

Achotines Laboratory
ⓘ *T995-8166, www.iattc.org. Tours of the facilities are by scientific staff, Mon-Thu and by appointment only, US$1; call ahead.*

Managed by the **Inter-American Tropical Tuna Commission**, the Achotines laboratory is primarily engaged with the scientific study of tropical tuna fish. Using tanks and incubation pools to hatch harvested eggs, the lab is one of the few places in the world that rears live tuna in order to study their growth and development. Nestled inside a protected bay, the facility is ideally located for the task. Around 8 km offshore, the continental shelf drops to a depth of 200 m, providing fertile spawning ground for numerous pelagic species. So far 150 types of fish have been collected in the bay, including at least 10 species of tuna. The laboratory works in close association with the prestigious Smithsonian Tropical Research Institute.

Playa Venado and around → *Colour map 1, C6.*

Playa Venado (also known as Playa Venao) is the Azuero Peninsula's premier surf destination, a regular stop on the international tournament circuit and one of the country's finest beaches. Sadly, it has also been sold out to grandiose developers who intend to plant a casino and gated community right on its flank. For the moment it's unspoilt, but it won't stay that way for long – see it while you can. The beach is 4 km long and set in a perfect horseshoe cove with vast tubes that break left and right with perfect consistency. Around 4 km east of Playa Venado is **Playa Ciruelo**, rarely visited but also recommended for its rock bottom left break. A few kilometres further, **La Playita** has calm waters good for snorkelling or swimming, and a small, rustic resort that serves day-trippers. To the west of Playa Venado, the waves of **Playa Madroño** are also fit for surfing.

Reserva de Vida Silvestre Isla Caña → *Colour map 1, C6.*

ⓘ *From Pedasí, take a bus to Cañas, then to Tonosí, asking to be let out at the turning for Isla Cana. It's an 8-km hike from the bus drop-off. October, full moon. No flash photos, flash lights, etc. Admission US$10.*

The remote and tranquil shores of Isla Caña are frequented by five species of endangered marine turtles. Among them, olive ridleys have been nesting in the dark grey sands for centuries, if not millennia, and the 14-km-long beach sees up to 5000 arrivals each year between July and November. Swept with thorny vegetation and tropical savannah, Isla Caña has an area of 832.5 ha. Its 900 inhabitants are closely involved with conservation and maintain a modest tourism programme for those who would like to witness the nocturnal spectacle of turtles arriving to lay their eggs. Contact the ANAM-trained **Grupo de Ecoturismo** ⓘ *T6718-0032*, who offer *cabañas*, homestays and tours. There are a few simple restaurants on the island and it is a peaceful, pleasant place to hang out. On the mainland, there are 1300 ha of mangrove forests, where you might spot caiman, boas and waterbirds.

Tonosí and around

The tiny and decidedly remote cowboy town of Tonosí, 48 km west of Pedasí, is a picture of Azuero indolence. Day by day, life ambles up and down a single strip, distracted only infrequently by the lively drama of a spirited fiesta or rodeo. There isn't much to do in town itself, but surfers may want to head out to one of the region's fantastic beaches, including **Playa Guánico** and **Playa Cambutal**. From Tonosí, a highway bears north and eventually connects with the village of **Macaracas**, the site of a well-attended folklore festival in January. From there, a web of roads connects with Las Tablas and Chitré, completing a circuitous tour of the peninsula.

For sleeping and eating price codes and other relevant information, see pages 16-19.

● Where to stay

Chitré *p168, map p169*
Prices can rise by 50-100% during festivals.
$$$ Gran Hotel Azuero, Paseo Enrique Geenzier, T970-1000, www.hotelazuero.com. A large, new hotel on the outskirts of town, boasting a range of amenities including gym, pool, restaurant and bar. Rooms are modern, immaculately clean and kitted with a/c, cable TV, hot water, phone and safe. Professional service and the best hotel in Chitré. A 5- to 10-min walk from the centre.
$$$ Hotel Los Guayacanes, Vía Circunvalación, T996-9758, www.los guayacanes.com. A large 'country-club'-style hotel with generous grounds, casino, pool, tennis court, restaurants and artificial lagoon. Not as sophisticated as it would like to be, but reasonably quiet and isolated. Some mixed reports – ask to see a room before accepting.
$$ Hotel Bali Panama, Av Herrera and Calle Correa, T996-4620, www.hotelbalipanama. com. This friendly, helpful hotel has 28 clean, functional, windowless rooms with a/c, cable TV, safe and hot water. There's Wi-Fi in the lobby and a restaurant attached. Good coffee and parking available.
$$ Rex, Calle Melitón Martín by main plaza, T996-4310, hotelrex@hotmail.com. Hotel Rex has an excellent location on the plaza and great views from its shared balcony. Rooms are smallish, have a/c and cable TV. Wi-Fi is available in the lobby and restaurant. Breakfast included.
$$ Versalles, Paseo Enrique Geensier, near entry to Chitré, T996-4422, www.hotel versalles.com. An uninspired modern exterior gives way to a pleasant interior complete with cool, lush gardens and pool. Rooms are bland, but ultimately

decent and comfortable. It's a 5- to 10-min walk from the city centre.
$ Hotel La Amistad Backpacker Inn, Calle Francisco Corro, next to the stadium, T996-9509. Plenty of rooms at this newly renovated and functional budget hotel, all equipped with cable TV, hot water and a/c. Mattresses are hard, but rooms are clean and generally excellent value. Note they vary in size, so ask to see beforehand. There's a pool for cooling off.
$ Miami Mike's Backpackers Hostel, Av Herrera and Calle Manuel Correa, T910-0628, www.miamimikeshostel.com. A friendly and laid-back budget hostel with mixed and single-sex dorms, all strikingly adorned with murals of history's greats, Marilyn Monroe, Che Guevara and Bob Marley among them. Amenities include a fully equipped kitchen, lounge, Wi-Fi and lots of information. Located right on the Carnaval parade route with unsurpassed views from the breezy rooftop bar and terrace. You're welcome to sling a hammock. Highly recommended for budget travellers.
$ Pensión Central, Av Herrera, T996-0059. Clean and basic with soft beds, but OK. Get a quieter room at the back. Rooms have a/c, fridge and cable TV. Bustling economical restaurant downstairs.
$ Santa Rita, Calle Manuel Correa y Av Herrera, T996-4610. Built in 1930, this landmark hotel is definitely past its heyday, but it has great character. Simple rooms include cable TV, a/c and hot water. The cheapest ones have fan and no hot water. There's also Wi-Fi in the lobby, a microwave and a communal fridge. Old and weary, but clean and friendly. Recommended for budget travellers.

Villa de los Santos *p173*
$$ Hotel La Villa, Carretera Nacional, T966-8201, www.hotellavillapanama.com. A pleasant, well-kept hotel with a relaxing

outdoor patio and lots of ornamental plants, flowers and artwork. Rooms are clean, quiet, comfortable and equipped with a/c, hot water and TV. Amenities include a pool and a good restaurant serving *comida típica*.

Guararé *p175*
$$-$ Hotel Residencial La Mejorana, Vía Nacional, T994-5794, hotelmejorana@ hotmail.com. Clean, simple, straightforward rooms with a/c and hot water. A convenient spot on the highway.

Las Tablas *p176*
$$-$ Hotel Piamonte, Av Belisario Porras, T923-1903, hotelpiamonte@hotmail.com. A clean, friendly, helpful hotel with 2 buildings and 34 rooms; those with hot water cost slightly more. Amenities include a/c, cable TV, Wi-Fi, restaurant-bar, parking and safe deposit. They run a wide range of tours, including folkloric, agro-touristic, beach and islands.
$$ Hotel Don Jesús, Vía al Montero, Entrada Bda La Ermita, T994-5693, www.hoteldon jesus.com. A pleasant and well-kept lodging with 21 homely rooms, all equipped with a/c, fan, hot water, cable TV, phone and Wi-Fi. There's also a shared terrace, restaurant, pool and private parking. Not bad.
$$ Hotel Sol de Pacífico, Calle Agustín Cano, T994-1280, hsoldelpacifico@hotmail. com. The **Sol de Pacífico** is a fairly large hotel with 46 simple rooms. They come with a/c and national TV; some have hot water and kitchenette. OK.

Around Las Tablas *p178*
$$$ Hotel La Luna, Playa El Uverito, over-looking the beach, T6525-9410, www.hotel-laluna.com. A modern and stylish building that manages to keep in harmony with the traditional character of the Azuero. Rooms are clean, comfortable, well appointed and fully equipped with a/c, hot water and TV. There's also a pool.

Pedasí *p178, map p179*
$$$ Casa de Campo, Calle Principal, T6780-5280, www.casacampopedasi.com. Impeccable interior design with rich wooden finishes, solid furniture, earth tones and hints of colonial Spain. This villa-style boutique hotel features 5 extremely comfortable and well-presented rooms along with an attractive garden, pool, palapa and stylish dining hall.
$$$ Casita Margarita, Calle Principal, T995-2898, pedasihotel.com. A very handsome boutique hotel in an artfully remodelled colonial building. They have 6 comfortable, well-attired rooms and a host of amenities including Wi-Fi, restaurant and tour. Lots of attention to detail with very tasteful furnishings. Breakfast included. The best in town, recommended.
$$$ Hostal Lajagua, Vía El Arenal, after Buzo Azuero scuba centre, T995-2912, www.casalajagua.com. A stylish property with long, shady verandas, colonial-style walkways, rustic wooden furniture, a lush green garden and refreshing circular pool. Rooms are simply furnished but large and restful. Lajagua can organize a range of activities from ATV rental to fishing. Great hosts, good reports.
$$$-$$ Corner House, Frente a la Plaza Central, T995-2776, www.peakhostel.com. A small and intimate surf hotel with clean, modern, comfortable rooms. Amenities include bike rental, restaurant-bar and Wi-Fi. Helpful.
$$$-$$ Pedasí Sports Club, Calle Principal, frente de Policía, T995-2894, www.pedasisportsclub.biz. Fun motel-style lodgings and 'one stop shop' for adventure tours, including diving, snorkelling, hiking, spear-fishing and more. Clean, modern rooms and good suites with a host of amenities including pool, Wi-Fi, restaurant and bar. Rates include breakfast.
$$ Dim's Hostel, Calle Principal, T995-2303. A lovely hostel with a peaceful leafy garden, hammocks, restaurant, internet and good

clean rooms. Transportation to Playa Venado and Isla Iguana available. Very friendly and hospitable. Highly recommended.

$$ Hospedaje Francisca, Calle Principal, T995-2773, www.hospedajefrancisca.com. Friendly, local, family-run lodgings. Rooms are clean, simple, homely and equipped with Wi-Fi, hot water and a/c. They offer tours to Isla Iguana and other surrounding attractions.

$$ Hostal Doña María, Calle Principal, T995-2916, www.hostaldonamaria.com. A friendly guesthouse with 6 rooms and lots of lounge space, including a pleasant balcony and tranquil garden with hammocks and barbecue pit. Rooms have TV, internet, fan and hot water. Friendly and hospitable. Good reports.

$$ Hostal Pedasito, Calle Agustín Moscoso, Casa 2, T995-2121, www.pedasitohotel.com. Clean, contemporary furnishings and spa facilities, including several types of massage and aromatherapy. Other amenities include garden, pool, good restaurant and lounge-bar. Boutique rooms cost more (**$$$**). Tours and packages available.

$$ La Rosa de los Vientos, Camino a Playa de Toro, 2 km out of town, T6778-0627, www.bedandbreakfastpedasi.com. You'll find tranquil tropical grounds and stunning ocean views at this intimate and well-presented B&B. Rooms are comfortable and tasteful and feature sliding doors with shady verandas. Very romantic and reasonably priced. Recommended.

$$-$ Hotel Residencial Pedasí, Av Central, at the entrance to town, T995-2490, info@ residencialpedasi.com. This terracotta building has simple, straightforward rooms with hot water, a/c and cable TV. Secure parking, internet, restaurant and tours to Isla Iguana are also available. Friendly.

$ Residencial Moscoso, Av Central, T995-2203. Very basic, family-run lodgings for cash-strapped budget travellers and backpackers. Rooms with fan are cheaper. No hot water.

Playa Los Destiladeros and around
p180

$$$$ Azueros, T232-0171, www.azueros. com. A very tranquil and exclusive lodging that draws international celebrities and very wealthy vacationers. Options include boutique rooms at the **Villa Camilla** hotel or private, 2-level 'Ocean Loft' properties. Scores of amenities, including Wi-Fi, spa, riding stables and more.

$$$$-$$$ Hotel Villa Romana, Puerto Escondido, T995-2922, www.villapedasi.com. A very romantic boutique hotel with rustic Italian architecture and stunning ocean views. They offer a range of very comfortable and well-attired suites, all with therapeutic queen-size beds, a/c, Wi-Fi and minibar. Amenities include pool and restaurant.

$$$ Posada Los Destiladeros, T995-2771, www.panamabambu.net. Set in 8 ha of green, leafy grounds, Posada Los Destiladeros features a range of 15 traditionally built surfers' bungalows and houses that keep to the rural style of the Azuero. The interiors are chic but rustic. Direct beach access and restaurant on site.

Playa Venado and around *p181*

$$$$ Villa Marina, Playa Venado, T397-1058, www.villamarinapanama.com. A handsome colonial-style lodging set on 2 km of privately owned beachfront property with lush grounds. It has 9 rooms with a/c, French windows and wrap-around porches with stunning sea views.

$$$ Hotel El Sitio, Playa Venado, T832-1010, www.elsitiohotel.com. El Sitio has 14 modern rooms with solid contemporary furnishings and attractive wooden balconies overlooking the ocean. Activities include yoga, horse riding and fishing. Good restaurant serves dishes such as shrimps in tartar sauce and basil pesto pasta.

$$$ Playita Resort, La Playita, T996-6727, www.playitaresort.com. Rustic and inviting with lots of character and creative furniture fashioned from driftwood. Direct access to the beach and lush, rambling grounds

with peacocks, parrots and other wildlife. Cabins are modern and comfortable. The restaurant is open all day and popular with day-trippers, especially at weekends.
$$$ Sereia do Mar, Playa Ciruelo, sereiadomar.net. An attractive fishing and surfing lodge with 4 comfortable, well-equipped rooms with orthopaedic mattresses, a/c, TV, DVD and fridge. Garden hammocks and a fine veranda with striking ocean views – a great place to bask in the sunset. Good staff, friendly and hospitable.
$$$-$ Hostal Eco Venao, Playa Venado, T832-0530, www.ecovenao.com. Set in 140 ha of lush, reforested grounds, this self-styled surf lodge caters to a range of budgets. It features attractive and well-furnished guesthouses (**$$$**), romantic wooden *cabañas* on stilts (**$$**), a rustic hostel complete with dorm beds (**$**) and, for the truly adventurous, camping (**$**). Ecologically minded and recommended.
$$ Casa Estrella, Playa Ciruelo, T6471-3090, www.casadeestrella.com. A friendly B&B by the beach with clean, comfortable rooms and lots of wildlife in the grounds. They can help organize tours and other activities. Accommodation with balcony costs extra (**$$$**).

Tonosí and around *p181*
$$$ Hostal Boom Shiva, Playa Cambutal, no phone, www.boomshivapanama.com. An Eastern-flavoured surf lodge with 2-storey wooden bungalows on the beach, an authentic Italian restaurant and a spa offering massage therapy. Contributes to local turtle conservation.
$$$ Hotel Playa Cambutal, Playa Cambutal, T832-0948, www.hotelplaya cambutal.net. Clean, modern luxury lodging in the remote environs of Playa Cambutal. Rooms are comfortable and well attired with a/c, hot water and Wi-Fi. They can help with a host of activities including surfing, horse riding and sports fishing.

● Restaurants

Chitré *p168, map p169*
Dining in Chitré is more grub than gourmet. You'll find plenty of wholesome economical eateries, but few places of outstanding quality.
$$$-$$ Memories, Paseo Enrique Geenzier, western outskirts of town. American-style sports-themed restaurant-bar with big-screen TVs and artery-hardening comfort food, including burgers, fried chicken, enchiladas and kebabs.
$$ Ebeneezer, Julio Botello, near the stadium. A friendly and unpretentious family restaurant serving burgers, pizzas, pasta and other international fare. Good specials and a small café-bar for caffeinated drinks on the go. Some outdoor seating too. Recommended.
$$ El Anzuelo, Paseo Enrique Geenzier, western outskirts of town. Rancho-style outdoor restaurant with a convivial evening atmosphere. They serve very good fresh seafood and some tasty burgers. Friendly and popular, but service may be slow at busy times. Recommended.
$$ El Mesón, in the **Hotel Rex**, on the plaza. A wide range of national and international dishes, including burritos, nachos and a platter of grilled meats. The portions are generous, but the cooking could really use some love. Wi-Fi enabled.
$ El Aire Libre, on the plaza. Popular little locals' place that's always busy. They serve good cheap breakfasts and reliable *comida del día* for a few dollars. Friendly service and consistent quality. Recommended.
$ La Estrella, on the plaza, opposite the cathedral. Atmospheric, rough 'n' ready dining hall with plastic furniture and a lofty ceiling. Cheap, passable buffet fare and high-carb economical eats. OK.

Bakeries and cafés
Panadería Chiquita, Av Herrera. A big, lofty old-style bakery with lots of sweet and savoury treats. Unpretentious and bustling.
Pan and Cake, Nueva Provincia. Excellent, cheap and tasty sweet treats and snacks,

including good-value pizzas. The *maracuyá* (passion-fruit) ice cream is sensational. Highly recommended.

Villa de los Santos *p173*
The food stalls on the highway south of Los Santos are great places to sample the Azuero's *comida típica*.

Las Tablas *p176*
Dining options aren't extensive. You'll find cheap and cheerful bakeries scattered around town, along with some economical locals' eateries concentrated near the market on Av Belisarrio Porras.

$$-$ El Caserón, A good clean place, the best in town. They serve chicken, meat, pork and seafood, including lobster. Indoor and outdoor seating and attentive service. Not bad.

$ Los Portales, Av Belisarrio Porras. A great old colonial building with indoor and outdoor seating. They serve economical home-cooked fare and *comida típica*. Rustic ambience.

Pedasí *p178, map p179*
$$ El Patio, 2 blocks east and 1½ blocks south of the Plaza Central. An intimate and friendly restaurant serving excellent Spanish-flavoured cuisine, including fresh fish fillet, shrimp, paella, steaks and other tasty, well-seasoned fare. Good wine and sangría. Recommended.

$$ La Granja, Vía El Arenal, inside the Pedasí Sports Club. Locals rave about La Granja and its tasty seafood offerings, its generous portions and its scintillating home-made desserts. Open for breakfast and dinner. Recommended.

$$ Restaurante Isla Iguana, Calle Principal, southern exit of town. A large restaurant with some seating outside by the road. They serve great seafood, including very tasty fish fillets. Friendly service. Recommended.

$$-$ Chili Reef, 2 blocks north of the Plaza Central. Rancho-style eatery serving predominantly Mexican grub, including tacos, enchiladas and burritos, but some Panamanian classics too.

$$-$ Pasta e Vino, 4 blocks east of the Plaza Central, T6695-2689. Tue-Sun, dinner only. Simple, authentic Italian food served in the home of the owners, Danilo and Elena. A changing menu includes a selection of pasta, salads and wines. Good service and desserts. Paella is available, but give advance notice earlier in the day. Only a few tables, make advance reservations. Good reports.

$$-$ Smiley's, Calle Principal, northern entrance to town. American comfort food including burgers, chicken wings and fries. A popular expat hang-out and good for a beer with live music and buzzing atmosphere on Tue and Fri. Friendly and hospitable.

$ Pizzeria Tiesto, Plaza Central, closed Tue. A cheerful, unpretentious eatery serving tasty wood-fired pizzas, sandwiches and other wholesome snack food. Economical and popular.

$ Restaurante Ejecutivo, Plaza Central. Extremely unpretentious locals' haunt serving very cheap high-carb buffet food and *comida típica*. A bit charmless, but suitable for thrifty travellers.

Cafés and bakeries
The Bakery, Calle Principal. A good stop for fresh baked bread and sweet treats. They also do popular (if pricey) breakfasts and snack food at lunch-time. Some outdoor seating.

Dulcería Yely, Calle Ofelia Reluz, just off Calle Principal. A Pedasí institution that's been visited by politicians and dignitaries from afar. A good place for sweet cakes and coffee. Breakfast served.

Maudy's, Calle Principal. A very cute little café with some outdoor seats and a good notice board. They serve the best smoothies on the Azuero. Wi-Fi enabled. Recommended.

⊕ Bars and clubs

Chitré *p168, map p169*
If you're up for a good drink, you'll find several rough-and-ready cantinas and

The pollera: Panama's national dress

Panama's national dress, the *pollera*, is an intricate ensemble consisting of elaborate blouses, flowing skirts and precious ornaments. Produced mainly in the province of Los Santos, it is widely regarded as one of the most beautiful national costumes in the world. Shapes and styles of *pollera* vary between villages, but the blouse is usually worn off the shoulders with two lace-trimmed ruffles and a wealth of embroidered floral patterns. The lower part normally consists of an ornate petticoat and a sweeping ruffled skirt trimmed with lace and adorned with colourful streamers. The hair ornaments, or *tembleques*, are equally flamboyant and comprise dazzling pearl-encrusted combs and gold hair pins. A wealth of gold chains, bracelets and earrings complement the outfit. The exact origin of the *pollera* is unknown, but it is generally believed to have evolved from the simple Spanish house dress of the 16th and 17th centuries. The heavy velvet court dresses of the Spanish

aristocracy would not have fared well in the heat and humidity of the tropics, but the simple cotton skirts of the servant class would. Appropriated by the Spanish colonists, these dresses acquired lavish new details as they were adapted to reflect their wealth and status. Today, the *pollera* is a source of great Panamanian pride, but generally reserved for special occasions such as weddings, national events or festivals. Most women own at least two *polleras* – one for childhood and one for adulthood – along with special items passed down between generations, particularly jewellery. *Polleras* can cost anything from a few hundred to several thousand dollars. At their most extravagant and detailed, they can take over a year to create. *Polleras* are made in villages near Las Tablas, the most beautiful coming from Santo Domingo (5 km east).

If you are interested in purchasing a *pollera*, the ATP has released a useful directory of *artesanías* entitled *Ruta de la Pollera Santeña*.

---

a small casino in Chitré. Particularly recommended is:

The Spider Bar, in the suburb of Monagrillo, main plaza, take a taxi. A grungy leftist bar with lots of personality and giant spiders' web hanging from the ceiling. Totally unexpected and a great spot for a several thirst-quenching beers.

☸ Festivals

Chitré *p168, map p169*
Feb/Mar Chitré's raucous carnival celebrations are second only to Las Tablas. Expect non-stop party action and bring a spare liver. See also box, page 177.
24 Jun Chitré's patron saint is honoured in the Fiesta de San Juan Bautista. Also in the preceding week.

19 Oct The foundation of Chitré (1848) is celebrated with colourful performances and historically themed parades.

Parita *p171*
3-7 Aug Parita's patron saint, Santo Domingo, has a lengthy and well-attended festival with lots of bullfighting, dancing and merry-making.
18 Aug Colourful processions commemorate Parita's founding in 1558.

Pesé *p172*
Mar/Apr Pesé sees a dramatic re-enactment of Christ's Passion and Crucifixion during annual **Semana Santa** celebrations.

Ocú *p173*

18-23 Jan San Sebastían, the district's patron saint, is celebrated in Ocú with costumed folklore groups and the ritual burning of his effigy.

Aug Festival del Manito is a 3-day festival straight from medieval Spain and well worth attending. Dramatic performances include the Duelo del Tamarindo and the Penitente de la Otra Vida.

Villa de los Santos *p173*

End Apr The Feria de Azuero takes place in its own grounds just outside Villa de los Santos. It is an important and well-attended event that showcases the region's agriculture, culture, crafts and gastronomy.

May/Jun Corpus Christi (40 days after Easter) is a 4-day Catholic feast celebrated with astonishing vigour in Los Santos. Lots of firecrackers, processions, theatrical performances and dance contèsts, especially from the grotesque *diablos sucios* (dirty devils). Very popular and a glorious distillation of the peninsula's Spanish roots. See box, page 174.

10 Nov Hearty celebrations commemorate Los Santos's Grito de Independencia.

Guararé *p175*

23-28 Sep The Feria de la Mejorana is an important folk music festival that attracts great crowds to Guararé. A *mejorana* is a stringed instrument, much like a guitar.

Las Tablas *p176*

Feb/Mar Commencing the Sat before Ash Wed, Carnaval is celebrated all over the Azuero Peninsula with great gusto, but Las Tablas takes the crown. Expect 5 days of spirited celebrations, with lots of dancing, drinking and water fights. Calle Arriba and Calle Abajo famously compete for the best floats and beauty queens (see box, page 177).

19-23 Jul The Fiesta de Santa Librada is a very important patron saint feast that draws thousands of pilgrims from all over the country. It combines religious services and street parties and is now incorporated into the Fiesta de la Pollera, a competitive celebration of Panama's intricately embroidered national dress (see box, page 187).

Pedasí *p178, map p179*

29 Jun Celebrations with folkloric dancing honour the patron saint of Pedasí.

16 Jul Playa El Arenal, near Pedasí, is the site of an annual fishing tournament.

25 Nov More music and dancing in honour of the patron saint.

☉ What to do

Pedasí *p178, map p179*
Diving, snorkelling and fishing
Buzos de Azuero, Vía El Arenal, inside Pedasí Sports Club, T995-2894, www.pedasisports club.biz. Dive and snorkel trips to Isla Iguana and Isla Frailes, as well as PADI certification up to Dive Master. They also offer sports fishing, spear-fishing, kayaking, turtle observation and whale watching. Very experienced.

Kite-surfing
Shokogi, T6701-5476, www.shokogi.com. Playa El Arenal is a popular kitesurfing spot Dec-Apr. If you've never tried it before, Shokogi offer a 4-day training course to get you started, including safety and kite control, as well as equipment rental and second-hand sales for experienced kitesurfers. Contact Gigi.

☉ Transport

Chitré *p168, map p169*
Bus
Chitré is the transport hub of the peninsula. The bus terminal is on Vía Circunvalación on the south side of town; taxi to/from the centre US$2. Most buses run from sunrise to sunset. For **Las Arenas** and **Playa Aguallito**, use city buses.

To **Las Tablas**, every 15 mins, 1 hr, US$1.50; to **Parita**, every 30 mins, 15 mins,

US$1; to **Pesé**, every 20 mins, 20 mins, US$1.20; to **Pedasí**, go to Las Tablas and change; to **Ocú**, 0430-1900, every 30 mins, US$3; to **Panama City** (250 km), every 1-2 hrs or when full, 0600-2300, 4 hrs, US$9.05; to **Santiago**, every 30 mins, 1½ hrs, US$3; to **Villa de Los Santos**, every 15 mins, take a Las Tablas bus, 10 mins, US$0.35.

Car hire
The Azuero is perfect for driving, but you may need a 4WD to reach its most remote stretches. There are few rental agencies in town, try: **Hertz**, T996-2256, www.rentacar panama.com; **Thrifty Car Rental**, T996-9565, www.thrifty.com.

Ocú *p173*
Car
Ocú can be reached directly from the Interamericana (19 km) by a paved turn-off south just past the Río Conaca bridge (11 km west of Divisa); *colectivos* run from here for US$1.20. Alternatively, a mostly gravel road runs west from Parita along the Río Parita valley, giving good views of the fertile landscapes of the northern peninsula.

Las Tablas *p176*
Bus
Buses to **Panama City** depart from their own bus station on Av 8 de Noviembre and Calle Emilio Castro, hourly, 0600-1630, 5 hrs, US$9.70. To **Chitré** (including **Guararé** and other destinations north on the highway) wait for passing services on Av 8 de Noviembre, 0600-1900, every 10-20 mins, 45 mins, US$1.50. Buses to **Pedasí** depart from the market on Av Belisarrio Porras, 0600-1900, every 45 mins, 1 hr, US$2.40.

Pedasí *p178, map p179*
Boat
Boats to **Isla Iguana** depart from Playa El Arena, around US$60-70 return; prices negotiable. Always pay upon return.

Bus
Buses to **Las Tablas** depart from Calle Principal outside The Bakery, 0600-1615, every 45 mins, 1 hr, US$2.40. For **Playa Los Destiladeros**, **Achitones Laboratory** and **Playa Venado** and around, take a bus bound for Las Cañas, 0700, 1200, 1500 (Las Tablas service), 45 mins, US$2.40, and inform the driver of your intended destination. Buses return from **Las Cañas to Pedasí** at 0700 (Las Tablas service), 0900, 1500. If travelling in a group, it may be better to share the cost of a taxi (see below).

For **Reserva de Vida Silvestre Isla Caña** and **Tonosí**, you must take the 0700 bus to Las Cañas and catch a connecting service towards Tonosí, hourly, 1 hr, US$2 – the last one leaves Las Cañas at 1200 (the last returns to Las Cañas at 1400).

Taxi
Due to irregular bus timetables, taxis are often the easiest way to get to and from the beaches. To **Playa Los Destiladeros**, US$10; to **Playa Venado**, US$20; to **Reserva de Vida Silvestre Isla Caña**, US$30; to **Tonosí/ Playa Cambutal**, US$40.

❶ Directory

Chitré *p168, map p169*
Hospitals Hospital Cecilio Castillero, Camelo Spadafora, several blocks south of the plaza. **Laundry** Lavandería Azuero, Carmelo Spadafora, Mon-Sat 0700-1800, drop-off service, around US$3 medium load.

Pedasí *p178, map p179*
Language schools Buena Vida, T6886-1022, www.pedasispanishschool. com. Individual instruction from US$12-15 per class; or group lessons, US$230 per week. All teachers have university degrees in education. **Volunteering** Proyecto Ecológico Azuero, www.proecoazuero.org.

Veraguas

Veraguas is one of the least populated, least developed and least visited provinces in Panama, and the only one to touch both Caribbean and Pacific shores. Its coastline is staggering and blissfully remote, the preserve of intrepid wave-seekers who congregate at the fabled surf haunt of Santa Catalina. Offshore, adventurous divers head to the pristine waters of Isla Coiba, where a scintillating underwater world plays host to really big marine species like hammerhead sharks, sailfish, bottlenose dolphins and humpback whales. Inland, hikers head to the lofty peaks of Santa Fe, rich in cloud forests, colourful birdlife, remote communities and delicate orchids. Veraguas boasts truly world-class adventure potential, but it remains largely ignored by the mainstream. ▸▸ *For listings, see pages 199-202.*

Santiago and around → *For listings, see pages 199-202. Colour map 1, B4.*

Santiago, the provincial capital of Veraguas, was founded in 1632 by migrant families from Santa Fe and Montijo. It is home to approximately 75,000 inhabitants and boasts a thriving economy grounded in agriculture, livestock and banking. Although rapidly modernizing, it is a hot, grungy and terminally humdrum place with little to offer the casual explorer. Located halfway between Panama City and David, it serves as a major transport hub and pit-stop for motorists and long-distance buses, which often pause for fuel, food and refreshments on the Interamericana highway. Unless you have business to conduct in the centre, your experience of Santiago is likely to be transitory and forgettable. For those who take the time, there are a handful of mildly diverting attractions in and around town.

Arriving in Santiago
Public transport to Santiago is frequent. International and long-distance **buses** travelling between Panama City and David/Costa Rica stop next to the Hotel Piramidal on the Interamericana or, less frequently, at Los Tucanes restaurant, 750 m further north. Direct and local buses with a final destination of Santiago arrive in the regional bus station on Calle 10a Norte (also known as Polidoro Pinzón). The downtown and commercial areas are compact and can be easily explored on foot. However, if you're lodging on the Interamericana, it's a 2- to 3-km walk to the centre of town. Taxis are ubiquitous and fares rarely exceed US$2. For tourist information, Santiago has a regional **ATP**, on Avenida Central, with limited help and flyers. If you're planning to visit **Isla Coiba** independently, don't forget to consult the environment agency, **ANAM**, Carretera Interamericana, who will supply the necessary permission and advice.

Plaza San Juan de Dios
Located at the west end of Avenida Central, the well-tended and tranquil Plaza San Juan de Dios is the historic heart of the city. Punctuated by tidy paths, trees and flowering archways, it's a relaxing place to sit, read or otherwise take a breather. The city cathedral – properly known as the **Catedral Santiago Apóstol** – Is on south side of the plaza. It is a fairly unremarkable white and mustard-coloured structure, mostly dating from the 1930s.

Museo Regional de Veraguas

ⓘ *Plaza San Juan de Dios, Mon-Sat 0900-1600, free.*

Situated on the north side of the plaza, the Museo Regional de Veraguas contains a small and mildly diverting collection of historical artefacts – good for killing time but strictly non-essential viewing. Exhibits explore the development of the region from its ancient geological formation through to the colonial era and early republic. There is a particular emphasis on pre-Columbian history and indigenous cultures, with various archaeological artefacts and examples of ceramics from different developmental phases. The museum itself is housed in an attractive colonial building that once served as an old prison – Belisario Porras found himself interred there during Panama's struggle for Independence from Colombia.

Escuela Normal Superior Juan Demónstrenes Arosemena

ⓘ *Calle 6 y Calle 7, not open to the public, but politely ask security and they should allow you inside.*

Opened in 1938 as a model education institution and national teaching college, Santiago's Escuela Normal is one of the most aesthetic buildings in all Panama. Engineered by Louis Caselli, its baroque-style exterior features an ornate façade of sculpted vines, pillars, saints and sensual female figurines. The main hallway boasts twin staircases, yet more elaborate frontage and an interesting clock set into sculpted stone. Ask the security guard to open the assembly hall, where stunning murals depict the evolution of civilization through discoveries in art, technology and trade. The Escuela Normal was declared a national historic landmark in 1984.

Iglesia San Francisco de Asís de la Montaña

The small agricultural community of **San Francisco**, founded in 1621 by Fray Pedro Rodríguez and Valderas of the Santo Domingo order, lies 16 km north of Santiago. It is well known for its ancient church, the Iglesia San Francisco de Asís de la Montaña, which steadily draws pilgrims from afar. Completed in 1727, the church features striking frescoes and several altars which blend indigenous and Catholic motifs. It was declared a national monument in 1937 and remains one of the best places in the continent to see very early colonial and baroque artwork. Just behind the church, a path leads a few hundred metres away to the **Chorro del Espíritu Santo**, the Holy Ghost Waterfall, a popular and refreshing swimming hole. To get to San Francisco, take a bus from Santiago's regional bus station, every 15 minutes, 20 minutes, US$0.65.

Atalaya

A few kilometres east of Santiago lies the diminutive village of Atalaya. It's best known for its church of **Jesús Nazareno de la Atalaya**, which is the focus of fervent and well-attended Lent celebrations. Each year, thousands of pilgrims descend on the village to participate in the event or otherwise pay homage to the image of the Nazarene. Outside of religious festivities, Atalaya is a calm, quiet, tidy place that sees few visitors or drama. The church, situated on the village plaza, is a simple structure with an interesting bell tower positioned directly over the entrance.

Santa Fe → *For listings, see pages 199-202.* → *Colour map 1, B4.*

Nestled in the shadow of the continental divide, the obscure highland town of Santa Fe enjoys striking mountain vistas and a refreshing spring-like climate. Founded by

The tragic tale of Father Héctor Gallego

Few places in Panama were as wretched and downtrodden as the highlands of Veraguas in the mid-20th century. Once a bastion of great colonial power, the region had long since descended into feudal obscurity, where very ancient and unpleasant ideas of privilege persisted in spite of the modern world outside. In the rugged hills and mountains of Santa Fe, an oligarchy of wealthy landowners maintained sway over some 10,000 impoverished *campesinos*, who lived in scattered hamlets with no access to schools, roads, markets or hospitals. They endured the country's lowest rate of per capita income and the highest rates of illiteracy. Any produce they managed to reap from the tired mountainous soil was sold at cut prices to the stores in town, who in turn hawked dried grains and other sundries back to them at inflated rates. Many were forced into a lifetime of debt servitude and, since the oligarchy controlled the local police and judiciary, anyone who didn't pay up or play by the game found himself in jail.

Unsurprisingly, Veraguas was a hotbed of socialist activity and the church was only too keen to encourage it. In 1967, the town of Santa Fe received its first priest, a 30-year-old Colombian named Héctor Gallego. He was a humble man, extraordinarily charitable and given to great self-denial. Dwelling in a simple shack, he expended enormous energy reaching out to his far-flung parish, organizing them into Bible study groups and, later, co-operatives. He expounded the virtues of Liberation Theology, which stressed the overthrow of unjust economic relations along with the guiding Christian values of love, brotherhood and community. Soon his parishioners boasted their own co-op store where their produce could be sold directly to the public at fair and reasonable rates. The townsfolk were displeased and rewarded the priest's efforts by stealing building materials for the village church and, on the town's patron saint's day, drunkenly beating him up.

Worse was to come. Gallego found his most deadly enemy in Alvaro Vernaza, a cousin of the Maximum Leader, Omar Torrijos, and the owner of the largest store in town. He had Gallego arrested on trumped-up charges and attacked him with a metal cable when the Bishop of Veraguas intervened to have him released. Relations escalated in May 1971 when *campesinos* in the hamlet of Cerro dared to defend a local woman, Juana González, who was under threat of having her house demolished. The townsfolk blamed Gallego for their insolence and burned down his shack on 22 May. When the priest wrote directly to Omar Torrijos, he was mysteriously spirited away by Guardia troops on 9 June. The rumour is that Manuel Noriega, under direct orders from Torrijos, murdered the priest by dropping him from a helicopter into the ocean. Today, Santa Fe is much transformed and Gallego is feted as a local hero. No doubt his tireless followers took his words to heart: "If I disappear, do not look for me. Keep fighting."

Francisco Vásquez in 1557, the settlement first flourished as a gold-mining camp. Today it is better known for agriculture, especially coffee, but it is also earning a reputation as an 'undiscovered' outdoors destination. Filled with rugged peaks, rolling valleys, pine trees, cloud forests and innumerable waterfalls, the surrounding landscapes make for superb walking country. The truly adventurous (and physically fit) can even cross the continental divide all the way to the Caribbean coast. Panama's principal birdwatching association, the Audubon Society, has known about Santa Fe for years and regularly organizes trips to observe the region's 400 bird species. Horticulturalists, too, flock to the town in an annual orchid festival. Now it seems Santa Fe is poised to enter the mainstream. Foreign developers are buying up large tracts of the countryside and, much to the concern of the locals, are marketing Santa Fe as 'the next Boquete'.

Arriving in Santa Fe
ⓘ *Santa Fe lies 52 km north of Santiago. The road is paved and in good repair with buses departing the main bus station every 30 mins, 1½ hrs, US$2.90. Buses arrive at a small terminal on the north side of town.*

Santa Fe is a very small place that can be easily covered on foot. Nonetheless, a lack of straight, flat roads mean it can be strangely disorientating. Keep a map handy until you are familiar with the layout. According to locals, Santa Fe's privately operated **tourist information centre** has been closed for some time, leaving hotels, hostels and tour operators as your best source of local information. There is a small **ANAM station** ⓘ *on the road to Alto de Piedra, Mon-Fri 0800-1600*, which supplies details on the Santa Fe National Park. There is no bank or ATM in Santa Fe.

Orchid gardens
Berta de Castrellón ⓘ *T954-0910*, is the most experienced and creative horticulturalist in Santa Fe. She keeps a collection of over 250 orchids in her garden, all quite stunning and unique to the surrounding highlands. October to November are the best months for seeing them in bloom. Berta also paints flowers, birds and butterflies and is happy to sell her artwork. A few doors down, **Anayansi Vernaza** ⓘ *T6129-2991*, maintains a smaller but equally lively orchid collection. She also creates attractive jewellery from wild seeds and sells them in a gift shop adjoining her house. Occasional workshops are available if you would like to try your hand at making them. If you're in the market for *artesanías*, check the **Mercado** in the centre of town – it contains Ngäbe crafts, *sombreros pintados* and other locally produced work.

Café El Tute
The working coffee-processing plant of Café El Tute is managed by the **Co-operativa La Esperanza de los Campesinos**, a famous collective established in 1969 by the good Father Héctor Gallego (see box, page 192). Both the co-op and the plant remain powerful economic forces in town, although their coffee is sold for domestic consumption only. Tours of the aromatic roasting facilities are in Spanish, just turn up and enquire, US$5 per person. If you would like to combine your visit with a tour of a *finca*, contact the **Fundación Héctor Gallego** ⓘ *near Hostal La Qhia, T954-0737*. **Café El Tute** coffee is 100% organic and quite delicious – bags are available in the market if you would like to take some away.

Around Santa Fe → *For listings, see pages 199-202.*

Quebrada Bulavá
On a hot day, there's no better way to cool off than visiting the swimming hole of Quebrada Bulavá. If you're feeling lazy, you can hire an innertube and drift through the creek, which eventually merges with the **Río Santa María**. A local entrepreneur, **William Abrego**, rents them for US$5 including a life jacket. He can also arrange a taxi to pick you up downstream.

Quebrada Bulavá is located about 20 minutes out of town. To get there, cross over the bridge on the east side of the village, then take the second dirt road on the right. On the other side of the bridge, you'll see a sign for 'William's Inner Tubes'.

El Bermejo

El Bermejo is the highest and most spectacular of the region's many waterfalls. It is a great place to spend the day, very refreshing and otherwise impressive. To get there, cross over the Río Bulavá and continue past William's Inner Tubes. When the road divides, turn left and begin climbing uphill, following the signs for 'Cascada de Bermejo'. When you arrive at the trailhead, look out for the yellow arrows and be prepared to cross several streams. Stick to the left whenever the trail divides. Note that accidents have occurred at the falls so it is recommended you visit with at least one other person. Beware slippery rocks and strong currents and seek local advice before setting out in the wet season.

El Salto

Several kilometres south of Santa Fe, El Salto consists of three enchanting side-by-side waterfalls. There are lots of petroglyphs in the area and the local *campesino* community is famed for its organic gardens. To get there, take a bus towards Santiago and exit at the bridge over the Río Santa María. Take the road towards El Carmen/El Alto for around 1 km until you see El Salto signed on the right. After another kilometre, the road forks – take the right path. The road will continue climbing for around 5 km and you'll cross several streams. Look out for the waterfalls on your left, or descend to the village, where **Egberto Soto** will be happy to take you on a tour of the community. This hike should not be attempted unguided in the wet season when streams are deeper and more powerful.

Alto de Piedra

It's easy to spot hawks and other birds of prey hunting over the pastures around the hamlet of Alto de Piedra, around 7 km from Santa Fe. The area is famous for its three waterfalls, each higher and more magnificent than the last. To get to there on foot, take the road heading west from the mobile phone tower. It winds uphill for several kilometres offering pleasant views of the valley before arriving at an *agroforestal* school, where it deteriorates into a dirt track. To reach the waterfalls, follow the track for a few hundred metres past the **Centro Turístico Alto de Piedra** until you see the trailhead marked with a sign on the left-hand side. Each waterfall can be visited in succession (backtrack slightly after the first one), but you will need to ascend some steep and muddy paths; a guide is strongly recommended. Please take extreme care on the rocks, which are very slippery. After the final waterfall, you can return to Santa Fe on a different route. Backtrack on the dirt road and take the right-hand path when you pass the pond. Walk through the forest for 1 km until you meet the main road back to Santa Fe. Note that trails may be washed out or dangerous in the wet season; always seek local advice before setting out.

Parque Nacional Santa Fe → *Colour map 1, B5.*

Encompassing 72,636 ha of mountains and cloud forests, the Parque Nacional Santa Fe is an extensive and somewhat remote protected area adjoining the Parque Nacional Omar Torrijos to the east (see page 159). It is home to some particularly rare (if infrequently sighted) animal species, including tapirs, jaguars and pumas, with magnificent harpy eagles among the park's 300 bird species. The park has next to no infrastructure and you will certainly need an experienced guide to navigate its inscrutable trails and rugged expanses. Truly hard-core adventurers can attempt a hike over the continental divide to **Calovébora** on the Caribbean coast. It is also possible to drive, but the road is extremely rough and you will require a 4WD with high clearance and a winch, a spare tyre or two and excellent off-road skills and experience – please seek local advice before attempting this. Casual birdwatchers may want to try some less ambitious destinations outside the park's boundaries, such as the popular walking trails of **Cerro Tute**.

The Gulf of Montijo and around → *For listings, see pages 199-202. Colour map 1, C4.*

Embracing the convoluted coastline between the Las Palmas and Azuero peninsulas, the Gulf of Montijo is an ecologically rich area that includes steamy marshes, mangroves, estuaries and Ramsar-listed wetlands. Once upon a time, the region enjoyed considerable prosperity thanks to its ports, its bustling commercial centres and a highway that connected it with the rest of the country. Today, the modern Interamericana completely bypasses the area and has left many of its towns dwindling in obscurity. Their fortunes may be set to change, however, as mainstream developers rally the vast tourist potential of the gulf, its waters and its adjoining peninsulas, which include several pristine islands and a succession of arresting beaches. Thankfully, it will take several years for them to fully capitalize on the region, and for now it remains reasonably remote and blissfully unspoilt.

The old Panamerican Highway

The old highway, although quite dishevelled in parts, offers the opportunity to get off the beaten track and experience Panama's evocative back-country. Its string of obscure old towns, verdant pastures, weathered farmhouses and iron bridges are faintly reminiscent of the Old West. The highway is great for cycling or driving, but you should start early and come prepared. A 4WD is highly recommended, along with a spare tyre (or puncture repair kit, if cycling), a road map and plenty of water. You can access the old highway a few kilometres west of Santiago. It dips south within several kilometres of the gulf, then rambles west to Chiriquí province, where it finally emerges on the Interamericana at **Guabalá**. If you need to exit before then, look for a northbound road near El María, which passes the town of **Las Palmas**, well known for its beautiful waterfalls (ask directions).

Soná → *Colour map 1, C4.*

The town of Soná, probably named after a local indigenous chief, is located roughly halfway along the old Panamerican Highway. It is surrounded by rivers and once served as an important trade centre. Today it's better known for its cantinas and its attractive wooden houses – some of them are quite old and look as if they've been lifted straight from the set of a Western. If you're heading towards Santa Catalina (see below), you will need to change buses or turn south in Soná. It is also your last stop for all kinds of amenities, including gasoline, so stock up if you need to.

Santa Catalina → *For listings, see pages 199-202. Colour map 1, C4.*

'Discovered' in the 1970s by intrepid vagabond surfers, the obscure fishing village of Santa Catalina was a closely guarded secret for over three decades. Blessed with indolent beaches and enormous Hawaiian-style waves, it was only a matter of time before word got out: Santa Catalina is hot. Today, many are predicting the village's imminent emergence as a major surfing mecca and recent developments tend to support that. Rising land values, a string of construction projects, the entry of upscale surf lodges and an established international tournament all point to the village's growing prestige. Santa Catalina has also become the favoured departure point for trips to Isla Coiba, drawing divers and wildlife enthusiasts, along with sports fishers, who arrive in search of snapper, grouper, marlin, sailfish and other valued game. It's only a matter of time before everything changes – hold on tight Santa Catalina.

Arriving in Santa Catalina

To get to Santa Catalina from Santiago, first take a bus to Soná, every 30 minutes (one hour) US$1.10, then take a connecting bus, 0700, 1200, 1600, two hours, US$4.25. If driving, look for signs and a turn-off near the Shell station in Soná. Once you arrive, Santa Catalina is very small and easy to get around on foot. For tourist information, consult your local hotel, or go online – the best source is www.santacatalinabeach.com. There is no ATM in Santa Catalina.

Beaches and breaks

Although Santa Catalina has a small place for beginners, it is generally the preserve of moderately advanced and more experienced surfers. If you are still learning, head to **Playa El Estero** at the end of a dirt road on the edge of town – the waves are easy and break left and right over the sand. Confident surfers congregate at the town's other beach, **Playa Santa Catalina**, where you'll find strong, consistent left and right hollows breaking over volcanic rocks. The waves are best surfed at high and medium tide, although those with lots of local experience also surf when the tide is low. As the closest beach to town and the departure point for numerous offshore expeditions, it is sometimes busy. If you're prepared to travel, there are plenty of quieter and equally awesome local breaks. **Punta Brava**, about half an hour southwest of Santa Catalina, has two left breaks and one right – the main break is a left over a rocky bottom. About 45 minutes northeast, or 10 minutes by boat, **Punta Roca** offers similar waves to Santa Catalina with a hollow left break over rocks. **San Pedrillo**, 20 minutes from Santa Catalina by boat, has powerful left and rights. There are numerous other sites, some of them secret, that local hotels and operators (see page 199) will be happy to guide you to – just ask. Note the waves in Santa Catalina are highest between February and August, when they can reach a staggering 9 m.

Parque Nacional Isla Coiba → For listings, see pages 199-202. Colour map 1, C3.

Isla Coiba is the largest and most resplendent of Panama's islands. It is almost entirely covered in virgin rainforests and so biologically diverse it is often compared to the Galápagos of Ecuador. Once described by the Smithsonian Tropical Research Institute as "an unparalleled destination for discovering new species", the island shelters some 20 endemic bird species and numerous mammals, including the Coiba agouti, howler monkey, possum and white-tailed deer. But it is offshore, where warm ocean currents and stunning geological formations converge, that Coiba becomes truly extraordinary. Among the marine species that frequent Coiba's waters are 23 species of whale and dolphin – bottle-nose dolphins, hump-back, killer and sperm whales among them – and prolific sharks – including white-tip and black-tip, bull, tiger, whale and reef sharks, and truly awesome pods of hammerheads. Add four types of turtle, untold manta rays, vast schools of snapper, jacks and barracuda – not to mention the second largest coral reef in the Eastern Pacific Ocean – and you'll understand why Coiba has earned its reputation as an underwater wonderland. The island owes much of its pristine state to its former role as a penal colony, which kept settlers out as much as prisoners in. Official protection of the island's natural heritage was realized in 1991 with the creation of the Parque Nacional Coiba. In 2004, the park boundaries were extended to cover 503 sq km and numerous small islands that comprise its archipelago. In 2005, UNESCO granted the park World Heritage status. Sadly, there is shameful on-going talk of building a resort on the island.

Arriving at Parque Nacional Isla Coiba

Isla Coiba lies 20 km offshore and is most frequently accessed from Santa Catalina and Puerto Mutis (see below). You can travel to the island independently, but there have been reports of visitors being denied access by ANAM – a professional tour operator is highly advised. If you do decide to go it alone, be sure to visit ANAM offices in Santiago to pay park fees and acquire the appropriate paperwork. They may be able to give you a ride (you will still be required to pay substantial costs), but otherwise expect to pay US\$150-250 for the round trip. Be sensible and thorough when selecting a boat and captain, and be aware the sea can be rough. Simple lodging is available on the island; bring insect repellent and a sheet sleeper, and your own food for cooking. Camping is possible. A good source of online information is www.coibapanama.com.

Visiting Parque Nacional Isla Coiba

The northeast shores of Isla Coiba are home to an **ANAM station** and the old penal colony prison cells. During the years of Guardia dictatorship, numerous political prisoners were interred on Coiba and many of them ended up as shark fodder. Towards the end of the prison's 92-year life, Coiba was exclusively used to incarcerate the country's most violent and dangerous offenders. It closed completely in 2004 and has since been crumbling into ruin. Nearby, you'll find fine white-sand beaches and access to several other islands, including **Ranchería** and **Canales**. From the ANAM station, several hiking trails wind through the forests and offer rewarding opportunities for viewing animals and birdlife, including crested eagles and numerous red macaws. The **Sendero Observatorio** is a 500-m trail which ascends a hill for views of neighbouring Isla Coibita and concludes at a birdwatching platform. **Sendero Los Monos** is accessible only by boat. It provides access to several beaches and, as the name suggests, views of monkeys. Other trails include **Sendero Los Pozos**, which concludes at a thermal bath, and the two-hour **Sendero de Santa Cruz**. An alternative way to spot wildlife is to kayak among the mangroves and jungle-shrouded rivers, where dazzling poison dart frogs, giant boa constrictors and crocodiles are reported to lurk. In the water, Coiba's famous coral reef, **Bahía Damas**, covers an area of 135 ha off the eastern shore; the diving and snorkelling are first class. The great ocean canyons, which are so often frequented by large sea mammals and pelagic species, lie off the untouched southern coast, where you'll also find pristine sandy beaches and giant waves to please any surfer. Sports fishers will not be disappointed by Coiba. The giant underwater cliffs of **Hannibal Bank**, which mark the edge between ocean environments, are reportedly home to giant marlin. Don't forget to acquire a catch-and-release permit from ANAM for fishing within the park boundaries, US\$50, valid for one week.

Puerto Mutis and around → *For listings, see pages 199-202. Colour map 1, C4.*

Located 18 km south of Santiago, Puerto Mutis is a sleepy port and fishing town perched on the banks of the Río San Pedro. It is a warm and languid place, surrounded by teeming mangroves and diminutive farming communities. There's little to do in town, but it is home to a few simple restaurants where you can sample wonderfully fresh local sea food prepared in home-cooked style. The dock is an interesting place to watch the comings and goings of local life. Many tour operators depart for Isla Coiba from Puerto Mutis as it's easier to reach than the more popular gateway of Santa Catalina. The boat trip is at least one hour longer, however. For organizing transport to Isla Coiba, contact **Rómulo Pineda** (T6471-9173, romulopromero@hotmail.com) well in advance of your trip.

El Pilón

Situated a few kilometres north of Puerto Mutis, the friendly rural hamlet of El Pilón is home to around 200 households. Rice, yucca, corn, cattle and chicken are the staples of the local economy, which is now supplemented by a promising ecotourism project. **Grupo Avicennia** offers guided tours of the protected mangroves, home to a stunning 70 species of migratory and non-migratory avifauna, numerous molluscs, crabs, amphibians and monkeys. The tour costs just US$10 and includes a spin around the mangroves in a boat where, if you're very lucky, you might glimpse caiman, boas, turtles and other marine life. For an extra US$2.50 you can enjoy a tasty natural lunch in an open-air palapa. Birdwatchers should ask for local expert **Alonso Herrera** or **Rómulo Pineda** (see above), who will take you to the prime sites, US$8 for half a day. For a taste of country life, head to **Rancho Nueva York**, which offers fantastic farm tours and, soon, restful accommodation in new *cabañas*.

Western Azuero Peninsula → *For listings, see pages 199-202. Colour map 1, C5.*

Southeast of Santiago, a highway branches into the Azuero Peninsula. Separated from the rest of the peninsula by a chain of mountains, this narrow sliver of land technically belongs to Veraguas province and is distinct from its neighbours, Herrera and Los Santos. The highway, infrequently travelled by outsiders, skirts the Azuero's western shore, winding through rolling cattle pastures and a string of rural towns and villages, including **Malena** ① *www.playamalena.org*, where you'll find an excellent ecotourism and turtle conservation project. They offer a range of tours in the surrounding countryside and welcome volunteers. Nearby, **Palmilla** is home to refreshing waterfalls and the ecotourism operator **Tanager Tourism** (see page 202), who specialize in trips to Parque Nacional Cerro Hoya (see below).

Parque Nacional Cerro Hoya → *Colour map 1, C5.*
① *The road ends at Restigue, a village just south of Arenas, from where you must walk. You will need a 4WD to get there. Alternatively, you can enter the park via the coastal village of Cambutal, boat hire US$70. For a reputable guide, speak to Tanager Tourism (see page 202).*
A bastion of rugged natural beauty in an otherwise heavily deforested and intensively farmed peninsula, the Parque Nacional Cerro Hoya protects 326 sq km of diverse and challenging terrain, including the highest peak in the Azuero, **Cerro Hoya** (1559 m). Elsewhere, you'll find mangrove swamps, coastal cliffs, offshore reefs, islands and uplands. Cerro Hoya is home to lower montane wet forests, pre-montane forests and tropical rainforests, and is the largest forested area on the Pacific. Much of the vegetation, however, is secondary growth. Prior to the park's establishment in 1984, the area suffered significant damage through logging, deforestation and other human activities. Today, it appears to be recovering well. Some 30 endemic plant species have been recorded inside the park, along with 95 bird species – ospreys, hawks and scarlet macaws among them. Cerro Hoya is reasonably remote and there is poor infrastructure in the area. Hiking is tough and a guide is absolutely necessary. If you plan to stay overnight, bring food, tents and plenty of insect repellent.

For sleeping and eating price codes and other relevant information, see pages 16-19.

🛏 Where to stay

Santiago *p190*

$$ Gran David, Carretera Interamericana, T998-4510. A reliable highway lodging close to the centre of town, but not as economical as it once was. Rooms are clean and comfortable with private bath, a/c and hot water. There's a reasonable restaurant with good set-price lunches. Wi-Fi in some areas. Recommended.

$$ Piramidal, Carretera Interamericana, T998-3123. A rather cold, grey building, but friendly inside, and conveniently located for the Panama City–David bus, which stops right by it. Rooms have a/c, TV, and shower. There's a good pool. Recommended.

$$-$ Hotel Plaza Gran David, Carretera Interamericana, T998-3433, hotelplaza grandavid_@hotmail.com. This hotel is inconveniently located on the eastern edge of town with very few restaurants nearby. There is an excellent pool, however, and all rooms are fitted with a/c, hot water and cable TV. OK for a night.

$ Santiago, Calle 2, near the cathedral, T998-4824. This old wooden hotel is quite shabby and run-down, but friendly and very cheap. Rooms have a/c and private bath, but no TV or hot water. Rooms with no a/c or fan, if you can stand the warmth, are even cheaper.

Santa Fe *p191*

$$-$ Hostal La Qhía, T954-0903, www. panamamountainhouse.com. A popular international hostel in the style of a handsome highland lodge. They offer dorms (**$**) and private rooms (**$$**) with shared bath, cane walls and little privacy. Rooms with stone walls cost extra and include own bath with attractive tile-work. There is a tidy outdoor kitchen with fridge; breakfast available at extra cost. Good local

information, book exchange and videos. Green grounds and a great palapa with hammocks, perfect for chilling out.

$$-$ Hotel Santa Fe, 500 m south of the entrance to town, T954-0941, www.hotel santafepanama.com. This hospitable motel-style lodging on the outskirts of town boasts superb mountain views and a very good restaurant. Rooms are clean, comfortable and generally good value; one has a/c and hot water. Friendly and helpful management with lots of excellent local information. Relaxed, professional and recommended.

$ Tierra Libre, behind the Iglesia de Santa Fe, T6911-4848, www.santafepanama.info. Friendly, low-key hostel with a clean 6-bed dorm and some very spacious private rooms with own bathroom and hot water. Great food at the restaurant, including breakfast for US$5. Laundry, restaurant, bar and reference books on the region. Clean and quiet.

Santa Catalina *p195*

$$$ Hotel Santa Catalina at Kenny's, road to Playa El Estero, T6781-4847, www.hotel santacatalinapanama.com. A friendly, long-running surf hotel originally established by Kenny Myers, one of Catalina's early pilgrims and a local legend. It boasts a low-impact design and a handful of clean, comfortable rooms, all equipped with hot water, a/c, fan, mini-fridge, terrace and hammock. Good location by the beach. Recommended.

$$$ On the Reef, road to Playa El Estero, T6491-7057, www.onthereefpanama.com. As the name suggests, right on the reef, with unrivalled sea views and access to the best break in town. They offer 3 stylish oceanfront suites complete with direct TV, Wi-Fi, ocean views and pool. Owner Ricardo Espriella is from a prominent Panamanian family and has lots of interesting stories. Long-established and reputable. "Not a surf camp".

$$$ Sol y Mar, Calle Principal, near the entrance to town, T6920-2631, www.soly marpanama.com. Perched on a hill with superb sea views, laid-back **Sol y Mar** has clean, comfortable cabins, all equipped with a/c, satellite TV, hot water and mini-fridge. Facilities include pool, ping-pong and a good restaurant serving tasty seafood. The owner, Luis, is very helpful and a great host. Lots of good reports, recommended.

$$ Blue Zone, T6981-9679, www.blue zonepanama.com. Self-styled surf and dive hostel with rustic fixtures, adobe walls and earth-coloured tones, all quite attractive and faintly reminiscent of Santa Fe, New Mexico. Rooms are simple and economical, including shared bathroom and kitchen facilities. Sociable and friendly.

$$ Hibiscus Garden, Playa Lagartero, 10 km before Santa Catalina, T6615-6097, www.hibiscusgarden.com. Simple, friendly guesthouse with clean, comfortable rooms, all equipped with a/c, fan, private bath, hot water and private terrace. Located out of town close to a good swimming beach. Tranquil, helpful and very hospitable, good reports.

$$ Rancho Estero, Playa Estero, T6415-6595, www.ranchoestero.com. Situated on a bluff overlooking the beach, Rancho Estero offers simple cane-and-thatch 'Tiki' cabins. Most facilities are shared, including hot-water showers and sun terrace. Great views, with lots of hammocks and chill-out spaces.

$$ Santa Catalina Inn, Centre of town, 5 mins from the beach, T6571-3125, www.santacatalinainn.com. A new hotel, home to **Scuba Coiba Dive** shop and the very good **Chili Rojo** restaurant. They offer comfortable, simple, straightforward rooms with good balconies, a/c, fan and hot water. Good central location and friendly owner. Not bad.

Into the Azuero Peninsula *p198*
$$ Hotel Heliconia B&B, Palmilla, T6676-0220, www.hotelheliconiapanama.com. Offering easy access to stunning attractions such as the Cerro Hoya National Park, Isla Coiba and Isla Cebaco, this excellent new B&B has 4 clean, comfortable guestrooms, all with hot water and fan, 1 with a/c. Owned and operated by 2 Dutch biologists,

Kees Groenedijk and Loes Roos, who also offer a range of nature and community tours (see What to do, page 202). Beautiful lush grounds filled with wildlife and great food in the restaurant. Highly recommended.

Restaurants

Santiago *p190*
$$$-$$ Puerto Perú, Carretera Interamericana, opposite Hotel Piramidal, T998-1264, www.restaurantepuertoperu.com. Closed Mon. One of Santiago's best restaurants. They serve delicious and authentic Peruvian cuisine, including sumptuous shrimp and lobster. A smart setting and pleasant ambience.

$ Los Tucanes, Carretera Interamericana. Large, bustling, buffet place, economical and popular with the locals. They serve reasonable carb-rich *comida típica* and are sometimes full with itinerant bus passengers. There's a bakery next door for a cheap snack. OK.

$ Restaurante Tropicalisimo, Av Central y Calle 17. Cheap and cheerful set meals, including a handful of Cuban specials. OK, filling and economical, but nothing special.

Cafés
Danny's, Av Central, near the junction with the Interamericana. A little roadside café serving fresh coffee, juice, snacks and breakfasts.

Santa Fe *p191*
$ El Terminal, at the bus terminal. Simple grub, locals' fare and carb-rich offerings, including ultra-economical breakfasts and lunch, best washed down with a sugary cup of instant coffee.

$ Hotel Santa Fe, 500 m south of the entrance to town. Tasty and reasonably priced local and international fare made with fresh, locally sourced ingredients. Dishes include chicken, pork, beef and fish specials, and a refreshing wild lemongrass tea. Open for breakfast, lunch and dinner. Recommended.

$ Tierra Libre, behind the church. Tue-Sun lunchtime only. Really excellent chicken sandwiches, falafels, lunchtime snacks, fresh fruit smoothies and other tasty delights, all prepared with love and highly recommended.

Santa Catalina *p195*
$$-$ Los Pibes, towards Playa Estero, 2nd dirt road on the right. Friendly, funky open-air restaurant serving wholesome Argentine fare including tasty grilled steaks, burgers and delicious fresh fish. Recommended.
$ Donde Viancka's, on the road to Playa Estero. Friendly open-air restaurant serving ultra-fresh seafood and catch of the day, including lobster (if in season), shrimps and tasty corvina. Panamanian and locally flavoured.
$ Jammin' Pizza, towards Playa Estero, 1st dirt road on the right. Buzzing little eatery serving tasty stone-baked pizza and ice cold beer. Well established and very popular in the evenings, recommended.
$ Restaurante Vásquez, towards Playa Estero, next to the general store. Cheap *comida típica* and other local grub. Simple, unpretentious and good for a scrambled egg breakfast in the morning.

⊛ Festivals

Santiago and around *p190*
Feb Celebrations dedicated to Jesus of Nazareth, Atalaya. A major religious festival that sees around 50,000 pilgrims arrive in the village.
25 Jul Santiago's patron saint festival, including folk parades, dancing and religious service. Well attended and very festive.
4 Oct Patron saint feast in the village of San Francisco.

Santa Fe *p191*
Aug Santa Fe's **Feria de Orquídeas** sees beautiful presentations of highland orchids and thousands of horticulturists from all the over country.

⊙ What to do

Santa Fe *p191*
Agro-tourism
Chon and María, T6525-4832. Friendly Chon and Maria offer intriguing and personable tours of their organic gardens and farm. Most visitors leave with a smile on their face.

Hiking and birding
Aventuras Cesama, T6792-0571, www.aventurascesamo.blogspot.com. Managed by experienced guide César Miranda, who knows the mountains intimately. He offers a wide range of walking and riding tours to local waterfalls, forests and rural communities, including **Alto de Piedra**, where he maintains a pleasant finca.
Nicolás Alvarado, T6087-0754, nikito 112009@hotmail.com. Good lad, will show you **Alto de Piedra** and other places, but much more of chauffeur than a guide. Car hire US$20-30.

Whitewater rafting
Veraguas Expeditions, T6714-2094, www.veraguas-expeditions.com. The only known tour operator offering whitewater rafting on the Río Santa María, including rapids up to Class IV. They also offer hiking, and horse riding, tours and sailboat charters.

Santa Catalina *p195*
Diving
A 2-tank dive in Coiba National Park costs around US$115; 3-tanks US$140. A snorkel tour costs US$55-65 per person, 4-5 person minimum. Multi-day trips cost upwards of US$500; consult individual operators for schedules. Open-water PADI certification is comparable to other places in Panama; around US$325 including all materials. All prices are exclusive of park entrance fees, US$20-35 depending on length of visit.
Coiba Dive Center, Calle Principal, T6780-1141, www.coibadivecenter.com. Well established and reputable, **Coiba Dive Center** offers 2-tank and 3-tank dives, multi-day

expedities (consult website), snorkelling and certification up to Dive Master. Owned by Canadian Glenn Massingham.

Scuba Coiba, Calle Principal, T6980-7122, www.scubacoiba.com. Managed by Austrian Herbie Sunk, Scuba Coiba is Santa Catalina's 1st dive shop. They offer 2-tank dives to Coiba, snorkelling trips and multi-day expeditions, including an overnight stay on the island. Certification is available from Open Water to Dive Master.

Sea kayaking
Fluid Adventures, Calle Principal, T6560-6558, www.fluidadventurespanama.com. Day trips and multi-day trips to Isla Coiba and beyond. Very well equipped and professional with rental of high-quality single and tandem kayaks and other equipment, including surfboards. Lessons are available.

Into the Azuero Peninsula *p198*
Tanager Tourism, Palmilla, T6676-0220, www.tanagertourism.com. This socially and environmentally aware ecotourism project is operated by 2 knowledgeable Dutch biologists. They offer a diverse range of interesting tours including snorkelling trips to Isla Cebaco and Isla Coiba, hiking in Cerro Hoya National Park, turtle watching on the beach, community tourism, birdwatching and swimming in local waterfalls. Very professional and experienced. Highly recommended.

Ⓣ Transport

Santiago *p190*
Bus
Santiago's bus station is located on Calle 10, 15-30 mins walking from the Interamericana; taxi US$1.50. To **Panama City**, www.playamalena.org, 0600-2300, 3½ hrs, US$9.10; for **David**, buses stop outside the **Hotel Piramidal**, hourly, 3½ hrs, US$9; to **Chitré**, every 30 mins, 0600-1700, 1½ hrs, US$3; to **San Francisco**, every 30 mins, 0700-1600, 1 hr, US$0.90; to **Santa Fe**, every hour, 0700-1600, 30 mins, US$2.90; to **Palmilla**, 10 daily, 0600-1730, 2 hrs, US$4.25; for **Santa Catalina** first go to Soná, every 30 mins, 1 hr, US$1.10, then take a connecting bus, 0700, 1200, 1600, 2 hrs, US$4.25.

Santa Catalina *p195*
Bus
Return service to **Soná** departs at 0700, 0800, 1400, 2 hrs, US$4.25; subject to change, check times locally.

Contents

Border crossings

Chiriquí & the Comarca Ngäbe-Buglé

At a glance

Getting around Buses, trucks, 4WD and horses. Offshore, you will need a motorboat.

Time required 7-14 days.

Weather The dry months are Dec-Apr, great for most outdoor activities. The so-called *bajareque* is a fine mist that often engulfs Boquete in the early afternoon.

When not to go The wet months, May-Nov, are fierce with torrential rain in the mountains, but it's a good time for whitewater rafting. Flooding is common Sep-Nov, when you should avoid hiking.

Chiriquí is a friendly and prosperous province with a distinctive regional identity rooted in trade and agriculture. Historic dealings with the United Fruit Company, foreign coffee barons, cattle ranchers and the oil industry have long brought economic stability to the region, which is today rediscovering itself as a world-class tourist destination. On the Pacific coast, the rambling Gulf of Chiriquí embraces a procession of surf-swept beaches and deserted offshore islets. Rolling inland, the steamy lowlands relent to a rugged canopy of rambling hills, mist-swathed valleys, teeming forests, whitewater rivers and formidable peaks, including Volcán Barú, the highest mountain in Panama. Some Chircanos are so proud of their province they would like to see it become an independent republic – and understandably so, for Chiriquí is special. But sadly, the region's unique promise is today being overshadowed by a glut of aggressive hydroelectric concessions, which threaten to devastate its watershed. Similarly, to the east, the semi-autonomous Comarca Ngäbe-Buglé has become the frontline in an on-going conflict over government plans to mine the area. Encompassing 7000 sq km of remote mountainous terrain, the Comarca is the largest indigenous landholding in Panama, home to immense mineral deposits and one of the most solitary places in Central America. Devoid of roads or electricity, its Ngäbe and Buglé inhabitants maintain an intimate and isolated relationship with the natural world. Scores of diverse plants are used in their traditional forms of medicine, craft and construction, while daily survival is contingent upon the cultivation of yucca, maize, beans, plantain and other staples. Thus the land symbolizes much more than its staggering highland vistas and pristine cloud forests, and more than a foundation for work and activity. It symbolizes life itself, and in the spiritually charged Comarca Ngäbe-Buglé, land, people and life are one single indivisible entity. No wonder they fight so fiercely to protect it.

Chiriquí lowlands

The sweltering lowlands of Chiriquí are punctuated with an arresting labyrinth of scattered green islets, vast sandy beaches, tangled mangroves, teeming estuaries, marshlands, tropical forests and swamps. The grungy city of David, the second largest urban settlement in the country, is fast evolving from a humdrum backwater into a dynamic hub of business and enterprise. On the Burica Peninsula, the offbeat and slightly dilapidated port of Armuelles wistfully recalls its glory days as the banana and oil capital of Panama, while further east, the diminutive fishing village of Boca Chica patiently awaits the tourist boom that's sure to soon engulf it. Offshore, scores of dazzling emerald islands await exploration, as densely vegetated as they are blissfully uninhabited. Coral reefs conceal pockets of colourful marine life and large sea animals, including dolphins, sharks and whales, ply the waters too. ▶▶ For listings, see pages 211-215.

David and around → *For listings, see pages 211-215. Colour map 1, B2.*

David is the perpetually steamy capital of Chiriquí and a thriving centre of commerce where the province's coffee, cacao, sugar, timber, bananas and cattle are bought and sold. International trade with Costa Rica, a mere hour away, has long brought cheap imports and a special prosperity to the city, whose affluence is only intensifying thanks to a property boom in the surrounding countryside. Nonetheless, it remains a slow-paced city with few cultural diversions and modest aesthetic charms. David is very much a working place, visceral, unrefined and coloured by intriguing day-to-day graft. Its abundance of banks, shops, hotels, restaurants and other useful amenities – along with its transportation links and location halfway between Panama City and San José, Costa Rica – make it a very practical place to pause.

Arriving in David
David is framed by the Interamericana highway, where international buses bound for Panama City make a stop. Most inter-urban routes arrive in the city's downtown **bus station**, Paseo Estudiante, a five-minute walk from Plaza Cervantes; **Tracopa buses** (David–San José) have their own terminal next to the main bus station. David's airport, **Aeropuerto Internacional Enrique Malek (DAV)** ① *Vía Aeropuerto, T721-1072*, receives flights from Panama City and Costa Rica. It is located 5 km south of the city centre and serviced by ample taxis, US$3-4. Although David's downtown area is easily explored on foot, it can nonetheless pose navigational challenges. The central plaza is not central, there are few street signs, some streets have two names, or no pavements, and sometimes the locals prefer to use nostalgic points of reference when giving directions (eg two blocks from where the oak tree used to be). **Taxis** are helpful and the easiest method of covering long distances; most fares rarely exceed US$3. City bus routes are circuitous and can generate additional confusion. For information, the **ATP office** ① *Calle Central, between Av 5a Este and Av 6a Este, T775-4120, www.visitpanama.com, Mon-Fri 0900-1600*, is friendly and helpful. Several blogs and websites also provide useful information, including **Chiriquí Chatter** ① *www.chiriquichatter.com*.

Background
Portuguese governor and Jewish convert, Juan López Sequeira, ordered the construction of David in the area of today's Barrio Bolívar. The city's name is a Hebraic reference to King

David of Israel, and possibly the reason why the Catholic Audiencia of Panama neglected to bestow on it official recognition until 1736, when it was belatedly inaugurated San José de David. By then, many powerful landowners and political figures from nearby Santiago de Alanje had established homes in the settlement. In 1849, when the province of Chiriquí was created, David was designated its capital. In 1860 it was granted city status. Starting with the Chiriquí National Railway in 1916 – which connected David with Pedregal, La Concepción, Boquete, Potrerillos and, later, Puerto Armuelles and San Andrés – the 20th century brought exciting new infrastructure to the city. Electricity arrived in 1920, the national highway in 1931, and the Interamericana highway in 1967. The iconic Chiriquí National Railway ceased functioning completely on 31 December 2008.

David

Where to stay 🛏
Alcalá **6**
Bambú Hostel **1**
Castilla **2**
Ciudad de David **3**
Gran Hotel Nacional **4**
Iris **7**
Occidental & Multi-Café **5**
Pensión Costa Rica **8**
Pensión Fanita **9**
Puerta del Sol **10**
Purple House **11**
Residencial La Avenida **13**

Restaurants 🍴
Café Katowa **1**
Casa Vegetariana **2**
El Churrasco **6**
El Fogón **4**
El Rincón Libanés **10**
Helados Jackelita **3**
La Nueva China **5**
Mosto Bistro **7**
Rosa Luz **8**
Tambú Country **9**

Bars & clubs 🍸
Opium **11**

Don't miss ...

Parque Cervantes

Although geographically off-centre, Parque Miguel de Cervantes Saavedra (known simply as El Parque or Parque Cervantes) is the social and commercial heart of David. Filled with ornamental flowers, palms and shady trees, it is one of the city's most verdant and calming spaces – an ideal place to unwind and quietly observe the comings and goings of daily Davidian life. At its centre stands a blue-grey diamond-shaped fountain, designed by Osmeida Ferguson in 2007, which contributes much to the general air-conditioning of the plaza.

Barrio Bolívar

Barrio Bolívar, formerly known as Barrio El Peligro, occupies a few square blocks southeast of Plaza Cervantes. There's not much to see beyond a handful of historic buildings, but strolling around is pleasant and with enough imagination you can get a sense of old David. The barrio's geographic centre is the sedate **Plaza Bolívar**. On its northwest side, the **Catedral de San José** is a modern structure with a separate and beautifully textured stone bell tower built by Italian architect José Belli in 1892. A block northwest of Plaza Bolívar, on Avenida 8a Este, you'll find one of the city's oldest and most aesthetically pleasing buildings – the former 19th-century home of Chiriquí's founder, José de Obaldía y Orejuela. The building, complete with a rustic red-tile roof and attractively landscaped garden, was undergoing restoration at the time of research, but should soon return to its long-running function as a museum of archaeology, religious art and local history. Next door, an equally handsome structure houses the **Fundación Cultural Gallegos**, created in 1988 for the promotion of David's art and culture. Around the corner on the same block, you'll find the tiny **Museo La Casona** ⓘ *Calle Central, between Av 6a Este and 7a Este, T775-2239, open 0900-1200 and 1500-1800*, with a small but compelling art and antique collection, some of which is for sale. The curator, Dr Mario José Molina Castilla, is a local historian who has written a book about David.

Puerto Pedregal

The diminutive port of Pedregal, 8 km south of David's city centre, is perched on the serpentine **Río Platanal**, close to the estuary of the mighty Río Chiriquí. The port acquired brief commercial importance after the construction of the Chiriquí railway in 1916. Its shallow waters, however, have always rendered it unsuitable for large-scale industrial development (a fate ultimately fulfilled by Puerto Armuelles). Today, Pedregal hosts a modest marina with mooring and basic facilities, as well as a yacht club and a scattering of restaurants. To get there, take a bus from the corner of Parque Cervantes, US$0.50, 20 minutes; or a taxi, US$4-5.

Dolega

The small town of Dolega, whose name means 'place of winter', lies 13 km north of David on the highway to Boquete. The date of its foundation is disputed, but many believe Franciscan monks established the settlement in 1795. The town is known principally for its hydroelectric plant, its church, its orchids, and the **Bookmark Secondhand Bookshop** ⓘ *David–Boquete highway, T776-1688, Tue-Sun 0900-1700*, which contains one of the country's best collections of second-hand English-language books. Roughly 4 km south of town on the highway you'll find the entrance to the refreshing **El Majagua** waterfall, part of a popular resort complex that opens only during high season (off season it's best avoided).

Playa Barqueta → *For listings, see pages 211-215.*

Pounded by strong waves, Playa Barqueta is the closest beach to David. It is infrequently visited off-season when there may not be another soul in sight for miles along its grey-black sands. The beach is backed by a string of wealthy vacation homes, but has few public facilities. Around 300 m west of **Las Olas** resort you'll find a beachfront restaurant with showers and toilets, US$0.25. The food isn't great, so pack a picnic or splash out at **Las Olas** instead. Getting to Playa Barqueta by public transport is tricky; take a taxi, US$10-15 one way.

Refugio de Vida Silvestre Playa de la Barqueta Agrícola → *Colour map 1, B2.*

Six species of sea turtles visit the 5935-ha Refugio de Vida Silvestre Playa de la Barqueta Agrícola, including olive ridley, green, black, hawksbill, loggerhead and leatherback. Inland, alternating habitats of grassland, freshwater marshes, mangrove swamps and forests are home to bird species such as orange-chinned parakeets, yellow-fronted amazons, keel-billed toucans, black-bellied whistling ducks and pale-vented pigeons. Access to the reserve is officially via a long dirt road that follows the coast until it ends close to an ANAM ranger station; you will need a sturdy 4WD to traverse it. Alternatively, you can just keep walking east on the beach, but pack water, start early and dress for the heat.

David to Costa Rica → *For listings, see pages 211-215.*

La Concepción → *Colour map 1, B1.*

La Concepción lies 25 km west of David on the Interamericana highway, roughly halfway between David and the border crossing of Paso Canoas. Sometimes referred to as **Bugaba**, after the district of which it is the capital, La Concepción is an important agricultural shipping point, widely known for its handmade saddles. It is also the gateway to the town of Volcán and the western Chiriquí highlands, from where it's also possible to reach the far-flung and lesser visited border crossing of **Río Sereno** (see box, page 234).

Paso Canoas → *Colour map 1, B1.*

Paso Canoas, 52 km from David, is Panama's most important border crossing. It's a busy town with many places to eat and shop. Informally crossing back and forth between stores and business areas is easy, but travellers intending to leave one country for the other must submit to formalities before proceeding (see box, page 209). At **Gariche**, a few kilometres east of Paso Canoas, there is a secondary checkpoint where cars and buses coming from Costa Rica are checked. Have passport, vehicle permit and driver's licence handy in case they are asked for (usually hassle-free).

Border crossing: Panama–Costa Rica

Paso Canoas

Paso Canoas is the main border crossing with Costa Rica. It is a grimy and hectic place with an insalubrious atmosphere, but easy enough to navigate. There are plenty of restaurants, fast-food joints, cheap hotels and duty-free shops. The crossing is relatively quick and painless unless an international bus has arrived just before you. Try to arrive after 1000 and before 1700.

Panamanian immigration Open 0500-2230. You will be taxed US$1 by the Alcadía when submitting your passport. Regulations are strict when entering. You must present US$500 as proof of funds (or a credit card) and an onward ticket – buy one from the Tracopa bus station if you don't have one, US$10-15. For more on entry requirements, see page 34.

Costa Rican immigration Open 0600-2130 (Costa Rica time). Located 400 m up the road from the Panamanian office. Generally efficient and relaxed.

Currency exchange Money changers will exchange colones and dollars at poor to average rates. There are ATMs at the Banco Nacional de Panamá and others.

Onwards to Costa Rica Tracopa buses to San José and other Costa Rica destinations including the central Pacific coast and Burica Peninsula; departures every hour or two.

Onwards to Panama Buses to David depart every 15 minutes; for Volcán/Cerro Punta, change in La Concepción. Long-distance buses to Panama City with **Padafront**, every hour or two (or go to David and change).

Time Panama is one hour ahead of Costa Rica.

Puerto Armuelles → *Colour map 1, B1.*

Puerto Armuelles is a super-hot industrial city with an abundance of attractive clapboard housing but little to offer the casual visitor. Perched on the eastern flank of the **Burica Peninsula**, the city was founded in 1928 and named after Tomás Armuelles, a Panamanian soldier who died in the 1920s Coto War with Costa Rica. Previously, the area was known as 'Rabo de Puerco' (Pig Tail). It is the second largest city in the province and, for over 70 years, the Pacific headquarters of the **United Fruit Company**, which constructed one of the city's two deep-water ports. By the 1990s, the city was quite economically depressed because of its inability to compete with cheap Ecuadorian bananas. In 2001, **Chiquita** (as the United Fruit Company was then known) pulled out of the area completely, leaving thousands unemployed and deepening the port's decline. Also known as the oil capital of Panama, the city gained prominence as a super-tanker port in the 1970s with its own deep-water facility at the nearby settlement of **Charco Azul**. In the 1980s, Puerto became the Pacific terminus of a transoceanic pipeline to the Caribbean port of Chiriquí Grande. However, little oil wealth has ever reached the city itself and unemployment remains stubbornly high.

Boca Chica and around → *For listings, see pages 211-215. Colour map 1, B2.*

Surrounded by green islands and mangroves, the obscure fishing village of Boca Chica lies on the Bahía de Muertos, just east of the Río Chiriquí's yawning estuarine outlet. Until recently, the only way into this sleepy town was by boat or 4WD, but now a paved road conveniently connects it with the outside world. Amenities comprise some hotels, a few roads, a school and a handful of stores; as a result, there's not much to do in Boca Chica but do as the locals and drink. The village is also the gateway to some stunning destinations further afield, including the soporific Isla Boca Brava, the pristine Parque Nacional Marino Gulfo de Chiriquí or any of the bay's idyllic islands, whose waters are rich in prized game like marlin, sailfish and dorado.

Arriving in Boca Chica
To get to Boca Chica from David, take a bus to **Horconcitos**, 39 km away. If there are no direct buses, you can catch any eastbound service and ask to be let out at the Horconcitos turning. From there you must take a taxi into the village, US$3. Once in Horconcitos, infrequent buses travel an extra 13 km to Boca Chica, US$3. If there's no bus, the restaurant opposite the Boca Chica turning can call you a taxi, US$8. You can also boat it to Boca Chica from Pedregal in 30-60 minutes.

Isla Boca Brava → *Colour map 1, B2.*
ⓘ *Water taxis cross the narrow channel between Boca Chica and Isla Boca Brava, 5-10 mins, US$2-3.*
Just across the water from Boca Chica, Isla Boca Brava is a tranquil offshore retreat swathed in tropical foliage. There are dirt roads, good for hiking, and several kilometres of walking trails, some of which are overgrown and hard to follow. Two decent crescent-shaped beaches can be found on the southern side of the island; those on the northern side are rocky and less pleasant. Around 280 bird species make their home on Isla Boca Brava, including the lance-tailed manakin, whose local populations continue to fascinate biologists. The species is renowned for its courtship dances, uniquely performed by pairs of cooperative males. If the pair is successful in attracting a female, only the dominant alpha male will go on to mate. The beta male may spend up to five years as an 'apprentice' until he becomes an alpha himself.

Parque Nacional Marino Golfo de Chiriquí → *Colour map 1, B2.*
Created in 1994, the ladle-shaped Parque Nacional Marino Gulfo de Chiriquí protects 14,740 ha of ocean space. It is a highlight of any trip to the region and home to diverse marine species like white-tipped sharks, angel kingfish, leatherback and hawksbill turtles, bicoloured parrot fish, moray eels, lobsters, dolphins and, between September and November, migrating humpback whales. The park protects more than a dozen coral reefs and includes the 22 densely vegetated islands of the Parida archipelago. The largest, **Isla Parida**, has a source of fresh water and some lodgings. The others are uninhabited, but easily visited. Several of them, such as **Isla Bolaños**, boast scintillating white-sand beaches and verdant forests replete with oak, cedar, wild cashew and guanacaste trees. On the larger islands you might spot howler monkeys, agoutis, green and black frogs and iguanas.

Islas Secas → *Colour map 1, C2.*
The Islas Secas are a chain of 16 remote islands, all swathed in jungle and barely inhabited. Formerly owned by American entrepreneur Michael Klein, who tragically died in a plane crash in 2007, the islands are very secluded and offer exclusive resort-style lodging for those who can afford it. Access is by private charter plane from Panama City, or a 45-minute boat ride from Boca Chica; make advance arrangements with the resort. For more information, see listings, page 213.

Playa Las Lajas → *For listings, see pages 211-215. Colour map 1, B3.*

ⓘ *To get there from David, catch a Las Lajas bus, or any eastbound service that passes Las Lajas. Exit at the beach turn-off and take a taxi south, US$6.*

Located 62 km east of David and 13 km south of the Interamericana highway, the broad expanse of Playa Las Lajas stretches for 14 km with grey sands, palm trees and burgeoning beachfront developments. It has large waves which might suit beginner body-boarders, but little for the surfing pro. During high season, especially on Sundays, Panamanian day-trippers descend on the area to eat, drink or otherwise party. During low season, particularly on weekdays, it's blissfully deserted. Be warned, high tide consumes most of the sand.

◉ Chiriquí lowlands listings

For sleeping and eating price codes and other relevant information, see pages 16-19.

◉ Where to stay

David *p205, map p206*

$$$$ Ciudad de David, Calle D Norte and Av 2a Este, T774-3333, www.hotelciudad dedavid.com. This slick new business hotel has 103 impeccably attired rooms, pool, gym, spa, restaurant and business centre. Rack rates are high, but they often offer discounts of nearly 50%. The breakfast buffet, US$10 for non-guests, is worth sampling. The best in town. Recommended.

$$$ Gran Hotel Nacional, Av Central and Calle Central, T775-2221, www.hotelnacional panama.com. A landmark David hotel. Rooms are comfortable, generic and overpriced. New rooms and poolside rooms cost extra. The amenities are generally excellent, including garden, pool, casino and 3 restaurants. The lunch buffet isn't bad, US$7.25.

$$ Alacalá, Av 3a Este and Calle D Norte, T774-9018, www.hotelalcalapanama.com. Rooms are clean, pleasant and functional, if unexciting. All are equipped with a/c, telephone, Wi-Fi, hot water and cable TV. General amenities include restaurant, bar, parking and room service. Discounts available.

$$ Castilla, Calle A Norte, between Av 2a Este and Av 3a Este, T774-5260, www.hotel castillapanama.com. A clean, quiet hotel with an attractive lobby and 68 well-appointed rooms. Services include Wi-Fi,

parking, a/c, cable TV and hot water. The restaurant serves Spanish and Panamanian food. Friendly, helpful staff and discounts off-season. Recommended.

$$ Iris, Calle A Norte on Parque Cervantes, T775-2251, hotel_irispanama@hotmail.com. Rooms here are on the small side, but they come with a/c, cable TV, Wi-Fi, hot water and phone; cheaper rooms have fan (**$**). Friendly and reasonable.

$$ Occidental, Calle 4a on Parque Cervantes, T755-4068. This weathered old favourite overlooking the plaza is on the musty side, but most rooms are good and comfortable. They come equipped with a/c, cable TV and hot water. Some rooms are exceptionally large and excellent value; others smell of cooking oil – ask to see a few.

$$ Puerta del Sol, Av 3a Este and Calle Central, T774-8422, www.hotelpuertadelsol. com.pa. This hotel has clean, comfortable rooms with leather armchairs, cable TV, writing desks, hot water and a/c. The lobby is decked out with contemporary furnishings. Friendly and helpful. Not bad.

$ Bambú Hostel, Calle de la Virgencita, San Mateo Abajo, T730-2961, www.bambu hostel.com. A friendly, sociable hostel with a pleasant landscaped garden, pool and 'Mayan-style' rancho bar. Small dorms and a few well-equipped double rooms are available. Lots of amenities, including TV, DVD, Wi-Fi, gym, BBQ and ping-pong, lockers and hot shower, to name a few. Located in the suburbs; take a taxi to get there.

$ Pensión Costa Rica, Av 5a Este and Calle A Sur, T775-1241. An interesting old house with a good outside porch and lots of local character. Rooms are basic and equipped with fan and shower. The TV is shared. Run-down and suitable for hardened travellers.

$ Pensión Fanita, Calle B Norte, between Av 5a and Av 6a, T775-3718, pensionfanita@hotmail.com. A friendly, ramshackle cheapie with smallish, dusty rooms. A range of options are available. The most expensive have private bath, a/c and TV; the cheapest have just a bed and shared bath. The restaurant serves cheap food (**$**).

$ The Purple House, Calle C Sur and Av 6a Oeste, T774-4059, www.purplehousehostel.com. Hostel close to the town centre with private rooms (**$$-$**) and dorms, all equipped with orthopaedic mattresses. A wealth of amenities include book exchange, *artesanías*, DVD, kitchen, Wi-Fi and stacks of travel information. Very helpful, but a few mixed reports. Located away from the centre; take a taxi.

$ Residencial La Avenida, Av 3a Este and Calle D Norte, T774-0451, residencialavenida@hotmail.com. One of David's best budget hotels. It has clean, pleasant rooms with lots of space and natural light. They come equipped with a/c, cable TV, phone and Wi-Fi. Cheaper quarters have fan. Quiet, relaxed and good value.

Playa Barqueta *p208*

$$$ Las Olas, T772-3000, www.beachresort panama.com. If the chaos and humidity of downtown David isn't to your taste, this large, well-attired oceanfront resort is a quiet and out-of-the-way alternative. It boasts a wealth of amenities including pool, spa services, tour operator, restaurants and bar. Rooms are comfortable and modern. Good reports.

Boca Chica *p209*

$$$$ Seagull Cove Lodge, T851-0036, www.seagullcovelodge.com. The secluded and tasteful Seagull Cove Lodge enjoys a peaceful, natural setting overlooking a bay.

The grounds are leafy and rambling with 5 comfortable bungalows, restaurant, pool and pier on the water. Very gracious and hospitable with lots of excellent reports. Recommended.

$$$ Gone Fishing, T851-0104, www.gone fishingpanama.com. This comfortable and relaxing lodging on a cliff-top boasts awesome views of the ocean. They can organize a range of outdoor activities, including fishing (as the name suggests). Amenities include infinity pool, garden, and a restaurant serving catch of the day.

Isla Boca Brava *p210*

$$$$ Boutique Hotel Cala Mia, T851-0059, www.boutiquehotelcalamia.com. A beautifully presented and exclusive boutique lodging with 11 elegant bungalows with handmade furniture, ocean views and outdoor rancho terraces. Some have direct access to the beach. Amenities include spa treatment, infinity pool and a fine restaurant serving organic food sourced from their own farm. Completely powered by solar. Good reports.

$$ Hotel Boca Brava, T851-0017, www.hotelbocabrava.com. Hotel Boca Brava boasts a range of quirky rooms and bungalows, some much better than others. The grounds are rambling and leafy and offer access to the island's main trails. The restaurant has superb views and breezes. Various tours available, including surfing, whale watching and fishing. Hospitable and helpful owners. Recommended.

Parque Nacional Marino Golfo de Chiriquí *p210*

$$$$ Propiedad de Paradise, T573-7888, www.fishpanamatoday.com. For the discerning sports fisherman, **Propiedad de Paradise** offers deep-sea fishing expeditions and homely accommodation in its remote island lodge. Rooms are well equipped with flat-screen TVs, fans, hardwood furniture and refrigerator. Close to some prime sites. Recommended.

Islas Secas p210

$$$$ Islas Secas Resort, T646-837-0705, www.islassecas.com. An exclusive lodging with capacity for just 14 guests. Accommodation is in luxury yurt-style *casitas* with superb views of the ocean. Diving, fishing and spa services are available. One of the best, but not cheap.

Playa Las Lajas p211

$$$ Las Lajas Beach Resort, T832-5462, www.laslajasbeachresort.com. A breezy beachfront hotel with 12 clean, comfortable rooms, all equipped with a/c, hot water, safe, fan and Wi-Fi. Amenities include a pool with a waterfall and a good open-air bar-restaurant serving tasty fish and chips. The grounds are green and tranquil. Recommended.

$ La Spiazza, T6620-6431, www.laspiazapanama.com. Laid-back and rustic Italian-run hostel with private rooms, dorms, shared kitchen and restaurant serving genuine wood-fired pizza. There's a small 'eco-shop' selling fruit, vegetables and souvenirs. Green-themed and friendly.

🍴 Restaurants

David p205, map p206

$$$ Mosto Bistro, Plaza Real, Calle D Norte, between Av Central and Av 1a Este. This fine dining establishment serves well-seasoned steaks, tasty fillet of trout, lobster and wine. Wed night is sushi night and reportedly very good. A little pretentious, but full of flavour and well presented. Good service. Not cheap.

$$ El Churrasco, Av Central, between Calle C Norte and Calle D Norte. This popular restaurant serves a very decent lunch buffet with a broad selection of wholesome, economical Panamanian fare. In the evening there are stone-baked pizzas, as well as the restaurant's namesake, beef churrasco. Highly recommended.

$$ El Fogón, Calle D Norte and Av 2a Oeste. A popular, brightly decorated David institution. They serve Panamanian and

international food, such as ceviche, burgers, whole chicken and pasta. The seafood menu is extensive with a range of lobster, prawn, fish fillet and octopus dishes.

$$ El Rincón Libanés, Calle F Sur, between Av Central and Av 1a Este. Arabic and Lebanese cuisine, including kebabs and other grilled meat, tasty hummus and tsatsiki. They have shisha pipes and molasses tobacco, if you fancy an after-dinner smoke. Recommended.

$$ La Nueva China, Av Olbadía. The best Chinese restaurant in David. Try the *pescado con hojas* (fish in black bean sauce served on a bed of pak choi). The sweet and sour chicken isn't bad either. Recommended.

$$ Tambu Country, Av 4a Este (3 de Noviembre) and Av E Sur. Reasonable pizzas, burgers and other wholesome American-style fare. Indoor or outdoor seating and buttons to summon the waiter. Not bad.

$ Casa Vegetariana, Av 2a Este and Calle Central. A great little vegetarian buffet serving economical Chinese fare. Fill your plate with noodles and other grub for US$1.50 or less. Open for lunch only. Recommended.

$ Multi-Café, Plaza Cervantes, Av 4a. Economical breakfasts, lunches and dinners served from a buffet. Cheap and filling, but pick something that looks fresh and hot. OK for a quick meal, but nothing special. Popular with locals.

$ Rosa Luz, Av 2a Este and Calle E Sur. Unpretentious outdoor dining at this popular locals' haunt. Take your pick of simple breakfast, lunch and dinner dishes. Economical, rough, ready and reliable.

Cafés, bakeries and juice bars

Café Katowa, Plaza Real, Calle D Norte, between Av Central and Av 1a Este. Pricey but good coffees, cappuccinos and espressos. Western coffeehouse ambience.

Helados Jackelita, Calle E Norte, between Av Central and Av 1a Oeste. Very good fresh fruit ice creams and smoothies. Recommended.

🎭 Entertainment

David *p205, map p206*
Bars and clubs
Opium, Av 4a Oeste and Calle Miguel A Brenes. Bright, flashy young disco and David's premier night spot. Dress to impress.

Cinemas
Cine Moderno, Chiriquí Mall, Vía Interamericana, T774-9895.
Culturama, Av 6a Este, between Calle Central and Calle A Norte, T730-4010, www.semanarioculturama.com. Shows alternative films on Mon nights, 1900.
Multi-Cines Nacional, Hotel Gran Nacional, Av Central and Calle Central, T774-7887.

🎉 Festival and events

David *p205, map p206*
Mid-Mar, Fería Internacional de David. A major 10-day festival that sees over 300,000 visitors and over 500 exhibitors in the fields of industry, commerce and agriculture. Everything from heavy machinery to *artesanías* to flowers and livestock is sold. The entrance to the festival is marked by a large traditional gate specifically built for the occasion. Dates change each year, but always include the city's patron saint's day on 19 Mar. For more information, see www.feriadedavid.com.

La Concepción *p208*
Late Jan-early Feb, Fiesta de Candelaria. A very large and popular 10-day Catholic Candelmas festival in honour of the city's Virgen de la Candelaria. Lots of dancing, drinking, feasting, horse riding, fireworks and bullfights.

🛍 Shopping

David *p205, map p206*
David is a major commercial centre with no shortage of shopping options. For cheap clothing, follow Av 4a Este northeast from Plaza Cervantes to arrive in a bustling neighbourhood filled with cut-price stores. This activity culminates in a small but colourful market district close to the bus station. If you're looking for mall shopping, try **Plaza Terronal** on the Interamericana highway. Camping supplies are available in the **Do-it Centre**.

🌙 What to do

Isla Boca Brava *p210*
Diving
Boca Brava Divers, T775-3185, www.scuba diving-panama.com. Managed by reputable dive expert Carlos Spragge, who has many years of experience in the waters of Chiriquí. His dive packages start at US$150 per day, 4-person minimum, including boat, tanks, weight and lunch. Tours to Isla Coiba are also available.

Parque Nacional Marino Golfo de Chiriquí *p210*
Fishing
Casual fishing is as easy as finding a boatman to take you out for the day. Prices vary with the amount of fuel used, but you should expect to pay around US$100-150 for around 6 hrs. If you don't have your own equipment, or if you want to conduct a serious deep-sea expedition, contact one of the fishing lodges mentioned above.

Whale watching
Whale watching is possible Sep-Nov. Any hotel should be able to hook you up with a boatman; most charge around US$50-60 per person, 4-person minimum. Trips include a 1- to 2-hr stopover on a secluded beach and can usually be combined with snorkelling/fishing.

⊖ Transport

David *p205, map p206*
Air
Aeropuerto Internacional Enrique Malek (DAV), Vía Aeropuerto, 5 km from centre, is being expanded and will soon handle long-haul international flights. To **San José** (Costa Rica), **Air Panama**, 1030, US$125 one-way. To **Panama City**, Air Panama, 0800, 1400, 1800, US$80 one-way. All fares exclude tax. You can acquire tickets at the airport, or downtown at **Air Panama**, Av 2a Este and Calle D Norte, T775-0812, www.flyairpanama.com. To get to the airport, take a taxi, US$3; or a Pedregal bus from the corner of Parque Cervantes, US$0.30.

Bus
Long distance David's long-distance bus station is located on Paseo Estudiante, 1 block north of Av Obaldía. Taxi to city centre, US$1. Padafront has its own terminal at Av 2a Este and Av Obaldía. To **Almirante**, every 30 mins, 0300-1900, 4-5 hrs, US$8.45; to **Boquete**, every 20 mins, 0525-2125, 1 hr, US$1.75; to **Caldera**, every 1-2 hrs, 0610-1915, 1 hr, US$2.45; to **Changuinola**, every 30 mins, 0300-1900, 5-6 hrs, US$9.70; to **Cerro Punta**, every 15 mins, 0445-2030, 2 hrs, US$3.50; to **Dolega**, every 10 mins, 0520-2330, 30 mins, US$1.35; to **Panama City**, Terminales David–Panamá, 16 daily, 0300-0000, 7-8 hrs, US$15.25; Express 2245 and 0000, 5-6 hrs, US$18.50; Padafront, 5 daily, 0500-2000, US$15; to **Paso Canoas**, every 15 mins, 0600-2130, 1 hr, US$2.15; to **Puerto Armuelles**, every 20 mins, 0600-2130, 1½ hrs, US$3.75; to **Río Sereno**, every 40 mins, 0430-1800, 2½ hrs, US$5.25; to **San Félix**, hourly, 0700-1820, 1½ hrs, US$2.70; to **Soloy**, hourly, 0800-1200 and 1400-1700, 1½ hrs, US$3; to **Tolé**, every 40 mins, 0700-1945, 1½ hrs, US$3.35; to **Volcán**, every 15 mins, 0445-2030, 1½ hrs, US$3.

International Expreso Panamá (formerly Panalines) and Ticabus services travelling from San José (Costa Rica) to Panama City drop off passengers on the Interamericana in David, but there is no way to board a bus. The quickest and cheapest way of reaching Costa Rica is to take a bus to Paso Canoas, cross the border on foot and pick up a bus on the other side. If you don't want to change buses, Tracopa offer services David–San José, 0830, US$14, 8 hrs, but you will have to queue 2-4 hrs for immigration and customs with your fellow passengers.

Car hire
Alamo, Aeropuerto Enrique Malek, T721-0101, www.alamopanama.com. **Express rent-a-car**, Calle 3a and Av F Sur, T777-3200, www.expressrentpanama.com. **Hertz**, Aeropuerto Enrique Malek, T721-8471, www.rentacarpanama.com. **Nacional**, Aeropuerto Enrique Malek, T721-0000, www.nationalpanama.com.

Boca Chica *p209*
Boat
Private water taxis run to **Isla Boca Brava** for around US$5 one way. If no one is waiting at the main pier, enquire at a local bar or store and they should call in a boatman.

Bus
Buses run infrequently to **Horconcitos**, US$3. Alternatively, take a taxi, US$8.

⊙ Directory

David *p205, map p206*
Cultural centres Culturama, Av 6a Este, between Calle Central and Calle A Norte, T730-4010, www.semanarioculturama.com, is an interesting NGO that has been distributing reading material to distant Chiricano communities for some 20 years; they produce a newsletter and have a selection of books on the province. **Dentist** Clínica Spiegel, Av Belisario Porras, T775-2683, good reports. **Hospitals** The best private hospital is Hospital Mae Lewis, Carretera Interamericana,

T755-4616, www.maelewis.net. **Hospital Chiriquí**, Av 3a and Calle Central, T774-0128, www.hospitalchiriqui.net, provides good care, but is alleged to overcharge. Several laboratories for blood and stool tests, including **Laboratorio Clínico Bio Médica**, Av 3a Este and Calle D Norte. **Immigration** Immigration office, opposite the Policlínica Edif Malami Altos Oficentro Vega Oficina No 9, T774-1923, Mon-Fri 0800-1500. **Laundry** A few *lavomáticos* are clustered on Av 2a Este, between Calle F Sur and Calle D sur. **Libraries** Biblioteca Pública Santiago Anguizola, Calle A Sur, between Av 1a and 2a Este. Small collection, housed in the old train station.

Boquete and around

Nestled in the verdant valley of Caldera, the highland town of Boquete has always been an important centre of trade and agriculture. The surrounding mountains are green and rugged, thickly forested in parts, home to thunderous rivers, piping hot springs and abundant birdlife. At 1060 m, the cool climate allows for the production of orchids, strawberries, root vegetables and, most importantly, coffee. But times are changing in Boquete. Since the 1990s, the town has been the focus of a formidable real estate boom with an unprecedented influx of foreign baby-boomers arriving to live out their retirement. Increasingly, Boquete looks and feels like a well-heeled North American suburb. The region's changing demographics, along with rock-bottom coffee prices, mean many locals are turning to tourism as an alternative source of income. Today, Boquete is feted as Panama's premier outdoors destination. Its lodgings run the gamut from backpacker hostels to luxury spas and it is a great base for organizing whitewater rafting, hiking, horse riding, birding and other adventures. ▶▶ *For listings, see pages 221-227.*

Arriving in Boquete → *Colour map 1, B2.*

Boquete lies 38 km north of David on a paved and newly expanded four-lane highway. **Buses** depart from David's bus terminal every 20 minutes, 0525-2125, US$1.75, and reach Boquete's main plaza roughly one hour later. Boquete is small and easily navigated on foot. The town's principal artery is **Avenida Central**, where you'll find most shops, hotels, restaurants and the plaza. Taxis are a feasible way to reach some remote locations, but in some cases you will need a 4WD, or the services of a tour operator. The stunningly positioned **CEFATI visitor centre** ① *1 km south of Boquete on the highway, T720-4060, Mon-Fri 0900-1700,* provides local information and has a coffee shop attached. The building is reminiscent of an Alpine mountain lodge; if coming from David, look out for it on the right-hand side. Around town, pick up a copy of *The Bajareque Times.* Online, several blogs and websites offer insider information, including **Boquete Panama Guide**, www.boqueteguide.com.

Places in Boquete

Boquete is a tranquil, predominantly wood-built town with several landscaped gardens and meandering streams. At its heart lies the recently renovated **Parque de las Madres**, also known as the Parque Central, a shady plaza complete with trees, bandstand and old-fashioned lamp posts. It is not unusual to see lots of Ngäbe people about town, the men sporting straw hats and machetes, the women in their distinctive brightly coloured dresses. Many of them come from nearby villages to work in Boquete's fincas, or otherwise stock up on supplies. Cross over the Río Caldera and you'll arrive at the fairgrounds of the

Boquete

annual **Feria de las Flores y del Café**, usually held mid-January (see Festivals, page 225).

Mi Jardín Es Su Jardín

ⓘ *Av Central, roughly 500 m north of the plaza, T720-2040, 0900-1800, free.*

Home to over 200 species of flower, the internationally acclaimed Mi Jardín es su Jardín is Boquete's most famous and striking botanical garden. Owned by the González family, the gardens officially opened to the public in 1995. Some 8000 sq m of imaginatively landscaped grounds contain a variety of colourful flower beds, bubbling creeks, teeming carp ponds and trickling man-made waterfalls. A procession of wacky ornaments add a surreal touch to the gardens, including gaudy painted flamingos and giant psychedelic cows.

Boquete Tree Trek

ⓘ *Plaza los Establos, Av Central, www.boquete treetrek.com, T720-1635.*

The adrenalin-charged thrill of traversing a tropical forest on a high-speed zip-line never fails to invigorate those who try it. The Boquete Tree Trek is the second longest canopy tour in Central America and former customers have reported decent, professional service with a strong emphasis on safety. Hold on tight for a racy ride between 14 high-level platforms, a giant Tarzan swing and a exhilarating rappel back to earth. Photos are available if you wish to capture your excitement – or terror – for all time.

El Explorador

ⓘ *Jaramillo, 3 km northeast of town, T720-1989, daily 0900-1800, US$3. To get there take a taxi, 5-10 mins, US$3, or walk, 45 mins.*

The quirky and good-natured El Explorador gardens have been designed to instil a sense of tranquillity and well-being. Fine horticultural displays of roses and fruit trees are punctuated by an array of eccentric ornaments, including recycled household items. Throughout the 2 ha of landscaped

Coffee fincas around Boquete

The mountains and hills around Boquete are the misty heartland of Panama's coffee industry. Fans of the black stuff should not miss the opportunity to visit one of the many local fincas and learn about the processes of production, from cherry to cup. Each producer has a slightly different approach and there are too many to list entirely.

The most famous is **Café Ruiz**, 500 m north of the plaza in Boquete, T720-1000, www.caferuiz-boquete.com, daily tours US$9-30, advance reservation necessary. Established in 1979 as a family business, the company has won numerous international awards, including the prestigious Coffee World Cup in 2001. Today, **Café Ruiz** is the largest exporter of speciality coffee in Panama with some 90% of its beans shipped to Europe and the United States for roasting. You can take a full tour of the facilities, three hours, US$30, or stop for a quick 'coffee appreciation' taster session, 45 minutes, US$9.

If you'd like to combine your coffee tasting with some world-class birdwatching, head to **Finca Lérida**, northwest of town, T720-2285, www.fincalerida.com, tours two hours, US$31, reserve in advance. The sprawling estate, established by Tollef Monniche in 1922 and bought by Alfred Collins in 1957, features moss-draped cloud forests that are home to hundreds of bird species, including the rare resplendent quetzal. Luxury lodgings are available if you want to make a dawn start on the trails. The fincas itself is one of the oldest coffee operations in Boquete and its beans are still processed in the pioneering plant designed by Mr Monniche.

Those familiar with the streets of Boquete or David may have already noticed the Western-style coffee houses of **Kotowa Coffee**, www.kotowacoffee. com. The Kotowa estate was founded in 1918 by Canadian entrepeneur Alexander MacIntyre, who notably channelled the Río Cristal to drive his hydraulic mill. Kotowa coffee, grown without pesticides, has a good body, chocolatey taste and sweet acidity. Tours of the estate are offered by **Coffee Adventures**, T730-3852, www.coffeeadventures.net, Monday to Saturday 1400, US$29.50, advance reservation necessary. They include a visit to the historic processing mill and end with a tasting session.

grounds, wooden signs proclaim philosophical truths and classical music is piped through loud-speakers. There is a café and bakery on site, should all that otherworldly contemplation leave you peckish.

Hikes around Boquete

There's a wide of variety of potential hikes in Boquete's bucolic surroundings, far more than can be mentioned here. Locals will know secret routes and should be able to point you in the right direction. Many short trips can be undertaken without a guide, but guides can also be very useful for spotting wildlife. Whatever your plans, it's a good idea to start early to avoid getting caught in afternoon showers. Bring water, sunscreen, waterproofs and food. The most popular walking is in the **Parque Nacional Volcán Barú**, with one awesome trail leading to the summit and another to **Cerro Punta** (see page 231). Planning is required for both trips and, if you're inexperienced, so is a guide. True adventurers should consider the four-day odyssey to **Bocas del Toro**. The trip, which should only be accomplished with a qualified guide, crosses over the continental divide and is not for the faint of heart. Less demanding are the various paved loop roads snaking around the hillsides. They're usually quite empty of traffic and great for biking too, especially on the downhill stretches. Allow three to four leisurely hours to walk the scenic **Volancito loop** up and around the western flank of the Caldera Valley. It begins at the CEFATI visitor centre on the south side of town: just follow the sign to Volcancito and enjoy the views. Likewise, the **Jaramillo loop** offers expansive views from the eastern side of the valley. Cross over the bridge towards the festival grounds and bear right up the hill, sticking to the left when passing any major forks or junctions; three to four hours. The **Alto Lino loop** begins a few kilometres north of the town on an eastbound road heading uphill. Roughly halfway along the road you'll arrive at the **Sendero El Pianista** (Pianist trail), a good but strenuous birdwatching trail which leads uphill from the cattle pastures into mist-swathed cloud forest and the provincial border with Bocas del Toro. The trail is a four- to five-hour round-trip, so you might want to get a taxi (US\$3) to shuttle you to and from the trailhead rather than walk all the way from Boquete.

Around Boquete

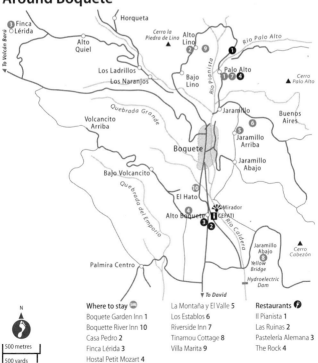

N
500 metres
500 yards

Where to stay 🛏
Boquete Garden Inn 1
Boquette River Inn 10
Casa Pedro 2
Finca Lérida 3
Hostal Petit Mozart 4

La Montaña y El Valle 5
Los Establos 6
Riverside Inn 7
Tinamou Cottage 8
Villa Marita 9

Restaurants 🍴
Il Pianista 1
Las Ruinas 2
Pastelería Alemana 3
The Rock 4

Parque Nacional Volcán Barú → *For listings, see pages 221-227. Colour map 1, B2.*

At 3474 m, **Volcán Barú** is Panama's highest peak and the views from its summit are astounding. On an exceptional day, you can glimpse both Pacific and Atlantic oceans and breathe in one of the most expansive vistas anywhere. Since 1976, the volcano has been protected as part of the extensive Parque Nacional Volcán Barú. The park shelters seven craters and no less than 10 different rivers, including the Río Caldera and Río Chiriquí, both vital to Chiriquí's agriculture. Local fauna includes some 40 endemic species, five species of big cat, numerous endangered mammals, amphibians, reptiles and over 400 species of bird, including black and white hawk eagles, volcano juncos and, between January and May, numerous resplendent quetzals. Average temperatures in the park range from a subtropical 20°C on the lower slopes to a distinctly chilly 10°C higher up. During the dry season, frost is not unusual on the summit, or even an occasional flurry of snow. Although dormant for the last 600 years, Volcán Barú is technically active. In 2006, seismic activity was detected, causing some scientists to warn of an imminent eruption.

Arriving at the Parque Nacional Volcán Barú

The park can be accessed from Boquete on Barú's east slope, or from Volcán or Cerro Punta in the west. It is easiest to reach the summit from the east side as the trail on the west face is dicey and unclear; if you do choose to begin your trek in Volcán, you are strongly advised to use a guide. On the lower slopes, the famous **Sendero Los Quetzales** is much easier to follow from west to east, starting in **Cerro Punta** (for more information see page 231).

To the summit

Only experienced hikers should attempt to climb Volcán Barú unguided. Departing from Boquete, it takes six to eight hours to complete the strenuous 21-km trail to the summit, and another five to six hours to return. Begin your ascent at 0500 if you want to make it back before dark. Alternatively, camp halfway and climb to the summit early the next morning – you will have a better chance of seeing both oceans at dawn anyway. Pack dried food, 4-5 litres of water per person, compass, waterproofs and plenty of warm clothing. **Explora Ya** in Boquete can provide tents and sleeping bags. For other camping equipment, try the **Do-it Center**, Plaza Terronal in David. Take all the usual precautions and inform your hotel of your intentions before you set out.

The first 7 km of the ascent is paved, passing through rich coffee groves and forests of aromatic pines. It concludes at the ANAM office where you must pay admission. Note you can take a taxi this far, US$3-5. From the park entrance, the trail climbs through cloud forest draped with creepers, lichen and bromeliads. It's possible to spot many bird species and, as the road rises, you'll be rewarded with views of the valley, the Río Caldera and the Pacific beyond. Around 9 km from the ANAM office there's a sign, 'La Nevera', indicating a small side trail which leads to a mossy gully with a stream for water, but no flat ground to camp. At the summit you'll find a forest of TV and radio aerials in a fenced enclosure. A small path leads to a cross and trigonometric point where you'll enjoy the best views of the craters, and sometimes, rainbows formed by the *bajareque* drizzle.

Caldera → *For listings, see pages 221-227. Colour map 1, B2.*

The village of Caldera, 18 km from Boquete, is one of the oldest inhabited settlements in Chiriquí. You can access the village from either Boquete or David, but direct buses are infrequent. The David–Boquete bus passes the Caldera turning (marked Chiriquitos), 11 km south of downtown Boquete; from there it's a 7-km hike. Its name, which means 'cauldron', is said to derive from features of the landscape which resemble a giant cooking pot. Caldera is famous for its large boulder covered in pre-Columbian petroglyphs. Some of the designs are geometric, others are suggestive of animals, plants and people, but the exact purpose of the painted rock, or **Piedra Pintada**, is an anthropological mystery. The land around Caldera is flat, grassy, wide open and ideal for horse riding.

Los Pozos de Caldera

ⓘ *Daily 0800-1900, US$2. Follow the signs from Caldera village. A 60-min hike on dirt roads; driving is possible with 4WD. A taxi from Boquete should cost US$40 return, including a wait.*
The hot springs of Caldera are the perfect restorative for weary limbs and bones. Four thermally heated pools of differing temperatures, most of them enclosed by foliage and rustic walls of rocks, are said to alleviate rheumatism, arthritis and skin problems. At 38-45°C, their mineral-rich waters certainly make a relaxing end to a vigorous day of hiking. The springs are located on the banks of the Río Chiriquí where it's possible to cool off in the dry season (extremely dangerous in the wet season!). Wandering peacocks and a cheeky spider monkey add an exotic flavour to the site, and the owner offers horse tours and buffalo rides.

⊚ Boquete and around listings

For sleeping and eating price codes and other relevant information, see pages 16-19.

⊜ Where to stay

Boquete and around *p216, maps p217 and p219*

$$$$ Finca Lérida, T720-2285, www.finca lerida.com. One of Boquete's most famous and elegant 'ecolodges' and a destination in itself. Finca Lérida has a wide range of rooms and suites, many in classic Scandinavian style, after the lodge's original owners. The grounds are vast and rambling and a birders' delight.
$$$$ La Montaña y el Valle – The Coffee Estate Inn, Jaramillo Arriba, 2.5 km from central Boquete, T720-2211, www.coffee estateinn.com. Deluxe cottages nestled in 2.5 ha of gorgeous, verdant grounds. Units are fully equipped with kitchen and living area, and deliver great views of the countryside. Delicious gourmet food is available, including freshly roasted coffee from their farm. Breakfast and tour included. Recommended.
$$$$ The Riverside Inn, Palo Alto, T720-1076, www.riversideinnboquete.com. One of Boquete's most exclusive lodgings, complete

with beautifully decorated rooms and a handsome master suite with a 4-poster bed and jacuzzi. 'Standard' rooms have superb mattresses, Egyptian cotton linen and a wealth of kit such as TV, DVD, coffee-makers and Wi-Fi.
$$$ Apart-Hotel Kadini, Av Central, Bajo Boquete, T730-9314, aparthotelkadini.com. Conveniently located in downtown Boquete, Apart-Hotel Kadini has 8 modern apartments for daily, weekly or monthly rental. Each has 2 bedrooms, fully fitted kitchen, living room, bathrooms, cable TV, Wi-Fi and hot water.
$$$ Boquete Garden Inn, Palo Alto, T720-2376, www.boquetegardeninn.com. Perched on the banks of the Río Palo Alto, the hospitable Boquete Garden Inn has received glowing reports from previous guests. It has 5 spacious *cabañas*, all tastefully decorated and well equipped with cable TV, Wi-Fi and kitchenette. Beautiful, tranquil, flowery grounds, plentiful birdlife and super-friendly owners. Excellent, one of the best and highly recommended.
$$$ Boquete River Inn, T720-4385, www.momentum-panama.com. Large, fully equipped, wheelchair accessible

cabins set on a plateau overlooking the valley of the Río Cochea. Amenities include a pool, gym, volleyball court and walking trails. Slightly cheaper B&B lodging is also available. Verdant flower-filled grounds and a peaceful location.

$$$ Cabañas Isla Verde, on main street, follow signs posted just before the **Casona Mexi** restaurant, Bajo Boquete, T720-2533, www.islaverde panama.com. An interesting option with 6 imaginatively designed 2-storey 'roundhouse' *cabañas* and 4 suites overlooking a small stream. German owner Eva Kipp is friendly and knowledgeable. Discounts available in the low season.

$$$ El Oasis, Av Buenos Aires, just over the bridge, Bajo Boquete, T720-1586, www.oasis boquete.com. This attractive hotel overlooks the Río Caldera close to the flower fair. They have 11 clean, decent rooms and 6 stylish suites with lots of natural light, comfortable furnishings, TV, hot water and Wi-Fi. Pleasant gardens and good views over the valley. The restaurant is recommended.

$$$ Los Establos, T720-2685, Jaramillo Arriba, www.losestablos.net. Very elegant and secluded lodgings in the style of a traditional coffee hacienda. They offer a range of deluxe rooms, suites and cottages, all well attired with local art and solid wood furnishings. Breakfast, coffee and wine are included in the rates.

$$$ Panamonte, Av 11 de Abril, Bajo Boquete, T720-1324, www.panamonte.com. Built in 1919, this highly attractive hotel is today managed by the Collins family (Swedish-American). The rooms are elegant and comfortable and the garden is home to over 200 varieties of orchid. New developments include a day spa and various tours are available. Charming and recommended.

$$$ Tinamou Cottage, Jaramillo Abajo, 10 mins from town, T720-3852, www.coffee adventures.net/tinamou.html. A tastefully presented B&B with 3 comfortable, well-equipped and secluded cottages on a private coffee finca. Perfect for nature-lovers, with expert hosts and good walking trails. Rates include breakfast and owners can arrange pickup in town. Discounts with internet bookings.

$$$ Villa Lorena Cabañas, Av 11 de Abril, near the **Panamonte**, Bajo Boquete, T720-1848. Comfortable whitewashed cottages for 4-6 persons, all overlooking the Río Caldera. Each has TV, bath, hot water, kitchenette, sofas, Wi-Fi and back porch with hammocks. Not bad.

$$$ Villa Marita, El Santuario, 5 mins' drive from central Boquete, T720-2165, www.villamarita.com. This self-styled 'ecolodge' has 7 attractive, well-equipped cottages and 3 rooms (**$$**) complete with satellite TV, Wi-Fi, hot water and refrigerator. There's lots of birdlife in the garden, including green parrots and a friendly toucan. Tours of their hydroponic greenhouse on request. Comfortable and well presented.

$$ Casa Pedro, Alto Lino, Diagonal a Clínica Dental del Dr Rivera, T720-2402, www.casapedroboquete.com. A pleasant mid-range option managed by a friendly American-Panamanian family. Clean, comfortable, homely double rooms have shared hot-water bath. There's also a suite with a great wooden viewing deck and some fully equipped cottages (**$$$**).

$$ Hostal Boquete, just off Calle 4 Sur to left of bridge, Bajo Boquete, T720-2573, www.hostalboquete.com. This lovely hostel has great views of the river and a pleasant, sociable atmosphere. Various brightly coloured rooms are available, all with private bath, Wi-Fi and cable TV; some have balconies and good vistas. Laundry service, *artesanías*, BBQ pit and tours also available.

$$ Hostal Petit Mozart, on the Volcancito road, 5 mins' drive from central Boquete, T720-3764. Charming, brightly decorated house with an outside patio offering nice views. Friendly owner Lorenza speaks German, English and Spanish. Breakfast and dinners are delicious. Camping also available.

$$ Pensión Topas, Av Belisario Porras, Bajo Boquete, T720-1005, www.pension-topas.

com. Brightly coloured hotel run by the Schöb family. The garden has views of Volcán Barú, a small pool, volleyball court, patio and an inquisitive toucan. Large, comfortable rooms have cable TV, bath and Wi-Fi; there's also a handful of cheaper rooms with shared bath (**$**). Good breakfasts (extra cost) with fresh coffee straight from their private finca. Friendly.

$$ Rebequet, Calle 7 Sur and Av B Este, Bajo Boquete, T720-1365, www.rebequet.com. Excellent spacious rooms and a handful of comfortable cabins around the garden. The rooms are well equipped with tasteful furniture, hammocks, plasma TV, fridge and bath. There is also an Italian restaurant, breakfast included and 50% reduction in low season. Popular, friendly and helpful.

$$-$ Hostal Refugio del Río, From Plaza Los Establos, 1 block west, ½ block north, Bajo Boquete, T720-2088, www.refugio delrio.com. The friendly **Refugio del Río** has comfortable annexed private rooms (**$$**) with pleasant riverside porches. For budget travellers, there are 2 dorms (**$**) inside the main house, complete with communal kitchen, internet, laundry facilities, dining room and TV. Motorbike, cycle and ATV rental available. Recommended.

$ Hostal Beiro, Av Belisario Porras, Bajo Boquete, T720-1679, hostal.beiro@hotmail. com. This simple, comfortable *hostal* has just 4 plain, private rooms with hot water, cable TV and Wi-Fi. Friendly family atmosphere – 'whatever you want, just ask'.

$ Hostal Colibrí, Av Belisario Porras, Bajo Boquete, T720-1024, www.colibrilodging. com. This economical family-run *hostal* has a handful of clean, comfortable and annexed private rooms. All are equipped with private bath, cable TV, Wi-Fi and hot water. Reasonable.

$ Hostal Gaia, Av Central, behind **Sugar and Spice** bakery, Bajo Boquete, T720-1952, www.hostalgaia.com. Friendly, intimate little *hostal* with small dorms for 4-6 persons, fully equipped kitchen, games, books, laundry, lockers and free coffee. 2 private

rooms are also available (**$$**). New, clean, pleasant and recommended.

$ Hostal Mamallena, Parque Central, Bajo Boquete, T720-1260, www.mamallena boquete.com. A new and popular back-packers' joint with a convenient central location on the plaza. Opened by the same team who own **Mamallena** in Panama City, the hostel boasts 17 private rooms and 5 dorms of different sizes. Plenty of amenities including kitchen, luggage storage, Wi-Fi, bar and restaurant. Free tea and coffee and all-day pancake breakfast included. Friendly, helpful and English-speaking.

$ Hostal Nomba, 100 m west of Parque Central, behind **Bistro Boquete**, Bajo Boquete, T720-2864, www.nombapanama. com. Sociable self-styled 'adventure hostel' that's very popular with backpackers. They offer simple but comfortable dorms and private rooms, communal kitchen, library, in-room security lockers and bike rental. Their on-site tour agency can organize a range of excursions.

$ Pensión Marilós, Calle 7 Sur and Av B Este, opposite **Rebequet**, Bajo Boquete, T720-1380. A friendly, economical place with an agreeable home ambience. Rooms are very clean and comfortable with bath and hot water. Guests have use of the kitchen and living areas. The English-speaking management can also organize tours or store luggage. Often full but sharing is permitted. Good value and recommended.

Caldera p220

$$$$ Rancho de Caldera, T720-4225, www. ranchodecaldera.com. A very handsome and tasteful property overlooking the rolling landscapes of Caldera. Accommodation includes comfortable rooms and suites, all fully equipped with fridge, microwave, Wi-Fi, toaster, coffee-maker and more. 2 no-frills rooms available (**$$**). The hotel is self-powered with wind, solar and hydro, and boasts an infinity pool with stunning mountain views, a fantastic restaurant and horses. Lots of good reviews. Recommended.

Restaurants

Boquete and around *p216, maps p217 and p219*

$$$-$$ Art Café La Crepe, Av Central, near San Juan Bautista. Tasty French crêpes are served at this jazzy, continental eatery, including some very creative ones. Classic French cooking is the house speciality, and dishes include fresh rainbow trout and crayfish in brandy and liqueur. Recommended.

$$$-$$ El Oasis, Av Buenos Aires, just over the bridge, Bajo Boquete, T720-1586, www.oasisboquete.com. Gourmet dining in a vibrant and sophisticated setting. Tasty offerings include ceviche, king prawn cocktail, Waldorf salad, and tricolour mousse. They have an extensive pasta, sandwich and vegetarian menu, and plenty of meat dishes too. Good service, but mixed reports on the lamb.

$$$-$$ Restaurante Hotel Panamonte, Av Central, north end of Boquete. This restaurant is quaint and charming and the meals are fantastic – pricey, but worth the treat. Open for breakfast, lunch and dinner, serving succulent trout, fresh juices and delicious desserts, among others.

$$$-$$ The Rock, Av 11 de Avril, Palo Alto, inside the Riverside Inn, www.therock boquete.com. The Rock enjoys a reputation as one of Boquete's best. Their gourmet offerings include delicious onion soup, trout fillet, pork ribs, Thai chicken and steak, all beautifully prepared and presented. Beverages include artisan beers and a selection of fine wines. Great service, pleasant setting and highly recommended.

$$ Antojitos Mexicanos, Av Central, Bajo Boquete. One of a handful of Mexican restaurants in town, but this one is undisputedly the best. They serve tasty, home-cooked fare including tacos, burritos and *chilaquiles*. The interior is brightly painted in typical Mexican style and the friendly owners are from Guadalajara. Authentic and recommended.

$$ Bistro Boquete, Av Central, Boquete. US owner Loretta once cooked for a US president in her previous establishment in Colorado. Her bistro here is renowned for excellent filet mignon, good breakfasts, tasty lunches and dinners.

$$ Il Pianista, Palo Alto, near Boquete Paradise. Located on a hill close to the entrance of the Pianista hiking trail, this oft-praised restaurant serves large, tasty Italian dishes including pizza and calzone. Good for a lunch stop after completing the hike. Romantic and cosy setting, friendly service and reasonable prices. Recommended.

$$ Las Ruinas, Boquete–David Highway, Alto Boquete. This rancho-style open-air eatery by the highway is a winner among the local expat crowd. They serve a range of tasty, artery-hardening comfort food, including baby back ribs, fried shrimps, tuna steaks, burgers and blackberry cobbler. Good for a cold beer too.

$$ Machu Picchu, Av Belisario, Porras. Fantastic Peruvian food cooked by a very friendly Peruvian. Pleasant interior, impressive menu, mostly meat, fish and seafood. Heartily recommended by locals as one of the best in town.

$$ Tammy's, at the entrance to the cemetery, opposite the Texaco on Av Central, Bajo Boquete, www.tammysboquete.com. Firewood-roasted chicken, kebabs, falafels, hummus, wraps, sandwiches, pizza and flame-grilled burgers are just some of the offerings. Popular with expats.

$ Central Park, Parque Central, Bajo Boquete. Intimate but casual little restaurant and coffeeshop on the plaza. They offer economical fare, including hearty breakfasts and set lunches, as well as *comida típica*, such as stewed meat, grilled pork and pan-fried fish.

$ Jardines de Boquete, Calle 5 Sur, opposite Plaza Los Establos, Bajo Boquete. Cheap and cheerful Panamanian fare, including a variety of meat and chicken dishes. Lunchtime specials are ultra-economical. Great for budget wanderers.

$ Nelvis, Av A Oeste, behind Plaza Los Establos, Bajo Boquete. Very popular with locals at lunchtime, cheap and cheerful Nelvis sees crowds queue up for the economical Panamanian buffet. The fried chicken is reportedly the best in town.

$ Pizzería La Volcánica, Av Central, ½ block from main plaza. Reasonable pizzas and pasta at economical prices. Casual and popular.

$ Punto de Encuentro, Av A Este, near Pensión Marilós. Cosy little café with a garden and notice board. Breakfast only; pancakes, fruit salad and juices.

$ Sabrosón, on Av Central near church. High-carb Panamanian fare. Fair quality and value – the best place for budget dining.

Bakeries, cafés and delis

Deli Barú, Av Central, Bajo Boquete. A popular deli selling tasty imports and hard-to-acquire sundries such as smoked salmon, fine ham and cheese.

Pastelería Alemana, south of the arch at the entrance to town. Delicious coffee and pastries.

Sugar and Spice, Av Central, Bajo Boquete. The best café and bakery in town, serving truly delicious fresh bread, pies, cakes, sandwiches, soups and other tasty fare. Highly recommended, don't miss it.

⊕ Entertainment

Boquete and around *p216, maps p217 and p219*

Bars and clubs

Not renowned for its nightlife, Boquete is usually a ghost-town after 2200. You might find boozy gatherings at some of the hostels or expat restaurants mentioned above, otherwise most revellers head to the popular Canadian-run **Amigos Bar**, Plaza Central, which features live music and lashings of beer. The African-themed jazz haunt of **Zanzibar**, Av Central (closed Mon), is another good option.

Theatre

Boquete Community Players Theatre, across the river near the *feria* grounds, www.bcpboquete.com. Popular plays and theatrical events from Boquete's expat crowd. Check their website for the latest.

⊛ Festivals

Boquete and around *p216, maps p217 and p219*

Jan Thousands of visitors descend on Boquete for its annual **Feria de las Flores y del Café** (Flower and Coffee Fair), www.feriadeboquete.com, a 10-day festival showcasing the region's abundance of exotic and colourful flowers. Coffee harvesting is also in full swing and the occasion draws tradesmen from all over Central America. Usually commences 2nd week of Jan and lodgings fill up quickly; book in advance.

Mar Founded in 2007, the Boquete **Jazz and Blues Festival**, www.boquetejazzand bluesfestival.com, sees a convergence of musical talent. The 2nd most important musical festival in the country after the **Panama City Jazz Festival** (see page 70).

Apr The **Feria de las Orquídeas** (Orchid Fair) is the time and place to shop for orchids, which grow in abundance throughout the Chiriquí highlands. A hit with horticulturalists and a good place to share tips and expertise.

⊙ What to do

Boquete and around *p216, maps p217 and p219*

Kayaking and whitewater rafting

For more information about whitewater rafting in Chiriquí and the Comarca Ngäbe-Buglé, see box, page 226.

Boquete Outdoor Adventures, Plaza los Establos, Av Central, T720-2284, www.boqueteoutdooradventures.com. Various 1-day and multi-day adventure packages in Chiriquí and beyond. Specializes in

Whitewater rafting

Western Panama's rugged terrain offers some of the most accessible and challenging whitewater rapids in Central America. Everything from gentle Grade II jaunts to heart-racing encounters with Grade V monsters are possible on the region's extensive river system. Nearly all specialized tour operators are based in Boquete and the best year-round rafting is on the **Río Chiriquí Viejo**, although this fantastic 128-km waterway is now under threat from hydroelectric projects – enjoy it while you can. The **Sabo section** is very good for cautious beginners with its relatively tame Grade II and III rapids. More adventurous types can try the Grade III and IV rapids on the **Palón section**, while the Grade IV **Jaguar section** is a highly popular stretch with its 73 rapids and 16 km of canyons and waterfalls. There are several very technical Grade V and VI rapids on the Chiriquí Viejo that require experience and preparation, including the **Puma section** near Volcán. The region's rapids become more powerful in the wet season, May to November, rising a grade or two during the torrential final months. They usually supply enough water for some more subdued rapids, including the Grade III **Witches section** of the **Río Chiriquí**, the second most popular river in the province. In the Comarca Ngäbe-Buglé, often overlooked by travellers, the powerful Río Fonseca has plentiful rapids ranging from Grade I to IV. You'll find an excellent and professional outfit operating in Soloy; contact **Eusebio Bejerano**, T6868-3433. Whatever river you choose to ride, be sure to discuss your options thoroughly with your chosen operator and check your insurance cover before setting out.

whitewater kayaking but also offers rafting and sea kayaking.
Chiriqui River Rafting, Av Central, next to Lourdes, T6897-4382, www.panama-rafting. com. Open 0830-1730. Bilingual father-and-son team Héctor and Ian Sánchez, offer 2- to 4-hr Grade II, III and IV trips with modern equipment. Recommended.
Panama Rafters, just below the square on Av Central, T720-2712, www.panama rafter.com. Good, solid rafting operation with quality gear, guides and a strong emphasis on safety. Kayak and multi-day trips are available, but most trips are run on the excellent Río Chiriquí Viejo.

Tour operators
Boquete Mountain Safari Tours, Plaza Los Establos, Av Central, T6627-8829, www.boquetemountainsafari tours.com. From short hikes to full-on adventures, **Boquete Mountain Safari Tours** offers a good selection of half- and full-day tours, including horse riding, hot springs, coffee farms, hiking and birdwatching. Uses distinctive vintage Land Rovers. Helpful and friendly with lots of good reports.
Boquete Tree Trek, Plaza los Establos, Av Central, T720-1635, www.boquetetree trek.com. Known for their high-speed zip-line tours of the forest canopy, **Boquete Tree Trek** also offers hiking, birdwatching, biking and other outdoor adventures, as well as overnight stays on their rural property.
Coffee Adventures, T720-3852, www.coffee adventures.net. A diverse range of hiking, birdwatching and community tours of the areas surrounding Boquete, as well as visits to the Kotowa coffee estate. Expertly run by Terry Van Niekerk, who speaks English, Spanish and Dutch. Good reports and highly recommended, especially if hiking the Sendero Los Quetzales.
Explora Ya, Plaza Los Establos, Av Central, T730-8344, www.exploraya.com. Excellent and well-presented new operator that

offers a creative range of local adventures, including hiking, rafting, hot springs, horse riding, rocking climbing and ascents of Volcán Barú. Affiliated with the popular **Habla Ya** Spanish school. Very popular, professional and highly recommended.

❷ Transport

Boquete and around *p216,*
maps p217 and p219
Buses to **David** depart from the southeast corner of the plaza, every 20 mins, 1 hr, US$1.75, and travel south along Av Belisarrio Porras. Local buses ply the hills around town and collect passengers along Av Central, irregular schedules, US$0.50-2. The easiest way to reach hotels in the surrounding suburbs – including Palo Alto, Jaramillo

Arriba, Jaramillo Abajo – is by taxi; most one-way fares are US$2-5.

❶ Directory

Boquete and around *p216,*
maps p217 and p219
Language schools Habla Ya, Plaza Los Establos, Av Central, T720-1294, www.hablaya panama.com. Very good, professional school that receives good reviews from former students. Class sizes are small and teachers are well trained. Recommended. Spanish by the River, Alto Boquete, T720-3456, www.spanishat locations.com. A little out of town but has also received very good reviews. **Laundry** Lavomático Las Burbujas, just south of church, very friendly, US$1 to wash.

Western Chiriquí Highlands

The calm, refreshing tierras altas *west of Volcán Barú are the setting for a disparate network of bucolic villages, all traditionally grounded in the trade of vegetables, fruit, flowers, coffee, cattle and race horses. Bound by the Cordillera Talamanca to the north and the Costa Rican border to the west, the region boasts a surprising diversity of natural landscapes. Rolling green pastures, desolate lava fields, misty cloud forest and jagged mountain peaks provide endless opportunities for birdwatching, horse riding or idle rambling through the wilderness. Despite the region's vast outdoors potential – including two world-class national parks – Chiriquí's western highlands are far less visited than the sites around Boquete. As a result, the region offers an authentic taste of highland life, for the moment unsullied by grasping international developers.* ➽ *For listings, see pages 235-237.*

Volcán and around → *For listings, see pages 235-237. Colour map 1, B1.*

Nestled in a high plateau formed by an ancient eruption, the highland town of Volcán basks in the shifting moods of rugged Volcán Barú. The town, 32 km north of La Concepción, is stretched out over a sparse strip of highway where you'll find shops, restaurants, banks, petrol stations and other amenities. Venture off the main thoroughfare and a criss-cross grid of backroads peters out amid fields and scrubland. Perched on the western, leeward flank of the volcano, Volcán has highly porous pumice soil that dries within minutes of draining. Wiry shrubs, pine trees, rough grasses and tough wild flowers proliferate in the immediate surroundings. Elsewhere, much of the landscape is filled with rolling pastures and dairy farms, a joy to hike and often resplendent with chattering birds. Volcán is located 1450 m above sea level and often chilly after dark. It is a quiet, friendly and underrated place.

Arriving in Volcán

Buses to Volcán (marked Cerro Punta or Río Sereno) depart regularly from David's bus terminal, pausing at La Concepción en route. You can get around town on foot, but its sprawling layout means buses, every five to 15 minutes, are a more convenient option if you need to get from one side of town to the other. There is no ATP office in Volcán but tour operators may be able to supply advice, along with the ANAM office on the highway to Cerro Punta.

Lagunas de Volcán

ⓘ *4 km from central Volcán. Take a taxi to the old airport, US$2.50 then follow the dirt road for 2 km. In the forest, a left branch leads to the lakes. Arrange a return time with the driver.*

Backed by verdant and hills and teeming forests, the tranquil waters of Lagunas de Volcán will please birders and landscape photographers alike. Opened to the public in 1994, the

Volcán

Where to stay 🛏		Guatoso 3
Cabañas Dr Esquivel 1	Las Huacas 6	Il Forno 4
Cabañas Reis 2	Motel California 7	Maná 5
Don Tavo 3	Volcán Lodge 8	Panadería Ortega 6
Dos Ríos 4		Restaurante Mary 7
Hospedaje Brisas	Restaurants 🍴	Valley of the Moon 8
de California 5	Cerro Brujo Gourmet 1	
	Dalys's 2	

N
Not to scale

Daring and defiance in the Chiriquí Highlands

An hour before midnight on 12 October 1968, the first shots rang out in a spontaneous uprising against Panama's military junta, who had seized control of the country just 24 hours earlier. Around 10 *campesinos* fired at a Guardia patrol truck near Volcán before fleeing over the border into Costa Rica. The Guardia responded by posting over 100 reinforcements and burning down the houses of known troublemakers. But the rebels, who had close ties to recently deposed President Arnulfo Arias, were granted refuge by Costa Rican authorities. They began acquiring submachine guns, shotguns and pistols and, on 22 November, crossed back into Panama. The band of 30 armed *campesino* guerrillas were soon assisted by an American Vietnam vet called Kimball, who provided them with some rudimentary military training. On 30 November they ran their first ambush at Piedra Candela. It was a botched affair, but they managed to kill 12 *guardias* before escaping along the mountain trails. Nonetheless, the confrontation left many of them rattled, including Kimball, who left the group only to be arrested in Bambito the next day. According to rumours, he was held in solitary confinement for five months, rigorously tortured and finally hanged in his cell.

On 5 December, Manuel Noriega was placed in military command of Chiriquí. Notorious for his love of other people's pain – the sicker and more degrading the better – nothing could have been worse for the incipient guerrilla band… or the people of Chiriquí. Several hundred innocent *campesinos* were rounded up and summarily 'interrogated'. Several hundred more fled across the border. As Noriega systematically stamped out the insurgency, a darkness fell over the province. Using pilfered whiskey from the Colón Free Trade Zone, Costa Rica was bribed on side by Maximum Leader Omar Torrijos. The rebels were forced into Panama and split into two groups but, on 24 January 1969, one of their most important commanders, Ariosto González, was captured and killed by Guardia forces. The insurgency bravely fought on under the leadership of a Uruguayan called Sardiñas, but by October, the Chiriquí resistance movement had been all but crushed. Sardiñas retreated to Costa Rica where he was assassinated the following year. Throughout the conflict, the Guardia maintained strict control over the press and few people outside of Chiriquí ever heard about Panama's short-lived but highly spirited guerrilla movement. Who knows how things might have turned out otherwise.

13-ha area features two large lakes rich in waders and waterfowl, including many ducks, herons, geese and jacanas. The surrounding vegetation, great for casual strolling, is home to woodpeckers, antbirds, fly-catchers, warblers and scores of other species. At 1240 m, the lagunas are the highest lake system in Panama. They fall under the private property of the Janson family, who operate one of the finest coffee fincas in the country (see below).

Torcaza Coffee Estate

ⓘ *Next to the old airport, T771-4306, www.estatecoffee.com, Mon-Fri 0800-1630, Sat 0830-1330. Tours in Spanish or English, US$10 per person, arrange 24 hrs in advance.*

The Torcaza Coffee Estate – managed by Peter, Maico, Carl and Ricardo Janson, third generation Panamanians descended from European and North American immigrants –

produces some of the finest gourmet coffee in the world. The high-altitude plantations enjoy a long growing season that gives their beans a special complexity of flavours, including a unique butterscotch tang that pulls together all the disparate elements of a standard cup of Janson coffee. Organic farming methods and traditional production techniques supplement a meticulous picking and sorting process that the brothers say helps distinguish their product from that of the competition.

Sitio Arqueológico Barriles
ⓘ *Daily 0900-1700, US$1, 6 km from town on the road to Caizán, several buses daily, US$0.50; or take a taxi, US$4.*

The Barriles archaeological site is modest compared to the grand Mayan metropolises further north in Central America, but it is intriguing nonetheless, especially if the curator, Edna Houx, is on hand to bring the exhibitions to life. Thought to have been a socio-ceremonial centre with a population of up to 1000 inhabitants, Barriles was part of the Gran Chiriquí culture, which included Western Panama and large parts of southern Costa Rica. It peaked AD 300-900 and mysteriously declined, some say after a massive volcanic eruption. The site's name, which means 'barrels', is derived from several large cylindrical stones. It is believed that they were used to transport volcanic boulders from the foot of the Volcán Barú, some 20 km away. Barriles was first uncovered by the Houx family in 1924. It was abandoned during the Second World War and, when the family returned in 1942, the site had been badly damaged by *campesino* squatters. In 1949, National Geographic conducted a major excavation of the area and uncovered a giant ceremonial *metate* (grinding stone) that featured 48 carved human heads – a motif almost certainly connecting the site to human sacrifice. Other important finds included 14 humanoid statues.

Even today, relatively little is known about the site. A popular myth suggests that it was once occupied by African and Asian immigrants, evidenced by the physical characteristics of the statues, which are said to be more Asiatic and Negroid than Amerindian. This is likely to be untrue, as ceramic styles dating to the same era show a clear lineage from previous cultures with no dramatic interruptions. In any case, the statues themselves are highly stylized and unrepresentative of a true human form. Many of the best finds at Barriles are now under the care of the **Reina Torres de Araúz Anthropological Museum** in Panama City (see page 56). The landscaped grounds are still interesting to stroll around and are filled with more fiery heliconias than you're likely to see anywhere else. The recently excavated foundations of a homestead lie at the end of a meandering trail, while a small building conceals a wealth of ceramic artefacts including funerary urns, obsidian knives, *metates*, three-legged incense burners and a very ancient medicine jar. There is also an interesting petroglyph near the house, which researchers say is a map of the area – spirals signify mountains, circles are towns and rectangles are temples.

Paso Ancho
Flanked by wide open spaces and sparsely vegetated lava fields, the settlement of Paso Ancho lies roughly a kilometre beyond Volcán on the highway to Cerro Punta. If you have your own vehicle, you can experience the strange optical illusion for which the area is known. Stop the engine and put the car in neutral, then watch as it mysteriously rolls uphill, defying the laws of gravity. Paso Ancho is the starting point of an important trail to the summit of Volcán Barú. The trail is beautiful, climbing through lush cloud forests and then ascending steeply over loose volcanic rock and scree. It is poorly marked near the top, however, and for that reason a guide is recommended. Note the climb requires seven

to nine hours one way and most people use an alternative trail from Boquete, which is considered a shorter and easier ascent (see page 220). Paso Ancho is home to the **Carmen Estate**, which is not open to the public but produces excellent, award-winning coffee.

Bambito

The diminutive settlement of Bambito lies roughly halfway between Volcán and Cerro Punta. It is a tranquil and sparsely inhabited destination backed by volcanic cliffs and pine forests. Several comfortable hotels dot the area including the reputable **Hotel Bambito**, which manages a famous trout farm beside the highway. **Venta de Truchas** ① *0700-1600, offer fresh fish straight from the pools at US$2.60 per pound*. You can rent a rod to catch them, US$5, or use your own, US$2.60, or just ask the guards to snare one. Trout are not native to Panama; they were introduced in 1925 and make a delicious addition to local rivers and dinner menus.

Cerro Punta and around → *For listings, see pages 235-237. Colour map 1, B1.*

Surrounded by a patchwork of diminutive fields, the sleepy town of Cerro Punta lies at the heart of a vegetable- and flower-growing zone known as 'Little Switzerland'. Many of the town's Alpine-style houses faithfully reflect the influence of former Swiss and Yugoslav settlers – there is even a small settlement nearby called Nueva Suiza. At an altitude of 2130 m, the countryside around Cerro Punta is cool, lush, green and reminiscent of rural England. Dairy farms and race-horse stables supplement the traditional economy of 'cold' produce, such as strawberries, cabbages, potatoes and carrots. It is an excellent area for walking and birdwatching, but economic pressures have sadly pushed the crops high up the hillsides, at the expense of wooded areas. The use of agro-chemicals is extensive too and on a bad day the smell of synthetic fertilizer hangs in the air. Don't let that deter you from exploring the area, though, as it is home to super-friendly villages, stunning forests and hiking trails. The flower-festooned village of **Guadalupe** lies around 3 km north of Cerro Punta at the end of the road. It is a quiet, friendly place filled with well-tended gardens, strawberry stands and flower stores.

Arriving in Cerro Punta

Cerro Punta lies 25 km north of Volcán on a paved highway. It is served by frequent buses from David, which pass through La Concepción and Volcán and eventually terminate at Guadalupe just beyond Cerro Punta. There are a few taxis around town, otherwise most attractions lie a short hike away. There is no tourist office in Cerro Punta but Hotel Los Quetzales in Guadalupe sells maps and can hook you up with their guides.

Race-horse stables

Cerro Punta is a renowned centre of race-horse breeding and training. Some claim the high altitude and fresh air encourage the horses to develop strong lungs and hearts. Established in 1977, **Haras Cerro Punta** ① *T227-3371, www.harascerropunta.com*, is the largest stud stable in town and has a reputation for turning out award-winning thoroughbreds. Tours of the stables are possible with advance notice. An alternative is **Haras Carinthia** ① *T771-2066*.

Sendero Los Quetzales

① *To get to the trail, head north out of Cerro Punta, cross over the bridge and follow the signs to the ANAM station at Alto Respingo, 4 km away; alternatively, take a 4WD taxi, US$10. Park* *entrance US$5. Total journey time, 5-8 hrs one way. Note: the trail was closed at the time of research but should be re-opening in later 2012; enquire locally on its status before setting out.*

Meandering through pristine cloud forests at the foot of **Volcán Barú**, the Sendero Los Quetzales is widely regarded as one of Central America's most stunning hiking trails. Connecting **Cerro Punta** and **Boquete**, the 10-km *sendero* can be followed in either direction, but it is quicker and less strenuous when followed west to east. Note you will have to cover some extra ground between the towns and the rangers' stations, bringing the total distance to 22 km (this can be reduced with 4WD taxis). Commencing at the rangers' station in **Alto Respingo**, 4 km from Cerro Punta, the trail climbs briefly before continuing through the forest in a general downhill fashion. After a few hours, you will arrive at **Mirador La Roca**, a rest point with picnic tables, campsite and expansive views. The final stretch follows the Río Caldera and some roughly hewn dirt tracks as far as the second rangers' station at **Alto Chiquero**. From there, it is another 8 km to Boquete. The trail is much easier in the dry season, but can be enjoyed throughout the year, if properly kitted with rubber boots and raincoat. During the wet season, it can make sense to begin in Boquete, where you have a better chance of a dry morning.

Finca Drácula

ⓘ *Guadalupe, T771-2070, www.fincadracula.com. Mon-Fri 0800-1130, 1300-1700; entrance US$7, entrance + guided tours US$10 (reserve in advance). To get there, follow the signs past Hotel Quetzales, 10-15 mins uphill.*

There's no sign of Transylvanian vampires at Finca Drácula, a superb orchid sanctuary named after the *Telipogon vampirus* flower. Said to be the largest collection of orchids in Latin America, the finca is home to 2200 species, some of them very rare and endangered. The sanctuary is particularly renowned for its efforts to protect and propagate native species threatened by temperature change, deforestation or the disappearance of pollinating insects. Their scientific work includes the discovery of 150 previously unknown species. Finca Drácula was established by Andrew Maduro in 1969. Formerly home to extensive cattle pastures, the 10-ha grounds are today immaculately landscaped with winding trails, trees, lakes, ponds and streams. The main house was built by Swiss-German immigrants around 1920 and has been reconstructed using cedar. Finca Drácula offers month-long internships for students from diverse academic backgrounds.

Parque Internacional La Amistad (PILA) → For listings, see pages 235-237.
Colour map 1, A1.

Encompassing 401,000 ha of diverse life zones, the Parque Internacional La Amistad is jointly administered by Costa Rica and Panama. It is home to some of the last remaining highland virgin forests in Central America, including areas that have been untouched for 25,000 years. The park is a designated UNESCO World Heritage Site and enjoys particularly high rates of endemism. Some 180 endemic plant species and 40 endemic bird species have been recorded in the region. The Panamanian section of the park covers approximately 207,000 ha of complex volcanic terrain including the numerous peaks, valleys and cliffs of the **Talamanca** mountain range. Temperatures and altitudes vary greatly, encouraging high biodiversity. Some 400 bird species inhabit La Amistad, including harpy eagles, quetzals, crested eagles and bare-necked umbrella birds. Mammal species number about 100 and include tapirs, ocelots and jaguars. In 2006, the **Darwin Initiative** funded a collaborative research project led by the **Natural History Museum**,

INBio and ANAM. They discovered many new species including 12 plant, one beetle, 15 amphibian and three reptile species.

Arriving at the Parque Internacional La Amistad

In Panama, there are three entrances to the Parque Internacional La Amistad. On the lesser visited Caribbean side, access is via the Naso-run **Weckso** project (for more information, see page 251). Dominated by dense lowland rainforests, the trails and infrastructure on this side are generally undeveloped – you will require a guide for any serious exploration. On the Pacific side, the main entrance is at **Las Nubes**, around 7 km northwest of Cerro Punta, 0800-1600, US$5, where well-maintained trails snake through highland cloud forests, great for casual walking. If you wish to stay overnight, there is a basic rangers' station with beds, US$12; bring your own sleeping bag and book in advance through **ANAM**. A third entrance can be found in **Guadalupe**, 3 km northeast of Cerro Punta. It is normally only used by guests of **Cabañas Los Quetzales** – a collection of beautiful eco-cabins located a few kilometres inside the park's cloud forests (see below).

Hiking trails

Several trails commence at the Las Nubes entrance. For a casual 500-m stroll through the forest, head to **Sendero Puma Verde**. Nearby, **Sendero El Retoño** is a 2.1-km loop trail, also flat and very easy. It crosses streams and rivers and offers good birdwatching opportunities. For a moderately strenuous two- to three-hour hike, the **Sendero La Cascada** leads uphill to a series of miradors with expansive views over the valleys. It concludes at an impressive 50-m-high waterfall. **Vereda la Montaña** is a fairly strenuous 4-km hike up **Cerro Picacho**. It take around six hours to complete the round trip (guide necessary) and you will be rewarded with fine views of the Caribbean. There is a rangers' station at the summit, if you want to stay overnight.

Cabañas Los Quetzales

Constructed long before the cloud forests of La Amistad were protected as a nature reserve, the Swiss-style chalets of Cabañas Los Quetzales offer excellent opportunities for close-up encounters with wildlife. Encounters with countless buzzing hummingbirds, inquisitive racoons and friendly kinkajous are virtually guaranteed if you decide to stay overnight. Resplendent quetzals are fairly easy to spot too. Located at the end of a rough dirt track 1.5 km from Guadalupe, the cosy cabins are well positioned for early morning hikes when birds and other beasts are most active. They are equipped with hot water, wood fires and gas lanterns, but no electricity. The setting is very romantic.

Volcán to Costa Rica → *For listings, see pages 235-237. Colour map 1, A1.*

From the police station in Volcán, a paved highway winds west towards the Costa Rican border, climbing over Cerro Pando and passing scenic coffee plantations and cattle country. **Los Pozos**, an area of rustic hot springs beside a rushing river, lies about 8.5 km from town, but the dirt road is unsigned and you will need a 4WD to reach it. At **Río Colorado**, 15 km from Volcán, **Beneficio Café Durán** ① *www.cafeduran.com*, is a famous coffee-processing plant.

Finca Hartmann

① *Santa Clara, T6450-1853, www.fincahartmann.com. To get there, take a bus or drive 27 km from Volcán along the Río Sereno highway and look for the sign on the left, a few hundred*

Border crossing: Panama–Costa Rica

Río Sereno

Río Sereno sees comparatively little international traffic. It is a very scenic crossing with convenient access to and from the Western Chiriquí highlands, but otherwise out of the way. There are numerous general shops and a few cheap restaurants. Note vehicle formalities cannot be completed on the Costa Rican side.

Panamanian immigration Open Mon-Sat 0900-1700; Sun 0900-1500.
Costa Rican immigration Open Mon-Sat 0800-1600; Sun 0900-1400.
Currency exchange There is a bank near the main plaza with an ATM, but no exchange; bring currency or enquire locally where you can acquire colones/dollars.
Onwards to Costa Rica Frequent buses to San Vito via Sabillito with numerous onward connections.
Onwards to Panama Dawn to dusk bus services to Volcán, La Concepción and David, every 15 minutes.
Time Panama is one hour ahead of Costa Rica.

metres after the gas station. Coffee tours cost US$10, all other tours, including hiking and birding, are individually priced; enquire in advance.
Specializing in the production of shade-grown boutique coffee, Finca Hartmann, 27 km from Volcán, was founded in 1940. The plantations, which are sustained through robust organic practices, occupy the buffer zone of the Parque Internacional La Amistad, enjoying the cover of large rainforest trees. Numerous hiking trails criss-cross the property, highly renowned as a birdwatching and wildlife mecca. Based on observations made by the **Smithsonian Tropical Research Institute**, 282 bird species and 62 mammal species can be spotted on the densely wooded finca. A small museum pays tribute to local insect life with some enormous beetles and cockroaches (no longer alive and safely behind display glass). Visitors are welcome and there are rustic cabins too.

Río Sereno → *Colour map 1, A1.*

The international crossing at Río Sereno, 45 km from Volcán, is extremely quiet, friendly and usually easy, but not recommended if you are entering Costa Rica with your own vehicle (see box, above). Approaching the village from Volcán, abandoned military installations are visible on the right. The bus will drop you a short walk from the border. A small handful of Panamanian businesses, including the **Banco Nacional**, are centred around the plaza. South of Río Sereno, a winding road runs 50 km to Paso Canoas, some 2½ hours away by bus. It is in poor shape, however, and rarely used.

For sleeping and eating price codes and other relevant information, see pages 16-19.

◉ Where to stay

Volcán *p227, map p228*

$$$ Dos Ríos, Río Sereno Highway, on the edge of town, T771-4271, www.dosrios.com. pa. A long-standing motel-style place with beautiful lush grounds and slightly tired rooms. Noise is reportedly an issue – get a room upstairs so you don't have to hear the creaky floorboards. OK, good staff, but not great value.

$$$ Las Huacas, Río Sereno Highway, on the edge of town, T771-4363, www.huacas cabins.com. Pleasant cottages with full kitchens, hot water, bedrooms, living and dining areas. The largest sleeps up to 8. The ground are rambling and fabulous, home to lots of shady trees, streams, pond and geese.

$$ Cabañas Dr Esquivel, behind Supermarcado Bérad, follow the signs, northwest side of town, T771-4770, www. cabanasdresquivel.com. Several large cabins in a row, all comfortable, clean and fully equipped with kitchens, sofas, hot water, Wi-Fi and TV. Friendly and helpful.

$$ Cabañas Reis, at the entrance to Volcán, T771-5153, www.cabanasreis.com. Formerly Cabañas Señorials, this pleasant road-side lodging has a row of 10 clean, tidy, concrete cabins, fully kitted with cable TV, Wi-Fi, hot water and comfortable furnishings. Friendly, English-speaking management.

$$ Hotel Don Tavo, Av Central, northwest side of town, T/F771-5144, www.volcanbaru. com/hoteldontavo/index.htm. A convenient main street location but rooms are a bit run-down and not great value. Ask to see a room first. On the plus side, there's a tranquil green lawn, restaurant and internet café.

$$ Volcán Lodge, Calle 1, near the entrance to Volcán, southeast side of town, T771-4709, www.volcanlodge.webs.com. A very cosy, historic and well-restored wooden guesthouse with a handful of clean, simple, comfortable rooms. The restaurant is one of the best places in town. Warm, friendly and recommended.

$ Hospedaje Brisas de California, Calle 11, Nueva California, T771-4323. Budget guest-house managed by a very friendly and helpful Panamanian couple, Efraín and Mariela, who do everything they can to make you feel at home. Rooms are simple but pleasant, equipped with TV, hot water, Wi-Fi and a simple outdoor cooking area. Recommended.

$ Motel California, 1 block west of Av Central, look for signs, T771-4272. Quiet, motel-style place off the main drag. They have a range of basic rooms, some in better repair than others, check before accepting. Hot water, parking and limited Wi-Fi available. Good green lawn with lots of birdlife around. Friendly.

Paso Ancho *p230*

$$$-$$ Las Plumas, Paso Ancho, T771-5541, www.las-plumas.com. Set in 2.4 ha of leafy grounds, Dutch-owned Las Plumas offers 4 comfortable, well-equipped cottages available on a daily, weekly or monthly basis. Amenities include hot water, laundry room, satellite TV, high-speed internet, living room and kitchen.

Bambito *p231*

$$$ Cabañas Kucikas, Bambito, www. kucikas.com, T771-4245. Perched on the banks of Chiriquí Viejo, Cabañas Kucikas offers a range of comfortable cottages complete with fully equipped kitchens, lounges, dining areas and bedrooms. Some of them have capacity for up to 10 people. A pleasant setting.

$$$ Hotel Bambito, Vía Cerro Punta, T215-9448, www.hotelbambito.com. Alpine-style resort with 47 rooms and natural landscapes. Luxury amenities include an indoor swimming pool, jacuzzi, sauna, spa facilities, tennis court, health club, restaurant and lounge. Rooms are comfortable, well equipped and decorated in relaxing earthy hues. Breakfast included, packages available.

Cerro Punta *p231*

$$$$-$$$ Hostal Cielito Sur, Nueva Suiza, 2 km before Cerro Punta, T771-2038, www.cielitosur.com. A very comfortable and hospitable B&B operated by Janet and Glenn Lee. Rooms are comfortable and creatively decorated; some are equipped with refrigerator and microwave. Amenities include restaurant, porch and communal area with soft sofas and fireplace, great for unwinding after a day on the trails.
$ Hotel Cerro Punta, Calle Principal, T771-2020, www.cerropunta.zxq.net. Needs a lick of paint. 10 tired, slightly cramped rooms with hot water and no TV. There's a dated wood-panelled restaurant offering hot meals. Past its heyday but quite friendly, helpful and OK for budget travellers.

Guadalupe *p231*

$$$$-$$ Los Quetzales Lodge & Spa, T771-2182, www.losquetzales.com. A true forest hideaway with self-contained cabins inside Parque Amistad. A multitude of animals and birds, including quetzals, can be seen from the porches. Back in town, there are dormitories, chalets and some economical rooms, all comfortable and pleasant. Spa facilities and restaurant are excellent. Very special and highly recommended.

Volcán to Costa Rica *p233*

$$$ The Hartmanns, 1 km beyond the end of the dirt road, Santa Clara, T775-5223, www.fincahartmann.com, have comfortable wooden cabins available in the woods, no electricity but with bath and hot water on a working coffee finca. Also some bunks (**$**).

❷ Restaurants

Volcán *p227, map p228*

$$$ Cerro Brujo Gourmet, Av 6 y Calle 7a, Brisas del Norte, T6669-9196. Very tasty and creative cooking from chef Patricia Miranda. The menu is constantly changing and features home-grown organic produce from her garden. Lots of praise and good reports.
$$ Il Forno, off Av Central, turn left at the Hotel California sign. Open Thu-Sun. Authentic stone-baked pizzas, minestrone soup, lasagne and other fine Italian fare at this rustic favourite. A friendly owner and convivial atmosphere. A good selection of wines too.
$$ Maná, Calle 1, inside **Volcán Lodge**, near the entrance to town, T771-4709, www.volcanlodge.webs.com. Delicious home-cooked comfort food including soups, salads, sandwiches and hearty specialities such as filet mignon, beer-battered shrimps and fish of the day. An attractive setting in a historic wooden guesthouse. Affordable prices and highly recommended.
$$ Valley of the Moon, off Av Central, near southern entrance to town. Closed Tue. Part of the Natural Solutions alternative health centre. They serve soups, cakes and fine organic fare. Seating indoors and out, including a tranquil terrace with a bubbling fountain. Open breakfast, lunch and dinner.
$$-$ Gustoso, Av Central. Bright, young, bohemian place managed by a pair of friendly girls from Panama and Brazil. They serve good burgers, crêpes, grilled dishes, sandwiches and specials, such as coconut curry. Pleasant and recommended.
$ Dalys's, Av Central, at the southern entrance to town inside an old gas station. Generous cooked breakfasts to fuel up before a long day hiking. They also serve sandwiches, cakes, coffee and other light snacks. Casual, friendly and popular with expats.
$ Restaurante Mary, Av Central. A popular lunchtime haunt where you can pick up a good, economical, wholesome set meals, such as *pollo frito* and *pollo guisado*. A la carte dishes **$$** are OK, but not as good value.

Cafés and bakeries

There are lots of bakeries in town, great for a cheap breakfast, coffee or snack.

Panadería Ortega, Av Central. Serves a good selection of cakes and cookies. A nice place to warm up with hot chocolate or coffee when the chill twilight sets in.

Cerro Punta *p231*
$ Restaurant Cerro Punta, Calle Principal. One of a handful of cosy eateries in town. They serve economical local fare.

Guadalupe *p231*
Look out for the kiosks selling sweet strawberries fresh from the farms. For the best sit-down meal in the village, head to Los Quetzales Lodge; other dining options consist of unpretentious cafés.
$ Restaurante Mónica, next to Los Quetzales Lodge. A friendly, economical locals' café serving simple cooked breakfasts and lunches.

⊕ Festivals

Volcán *p227, map p228*
Dec The Feria de las Tierras Altas is held during the 2nd week of Dec. Festivities include dancing, a craft fair and general merriment.

⊙ What to do

Despite Volcán's incredible touristic potential, there are few tour operators in town – Boquete remains the main hub of action. Your hotel should be able to recommend a reputable guide (essential for climbing Barú), otherwise try:
Green Mountain Adventures, Av Central, at the northwest exit to town, near Hotel Dos Ríos, T6457-6080. A good range of outdoor activities, including hiking, biking, rock climbing, agro-tourism and horse riding.

⊖ Transport

Volcán *p227, map p228*
Buses to **David** run southeast along Av Central every 15-20 mins, US$3. For **Cerro Punta** and destinations north, buses turn north outside the police station, every 20-30 mins, US$1. To **Río Sereno**, wait for a passing bus on Av Central, every 30 mins, US$2.25. To **Los Barriles**, take a Caizán bus from the station next to Panadería Ortega, about 1 km northwest of the police station on Av Central; every 30 mins, 15 mins, US$0.70.

Cerro Punta *p231*
Buses to **David** depart every 30 mins, US$3.50, passing through Volcán and Concepción (Bugaba) en route. A **taxi** is recommended to reach **Parque Nacional La Amistad**, US$5.

Comarca Ngäbe-Buglé

Life in the Comarca Ngäbe-Buglé obeys its own laws and innate natural rhythms. It is an extraordinarily peaceful place filled with rugged, earthy tones and scenes of rural easiness. The sounds of birdsong, crickets and clicking cicadas permeate the air, interrupted only by the crackled violins of Ngäbe community radio or the occasional thwack of machetes on the undergrowth. The aroma of burning wood, bubbling stew and fresh-brewed coffee draws fieldworkers and hungry dogs alike, while horses stroll along the dirt roads, with or without riders, and wandering chickens scratch nonchalantly in the dust. But beyond the Comarca's disarming sense of serenity, life in its dispersed highland communities is relentlessly tough. Punctuated by vast mountainous folds and powerful rivers, few landscapes in Panama are as daunting or difficult to traverse, especially in the absence of developed infrastructure. The Ngäbe and Buglé are among the poorest people in Latin America and largely ignored by the world outside. The strength and tranquillity of their communities is a true testament to their fortitude and character. ⮞ *For listings, see page 242.*

Arriving in the Comarca Ngäbe-Buglé → *Colour map 1, B2-B4.*

Getting there
Getting to the Comarca independently has never been easier. If **driving**, the Interamericana highway runs parallel to the Cordillera Central with several paved access roads. If using public transport, regular **buses** now run directly to numerous Ngäbe towns and villages. To some extent, **taxis** to the Comarca are possible from populated areas on its outskirts, including Tolé.

Getting around
Getting into the Comarca is much less of a challenge than getting around. Beyond the main communities, there are very few paved roads and even a 4WD has its limits, especially in the wet season. Most of the time you'll have to rely on old-fashioned methods – **walking** and **horse riding**.

Tourist information
Panama's tourist board, the **ATP**, is now starting to support the Comarca in its efforts to draw visitors. The office in David may have some basic information, but don't count on it. Your best source of up-to-date advice is the **Peace Corps**, which has English-speaking volunteers working in numerous communities, some of them specifically in tourism. If you can't find the Peace Corps, you'll have to rely on your own skills of enquiry. Priests are usually trustworthy and helpful, and shop owners know everyone and everything about the community. Useful **tourism co-ops** and NGOs can sometimes be found in larger communities.

What to expect
The Comarca is a semi-autonomous indigenous territory similar to a Native American reservation. Tourism is in its very earliest stages, and infrastructure, where it exists, is extremely basic. Although a number of lodgings are under construction, at present there are no hostels; accommodation is in private homes or volunteer projects. Restaurants, where available, consist of simple cafés serving home-cooked grub. There is no electricity: a torch is essential if you plan to stay overnight. Be prepared for the possibility of bats and bugs in your room, bring a sheet sleeper (or sleeping bag for higher altitudes) and a mosquito net. Do not drink the water without first boiling or sterilizing it. Larger communities have simple shops selling bottled water, sodas, snacks and sundries. Rubber boots are essential for hiking in the wet season.

Customs and etiquette
The Ngäbe and Buglé are friendly people, but also quite reserved. Men are much more likely to strike up a casual conversation than women. Please understand that most outsiders are either volunteers, missionaries or representatives of mining or hydroelectric corporations and, for now, tourists and travellers are an unknown quantity. Women should dress conservatively and bathe in the rivers fully clothed. Men should not bare their chests. Some people, including children, may try to beg change from you and you are asked not to encourage it. If you would like to contribute something practical to your host or the community – for example, school books and stationery – it is always welcome. You should never travel to remote areas of the Comarca without a trustworthy guide. Even short trips out of the community may require accompaniment, so please seek advice before casually striking out on any trails. As ever, no photographs should be taken without permission, although many people will be happy to pose. It may be better if you don't bring alcohol into the Comarca.

Background

The Spanish conquest and resistance

At the time of the Spanish conquest in the 16th century, western Panama was home to numerous indigenous groups, including the Ngäbe and the Buglé, two linguistically separate but closely related cultures. Both groups fiercely resisted Spanish domination, especially the Buglé, who fought for years under the leadership of **Chief Urraca**. Both survived the conquest, but were systematically driven from the lowlands up into the less productive mountains of the Cordillera Central. The Ngäbe and Buglé led semi-nomadic lifestyles until the 1970s, when **General Omar Torrijos** encouraged them to settle into permanent communities in exchange for cattle, schools, clinics and other civic amenities.

Birth of the Comarca

The Ngäbe and Buglé won the right to establish their own semi-autonomous comarca in 1997. The signing of Law 10 by **President Ernesto Balladares** marked the end of a 40-year campaign that had included dedicated petitioning, hunger strikes and an extraordinary 400-km march to the capital. The new Comarca comprised land formerly belonging to Bocas del Toro, Chiriquí and Veraguas provinces. It continues to be self-governing with its own system of regional and general chiefs, although central government in Panama City maintains control over tax and expenditure. The Comarca's Ngäbe population stands at around 150,000 – up from around 110,000 a decade earlier. Its Buglé population is much smaller.

Recent struggles

Since 2009, regional tensions have been mounting over government plans to sell off the Comarca's mineral wealth, including **Cerro Colorado**, the second largest copper deposit in the world. Early in 2011, the Martinelli administration passed **Law 8**, which provided foreign companies bold new rights of exploration and exploitation. The Ngäbe responded by coordinating a series of disruptive protests and blocking the flow of traffic on the Interamericana. After violent confrontations between police and protestors, the government dropped Law 8 and promised to insert new protective articles into current mining legislation. In September 2011, Martinelli ran a rigged election in the Comarca after disenfranchising nearly half of its voters. There was a 28% turnout with 20% of the ballots spoiled. Nonetheless, an anti-mining candidate, **Silvia Carrera**, was appointed Cacique General after winning under 5000 votes.

Martinelli's failure to install his chosen candidate did not deter him from pressing ahead with his mining plans. In late 2011, the government tabled a series of amendments to **Mining Code 415**, which included dropping their promised protection for the Comarca. In response, Ngäbe protestors once again shut down the Interamericana, inspiring similar protests in other parts of the country. By March 2012, a fragile truce was in place and Silvia Carrera was negotiating with the government.

Culture and community

Settlements in the Comarca consist of dispersed hamlets and villages connected by rambling dirt roads and mule trails. Community life tends to be dominated by a handful of extended families bound by kinship ties. Slash-and-burn agriculture, livestock and fishing are supplemented by seasonal work in commercial coffee, fruit and vegetable plantations. Wages and conditions tend to be poor. Traditional housing is increasingly rare and

Mama Tata: the prophetic visions of Besikö

The religion of *Mama Tata*, which means 'Mother Father' in Ngäbere, began in 1961 after the prophetic dream of a young Ngäbe girl called Besikö. In her vision, an old man advised her that her traditional culture would be lost forever if the Ngäbe people did not strictly adhere to his demands. Alcohol should be banned in all Ngäbe communities, said the old man, along with the promiscuous festivals where it was so heavily consumed. Furthermore, the Ngäbere language should be rigorously practised and celebrated, along with traditional forms of dress, dance and craft. Versions of Besikö's vision vary from village to village, where one describes an encounter with the Virgin Mary and another a meeting with Jesus Christ on a motorbike. Whatever the source and nature of Besikö's vision, it became the inspiration for the deeply popular revivalist religion of Mama Tata. Fusing ancient animist philosophy and Christian spirituality, it roused, revitalized and unified the Ngäbe population. Today, Mama Tata has declined in popularity, but it has left a lasting and important cultural legacy. Besikö herself passed away years ago, but one of the Comarca's seven districts is named after her.

consists of cane-and-thatch roundhouses with conical roofs. Rectangular houses made from wooden planks or concrete are more common and, on the Caribbean side, you'll see houses raised on stilts. Households will typically shelter large extended families, but the nuclear structure is also common. In times past, the Ngäbe practised polygamy (the Buglé less so) but are now monogamous.

Rituals and traditions

Women continue to wear colourful traditional dresses called *naguas*. Their striking zig-zag patterns are said to symbolize the mountains and rivers of the Comarca or, according to some accounts, an ancient mythical snake. Intricate necklaces called *chakiras* are reserved for special occasions. Most men dress like typical *campesinos*, but some wear special shirts with trademark zig-zags and, at important events, traditional hats adorned with feathers. Several ancient traditions have survived the ages, including a feminine rite of passage called the *Mogon*, which marks the onset of puberty and the transition to womanhood. Important practical and traditional knowledge is imparted during the four-day ceremony, which includes social isolation, strict dietary provisions, ritual bathing, the cutting of hair and, after four weeks, a large and spirited feast. A host of interesting ceremonies are connected to the moon and its cycles, including the harvesting of fibres for making traditional bags called *chakras*. The most famous Ngäbe festival is the Balsería, a four-day event that involves throwing large balsa logs and ritual boxing matches. The traditional Ngäbe dance is the *jeki* and it is performed in a procession to the music of flutes, drums and conches.

Soloy → *For listings, see page 242. Colour map 1, B2.*

Surrounded by thundering waterfalls and powerful whitewater rivers, the rustic village of Soloy is home to around 6000 Ngäbe inhabitants, most of them subsistence farmers. Thanks to the efforts of grassroots NGOs and Peace Corps volunteers, the community has some rudimentary tourist infrastructure and makes a very practical and friendly introduction to the Comarca. Located in the western district of **Besiko**, it is considered a fairly commercial settlement that sees plenty of travellers from surrounding communities. It is also one of the most accessible places in the region, with paved road access from the Interamericana highway and public transport direct from David. It boasts numerous amenities including mobile phone reception, running water (not potable), a handful of simple lodgings, restaurants and basic stores. There is talk of electricity arriving in town, but for now, it is assuredly off the grid. Soloy is the gateway to numerous remote destinations, including a very challenging trail that leads all the way over the continental divide.

Arriving in Soloy

Direct **buses** run from David to Soloy, 0800-1200 and 1400-1700, 1¾ hours, US$3, arriving at a small plaza at the heart of the village. Alternatively, **trucks** depart from the turning on the Interamericana highway (opposite the turning for Horconcitos), one hour, US$1.50. The village is quite dispersed and bisected by a single paved road. You won't get lost, but exploring Soloy can involve a lot of walking. You are strongly advised to make contact with the village before your visit; call **Eusebio**, T6868-3433 or **Juan Carlos**, T6638-0944, who belong to the **OCAB** community tourism group. Alternatively, try the excellent **NGO Medo** ⓘ www.medo.awardspace.com, run by Adán Bejerano, T6468-5249 (English-speaking). Peace Corps volunteers are a great source of help once you've arrived. Online, try the community's website, www.comarcangobebugle.com.

Around Soloy

Soloy is a very relaxed place, great for strolling and striking up idle conversations with strangers. Adventurous souls can enjoy a thrilling rafting trip on the **Río Fonseca**, which courses past the community with Grade III-IV whitewater rapids; contact **Eusebio Bejerano**, T6868-3433, US$30-75 including all safety equipment. Cultural presentations can be arranged through OCAB or Medo (see above) and include *artesenía* presentations, a traditional *jeki* dance and *balsería* log-throwing, US$25. **Horacio Bejerano**, T6598-3325, maintains an excellent botanical garden with all kinds of rare orchids and interesting medicinal plants; tours US$5. There are several co-op stores around town where you can pick up local *artesanías* and produce – Soloy's coffee is organically grown and particularly good.

There are plenty of hikes in the countryside around the village. The **Sendero La Esperanza** is a light walk, 1½ hours' round trip, that offers fine views of the mountains before concluding at a double waterfall. The **Sendero Salto Mono**, three hours' round trip, leads to a sheer cliff with a powerful waterfall and, if in bloom, swathes of *chichica* (heliconia) flowers. For views of the Pacific Ocean, **Sendero Cerro Miel** is a moderately strenuous uphill hike, three to four hours' round trip. The most impressive of Soloy's many waterfalls is the **Cascada Kiki**, which some say is the highest in the country. The hike is only moderately strenuous, but the final descent into the canyon on a rope is not for the faint of heart; three to four hours' round trip, US$2 entrance. The hike to the Caribbean coast is a fascinating odyssey that leads deep into the Comarca. If the trail is open, it requires several challenging days of walking and lots of planning. Guides are US$15 per day and horses, particularly good for the trail to Kiki, are US$15 per person per day; arrange through Medo or OCAB (see above).

San Félix → *Colour map 1, B3.*

Nestled in a verdant river valley, the farming town of San Félix lies 64 km east of David on the Interamericana highway. Although it is technically located outside the Comarca, it is home to a significant Ngäbe population and is also a major gateway to remote Ngäbe communities beyond. San Félix has often been a flashpoint in anti-mining protests, with violent clashes between protestors and police taking place on the highway. Vehemently opposed to any form of mineral extraction in the region, the town is situated in the shadow of Cerro Colorado, a major copper deposit 30 km north. The 3-km access road to San Félix is opposite the turning to Las Lajas; look out for the Centro Commerical Oriente. Any bus heading east or west on the highway should be able to drop you there.

Around San Félix

Around 4 km east of San Félix, you'll find **Los Pozos del Galique**, a collection of three modest, curative hot springs. The turning is signed (not obvious) with a very rough 4-km access road; 4WD is necessary. There are no facilities at the springs; bring water, food and other sundries. In the Comarca, north of San Félix, the rugged and very traditional community of **Hato Chami** is making great strides with its community tourism programme. Visitors can enjoy really excellent birding and hiking in the surrounding hills and cloud forests, as well as horse riding, waterfalls and petroglyphs. Cultural presentations can also be arranged along with tours of local bee hives, coffee farms and a medicinal garden. **Buses** and **trucks** to Hato Chami leave every one to three hours from San Félix, two hours, US$2-4; start travelling as early in the day as possible.

Tolé and around → *Colour map 1, B3.*

Located 23 km east of San Félix on the Interamericana, the sleepy mestizo town of Tolé is a minor trade and administrative hub. Look out for the large arch marking the access road, from where it's a gentle 3- to 4-km walk uphill. The town is home to many Ngäbe but, like San Félix, it is actually outside the Comarca. Around 45 minutes north of Tolé on a paved road, the community of **Chichica** occupies a particularly striking location on a mountain ridge; buses every two to three hours. They offer a host of artisan and cultural presentations, as well as tours of sugar and coffee farms. It is a very friendly and easy-to-access community – ask around for the Peace Corps. Around 5 km west of Tolé on the Interamericana, a 3-km access road leads to the petroglyphs of **Nancito**; follow the road north until you reach the Cantina Oriente, then head west for 80 m or so.

⊙ Comarca Ngäbe-Buglé listings

For sleeping and eating price codes and other relevant information, see pages 16-19.

⊕ Where to stay

Soloy *p240*
At the time of research, a hostel was under construction in Soloy, but it was unclear when it would be open to the public.
The excellent NGO Medo, T6468-5249, has 1 clean, rustic room with 2 single beds and a shared outdoor latrine (**$**). Economical homestays can also be arranged through Medo, T6468-5249, or Horacio Bejerano, T6124-3686, on a daily or weekly basis, including 3 traditional meals.

Contents

Footprint features

Border crossings

At a glance

⊖ **Getting around** Buses, trucks and *piraguas* (river boats) on the mainland. High-speed *pangas* and water taxis on the islands.

⦿ **Time required** 7-14 days.

☼ **Weather** It rains frequently in Bocas del Toro with short torrential downpours possible at any time of the year. The region has its own microclimate and the driest months are Feb, Mar, Sep and Oct, which are best for diving.

✕ **When not to go** Although often busy with Christmas vacationers, the months of Nov and Dec can be filled with days of driving rain and mud. Due to poor visibility at those times, diving is unpredictable.

An obscure Caribbean province of scattered islands and secret enclaves, the remote and sparsely settled backwater of Bocas del Toro plays host to a dazzling profusion of ecological niches. Steamy lowland rainforests, misty highland cloud forests, teeming coastal lagoons, kaleidoscopic coral reefs and rambling jungle rivers all punctuate the region, home to rare and endlessly exuberant flora and fauna. Bocas del Toro owes all its pristine natural beauty to millennia of obscurity and isolation. While neighbouring territories succumbed to the works programme of imperial Spain, Bocas was barely colonized or evangelized, let alone installed with working infrastructure. For centuries, foreign intrusion was fleeting – only itinerant pirates washed up on the shores with any regularity. But in the late 19th century, the United Fruit Company struck 'green gold' and nothing was ever the same again. Destined to become one of the world's most powerful multinational corporations, the UFCO set about radically transforming the region by installing prolific banana plantations, sea ports, railways and urban settlements. West Indian labourers arrived en masse, followed later by Latino and Ngäbe settlers from highland Chiriquí, all permanently altering the region's cultural composition. Today, the UFCO's operations are scaled back, but the inhabitants of Bocas del Toro continue to trace their ancestry to such disparate homelands as Jamaica, China, Europe and North America. The local dialect – Guari-Guari – is assuredly multicultural too, fusing elements of the English, Spanish and Ngäbere languages. But despite its international pretensions, Bocas del Toro remains decidedly insular. Hemmed in between mountains, sea and jungle, road connections to Panama's interior were only completed towards the end of the 20th century. From the forests of the mainland to the scattered islands of its archipelago, Bocas del Toro remains a colourful patchwork of isolated, culturally distinct communities, as vivid and varied as the natural world they echo.

Mainland Bocas del Toro

Mainland Bocas del Toro is a land of few roads and fewer travellers. You'll need sturdy boots and a strong machete to explore this wilderness of tangled mangrove swamps, pristine rainforests and isolated indigenous villages. Stamped with the blue marks of Chiquita Brands, bananas continue to play a major role in the local economy. The grungy city of Changuinola, the largest urban settlement in the province, is enveloped in steamy plantations and remains an important centre of cultivation and export. Other communities, such as Chiriquí Grande, are less fortunate. Neglected by the fruit giants, they dwindle in depression and obscurity, old fincas consumed by the forests and railway lines rusting in the undergrowth. But beyond the dilapidation, mainland Bocas del Toro is interspersed with intriguing indigenous communities. The lowlands, traversed by a single paved road as far as the Costa Rican border, are the preserve of the Ngäbe and Buglé. Further inland, where the Parque Internacional La Amistad rolls upwards to meet the cloud-drenched peaks of the Talamanca mountain range, you'll find determined communities of Naso and Bri Bri. An expedition to their heartland is one of the most rewarding adventures Panama has to offer. ➤➤ *For listings, see pages 253-254.*

Chiriquí to Bocas del Toro → *For listings, see pages 253-254. Colour map 1, B2-A2.*

Around 14 km east of David, a paved road branches north off the Carretera Interamericana to provide overland access to Bocas del Toro. The wending journey over the Talamanca mountains is captivating and a cyclist's delight with astounding vistas and very little traffic. As you climb steeply towards the cool and often misty peaks, you will be rewarded with views of the Pacific Ocean and Chiriquí lowlands. Soon after, you'll enter the forested zones of the Fortuna Reserve.

Reserva Forestal Fortuna
The 19,500-ha Reserva Forestal Fortuna was created in 1976 to protect the river basin of the **Lago Fortuna**. It a very wet place, receiving 8000 mm of rain annually. The reserve is co-managed with ANAM by the **Fortuna Hydroelectric Company** and it is home to some captivating flora and fauna. The Smithsonian Tropical Research Institute has a long history of conducting research in the area, where many species of rare birds and amphibians live. There are multiple paths through the cloud forests and the best way to experience them is by spending a night or two at one of the area's interesting lodges (see listings, page 253).

Into Bocas del Toro
After crossing the continental divide, the road winds precariously down to sea level, passing the **Fortuna Hydroelectric Plant** and its vast artificial lake, where some people park their cars to take photos. As you descend towards the steamy, flood-prone lowlands of Bocas del Toro, there is a significant shift in humidity and architecture. You will pass villages with clusters of wooden houses raised on stilts, very typical of the Caribbean. If travelling by bus to Almirante/Changuinola, you will pause for a break at Chiriquí Grande junction, where there is a busy roadside restaurant.

Don't miss ...

The Banana Coast → *For listings, see pages 253-254.*

It's hard to believe that the jungle-cloaked coast of Bocas del Toro was once the thriving economic engine of a banana republic. At the height of its glory, great steamships would ply the waters offshore, heavily laden with fruit and migrant workers. Today, the plantations have been abandoned, the 'great white fleet' has been sold, and most of the old banana towns are dwindling as younger generations flee in search of a better life. Only the city of Changuinola retains a modest base of operations; in every other way, the region remains obscure. For those willing to dig beneath the surface, however, a journey to Panama's Banana Coast can be an intriguing adventure.

Background

Opinions are divided over the legacy of the United Fruit Company (UFCO), one of the world's oldest and most controversial transnational corporations. Defenders say it has provided gainful employment for thousands of working families, contributed modern infrastructure, houses, schools and hospitals, and rendered vast swathes of land cultivable. Critics point to the company's long record of political interference and abuses – a military coup in Guatemala and the massacre of striking workers in Colombia are among the darkest chapters in its history. Whatever the final judgement, the UFCO has left an indelible mark on Bocas del Toro, the place where it all began in the late 19th century. Its base of operations was in Bocas Town on Isla Colón and a former railway tycoon, Minor Keith, was in charge.

In 1903, Michael Snyder completed a shipping canal between Boca del Drago on Isla Colón and Changuinola on the mainland, where plantations and infrastructure rapidly expanded. Three years later, the UFCO built a wharf at Almirante, and by 1912, the burgeoning settlement emerged as the company's headquarters. Infrastructure continued to expand with the construction of an electric power plant, telegraph systems and a new railway connecting Almirante with Changuinola and the Costa Rica border. Through the 1920s, a destructive fungus called 'Panama disease' swept through the region, devastating harvests and forcing the plantations ever northwards. By 1929 the UFCO was forced to close shop and relocate to Puerto Armuelles on the Pacific. Bocas was bust and the global depression of the 1930s only compounded its woes. Many left the region in search of work elsewhere.

In the 1950s, the UFCO restarted operations in Bocas, initiating an ambitious revitalization programme that included the extensive treatment of soils. Within a few years Panama disease had once again obliterated the crops and the company decided to use disease resistant varieties of fruit thereafter. In 1968, Eli Black acquired a controlling stake in United Fruit and merged it with his own company, AMK, to form United Brands. Operations were

Sixaola–Guabito

A straightforward and interesting crossing with a decrepit old United Fruit Company railway bridge over the Río Sixaola. Basic hotel accommodation is available, but undesirable.

Panamanian immigration Open 0900-1700, but sometimes closes early.

Costa Rican immigration Open 0800-1600 (Costa Rica time); shut for lunch at weekends. Office is just before the bridge.

Currency exchange No banks; try money-changers or the supermarket. Poor rates.

Onwards to Costa Rica Hourly connections to Puerto Limón and the Caribbean coast. Four direct buses daily to San José, 5½ hours.

Onwards to Panama To reach the Bocas del Toro archipelago, take a bus from Guabito to Almirante, 1½ hours, then a boat to Isla Colón, 20 minutes. If there are no direct buses, change in Changuinola.

Time Panama is one hour ahead of Costa Rica.

relocated from Almirante to Finca 8 in Changuinola. Seven years later, crippled by debt and mired in political intrigue, Black threw himself off the 44th floor of the Pan Am Building in New York. The American Financial Group, headed by billionaire Carl Lindner, took control of United Brands in 1984 and renamed it Chiquita Brands. Under the subsidiary Bocas Fruit, they maintained scaled-back operations in Changuinola with around 4000 employees.

Chiriquí Grande → Colour map 1, A2.

Perched on the shores of **Laguna de Chiriquí**, the salty town of Chiriquí Grande has weathered boom and bust cycles like a stubborn old sailor. Flourishing and withering as a banana town, a major port and, in the early 1980s, as the Caribbean terminus for a transoceanic oil pipeline, it has again fallen on hard times and is today quite depressed. Some exports are still hauled through its docks, but it is generally a place without purpose since the completion of the paved road linking the coast with Costa Rica and the Panamanian interior.

Silico Creek → Colour map 1, A2.

Located at Km 25 on the highway to Almirante, the welcoming Ngäbe community of Silico Creek is home to 500 inhabitants. Founded in 1961 by José Quiroz, part of the village is located in the Comarca Ngäbe-Buglé and part is located in Bocas del Toro province. Not to be missed, the **Urari Community Tourism Project** ① *T6233-8706, www.urari.org*, offers an excellent cacao tour, US$10, where you'll be led through the process of chocolate production from finca to factory. The tour concludes with tastings of delicious organic chocolate and home-made coconut bread. Urari also offers rustic accommodation in traditional wood and thatch cabins and can coordinate a range of cultural and adventure activities, including explanations of *artesanía* and agricultural production, and hiking in the rainforests of the **Bosque Protector Palo Seco**.

Almirante → Colour map 1, A2.

Dredged from malaria-infested swamps in the early 20th century, the sluggish and often sketchy port town of Almirante served as the UFCO headquarters between 1912 and 1929. Today utilized for exports by Chiquita Brands, whose blue and white containers can be

Life is sweet: Oreba chocolate

The cultivation of cacao – the raw ingredient in chocolate – is a very ancient indigenous practice. Cacao farmers were once among the wealthiest people in pre-Columbian society, partly due to the widespread use of cacao beans as a form of currency. Chocolate itself was considered a delicacy, consumed on special occasions by the nobility and merchant classes. The ancients knew they were handling treasure and, even today, the dark stuff continues to be held in the highest regard. Not only delicious and versatile, chocolate also has proven health benefits, including lowering blood pressure, slowing the effects of ageing and reducing cholesterol. It makes you feel good too, delivering mild stimulants to the brain and acting directly on serotonin and endorphin pathways. The art of chocolate making continues to be practised widely, but few places are as expert or accomplished as the Ngäbe-owned Oreba chocolate farm. Their organic shade-grown cacao is among the best quality in the world, and anyone with a passing interest in chocolate, sustainable agriculture or indigenous culture shouldn't miss the opportunity

to visit their network of co-operatives. Tours include a two- to three-hour hike through the grounds, home to over 100 different species of cacao trees arranged in an ingenious permaculture system. Wildlife is prolific and you're likely to encounter sloths, poison dart frogs and vociferous toucans. After an explanation of the processes of growing, harvesting, fermenting and drying, you'll be treated to a hands-on demonstration of the roasting and grinding process, concluding with a tasting. Oreba chocolate is 100% cocoa, dark, sweet, strong and incredibly flavoursome. No wonder prestigious Swiss chocolate makers are among their clients.

ⓘ *The Oreba chocolate farm, T6649-1457, is located in the community of Río Oestre Arriba, outside Almirante on the mainland. Three-hour tours depart twice daily from Bocas Island, 0900 and 1300 – book ahead with the Info Bocas Kiosk, Hotel Heike or Casa Verde, US$30 per person. Wear good hiking boots, not flip-flops. Note you'll need to take the boat to Almirante where a taxi will meet you. Costs include a traditional Ngäbe lunch and a sample of chocolate to take home. All proceeds go to the community.*

seen stacked high on the docks, Almirante is as rough and seedy as any other desperate backwater. Despite its vaguely criminal pretensions, the town sees a steady stream of visitors – almost all of them on their way to the Bocas del Toro archipelago. You are advised to follow, and as quickly as possible. Water taxis to **Isla Colón** depart half hourly from the docks, 0600-1830, 25 minutes, US$4, and cross the bay of Almirante at high speed.

Changuinola → *Colour map 1, A2.*

The scruffy, sultry city of Changuinola is the headquarters of the **Bocas Fruit Company**, a subsidiary of Chiquita Brands. It is the only place of any real size in the province and most of its 50,000 inhabitants find employment in the surrounding sprawl of banana fincas. Work in the plantations – mostly fulfilled by indigenous Ngäbes – is hot, tiring, poorly paid, and now unhealthy due to pesticides. As a regional hub of commerce and transportation, many travellers stop in Changuinola on their way to and from Costa Rica (see box, page 247). The main street, **17 de Abril**, is busy with pedestrians and cut-price stores where you can stock up on cheap supplies. There are also several banks, a good general market, restaurants, hotels and other useful amenities. Until recently, boats to the Bocas del Toro archipelago departed from Changuinola's Finca 60, memorably traversing the jungle-shrouded **Snyder Canal**. At the time of research the canal was closed due to flood damage.

Humedal San San Pond Sak → *Colour map 1, A2.*

ⓘ *The reserve is managed by ANAM, but you are advised to organize your visit 24 hrs in advance through the Asociación de Amigos y Vecinos de la Costa y la Naturaleza (AAMVECONA), offices at the reserve's entrance, 5 km north of Changuinola on the highway to Guabito, T6666-0892, www.aamvecona.com. To get there, catch a bus bound for Las Tablas, US$0.70, 10 mins, and ask to be dropped off at the entrance; or take a taxi, US$4.*

Established as a protected area in 1994, the Humedal San San Pond Sak encompasses 16,125 ha of vitally important wetlands. It is home to a large population of critically endangered manatees, who dwell all year round among the brackish waters and tangled roots of the mangrove swamps. The slow-moving and good-natured creatures can live up to 60 years and their proportions are impressive – some grow up to 4 m in length and 900 kg in weight. Endangered sea turtles, including green and hawksbill, are also provided refuge by San San Pond Sak. They nest on the reserve's beach every year from March to July, but face continued threats from egg poachers – a situation helped neither by local economic conditions nor by the reserve's lack of resources (just six rangers maintain the entire reserve). The best way to experience the wetlands is through the **Asociación de Amigos y Vecinos de la Costa y la Naturaleza (AAMVECONA)**, who monitor the wildlife, raise international awareness and generally involve local communities in protecting their environment. They offer a half-day manatee tour, US$70 per group, including transportation by boat and Spanish-speaking guide. They promise a 90% chance of seeing the peaceful creatures from an observation platform where bunches of plantain are lowered into the water as bait. You can also take a two-hour aquatic tour by kayak, or visit the turtle beach, if in season, for an additional US$10 per person. AAMVECONA manage a simple wooden ecolodge within the reserve with bunk beds and a shared kitchen, US$10 per person per night plus US$5 for each cooked meal. The organization welcomes volunteers in the tasks of reforestation, beach cleaning, patrols, and the tagging and monitoring of wildlife. A minimum commitment of eight days is required and costs include a one-off registration fee of US$35, plus a daily fee of US$25, which includes all food and lodging. **Felix de León**, who manages San San tourism and volunteer activities, is helpful, friendly and very knowledgeable about the reserve – talk to him about your plans. ANAM, who officially manage the wetlands, have built a walkway through the swamps, **Camino 44**, but it is broken in many parts, generally foul-smelling, snake-infested and dangerous – it is utilized more by poachers than tourists.

The Naso Kingdom → *For listings, see pages 253-254.*

The Río Teribe, known as *Tjer Di* ('Grandmother Water') in Naso, is the central axis and spiritual heart of the Naso Kingdom – one of indigenous America's last remaining monarchies. The 4000-strong tribe, who occupy 11 communities on or around the riverbanks, consider themselves guardians of the rainforest. Their ancestral lands encompass the remote **Parque Internacional La Amistad** and the **Bosque Protector Palo Seco**, home to over 400 brilliant bird species, scores of rare mammals, reptiles and amphibians, and more plant and tree species than can be found in the entire European continent. Unsurprisingly, the Naso are masters of bushcraft and jungle medicine, not to mention hunting and fishing.

Martinelli's rotten sausage

Rushed through the legislative assembly in June 2010, Martinelli's now infamous Sausage Law had nothing whatsoever to do with the regulation of processed meat. Law 30, as it was properly known, was actually an innocuous civil aviation bill – but only on the outside. On the inside, it concealed an unpalatable mix of broad-reaching reforms that amended no less than nine different laws. The changes affecting the airline industry were fairly pedestrian, and others, including those establishing criminal penalties for human trafficking, were eminently wise. But among the mish-mash of reconstituted directives were several deeply controversial articles. Under Law 30, development projects deemed to have a 'social interest' were exempt from submitting an Environmental Impact Study. In changes to the judicial code, the police were granted new rights of impunity, while reforms to the labour code were perceived as a direct attack on the unions. Among them was the abolition of obligatory union fees and new rights to hire and fire at will in the event of industrial action. As far as the unions were concerned, Martinelli had cooked up a truly rotten sausage – and they were not about to eat it. On 2 July 2010, when the Changuinola-based Bocas Fruit company announced it would no longer be collecting union fees, the Sindicato de Trabajadores de la Industria de Banano (SITRAIBANA) responded with a 48-hour strike. In retaliation, Bocas Fruit declared the strike illegal and docked its entire workforce two weeks' wages for 'spoiled fruit'. SITRAIBANA reacted by extending the strike indefinitely and demanding the complete repeal of Law 30. On 6 July, the government mediated talks between the union and the fruit company but they failed to reach an agreement. The strikers began blocking the Changuinola–Almirante highway with fallen trees, and, on 7 July, riot squads opened fire with rubber bullets and bird shot. Armed with rocks and sling-shots, a large contingent of indigenous protestors arrived on the scene to express solidarity, many of them outraged by government-sanctioned mega-projects in their homelands. The conflict rapidly escalated when four policemen were taken hostage and a police station was burned to the ground. Curfew was declared as riot squads began pelting residential neighbourhoods with tear gas, killing five children in their homes. By 12 July, 10 people were dead and dozens had lost their eyesight, partially or fully, when police fired bird shot straight into their faces. Several hundred more were incarcerated or hospitalized. Amid plummeting approval ratings, Law 30 was provisionally suspended, and after lengthy negotiations, repealed later in the year. The clashes marked the first of many such conflicts for President Ricardo Martinelli, who has since consolidated his reputation for autocracy, insensitivity and blundering heavy-handedness. Memories of the 2010 Changuinola riots will live forever in local lore.

Arriving in the Naso Kingdom

To get to the **Río Teribe**, first catch a bus from Changuinola to El Silencio, every 20 minutes, US$0.65, 30 minutes. From El Silencio you can hire a boatman to take you upstream, US$35-50, or more economically (and less scenically), catch a truck on the new road as far as Bonyic or Weckso, every 30 minutes, US$1, 20 minutes. Beyond Bonyic, where the El Silencio road terminates, transit along the Río Teribe is by punted rafts and motor-powered longboats. There are no public or scheduled services, so you will need to hire a boatman or enquire locally about the possibility of sharing a ride with locals. Many communities are connected by forest trails and you will need a guide or wilderness skills to navigate these. For information, the **Organización de Desarrollo Ecoturismo Naso (ODESEN)** manage the pioneering **Wekso Ecolodge** and are the foremost touristic authority in the region (see below). Nearby, at Bonyic, the **Organización Naso de Ecoturismo (OCEN)**, is another reliable source of information (see page 252). During your visit, take precautions against mosquitoes, ticks, leeches, scorpions, water-borne pathogens and all the usual beasties. Electricity is very limited or non-existent and torches are essential. Rubber boots are vital for crossing streams and waterlogged trails. The river is sometimes fierce and generally fraught with rapids, so ensure you are kitted with a life jacket and your electronic items are well protected in sealed plastic bags.

Background

The war-like Naso flourished for centuries in western Panama until Spanish contact in the 17th century brought devastating diseases. Their numbers significantly reduced, the Naso continued to dwell in the isolation and obscurity of the rainforests, resisting attempts at forced integration and evangelization. As such, they successfully retained many structures of their pre-Columbian culture. Today, most Naso live like their forebears, surviving on subsistence agriculture, hunting and fishing. Cattle are also reared, but not extensively. Most community housing consists of traditional wood and thatch structures, although zinc is increasingly used for roofing. In recent years, missionary and Western influences have intensified and the role of the shaman has been marginalized by pastors, ministers, priests and doctors. Traditional clothing has been largely exchanged for Western attire and the Naso language, belonging to the Chibchan family, is now declining. The main governing structure of the Naso Kingdom is the monarchy, headed by a king or queen and supported by a *consejo* (council) of 30 elders. Since the 1980s, power has been transferred by election, although only candidates from the royal Santana family may occupy the top position. In 2004, King Tito Santana caused a schism in Naso society by signing away the Bonyic River to Colombian hydroelectric interests. He was subsequently deposed and replaced by King Valentín. However, the Panamanian government refuses to acknowledge the new king and continues to strike hydroelectric deals with Tito, now in exile. Today, the Naso are lobbying for the formation of 130,000 ha of semi-autonomous *comarca*; sadly this outcome looks unlikely under the Martinelli administration.

El Silencio

Home to increasing numbers of Naso, the jungle gateway of El Silencio is slung along a muddy river bank at the confluence of the Río Chaguinola and the Río Teribe. There's nothing to do here, but there are a handful of simple restaurants and a reasonably well-stocked 'super' where you can pick up food, water and sundry items, such as candles, torches, batteries, matches, insect repellent and rubber boots. A new bridge, constructed by the controversial **Empresas Públicas de Medellín** hydroelectric company, now crosses the Río Teribe to connect with a new road to Bonyic.

Wekso Ecolodge

ⓘ *On the northern bank of the Río Teribe, opposite the community of Bonyic, T6569-2844, www.odesen.bocas.com. If arriving by road, you will need to cross the river; call ahead to arrange a pickup or ask for assistance in Bonyic.*

Established in 1995 by the Naso-led tourism initiative **ODESEN**, the Wekso Ecolodge is an essential stop for anyone wishing to penetrate the mysteries of Naso land and culture. The lodge is conveniently located at the entrance to the Parque Internacional La Amistad (see below) and Adolfo Villagra, ODESEN's highly regarded founder, can expertly organize, assist or advise on a wide range of activities. Popular options include guided hikes in the rainforest, river trips to the Naso heartland, traditional fishing with bows and arrows, community tours of Sieyic and Sieykin, stays with local families, and for the truly adventurous, week-long expeditions to sacred mountains and beyond. Wekso's guides cost US$20 per day (plus tip and, if applicable, transportation costs) and are excellent and informative – **Edwin Sánchez**, T6574-9874, is particularly recommended. If you decide to make your base at Wekso, the lodge offers rustic accommodation for up to 30 guests in traditional thatch and wood or concrete houses (see Where to stay, page 254). Built on the site of a former 'Pana-Jungla' Panamanian Defence Force training camp, the grounds are littered with intriguing sights. Check out the overgrown helipad where General Noriega touched down, the weathered 'animal warrior' statuary and the crumbling mural where painted verses extol the hardened glories of the Pana-Jungla life.

Parque Internacional La Amistad → *Colour map 1, A1.*
ⓘ *Managed by ANAM at Wekso, entrance US$5 plus guide.*

The immense Parque Internacional La Amistad spans both sides of the Panama–Costa Rica border and encompasses 207,000 ha of diverse territory, including 12 life zones, two mountain ranges and the largest unbroken forest in Central America. In Bocas del Toro, the official **ANAM** park entrance is in the grounds of Wekso, where a former Pana-Jungla cross-country training circuit has been converted into a 2.5-km hiking trail, **Sendero Heliconias.** The trail snakes through secondary and primary rainforest where sloths, monkeys, agoutis and any number of birds are commonly spotted. Good guides will point out plants and trees and explain their traditional uses in building, tool-making and medicine. Much deeper into the forest, one day away, tapirs can be seen. Note the southern entrance to the biosphere reserve is a more popular access point. It is located in Chiriquí province, close to the highland town of Cerro Punta (for more information, see page 231).

Bonyic → *Colour map 1, A1.*

Perched at the confluence of the Río Bonyic and Río Teribe, the community of Bonyic is home to approximately 300 people. Public amenities include a small health centre, a school, a football pitch and a community hall. Bonyic is the base of operations for **OCEN** ⓘ *www.ocen.bocas.com, T6569-3869,* who offer accommodation, guides, tours and transportation; ask around for Raúl Quintero, the project manager. Colombian workers from the **Empresa de Medellín** hydroelectric company are a visible and not entirely welcome presence around Bonyic. They are allegedly armed, but pose no threat to foreign travellers. The site of the **Bonyic Hydroelectric Plant**, scheduled for completion in 2013, is in an area of great natural beauty and can be discreetly visited with a guide.

Sieyic

Upstream from Bonyic the river winds through forested hills and past pebble-strewn banks. The waters are choppy and heavily laden boats may struggle. Wending your way south, you will pass the communities of **Solón** and **Tres Piedras**, home to a combined population of 300, before arriving, approximately one hour later, in the community of Sieyic. Home to around 800 people, Sieyic is the seat of power for King Valentín

Santana, who governs the 11 communities of the Naso Kingdom from his royal palace. The community is an excellent place to learn about cultural traditions and agricultural practices, or simply observe day-to-day Naso life. Activities include displays of traditional dancing, farm visits, tours of botanical gardens, lessons in the Naso language, storytelling, instruction in *artesanía* production, horse riding and guided hikes.

Sieykin

Home to 700 inhabitants and divided into 'Sieykin arriba' and 'Sieykin abajo', the sprawling community of Sieykin is an important centre of culture and commerce. The village was founded approximately 60 years ago by the Sánchez, Torres and Villagra families and is located on the opposite riverbank to Sieyic. Modest municipal buildings dot the centre, where several paths trail away into dense banana, maize and cacao plantations. Sieykin makes a good base for extended adventures in the Amistad Biosphere and offers broadly similar cultural activities to Sieyic, including language lessons, community tours and *artesanía* presentation. **Señor Héctor Sánchez** is a highly respected local shaman who leads traditional dance groups and can sing songs on the popular Naso themes of nature, history and heroes. Sieykin is home to a very interesting botanical garden maintained by an educational group called **ASOMETRAN**, who train local students in medicinal plants. The Naso system of traditional medicine utilizes over 2000 botanical species and requires a minimum of four years of study to master. Approximately 400 species are represented in the ASOMETRAN garden, which appears like a patch of jungle to the untrained eye. Many species have been transplanted from remote locations in the mountains, others from as far as the Darién. **Rafael Sánchez**, an ASOMETRAN student, offers guided tours of the garden, US$30 for a group of five.

◉ Mainland Bocas del Toro listings

For sleeping and eating price codes and other relevant information, see pages 16-19.

● Where to stay

Reserva Forestal Fortuna *p245*
$$ Finca La Suiza, Hornito, 4 km north of Los Planes, T774-4030. A very comfortable and hospitable highland lodge managed by Herbert Brullman and Monika Kohler. Several excellent hiking trails begin in their property where you'll see plentiful birdlife. Excellent organic food and all-round good reports. Recommended.
$ Lost and Found, T6432-8182, near Valle de la Mina, www.lostandfoundlodge.com. A very popular and successful youth hostel located high up on the edge of the continental divide. Verdant grounds encompass 12 ha of rainforest with a

variety of tours and volunteer opportunities. Accommodation includes dorms and simple private rooms. Recommended.

Changuinola *p248*
$$ Alhambra, Calle 17 de Abril, T758-9819. A range of 32 rooms, some quite large, and all equipped with bath, hot water, a/c, telephone and TV. Those overlooking the street may be noisy.
$ Residencial Carol, Calle 17 de Abril, next to Semiramis, T758-8731. Small dark rooms with bath, hot water, TV and a/c (cheaper rooms without). Quiet and simple.
$ Semiramis, Calle 17 de Abril, diagonally opposite the **Alhambra**, T758-6006. Offers 29 dark rooms with outstandingly kitsch pictures, a/c, hot water, TV, and Wi-Fi in the lobby. The restaurant serves seafood. Parking available. Friendly.

Wekso *p251*

$ Wekso Ecolodge, across the river from Bonyic, T6569-2844, www.odesen.bocas. com. Built in the grounds of a former Pana-Jungla military training camp, Wekso offers both concrete and traditional wooden lodgings, all with mosquito nets, limited electricity and shared bath. Meals cost extra, US$4-5. Attractive, peaceful grounds on the edge of the rainforest, good attention and personalized service. Highly recommended.

Bonyic *p252*

$ OCEN, Bonyic, T6569-3869, www.ocen. bocas.com. Managed by Raúl Quintero, this community tourism project offers 2 separate facilities with a total capacity for 18 people. The concrete house has a living room, bathroom and working area. The 'blue house' is wooden and much simpler. The cost of 3 meals is US$13 per person per day.

$ Soposo Rainforest Adventures, Soposo, T6631-2222, www.soposo.com. Traditional wooden huts set in pleasant grounds with numerous fruit trees. Locally operated **Soposo Rainforest Adventures** offers all-in-one packages that include pickup, transport, tours, accommodation and meals.

Sieykin *p253*

$ Casa Edwin Sánchez, Zona Sánchez, T6574-9874, edwinsanchez_47@hotmail. com. Simple wood and thatch housing in the community of Sieyking. Good for adventurers planning forays deep into Amistad. Arrange in advance.

❼ Restaurants

Changuinola *p248*

$$ Casa Roma, Calle 17 de Abril, next to **Residencial Carol**. Casa Roma serves reasonably priced Turkish and Italian fare,

including pizzas, kebabs and hummus. Clean and friendly. Not bad.

$$ Restaurante Ebony, Calle 17 de Abril. Authentic Afro-Antillean fare served in an equally authentic, laid-back setting. Lots of tributes to Bob Marley.

$ Restaurante La Herrerana, Calle 17 de Abril, opposite Hotel Alhambra. A large open-front dining hall where they serve the usual high-carb buffet fare. Cheap and cheerful.

❷ Transport

Almirante *p247*

Boat Water taxi to **Bocas** 0600-1830, 25 mins, US$4. Several companies at the *muelle* compete for your custom, including **Jampan** and **Bocas Marine Tours**. A *colectivo* taxi from the bus station to the *muelle* is US$1, or it can be walked in 5-10 mins. Unofficial guides may request 'tips'.

Bus To **David**, every 40 mins, 4-5 hrs, US$8.45; **Changuinola**, every 30 mins, 30 mins, US$1.50.

Changuinola *p248*

Bus The SINCOTAVECOP bus station is 1 block behind 17 de Abril, turn up from the Shell station. To **Almirante**, every 30 mins till 2000, 30 mins, US$1.75; to **El Silencio**, every 20 mins, 20 mins, US$0.65; to **Costa Rica**, catch a Las Tablas bus to Guabito, every 20 mins till 2000, 30 mins, US$0.80, cross the border on foot and catch a service from Sixaola on to Limón. There is also a non-stop service to **San José** 1 daily, 1000 (no office, pay on bus) US$10, 6-7 hrs, but many police checks (note this bus may not always run). For long-distance buses south and east, head to the Terminal Urracá at the north end of town; to **Panama City**, 0700, 10-12 hrs, US$28; to **David**, 4-5 hrs, US$8.45.

Bocas del Toro archipelago

The far-flung islands of the Bocas del Toro archipelago have long drawn adventurers to their languid shores, Christopher Columbus first and foremost among them. When he became the first European to explore the region in 1502, he failed to find gold or a passage to Asia, but he did lay eyes on a pristine natural bounty that has some naturalists drawing comparisons with the Galapagos Islands of Ecuador. Tangled rainforests teem with exuberant and uniquely evolved flora and fauna, including dazzling neon-coloured frogs, clambering sloths, orchids and butterflies. Endangered turtles arrive en masse each year between March and September, while vast coral reefs play host to swirling schools of multicoloured fish. Add the lure of white-sand beaches, world-class waves, authentic Caribbean communities and a robust party scene, and you'll soon understand why increasing numbers of foreigners are coming here to retire, open businesses or otherwise bask in the laid-back local lifestyle. Sadly, the flurry of international interest has also attracted less benign forces, including aggressive property developers with grandiose plans for gated communities. Thanks to their mercenary ambitions, a rather venal land grab has precipitated sky-high property prices and, in some cases, the destruction of local ecosystems. Please tread carefully, life is fragile. ►► *For listings, see pages 264-274.*

Isla Colón → *For listings, see pages 264-274. Colour map 1, A2.*

Isla Colón is the most heavily populated of the archipelago's islands and home to the province's jaunty capital, Bocas Town. As a hub of transport, commerce and unfettered hedonism, most visitors wash up on its streets at some stage. But beyond the multicultural hustle of its capital, the island's interior is quiet and remote, consumed by verdant cattle ranches and steamy tropical forests. A rambling coastline boasts a variety of beaches to suit swimmers, surfers and party-goers, and for nature-lovers there are teeming mangroves, turtles and bird sanctuaries.

Arriving on Isla Colón

Getting there Bocas del Toro Airport ① *Av E and Calle 6a*, on the edge of the downtown area, receives daily **Air Panama** flights from Panama City, as well as international services from Costa Rica's **Nature Air**. Overland access to the archipelago is by water taxi from the mainland port of Almirante. All services arrive at the piers on Calle Primera, in the heart of Bocas Town.

Getting around Water taxis ply the islands and rarely cost more than US$5 per person per journey. On Isla Colón, you can hail a ride from a variety of waterfront piers along **Calle Primera**. On other islands, waving a large flag (often provided at piers) should summon a passing taxi, or simply ask the nearest restaurant or hotel to call up a boatman. **Bicycles** are a good way to get around, as are **taxis**, which cost US$0.50 *colectivo*, or US$1 at night.

Information In Bocas Town you'll find an **IPAT office** ① *Calle 1a, T757-9642, 0900-1200 and 1300-1700*, with limited tourist information and fading exhibits on Bocas' history and ecology. The environment agency, **ANAM** ① *Calle 1a, T757-9244, Mon-Fri 0800-1200 and 1300-1600*, can supply details on national parks and visitor permits, if required. The monthly magazine, *Bocas Breeze*, www.thebocasbreeze.com, is an expat-led effort and a good source of local news. You can find it in hotels and restaurants throughout Bocas town.

Safety Most crimes in Bocas are opportunistic. Never leave valuables unattended on the beach and do not wander empty or unlit roads after dark. Take particular care at the bars if you drink too much. Increasingly, young hustlers are arriving from Almirante to work over visitors for tips or commissions – these should be considered an annoyance rather than a threat. The single greatest danger to travellers comes from the ocean itself in the form of rip tides – please familiarize yourself with their hazards (see Essentials, page 31). Visitors should not drink the tap water.

Background

In 1899, the United Fruit Company established its headquarters in Bocas Town inside a large wooden mansion that is today the Hotel Bahía. As Bocas boomed, it expanded with wooden walkways over the mangrove swamps, gradually incorporating modern infrastructure. The population was broadly multicultural, consisting of Afro-Antillean migrant workers, European farmers, North American businessmen and others. Baseball and cricket were widely enjoyed, as was horse racing on the beach. As the town consolidated its important economic role, embassies and consulates were constructed. In 1904, 1907 and 1918, a series of fires destroyed much of the town's original architecture and it was reconstructed to include working sewage systems, a central plaza and more logical street layout. By 1929, however, Panama disease had ruined fruit agriculture in the region and the UFCO shut up shop. For decades, Bocas dwindled as a far-flung provincial capital with no industry and little purpose.

In 1989, at the close of the Noriega years, there were just three hotels in town – a situation that would soon be transformed by the *Tico Times* and other gringo media, who

1 Bocas del Toro Archipelago

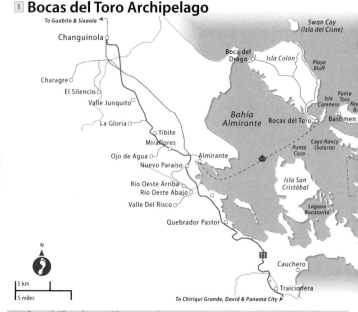

instigated a frenzied land grab of the archipelago's 'paradise islands'. Within two decades, most prime real estate, including all beach-front lots, had been acquired by foreign investors. Today, tourism is the backbone of the local economy and provides hundreds of jobs in an otherwise neglected backwater. However, a major conflict has developed between conservation groups and foreign investment interests. In the construction boom of the last 20 years, many pristine areas have been cleared for construction or otherwise plundered for their precious hardwoods. Numerous unique ecosystems have been damaged or destroyed in processes often expedited by local corruption. Long-term sustainable development plans were formulated in a 1993 forum entitled, 'Ecological and Social Agenda for Bocas del Toro', but these have now been abandoned.

Bocas Town

Like all good port towns, Bocas manages to exude charm and sleaze in equal measure. Beneath a gentle exterior of brightly painted wooden houses, the town nurtures a dark and feisty predilection for pleasure. Life ambles up and down **Main Street**, also known as **Calle Tercera**, where scores of waterfront restaurants, hotels, bars, cafés and water-taxis vigorously compete for your tourist dollars. Those expecting the Caribbean of times gone by may be disappointed. Crowds of sun-bleached wave-seekers, inebriated frat boys and scraggly backpackers dominate the scene, especially in high season, giving Bocas a resort-style ambience. But, despite its gaudy marriage to the entrepreneurial expat crowd, the town remains low-key and home to plentiful Afro-Caribbean, indigenous, Latino and Chinese communities. Beyond drinking, there isn't much to see or do, but a handful of buildings recall the glory days when the banana business was booming – check out the old **United Fruit Company Headquarters** at the end of Main Street, now the Hotel Bahía. The geographic and social heart of town is the shady **Plaza Simón Bolívar**, otherwise known as El Parque, which is flanked by the commercial arteries of Main Street and **Calle Primera**, as well as the **Palacio Municipal**. El Parque is a great spot for people-watching and local interaction. Spark up a conversation and you're likely to meet any number of friendly, talkative, off-the-wall or on-the-edge characters.

> → **Bocas del Toro maps**
> 1 Bocas del Toro Archipelago, page 256
> 2 Bocas Town, page 259

Caribbean Sea

Playa Larga
National Marine Park
Isla Bastimentos
Punta Vieja
Zapatilla Norte
Zapatilla Sur
Cayo Crawl
Isla Popa
Cayo del Agua

Playa Istmito

Perched on the outskirts of town, Playa Istmito – also known as **La Cabaña** – overlooks the sea with yellow-grey sands and a string of colourful cabins that are empty until the annual **Feria del Mar** celebrations (see page 272). Although cleaner than it's been in many years, the beach is far from pristine. It is quite popular with locals, however, who often gather to play volleyball or sip *cervezas* under the thatched palapas. There are

The rainbow frogs of Bocas del Toro

The dazzling poison dart frogs of Bocas del Toro include a rainbow array of more than a dozen multi-coloured morphs. Their vivid colouration, believed to result from sexual selection rather than mutation, serves as a toxicity warning to would-be predators. Scientists believe their poisons are not synthesized internally, but gathered from alkaloids in their diet, which typically includes ants and beetles. Poison dart frogs bred in captivity and fed on non-alkaloids do not develop toxic characteristics, making them popular exotic pets. The name 'poison dart' is a reference to the traditional use of their chemicals in indigenous blow darts. The strength of the toxins varies between species and recent research suggests they show pharmaceutical potential as painkillers, muscle relaxants and appetite suppressants. The Bocas del Toro frogs all belong to the species *Dendrobatidae pumilio*, commonly known as the strawberry poison dart frog. Females outnumber males, causing the males to show more colour and territorial aggression. Fierce wrestling matches over roosts and mates are quite common. The female's eggs are fertilized externally after she has laid them and, intriguingly, once they hatch into tadpoles, she will carry them to a nest on her hind leg. She will guard the nest – often the watery heart of an epiphyte, a puddle or a small hollow in a tree – and feed the clutch for up to six or eight weeks until metamorphosis is complete. The male will also water and protect the tadpoles for around 10 to 12 days before disappearing to find another mate. The frogs are very easy to spot near the base of trees or in the moist leaf litter on the forest floor. They rarely exceed a centimetre or two in size – watch your step!

several restaurants skirting the beach, as well as some rowdy macho bars that kick off after nightfall. As the name suggests, Playa Istmito is situated on a slender isthmus. On the opposite flank is the poor, polluted but authentic neighbourhood of **Saigon**.

STRI Bocas del Toro Research Station
ⓘ *El Istmito, 1 km north of the feria, T757-9794, www.stri.si.edu, Thu-Fri 1400-1700, free.*
The **Smithsonian Tropical Research Institute** maintains an excellent research station for the study of the archipelago's diverse marine and terrestrial ecosystems – seagrass meadows, coral reefs, mangroves and sand beaches among them. The institute is particularly concerned with sustainable use and the environmental impact of multiple activities such as fishing, tourism and agriculture. The institute receives over 175 visiting scientists per year and is highly regarded as a centre of research and education. Previous STRI studies have examined coral spawning and turtle nesting. Members of the public visiting the station can enjoy tours of the laboratories, a nature trail, aquariums, a bookshop and various interpretive displays on local ecology.

Finca Los Monos
ⓘ *El Istmito, north of the STRI Research Centre, T757-9461, www.bocasdeltorobotanical garden.com. Tours depart Mon 1300 and Fri 0830, or by appointment, 2 hrs, US$10, sturdy footwear recommended.*
A lot of love and hard work has gone into Finca Los Monos, a 9.3-ha tropical botanical garden created by plant enthusiasts David and Lin Gillingham. Hundreds of brilliantly coloured

2 Bocas del Toro

To ② Playa Bluff, Playa El Ismito, La Gruta & Boca del Drago

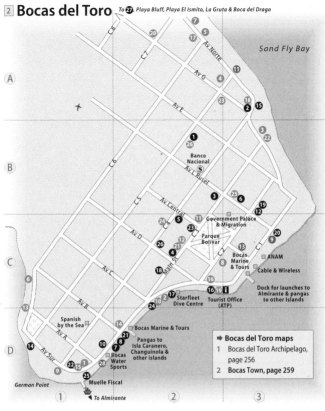

Bocas del Toro maps

1 Bocas del Toro Archipelago, page 256
2 Bocas Town, page 259

100 metres
100 yards

Where to stay
Angela/Sol y Sombra **5** *A2*
Bahía **1** *D1*
Bocas del Toro **2** *C2*
Bocas Inn Lodge **3** *B3*
Casa Amarilla **4** *A2*
Cala Luna **26** *B2*
Casa Verde/
  La Mama Loca **9** *D1*
Cayos Zapatillas **12** *C2*
Cocomo-on-the-Sea **7** *A2*
Del Parque **8** *C2*
Dos Palmas **13** *D1*
El Limbo **10** *C2*
Gran Kahuna Hostel **14** *D2*
Heike **11** *C2*
Hotelito del Mar **16** *C2*
La Veranda **20** *A2*
Laguna **21** *C2*
Las Brisas **22** *B3*
Lula's B&B **17** *A2*
Mondo Taitu **18** *A3*
Olas de la Madrugada **6** *C1*
Palma Royale **15** *D1*
Posada Los Delfines **23** *A2*
Sagitarius **24** *C2*
Swan's Cay **25** *B3*
Tropical Suites **19** *C2*

Restaurants 🍴
9 degrees **20** *C3*
Alberto's **1** *B2*
Barracuda **21** *D2*
Bocas Blended **2** *A3*
Buena Vista Bar
  & Grill **17** *C2*
Casbah **15** *A3*
Chitre **18** *C2*
El Lorito **3** *B2*
El Pecado **4** *C2*
El Ultimo
  Refugio **14** *D1*
Gringos **5** *C2*
La Ballena **6** *B3*
La Buguita **7** *D2*
Lemongrass **17** *C2*
Lili's Café **16** *C2*
McDouglas Golden
  Grill **23** *C2*
Natural Mystic **10** *D1*
Om Café **12** *B3*
Panadería Dulcería
  Alemana **19** *B3*
Pirate **24** *C2*
Reef **25** *D1*
Shelly's BBQ **26** *C2*
Starfish Coffee **8** *D2*
Super Gourmet **22** *D1*
Viva y deja vivir **27** *A2*

Bars & clubs 🍸
Barco Hundido **9** *C3*
El Encanto **28** *D1*
Rip Tide **11** *A3*
Toro Loco **13** *C3*

species are represented in the grounds, rainforest heliconias, ornamentals, gingers, palms, fruit and spice trees among them. The interpretive trails – punctuated by delicate lily-strewn ponds, fairytale bridges and hibiscus-drenched tunnels – are well-labelled and provide interesting ethno-botanical insights. The garden attracts plenty of wildlife too. Howler monkeys, sloths, iguanas, frogs and scores of bird species are resident and easily spotted.

Playa Big Creek to Playa Bluff

Several beaches skirt the eastern flank of Isla Colón, accessible from a paved road that begins to deteriorate after the small, moneyed community of **Big Creek**. Most of these beaches are fraught with monster waves that make them bad for swimming but good for surfing. **Playa Paunch** has three lefts and a right-hand break that are suitable for all levels; wear boots and beware sharp coral. Further north, the unattractively named **Dumpers** (it faces the city dump) has a powerful bottom left break over a reef and waves up to 3 m high; for advanced surfers only. **Playa Bluff**, 7 km from downtown, is several kilometres long and has hard, fast waves. It is one of the most popular surf spots on the island, but also unsuitable for the inexperienced. Note leatherback turtles lay eggs on Playa Bluff between May and September, when you should take care not to disturb nests. It is possible to cycle to Playa Bluff, but the road is rough, hot and rather impractical with a surf board. Taxis are expensive, US\$10-20, 25-30 minutes, depending on which end of the beach you want.

La Gruta

ⓘ *Signposted at Colonia Santeña, US\$1. A small house at the turn-off sells soft drinks, if open.*
Halfway between Bocas Town and Boca del Drago, the tiny hamlet of **Colonia Santeña** is home to a small, dark cave known as 'La Gruta'. Decorated with a statue of the Virgin Mary at the entrance, the cave is revered as a shrine. Inside, however, the air is thick with the rather unholy and unpleasant stench of guano. Many thousands of bats live inside the darkened recesses of La Gruta and pose something of a health risk to visitors. If you still wish to see the colony, follow the stream a short way and shine a torch on the ceiling. The sight of them quivering between the stalactites is either creepy or beautiful, depending on your sense of aesthetics.

Boca del Drago

The best swimming beach on Isla Colón is at Boca del Drago, 25 km from Bocas Town at the end of the road through the interior. Nearby, the ever-popular **Playa Estrella** is a winner with its large starfish population and fine white sands backed by mangroves; please do not handle the starfish. Boca del Drago is also the site of a private biological research station, the **Institute for Tropical Ecology and Education** (ITEC), www.itec-edu.org, which offers courses in field work and often has research opportunities available. Perched on the island's northwest tip, Boca del Drago is easily reached by water taxi, US\$3, and is a popular destination with tour operators. You can get there overland by bicycle (expect a hot, tough ride) or more easily by bus, US\$2.50, 30 minutes.

Swan's Cay

The jagged outcrop and wildlife reserve of Swan's Cay (or **Isla del Cisne** or **Isla Pájaros**) is an important ground-nesting site for many indigenous and migratory seabirds including frigates, pelicans, boobies, gulls and the famous red-billed tropic birds. During the golden age of the **United Fruit Company**, people would shoot the birds for sport, but today they are protected. Located a short distance northeast of Boca del Drago, you'll need to join a tour or hire a boat to get up close. As there's a risk of disturbing the nests and other important elements of the habitat, you'll need ANAM permission to go ashore and you should definitely be accompanied by a qualified naturalist if you choose to do so.

Isla Caranero → *For listings, see pages 264-274. Colour map 1, A2.*

Isla Caranero, or **Careening Cay**, is the site where Christopher Columbus careened his vessels (ie tilted them on their side for the purposes of cleaning or repair) during his fourth exploration of the Americas. The island is visible from the waterfront in Bocas Town and just two minutes away by water taxi, US$1-1.50. It is considerably smaller and calmer than its feisty neighbour and a tranquil alternative for those who want to be close to the action, but not completely immersed in it. A string of comfortable hotels flank the island's shores, any of which are good for slinging a hammock. Among them is the popular **Aqua Lounge**, which hosts a raucous twice-weekly party with 300 revellers or more (meaning it's not all peace and quiet on Caranero). The island's beaches aren't dazzling, but good enough for lolling quietly – bring insect repellent to combat sandflies. More popular with surfers than beachcombers, the island's reef point breaks – most notably **Caranero Point** – are suitable for intermediate and advanced surfers. There are also some less challenging 'beginner' waves, including **Black Rock**. Isla Caranero is the site of the new 40-slip **Careening Cay Marina** ① *T757-9242, www.careeningcaymarina.com.*

Isla Bastimentos → *For listings, see pages 264-274. Colour map 1, A2.*

For verdant nature and swashbuckling adventure, you can't do much better than Isla Bastimentos. Named after an old Spanish word for 'supplies', Bastimentos is where Christopher Columbus re-stocked his ships with provisions in 1502. Thick with rainforests and mangroves, it is the second largest island in the archipelago and boasts a procession of wave-lashed beaches, including **Playa Wizard**. A large area of Bastimentos falls within the scope of the **Parque Marino Bastimentos**, Panama's first marine park, which extends far offshore and encompasses a dazzling underwater world of teeming coral reefs. The island's principal community, **Old Bank**, is a ramshackle Afro-Caribbean settlement of strutting roosters, lilting Calypso rhythms and talkative, terminally idle characters. The pace of life remains authentically unhurried with little danger of modernity intruding – at least not any time soon. The island's indigenous Ngäbe communities, **Bahía Honda** and **Salt Creek**, offer equally intriguing glimpses of Bastimentos culture.

Old Bank

The indolent, rum-soaked village of Old Bank clings to the Bastimentos shoreline with a helter-skelter profusion of rickety old piers and teetering clapboard houses. It appears to be sliding, slowly, nonchalantly and inexorably into the waves. Predominantly Afro-Caribbean and English-speaking, Old Bank, also known as **Bastimentos Town**, is the largest settlement on the island and a bastion of Bocatorean authenticity. Between impassioned rounds of dominoes, its population appears to be engaged in life's more civilized pursuits – drinking, smoking and idle conversation. There's not much to do but join them, or else sling a hammock and simply soak up the carefree vibe. If you need to stretch your legs, a 15-minute uphill walk from the police station leads to an interesting organic farm, **Up In the Hill** ① *T6607-8962, www.upinthehill.com*, where they produce a range of cacao-based products, and coconut oil infused with herbs and wild flowers.

Silverbacks to Playa Larga

The searing northern coastline boasts a shifting succession of broad sandy beaches, forested headlands, rugged coves, sheltered bays, teeming coral reefs and awesome surf breaks. The legendary site of Silverbacks, close to the northwest tip of the island, sees spectacular 7-m Hawaiian-style waves, suitable for advanced surfers only (peaks December to February); take a water taxi to get there, US$3-5. Further east, **Playa Wizard**, also known as Playa Primera, is the first in a series of beaches. To get there from Old Bank follow a path over the hill that starts at the east side of the village, 25 minutes; wear proper shoes as the trail can be muddy. The waves at Playa Wizard are powerful and good for intermediate surfers, but also filled with rip-tides and unsuitable for swimming. Do not leave valuables unattended. From Playa Wizard, an interesting **hiking trail** heads east, skirting the shore and occasionally ducking into the rainforest. It is overgrown in parts, and also muddy and waterlogged if it has been raining much (rubber boots are best). The trail is an excellent opportunity to spot the tiny, vociferous strawberry poison dart frogs that inhabit the island in great numbers (see box, page 258). After approximately 20 minutes, the trail passes **Playa Segunda** or Second Beach, followed shortly after by **Red Frog Beach**, the site of a controversial new resort and residential complex. Whatever its claims to ecological sensitivity, the **Red Frog Beach Rainforest Resort**, www.redfrogbeach.com, is a heavily invested commercial proposition – and a cynical one. It includes a modern **marina** to help speed your escape. Overland, the trail continues its eastward ramble, soon arriving at **Magic Bay** and then to the sheltered waters of **Playa Polo**, where several coral reefs can be explored and the waters are generally calm. **Playa Larga** lies another half-hour away and is an important nesting site for leatherback and hawksbill turtles, who arrive en masse from March to September. Sea access to this final stretch of coast is generally restricted to the calm months of March to April and September to October.

Parque Nacional Marino Isla Bastimentos

ⓘ *Managed by ANAM, who maintain a rangers' station on Cayos Zapatillas. Admission to the islands is US$10, sometimes included in tour costs. On Bastimentos, the rainforest trails are poorly maintained and overgrown – use a guide or risk getting lost.*

Created in 1988, the Parque Nacional Marino Isla Bastimentos encompasses an area of 13,226 ha, over 85% of it marine. Arcing over the island in a rough 'R' shape, the park protects a range of terrestrial habitats including approximately half of the island's total land mass. Its tropical forests, sandy beaches and mangroves provide refuge for 68 species of bird, 32 species of mammal and 28 species of mostly endangered reptiles and amphibians. Offshore, the scintillating **Cayos Zapatillas** – a pair of pristine 'desert isles' fringed by white-sand beaches – are one of the most stunning attractions in the entire archipelago. The snorkelling and diving in the surrounding waters is quite diverting, with vast shelves of teeming coral, dolphins, sharks, rays and many diverse fish species. The islands' shores are also nesting sites for hawksbill and leatherback turtles and the easternmost island has an easy walking trail.

Quebrada Sal

The friendly Ngäbe village of Quebrada Sal (Salt Creek) is perched on the eastern shore of Isla Bastimentos. Visitors can enjoy traditional food, dances and *artesanía* presentations, as well as guided hikes on four different trails, each lasting up to an hour. The surrounding forests and wetlands are rich in wildlife, including caimans, poison dart frogs, toucans, monkeys and sloths. Near the community you will find the coral reefs of **Punta Vieja** and the broad sands of **Playa Larga** to the north; guides and boatmen can help you reach them. Community tourism in Salt Creek is managed by the **Alianza de Turismo de Salt Creek** ⓘ *T6092-7259, www.aliatur.bocas.com; please call ahead to arrange your visit.*

Cayo Crawl

Located off the southeast tip of the island, Cayo Crawl, also known as **Coral Cay**, is actually a narrow channel between Isla Bastimentos and Isla Popa. It offers excellent snorkelling in the calm waters of a coral garden. Popular with Bocas tour operators, many groups pause for a lunch at Cayo Crawl, mooring at one of the rickety and locally famous restaurants. Perched over the water, they supply interesting views of the brightly coloured marine life; however, better coral gardens can be found a short distance away.

Bahía Honda

The Ngäbe village at Bahía Honda is home to a small community meeting hall, a chapel, primary school and restaurant. Plentiful *artesanías* are available and you are welcome to stay for lunch, but most people come to experience the **Trail of the Sloth**. Managed by the **Timorogo community tourism project** ⓘ *T6726-0968, www.timorogo.org*, the trail takes visitors along a mangrove creek by traditional dugout *cayuco* (kayak). Sloths and monkeys are easily spotted in the trees along with the occasional caiman on the riverbank. Back on land, the trail winds through an old cacao plantation and rainforest before concluding at a large cave and bat colony.

Isla Solarte → *For listings, see pages 264-274. Colour map 1, A2.*

Isla Solarte, also known as **Nancy Cay**, is a small, quiet, verdant island inhabited by a handful of expats and a community of Ngäbe fishermen. At its westernmost tip lies Hospital Point, named after the old UFCO medical facilities built in 1899 by Minor Keith and the Snyder brothers. The pioneering hospital treated many thousands of banana workers for malaria and other tropical diseases, before it was decommissioned and removed to Almirante in 1920. Today, a local historian and former United Fruit researcher, Clyde Stephens, owns the plot where it once stood. Clyde has written some interesting books on the history of Bocas del Toro, Hospital Point and the UFCO, available to purchase in **Bocas Books** on Isla Colón (see Shopping, page 272). There are a couple of walking trails that snake Isla Solarte's length, and the surrounding waters are sheltered, rich in coral and particularly good for diving and snorkelling (see box, page 273).

Isla San Cristóbal → *For listings, see pages 264-274. Colour map 1, A2.*

Isla San Cristóbal covers an area of 37 sq km and is home to one of the largest Ngäbe villages in the region, **San Cristóbal**, where fishing and subsistence farming are the mainstay of local life. Located on the north side of the island, the community welcomes visitors and can supply guides or boatmen for fishing, hiking and snorkelling expeditions (bring your own equipment). A trail connects San Cristóbal with the smaller community of **Valle Escondido**, which can also be reached by boating down a creek. On the southeast shores of the Isla San Cristóbal lies **Laguna Bocatorito**, or **Dolphin Bay**, a bottlenose dolphin breeding ground. The clever creatures, who enjoy splashing and frolicking near the surface, can be observed all year, but June to September are best. In high season, boatloads of tourists often arrive together in the morning and chase the pods around in what must be a very familiar (and perhaps tedious) ritual for the animals. Try to time your visit outside of conventional visiting hours. Although they are friendly, it's not a good idea to go diving with the dolphins as the bubbles from the regulator tend to freak them out.

Isla Popa → *For listings, see pages 264-274. Colour map 1, A2.*

Isla Popa is one of the largest islands in the archipelago and home to rustic Ngäbe communities who are rarely visited but keen to attract interest. Perched on the island's northwest flank, the village of **Popa 1** is the oldest and most populous of its communities and a good place to start your explorations. Further south, the slightly smaller and younger community of **Popa 2** is composed of Ngäbe migrants from all over the province. Intriguing mangrove and rainforest trails commence in the village, also home to the **Meri Ngobe Community Tourism Project** ① *www.meri-ngobe.org*, which offers simple (but comfortable) accommodation, guides and *artesanías*. On the southwest side of the island, a small channel divides Popa from **Split Hill Island** where some 300 Ngäbe live in the diminutive ranching community of **Loma Partida**. On Popa's southern shores, the community of **Punta Laurel** overlooks teeming coral reefs, while **Cayo Agua** – a separate island off Popa's eastern flank – is home to a notable community, hiking trails and a rainforest.

◉ The Bocas del Toro archipelago listings

For sleeping and eating price codes and other relevant information, see pages 16-19.

🛏 Where to stay

Isla Colón *p255, maps p256 and p259*
Bocas Town
$$$$-$$$ Bocas del Toro, Calle 2a, T757-9771, www.hotelbocasdeltoro.com. This attractive boutique hotel on the seafront has been constructed with 11 types of hardwood. It boasts large clean, comfortable rooms, some with excellent sea views. There's a restaurant, kayak rental, tours by arrangement and Wi-Fi. Rooms are well equipped with flatscreen TVs, a/c, orthopaedic mattresses, electronic safes, telephones, coffee-makers and a complimentary bag of organic coffee. Recommended.
$$$$-$$$ El Limbo, Calle 2a, T757-9062, www.ellimbo. com. This boutique hotel has a great location overlooking the channel between Isla Colón and Isla Caranero. The business-like rooms have nice wooden floors and walls, a/c, TV, Wi-Fi and fridge. Those with balconies and sea views are

better, and more expensive. The restaurant is good but pricey. They also have a place on Isla Bastimentos (**$$$**).
$$$$-$$$ Tropical Suites, Calle 1a, T757-9880. Boutique hotel located in the heart of downtown Bocas. A range of suites boast fully equipped kitchens, attractive wood furnishings, Wi-Fi, a/c, flatscreen TVs and, in some cases, jacuzzis. Rates vary with views and season. Sometimes good internet rates are available. Breakfast included.
$$$ Bahía, south end of Main St, T757-9626, www.ghbahia.com. Built in 1905, this interesting historic building was the former HQ of the **United Fruit Company** – check out the intriguing old photos on the walls. All rooms have hot water, TV, a/c, and the remodelled rooms are more expensive. There's a new Peruvian restaurant in front and Wi-Fi is available. Ask to see a room before accepting.
$$$ Bocas Inn Lodge, north end of Main St, T757-9600, www.anconexpeditions.com. Run by tour operator **Ancon Expeditions** (see page 72). Comfortable and simple with pleasant, spacious bar and terrace, communal veranda upstairs and platform

for swimming. The water is heated with solar panels. Crab and lobster off the menu due to overfishing concerns. Prices include breakfast. Good reviews.

$$$ Cocomo-on-the-Sea, Av Norte y Calle 6a, T757-9259, www.cocomoonthesea.com. A lovely B&B on the seafront with a lush tropical garden, sundeck and 4 clean, simple rooms with a/c and private bath. A huge all-you-can-eat breakfast is included, book swap, Wi-Fi, laundry service, free use of kayaks, refrigerator and beach towels. US owner Douglas is a superb fellow and very helpful – he can hook you up with some of the best guides on the island. Nice place and recommended.

$$$ Laguna, Calle 3a and Av D, T757-9091, www.thehotellagunabocas.htm. This centrally located 3-star hotel has 20 attractive wooden rooms and 2 suites with a/c, hot water, cable TV, electronic safes, Wi-Fi and orthopaedic mattresses. There's a terrace and bar downstairs, breakfast is included and good reductions are available in low season.

$$$ Palma Royale, Main St, www.palmaroyale.com. A new condo-style establishment that's received good reviews from guests. They offer a range of designer suites (**$$$**), studios (**$$$$**) and a penthouse (**$$$$**) with handsome hand-crafted wood furniture, flatscreen TVs, Wi-Fi and all the usual amenities.

$$$ Swan's Cay, opposite the municipal building on Main St, T757-9090, www.swanscayhotel.com. A smart, upmarket hotel with an elegant lobby, 2 pools, 2 restaurants, Wi-Fi and comfortable rooms with hot water, a/c, cable TV and the usual amenities. Perhaps not quite as luxurious as it would like to be.

$$ Cala Luna, behind **Alberto's Restaurant**, Calle 5a and Av E, T757-9066, www.calalunabocas.com. Hidden in the backstreets, rooms are spacious with a sparse, appealing style. All are equipped with a/c, fan, fridge, cable TV, safe, orthopaedic mattresses, private bath and hot water. Shared balconies with hammocks and Wi-Fi for chilling out, ping-

pong downstairs. Clean, pleasant, family-run. Same owners as **Alberto's** (see page 269).

$$ Casa Amarilla, Calle 5a and Av G, T757-9938, www.casaamarilla.org. 4 large airy rooms with good beds, a/c, fridge, digital safe, laptops, Wi-Fi and large flatscreen cable TVs. Owner Dennis Fischer lives upstairs and is a very sound fellow – helpful and interesting to chat to. Free coffee and tea all day. A good place and recommended. Space is limited, so book in advance.

$$ Del Parque, Calle 2a, on the plaza, T757-9008, hdelparque.webs.com. Well-kept old townhouse with light wooden rooms and good beds, a/c, pleasant shared balconies, good views, hammocks, hot water, use of kitchen, Wi-Fi, free coffee and fruit. Dorm beds are also now available (**$**), discounts in low season, and can help arrange tours. Much better upstairs.

$$ Dos Palmas, Av Sur y Calle 6a, Bocas, T757-9906, hoteldospalmas@yahoo.com. A quaint, quiet, family-owned hotel with lots of local charm. Clean rooms have hot water, TV and a/c; cheaper with fan. Built over the water with a good swimming platform at back. Free coffee before midday. Pleasant management.

$$ Hotel Angela, Av Norte and Calle 6a, T757-9813, www.hotelangela.com. Managed by Claudio from Memphis, who is a true gentleman and very helpful. Hotel Angela has 12 rooms with a/c, private bath, hot water and Wi-Fi. TVs and orthopaedic mattresses are planned for the near future. There is also a comfortable apartment with a full kitchen and jacuzzi (**$$$**). Recommended.

$$ Hotelito del Mar, Calle 1a, T757-9861, www.hotelitodelmar.com. Rooms are quiet, sparklingly clean and adorned with vibrant artwork. They all have private bath, hot water, cable TV, Wi-Fi and a/c. Tourist information is available and tours by arrangement. The owner is friendly. Good central location. Continental breakfast included.

$$ Hotel Olas de la Madrugada, Av Sur, T757-9930, www.hotelolas.com. This popular hotel built over the water has 24 clean, bright rooms, all with a/c, cable TV and private hot water shower. Wakeboard rental available. Wi-Fi and breakfast included. Friendly, with good attention.

$$ La Veranda, Calle 7a y Av G, T757-9211, www.bocasdeltorohotel.yolasite.com. Original wooden Bocas-style house with history. Rooms come with a/c and private bath or fan and shared bath (**$**). Large veranda on 1st floor has a communal kitchen and an area to eat or relax. One room has capacity for 5 people and Wi-Fi is available for guests.

$$ Lula's B&B, Av Norte, across street from Cocomo-on-the-Sea, T757-9057, www.lula bb.com. Old-style, family-run place with a kitchenette and deck upstairs and a living area downstairs. This is the base of operations for **Bocas Surf School**. All rooms come with a/c, private bath, safe and hot water; Wi-Fi and full breakfast are included. Owners Bryan and Jana Hudson are friendly and helpful. Homely, clean, quiet, safe and very secure.

$$ Posada Los Delfines, Av G y Calle 5a, T757-9963, www.posadalosdelfines.net. A big, blue building with clean, reasonably sized rooms with cable TV, Wi-Fi, hot water and a/c. Dorm beds (**$**) and a shared kitchen were under construction at the time of research. Tours and transportation offered, including to Costa Rica. Popular with groups. Simple breakfast included.

$ Casa Verde, Av Sur, T6633-8050, www. casaverdebocas.com. This small, friendly hostel have a range of simple private rooms, all kitted with a/c, fridge, electronic safe and shared bath with hot water. Various economical dorm beds are also available. General amenities include a communal kitchen, Wi-Fi, internet terminal, a sea deck for swimming, inner tubes, and a buzzing little bar-restaurant where you can pick up quesadillas and other snacks. Affordable tours depart daily. Recommended.

$ Gran Kahuna Hostel, Calle 3a, T757-9038, www.grankahunabocas.com. A large, popular surf hostel located at the heart of the action on main street, **Gran Kahuna** offers a range of economical dorms, Wi-Fi,

games, communal TV, surfboard rental, classes, transportation to the breaks and various surf-and-stay packages. Clean, well established and sociable.

$ Heike, Calle 3a, on the plaza, T757-9708, www.hostelheike.com. A friendly, inexpensive backpackers' hostel with 2 private rooms, 6 dorms, shared bathrooms, kitchen, communal veranda, coffee all day and a cosy sun terrace complete with hammocks, internet terminals, good breezes and sofas. Surfboards are available for rent, free use of the guitars, filtered water and pancake breakfast included.

$ Hotel Cayos Zapatillas, Calle 3a, on the plaza, T757-9844. This popular cheapie has a handy central location. It offers scores of simple, occasionally scruffy rooms with private hot water shower, cable TV and fan. Rooms with a/c cost more. Simple and economical, although noise may be an issue at times. Wi-Fi and kitchen are available for guests.

$ Las Brisas, on the sea at north end of Calle 3a, T757-9549, www.brisasbocas.com. Marketed as a surf 'n' sports lodge, this wooden building on stilts has a nice veranda over the sea, but has seen better days. All rooms have a/c and private bath, although those upstairs have thin walls, and some rooms are quite musty. Discounts available if several days are purchased up front. Good for rough-and-ready groups, but check the room before accepting. Kitchen and Wi-Fi available.

$ Mondo Taitu, Av G, T757-9425, www. mondotaitu.com. Ramshackle party hostel that vaguely resembles a shipwreck. The bar is busy (and noisy) in the evenings, happy hour 1900-2000. Amenities include kitchen, bikes (including tandems), guitars, surfboards, free coffee and tea, and a pancake breakfast. A handful of 'treehouse rooms' and various dorms available. Friendly and popular with surfers, backpackers and whippersnappers.

$ Sagitarius, Calle 4a, T757-9578, hsagitario@ cwpanama.net. Simple, reasonably priced wooden rooms with hot water, bath, TV and a/c (cheaper with fan). Locally owned, clean and good for budget wanderers.

Around Isla Colón

$$$$ Punta Caracol, western side of the island, T757-9410, www.puntacaracol.com. Located in a secluded enclave on the western side of the island, **Punta Caracol** is an exclusive and famous eco-resort consisting of a string of thatched luxury bungalows arcing over the water on their own private pier. The most expensive lodgings in the area, 1st class and very attentive.

Isla Caranero *p261*

$$$ Buccaneer Resort, east side, T757-9042, www.bocasbuccaneer.com. Situated close to good surf breaks, swimming areas and coral reef, **Buccaneer** offers a range of simple, wooden lodgings to suit families, groups and couples. Their suites sleep 4 and include great sea views, a/c, fridge, hammocks, balcony and private bath with hot water. Smaller, cheaper bungalows sleep 3 and include similar amenities. For more adventurous types there are rustic *cabañas*. Wi-Fi available and breakfast included. Friendly, helpful management.
$$$ Doña Mara, T757-9551, www.hotel donamara.com. Located by a small white-sand beach, this comfortable hotel offers 6 clean, quiet rooms with hot water, a/c, Wi-Fi and cable TV. Prices include breakfast. The attached restaurant does very good Caribbean seafood, good music, and happy hour 1600-1900.
$$$ Hotel Tierra Verde, T757-9903, www.hoteltierraverde.com. A well-maintained hotel situated among coconut palms, a stone's throw from the shore. Rooms have private showers, hot water and Wi-Fi. Those with ocean view cost US$10 more. The hotel can arrange tours and sometimes walk-in rates apply. Continental breakfast included. Comfortable and friendly.
$$$-$$ Careening Cay Resort, north side of the island, T757-9157, www.careeningcay. com. Very attractive wooden *cabañas* in a tranquil location; some are equipped with stove, microwave and fridge, all have a/c, TV, DVD and bath. The family suite is particularly good, with a 10-person capacity, sofas, kitchen, loft and hammocks. Their restaurant, the **Cosmic Crab Café**, is excellent, and the *artesanía* store has some interesting international crafts.
$ Aqua Lounge Hostel and Bar, T6456-4659, www.bocasaqualounge.info. A very cool and popular hostel that flies in DJs for their famous twice-weekly parties. At most other times the hostel is quiet. Plenty of useful amenities including a chill-out terrace on the water, swimming area, hammocks, movie theatre, ping-pong, water trampoline, Wi-Fi, restaurant, kitchen, laundry and bar. Lodgings consist of large dorms and 6 simple private rooms with shared bath. Happy hour runs all day and the hostel regularly hosts special events like BBQs and 'Beer Olympics'. Prices include buffet breakfast.

Isla Bastimentos *p261*

$$$$ Al Natural, Old Point, T757-9004, www.alnaturalresort.com. Belgian-owned solar-powered ecolodge bungalows built using traditional techniques and native fallen trees. Bungalows consist of 3 walls, leaving 1 side open and exposed to a spectacular view of the ocean and Zapatillas in the distance – a truly natural experience. Price includes transport from Isla Colón, 3 lovingly prepared meals with wine, use of kayaks and snorkelling gear. Email reservations in advance. Highly recommended.
$$$$ Eclypse de Mar, offshore, near Old Bank, T6611-4581, www.eclypsedemar.com. Attractive 'Acqua-Lodge' in the same vein as the famous **Punta Caracol**. Secluded bungalows built over the water, all fully equipped and with stunning sunset views.
$$$ Coral Cay, east of Isla Bastimentos, T6626-1919, www.bocas.com/coralcay.htm. Peaceful, rustic cabins built over the water. Beautiful surroundings and outstanding seafood. Price includes 2 meals per day, snorkelling equipment and the use of a traditional dugout canoe. Watch out for the sandflies.

$$ Caribbean View Hotel, Old Bank, T757-9442, hotelcaribbeanview@yahoo.com. Wooden, traditional-style hotel with lovely local owners and quite upmarket for rustic Bastimentos Town. Rooms have a/c or fan, private shower, hot water and TV. Wi-Fi, kayaks, boat and cave tours also available. There is a communal deck over the water.

$$ El Limbo, T757-9062, www.ellimbo.com. Close to the national park with a handsome beachfront location. Rooms are clean and comfortable. They offer a good mix of activities. However, it's a little pricey for the package and reviews have been mixed.

$$ The Point, Old Bank, at the end of the road, northern tip of the island, T757-9704, sloopj4@yahoo.com. **The Point** boasts superb views, breezes and great access to local reef breaks. Rooms are modest, comfortable and equipped with fridge, coffee-maker, fan and bath. Clients may also use surfboards, kayaks, book exchange and snorkel gear. The balcony is a great spot to relax in a hammock. Friendly and recommended.

$ Hostal Bastimentos, Old Bank, T757-9053, www.hostalbastimento.com. This long-established budget hostel has lots of interesting statues in the garden and an elevated position overlooking the town. Lodgings include ultra-cheap dorm beds and a wide range of double rooms, cheaper without private bath and more expensive with hot water and fridge (**$$**). Amenities include 2 shared kitchens, Wi-Fi, internet terminal and free kayaks.

$ Tío Tom's Guesthouse, Old Bank, T757-9831, www.tiotomsguesthouse.com. Dutch adventurer Tío Tom is a Bastimentos institution. He offers rustic wooden rooms on the water, all with private bath, and a pleasant bungalow with its own terrace (**$$**). Interesting extras include a small orchid garden, hydroponic crops, own produce, dive school, kayak rental, book exchange, and an evening 'family meal' that uses local ingredients as much as possible. Very knowledgeable about Panama and the islands. Recommended.

$ Yellow Jack, Old Bank, T6908-3621, www.yellow-jack.com. A very cool, secluded budget hotel with 4 simple private rooms and a small house with a 5-person capacity (**$$$**). Amenities include use of the fridge, dive school and a pleasant communal area built over the water. Friendly Argentine management and chilled-out atmosphere. Recommended.

Isla Solarte p263

$$$ Solarte del Caribe, T6488-4775, www.solarteinn.com. B&B on the southern side of the island. Comfortable beds, colourful, tropical surroundings and good food. Breakfast and round-trip transport included.

Isla Popa p264

$$$$ Popa Paradise Beach Resort, Isla Popa, T832-1498, www.popaparadisebeach resort.com. High-end cabins and casitas with TV, a/c and balconies. 2 'penthouse' suites are also available, with kitchen, balcony, living room and dining area. Personal, professional attention and 'barefoot luxury'.

● Restaurants

Isla Colón p255, map p259
Bocas Town

$$$ 9 Degree, Calle 1a, inside the Tropical Market. Upmarket restaurant that might appeal to moneyed urban types. Creative dishes include prawn penne and Indonesian pork tenderloin. Smart, sophisticated and overlooking the water.

$$$ Barracuda, Calle 3a. This pleasant dining option perched on the water serves Italian and seafood specials like fettuccine with shrimp, tuna steak and ricotta and spinach ravioli. Wi-Fi for checking your emails.

$$$ La Ballena, Av E, next to Swan Cay Hotel. Delicious Italian seafood pastas and cappuccinos, good for breakfast with tables outside. On the pricey side but has a good reputation.

$$$ La Casbah, Av G. Popular and intimate evening restaurant with seating inside and out. Dishes are fresh, creative and tasty with both local and Mediterranean inspiration. Catch of the day is good.

$$$ El Pecado, Calle 3a, under Hotel Laguna. Panamanian and international food, including Lebanese. One of the best restaurants in town, and not too expensive. Great drinks and good wines worth splashing out on, also try their early-evening hummous with warm Johnny Cakes (coconut bread). Recommended.

$$ Alberto's Restaurant, Calle 5a. Authentic Italian cuisine including great pizza, pasta and lasagne. There's also BBQ meat and fish. Wine is served. Reasonable prices.

$$ Bar y Restaurante The Pirate, Calle 3a, next to **El Limbo Hotel**. Long-standing wooden restaurant built over the water. They serve good seafood, breakfasts, smoothies and wine. There's also a full bar and happy hour.

$$ Buena Vista Bar and Grill, Calle 2a. Long-standing restaurant/bar run by a very friendly Panamanian and his American girlfriend. Good menu for both bar snacks and main meals, grills, tacos, fish and veggie options. Nice spot over the water to relax with a beer or cocktail.

$$ El Ultimo Refugio, Av Sur and Calle 5a. A ramshackle and romantic setting on the water with lots of candlelight and a plant-covered wooden deck. Creative dishes include Peruvian ceviche, marlin fillet, pork tenderloin, pineapple and ginger shrimp. Popular and recommended.

$$ Gringos, Calle 4a, behind Golden Grill. Authentic Tex-Mex menu with some classic recipes imported from Baja California. The nachos and salsa are excellent, the burritos rich and filling. Wholesome comfort food, popular with expats and recommended.

$$ Lemongrass, Calle 2a, next to **Buena Vista**, upstairs. One of the best in Bocas. The hospitable English owner has experience of cooking in Asia so expect good, authentic Thai curries and lots of fresh seafood. Good views over the bay and excellent bar for cocktails. Friendly, buzzing and recommended.

$$ Natural Mystic, Calle 3a. As the name might suggest, mystically themed with oriental artwork and a decidedly bohemian vibe. The changing menu often features affordable fish and shrimp dishes. Sometimes there are live music acts too.

$$ The Reef, end of Calle 3a, opposite **Super Gourmet**. Big wooden structure with a terrace over the water. They serve local food, seafood specials and cocktails. Popular with Panamanians but inconsistent.

$$ Shelly's BBQ Mexican Food, behind Hotel Laguna (see Where to stay), T757-9779. First Mexican eatery in Bocas, with enchiladas, mole, guacamole and barbecued meats. They also do home delivery (plus taxi cost) and sell a range of frozen specials in Bocas' **Super Gourmet** store.

$$ Sol y Sombra, Av Norte y Calle 6a, inside **Hotel Angela** (see Where to stay). This relaxed waterside restaurant has a fine local reputation. The changing menu includes specials like ceviche, prawn cakes, prime ribs and passion fruit crème brûlée. The filet mignon is outstanding. Only open for dinner at the time of research, but there are plans to open for lunch too. Highly recommended.

$$-$ La Buguita, Calle 3a, attached to La Buga dive shop. Popular with backpackers and divers, this little café on the water serves fish tacos, deli sandwiches, breakfast burritos, smoothies and mini-pizzas.

$$-$ Lili's Café, Calle 1a, next to **Tropical Suites Hotel**. Chilled-out and friendly café on the water serving Caribbean cuisine with a healthfood twist. A good range of breakfasts and mains, including pastas, soups, salads and sandwiches. Open for breakfast and lunch only.

$$-$ Om Café, Av E, closed Wed and Thu. Excellent, home-made Indian food served in very relaxing and ambient surroundings. Tables are available on the balcony or private rooms for larger parties. **Om** also serves good breakfasts with home-made granola and yoghurt, lassis, fruit salads and bagels. Recommended.

$ El Lorito, Calle 3a. Most popular – and oldest – local café in town, serving cheap, wholesome buffet food and cakes. Ask for the pudding – unique to Bocas – and their malted milkshakes.

$ McDouglas Golden Grill, Calle 3a, opposite the park. The fast-food emporium of Bocas – cheap burgers, chips and hot dogs. Also pizzas with loads of cheese, and breakfast eggs and pancakes – good for those on a budget, but not on a diet. Free Wi-Fi for clients.

$ Restaurant Chitré, Calle 3a. Long-running *fonda* serving cheap and cheerful buffet fare. Nice owners, and a good spot for watching street traffic.

$ Vive y Deja Vivir, Calle 3a, several blocks from the centre. Economical home-cooked Caribbean breakfasts and lunches, including fish and meat dishes. Very friendly, tasty and good value. A little walk out of the centre, but recommended.

Cafés, bakeries, delis and juice bars
Bocas Blended, Calle Norte, on the corner opposite Casa Max. Quirky old bus converted into a juice bar. There's conspicuous seating on the roof where you can watch the world go by. Juices are good and rich in vitamins, but not cheap. They also do wraps and other snacks.
Panadería Dulcería Alemana, Calle 2a. This small German bakery does tasty cakes, delicious fresh bread, good coffee and light snacks. Very good, but not cheap, and service is sometimes slow.
Starfish Coffee, Calle 3a, just before **Bocas Water Sports**, Bocas del Toro. Cappuccino, pastries, croissants and brownies. Excellent breakfast deals at reasonable prices. Owner offers yoga classes in the morning and tours of their environmentally friendly coffee plantation on the mainland on request.
Super Gourmet, Calle 1a, near the ferry for Almirante. Deli and gourmet supermarket that does very good, if pricey, sandwiches, pastas and salads. You'll also find tasty local produce and plenty of foreign imports here.

Isla Caranero *p261*
$$$-$$ Cosmic Crab Café, north side of the island, facing Isla Colón. Managed by a friendly American couple, Joan and Steve, who offer a creative menu with diverse international influences including Greek, Thai, Indian and Caribbean. Dishes include seafood lasagne, baby back ribs in mango chutney sauce, seafood bisque and key lime pie. Their cocktails and fresh fruit smoothies are exceptional, and they have an entire menu devoted just to Martinis.
$$ Bibi's on the Beach, part of the **Buccaneer Resort**, east side of the island near Black Rock, T6785-7984, www.bibisonthebeach.com. Managed by friendly Argentine Luis Bertone, Bibi's has a great location overlooking Bastimentos and Solarte islands. They specialize in fresh, tasty, Creole-style seafood, including ceviche, prawns, lobster, whole fish, fillets, octopus and seafood platters. Salads, pastas, burgers and chicken dishes are also available. Open for breakfast, lunch and dinner every day except Tue. Good ambience. Recommended.
$$ The Pickled Parrot, facing Isla Bastimentos. Draught beers, Thai soups and American BBQs, with a daily happy hour 1500-1700. Owner George is a world-class raconteur and host. Lovely at sunset and great for drinking after dark.
$$ Restaurant Doña Mara, facing Isla Colón. Excellent Caribbean seafood including octopus, shrimp and conch meat. The house speciality is Caribbean whole fish. Good music and happy hour 1600-1900. They also do typical Panamanian food.

Isla Bastimentos *p261*
$$ Mantis, on the hill, 5-10 mins from Old Bank, follow the path next to the police station. Excellent, authentic Thai curries, soups and noodles served on a pleasant deck overlooking the jungle and ocean. Good service, reasonable prices and easily the best restaurant on the island. Very satisfying and highly recommended.

$ Kechas, Old Bank, north of the police station. Reliable Caribbean eatery on the water also known as Alvin's. They serve large plates of hearty local fare, including seafood, chicken and meat, all invariably accompanied by rice and plantain. Good value.

$ Puntai Pizza, Old Bank, south of the police station. Run by Nicole, **Puntai** serves sandwiches, coffee, breakfasts, juices and, of course, fresh-baked pizza. Good local reports and worth a look. Breakfast and dinner only.

$ Roots, Old Bank. Locally famous bar and restaurant with a nice terrace over the water. They serve Caribbean seafood and other local fare. Closed for a while but now under new management, back on its feet and doing well.

$ Sonrisas del Mar, Old Bank, close to the northern tip. Perched on the water, this locals' favourite serves seafood and smoked chicken, as well as occasional 'exotics' and 'bush' meat, which may or may not be ethical depending on the species, source and season. Please order wisely.

Cafés

Up in the Hill, 15 mins from Old Bank, follow the path next to the police station. Intimate and ramshackle café attached to an interesting cacao and coconut farm. They serve hot coffee, fresh herbal teas, juices, brownies and exquisite truffles.

Bars and clubs

Isla Colón *p255, map p259*
Bocas Town
Barco Hundido, Calle 1a, next to Cable & Wireless office. The **Wreck Deck** (its original name) is built over a wrecked, sunken boat. Once very popular, there have been some negative reports lately.

El Encanto, Calle 3a. One of the few truly local spots in the downtown area. Salsa is played at volume and there is a pool hall. An interesting change from the gringo haunts, but take care.

La Mama Loca, inside **Casa Verde** (see Where to stay). A nice little crowd at the

time of research. Beer, cocktails, shooters and shots by the waters' edge, and usually live music from 1800, including reggae. Friendly and recommended.

Mondo Taitu, Av G, T757-9425 (see Where to stay). Busy and often buzzing bar in a backpackers' hostel. Good for beer, cocktails, hukka pipes and meeting other travellers. A young, brazen, party-loving crowd.

Rip Tide, Calle Norte, the waterfront. A famous and popular expat bar built into a big old boat on the water. Good for a beer, an interesting conversation and a laugh, but not for innocents. They also do filling grub, including chicken wings, should you get peckish.

Toro Loco, Av Central, between Calle 1a and 2a. A US-style grill and bar with loud music, sports TV, dartboard and various dark little corners. Popular with expats and praised as one of the best watering holes in town.

Isla Caranero *p261*
Aqua Lounge, 2 mins from Bocas. An estimated 300-400 people attend the legendary parties at the **Aqua Lounge**, hosted every weekend and on an additional night in the week. Happy hour runs all day, giving you plenty of warm-up time. Good security and admission by invitation only (invites are distributed at hostels in Bocas town; otherwise just show up on the night and ask for one). Highly recommended.

Isla Bastimentos *p261*
Every Mon everyone who wants to party heads over to Isla Bastimentos for **Blue Mondays**, a largely local event with live calypso music and the full Caribbean vibe. Hugely popular.

Festivals

Isla Colón *p255, maps p256 and p259*
Jul The Virgen del Carmen is honoured in the 3rd week of Jul with pilgrimages to La Gruta.

28 Sep-2 Oct The **Feria del Mar** is held on the Playa Istmito with lots of music, dancing and fun.
16 Nov Celebrations commemorating the foundation of Bocas del Toro.

Isla Bastimentos *p261*
23 Nov Bastimentos Day, featuring music, parades and good-natured revelry.

○ Shopping

Bocas Town *p257, map p259*
Bocas Books, Av E, under **Om Café**. One of the best English-language bookshops in Panama with a vast collection of second-hand fiction and non-fiction titles. The owner, Dave, is a convivial fellow with lots of interesting insights into island life. Stop by, browse the books, have a chat, drink a beer or two... Highly recommended.

○ What to do

Isla Colón *p255, map p259*
Diving and snorkelling
Sep-Oct and Mar-Apr are the best months for diving and snorkelling. Bocas is a good place for beginners and courses are competitively priced during the low season.
Bocas Watersports, Calle 3a, T757-9541, www.bocaswatersports.com. Dive courses, waterskiing and kayak rental. Local 2-tank dives cost US$50, with longer 2-tank trips to Tiger Rock and the Zapatilla Cayes running at around US$75. Snorkelling gear costs US$5 a day. They offer a day-long snorkelling tour to Dolphin Bay, Crawl Cay, Red Frog and Hospital Point, snacks included, US$20. Training from Open Water Diver to Dive Master.
La Buga Dive Center, Calle 3a, T757-9534, www.labugapanama.com. An expanding and popular outfit. They offer training from Open Water Diver, US$245, to Dive Master. Specialities include Deep Diver, Night Diver and Underwater Naturalist. They claim to have the biggest, fastest boat in

the area, and know special dive sites their competitors don't.
Starfleet, Calle 1a, next to Buena Vista, T757-9630, www.starfleetscuba.com. A very professional, PADI Gold Palm IDC centre, managed by Tony and Georgina Sanders from England. They offer training from Open Water Diver, US$175-235, right up to Instructor level. A 2-tank dive is US$60, a day-long snorkel tour, US$20. They have over 17 years' experience in Bocas waters and notably sponsored Panama's first and only native PADI course director. Impeccable safety record, with good instructors and equipment. Dive Master internships also available. Highly recommended.

Health and spa
Bocas Yoga, Calle 4a, the big purple building, www.bocasyoga.com. Dedicated Yoga studio with daily classes in Hatha, Vinyasa and Anusara-inspired yoga. Drop-in rates US$5 per class, multi-class packages also available. Teachers are certified and experienced. Suitable for all levels, check for the latest schedule.
Starfleet Massage and Day Spa, Calle 1a, inside Starfleet Scuba. A range of professional spa treatments including facials, waxes, hot-stone therapy and clinical massages from simple chair massages to full body massages. Qualified and licensed therapists.

Sailing
Catamaran Sailing Adventures, Av Sur y Calle 6a, next to Hotel Dos Palmas, T757-9710 or T6464-4242, www.bocassailing.com. Owner Marcel offers popular day sailing tours on his 12-m catamaran around the Bocas Islands for US$44, including lunch and snorkelling gear. Very knowledgeable when it comes to finding the best reef areas – you can also hire the whole boat from US$400 and do a customized trip. Trips leave daily at 0930, but you will need advance reservation. Environmentally aware and recommended.

Diving and snorkelling in Bocas del Toro

The real joy of diving and snorkelling in Bocas is in the details. Some wonderful intact coral gardens play host to a multitude of little gems, including brittle star fish, spotted morays, arrow crabs, toad-fish, squid, and a prolific variety of Caribbean reef fish. Larger marine creatures, including dolphins, sea turtles, rays and nurse sharks, are often spotted further offshore. If you've never dived before, the waters around Bocas del Toro are particularly calm and sheltered, making it a great place to learn. PADI Open Water Diver courses last three to four days and are comparatively cheap at around US$275. Be warned, the course is as demanding as it is rewarding, and when you're not in the water practising skills, you'll need to study your textbook and watch cheesy PADI DVDs. Four or five dives will be included in your training package and there's a multiple-choice exam at the end. Once you've passed, you'll be qualified to dive anywhere in the world and take your skills in new directions – underwater naturalist, photographer and deep diver are some of the immediate possibilities. Bocas' dive sites are varied and there are many more than can be listed here. Some are known to only a handful of veteran divers, others are waiting to be discovered. **Hospital Point** is a popular location at the northern side of Isla Solarte. It has a gently sloping shelf of coral that suddenly drops to a depth of 16 m. **The Wreck**, another popular site, is a ferry deliberately sunk in 2000 to create an artificial reef. In front of Bocas Town you'll find **The Playground**, a circle of reef where turtles are often spotted. **Cayo Crawl**, at the southern end of Bastimentos, is full of great corals but often frequented by tour boats. A handful of really excellent sites lie further afield, but are only accessible in the calm months of March to April and September to October. Among them, **La Gruta del Polo** has spooky underwater caverns and a swim-through. **Tiger Rock** is one of the best sites in Bocas and features underwater pinnacles. The **Cayos Zapatillas** are also highly regarded. If diving doesn't appeal, snorkelling is a feasible alternative. Most tour operators run snorkel trips to the major sites, but it might be worth using one of the dive shops to be sure of the best service.

Surfing

You can rent boards from hostels like Gran Kahuna, Mondo Taitu and Heike. There are 2 surf shops in town, **Tropix**, on Calle 3a (T757-9415) who make custom boards and **Flow**, located under **Om Café**. Bocas Surf School operates from Lula's B&B, Av H, T6482-4166, www.bocassurfschool.com.

Tour operators

There are numerous tour operators, most have maps and photos to help plan your day. Typical tours visit either Dolphin Bay, Hospital Point, Coral Cay and Red Frog Beach (Bastimentos), or Boca del Drago and Swans Cay (Bird Island). For a little extra you can add Cayos Zapatilla to the first tour. You are advised to use reputable operators rather than street touts.

Coopeguitour, Calle 1a, miguil1969@hotmail.es, T6477-7311. A local cooperative of guides and boatmen, **Coopeguitour** visits the major sites and offers a range of competitively priced packages. Some captains are bilingual, check before departure. **Jampan**, Calle 1a, T757-9619, www.jampantours.com. A professional, safe and well-established operator with quiet, fuel-efficient four-stroke motors and knowledgeable bilingual captains. They visit all the usual haunts and some different ones too, including medicine women on

Isla San Cristóbal, the jungles of Punta Solarte, Shepherd Isle and Cerutti's Green Acres Chocolate Farm. They also rent out a houseboat. Recommended.

Transparente Tours, Calle 3a, beside The Pirate, T757-9915, transparentetours@ hotmail.com. A long-running and reputable operator that offers boat tours of the islands and major sights, including Laguna Bocatorito, Coral Cay, Zapatillas, Red Frog Beach and Hospital Point. An interesting and original option is the far-flung and very beautiful island of Escudo de Veraguas.

Isla Caranero *p261*
Surfing, kayaking and snorkelling
Aqua Lounge Surf School, T6456-4659, www.bocasaqualounge.info. Surf coaching from US$40 half day; US$60 full day. A typical session includes surf theory, rules and etiquette, warm-up and actual surfing. They have a specialist surf photographer and your sessions can be combined with yoga lessons.
Escuela del Mar, part of the Buccaneer Resort, east side of the island near Black Rock, T6785-7984, luisbertone@gmail.com. Passionate surf instructor Luis Bertone has 20 years' experience riding waves. His surf school is perfectly positioned next to Black Rock, an ideal break for learners, and he offers instruction to all ages from US$45 for a half day to US$110 for 3 full days. Lessons can be 'kayak assisted' and rentals include long boards, short boards, body boards, kayaks (very affordable) and snorkel gear. Recommended.

Isla Bastimentos *p261*
Diving and snorkelling
Scuba 6 Dive Center, Old Bank, inside Tío Tom's Guesthouse, T6793-2722, www.scuba6diving.com. An enthusiastic new outfit managed by experienced and adventurous divers. They offer PADI Open Water certification, training up to Assistant Instructor and preparation for IDC. Groups

are kept small and course materials are available in German, English, Dutch or Spanish. Recommended.
Yellow Jack, Old Bank. Attached to a relaxed, Argentine hotel (see Where to stay), Yellow Jack offers Open Water certification (US$230) and training up to Dive Master level, in addition to regular 1-tank (US$30) and 2-tank (US$55) dives. Friendly and easy-going.

⊖ Transport

Isla Colón *p255, maps p256 and p259*
Air Bocas del Toro can be reached with Air Panama twice daily from Albrook Airport, US$103 one-way. To **David** Mon, Wed and Fri, US$65; to **Changuinola**, twice daily, US$37. **Nature Air** (Costa Rica, www.nature air.com) now operate flights between Bocas del Toro and San José, Costa Rica, US$140 one-way. Call **Bocas International Airport** for details, T757-9841.

Boat To **Almirante**, water taxis run daily 0530-1830, 30 mins, US$3. *Palanga*, the car ferry, runs between **Almirante** and Bocas every day, leaving at 0900 and returning from Bocas at 1200. US$15 per car (more for large vehicles), US$1 for foot passengers. If you're travelling to San José, Costa Rica, set off at dawn.

From Isla Colón to the other islands, including **Caranero**, **Bastimentos** and **Solarte**, water taxis depart from various points along the waterfront – ask around The Pirate, Taxi 25, near IPAT or the dock for Bocas Marine Tours. Fares are US$1-5 one-way and always rising with the cost of gasoline. From Caranero or Bastimentos Town it's easy to flag down a passing boat. If going to remote beaches, always arrange a pickup time. If hiring a boat, try to arrange it the day before, at least US$60-100 per day (4 hrs minimum, can take 9 people or more, depending on boat size).

Contents

Footprint features

Background

Panama history

Pre-Columbian history

Scholars are divided over when human beings first arrived in the Americas. Most theories trace their origins to the **Upper Paleolithic era** (late Stone Age), between 13,000 and 40,000 years ago. The most conventional hypothesis suggests that waves of Asiatic migrants crossed the frozen waters of the Bering Strait towards the end of the **Pleistocene epoch** (the last ice age), gradually spreading across the continents. Around 9000 BC, glaciers began melting and the early Americans enjoyed an era of Clovis culture when they were chiefly sustained by grubs, berries and woolly mammoths. By 2000 BC, thanks to generations of selective plant-breeding, a tiny-fruit bearing grass called teosinte had evolved into agricultural maize. It was the dawn of Mesoamerican history, the Formative era, when hunter-gatherers began settling into sedentary villages.

The Isthmian cultures

On the Azuero Peninsula, the site of **Monagrillo** (2500-1200 BC) is one of Panama's most ancient inhabited areas. Archaeological evidence from the site includes projectile points, stone tools and the oldest known pottery in Central America. Its population relied on fishing and hunting and there is also some limited evidence of maize and manioc cultivation. As yet, there is nothing suggesting that the isthmus ever developed the kind of vast city-states that appeared in the Mayan heartland further north. However, there is ample evidence of complex, varied, urban societies. The **Gran Coclé** culture, which lasted from 1200 BC until the 16th century, was a powerful chiefdom boasting grand ceremonial centres, stone houses, an elite caste of priests and nobles, and a wealthy merchant class that exploited extensive north-south trade routes. The economy was driven by hunting and gathering, as well as the cultivation of corn, cacao and root vegetables, and the production of ceramic vessels, tools, weapons and dazzling gold jewellery. The Gran Coclé belonged to a network of **Chibchán** cultures, which extended between Honduras and Colombia with dozens of distinct but related languages, still spoken by the present-day Ngäbe, Buglé, Guna and Naso. The **Chocoan** cultures – which include the ancestors of the Emberá and Wounaan – were another significant force on the isthmus with at least 10 different languages between them. Sadly, the arrival of the Spaniards signalled an extinction event and most of the Isthmian cultures were wiped out within a century of first contact.

Exploration, conquest and colonization

The age of exploration was already gathering pace when **Cristóbal Colón** (Christopher Columbus) set sail in 1492. He failed to discover a passage to Asia, but he did succeed in locating the islands of Cuba, Hispaniola and the West Indies. The 'discovery' of the so-called New World only intensified the European drive to explore uncharted territories. By royal decree, a cavalcade of Spanish and Portugese pioneers set forth in search of gold and glory, including a wealthy notary from Seville called **Rodrigo de Bastidas**, who sailed from Cádiz in 1500. Arriving off the coast of what is today Venezuela, he explored the shores of Colombia and became the first European to set eyes on the isthmus in 1501. He charted the gulfs and inlets of the Darién before sailing west, possibly as far as Portobelo, when his ships started leaking and he was forced to return to Hispaniola (present-day Dominican Republic and Haiti).

The fourth and final voyage of Cristóbal Colón

Since the conclusion of his third exploratory voyage, Cristóbal Colón had fallen on hard times. His governorship of Hispaniola had ended in scandal, he suffered agonizing arthritis and was otherwise widely regarded with contempt. Nonetheless, Queen Isabel of Spain remained his loyal admirer and granted him licence for one last voyage. He left Cádiz on 11 May 1502, sailed to the Caribbean and, seeing signs of an imminent hurricane, steered towards Hispaniola. He was not permitted to land, however, and, when his warnings about the incoming storm were ignored, the colony lost 28 of its treasure ships and 500 of its men. Colón himself weathered the hurricane in the sheltered mouth of the Río Jaina. He set sail for Central America soon after, exploring the coast from Honduras to Panama, naming and claiming new sites for the Spanish Crown. On 5 October, he arrived in **Almirante Bay** in Bocas del Toro and spent 10 days exploring the islands and shores. On 17 October, he encountered the land of Veragua, which, to his delight, was rich in gold. On 31 October, he located the **Río Chagres**, which he named Río de los Lagartos (Crocodile river). On 2 November he took refuge from a storm in **Puerto Bello**, and on 10 November, arrived in **Nombre de Dios**. He subsequently scoured the **Bay of Limón** for solid ground to build a settlement, found none and instead forged a garrison at **Santa María de Belén** in Veragua. On 16 April 1503, he was driven away by hostile natives and returned to Spain sick and empty-handed, becoming famously stranded for a year on Jamaica on the way. He died of heart failure in 1506.

First settlements, first disasters

By 1508, the newly discovered lands of **Tierra Firme** included a swathe of territories from Cabo de la Vela in eastern Colombia as far as **Cabo Gracias de Díos** on the Nicaragua-Honduras border. Two noblemen vied to colonize the region and the king decided to divide it between them. **Alonso de Ojeda** was granted governorship of **Nueva Andalucía**, which included all the lands east of the Río Atrato in the Darién. **Diego de Nicuesa** was granted **Veragua**, which included everything west of the same river. Having previously travelled with Cristóbal Colón, Ojeda had experience on his side, but he was not a wealthy man and was forced to seek outside financial backing. By contrast, Nicuesa was a man of great means, but he was also arrogant, foolish and ill-prepared for the rigours of tropical exploration. Both expeditions were destined to end ingloriously.

In Nueva Andalucía, Ojeda founded the colony of **San Sebastián** in 1510. It struggled under constant and debilitating attacks from local tribes and was finally abandoned when Ojeda departed for Hispaniola and promptly disappeared. He was actually marooned on Cuba, but his colony had been ordered to disband failing his return. In Veragua, Nicuesa established the miserable colony of **Nombre de Dios** only after great privation and the loss of most of his men. It was already dwindling when one of Ojeda's financial backers, a lawyer called **Martín Fernández de Enciso** (who had also been appointed Alcalde of Nueva Andalucía), arrived to establish the colony of **Santa María de Antigua**. Unfortunately, the new settlement fell under Nicuesa's jurisdiction and when he heard about it he threatened to punish the colonists and claim the site. But they were forewarned of his arrival, he was taken prisoner and exiled on a leaky ship, never to be seen again.

Vasco Núñez de Balboa

Among the founders of Santa María was Vasco Núñez de Balboa, a conquistador who had served in the original crew of Rodrigo de Bastidas. Balboa had spent nearly a decade in obscurity on Hispaniola, trying and failing to establish himself as a farmer. Heavily in debt and pursued by creditors, he stowed away on Enciso's ship. When he was discovered hiding inside a barrel, he was initially arrested, but Enciso later released him. After landing in the Darién, Balboa, who had already won the respect of the crew, expertly suggested the site of the new colony. A power struggle ensued. When Balboa emerged as governor he expelled Enciso and set about subjugating the region through brute force and a carefully garnered network of indigenous allegiances. In 1513, he became the first European to cross the isthmus and set eyes on the Pacific coast. A year later, Santa María was elevated to city status and granted its own cathedral.

Pedrarias the Cruel

Following the expulsion of both Nicuesa and Enciso, the king was compelled to replace Balboa as governor. On 30 June 1514, an unprecedented convoy of 18 galleons arrived in the New World carrying some 1500 men. Among them was **Pedro Arias de Avila**, Balboa's replacement and the officially appointed governor of the newly formed province of **Castilla de Oro**, which included sections of Veragua and Nueva Andalucía, along with the city of Santa María. Dubbed Pedrarias the Cruel, he was a ruthless and unscrupulous old man given to bloodthirsty bouts of violence. His first year was disastrous and saw over 500 men die from starvation and disease. The following year, he settled into the serious business of exploring the isthmus, raining terror on indigenous villages and plundering whatever gold he could. For his part, Balboa continued to command great respect and loyalty in Santa María and posed an uncomfortable threat to Pedrarias. In a deft political move, Pedrarias offered Balboa his own daughter in marriage. Relations between the two conquistadors seemed relaxed until 1516, when Balboa requested a licence to explore the South Sea (the Pacific Ocean). Pedrarias consented and Balboa relocated to the port of **Acla** where he had four ships built. After exploring the Pearl Islands and Pacific coast, he was arrested on the mainland on trumped-up charges of treason. On 17 January 1517, he was beheaded in Acla. Pedrarias went on to rule the province until 1527 and he lived out his final years terrorizing the population of León Viejo, Nicaragua, where he was sadly appointed governor.

Days of empire

Pedrarias's most important acts as governor were the founding of Panama City and the paving of the **Camino Real**, the first of several transisthmian trade routes that consolidated Tierra Firme's role as a commercial hub. Control of the isthmus and both its coastlines also gave the Spaniards a massive military advantage. In 1531, **Francisco Pizarro** and **Diego de Almagro** set out from Panama City to conduct their third and most deadly exploration of Perú, capturing and killing the Inca ruler, **Atahualpa**. Gold and other plundered riches began arriving in quantity and Spain rapidly expanded its colonial reach. On 26 February 1538, the business of civil administration was deferred to a new **Audiencia Real** in Panama City, which governed the region until it was finally abolished in 1739.

But as Spain managed its presence in the New World, a succession of threats arose. In 1544, **Vasco Núñez de Vela** arrived in Nombre de Dios to enact new laws forbidding slave labour. After confiscating a shipment of gold from Perú, **Gonzalo Pizarro**, a rebellious half-brother of Francisco Pizarro, seized control of Panama City, executed Núñez de Vela and roused a considerable rebel force. On 8 April 1548 he was finally captured and beheaded by **Pedro de Gasca**. But as European interests converged on the Caribbean, new threats came from pirates and privateers, starting in the 16th century with **Sir Francis Drake**, who looted the Spanish royal convoys and destroyed Nombre de Dios. In 1671, Panama City was completely obliterated during an attack by **Henry Morgan**, and in 1739, **Admiral Vernon** levelled the fortresses of Portobelo. Thereafter, as trade ships began rounding Cape Horn, the isthmus fell into decline.

The birth of a nation

The New World political landscape was undergoing radical transformations by the start of the 19th century. The United States had seceded from Britain in 1783 and Independence movements were gaining momentum across Latin America. In the Viceroyalty of New Granada – an administrative area broadly corresponding to present-day Colombia, Ecuador, Panama and Venezuela – **Simón Bolívar** led the struggle, winning de facto Independence from Spain in 1819. In 1820, the printing press arrived in Panama and began stirring separatist fervour with its first newspaper, *La Miscelánea*. On 10 November 1821, the famous *Grito* (cry) for Independence sounded from the town of Villa de los Santos, a historic hotbed of anti-royalist sentiment. On 28 November, one of Panama's most powerful military leaders, Colonel Fábrega, rallied the rebels in Panama City to express solidarity with Bolívar. Panama was free.

A new order

In 1822, Panama joined Bolívar's newly forged **United Provinces of New Granada**, a federal union geographically analogous to the old Viceroyalty. The isthmus was divided into two provinces, **Panamá** and **Veraguas**. In 1829, Venezuela seceded from the union, followed by Ecuador in 1830. In 1831, the Republic of New Granada was formed, consisting of just Colombia and Panama. In the same year, **Colonel Alzuru** led an uprising against the new order but was crushed by **Tomás de Herrera**. In 1832, another rebellion flared, but it too was put down. In 1840, Herrera changed sides and led a separatist movement culminating in the creation of the **Estado Libre del Ismo de Panamá** (Free State of the Isthmus of Panama). In December 1841, under vociferous threats from Bogotá, the isthmus was re-incorporated into New Granada. By the mid-19th century, thanks to advances in engineering, the international community began speculating on the possibility of a transisthmian canal or railway. On 12 December 1846, the signing of the **Bidlack-Mallarino Treaty** granted the US privileged transit rights on Panamanian soil, along with the right to intervene in any rebellion against Colombia. The US would exercise both rights over the coming years, breeding much local resentment. In 1848, the California gold rush sparked a massive migratory wave across Panama. The US responded by constructing the **Panama Railway** and several new townships, including the port of Colón. In 1878, **Lieutenant Lucien Napoleon Bonaparte Wyse** acquired the concession to build a transisthmian canal. The French effort was doomed to fail, but it opened the way for an American attempt (for a more detailed history of the canal construction, see page 86).

The War of a Thousand Days

By 1899, Colombia's political class was bitterly divided and irreconcilable. The Conservatives favoured a centralized system of government, selective suffrage and strong links between church and state. The Liberals campaigned for the polar opposite. When the Conservative Party took office amid accusations of electoral fraud, the Liberal Party saw their chance to foment a rebellion. Between them, the ensuing civil war lasted three years and claimed around 100,000 lives. Some of the bloodiest battles were fought in Panama, where the Liberals might have seized control had it not been for the United States exercising its famous rights of intervention. By November 1902, the US had resolved to purchase the failed French canal company and build its own transoceanic channel through the isthmus. It sent a warship, *USS Wisconsin*, to quell rebel activity and encourage both sides to sign a peace treaty.

Separation and sovereignty

Just one year later, the US withdrew its support for the Colombian government when Conservatives blocked their canal plan. Washington responded by opening secret negotiations with a Panamanian separatist group headed by Dr Manuel Amador Guerrero, General Obarrio, Ricardo Arias, Federico Boyd and others. Thanks to the backroom negotiations of Frenchman **Philippe Banau-Varilla**, a major stakeholder in the failed French Canal company, the US was able to secure favourable construction rights in exchange for supporting the rebels. On 3 November 1903, the *USS Nashville* arrived offshore and Panama declared itself Independent. On 13 November, the US formally recognized the new republic and, five days later, **John Hay**, on behalf of the US, and Banau-Varilla, on behalf of Panama, signed a treaty formalizing relations between the two nations. It included the controversial stipulation that the US should own and maintain a sovereign Canal Zone in perpetuity. The treaty was ratified by both parties and Panama's first constitutional president, **Manuel Amador Guerrero**, was elected in February 1904.

Militarism and dictatorship

In 1904, an attempted coup by **General Huertas** caused the United States to intervene in the interests of 'stability'. The coup was crushed and the Panamanian armed forces disbanded thereafter. As a result, a culture of militarism did not immediately take root in Panama, unlike some neighbouring countries, where decades of harsh social inequality were fomenting discontent. In the longer term, US foreign policy would prove highly detrimental to the region. As societies began breaking down, the old system of client states – and all the transnational businesses that relied upon it – threatened collapse. Propping up the oligarchies was no longer tenable so instead the US began forging allegiances with the emerging military classes. A firm hand, it was believed, would keep the 'red menace' at bay and ensure US economic dominance over the region. Eventually, this same strategy would be applied to Panama.

Enter Arnulfo Arias

In 1925, a middle-class doctor called **Arnulfo Arias** became leader of the **Patriotic Communal Action Association**, a group of grassroots xenophobes who rallied widespread anger against the United States. The group evolved into the staunchly nationalistic **Panamañista Party**, which led a successful coup to depose President Arosemena in 1931. **Harmodio Arias**, Arnulfo's brother, was installed as president with Arnulfo dispatched to Europe to fulfil a variety of diplomatic functions. Seemingly impressed by the rise of fascism, Arnulfo incorporated some of its more detestable tenets into his own political philosophy. In 1940 he was elected president – or *El Caudillo* (The Leader), as he liked to be known – and began making sweeping reforms. In some respects, he was surprisingly progressive, instituting a new system of social security and a new constitution that extended suffrage to women. But he was also harmful and regressive, waging a hate campaign against

Panama's ethnic minorities and openly expressing sympathy with the Axis forces in Europe. A year later, he was ousted in a US-backed coup. In 1948, he ran again for president as head of a coalition between his new **National Revolutionary Party** and the **Authentic Revolutionary Party**. He initially lost, but was installed a year later following a recount. He was soon up to his old tricks, setting up a secret police force, suspending the Supreme Court and dissolving the National Assembly. He was impeached in 1951 and stripped of his rights to hold office. Disgraced, he disappeared into obscurity, but not for long.

The rise of the Guardia

A former police commander and long-time enemy of Arias, **José Antonio Remón Cantera**, was elected president in 1952. He promptly renamed Panama's police force the **Guardia Nacional** and began reforming its structure along militaristic lines. Meanwhile, the United States had formalized its cold war strategy in the **US Mutual Security Act of 1951**, which provided 'aid' and technical assistance to its allies in order to build their defence forces. Panama signed up as a recipient and began channelling generous funds into the Guardia's expansion. Soon Panama was receiving US$3 million annually and had built up a military force of 5000 men. In a curious twist of fate, Arnulfo Arias was politically rehabilitated by Panama's upper classes and elected to office on 1 October 1968. He immediately stamped his authority on the Guardia, restructuring its ranks and casting several powerful figures into effective exile. He was president for just 11 days before **General Boris Martínez** staged a coup. Following a dramatic high-speed chase through the streets of Panama City, Arias took refuge in the US-governed Canal Zone. He was exiled to Miami soon afterwards and the Guardia retained control over the country.

Maximum Leader Omar Torrijos

When Martínez signalled his ambitions for tackling corruption in public life, he was rapidly ousted and replaced by **Colonel Omar Torrijos**, who served as de facto ruler from 1969 to 1981. Torrijos immediately promoted himself to Brigadier General, but came to prefer the grandiose title of 'Maximum Leader of the Revolution'. He spent a lot of time and energy trying to garner popular support, visiting numerous impoverished communities where he would make rousing speeches and hand out gifts. His performances were bolstered by a raft of leftist policies, including redistributing land to the rural poor and backing the Sandinista rebels in Nicaragua. It was enough to convince **Fidel Castro** of his Marxist credentials, along with left-leaning intellectuals such as **Graham Greene**, who were quite taken with the 'benevolent dictator'. But Torrijos was neither a revolutionary nor, as many like to think, a populist. If anything, he was a skilled manipulator.

Behind the scenes, he was heavily into drugs, arms and people trafficking. He was also a US stooge and otherwise highly intolerant, stamping out free speech, imprisoning his critics and ordering assassinations of his enemies. He and his colleagues notably extorted vast sums from the state's social security department and racked up a hefty national debt too. However, many continue to remember Torrijos warmly as the man who negotiated the handover of the Panama Canal. The historic 1977 **Torrijos-Carter Treaty** set forth a schedule for US military withdrawal along with the complete dissolution of the Canal Zone. It was essentially the same treaty that had been forged with Lyndon Johnson a decade earlier, but that did not stop Torrijos from using it to make political capital. Unfortunately for him, the treaty came at a significant price, with the US insisting on the restoration of civil liberties, including free elections. In 1978, Torrijos stepped down as head of government but retained his position as de facto ruler. The political wing of the

The return of Manuel Noriega

Manuel Noriega is no prodigal son and his return to Panama after 21 years in foreign captivity was met with a frenzy of concern and indignation – most of it from corporate media in the US and Europe, who were quite unused to analysing Panama's domestic affairs. In reality, most Panamanians responded to Noriega's return with a disinterested shrug. His arrival on 11 December 2011 was almost entirely eclipsed by the annual Christmas parade in Panama City, and although his on-going presence has political relevance – mainly as a distraction from presidential bungling and as a living public relations disaster for the Democratic Revolutionary Party (PRD) – the man himself has become something of an irrelevancy. On 16 September 1992, he was sentenced to 40 years in prison for his role in drug trafficking, racketeering and money laundering. He was released after just 17 years, but held in US custody while France arranged his extradition on charges of money laundering. On 7 July 2010, Noriega was convicted for a further seven years and dispatched to La Santé jail in Paris. Behind the scenes, Panama began petitioning for his extradition so he could face trial for murder and human rights abuses. A year later, following his return to Panama and incarceration in El Renacer prison, the first blurry images of the fallen dictator emerged. They revealed a withered old man in a wheelchair, who, having suffered a stroke in the US, was unable to walk properly or go to the bathroom unassisted. Since then, Noriega's health has declined even further and his lawyers now claim he is suffering from a brain tumour. Increasingly, it seems likely that Noriega will manage to live out his remaining years under house arrest – and without ever having stood trial for his crimes in Panama.

Guardia was formed soon after – the Democratic Revolutionary Party (PRD) – but on 31 July 1981, Panama was plunged into turmoil when Torrijos's private plane crashed into the mountains of the Cordillera Central, killing the Maximum Leader.

General Manuel Noriega

Manuel Noriega was born into poverty in Panama City in 1934. Despite modest beginnings, he was destined to become one of Latin America's most infamous dictators. After training at Chorrillos Military School in Lima, he returned home to climb the ranks of the Guardia, receiving intelligence training at Fort Gulick – also known as the **School of the Americas** – in 1967. He was placed on the CIA payroll thereafter and dispatched to **Fort Bragg**, North Carolina, for instruction in 'psychological operations'. In 1969, Noriega put down a coup attempt against Torrijos and was promoted to chief of military intelligence as a reward. He spent many years stationed in Chiriquí province, stamping out campesino insurrections with measured cruelty. He was also summoned to perform violent and unpleasant tasks on behalf of the Maximum Leader, who liked to refer to Noriega as 'mi gangster'. At the same time, he was increasingly regarded with some affection by his CIA paymasters. By 1983, less than two years after Torrijos's death, Noriega had manoeuvred into position as head of the Guardia and de facto ruler of Panama. He consolidated the various arms of the military into the Panamanian Defence Forces and promoted himself to the rank of General.

One of his first actions as commander-in-chief was to assist the CIA in their counter-revolutionary efforts in Nicaragua. The Pana-jungla military camp in Bocas del Toro

The Art of War: Operation 'Just Cause'

On 20 December 1989, the United States launched Operation Just Cause and levelled one of Panama City's oldest and poorest neighbourhoods: El Chorrillo. In an immense aerial bombardment involving hundreds of fighter jets, nearly all of the district's buildings were obliterated, including the homes of approximately 2700 working-class families. The historic and long-neglected barrio had been home to the headquarters of the Panamanian Defence Forces – *La Comandancia* – as well as the barbaric penal complex of El Modelo, well known for its torture and severity. The precise civilian death toll exacted by the US attack is unknown. The CIA puts the official number of deaths at 516, but the UN and several human rights organizations suggest a figure of 2000 to 4000. The confusion over death tolls is consistent with the government's propaganda strategy at the time, which tended to stress minimal 'collateral damage'. Throughout the siege, rolling news broadcasts emphasized the clean and surgical precision of the operation, as if the removal of Manuel Noriega were tantamount to lancing an unpleasant boil. Even its code name was a work of propaganda, as General Colin Powell once announced, "Even our severest critics would have to utter 'Just Cause' while denouncing us."

When the US struck, the press were strictly prohibited from accessing El Chorrillo or other affected sites. Almost no film footage survived the invasion, but eye-witnesses reported horrifying experiences in the flames and gun-fire. In the aftermath, there were grim discoveries of mass graves, including the bodies of hundreds of civilian men, women and children. CNN maintained its vigorous flag-waving, but the Spanish-language press was less squeamish about using words like 'massacre'. Survivors of the bombardment included 20,000 refugees and many of them wondered if a rich white neighbourhood would have been subjected to the same mistreatment. Today, apartment blocks and concrete tenements have risen from the rubble of US intervention, but most of them are in shameful states of dilapidation. In a final act of treachery, President Martinelli is seeking to 'regenerate' the neighbourhood with the usual slew of showy executive towers. If he get his way, the final destruction of El Chorrillo is grimly assured.

was relinquished for the training of Contra guerrillas, while Panamanian airstrips were provided to fly out Israeli weapons to Honduras and Costa Rica. At the same time, Noriega loaded the planes with consignments of cocaine and assisted the US in laundering its war funds through banks and shell corporations in Panama City. In 1984, Noriega foolishly held an open election and was forced to intervene when it seemed Arnulfo Arias was once again on his way to victory. Instead, he installed **Nicolás Barletta**, a US puppet handpicked by Secretary of State, **Charles Shultz**. In 1985, **Hugo Spadafora**, a Panamanian national, hero of the Sandinista revolution and outspoken critic of Noriega, was accosted in Chiriquí province, tortured and beheaded. Barletta publicly declared there would be a full investigation, causing Noriega to usurp him. A year later, the **Iran-Contra** scandal broke and Noriega's involvement in drug and arms trafficking became public record. In 1988, Panamanian **President Eric del Valle** attempted to dismiss Noriega, but failed. Amid deteriorating diplomatic relations, the US imposed economic sanctions on Panama.

The invasion of Panama

Behind the scenes, a broad-based anti-Noriega movement – **La Cruzada Civilista** (Civil Crusade) – had been gathering pace. Their May 1989 electoral candidate, **Guillermo Endara**, was poised to win in a landslide victory when Noriega disrupted the proceedings and declared the election void. The next day, Endara and his colleagues staged a victory cavalcade in Calidonia, Panama City, where they were violently attacked by a Dignity Batallion (Noriega's thuggish street militia). The episode was captured on film and the public clamour for Noriega's removal grew unbearable. Around six months later, on 15 December 1989, Noriega was declared Chief Executive Officer of the government and immediately began ranting about war with the United States. Meanwhile, **President George Bush** – former chief of the CIA – was under criticism for having failed to subdue the unruly dictator. Increasingly goaded as a 'wimp', he drew up plans for the invasion of Panama.

On 16 December 1989, four US military personnel were stopped by PDF guards at a roadblock near El Chorrillo. The confrontation led to the death of Second Lieutenant **Robert Paz** and gave the US moral justification for an attack. On 20 December, they initiated **Operation Just Cause**, levelling parts of the capital. The exact number of casualties is unknown, but estimates range from 220 to 4000, with an additional 20,000-30,000 civilians made homeless. On 29 December, the UN General Assembly voted overwhelmingly to condemn the invasion. Meanwhile, Noriega had fled the scene to take refuge in the Vatican Embassy. In a bid to dislodge him, the US launched **Operation Nifty Package**, which reportedly included bombarding the embassy with 24-hour high-volume heavy metal music. On 3 January 1990, Noriega surrendered. In April 1992, he was tried and convicted in the US on eight counts of drug trafficking, racketeering and money laundering. The court refused to let him admit evidence relating to his work for the CIA, saying it would "confuse the jury".

A new democracy

Following Noriega's capture and incarceration, Guillermo Endara was rightfully installed as president. He went far to rehabilitate the country's broken image, disbanding the military, imprisoning known offenders and replacing them with a civil police force. He was placed under considerable pressure by the US to sign a **Treaty of Mutual Legal Assistance**, designed to limit banking secrecy and enable investigations into drug traffickers. Investment improved thereafter with a one billion dollar US aid package and a further US$540 million in international aid. The economy grew at a brisk pace of 8% and unemployment fell. Nonetheless, Endara faced criticism as a US puppet and his tenure was marred by pro-military coup attempts, riots, rising crime and isolated bombings. His term ended in staunch disapproval, but history may yet remember him more warmly as the man who ushered in a new era of democracy.

Return of the old guard

In 1994, **Ernesto Pérez Balladares** – a founding member of the Democratic Revolutionary Party (PRD) – successfully revived his party's fortunes and swept to power in closely observed elections. By emphasizing his historic ties with the Maximum Leader (and distancing himself from Noriega) he was able to win widespread popular support. His term was characterized by infrastructure improvements and aggressive free market policies, including the privatization of telephone and electric companies, and the admission of Panama to the World Trade Organization. When he tried to amend the constitution to allow presidents to serve two successive terms, he was roundly defeated and forced to leave office in 1999. Since January 2010, he has been under house arrest for alleged money laundering during his tenure.

Into the new millennium

In 1999, **Mireya Moscoso**, the widow of former President Arnulfo Arias, was elected to power. She was the country's first female president and had the unique honour of overseeing the canal handover on 31 December 1999. To her credit, the canal has functioned without a hitch ever since. Nonetheless, her term was sullied by allegations of corruption, nepotism and bribery, starting with 'Christmas gifts' of Cartier watches distributed to all 72 members of the Legislative Assembly. In 2002, a scandal erupted involving the alleged vote-buying of Supreme Court justices, but all of them were immune from investigation under Panamanian law. To make matters worse, in 2003, Moscoso mysteriously vetoed legislation that would have toughened penalties for embezzlement, fraud and other white-collar crimes. Her unpopularity was only compounded by rising unemployment and a slowing economy. She ended office with one of the lowest approval ratings of any Panamanian president.

In 2004, **Martín Torrijos**, a son of Omar Torrijos, ran against Endara and his new breakaway **Solidarity Party**, easily beating him with 47% of the vote. Heading a coalition known as the **Patria Nueva** – which consisted of the PRD and the People's Party – Torrijos began by implementing hugely unpopular fiscal and social security reforms, including increasing the age of retirement. As protests paralysed life in the capital, his approval ratings plummeted and he was forced to rework his initiatives. Worse was to come when protests over a development project ended in the death of a labour activist. As ever, the spectre of corruption stalked the political scene with several justices of the Supreme Court accused of receiving kick-backs from drug traffickers. Towards the end of his term, Torrijos issued a number of controversial decrees aimed at reforming the security apparatus, which critics said would effectively re-militarize the police. Above, all Torrijos will be remembered as the president who initiated the expansion of the Panama Canal.

A vote for change?

The main contenders in the 2009 elections were **Balbina Herrera** of the PRD, and a wealthy businessman, **Ricardo Martinelli**, who fronted the **Democratic Change Party** as part of a broad right-wing coalition. It was a dirty fight with little substance. Herrera was accused of radicalism and of having links to Hugo Chávez. Martinelli was accused of having bipolar disorder. Ultimately, the people voted for change. Having positioned himself as the first and only presidential candidate without ties to the old political order, Martinelli won a landslide victory with 60% of the popular vote. The honeymoon did not last long, however, and commentators were soon beginning to question his autocratic style. Martinelli, who famously owns Panama's 'Super 99' supermarket chain, quickly earned a reputation for boardroom bullying, ordering the suspension and arrest of Attorney General Ana Matilde Gómez on trumped-up charges. Accusation of nepotism have also been roundly levelled at the president with appointments of his close friends and allies to the Supreme Court.

Meanwhile, the president has overseen an uncontrolled sell-off of Panama's natural resources, handing out new construction, hydroelectric and mining concessions with little regard for environmental protection. Conflicts between trade unions, indigenous protestors and the police – who critics say now resemble a military force in all but name –

have been periodic and violent. Add public relations bungling via the president's Twitter account, soaring public debt and inflation, and Martinelli's political reign is starting to seem as contemptuous as those that came before it. Worryingly, there are now disturbing rumours about an impending coup d'état.

Panama culture and customs

People

Panama's vibrant cultural diversity often gives it the feel of a Caribbean island. Some 75% of its 3.5 million inhabitants live in densely populated urban areas, including Panama City, the most cosmopolitan place in Central America, where you're likely to encounter an array of far-flung ancestries including Hispanic, European, Afro-descendent, Chinese, Amerindian and many others. Beyond the big cities, ethnic groups tend to be geographically concentrated, lending each region of the country its own unique cultural flavour. For more detailed information on culture and community, please see individual chapters.

European descendants
Panama is a very unequal society, with a class structure that broadly echoes the old colonial caste system. At the top are a handful of very old, racially pure European families descended from powerful landholders who bought their political influence during the colonial era. Known somewhat disparagingly as *rabiblancos* ('white-tails', a derogatory reference to their pale skin and a type of ruffled songbird), they continue to control most commerce and industry in the country. Two decades of Guardia dictatorship effectively interrupted their social standing, but they have since resumed their role as Panama's tightly cloistered oligarchy. Intermarriage below their ranks is uncommon, but several foreign families – including Greek, Jewish, Chinese and Arabic – have recently infiltrated their set.

Mestizos
The word *mestizo*, once derogatory but now acceptable usage, originated in the colonial era to describe those people of mixed European and indigenous heritage. Today, they form the overwhelming majority of Latin America's population, including more than 70% of Panamanian nationals. Mestizo culture is stereotypically Catholic, Spanish-speaking, hot-blooded, quick-tempered, sensual, stylish and grounded in the ancient institution of machismo, which can be chivalrous or chauvinistic by turns. Mestizos maintain hegemony over the nation, particularly in the central provinces, which are often inaccurately regarded as Panama's 'cultural heartland'. Degrees of genetic mix vary greatly within the mestizo community with virtually pure Spanish bloodlines hailing from the Azuero Peninsula.

African descendants
Beyond the capital, Panama's African-descendant communities tend to be concentrated on the Caribbean coast of Colón, the islands of Bocas del Toro and in the rainforests of the Darién. They are divided into two broad groups. The so-called Afro-colonials were first brought to the isthmus as slaves in the 16th century, where they served as porters, miners and plantation workers. Many of them escaped custody to form their own communities and intermarry with indigenous groups. Today, their Spanish-speaking descendants continue

Indigenous prospects

The struggle to conserve Panama's environmental resources is echoed by an equally critical struggle to safeguard its indigenous cultures. Panama's eight indigenous groups face a life-and-death struggle if they are to retain their traditional customs and languages in the long term. While the Ngäbe, Buglé, Emberá, Wounaan and Guna have won some measure of autonomy through the self-governing structures of their *comarcas* (reservations), they are still bound by edicts from central government and excluded from wider decision-making processes. The Naso, Bri-Bri and Bokota have yet to be awarded their own *comarca* and are among the most marginalized peoples in the country. Daily life for most of Panama's indigenous people is marred by extreme poverty, high infant mortality and a lack of access to public services, including schools and healthcare. Predictably, migration to urban spaces, including the capitals of Panama and Costa Rica, is on the rise, especially among the Guna. Urbanization may or may not solve the immediate problem of poverty and access, but it almost certainly disrupts links to traditional culture and language. Territorial violations are also becoming increasingly common, with on-going invasions from colonists and corporate-sponsored mega-projects. International trade agreements such as the Mesoamerican Integration and Development Project (formerly the Plan Puebla Panama) are only accelerating indigenous dispossession in what is surely a venal last grab for the earth's resources. Worst of all, Panama's indigenous people are contending with persistent racism on the part of Panama's political classes. President Martinelli has maintained the course of his predecessors with several legislative assaults on indigenous rights, including Law 30 and Law 415, which sparked protests all over the country. The police, who are well accustomed to serving as private bodyguards to Panama's extractive and hydroelectric industries, were dispatched to the scene with tragic and bloody consequences. Rather than act with the dignity befitting a world leader, the president has tended to opt for tawdry psychological tactics, using threats, false allegations, harassment and other 'divide and rule' strategies to discredit indigenous activists who are less than sympathetic to his development plans. Shamefully, Panama is one of the last Latin American countries not to have ratified the International Labour Organization (ILO) Convention 169, one of the key legal tools for protecting indigenous rights. On a more positive note, Law 88 was passed in Panama in 2010, allowing for the teaching of traditional indigenous languages in schools. This signifies a milestone victory for Panama's long-suffering indigenous communities, and it is hoped, the first of many to come.

to boast a vibrant cultural life replete with raucous festivals and Congo dances. The second group of Afro-descendants are the Afro-Antilleans, who arrived from the Caribbean in the 19th and 20th centuries to work as railway, canal and plantation labourers. They brought Protestant values of hard work, family, marriage and church service, and some of them, seeing their presence as transitory, maintained allegiance to the British crown. Today, most Afro-Antilleans continue to speak Creole English – or in Bocas del Toro, the dialect of Guari-Guari – along with a tiny group of Creole French speakers originally from the island of St Lucia. Since the dissolution of the Canal Zone, many younger Afro-Antilleans have been choosing to fully assimilate into Spanish-speaking culture. For many years, their communities suffered racism from both Hispanics and North Americans and, during the 1940s, crypto-fascist President Arias attempted to deprive them of their citizenship.

The Ngäbe
Distributed mainly across western Panama, the Ngäbe (pronounced 'NO-bay') are Panama's largest and fastest-growing indigenous group, numbering more than 260,000 according to the 2010 census. They and their closely related contemporaries, the Buglé, were once lumped together as the *guaymí*, but this term of Spanish origin is considered impolite and has fallen into disuse. Although some Ngäbe subsist in fishing communities in lowland Bocas del Toro, the majority are tough but friendly mountain-dwellers who maintain their own self-governing structures in the form of a semi-autonomous Comarca. They are among the poorest and most isolated people on the isthmus, with subsistence farming and plantation labour their main economies. They face on-going challenges from soil exhaustion, deforestation, malnutrition and a lack of modern infrastructure, as well as the direct threat of displacement from hydroelectric and mining exploitation. Once dubbed 'Panama's forgotten people', they have lately begun to assert themselves in interesting and lively ways, grappling with new media technologies to publicize their on-going resource conflicts. Due to foreign missionary work, the Ngäbe are today predominantly Catholic, but they maintain a spiritual reverence for nature consistent with their ancient roots. There is a broad division in Ngäbe society between traditionalists who want to limit contact with the outside world and progressives who seek to embrace it.

The Guna
Highly determined, fiercely independent and politically organized, the Guna (also known as Kuna) are the second largest indigenous group in Panama. Most of their 80,000-strong population live on the scattered Caribbean islands of their self-governing Comarca in eastern Panama. On the mainland, there are less concentrated communities on the coast, in the Darién and in Panama City. In some respects, the Guna have become the poster children for Panama's first-nation peoples, thanks in part to their striking photogenic appearance. Many Guna women still wear the traditional attire of brightly coloured *molas*, colourful skirts, gold jewellery and red headscarves. The Guna were the first of Panama's indigenous people to earn their own Comarca, but only after considerable bloodshed. Fishing and coconut cultivation remain the traditional staples of the Guna economy, now supplemented by lucrative and tightly managed eco-tourism. Despite the widespread influence of Christian missions, the Guna retain a rich ceremonial life. They have long been celebrated for their sea-faring skills and sense of commercial enterprise. They remain economically disadvantaged, however, and threatened in the long term by dwindling lobster stocks, rising sea levels and the intrusion of drug traffickers.

The Emberá
Emberá ancestral lands encompass the borderlands of Panama and Colombia but, due to the recent advance of the Interamericana highway, large-scale deforestation, new hydroelectric projects, as well as aggressive incursions from colonists, drug traffickers and armed paramilitaries, the Emberá are increasingly migrating to new communities in central Panama. They are the country's third most populous indigenous group and number 31,000. The Emberá are traditionally semi-nomadic hunter-gatherers and began settling

in permanent villages from the mid-20th century. They received a small Comarca in the 1980s which they share with the closely related Wounaan people. Despite extensive social restructuring, the Emberá maintain a rich body of traditional knowledge, including the use of rainforest plants for medicinal and construction purposes. Their communities are mostly situated on riverbanks, with local economies grounded in fishing and subsistence agriculture. Community tourism has become a vital staple for many Emberá living in national parks outside the capital, where hunting and agriculture are restricted by law.

The Buglé
The Buglé are often confused with the Ngäbe, or worse, erroneously compounded as a single group – the 'Ngäbe-Buglé' – a mistake that probably arises from the shared name of their Comarca. In fact, the 25,000-strong Buglé are a distinct group with their own language, most of them settled on the Caribbean shores of Veraguas. They are far less studied than the Ngäbe, but share many cultural similarities, including a reliance on subsistence farming, fishing and hunting. At the time of the Spanish conquest, the Buglé were one of largest and most powerful groups in central Panama, but their numbers were devastated during a protracted struggle against European domination. Thanks to Protestant missionary efforts, most Buglé now belong to Methodist, Evangelical or Seventh Day Adventist churches.

The Wounaan
The Wounaan are a small, colourful tribe with a population of nearly 7300, most living in the rainforests of the Darién. Although they are a linguistically distinct group, they share almost identical cultural forms with the Emberá tribe and, until 1969, anthropologists did not distinguish between the two. Thanks to the work of Robert Gunn and Ron Binder, the label Chocó – previously used to identify both Emberá and Wounaan – has been dropped, although it continues to refer to a family of related languages. Binder has suggested that the Wounaan are the originators of fine arts and philosophical ideas, while the Emberá are imitators. Whatever their historic relationship, the two continue to live in very close social and cultural proximity.

The Naso Tjerdi
The Naso Tjerdi, who live on the thickly forested banks of the Río Teribe in Bocas del Toro, are one of the last surviving monarchies in Latin America. Their traditional knowledge is sadly declining, but a few fierce proponents continue to champion it. The Naso language, which belongs to the Chibchan family, is also under threat of extinction, with only 500 native speakers out of a total population of 4000. In recent years, hydroelectric companies have aggressively divided Naso society and wrought massive changes to their local environment. Powerful cattle-barons and destructive loggers are also presenting sustained challenges to their ancestral lands. The Naso resisted inclusion in the Comarca Ngäbe-Buglé and continue to lobby for the creation of their own semi-autonomous province.

The Bokota
Populations of Bokota number less than 2000 and are gradually diminishing as they become assimilated into culturally related Ngäbe and Buglé groups. Their settlements are mainly concentrated on the banks of the Río Calvébora in eastern Bocas del Toro, but they are a poorly studied group with little exposure to the outside world. For many years, they went unrecognized and were confused with the Buglé, who speak a similar sounding but mutually unintelligible language.

The Bri-Bri

Also known as Talamanca, after the mountain range straddling western Panama, the Bri-Bri are Panama's least populous indigenous people. They number just 1068, all of them in Bocas del Toro, but many more live across the border in neighbouring Costa Rica. They are an intriguing people with vibrant spiritual philosophies, rich mythology, a long tradition of shamanism and many rituals that revolve around the preparation and ingestion of sacred cacao beans. They farm iguanas or otherwise work in the banana plantations of the lowlands.

Chinese peoples

Panama is home to the largest Chinese community in Central America. They began arriving on the isthmus with the construction of the Panama railway in the mid-19th century and they continue to arrive today. It is not known exactly how many Chinese are living in Panama, but some estimates put their population as high as 135,000. Nearly all of them speak Cantonese and originate from Guangdong province, but a few newer arrivals speak Hakka. Panama's Chinese people are known chiefly for their heavy involvement in the country's retail economy and they operate a vast network of convenience stores in all but the most remote places. Historically, they faced a series of political attacks throughout the first half of the 20th century, particularly under Arnulfo Arias, who sought to revoke their citizenship. Panama City's Chinatown peaked in the 1950s and 1960s, but has since declined. Today, the Republic of China and Taiwan compete for political influence over Panama's Chinese community, both making significant contributions to their communities.

North Americans

There has been a strong US presence in Panama since the Canal Zone days, and North Americans, affectionately known as gringos, form the bulk of Panama's expatriate community. Panama's long and sometimes tawdry affiliation with its much larger and richer cousin to the north is quite revealing. Today, Panama may be seriously jaded after more than a century of US interference, but it has also embraced American-style consumerism with abandon. Prolific shopping malls, high-rise towers, gas-guzzling vehicles and a love of baseball would all seem to hint at a private fixation on American culture. Even the tourism authority is keen to peddle Panama City as 'the new Miami'. Thus Panama's close relationship with the United States might best be described as love-hate. Since the 1990s, US citizens and investors have been arriving in Panama to retire or establish new businesses, most in hospitality. Today, there are an estimated 25,000 North Americans in Panama, most of them in Panama City, Boquete and Bocas Town.

Religion

Religion is an integral part of daily life in Panama and around 85% of the population is **Roman Catholic**. Mass conversions in the colonial era ensured a secure historical footing for the church, which has long influenced the nation's civil and political spheres, sometimes to their detriment. Its long-term support of the Guardia dictatorship, for example, was a particularly regressive decision. Nonetheless, Catholicism continues to be the spiritual life-blood of Panama, with religious feasts and festivals the mainstay of public celebrations. **Protestantism**, including Episcopal, Methodist and Baptist churches, is the second most popular religion in Panama, particularly among the Afro-Antillean population. **Jehovah's Witnesses** are becoming increasingly common, as are **Mormons**, who first arrived in Panama with US military personnel in the Canal Zone days.

Jewish influence dates from the colonial era and there remains a sizeable Jewish community in the capital, attending Orthodox synagogues. **Islam**, arriving with the first slaves brought from Africa, has grown in popularity since construction of the canal and continues to garner followers. Mosques are now appearing in most major cities. A large **Hindu** community in Panama City is served by a fantastic temple on Vía Ricardo Alfaro, one of the largest in Latin America. Meanwhile, the egg-shaped 'Mother Temple of Central America', about 10 km northeast of downtown Panama City on the Vía Transístmica, was built by the Bahá'í Church and serves as a major centre of worship. Traditional indigenous religions, including Ngäbe **Mama Tata** (see page 240) and Guna **Iberogun**, tend to incorporate animistic ideas about the spirit world, but these are declining due to the continued intrusion of missionaries. African-tinged **Santería** and **Voodoo** are popular in Panama, as is **New Ageism** and various forms of **Witchcraft**.

Music and dance

From the streets to the dance halls, music is everywhere in Panama. Thanks to the nation's long history of multiculturalism – and its unique position between the Americas and the Caribbean – it boasts some of the most diverse musical output in the world. Panama's dazzling creative portfolio spans a host of contemporary genres, including merengue, salsa, calypso, reggae, pop, dance, hip-hop, techno and many more. Without a doubt, music is the nation's chief cultural export and it is perhaps unsurprising that Panamanians are gifted dancers too. Whether stepping to the rustic melodies of *música típica* or letting loose to the raunchy rhythms of reggaeton, dance is a vital and expressive part of the nation's cultural life.

Traditional and folkloric

Combining African, Spanish and indigenous elements, folkloric performances are a central part of most fiestas and public gatherings, especially in the Central Provinces. A typical rendition will involve a host of unique musical instruments including a *mejorana* (a small guitar with five strings), a *socabón* (or *bocana* – a slightly smaller guitar with just four strings), a Creole violin, flutes, maracas and drums called *tambores*. Folkloric singers love to pepper their performances with a distinctive falsetto cry called a *saloma*. In Spanish, it sounds something like '*Ajuauuua*!' It is a common way for Panamanians to express approval, especially at sporting events. According to psychologists, the *saloma* has indigenous origins and may aid in the relief of heat exhaustion induced by hours of toiling in the fields. The accompanying folkloric dances are often performed by couples, or groups of couples, who will have been practising the steps since childhood. The women are invariably attired in elegant *polleras* (traditional dresses) and the handling of their voluminous skirts is an important element of most dances. For their part, the men make a great show of tipping their *sombreros pintados* (traditional Panama hats).

Panama's most famous folkloric dance is the *tamborito*, a regular feature of carnival festivities. It has a very African sound, despite its highly choreographed Spanish overtones. The performance is led by a female singer called a *cantalante* and accompanied by a trio of tall drums and backing singers who repeat a clapping chorus of four-line stanzas. Also popular, the *mejorana* is a male solo performance with lyrics in the form of *décimas*, a type of ancient Spanish poetic verse. Most *mejoranas* dwell on the themes of love, life and land, cheerfulness and celebration and, sometimes, the melancholy of heartbreak. The *cumbia*, not be missed, is a quintessential folklore dance closely related to the Colombian music genre. Performed by pairs of couples forming circles around the room, it is believed to be an old courtship rite. The *punto* is a slower, more stately, elegant and melodic variant performed by a single couple. If done well, they are traditionally rewarded with a shower of coins and applause. Several interesting folkloric dances originate with the Afro-colonial cultures. The *congo*, performed mainly on the Costa Arriba, is a feisty and theatrical dance that recalls the region's ancient slave trade. The related *bullerengue*, from the Darién, is usually dedicated to a huntsman as a sensual celebration of his athletic prowess.

Pindín

Pindín, also known as *típica*, is the contemporary successor to Panama's traditional school of folklore. Its origins can be traced to the late 19th and early 20th centuries, when the accordion first arrived on the isthmus and began replacing the Creole violin as a lead instrument. The genre's formative years saw several notable pioneers, including **Ricardo Fábrega**, who successfully fused Cuban *danzón* with *cumbia* and *tamborito* to form the sub-genre of *tamborera*. His most famous songs are 'Guararé' and 'Tambor de Alegría', both regarded with considerable affection. Today, *pindín* has evolved to incorporate several modern styles and instruments, such as electric guitar, keyboard and bass. Its most famous proponents include household names like **Victorio Vergara**, **Osvaldo Ayala** and **Ulpiano Vergara**. The highly celebrated brother and sister act, **Samy and Sandra Sandoval**, have lately produced some very fast-paced and pop-orientated numbers, but the old folkloric roots are still clearly discernible. Like its stylistic predecessor, *pindín* finds its heart and soul in the rustic villages of the Central Provinces.

Salsa

Blending Spanish and African influences, salsa was always going to be a good fit for Panama. Having first emerged from Cuba in the 1930s, Latino communities in New York did much to popularize the genre throughout the 1960s and 70s. Soon salsa's infectious rhythms and feisty melodies had spread throughout Latin America, where a new generation of musicians developed variations on the classic Cuban *son*. In Panama, **Rubén Blades** – widely regarded as the nation's most important and influential artist – pioneered new lyrical forms that addressed controversial themes like oppression and imperialism. Until then, salsa lyrics had mostly focused on the 'call to dance', or the oft-explored themes of machismo and virility. Blades worked extensively with salsa legend **Willie Colón** of New York and went on to pen the song 'Parita', regarded by many as Panama's second national anthem. In recent years, salsa has spawned several new subgenres, including soppy *romántica* and its more steamy cousin, *erótica*.

Jazz

During the 1940s, in what is now regarded as Panama's golden age of jazz, numerous fine musicians emerged from the country's Afro-Antillean community. Born on Careening Cay in Bocas del Toro, pianist and composer **Luis Russell** famously made his name playing in Chicago and New York alongside legends like Louis Armstrong. Meanwhile, the Caribbean coast city of Colón evolved into the epicentre of Panama's thriving jazz scene, home to names like **Víctor Vitín Paz**, **Clarence Martin**, and **Barbara Wilson**, who was once dubbed 'Panama's Billie Holiday'. Few were as formidable and greatly admired as pianist and composer **Víctor Boa**, known as 'Electric Man' and the 'High Priest of Jazz'. He successfully advanced his own style of **tambo jazz** and was once the subject of an intriguing documentary by Professor Gerardo Maloney. In recent years, Panama has sadly experienced the passing away of many of its jazz legends, but a prestigious new annual festival is helping to inspire new talent and drive an exciting renaissance of the genre (for more information see box, page 70).

Plena and reggaeton

After the lilting rhythms of reggae emerged from Jamaica in the 1960s, a closely related Spanish-language counterpart emerged in Panama. Essentially a Latinized form of reggae, it was known simply as *plena* or *reggae en español*, and it blended classic reggae, soca, calypso, Jamaican dancehall and other styles. Its founding father is generally credited as **El General**, but artists like **El Maleante**, **Renato** and **Nando Boom** were also highly formative and influential. *Plena* was subsequently picked up in Puerto Rico where it spawned its mean and hugely popular urban offspring, reggaeton. Drawing influence from US rap and hip-hop, its lyrics are recited rather than sung, and usually dwell on violent or explicit themes. Reggaeton's syncopated rhythm – or in Creole, 'riddim' – is better known as **Dem Bow**. It is characterized by aggressive growling bass and snare drums, often heard pumping out of Panama City buses at ridiculously high volumes. On the dance floor, reggaeton is accompanied by the *perrero*, a steamy dance involving lots of sexualized hip-grinding and booty shakes.

Visual arts

The genesis of Panama's artistic traditions can be traced to the early 20th century, when **Roberto Lewis** (1874-1949) was commissioned to paint frescos on the great neoclassical structures of the new Republic, including the National Theatre in Panama City and the Escuela Normal in Santiago. He went on to paint portraits of the political elite and train a whole generation of artists at the National School of Painting. **Humberto Ivaldi** (1909-1947) is Panama's most celebrated landscape artist, revered for his dynamic and impressionistic style. **Juan Manuel Cedeño** (1914-1997), who continued Lewis's role of painting prestigious political portraits, borrowed heavily from cubism and futurism, depicting rustic scenes from the Azuero Peninsula replete with geometric shapes and dynamic lines. He is considered the father of modernism in Panama. Many of Panama's artists drew inspiration from periods of travel and study in Europe and the United States. **Eudoro Silvera** (b1917) trained under Lewis and in New York and was also heavily influenced by cubism. **Alfredo Sinclair** (b1915) studied with Ivaldi and was the first Panamanian artist to explore abstraction. He was heavily influenced by Jackson Pollock and spent considerable time in Argentina, the epicentre of abstract art in Latin America. **Manuel Amador** (1869-1952) was a contemporary of Roberto Lewis, heavily influenced by European and American styles. He was well ahead of his time, but apart from painting the national flag, his work went largely unrecognized during his own life.

Current artists

Panama's current crop of top artists are a diverse crowd. **Coquí Calderón** (b1938) began as an expressionist but steered towards urban culture and political themes after spending time in 1960s New York. Her 'Winds of Rage' series notably addressed the military dictatorship during the 1980s. **Antonio Alvarado** (b1938), taught by Dutary in the early 1960s, is a purely abstract painter. **Mario Calvit** (b1933) began as an abstractionist but went on to become a sculptor and figurative artist. He is today renowned for his interesting installations. **Olga Sinclair** (b1957), daughter of Alfredo Sinclair, learned from her father and travelled extensively in Europe, Asia and Latin America. She now lives in Panama City and is a celebrated figure painter. **Amalia Tapia** (b1949) is known for her still-life work and her poetic interpretations of everyday objects. More recently, she has been painting impressionistic landscapes, especially of the canal and its locks. **David Solís** (b1953) began as a watercolour artist, but moved to oils after spending time in Paris. He is known for his distortions of space and perspective. **Tabo Toral** (b1950) is a revered muralist who started out as an abstract artist but was later influenced by graffiti and urban art. **Isabel de Obaldía** (b1957) was born in the US but now lives in Panama. She works mainly with figures and likes to depict decapitated male torsos. **Brooke Alfaro** (b1949) famously painted a scene of the invasion of Panama. His work is often grotesque, typically mocking political and religious power and focusing on the lives of the poor.

Photography
One of Panama's most famous photographers is **Iraida Icaza**, internationally renowned for her abstract compositions. **Sandra Eleta**, also widely known, studied photography at the International Center of Photography in New York and is celebrated for her striking images of life on the Caribbean coast. **Stuart Warner** is particularly revered for his portraits of indigenous people, while **José Luis Rodríguez Pittí** notably travelled through the Azuero Peninsula for five years gathering fascinating documentary images. **Antonio José Guzmán** is Dutch-Panamanian born in Panama City. He makes films, documentaries, photos and art installations with a strong travel component.

Literature

Panama's earliest literature was penned by chivalrous European chroniclers and typically depicted life and dramas as seen through the eyes of Spanish conquistadors. Later literature was more historical and factual, including several useful accounts by early missionaries, friars and explorers. A true literary genre did not emerge until the 19th century, when higher education became more commonplace and the region began to undergo considerable socio-political changes. Most of the output of the age clamoured for autonomy and nationhood. **Mariano Arosemana** (1794-1858), a formidable essayist, journalist and historian, notably founded Panama's first newspaper, *La Miscelánea del Istmo*, which he used to foment the Independence movement.

Romanticism
Invariably, the emergence of romantic poetry in Panama was framed by pressing political and social issues, including freedom and revolution. **Gil Colunje** (1831-1899) was a crucial figure in the genre, penning a seminal poem about Independence from Spain, *28 de Noviembre*, as well as the country's first true novel, *La Verdad Triunfante*. **Tomás Martín Feuillet** (1834-1862) continued the theme of nationalism with a moving ode to Panama's national flower, *Flor del Espiritú Santo*, while **Amelia Denis de Icaza** (1836-1911) wrote disparaging verse about the US presence in Panama, including the immortal *Al Cerro Ancón*. The next generation of writers were less romantic and more grounded in social realities, but continued to dwell on the same themes of autonomy and freedom. **Jerónimo Ossa** (1847-1907) notably wrote Panama's national anthem, while **Federico Escobar** (1861-1912), Panama's first Afro-descendent poet, explored pioneering themes of racial identity.

Modernism

It was not until Nicaraguan master **Rubén Darío** achieved massive acclaim that modernism bloomed into full creative force on the isthmus. The very greatest of Panama's modernists – and possibly the most celebrated Panamanian poet of all time – is **Ricardo Miró** (1883-1940), who penned the poem *Patria*, which is still read and memorized by schoolchildren all over the country. A prestigious literary prize was named in his honour and it has done much to encourage the development of Panama's literary scene. Other notable modernists include **Octavio Hernández** (1893-1918), a black author who wrote about social injustice and went on to become editor of *La Estrella* newspaper; **León Soto** (1874-1902), a revered master of sonnet; and **Darío Herrera** (1870-1914), who published Panama's first collection of short stories. As modernism started to evolve into the vanguard, writers began experimenting with new themes and forms. **María Olimpia de Obaldía** (1891-1985) is credited as Panama's first feminist author, while **Demetrio Korsi** (1899-1957) wrote compelling accounts of daily life in the poor parts of the capital.

The Vanguard and beyond

Panama's vanguard movement flourished in the inter-war years and signalled a break from traditional forms of literature. **Rogelio Sinán** (1902-1994) is celebrated as the genre's founding father and he took the literary scene by storm after publishing his ground-breaking novel *Onda*. Panamanian literature entered a prolific period thereafter, with scores of poets and novelists establishing distinct themes of endeavour. The so-called *regionalistas* focused on the realities of life in Panama's provinces, drawing inspiration from local legends, traditions and culture. Among them are left-leaning **Carlos Francisco Chang Marín** (b1920), whose work explores the themes of exploitation and revolution; **José María Sánchez** (1918-1973), who set his stories in Bocas del Toro; and **Carlos Candanedo** (1906-1986), who wrote about illegal immigrants in the Darién. Other authors chose to pen historical novels, including **Octavio Méndez**, who wrote a compelling biography of Vasco Núñez de Balboa, and **Julio Belisario Sosa** (1910-1946), who wrote about Urracá's resistance struggle against the conquistadors. Social realities, worker injustice and contemporary political life were the inspiration for many authors, including **Narciso Nava** and **Renato Ozores**. **Tristan Solarte** (the pen-name of Guillermo Sánchez Borbón) is notable for his 1957 gothic psychological thriller, *El Ahogado*. As ever, the Canal Zone and US occupation was rich material for many authors including **José Martínez** and **José Franco**. More recent writers, including some post-modernists, have tended to experiment with the narrative form. Names to look out for are **Consuleo Tomás**, **Gloria Guardia**, **Rosa María Britton**, **Enrique Jaramillo Levi**, **Jorge Tomás** and **Cristina Henríquez**.

Panama land and environment

Geography

Nestled between Costa Rica and Colombia, the slender, S-shaped isthmus of Panama is a vital land-bridge between the Americas. The most popular theory of its formation suggests that the collision of Pacific and Caribbean tectonic plates triggered Panama's emergence from the ocean around three million years ago, initially as a string of volcanic islands. The separation of the oceans by Panama was a significant geological event that established new patterns of oceanic circulation, including the Gulf Stream. The isthmus covers an area of approximately 75,417 sq km, making it only slightly larger than Ireland. It has a length of approximately 772 km, a width that varies from 55 km to 177 km, a combined coastline of 2490 km, and over 1500 islands.

Mountains

Roughly a third of Panama's terrain is composed of hills and mountains, but most are comparatively low and only a small fraction – approximately 3% of the national territory – are higher than 1500 m. West of the canal, a central spine of rugged uplands divides the watersheds of the Caribbean and the Pacific. Known as the **Cordillera Central**, it is composed of igneous, metamorphic and sedimentary rocks and includes several ranges, including the **Serranía de Tabasará** and **Serranía de Veraguas**. Near the Costa Rican border, the Cordillera Central merges with the **Cordillera Talamanca**, which is home to Panama's *tierras frías* (cold lands) and the highest mountain in the country, **Volcán Barú** (3475 m). East of the canal, an arc of low rambling mountains skirts the Caribbean shore, beginning with the **Serranía Llorana** in Portobelo and concluding with the **Serranía del Darién** near the Colombian border. On the Pacific side, the **Serranía de Majé** begins just south of Lago Bayano and runs east along the Interamericana highway as far as the Gulf of San Miguel. There are several steep, thickly forested ranges in the eastern borderlands of the Darién. The **Azuero Peninsula** is almost entirely flat, except for its southwest tip where you'll find rolling hills and the challenging peak of **Cerro Hoya** (1559 m).

Rivers

Panama is home to approximately 500 rivers – 350 on the Pacific side, 150 on the Caribbean. Most of them originate in the remote Cordillera Central, where they course through the mountains with considerable energy before gradually slowing, widening and meandering into deep lowland valleys. Many of them emerge at the ocean in wide coastal deltas or wetlands. Caribbean rivers tend to be shorter than Pacific rivers, but no less powerful. Due to alternating patterns of drought and deluge, water levels vary greatly throughout the year, with flooding extremely common at the height of the wet season. The most important river basins in Panama include the Sixaola, San San, Changuinola and Chagres on the Caribbean; the Chiriquí, Chiriquí Viejo, David, Tabasará, Pacora, Tuira and Sambú on the Pacific. In recent years, many rivers have been harnessed for their hydroelectric potential, including the Río Chagres, which supplies the water for Lake Gatún in the Panama Canal (see Environmental challenges, page 300).

Wildlife and vegetation

Around three million years ago, the merging of North and South America into a single landmass sparked a mass migration of animals between both continents. Known as the **Great American Faunal Interchange**, it was a significant moment in the earth's natural history and it heralded bold new patterns of species settlement, adaptation, predation and, in some cases, extinction. The event was accompanied by the so-called **Great American Schism**, which separated the oceans and set marine species on their own unique evolutionary paths. Today, Panama represents the range limit for numerous North and South American animal species, as well as a land bridge for dozens of types of migratory birds. Unsurprisingly, it is one of the most biologically diverse places on the planet, home to 231 species of mammal, 972 species of bird, 226 species of reptile, 164 species of amphibian, as well as 10,000 species of plant and over 300,000 varieties of insect. New species are always being discovered.

Lowland rainforests

Panama's lowland rainforests are home to an extraordinary cornucopia of biological life. They are densely vegetated and largely inhospitable places, characterized by high temperatures, humidity and rainfall. The borderlands of the Darién play host to the most spectacular virgin forests in Central America, but there are also fine tracts in the Panama Canal watershed and in the lowland areas of the Caribbean coast. Life in the rainforest is sustained by an intricate web of relationships, all invariably driven by the struggle for survival. Predation, particularly of nests, is intensive and widespread, as is competition for food and light. Anyone unfortunate enough to find themselves stranded in a rainforest may find little to sustain them. Symbiotic relationships are also very common, with plants often having creative methods of pollination and seed dispersal. For example, many flowers are uniquely shaped for pollination by specific types of hummingbird, bat or butterfly. Parasitic relationships are also prolific and often gruesome, including wasps that inject their eggs inside the living bodies of ants.

Rainforests incorporate several distinct layers commencing with the forest floor, which is usually clear of vegetation and quite dark due to the multiple canopies above it. The exception is the site of a recent tree fall, which is always worth scrutinizing for its new growth and activity. Despite the rainforest's profusion of plants, its topsoil is very thin and nutrient-poor, causing many trees to have sprawling, buttressed roots near the surface. When a plant or animal dies, it is rapidly broken down by bacteria and insects, and its nutrients taken up by living vegetation via a network of mycorrhizal fungi – brush away some topsoil to see it. The forest floor is also a good place to spot insects, especially ants, which till the earth, clear away dead material, disperse seeds and perform other vital functions. Leafcutter ants are very common and can be seen clambering in long files carrying cuttings of leaves, flowers, seeds and other vegetative material, which they use to cultivate a type of nutritious fungus. Army ants are rarer but no less impressive, especially when they sweep through the forest in great columns, tearing apart any small creature unfortunate enough to get in their way. Termites, a close relative of the ants, do much to strip down wood, and their bulbous black nests are a common sight on tree branches.

Between the canopy and the forest floor, the understorey is home to numerous small animals. It is still a relatively dark place and most of its plants – typically shrubs and palms – need large leaves to maximize photosynthesis. Rodents, including agoutis, pacas and coatis, are a fairly common sight, as are amphibians, including poison dart frogs,

The last frog song

The extinction of any animal species is always a tragedy, but there is something particularly dispiriting about the extinction of a national animal. Once revered as a harbinger of fertility and good luck, the golden frog – symbol of the nation – has today all but disappeared from the wild. It is just the latest victim in a worldwide plague that has annihilated at least 100 amphibian species and gravely impacted 100 more. Frog chytrid is a fast-spreading parasitic fungus that attacks amphibian skin to inhibit respiration and other vital functions. Human activity has been heavily implicated in its spread, particularly deforestation and the trade in exotic frogs. The disease has been sweeping south and east through Panama since the turn of the century and it is now making its way into the Darién, one of the world's last strongholds of frog diversity, including 120 species and many

undocumented varieties. Smithsonian scientists are dashing to collect specimens so, as with the golden frog, they may maintain their populations in captivity. It is hoped that an imminent cure or vaccination will enable many rare species to be re-introduced into the wild, but, sadly, there are only resources to protect a fraction of Panama's brilliantly coloured frog species – and no political will to provide more. Today, over 40% of the world's amphibian species are in decline and they are disappearing at 200 times the average rate of extinction. Worryingly, some scientists see the collapse of frog populations as part of a much wider and more profound extinction event.

If you would like to know more about efforts to save the world's frogs, contact the **Amphibian Rescue and Conservation Project in El Valle**, www.amphibianrescue.org.

marine toads, leaf-litter toads and golden frogs. Rivers, streams, ponds and other bodies of water tend to draw larger mammals, including tapirs, jaguars, pumas, peccaries and ocelots, but most are nocturnal and rarely seen by humans. The canopy itself is teeming with plant life as vines, orchids and epiphytes compete for every available ray of light. The strangler fig, which descends from tree branches with thick, woody creepers, is a type of parasite that gradually engulfs and suffocates its host tree. Animals can often be seen in the canopy, including iguanas and sloths, but monkeys especially, including white-faced capuchins, mantled howlers, spider monkeys and night monkeys. The rainforest's highest canopy – the emergent layer – contains just a few tall trees, the giants of the forest. They are home to rare bird species, such as harpy eagles.

Tropical dry forests

Low-lying tropical dry forests receive far less precipitation than rainforests. They are home to numerous deciduous trees that must shed their leaves in the dry season in order to conserve water. The loss of leaves opens many gaps in the forest canopy, encouraging the growth of prolific underbrush. Many plants and trees have found strategies to cope with the dry conditions, including some that have evolved chlorophyll in their bark and others with swollen roots and stems that act as reservoirs. Resident animal species are broadly comparable to those of the rainforests, but ultimately less numerous and biodiverse. Some of them, including a few amphibians and reptiles, practise *estivation* – a state of dormancy where they burrow deep into the mud and sleep out the summer.

The coming of the rains is a fascinating time in the tropical dry forest, when numerous creatures emerge, flowers start blooming and the vegetation turns green virtually overnight. Tropical dry forests were once extremely prolific in Central America, but they have now been devastated and are endangered. In Panama, you will find them on the Pacific side of the country.

Cloud forests

Highland cloud forests are characterized by persistent mist and cloud cover. They are considerably cooler than rainforests with daytime temperatures of around 10-20°C. Because of to the almost constant blanket of fog, sunlight is greatly reduced, but there is an immense amount of precipitation and cloud forests play a crucial role in maintaining highland drainage and watersheds. They are extremely lush places, home to scores of green mosses, lichens, ferns, fungi, orchids and bromeliads. Trees are generally short with dense, compact crowns that cause wind-driven clouds to condense. Cloud forests also boast reasonably high biodiversity and high rates of endemism thanks to their numerous valleys and ridges, which many animals find impassable. Jaguars, tapirs, quetzals and harpy eagles are all known to inhabit Panama's cloud forests, which are concentrated on the slopes of Volcán Barú in Chiriquí province.

Wetlands and mangrove forests

Wetlands can be found on both coasts of Panama and are endowed with an abundance of water in different forms: fresh, salty, flowing and stagnant. Wetlands offer a diversity of ecological niches including sedge marshes, swamps, bogs, flood plains, coastal lagoons and mangrove forests. Proliferating in intertidal or estuarine areas, mangroves include a broad family of *halophytic* (salt-tolerant) trees and are one of the most common and important types of vegetation in Panama. They serve a vital function by trapping sediment, protecting the shore from erosion and building land. The forests have a low canopy and a low diversity of trees, usually dominated by red mangroves, which can be recognized by their dark stilted roots that hold them above the surface of the water. Mangrove forests are important nurseries for fish, birds, amphibians and crustaceans, including numerous crabs and shrimps. Unsurprisingly, many hunters stalk the forests, including common caimans, American crocodiles and scores of snakes, especially boa constrictors. In Bocas del Toro province, endangered manatees are a common sight in the wetlands of San San Pond Sak.

Beaches and shores

Panama's shorelines can be rocky, sandy or muddy. Low tide often reveals rock pools filled with clams and mussels, or teeming mud flats strewn with crabs and shrimps, all drawing waders and hungry seabirds. Larger avian species, including pelicans and pterodactyl-like frigate birds, are a common sight on any shore. Some of Panama's beaches see impressive migrations of endangered sea turtles, including leatherback, hawksbill, loggerhead and olive ridley. Females will typically swim ashore at night, dig a nest, lay their eggs and depart. Some sites, such as Isla Caña on the Azuero Peninsula, see mass arrivals of many thousands, but these are increasingly rare. The temperature of the nest will determine the future sex of the hatchling – above 29°C female; below 29°C male. The eggs will hatch simultaneously and the young turtles will inundate the sea in an evolutionary mechanism believed to give them the best chances of survival.

Offshore habitats

The Pacific waters off Panama are comparatively shallow, reaching only 180 m outside the Gulf of Panama and the Gulf of Chiriquí. Tidal ranges are quite extreme, however, at around 7 m. By contrast, Caribbean tides vary by only 0.7 m. Both oceans are home to prolific coral reefs, thousands of fish and invertebrates, including sponges, shrimps, lobsters, starfish and many others. Coral reefs are incredibly colourful places, thanks in part to the algae which provide the coral with oxygen via photosynthesis. Sea-grasses are also quite prolific and tend to grow in the protected waters of bays, lagoons and estuaries. They help to trap sediment at their roots and act as nurseries for numerous marine animals. The so-called pelagic zones – including the shores off Isla Coiba – occur at much greater ocean depths and are the places to encounter large sea animals including giant squid, whales, dolphins and blue-fin tuna.

Environmental challenges

Panama faces a long and difficult battle to protect its natural spaces. Many mega-projects are now proceeding with little or no local consultation, falsified environmental impact assessments and little regard for the rule of law. Foreign-owned corporations, which are behind most of the environmental devastation, have developed sophisticated 'green-washing' techniques as part of their public relations armoury. These include setting up fake environmental groups to champion their 'green' credentials, especially on the contested spaces of the internet.

Deforestation

Deforestation continues to cause significant damage to Panama. In 1947, around 70% of the country was covered in forests. Today, this figure has dropped to 43.7%. Although the rate of devastation has slowed in recent years, it remains worryingly high – between 1990 and 2010, Panama lost 14.3% of its total forest cover. Damage to forested spaces has been most extensive in the Darién, where the advance of the Interamericana highway has facilitated the opening of an agrarian frontier. Slash-and-burn colonists clear the land for one or two seasons, until the topsoil has been exhausted or washed away, and then advance to new areas, leaving the land open to cattle ranchers. Meanwhile, logging, mining and hydroelectric operations are rapidly accelerating the deforestation, with damage to mangroves by uncontrolled touristic development also becoming common. Unfortunately, Panama's reforestation drive appears to be making matters worse. More than 75% of reforested spaces are commercial teak plantations and, despite vociferous claims for their 'sustainable' credentials, they are actually non-native and very harmful to Panama's environment. Their leaves contain tannins which degrade the soil and prevent anything else from growing and, curiously, the only animals that appear to seek shelter inside the forests are a few species of insect. Sadly, there have been instances of good native forests being cleared for teak plantations, which continue to be incentivized with generous tax breaks and the UN's Clean Development Mechanism (ie carbon credits).

Mining

The rush to extract Panama's mineral resources has recently accelerated due to high market demand for copper and gold. Environmentalists argue that Panama is too small and ecologically sensitive to permit both open-pit mining and eco-tourism, but the government appears to have made its choice. Around 26% of the national territory has now been sold out to foreign mining interests, who are in varying stages of exploration and exploitation. The environmental costs of open-pit mining are staggering – contamination of watersheds with heavy metals and acids, deforestation, and the real possibility of cyanide spills mean neighbouring Costa Rica has outlawed it entirely. The inglorious history of modern mining in Panama began in 2005 with **Petaquilla Minerals**, directed by the controversial self-styled 'Grandfather of Panamanian Mining', Richard Fifer. From the outset, his **Molejón** gold mine in Donoso district, Colón, was mired in scandal including allegations of fraud and the flagrant contravention of environmental protection laws. More recently, the government's dogged pursuit of **Cerro Colorado**, believed to be the second largest copper deposit in the world, has sparked a series of violent conflicts with the Ngäbe, whose communities rely heavily on local watersheds (see page 239). In 2011, an extremely scandalous concession went to Cobre, a copper mine now under construction by Canadian company **Inmet**. Since **Cobre** is located in pristine protected rainforests, the company sought an injunction to change the area's status as a nature reserve. The Supreme Court rejected their claim but deferred the final decision to Panama's environmental agency, ANAM. In a sickening moment of political collusion, ANAM gave the green light for Inmet to begin work.

Hydroelectricity

Erroneously regarded as a source of clean energy, hydroelectric plants are frequently implicated in deforestation, contamination of watersheds, destabilization of local ecosystems, displacement of communities and the diversion of precious water resources. Moreover, the scale and extent of Panama's hydroelectric industry is extremely concerning. The province of Chiriquí has been slated for no less than 63 hydro projects, most of them applied to just four watersheds. According to the Interamerican Development Bank, the **Río Chirquí Viejo** will soon be diverted through 24 run-of-the-river plants – one every 6.7 km – exhausting 98% of the river's output and leaving just 2% for agriculture, drinking water and other traditional uses. While the government insists that hydroelectric power is vital to the nation's growing energy needs, in fact, much of the electricity it produces is exported to other countries.

Worse yet, the destruction of Panama's watersheds is being subsidized by the UN's Clean Development Mechanism, a carbon-trading scheme which continues to reward bad companies for environmentally destructive behaviour. In eastern Chiriquí, the **Barro Blanco** hydroelectric dam, currently under construction by **Generadora del Istmo** (GENISA), is threatening to displace up to 5000 Ngäbe farmers, all of them vehemently opposed to the project. Despite a series of heated public protests, the organization responsible for assessing GENISA's application for carbon credits – the **Asociación Española de Normalización y Certificación** (AENOR) – claimed in its final report that "Most relevant communities involved in the area of the project were consulted [and] all of them supported the project activity." Consequently, GENISA was granted its claim.

Interestingly, the same certification company also failed to recognize the grotesque abuses of hydro giant AES, whose construction of the **Chan 75** hydroelectric plant in Bocas del Toro was steeped in allegations of violence, intimidation, torture and sexual assault at the hands of the police. Many Ngäbe landowners were reportedly bullied into selling their property at ultra-cheap rates and the UN special rapporteur for indigenous peoples, **James Anaya**, was so concerned by what he saw that he ordered an immediate suspension of the project. This was flatly ignored and in 2011 AES began flooding the homes of families who had chosen to remain in the region. They and many others have never been compensated for their losses.

Environmental organizations

Alianza para la Conservación y Desarllo (ACD), www.acdpanama.org. The Alliance for Conservation and Development has conducted several useful studies into resource management, hydroelectric projects and indigenous culture.

Asociación Nacional para la Conservación del Naturaleza (ANCON), www.ancon.org. A reputable and experienced NGO founded in 1985 for the conservation of Panama's biodiversity and natural resources.

Autoridad Nacional de Ambient (ANAM), www.anam.gob.pa. Panama's environment agency manages the country's system of national parks and protected areas.

Centro de Incidencia Ambiental (CIAM), www.ciampanama.org. The Environmental Advocacy Centre is a well-respected NGO and the only legal defence organization in Panama wholly dedicated to protecting its environment and cultural heritage.

Fundación Albatros Media, www.albatros media.net. Albatros Media are celebrated for their excellent wildlife documentaries.

Fundación Avifauna Eugene Eisenmann, www.avifauna.org.pa. An excellent Panamanian-American bird conservation NGO that built the Rainforest Discovery Center in Soberanía National Park.

Fundación Mar Viva, www.marviva.net. Dedicated to the protection of marine environments, Mar Viva patrols the Pacific coast off Panama and Costa Rica.

Sociedad Audubon de Panamá, www.audubonpanama.org. The highly respected Audubon Society has chapters around the world. It is among the foremost experts in birdlife.

Protected areas

Panama has around 50 protected areas, including 16 national parks and a variety of nature monuments, multiple use areas, wildlife reserves, protected forests and others. Together they comprise around a third of the national territory. The government agency responsible for their administration is the **Autoridad Nacional de Ambiente (ANAM)**, which is chronically underfunded and understaffed, and unfortunately, politically compromised at higher levels. Nonetheless, many of its staff are competent, dedicated and passionate about the environment – they do the best they can under difficult circumstances. Panama's national parks vary in style and scope, but most have at least a few decent trails that can be explored without a guide. Simple accommodation in cots or hammocks is often available too, along with camping (bring your own equipment), for US$5-10 per night. All national parks charge an entrance fee of US$5 (US$10-20 for marine parks) and guides can usually be arranged for US$10-20 per day. All cities and most towns of any size have an ANAM office, which you should always visit if you're planning extensive treks or overnight stays.

Lowland forests and wetlands

The majority of Panama's protected areas consist of lowland forests, including rainforests and dry forests. In Panama City, the **Parque Metropolitano** is a highly convenient place to begin. Just 10 minutes from the city centre, it is surprisingly rich in wildlife and features easy-to-follow interpretive trails. Adjoining the park are two excellent and well-maintained areas with good hiking and world-class birdwatching – the **Parque Nacional Soberanía** and the **Parque Nacional Camino de Cruces**. Nearby, the **Parque Nacional Chagres** is a more rugged and challenging forest environment that crosses the continental divide to connect with **Parque Nacional Portobelo**. Also on the Central Caribbean coast, the **Bosque Protector San Lorenzo** is home to the excellent **Achiote Road** birding trail. West of the capital, the **Parque Nacional Altos de Campana** is the oldest nature reserve in the country and features rolling hills and steep cliffs. The wildest and most pristine forests lie in the east. The **Parque Nacional Darién** is a true bastion of rainforest splendour, but it is also extremely remote and tricky to access. Nearby you'll find the protected areas of **Serranía del Darién** and **Filo de Tallo**. There are numerous wetlands throughout Panama and many provide the opportunity for river-bound excursions and encounters with unique aquatic fauna. **San San Pond Sak** in Bocas del Toro is the place to see beautiful manatees year round, while in the Azuero Peninsula, the multiple-use area of **Ciénaga de las Macanas** offers intriguing glimpses into rural life.

Beaches, islands and marine parks

Panama's stunning marine fauna is not to be missed. The **Parque Nacional Isla Coiba** is the largest of the country's islands and in almost perfect condition thanks to its former role as a penal colony. Offshore you'll discover scintillating coral reefs and large pelagic species, including whales, dolphins and sharks. The spectacle of nesting sea turtles is exhilarating and your best chance of experiencing it is at the **Reserva de Vida Silvestre Isla Caña** in Los Santos Province. In western Panama, the **Refugio de Vida Silvestre Playa de la Barqueta Agrícola** is also visited by turtles, but more difficult to get to. Offshore, the **Parque Nacional Golfo de Chiriquí** encompasses a stunning archipelago of pristine islands and coral reefs, a consistent hit with divers and sports fishermen. On the Caribbean, you'll find an equivalent in the **Parque Marino Bastimentos**, easily accessed from the popular pleasure town of Bocas. Close to the capital, the **Barro Colorado Nature Monument** in Lake Gatún is a wildlife refuge and centre of scientific research, and a great place to learn about tropical ecology. **Isla Taboga**, a short ferry ride from the city, is home to a large pelican colony.

Mountains and highlands

Panama's mountains and highlands are filled with challenging terrain, majestic cloud forests and, of course, endlessly expansive vistas. In western Panama, just outside Boquete, the **Parque Nacional Volcán Barú** is an extremely popular destination with scores of rewarding trails. The hike to the peak of Barú is particularly awesome, as is the **Sendero Quetzales**, which connects with the village of Cerro Punta. Further north, the **Parque Internacional La Amistad** is home to lush, cool cloud forests. It can be accessed from outside Cerro Punta, or on the Caribbean side, mainland Bocas del Toro, where you will encounter remote rainforests in the heart of the indigenous Naso Kingdom. East of Boquete, the **Reserva Forestal Fortuna** also features cloud forests, easily accessible from a handful of highland lodges. In the Central Provinces, the **Parque Nacional Santa Fe** is an extremely remote area straddling the continental divide. It is rich in wildlife, barely inhabited and very challenging. Adjoining it, the **Parque Nacional Omar Torrijos** features a mixture of highlands and rainforest. It is reasonably remote and yet its trails are well maintained. The **Parque Nacional Cerro Hoya** on the Azuero Peninsula is tough but rewarding, remote and only for seasoned adventurers.

Books and films on Panama

Books

Anthropology

Howe, J *A people who would not kneel: Panama, the United States and the San Blas Kuna* (Smithsonian Books 1998) A fascinating account of Guna history, politics and anthropology, with particular focus on the Guna revolution and the role of American explorer Richard Marsh in fomenting it.

Kane, S *The Phantom Gringo Boat: Shamanic discourse and development in Panama* (Smithsonian Institute, 1994) A groundbreaking ethnographic study of Emberá spiritual life, shamanic traditions and medicine. Very readable and highly regarded.

Perrin, M & Dusinbere, D *Magnificent molas: the art of the Kuna Indians* (Flammarion, 2001) An excellent and thorough analysis of Guna art, including examples of 300 molas complete with explanations of their symbolism, manufacture and use in daily life.

Salvador, M *The Art of Being Kuna: layers and meaning among the Kuna of Panama* (University of Washington Press, 1997) A very lively and reliable ethnographic account of Guna cultural life, including music, dance, storytelling and ceremony.

Schermer, N *The Best Baskets in the World* (Langdon Street Press, 2011) An eye-catching coffee-table book about Emberá and Wounaan basket-making. It includes excellent photographic spreads with explanations of designs and manufacture.

Young, P *Ngawbe: tradition and change among the western Guaymi of Panama* (University of Illinois Press, 1971) Phil Young is the world's leading academic expert on the Ngäbe and his books, if you can find them, provide unrivalled insights into Ngäbe culture and customs.

Ecology and natural history

Coates, A *Central America: A natural and cultural history* (Yale University Press, 1988) Insightful background reading that puts Central American development in context. Written by several experts who explore the historical relationship between people and land.

Forsyth, A & Miyata, K *Tropical nature: life and death in the rainforests of Central and South America* (Touchstone Books, 1987) A very readable and lively explanation of the workings of rainforest ecology, written by two field biologists. Useful, intriguing, entertaining and authoritative.

Giles, E *Tropical forest ecology: A view from Barro Colorado island* (Oxford University Press, 1999) An ecological case-study of Isla Barro Blanco and its forests, with emphasis on the wider themes of mutualism and biodiversity. Highly regarded and essential.

Hilty, S *Birds of Tropical America: A watcher's introduction to behaviour, breeding and diversity* (University of Texas Press, 2005) No self-respecting twitcher should leave home without this excellent natural history of tropical birds. Recently re-issued and hugely popular.

Kricher, J *The Neotropical Companion* (Princeton University Press, 1999) An excellent and essential introduction to the ecosystems of tropical America. Highly authoritative and widely praised by scientists and laymen alike. Possibly the best single volume on the subject.

Field guides

Angehr, G & Dean, R *The birds of Panama: A field guide* (Zona Tropical Publications, 2010) Only recently published but already receiving rave reviews from birders. This is now considered the best available field guide for birds and is highly recommended for its colour illustrations of more than 900 species.

Conduit, R et al *Trees of Panama and Costa Rica* (Princeton University Press, 2010) A very thorough and accessible botany field guide with a rigorous and ambitious scope. Undoubtedly the best available volume for casual explorers.

Dressler, R *A field guide to the orchids of Costa Rica and Panama* (Cornell University Press, 1993) A meticulous guide with detailed and sometimes technical instructions for the difficult task of wild orchid identification. Recommended for biologists or professional botanists.

Reid, F *A field guide to the mammals of Central America and southeast Mexico* (Oxford University Press, 1988) A good, solid field guide with 49 full-colour plates, distribution maps and coverage of both land- and water-based mammals.

Ridgley, R *A guide to the birds of Panama* (Princeton University Press, 1992) The 2nd edition of a classic guide. Very weighty, beautifully illustrated and comprehensive, but some readers say it is in need of an overhaul.

History and politics

Balf, T *The Darkest Jungle: the true story of the Darien Expedition and America's ill-fated race to connect the seas* (Crown, 2003) A gripping account of an American expedition to the Darién in the 19th century – and all the grisly disasters that befell it.

Dinge, J *Our Man in Panama: How General Noriega used the United States and made millions in drugs and arms* (Random House, 1990) A very detailed and thorough exposé of the obscure relationship between Noriega and the CIA. An important contribution and quite critical of the United States.

Earle, P *The Sack of Panama: Sir Henry Morgan's adventures on the Spanish Main* (Viking Press, 1982) A useful chronology of the age of piracy and especially Morgan's travels in the Caribbean. Interesting political background, but quite light on the brutal realities.

Eisner, P & Noriega, M *America's Prisoner: The Memoirs of Manuel Noriega* (Random House, 1997) Noriega's largely fictitious

and self-serving memoirs have divided audiences. It tries very hard to paint the dictator as a victim of US imperialism, but it has its moments of intrigue.

Espino, O *How Wall Street created a nation: JP Morgan, Teddy Roosevelt and the Panama Canal* (Four Walls Eight Windows, 2001) A very interesting account of the corrupt backroom dealings between Roosevelt, Morgan and Banau-Varilla. An original take on a well-explored subject.

Greene, G *Getting to know the General* (Random House, 1984) Graham Greene's shameless apology for Omar Torrijos is rather fascinating. The dictator comes across as rather likeable, if something of a drunk and a womanizer. Greene himself never suspects he is being carefully manipulated.

Kempe, F *Divorcing the dictator: America's bungled affair with Noriega* (Putnam Adult, 1990) A very authoritative and detailed exploration of the Noriega years, including 3-dimensional and well-researched character analyses. Eye-opening and well worth reading.

Koster, R & Sánchez, G *In the time of tyrants: Panama, 1968-1990* (W.W. Norton & Company, 1990) An entertaining and accessible history of Guardia dictatorship that begins with an account of Hugo Spadafora's murder. Good journalistic style and dashes of black humour.

Lindsay-Poland, J *Emperors in the Jungle* (Duke University Press, 2003) An intriguing investigation into US military involvement in Panama, including jungle training camps, chemical weapons testing and Operation Just Cause. Unfortunately, the anti-American tone detracts from the book's overall value.

McCullough, D *The path between the seas* (Simon & Schuster, 1978) A very gripping account of the construction of the canal, essential reading for all visitors to Panama and something of a masterpiece. Brilliantly written and clearly explained.

Parker, M *Panama Fever: the battle to build the canal* (Hutchinson, 2007) A more recent narration of the canal construction, highly readable and at times quite gripping. Lots of interesting social history enlivens the major events.

Sosa, I *In Defiance: The battle against General Noriega fought from Panama's embassy* (Francis Press, 1999) An insightful and unique analysis of US-Panamanian diplomatic relations from a former Panamanian ambassador who served in the last days of the Noriega regime.

Fiction and travel writing

Dyke, T & Winder, P *The Cloud Garden* (Lyons Press, 2005) The true story of a horticulturist and a banker who travel to the Darién Gap in search of rare orchids, only to be kidnapped by Colombian paramilitaries.

DuFord, D *Is there a hole in the boat? Tales of travel in Panama without a car* (Booklocker, 2006) A collection of lively travel stories from an award-winning writer. Good descriptions of Panama's off-the-beaten-track destinations.

Mitchinson, M *The Darien Gap: Travels in the Rainforest* (Harbour, 2008) An intrepid travelogue brimming with daring and adventure. The author follows Balboa's historic route across the isthmus. A must-read for lovers of the Darién.

Galbraith, D *Rising Sun* (Pub Group West, 2001) An evocative, fictionalized account of the failed attempt to found the Scottish colony of New Caledonia in the Darién.

Le Carré, J *The Tailor of Panama* (Sceptre, 1999) A readable and entertaining tale of diplomatic intrigue and deception on the eve of the Panama Canal handover. Hardly a triumph for spy-master Le Carré, but worth a quick look.

Films

Benaim, A *Chance* (Panama, 2009) Filmed in Panama City, a black comedy about two housekeepers who work for a snooty aristocratic family. Sharp dialogue and mixed, if mostly positive, reviews. Spanish-language.

Bollow, V *Burwadii Ebo* (Panama, 2008) Also known as *The Wind and the Water*. One of the best films to have emerged from Panama's nascent film industry. It tells the story of a young Guna man who travels to Panama City and falls in love with a girl from a wealthy family. Spanish-language.

Boorman, J *The Tailor of Panama* (USA, 2001) The film adaptation of Le Carré's novel (see above). Light and watchable with good castings of Geoffrey Rush as bumbling Harry Pendel and Pierce Brosnan as obnoxious bully-boy Andy Osnard.

Herrera, H *One dollar, el precio de vida* (Spain, 1992) A harsh award-winning documentary that looks at life in the ghettoes of Panama City, including the seamy world of street gangs and crack addiction. Spanish-language, but English subtitles available.

Jacome, J *Ruta de la Luna* (Panama, 2012) A promising Panamanian-Ecuadorian film about an albino loner who travels across Central America to participate in a bowling tournament. His father insists on joining him despite their long history of distant relations. Spanish-language.

Mislov, A *Curundú* (Panama, 2007) A very interesting 66-minute documentary about day-to-day life in the rough neighbourhood of Curundú.

Ortega-Heilbron, P *Los Puños de una Nación* (Panama, 2005) A documentary feature about Panama's most celebrated boxer, Roberto Durán. Critical reviews were generally positive.

Trent, B *The Panama Deception* (USA, 1992) A very insightful if occasionally unbalanced account of Operation Just Cause, its political implications and its impact on Panama. The film went on to win an Oscar but it continues to rile American patriots.

Wiseman, F *Canal Zone* (USA, 1977) An interesting and ultimately unflattering depiction of life in the Canal Zone. Very aesthetic and slow-moving, a lingering work of art to be savoured, but extreme patience is also required.

Contents

Footnotes

Basic Spanish for travellers

Learning Spanish is a useful part of the preparation for a trip to Latin America and no volumes of dictionaries, phrase books or word lists will provide the same enjoyment as being able to communicate directly with the people of the country you are visiting. It is a good idea to make an effort to grasp the basics before you go. As you travel you will pick up more of the language and the more you know, the more you will benefit from your stay.

General pronunciation

Whether you have been taught the 'Castilian' pronounciation (z and c followed by i or e are pronounced as the th in think) or the 'American' pronounciation (they are pronounced as s), you will encounter little difficulty in understanding either. Regional accents and usages vary, but the basic language is essentially the same everywhere.

Vowels

a	as in English cat
e	as in English best
i	as the ee in English feet
o	as in English shop
u	as the oo in English food
ai	as the i in English ride
ei	as ey in English they
oi	as oy in English toy

Consonants

Most consonants can be pronounced more or less as they are in English. The exceptions are:

g	before e or i is the same as j
h	is always silent (except in ch as in chair)
j	as the ch in Scottish loch
ll	as the y in yellow
ñ	as the ni in English onion
rr	trilled much more than in English
x	depending on its location, pronounced x, s, sh or j

Spanish words and phrases

Greetings, courtesies

hello	hola	I speak Spanish	hablo español
good morning	buenos días	I don't speak Spanish	no hablo español
good afternoon/ evening/night	buenas tardes/ noches	do you speak English?	¿habla inglés?
goodbye	adiós/chao	I don't understand	no entiendo/ no comprendo
pleased to meet you	mucho gusto	please speak slowly	hable despacio por favor
see you later	hasta luego		
how are you?	¿cómo está? ¿cómo estás?	I am very sorry	lo siento mucho/ disculpe
I'm fine, thanks	estoy muy bien, gracias	what do you want?	¿qué quiere? ¿qué quieres?
I'm called...	me llamo...		
what is your name?	¿cómo se llama? ¿cómo te llamas?	I want	quiero
		I don't want it	no lo quiero
yes/no	sí/no	leave me alone	déjeme en paz/ no me moleste
please	por favor		
thank you (very much)	(muchas) gracias	good/bad	bueno/malo

Questions and requests

Have you got a room for two people?
¿Tiene una habitación para dos personas?
I'd like to make a long-distance phone call
Quisiera hacer una llamada de larga distancia

How do I get to_?	*¿Cómo llego a_?*
How much does it cost?	*¿Cuánto cuesta?*
	¿cuánto es?
Is service included?	*¿Está incluido el servicio?*
Is tax included?	*¿Están incluidos los impuestos?*

When does the bus leave (arrive)?
¿A qué hora sale (llega) el autobús?
Where is the nearest petrol station?
¿Dónde está la gasolinera más cercana?

When?	*¿cuándo?*
Where is_?	*¿dónde está_?*
Where can I buy tickets?	*¿Dónde puedo comprar boletos?*
Why?	*¿por qué?*

Basics

bank	*el banco*	market	*el mercado*
bathroom/toilet	*el baño*	note/coin	*el billete/la moneda*
bill	*la factura/la cuenta*	police (policeman)	*la policía (el policía)*
cash	*el efectivo*	post office	*el correo*
cheap	*barato/a*	public telephone	*el teléfono público*
credit card	*la tarjeta de crédito*	supermarket	*el supermercado*
exchange house	*la casa de cambio*	ticket office	*la taquilla*
exchange rate	*el tipo de cambio*	traveller's cheques	*los cheques de viajero/los travelers*
expensive	*caro/a*		

Getting around

aeroplane	*el avión*	to insure yourself against	*asegurarse contra*
airport	*el aeropuerto*		
arrival/departure	*la llegada/salida*	luggage	*el equipaje*
avenue	*la avenida*	motorway, freeway	*el autopista/ la carretera*
block	*la cuadra*		
border	*la frontera*	north	*norte*
bus station	*la terminal de autobuses/camiones*	south	*sur*
		west	*oeste (occidente)*
bus	*el bus/el autobús/ el camión*	east	*este (oriente)*
		oil	*el aceite*
collective/fixed-route taxi	*el colectivo*	to park	*estacionarse*
		passport	*el pasaporte*
corner	*la esquina*	petrol/gasoline	*la gasolina*
customs	*la aduana*	puncture	*el pinchazo/ la ponchadura*
first/second class	*primera/segunda clase*		
		street	*la calle*
left/right	*izquierda/derecha*	that way	*por allí/por allá*
ticket	*el boleto*	this way	*por aquí/por acá*
empty/full	*vacío/lleno*	tourist card/visa	*la tarjeta de turista*
highway, main road	*la carretera*	tyre	*la llanta*
immigration	*la inmigración*	unleaded	*sin plomo*
insurance	*el seguro*	to walk	*caminar/andar*
insured person	*el/la asegurado/a*		

Accommodation

air conditioning	*el aire acondicionado*	power cut	*el apagón/corte*
all-inclusive	*todo incluido*	restaurant	*el restaurante*
bathroom, private	*el baño privado*	room/bedroom	*el cuarto/*
bed, double/single	*la cama matrimonial/*		*la habitación*
	sencilla	sheets	*las sábanas*
blankets	*las cobijas/mantas*	shower	*la ducha/regadera*
to clean	*limpiar*	soap	*el jabón*
dining room	*el comedor*	toilet	*el sanitario/excusado*
guesthouse	*la casa de huéspedes*	toilet paper	*el papel higiénico*
hotel	*el hotel*	towels, clean/dirty	*las toallas limpias/*
noisy	*ruidoso*		*sucias*
pillows	*las almohadas*	water, hot/cold	*el agua caliente/fría*

Health

aspirin	*la aspirina*	diarrhoea	*la diarrea*
blood	*la sangre*	doctor	*el médico*
chemist	*la farmacia*	fever/sweat	*la fiebre/el sudor*
condoms	*los preservativos,*	pain	*el dolor*
	los condones	head	*la cabeza*
contact lenses	*los lentes de contacto*	period/sanitary towels	*la regla/las toallas*
contraceptives	*los anticonceptivos*		*femeninas*
contraceptive pill	*la píldora anti-*	stomach	*el estómago*
	conceptiva	altitude sickness	*el soroche*

Family

family	*la familia*	husband/wife	*el esposo (marido)/*
brother/sister	*el hermano/*		*la esposa*
	la hermana	boyfriend/girlfriend	*el novio/la novia*
daughter/son	*la hija/el hijo*	friend	*el amigo/la amiga*
father/mother	*el padre/la madre*	married	*casado/a*
		single/unmarried	*soltero/a*

Months, days and time

January	*enero*	Monday	*lunes*
February	*febrero*	Tuesday	*martes*
March	*marzo*	Wednesday	*miércoles*
April	*abril*	Thursday	*jueves*
May	*mayo*	Friday	*viernes*
June	*junio*	Saturday	*sábado*
July	*julio*	Sunday	*domingo*
August	*agosto*		
September	*septiembre*	at one o'clock	*a la una*
October	*octubre*	at half past two	*a las dos y media*
November	*noviembre*	at a quarter to three	*a cuarto para las tres/*
December	*diciembre*		*a las tres menos*
			quince

it's one o'clock	*es la una*	in ten minutes	*en diez minutos*
it's seven o'clock	*son las siete*	five hours	*cinco horas*
it's six twenty	*son las seis y veinte*	does it take long?	*¿tarda mucho?*
it's five to nine	*son las nueve menos cinco*		

Numbers

one	*uno/una*	sixteen	*dieciséis*
two	*dos*	seventeen	*diecisiete*
three	*tres*	eighteen	*dieciocho*
four	*cuatro*	nineteen	*diecinueve*
five	*cinco*	twenty	*veinte*
six	*seis*	twenty-one	*veintiuno*
seven	*siete*	thirty	*treinta*
eight	*ocho*	forty	*cuarenta*
nine	*nueve*	fifty	*cincuenta*
ten	*diez*	sixty	*sesenta*
eleven	*once*	seventy	*setenta*
twelve	*doce*	eighty	*ochenta*
thirteen	*trece*	ninety	*noventa*
fourteen	*catorce*	hundred	*cien/ciento*
fifteen	*quince*	thousand	*mil*

Food

avocado	*el aguacate*	goat	*el chivo*
baked	*al horno*	grapefruit	*la toronja/el pomelo*
bakery	*la panadería*	grill	*la parrilla*
banana	*el plátano*	grilled/griddled	*a la plancha*
beans	*los frijoles/ las habichuelas*	guava	*la guayaba*
		ham	*el jamón*
beef	*la carne de res*	hamburger	*la hamburguesa*
beef steak or pork fillet	*el bistec*	hot, spicy	*picante*
boiled rice	*el arroz blanco*	ice cream	*el helado*
bread	*el pan*	jam	*la mermelada*
breakfast	*el desayuno*	knife	*el cuchillo*
butter	*la mantequilla*	lime	*el limón*
cake	*el pastel*	lobster	*la langosta*
chewing gum	*el chicle*	lunch	*el almuerzo/ la comida*
chicken	*el pollo*		
chilli or green pepper	*el ají/pimiento*	meal	*la comida*
clear soup, stock	*el caldo*	meat	*la carne*
cooked	*cocido*	minced meat	*el picadillo*
dining room	*el comedor*	onion	*la cebolla*
egg	*el huevo*	orange	*la naranja*
fish	*el pescado*	pepper	*el pimiento*
fork	*el tenedor*	pasty, turnover	*la empanada/ el pastelito*
fried	*frito*		
garlic	*el ajo*	pork	*el cerdo*

potato	la papa	spoon	la cuchara
prawns	los camarones	squash	la calabaza
raw	crudo	squid	los calamares
restaurant	el restaurante	supper	la cena
salad	la ensalada	sweet	dulce
salt	la sal	to eat	comer
sandwich	el bocadillo	toasted	tostado
sauce	la salsa	turkey	el pavo
sausage	la longaniza/	vegetables	los legumbres/
	el chorizo		vegetales
scrambled eggs	los huevos revueltos	without meat	sin carne
seafood	los mariscos	yam	el camote
soup	la sopa		

Drink

beer	la cerveza	juice	el jugo
boiled	hervido/a	lemonade	la limonada
bottled	en botella	milk	la leche
camomile tea	la manzanilla	mint	la menta
canned	en lata	rum	el ron
coffee	el café	soft drink	el refresco
coffee, white	el café con leche	sugar	el azúcar
cold	frío	tea	el té
cup	la taza	to drink	beber/tomar
drink	la bebida	water	el agua
drunk	borracho/a	water, carbonated	el agua mineral
firewater	el aguardiente		con gas
fruit milkshake	el batido/licuado	water, still mineral	el agua mineral
glass	el vaso		sin gas
hot	caliente	wine, red	el vino tinto
ice/without ice	el hielo/sin hielo	wine, white	el vino blanco

Key verbs

to go	**ir**	there is/are	*hay*
I go	*voy*	there isn't/aren't	*no hay*
you go (familiar)	*vas*		
he, she, it goes, you (formal) go	*va*	**to be**	**ser**	**estar**
		I am	soy	estoy
we go	*vamos*	you are	eres	estás
they, you (plural) go	*van*	he, she, it is, you (formal) are	es	está
		we are	somos	estamos
to have (possess)	**tener**	they, you (plural) are	son	están
I have	*tengo*		
you (familiar) have	*tienes*	
he, she, it, you (formal) have	*tiene*	
we have	*tenemos*	
they, you (plural) have	*tienen*	

This section has been assembled on the basis of glossaries compiled by André de Mendonça and David Gilmour of South American Experience, London, and the Latin American Travel Advisor, No 9, March 1996

Panamanian Spanish

Panamanian Spanish borrows many words from American and Creole English and is considered a variant of Caribbean Spanish. It is very fast, filled with slang and vulgarities and can be tricky to understand. The accent takes work to master and includes selectively dropping 's's and 'd's (eg *¿dónde está?* becomes *'ónde 'tá*). Contractions of conjunctions and prepositions are very common too (eg *vamos para la fiesta* becomes *vamo' pa' la fie'ta*). Dialects vary widely between the interior and Panama City and a complete list of Panamanian expressions would fill a book in itself. Some of the best ones are given below:

ahuevado literally egg-head; an idiot, but can also be a term of endearment

arranque to party

arroz con mango literally rice with mango; big problems

blanco literally a white one; a cigarette

bochinche gossip

botella literally a bottle; a person appointed to a position but who doesn't work, especially in the public sector

buco many, from the French *beaucoup*

camarón literally shrimp; illicit money-making on the side

chambón awkward

chantín house, home, from the English *shanty*

chen chen money

chilin relaxing, from Creole English *chillin'*

chiva literally a female goat; a rural bus

chonta head

chucha female genitals, but not necessarily vulgar, often used as an interjection or expression of surprise

chuleta literally pork chop; an expression of surprise

chupata a party, a drinking session

de alante excellent, cool

de ley literally the law; meaning something is set

en panga not cool

engomado hung over

firi-firi skinny

focop a mess, from the Creole *fuck up*

gallo tasteless, tacky

garra friend

guapin what's happening, from Creole

guaro hard liquor, especially fermented sugar cane

juego vivo the art of cheating, sharp practice

loco literally crazy; a term of affection for close friends

ofi OK, understood, from *oficial*

palante to go or leave, a contraction of *para adelante.*

pavo literally a turkey; a bus driver's assistant

picando fashionable

pinta fría a cold beer

pipi sweet literally a sweet dick; a womanizer

ponchera a chaos, a commotion

pretti nice, from the English *pretty*

¿qué sopa? What's up? an inversion of *¿qué pasó?*

quemar literally to burn; to cheat on

rabiblanco literally white-tail; a rich white aristocrat

racataca a female gangster, a ghetto-style or cheap look

rejeros a group of guys on the town, lads

sólido literally solid; cool

ta cruel very bad, terrible

tongo a policeman, a cop, usually of low rank

tranque a traffic jam

vaina a thing, could refer to anything

yapla beach, an inversion of *playa*

yeye a yuppie or a preppy rich kid

Index → *Entries in bold refer to maps*

About the author

Prior to becoming a writer and journalist, Richard Arghiris found employment in a variety of colourful, if mostly terminal work roles. He was, by turns, a croupier on a seedy Mediterranean cruiseship, an usher in a crumbling seafront cinema, a machine operator for a brutal Dutch factory, a clerk, a waiter, a chef and, extremely briefly, a double-glazing salesman. His past lives include bouts in London, Brighton, Amsterdam and at sea. Once Richard realized his chequered employment history was entirely consistent with a career in writing, he swapped his working boots for walking boots and took off on the road armed with a notebook and pen. He has since become a professional nomad, travelling the margins of Central America in search of off-beat stories. He maintains two blogs: Interamericana, www.interamericanhighway.com, which features everything from imaginative on-the-road musings to serious news reports about indigenous rights; and Unseen Americas, www.unseenamericas.com, which is a platform for his photographic portfolio, showcasing a mix of candid street photography and photojournalism. Richard is currently somewhere between Mexico and Panama. He has no way of returning home, even if he wanted to...

Acknowledgements

First and foremost, a big thanks to Pat Dawson and Alan Murphy for putting this book on the rails, and to Felicity Laughton for her careful editing, advice and patience. Thanks to Pepi Bluck for her work on the colour section, Kevin Feeney for his attentive mapping, Beverley Jollands for painstakingly proofreading the entire draft and Emma Bryers for putting it all together. At home, a special thanks to Jennifer Kennedy, for her patience throughout the whole process and for keeping me alive with good hot meals and love. So many people were helpful on the road, it would be impossible to list all of them. In no particular order, a big thanks to Annie Young, Raul Arias de Para and Carlos Alfaro for their kind hospitality and on-going dedication to eco-tourism. A special thanks to Oscar Sogandares for opening my eyes to the beauty of the critically endangered Río Tabasará, and to Italo Jiménez, the M10 movement and Miguel Angel, who hosted me during the 2011 protests at Barro Blanco. In mainland Bocas del Toro, thanks to Edwin Sánchez and Adolfo Villagra for their hospitality and revealing insights into the Naso world. In David, thanks to Paul Romano for his lucid conservation, his cordial friendship and for storing our book collection all those months. In Boquete, many thanks to Jason and Susan for their hospitality. Thanks to Eric Jackson for his excellent English-language coverage of current affairs and to Bruce Ruiz for his essays on Panamanian history – their websites were invaluable sources of insight and information. In Soloy, special thanks to Adán Bejerano, Eusevio and Juan Carlos, as well as dedicated Peace Corps volunteers Laura Geiken and Jack Fischl, who have done an excellent job of promoting sustainable tourism in the community. Several other Peace Corps volunteers deserve thanks for their contribution to ethical tourism in Panama and for otherwise getting in touch with useful information, especially Silvie Snow-Thomas, Glenise Rice, Andrea Kraus, Sara Taylor, Jessica Rudder, Jessica Kovarik, Dana Dallavalle, Emily Lange, Karen Lee, Carmen Fleming, Matthew Sutton, Adam Armstrong, Kate Douglas, Kim Woods and John Eckbert. Finally, I would like to thank friends and family further afield for their on-going love, support and conversations by Skype, including Terri Wright, Jo Arghiris, Alan Peacock-Johns, Dan Roberts, Charlie Roberts, Thea Roberts, Paul, Bev and Corin Wright, Peter McCallan and Sym Gharial.

Credits

Footprint credits
Project Editor: Felicity Laughton
Layout and production: Emma Bryers
Proofreader: Beverley Jollands
Cover and colour section: Pepi Bluck
Maps: Kevin Feeney

Managing Director: Andy Riddle
Content Director: Patrick Dawson
Publisher: Alan Murphy
Publishing Managers: Felicity Laughton, Jo Williams, Nicola Gibbs
Marketing and Partnerships Director: Liz Harper
Marketing Executive: Liz Eyles
Trade Product Manager: Diane McEntee
Account Managers: Paul Bew, Tania Ross
Advertising: Renu Sibal, Elizabeth Taylor

Photography credits
Front cover: Jane Sweeney / awl-images.com (Comarca Guna Yala)
Back cover: Gavriel Jecan / www.agefotostock.com (red-eyed tree frog in an orchid)

Colour section
Page i: Jane Sweeney / awl-images.com
Page ii: age fotostock / SuperStock
Page vi: Heeb Christian / www.agefotostock.com
Page vii: vilainecrevette / Shutterstock.com
Page viii: Melba / www.agefotostock.com
Page ix: vilainecrevette / Shutterstock.com
Page xiv: Prisma / SuperStock (top); Oyvind Martinsen / Alamy (bottom)

Printed in India by Replika Press Pvt Ltd

Publishing information
Footprint Panama
1st edition
© Footprint Handbooks Ltd
July 2012

ISBN: 978 1 907263 50 7
CIP DATA: A catalogue record for this book is available from the British Library

® Footprint Handbooks and the Footprint mark are a registered trademark of Footprint Handbooks Ltd

Published by Footprint
6 Riverside Court
Lower Bristol Road
Bath BA2 3DZ, UK
T +44 (0)1225 469141
F +44 (0)1225 469461
footprinttravelguides.com

Distributed in the USA by Globe Pequot Press, Guilford, Connecticut

THE BEST OF PANAMA chosen by millions of travellers

Casa del Horno

Boquete Outdoor Adventures

Mantis

Top-rated places to stay

La Montaña y el Valle Coffee Estate Inn, Boquete
ⓞⓞⓞⓞⓞ
"A rainbow view almost every day"

Casa del Horno
Panama City
ⓞⓞⓞⓞⓞ
"Cool and elegant"

Los Cuatro Tulipanes
Panama City
ⓞⓞⓞⓞⓞ
"Excellent service in the heart of Casco Viejo"

Amazing attractions

Habla Ya Spanish Courses & Ecotourism, Boquete
ⓞⓞⓞⓞⓞ
"The perfect language experience"

Spa Boquete at Isla Verde
Boquete
ⓞⓞⓞⓞⓞ
"A sanctuary for relaxation"

Boquete Outdoor Adventures, Boquete
ⓞⓞⓞⓞⓞ
"Our favorite experience in Panama"

Popular restaurants

Mantis
Isla Bastimentos
ⓞⓞⓞⓞⓞ
"Beach views and a resident sloth!"

Guari Guari
Isla Colón
ⓞⓞⓞⓞⓞ
"A gem in the jungle"

The Rock
Boquete
ⓞⓞⓞⓞⓞ
"Delicious soups, ribs and desserts!"

ⓥⓥ tripadvisor®

Plan your perfect trip with millions of candid traveller reviews.

tripadvisor.co.uk   tripadvisor.it   tripadvisor.es   tripadvisor.de   tripadvisor.fr   tripadvisor.se
tripadvisor.nl   tripadvisor.dk   tripadvisor.ie   no.tripadvisor.com   pl.tripadvisor.com   tripadvisor.ru

Ratings were accurate as of March 2012 and may change over time. Visit tripadvisor.co.uk for current ratings.

Tread your own path

Footprint Handbooks

Footprint
Surfing Europe

South American
Handbook 2013

Footprint story

It was 1921

Ireland had just been partitioned, the British miners were striking for more pay and the federation of British industry had an idea. Exports were booming in South America – how about a handbook for businessmen trading in that far away continent? The Anglo-South American Handbook was born that year, written by W Koebel, the most prolific writer on Latin America of his day.

1924

Two editions later the book was 'privatized' and in 1924, in the hands of Royal Mail, the steamship company for South America, it became The South American Handbook, subtitled 'South America in a nutshell'. This annual publication became the 'bible' for generations of travellers to South America and remains so to this day. In the early days travel was by sea and the Handbook gave all the details needed for the long voyage from Europe. What to wear for dinner; how to arrange a cricket match with the Cable & Wireless staff on the Cape Verde Islands and a full account of the journey from Liverpool up the Amazon to Manaus: 5898 miles without changing cabin!

1939

As the continent opened up, the South American Handbook reported the new Pan Am flying boat services, and the fortnightly airship service from Rio to Europe on the Graf Zeppelin. For reasons still unclear but with extraordinary determination, the annual editions continued through the Second World War.

1970s

Many more people discovered South America and the backpacking trail started to develop. All the while the Handbook was gathering fans, including literary vagabonds such as Paul Theroux and Graham Greene (who once sent some updates addressed to "The publishers of the best travel guide in the world, Bath, England").

1990s

During the 1990s the company set about developing a new travel guide series using this legendary title as the flagship. By 1997 there were over a dozen guides in the series and the Footprint imprint was launched.

2000s

The series grew quickly and there were soon Footprint travel guides covering more than 150 countries. In 2004, Footprint launched its first thematic guide: *Surfing Europe*, packed with colour photographs, maps and charts. This was followed by further thematic guides such as *Diving the World*, *Snowboarding the World*, *Body and Soul escapes*, *Travel with Kids* and *European City Breaks*.

2012

Today we continue the traditions of the last 90 years that have served legions of travellers so well. We believe that these help to make Footprint guides different. Our policy is to use authors who are genuine experts who write for independent travellers; people possessing a spirit of adventure, looking to get off the beaten track.